THIS BUSINESS OF TELEVISION

by Howard J. Blumenthal
and Oliver R. Goodenough

Billboard Books

An imprint of Watson-Guptill Publications / New York

To our wives, with
thanks for their support,
patience, and love.

Edited by Fred Weiler
Senior Editor: Tad Lathrop
Design and Composition: Publications Development Co. of Texas
Jacket Design: Areta Buk

First published 1991 by Billboard Books, an imprint of Watson-Guptill
Publications, a division of BPI Communications, Inc. 1515 Broadway,
New York, NY 10036.

Library of Congress Cataloging-in-Publication Data

Blumenthal, Howard J.
    This business of television / by Howard J. Blumenthal and Oliver R.
Goodenough.
      p.   cm.
    Includes bibliographical references and index.
    ISBN 0-8230-7762-4
    1. Television broadcasting—United States. 2. Television—Law and
legislation—United States. I. Goodenough, Oliver. II. Title.
HE8700.8.B58   1991
384.55'0973—dc20   91-29135
                                                    CIP

Manufactured in the United States of America
First printing, 1991

1 2 3 4 5 6 7 8 9 / 96 95 94 93 92 91

Acknowledgments

The authors wish to thank the following people and organizations for their assistance in preparing this book:

Bruce Apar, *Video Business*
Jonathan Arkin
Zane Bair, The Australian Television Network
Alan Banks, Saatchi & Saatchi
Norm Blumenthal
Bob Boden
Steve Brennan, *The Hollywood Reporter*
Don Brown, NBC News
Shelley Cagner, Arbitron
Candy Cazau
James Charne, Absolute Entertainment
Douglas Chia
Michael Collyer, Kay Collyer & Boose
John Crigler, Haley, Bader & Potts
Cliff Curley
Dorothy Curley
Peter Dean
Jacques DeSuze, McHugh and Hoffman, Inc.
Mark Devereaux, Simon Olswang & Co.
Julian Dickens, Simon Olswang & Co.
Greg Fagan, GFP Publishing Services
John Fisher
Paul Flattery, FYI
Betsy Frank, Saatchi & Saatchi
Mark Fratrick, National Association of Broadcasters
Ron Giles, QVC
Adrianne Gordon, WGA
Peter Haratonik, Hofstra University
Stanley Hubbard, Hubbard Broadcasting
Ned Kandel, Kandel Enterprises
Aki Kaneko, *Billboard*

Stu Kantor, PBS
James H. Kaye, WGA
Nick Ketchum, CRTC
Jeff Klein, Jaguar
Bart Kuperus, *World Radio & Television Handbook*
Jo LaVerde-Curcio, Nielsen Media Research
Robert Levi, TBS-Superstation
Richard Levy
Paul B. Lindstrom, Nielsen
Mark Mandel, ABC Sports
Francis Mooney, Saatchi & Saatchi
Ginny Morris, Hubbard Broadcasting
Charles Nace, Newtown Cablevision
Gary Needle, VidAmerica
Melinda Newman, *Billboard*
Cathy Nierle, Post-Newsweek Stations
Jeremy Nussbaum, Kay Collyer & Boose
Matt O'Connell, Osborne Communications
David Othmer, WHYY-Philadelphia
Shelton Leigh Palmer
Ethan Podell
Trevor Potter, Wiley Rein & Fielding
Francois Pouget
Jay Rayvid, WQED-Pittsburgh
Deborah Rodriguez, Group W Newsfeed
Peter Sailer
Ariel Schwartz
Andrew Sennitt, *World Radio & Television Handbook*
Bill Sheehan, Saatchi & Saatchi
Jim Snyder, Post-Newsweek Stations
Harry Somerfield
Randi Subarsky
Paul Sweeting, *Billboard*
Mike Tiglio, NABET
Danielle Trembley, City TV
Diane Vilagi, Laurel Entertainment
Gary Wald
Fred Weiler, Billboard Books
Ira Weinblatt, Saatchi & Saatchi
Dick Williams, WDCA-Washington, D.C.
Rick Young, News 12-Long Island
Jim Yukich, FYI

The authors also thank Hope Bernhard, for endless typing and coordination; George Mannes, for his skillful research; and Anne Robinson, for her ability to organize, keep things moving, and do so with a smile.

Preface

This Business of Television has several purposes.

First, the book is intended as a desktop reference work covering all facets of the television and video businesses. A producer who needs to learn about the workings of PBS will find a useful section here. A writer who is considering membership in WGA will find a summary of Writer's Guild activities, including jurisdiction, an explanation of key agreements and their terms, and membership information. An advertising sales executive making the move from traditional broadcast to a regional sports network will learn the basic structure of that business. Showing how video stores and direct-mail clubs work, outlining the basic terms of a studio rental deal, explaining how to hire an agent— *This Business of Television* should be the definitive source of basic information about the television and video industries.

The book's second purpose is to provide a legal overview of the television business. Lengthy sections on personal rights, the protection of creative properties, financing, and regulation should function as indispensable reference material. While a book like this cannot possibly detail all of the nuances of, for example, copyright law, it does discuss in plain language the legal underpinnings of television.

Third, *This Business of Television* includes a considerable number of useful forms and form agreements in the appendixes. We have provided concise "boilerplate" contracts for the most common business transactions in television, such as hiring production personnel, optioning rights to creative properties, and forming legal entities such as partnerships and corporations.

We sincerely hope that you find *This Business of Television* to be a useful work.

Howard J. Blumenthal
Oliver R. Goodenough
August 1991

Before Using the Information in This Book

We have sought to keep this book current through August 1991. Please note, however, that certain union figures based on variable contract years, may reflect an earlier date, and that the legal appendices have specified dates for including amendments.

The information and forms provided in *This Business of Television* are intended for background only. This book should *not* serve as a substitute for the expertise that can be provided only by an experienced specialist, such as an attorney or accountant. It is not our intention to transform an untrained individual into an "instant expert"—rather, our goal is to create an informed television or video professional. The reader is encouraged to hire a lawyer to review the final versions of forms and contracts, to secure an accountant for tax and accounting matters, and to retain the services of an expert financial advisor.

Contents

Foreword

In essence, television is the exhibition of moving images with synchronized sound over a cathode-ray screen to homes and other establishments. But as Howard Blumenthal and Oliver Goodenough make clear in this easy-to-understand book, television is much more than that—it is a business, and a business with the over-arching purpose of attracting and fulfilling an audience. For network and syndicated television, the consumer is the target, since the advertiser wants to reach a specific demographic group. In the case of pay cable, satisfying viewers who subscribe is the primary goal. *This Business of Television* explores the interrelationship of the artists who create the productions, the marketing of the television programs by distributors or advertisers, and the role of the audience in determining the success or failure of the end product.

These pages illuminate the artisanship involved in the production of any television program. Production is a labor-intensive undertaking, requiring a producer and/or writer who can shape a simple idea into a form that can be presented to an advertiser, network, or broadcaster. The steps from basic concept to polished program—be it comedy, drama, news, or game show—draw upon the skill and talent of countless writers, directors, and performers. Along the way, the business niceties must be observed, the "i"'s dotted and the "t"'s crossed. More importantly, the final product cannot infringe upon or violate the rights or interests of any other parties.

This Business of Television presents the creative side of the television business. At the same time, Messrs. Blumenthal and Goodenough never lose sight of the fact that just because television is part of the entertainment industry, it is not all fun and games. For producers, distributors, legal practitioners, business-affairs experts, advertisers, and even newcomers to the field, *This Business of Television* will undoubtedly become *the* working handbook.

Michael Collyer
Kay Collyer & Boose
Chairman, National Academy of Television Arts and Sciences

Introduction

The business of television is fast-paced and poised for rapid growth in the twenty-first century. Change has been the rule in the television industry since its inception, and the business will continue to evolve with global expansion and technological innovation. Still, traditional approaches and deeply-rooted customs—some dating from the time when radio ruled the airwaves—continue to dominate the industry.

EARLY HISTORY OF BROADCASTING

The invention called television is a half-century old, but its roots extend back to 1876, when Alexander Graham Bell first demonstrated his telephone to an astonished public. Bell's invention prompted the public to consider a future based in electronic communication media. Speculating wildly on things to come, magazines published illustrations showing wall-sized screens—the visual complement to Bell's audio-only telephone. Other inventors supplied pieces of the puzzle that eventually became television. Marconi discovered how to propagate radio waves; Fessenden, how to send radio signals on modulating wave forms; and DeForest, how to amplify and generate waves. Some inventors became fascinated with the idea of wireless transmission of visual images.

On the business side, American Telephone and Telegraph (AT&T) was formed to exploit Bell's patents and the other patents needed to provide commercial telephone service. Rather than building a single nationwide system, AT&T licensed the technology to local service franchises, and then connected them to supply national service. (AT&T licensed the technology to its franchises for stock rather than cash, so it owned majority positions in most of its franchises before the turn of the century.) AT&T's purchase of Western Electric as its manufacturing division completed the picture: now, a single company provided all aspects of telephone communication service.

Although the telephone was successful by 1900, and wireless communication was possible before World War I (inventor Reginald Fessenden successfully broadcast both voice and music as early as

1906), little consideration was given to possible public applications of the technology. Legend has it that young David Sarnoff—a middle-level manager at American Marconi, then a telegraph company with interests in wireless technology—wrote a memo describing a radio music box that could be sold to individual households in 1914. Whether or not this story is revisionist history, the commercial potential of radio broadcasting became clear almost immediately after World War I. Amateurs who had learned about wireless technology during the war started setting up their own stations in garages and attics. Officially, the Navy controlled wireless broadcasting—it was seen mainly as a form of maritime communication—but Westinghouse and General Electric, the companies who dominated the U.S. electric industry along with AT&T, were anxious to see the technology made available in the commercial marketplace. The Navy, realizing that it would not be able to retain control over broadcasting, removed the one foreign force in U.S. broadcasting by pressuring British Marconi to sell all the stock of its U.S. operation, American Marconi, to a new company owned by General Electric. That company was named the Radio Corporation of America, or RCA.

Westinghouse and GE started manufacturing radio receivers by 1918. In 1920, Westinghouse opened its first radio station, KDKA in Pittsburgh, and in 1921, the company started WJZ in New York City. In the same period, GE's WGY in Schenectady, New York (its hometown), went on the air. AT&T's first station, WEAF, went on the air in 1922. By 1925, most major cities were served by multiple radio stations, frequently affiliated with an emerging network.

The growth of radio stations did not proceed according to AT&T's plans. In general, AT&T, true to its origins, saw the entire notion of broadcasting as an outgrowth of telephone service. In one instance, AT&T denied competitive networks access to its long-distance phone lines. The conflict between common carrier and broadcaster became increasingly clear; eventually, under pressure from the government, AT&T sold its stations and technology to RCA, reserving only the right to provide the long lines service that connected one radio station to another. GE and Westinghouse also invested in RCA, became partners, and contributed their stations. By 1927, there was sufficient belief in the potential of network broadcasting to form an RCA subsidiary called the National Broadcasting Company, or NBC.

COMMERCIAL RADIO AND THE GROWTH OF THE NETWORKS

AT&T originated the idea of paid commercial advertising on radio with a real-estate commercial that aired on WEAF in 1922. Within just two more years, AT&T became a leading producer of programs for stations on its temporary network link-ups. AT&T married sponsors to programs: *The Ipana Troubadours, The A&P Gypsies,* and *The Eveready Hour* were among the more popular offerings. Westinghouse's WJZ presented programs sponsored by Rheingold Beer, Schrafft's Restaurants, and John Wanamaker, a department store. Other companies followed suit—but AT&T objected on the grounds that it was the only company permitted to charge for commercial use of electronic media. The ensuing battle resulted in AT&T's withdrawal from RCA.

As early as 1927, NBC, under the executive leadership of David Sarnoff, was operating two networks—the Red Network, fed by WEAF (later, WNBC), and the Blue Network, fed by WJZ (later, WABC). (The networks' names came from the patchboard's use of red and blue to keep them separate.) NBC was not the only owner of networks at that time, but it was the only one with stations in most of the largest cities. A year later, William Paley bought a struggling network called United Independent Broadcasters, renamed it the Columbia Broadcasting System (CBS), and began aggressively seeking affiliates in major cities.

ABC came much later, in 1943, when radio's golden age was already drawing to a close. NBC's dominance had long been a cause for concern at the Federal Communications Commission (FCC), and in 1941 the Commission finally required NBC to divest itself of one of its two networks. NBC sold the Blue network to Life Savers tycoon Edward J. Noble in 1943, who established the American Broadcasting Company. By 1951, Noble had sold out to United Paramount Theaters and the third of network television's pioneers: Leonard Goldenson.

THE TRANSITION FROM RADIO TO TELEVISION

The concept of transmitting pictures as well as sound dates back to the late 1800s. The technology needed to capture an image from real life via a camera's pickup tube, then transmit the image back to a television screen, took about 50 years to develop. In 1930, engineers at RCA were able to display 60 lines of resolution, resulting in a crude television image. Nine years later, that number had increased to 441. In 1941, the National Television Standards Committee (NTSC), representing 15 leading electronic manufacturers, approved the 525-line system that is still in use today in the U.S. and in many other countries.

World War II delayed the start-up of television broadcasting on a large scale. By 1943, however, NBC was broadcasting occasional boxing matches; by 1944, Gillette had agreed to sponsor three nights a week of NBC boxing and wrestling coverage. At about the same time, CBS debuted its first regularly-scheduled entry: a game show called *Missus Goes A'Shopping* (it had been a popular program on CBS radio). ABC, then called ABC-Blue, also started with a game show, *Ladies Be Seated.* A fourth network, DuMont, began with low-budget programs: cooking shows and travelogues. Naturally, at the outset, much of the programming was experimental, and the scheduling somewhat informal. As more television sets were sold and more viewers became available, the system became more organized.

By 1948, television broadcasting had changed dramatically. ABC, CBS, and NBC were programming nearly all of the hours from 7:00 P.M. until 11:00 P.M., with only occasional lapses for local programming. Essentially, DuMont operated only on weekdays, with one notable exception on Saturday nights: the *Original Amateur Hour*. Many of the network programs were low-priced filler or sports coverage, which was inexpensive to produce because the event did not have to be staged. There was also an abundance of public affairs, talk, and other low-cost formats—plus the beginnings of the hit shows that would soon drive the business. *Texaco Star Theater* (NBC) featuring Milton Berle became the top show, followed by *Toast of the Town* (CBS), later renamed *The Ed Sullivan Show*. Both debuted during the summer of 1948, prior to the introduction of the first full-fledged fall season. An early version of Sid Caesar's *Your Show of Shows* (NBC) also debuted in 1948.

By 1950, the pattern was set, and it would not change in any substantive way for the next thirty or more years. Each of the networks—reduced to three with the demise of DuMont in 1956—worked closely with advertisers and advertising agencies to develop programs that would reach the largest possible audience.

THE EVOLUTION OF NETWORK PROGRAMMING

In the 1950s, situation comedies tended to feature young urban couples (*The Honeymooners, I Love Lucy*); those adapted from radio frequently retained an ethnic twist (*The Goldbergs, Mama, Amos n' Andy*). In the 1960s, the young suburban families on sitcoms like *The Dick Van Dyke Show, Bewitched, My Three Sons, The Partridge Family*, and *The Brady Bunch* reflected changes in the American lifestyle. CBS had a long run with sitcoms that had a strong rural appeal: *Petticoat Junction, The Beverly Hillbillies, Green Acres, The Andy Griffith Show*. By the 1970s, though, the old formulas were no longer working. ABC introduced shows intended for younger viewers (*Laverne & Shirley, Happy Days, Three's Company*); CBS depended heavily upon Norman Lear for progressive sitcoms that featured social topics (*All in the Family, Maude, One Day at a Time*); and MTM produced sitcoms about independent women (*The Mary Tyler Moore Show, Rhoda*).

Programs based on certain themes have remained popular throughout the history of television. Sitcoms with military themes, for example—*Sergeant Bilko, McHale's Navy, M*A*S*H**—have been consistently popular. Shows whose families feature outspoken children have also been successful year after year, though some have been of higher quality than others—the best include *Leave It to Beaver, Make Room for Daddy, Family Ties, The Cosby Show*, and *Roseanne*.

Dramatic programs based on cops, lawyers, detectives, spies, medical, and military themes have been consistent performers, though some years find more of one type of program than another. In the 1950s and into the 1960s, westerns like *Gunsmoke, Have Gun Will Travel, Wagon Train, Peter Gunn,* and *Bat Masterson* were very popular, but since then, only a small number have succeeded. Anthology shows (*The Twilight Zone, Alfred Hitchcock Presents*) did well in the 1950s and 1960s, especially those that featured live drama (*Playhouse 90, Armstrong Circle Theater, Philco Television Playhouse*), but these formats have essentially disappeared from view. Shows about reporters (*Lou Grant, The Reporters*) have occasionally succeeded, and the reporter show is one of the few "occupational" genres outside of those listed above that seem worth a programmer's—or producer's—risk. Family soap operas (*The Big Valley, The Waltons, Family*) have been successful, particularly if there is a big-money business at the heart of the family (*Falcon Crest, Dallas*).

Other types of programs besides comedy and drama have come and gone in prime time as well. In the fall of 1958, there were twelve game shows on the network prime time schedules; by 1962, there were four; by 1967, the format was relegated to daytime. There have been some experiments since, mainly as summer replacements, but none of them has succeeded on the networks. Game shows have since found their place in daytime and fringe periods mainly as cable and syndicated programs. Variety shows featuring big stars were among the most popular shows in the 1950s and 1960s; in 1963, for example, the fall schedule included regularly-scheduled programs featuring Mitch Miller, Red Skelton, Jack Benny, Garry Moore, Andy Williams, Danny Kaye, Sid Caesar, Perry Como, Edie Adams, Bob Hope, Jack Paar, Lawrence Welk, Jerry Lewis, Jackie Gleason, Ed Sullivan, and Judy Garland. Ten years later, only Sonny & Cher, Flip Wilson, Dean Martin, and Carol Burnett were on the air with variety shows (Bob Hope also appeared regularly, but less often than before). A year after that, only Sonny (without Cher) and Carol Burnett remained.

Daytime schedules have also been dominated by a limited number of formats. Soaps began as fifteen-minute programs in the 1950s, and by the 1980s, many were an hour long. Roughly half of the daytime schedule has been occupied by soaps since the 1950s. The other half has been filled mainly with game shows, plus occasional talk and variety shows (*The Tennessee Ernie Ford Show, Art Linkletter's House Party, Dinah's Place,* and, more recently, *The Marsha Warfield Show*). Syndication has taken over a role once played by the networks—supplying talk shows to local stations (*Donahue!, The Oprah Winfrey Show*).*

---

* For a complete year-by-year analysis of network prime time programming through 1980, see *Watching TV: Four Decades of American Television,* by Harry Castleman and Walter J. Podrazik. The same authors have prepared *The TV Schedule Book,* which includes detailed daytime and weekend schedules through 1982.

OTHER TELEVISION BROADCASTERS

From the 1940s until the late 1960s, the term "television" described the activities of the three networks, plus an assortment of independent stations—located mostly in the larger cities—that were unaffiliated with any network. The independent stations showed plenty of movies and sports coverage as well as inexpensive cartoon programs and some low-cost syndicated fare. Later, as the syndication marketplace matured in the 1980s, independent stations became competitive, sometimes equaling or surpassing the ratings of network affiliates for popular shows.

EDUCATIONAL AND PUBLIC TELEVISION

Educational television stations were on the air in the early 1950s in some cities, but the present-day system of public television broadcasting did not take shape until the late 1960s. Attempts at networks, co-productions between stations, and even group program-buying were only occasionally successful. (National Educational Television, or NET, started as one of several organizations that sent tapes by mail from one station to another). Community groups, school boards, municipal organizations, and other local entities provided the stations with small budgets and limited funds. In 1967, the Carnegie Commission on Educational Television recommended that Congress establish a corporation for public television, as an expansion on earlier educational efforts. Later that year, Congress established the Corporation for Public Broadcasting (CPB) as both a funding source for public television stations as well as a buffer organization between Congress and a new public television network.

What began as a non-commercial network financed by the government and foundation grants has since become a confederation of independently-owned and -operated, non-profit stations that have become indispensable to certain audience segments. Public television is especially popular with pre-schoolers, and with viewers who enjoy documentaries, opera, classical music, ballet, and British comedy. With increasing competition from cable services that provide similar programming, PBS is in the process of rethinking its goals; centralizing its programming operations is one possible step in this change.

NON-BROADCAST TELEVISION

Television has long been considered to be a mass medium, but television has served a significant variety of non-broadcast functions since the 1970s—and since the invention of affordable video recorders and players. Sony's U-Matic format, the first to house videotape in a viable cassette format, was introduced in 1975. Colleges have videotaped classwork since that time (and earlier, for those who operated television studios). Some high schools have a long history with non-broadcast as well. Closed-circuit television services have also been a part of the picture since the 1950s—for surveillance, and, later, for the distribution of training and information programming throughout large organizations, such as corporations.

Still, non-broadcast television, now almost universally called video, did not blossom until the late 1970s, when a combination of more affordable equipment and the VHS cassette standard encouraged corporate managers to invest in small-scale video set-ups. Many of these operations have grown considerably, and most corporations now use video as a primary communications tool. Some companies have experimented with annual reports on video; others use it regularly for employee communication and training, merchandising, doing public relations (in the form of electronic news releases), presenting sales literature in a dynamic way, demonstrating products, and other applications. Closed-circuit services continue to grow as well, supplying hospitals and hotels with movie channels, for example. With the coming convergence of video and computer technology, multimedia applications will further increase the variety of non-broadcast activities.

THE 1970s AND THE RE-INVENTION OF THE TELEVISION INDUSTRY

From the early 1950s until the mid-1970s, television was a closed business, of limited interest to outside entrepreneurs. Television stations which had started as outgrowths of radio stations or newspapers changed hands, but not often. Since the demise of DuMont in 1956, talk of a fourth commercial network was initiated by many companies, but nearly every plan faltered for the same reason: limited channel capacity. After a brief freeze on commercial television licensing, the FCC had devised a plan in 1952 that would allow only the very largest markets to have five or six VHF stations; most large markets, in fact, were limited to four or five. Other stations were licensed to operate on the UHF band—channels 14 to 83—but this was a "no man's land" because many sets could not receive the signals, and even viewers who owned VHF/UHF sets rarely watched the UHF band. Stations on the VHF band were almost always affiliated with either ABC, CBS, NBC, or public television. In order to build a successful new network, most of the stations would have to be on the VHF band—and there simply weren't enough unaffiliated major-market VHF stations to support a fourth commercial network. Some independent stations grew, and some even affiliated in ad-hoc networks like Operation Prime Time, but limited channel capacity was the single greatest impediment to further growth of the television industry.

By the mid-1970s, three developments had conspired to change not only this situation, but the entire definition of television.

First, the FCC lifted several restrictions which limited the growth of cable television. Until early 1970s, the FCC routinely passed rules that limited the ability of cable operators to pursue business in the top 100 markets, taking the view that broadcast interests were to be protected, and that cable operators were attempting to make money unfairly with the broadcaster's product. By 1972, the FCC had changed its stance, and within five years, cable operators were fighting over the valuable franchises for communities of every size. In 1972, 6.5 million households were subscribers to cable; in 1982, the number had jumped to 29 million; in 1992, the projected subscriber count is roughly 60 million, or two-thirds of U.S. television households.*

The second development that has changed the nature of television follows from the first. With a system of distribution and a growing universe of potential viewers, corporations with interests in the television and/or entertainment industries created cable television networks. Time, Inc. developed HBO and, later, Cinemax and The Comedy Channel. Syndication leader Viacom launched Showtime, and later purchased several networks developed by Warner (later Warner-Amex): The Movie Channel, Nickelodeon, and other services. Smaller companies also succeeded: Georgia entrepreneur Ted Turner, who was already familiar with the cable business because of the success of his superstation, WTCG (later renamed WTBS), developed cable's first 24-hour news channel, CNN. Turner followed with a second news service and, after the purchase of the MGM film library, with Turner Network Television (TNT). Special-interest networks like The Weather Channel and ESPN have also done well. ABC owns ESPN, and large portions of Lifetime and A&E. NBC has begun its own service with CNBC, and is also a partner in Cablevision and Cablevision's Rainbow Program Holdings subsidiary, which owns SportsChannel, Bravo, and American Movie Classics. CBS tried its own ambitious cable network (CBS Cable), but failed, and the network has not tried again. The next generation of cable television can offer systems with up to 100 channels, sometimes more. New channels are in development, but because there is only a finite number of viewers, many of these channels will face a downward spiral of ratings. The latest limitation is not technological—it is possible to build a cable system with more than a 100 channels—it is economic. The high cost of construction at the local level, and the relatively small numbers of viewers per channel at the national level, suggest that new financing patterns are necessary if such systems are to succeed.

The third development is the videocassette recorder. The VCR is now a part of television viewing in over 70 percent of U.S. households. After a slow start, growth of the installed base of VCRs was brisk: 2.3 million by late 1981, 25 million by 1985, and 65 million by 1990. No

---

* Source: National Cable Television Association, *Cable Television Developments*, May 1990.

dependable method of measuring viewership patterns in video has been devised, but it seems likely that viewing of tapes from the local video store is having an impact on network viewing, particularly on weekend nights.

The videocassette business has evolved from a rental marketplace, where retail stores purchase copies of popular titles for subsequent rental to customers, to a combination of rental and sell-through (whereby consumers buy the tapes directly). A large number of titles are now available for under $30 and, frequently, under $20. Hollywood sells movies directly to consumers—each of the studios operates a home video label in the U.S., and most are directly involved internationally as well. Some other large entertainment companies own labels (HBO Video), while smaller entrepreneurial concerns—unable to compete for big box-office films—tend to specialize in particular genres (Kultur, in performing arts, for example).

CHANGES IN THE 1980s

The 1970s presented only a glimpse of the more fundamental shifts that were destined to alter the entire television industry in the following decade.

First, individual television stations began to change hands more often. Buying and selling stations became a big business in the 1980s, supported by a change in the government stance on license transfer (see page 113), and by Wall Street interest. In New York City, for example, WOR, long an RKO General station, was sold to MCA Universal; WNEW, the flagship station for the old Metromedia group, was sold to Rupert Murdoch as a key station in the new Fox group (it is now called WNYW). In Los Angeles, RKO's KHJ was sold to Disney, and became KCAL. Stations were sold for high cash values; new companies, such as Act III Broadcasting began to buy and operate independent stations and convert them into Fox affiliates.

As a result of Wall Street maneuvering, each of the networks changed hands in the 1980s. Previously, the buying or selling of a network seemed impossible because of tradition and government barriers. This changed when Capital Cities successfully merged with ABC. GE then purchased RCA, and with it, NBC. The change at CBS was engineered in the boardroom, as stockholder Laurence Tisch took over, supposedly with the blessing of patriarch William Paley.

Second, the Big Three—ABC, CBS, and NBC—have been joined by a new competitor, Fox Broadcasting Corporation. Fox has survived where others might have failed because the network was carefully anchored by VHF stations in several key markets. Furthermore, with cable, the old distinction between UHF and VHF is no longer as important, so Fox has been able to get by with UHF stations in large markets (the Fox affiliate in Philadelphia, for example, is WTXF, Channel 29).

Fox's programming strategy has also been key to its success. The network has followed some traditional patterns, but it has varied the target audience. *21 Jump Street,* for example, was a cop show for a younger audience; *Married . . . With Children* is a sitcom with an attitude. Like other network start-ups, low-cost programming (*The Reporters, America's Most Wanted*) was also a part of Fox's early strategy, but these programs were skillfully crafted, so their ratings were higher than might be expected from modestly-budgeted programs. Quirky shows are also part of the strategy; from the beginning, Fox has attempted to do things that the other networks do not. Variety has been an important form (*The Tracey Ullman Show, In Living Color*), and the network's first true hit, *The Simpsons,* has encouraged the other networks to rediscover animation in prime time.

Third, as a result of cable, home video, and Fox, the three original networks' share of total viewers has seriously eroded. ABC, CBS, and NBC now claim only 65 percent of the prime time audience; this situation is likely to grow more severe as households spend more time watching videocassettes, and as the viewing options available on cable stations expand.

THE FUTURE

New technologies, competition from existing distribution systems and new ones, and a changing regulatory environment, will force the television and video industries to evolve and grow.

Cable television's multichannel dominance is beginning to experience competition from direct-broadcast satellites (DBS). High-power satellites are calling for smaller and smaller satellite dishes, and several ventures (SkyPix, Primestar) now provide DBS service nationwide. Other ventures are in the works.

Fiber-optic cables can transmit hundreds of television channels, plus data and voice communication. With changes in regulation, the telephone companies may become more active in cable operations; the ultimate result could be a single, mixed-use cable system for some combination of television programs, audio programs, voice communication, picturephone, an advanced form of fax or still video, and computer data.

The viewing experience is changing as well. More than 2 million households now own projection screens larger than 45 inches (diagonally measured); several manufacturers sell screens over 100 inches. Surround sound, which mimics the superior three-dimensional effects heard in the best movie theaters, is available for home use for about $1,000. A variety of widescreen and high-definition television (HDTV) formats are also in development.

TVs and VCRs are being installed on increasing numbers of planes, boats, cars, buses, trains, and trucks; battery-operated portable video systems, such as Sony's Color Watchman (which includes a small TV and VCR), are likely to change viewer's perceptions of the medium as well.

Digital video is the long-term variable. As computer and video technology continue along their converging paths of development, the turn of the century will bring new program forms, new kinds of personal and office communications equipment, toys, video players and recorders, and telephones that are not yet the stuff of dreams. All of these developments may lead to a completely new definition of what we presently refer to as "television."

Figure 1. The Top 100 Television Markets, Ranked by Number of Television Households

RANK	MARKET	ADI TV HH
1	New York	7,075,000
2	Los Angeles	5,036,000
3	Chicago	3,135,900
4	Philadelphia	2,736,000
5	San Francisco-Oakland-San Jose	2,223,600
6	Boston	2,115,500
7	Dallas-Ft. Worth	1,757,700
8	Detroit	1,726,700
9	Washington, DC	1,718,600
10	Houston	1,483,200
11	Cleveland	1,445,100
12	Atlanta	1,421,300
13	Tampa-St. Petersburg	1,357,700
14	Minneapolis-St. Paul	1,355,000
15	Miami-Ft. Lauderdale	1,326,100
16	Seattle-Tacoma	1,311,600
17	Pittsburgh	1,156,800
18	St. Louis	1,111,600
19	Denver	1,048,400
20	Phoenix	1,029,900
21	Sacramento-Stockton	1,025,600
22	Baltimore	945,700
23	Hartford-New Haven	911,400
24	Orlando-Daytona Beach-Melbourne	909,100
25	San Diego	906,400
26	Indianapolis	873,800
27	Portland, OR	814,900
28	Milwaukee	773,400
29	Kansas City	763,500
30	Cincinnati	752,000
31	Charlotte	744,100
32	Nashville	711,900
33	Columbus, OH	690,600
34	Raleigh-Durham	683,000
35	Greenville-Spartanburg-Asheville	650,900
36	New Orleans	641,700
37	Buffalo	614,300
38	Memphis	609,600
39	Grand Rapids-Kalamazoo-Battle Creek	604,500
40	Oklahoma City	600,000
41	Salt Lake City	597,700
42	San Antonio	588,800
43	Norfolk-Portsmouth-Newport News-Hampton	577,000
44	Harrisburg-York-Lancaster-Lebanon	564,400
45	Providence-New Bedford	559,600
46	West Palm Beach-Ft. Pierce-Vero Beach	533,800
47	Louisville	530,400
48	Greensboro-Winston Salem-High Point	522,200
49	Birmingham	518,600
50	Charleston-Huntington	511,900

51	Dayton	506,300
52	Albuquerque	506,000
53	Wilkes Barre-Scranton	492,400
54	Albany-Schenectady-Troy	491,500
55	Jacksonville	474,300
56	Tulsa	471,300
57	Little Rock	461,200
58	Flint-Saginaw-Bay City	453,700
59	Fresno-Visalia	437,700
60	Wichita-Hutchinson	431,500
61	Mobile-Pensacola	419,000
62	Toledo	414,500
63	Richmond	410,800
64	Knoxville	402,800
65	Shreveport-Texarkana	389,600
66	Green Bay-Appleton	388,400
67	Des Moines	387,500
68	Roanoke-Lynchburg	376,300
69	Syracuse	373,600
70	Portland-Poland Spring	369,700
71	Omaha	363,400
72	Austin, TX	362,900
73	Lexington	358,800
74	Rochester, NY	354,100
75	Springfield-Decatur-Champaign	342,600
76	Paducah-Cape Girardeau-Harrisburg-Marion	332,800
77	South Bend-Elkhart	321,600
78	Spokane	321,300
79	Davenport-Rock Island-Moline: Quad City	316,400
80	Tucson	313,900
81	Chattanooga	310,800
82	Cedar Rapids-Waterloo-Dubuque	308,500
83	Springfield, MO	308,500
84	Bristol-Kingsport-Johnson City: Tri Cities	307,100
85	Huntsville-Decatur-Florence	302,500
86	Las Vegas	300,600
87	Columbia, SC	300,300
88	Jackson, MS	293,500
89	Johnstown-Altoona	285,800
90	Madison	280,100
91	Youngstown	277,000
92	Evansville	264,500
93	Ft. Myers-Naples	260,600
94	Baton Rouge	254,100
95	Greenville-New Bern-Washington	252,900
96	Waco-Temple-Bryan	249,000
97	Springfield, MA	246,100
98	Lincoln-Hastings-Kearney	243,900
99	Burlington-Plattsburgh	241,600
100	El Paso	237,700

SOURCE: The Arbitron Company, *ADI Market Rankings 1990–1991.*

Figure 2.   Sample Page from A.C. Nielsen's Pocketpiece

Nielsen NATIONAL TV AUDIENCE ESTIMATES   **EVE.THU. JAN.3, 1991**

TIME	7:00	7:15	7:30	7:45	8:00	8:15	8:30	8:45	9:00	9:15	9:30	9:45	10:00	10:15	10:30	10:45
HUT	61.0	62.1	62.6	63.9	65.5	66.5	66.0	65.9	65.9	65.8	65.8	63.5	62.9	61.7	60.4	58.9	56.3

ABC TV

PRIMETIME LIVE →

	8:00	8:15	8:30	8:45	9:00	9:15	9:30	9:45	10:00	10:15	10:30	10:45
HHLD AUDIENCE% & (000)	11.0	10,240		11.4*	7.8	8.6*	7,260	7.9*	9.4	8,750		9.5*
74%, AVG. AUD. 1/2 HR	14.5	10.7*				10.9	7.7*	7.7*	13.5	9.3*		16*
SHARE AUDIENCE %	17	16*		17*		12	12*	12*	16	15*		16*
AVG. AUD. BY 1/4 HR	10.7	10.7	11.7	11.2	8.1	8.1	7.4	7.9	9.2	9.4	9.8	9.2

← FATHER DOWLING MYSTERIES →   ← GABRIEL'S FIRE (R)(PAE) →   ← KNOTS LANDING →

CBS TV

	8:00	8:15	8:30	8:45	9:00	9:15	9:30	9:45	10:00	10:15	10:30	10:45
HHLD AUDIENCE% & (000)	8.2	7,630		8.3	7,730	8.6*	8.3	7,730	14.1	13,130		14.1*
74%, AVG. AUD. 1/2 HR	10.3	10.7*		12.7	8.1*	13*	10.0	7.9*	16.9	14.1*		24*
SHARE AUDIENCE %	12	13		13	12*	13*	13	12*	24	23*		24*
AVG. AUD. BY 1/4 HR	8.6	7.8		8.1	8.7	8.5	7.7	9.0	13.8	14.3	14.0	14.2

TOP COPS (R)   FLASH (R)   CHEERS   WINGS   DOCTOR, DOCTOR   ← L.A. LAW →

NBC TV

	8:00	8:15	8:30	8:45	9:00	9:15	9:30	9:45	10:00	10:15	10:30	10:45
HHLD AUDIENCE% & (000)	20.0	18,620		20.1	18,710	24.4	18.1	16,850	15.8	14,710		15.7*
74%, AVG. AUD. 1/2 HR	23.3	30		22.4	30	27.4	20.6	29	19.6	15.9*		27*
SHARE AUDIENCE %	30	30		30	20.2	37	29	17.4	27	26*		15.5
AVG. AUD. BY 1/4 HR	19.1	20.9		19.9		24.2	18.9		15.9	15.9	15.9	

BILL COSBY SHOW   BLOSSOM PREVIEW   ← BEVERLY HILLS,90210 →

FOX TV

	8:00	8:15	8:30	8:45	9:00	9:15	9:30	9:45
HHLD AUDIENCE% & (000)	11.5	10,710		6.5	6,050	5.1	4,750	5.4*
74%, AVG. AUD. 1/2 HR	13.4	18		7.5	10	7.5	4.8*	5.9*
SHARE AUDIENCE %	17			10	6.1	8	7	5.5
AVG. AUD. BY 1/4 HR	11.0	12.0		6.8		4.9	4.8	

SIMPSONS   BABES (R)

INDEPENDENTS (INCLUDING SUPERSTATIONS EXCEPT TBS)

	7:00	7:45	8:15	8:45	9:15	9:45	10:15	10:45
AVERAGE AUDIENCE %	14.3 (+F)	15.2 (+F)	5.6	6.1	6.2	6.7	9.8 (+F)	8.5 (+F)
SHARE AUDIENCE %	23	24	8	9	9	11	16	15

PBS

	7:00	7:45	8:15	8:45	9:15	9:45	10:15	10:45
AVERAGE AUDIENCE %	2.1	2.4	3.2	3.7	2.9	3.0	2.0	1.9
SHARE AUDIENCE %	3	4	5	6	4	5	3	3

CABLE ORIG. (INCLUDING TBS)

	7:00	7:45	8:15	8:45	9:15	9:45	10:15	10:45
AVERAGE AUDIENCE %	10.5	11.3	10.3	12.6	13.3	14.0	11.8	10.3
SHARE AUDIENCE %	17	18	16	19	20	22	19	18

PAY SERVICES

	7:00	7:45	8:15	8:45	9:15	9:45	10:15	10:45
AVERAGE AUDIENCE %	2.1	2.2	2.1	2.6	3.4	4.8	5.3	4.0
SHARE AUDIENCE %	3	3	3	4	5	8	9	7

U.S. TV Households: 93,100,000   For explanation of symbols. See page B.

Figure 3. Sample Page from A.C. Nielsen's Viewers in Profile Report
EASTVILLE

DAYPART SUMMARY	METRO HH		DAYPART TIME(ETZ) STATION	DMA HOUSEHOLD							DMA RATINGS																														PERCENT DISTRIBUTION					TV HH RATINGS IN ADJACENT DMA'S		
							SHARE			TREND		PERSONS												WOMEN							MEN							TNS	CHILD			MET	HOME DMA	ADJACENT DMA					
	RTG	SHR		RTG	SHR	IN MKT SHR	NOV 'XX	JUL 'XX	MAY 'XX	FEB 'XX	2+	12-24	12-34	18-34	18-49	21-49	25-54	35+	35-64	50+	18+	12-24	18-34	18-49	25-49	25-54	WKG	18+	18-34	18-49	21-49	25-49	25-54	12-17	2-11	6-11			#1	#2	#3	#1	#2	#3
	1	2		7	8	9	10	11	12	13	15	17	18	19	20	21	22	23	24	25	26	27	28	29	31	32	34	35	36	37	38	39	40	41	42	43	44	45	46	47	48	49	50	51
			MON.-FRI. 3:00P-5:00P																																									
	1	2	WAAA I	1	2	3	2		3	5								1	1	1	1																47	98	2					
	13	39	WBBB A	11	35	46	36	41	38	34	6	6	6	6	6	6	6	7	6	8	10	10	10	9	9	9	6	3	2	2	2	2	3	5	1	1	62	98	1	1				
	5	14	WCCC C	4	13	17	15	10	11	16	2	2	2	2	2	2	2	3	2	3	3	4	3	3	3	3	2	1	1	1	1	1	1	2			59	95	4			1	
	3	9	WDDD N	2	7	9	13	13	13	14	1	1	1	1	1	1	1	1	1	2	2	2	2	1	1	1		1	1	1	1	1	1	1			70	96	4			1	
	2	6	WEEE IF	2	5	7	5	6	6	6	1	1	1								1													2	5	4	53	88	12			1	
	5	15	WFFF I	5	14	19	14	9	11	11	3	3	2	1	1	1	1	1	1		1	3	1	1	1	1	1	1	2	1	1	1	1	6	14	13	51	87	8	1	1	2		1
	1	3	WGGG P	1	2		2	2		2														1												2	1	80	100						
	2	6	CNN	2	7		NR	NR	NR	NR	1						1	2	2	2	1		1	1	1	1	1	1	1	1	1	1	1										
	1	3	USA	1	3			3	3	3																																	
	34		H/P/T.*	33		25	30	28	31	36	19	19	16	15	14	14	14	18	16	21	22	24	21	20	19	19	13	11	8	9	8	8	9	21	28	25								
			4:00P-6:00P																																									
	1	3	WAAA I	1	3	4	2		3	4	1							1	1	1	1						1										1	53	99	1					
	15	35	WBBB A	13	32	42	33	35	33	28	7	4	4	4	6	6	7	10	8	13	11	5	7	8	9	9	7	5	2	3	3	3	4	3	1	1	62	97	2	1		1	
	8	18	WCCC C	7	17	22	21	20	17	17	4	3	3	3	3	3	4	5	4	6	5	4	4	5	5	5	4	3	2	2	2	2	2	2	1		60	97	2			1	
	4	10	WDDD N	3	8	11	10	13	15	21	2	1	1	2	2	2	2	3	2	4	3	1	2	2	2	1	1	2	1	1	1	1	1	1			70	97	3			1	
	2	5	WEEE IF	2	5	6	5	6	6	6	1	2	1	1	1	1					1	2	1	1	1	1		1						3	5	5	51	86	13			2	
	6	14	WFFF I	6	14	18	14	9	11	10	4	5	3	2	2	2	1	1		1	5	2	2	2	2	1	1	2	2	2	1	1	8	15	17	52	88	7	3	1	3		1
	2	4	WGGG P	1	3		2	2	2	3				1									1								1			4	1	82	100						
	2	6	CNN	3	6		NR	NR	NR	NR	1		1	1	1	1	2	2	2	2	2		1	1	1	1	1	2	1	2	2	2	2										
	1	2	USA	1	2																	1												1									
	44		H/P/T.*	42		32	38	34	37	44	25	20	18	17	18	18	19	26	23	32	27	23	22	23	23	24	18	18	12	13	13	13	14	23	34	32								

xxvii

#1-NORTHVILLE   277,130   #2-WESTVILLE   671,840   #3-SOUTHVILLE   151,970

Figure 4. World Television Markets

Market	TV Households	Population	Color TV System
U.S.A.	91,000,000	251,000,000	NTSC
China (PRC)	81,000,000	1,100,000,000	PAL
Japan	40,000,000	124,000,000	NTSC
Germany	24,000,000*	78,000,000	PAL/SECAM
Brazil	22,000,000	154,000,000	PAL
United Kingdom	21,000,000	57,000,000	PAL
Italy	20,000,000	58,000,000	PAL
India	20,000,000	833,000,000	PAL
France	20,000,000	56,000,000	SECAM
Spain	11,000,000	40,000,000	PAL
Argentina	10,000,000	33,000,000	PAL
Mexico	9,500,000	88,000,000	NTSC
Canada	9,500,000	27,000,000	NTSC
Netherlands	5,500,000	15,000,000	PAL
Australia	5,000,000	17,000,000	PAL
Colombia	4,500,000	32,000,000	NTSC
Belgium	3,500,000	15,000,000	PAL
Chile	3,500,000	13,000,000	NTSC
Venezuela	3,000,000	20,000,000	NTSC
Greece	3,000,000	10,000,000	SECAM
Sweden	3,000,000	8,500,000	PAL

* Does not include TV households in East German; no reliable statistics available.

SOURCES: TV Households figures, *TBI's World Guide 1990*; population figures, *World Almanac and Book of Facts 1990*. All figures rounded off to nearest 500,000.

NOTE: While they have large numbers of television viewers, the People's Republic of China and India are not generally recognized as significant markets for Western television programs because of language/cultural differences with the West.

Part 1

DISTRIBUTION SYSTEMS

$\boxed{1}$ Network Television

Domestic television programming is delivered in three principal ways: broadcast, cablecast, and direct to consumers in the form of videocassettes and videodiscs. Chapters 1 through 12 discuss the organization and structure of each of these distribution systems.

The first chapter in this distribution section deals with commercial network television. By definition, a television network is a group of television stations that carry the same program schedule to viewers; a network can reach national or regional audiences.

HISTORY

From a viewer's perspective, the differences between the three largest television networks—NBC, CBS, and ABC—are barely noticeable. Each supplies affiliates with a regular schedule of prime time, daytime, morning, late-night, news, and sports programming. With few exceptions, each network can be seen in every city and town in the U.S. And each is a giant corporation whose principal interest seems to be pleasing the largest possible audience—that is, supplying the largest possible number of desirable viewers to the advertisers who provide the networks with revenues and thus fund the programs. The newest network, Fox Broadcasting Company, is somewhat different: some of its programs are more adventurous than the offerings seen on the other networks, and because it is still new, it does not yet supply a full schedule. Fox is organized differently as well.

There are differences, however, in the history and the structure of each of the networks.

National Broadcasting Company (NBC)

When the television business began in the mid-1940s, NBC was in the best position to exploit the new medium. It was, after all, owned by RCA, the electronics manufacturer that pioneered the development of television studio equipment and led the industry in its manufacture of transmitters and home receivers. NBC made its first experimental television broadcast in 1931, and its first regularly-scheduled broadcasts in 1943.

Because it possessed the technology plus the stars who could bring their popularity from radio to television, NBC was able to build an affiliate network of local television stations more quickly than CBS or ABC. Its programs immediately reached a larger audience; this led to higher advertising rates, which in turn permitted innovation and expansion. NBC was the first network with a regularly-scheduled morning program (*Today*) and a late-night program (*Broadway Open House* and, later, *The Steve Allen Show*; the latter pioneered the now-familiar *Tonight Show* format). NBC was also an early leader in news and sports coverage. Many of its programs have been innovative, unusual, and especially appealing to specific demographic groups. If the network did not lead a particular time period, it frequently delivered a large number of viewers in a specific group. The police drama *Hill Street Blues*, which was especially strong among men and women aged 18–49, is one of many examples. NBC has also generated a wide range of risk-taking comedies: *Rowan & Martin's Laugh-In*, *Saturday Night Live*, and *Late Night with David Letterman*, for example. Largely as a result of the RCA connection, NBC's firsts include *Wide Wide World*, an early globe-trotting magazine series; first television coverage of the Oscar and Emmy awards; first color coverage of the World Series (September 28, 1955); and many other events. Nonetheless, NBC has historically been the number two network to CBS.

NBC operated as a unit of RCA until 1985, when RCA was sold to General Electric; RCA's unsuccessful ventures in the CED videodisc system and computer hardware had weakened the company. GE sold NBC's radio stations, and has since allowed NBC to expand into cable (CNBC, a partnership with Cablevision in SportsChannel, and other ventures).

Columbia Broadcasting System (CBS)

CBS radio went on the air in 1927 as the Columbia Phonograph Broadcasting System, but in less than two years, William S. Paley, whose father's cigar company had been advertising on the network, bought it. At the time, it was a fledgling organization, but Paley, Frank Stanton, and a team of talented executives built CBS into a strong competitor to NBC.

Heading into the television age, CBS had two big problems. First, because it had concentrated on the development of a color TV system, CBS had not applied for television licenses; as late as 1951, CBS owned just one TV station. Second, it lacked the star power of NBC. In a remarkable series of tactical maneuvers (CBS lawyers came up with a capital-gains-tax loophole as part of an inducement for stars to sign with the network), Paley lured many successful shows and performers from NBC radio, notably Amos n' Andy, Jack Benny, Red Skelton, and Burns & Allen.

CBS became television's "Tiffany network": consistently profitable, well-managed, and classy. CBS nurtured its reputation as the network where the biggest stars could be seen (Lucille Ball, Jackie Gleason,

Danny Kaye, Arthur Godfrey, Carol Burnett). It was also the network of Edwin R. Murrow, Walter Cronkite, and a powerful group of CBS News correspondents—and of Captain Kangaroo, for years the most popular personality in children's television.

In its long history, CBS has never been especially lucky with television or video technology. Its attempts at developing a color television standard were costly and, despite its technical superiority over competing systems, the CBS color standard was not adopted. CBS also developed some early home video recorders and other devices that appeared promising but did not result in profitable products. (The technical strength of CBS was in audio; CBS engineers developed the long-playing record album, a standard for more than two decades.)

Strictly speaking, CBS is the only network that has not changed hands. Real control of CBS has shifted, however; the network was taken over in 1986 by a large stockholder, Laurence Tisch. In the Tisch era, CBS has concentrated only on broadcasting. CBS Records was sold to Sony in 1988 for $2 billion; the magazine group was sold to the company's president, Peter Diamandis, who formed Diamandis Communications. Other non-broadcasting ventures have been sold or scrapped.

American Broadcasting Company (ABC)

ABC was formed as a result of a Justice Department ruling that required NBC to divest itself of one of its two radio networks—NBC Red or NBC Blue. Since NBC Blue was the weaker network, it was sold in 1943. The buyer was Life Savers magnate Edward J. Noble, who came into broadcasting at a time when his competitors were diverting radio profits to build expensive television stations. Lacking stars, programs, and cash, Noble carefully managed his resources and focused on building television stations in five major markets: New York, Los Angeles, Chicago, San Francisco, and Detroit.

Building the stations was financially draining, but building an entire network was simply beyond Noble's capability. In 1951, after being romanced by CBS (which wanted ABC's stations but planned to disband the network), Noble sold ABC to United Paramount Theatres—the theater chain resulting from an antitrust divestiture by Paramount Pictures. Leonard Goldenson, a Paramount executive, took charge.

Throughout its first two decades, until the early 1970s, ABC struggled to remain afloat. The network had fewer affiliates than CBS or NBC, so it reached a smaller audience, and received a smaller share of advertising revenues. This difficult condition forced ABC to innovate, so ABC has a proud tradition of notable firsts. ABC was the first to look to Hollywood, mostly for programming produced on film—specifically, to Warner Brothers for *77 Sunset Strip, Maverick,* and *Cheyenne,* and to the Disney studio for *The Mickey Mouse Club* and *Disneyland* (the latter, which shifted to NBC in 1961, was later known as both *Walt Disney's Wonderful World of Color* and *The Wonderful World of Disney*). ABC's move prompted NBC to begin a long relationship with Universal, while CBS started working with all of the film studios. ABC also leaned heavily on gimmicky exploitation shows (*Batman*), low-cost sports coverage (*Wide World of Sports*), late-night rock concerts in the 1970s (*In Concert*), and new forms, like the mini-series (*Roots*). By the mid-1970s, ABC had developed a sufficiently strong schedule to woo a number of affiliates and finally gain parity with CBS and NBC. Since then, ABC has built up its once cash-poor sports and news divisions to compete successfully against CBS and NBC's traditionally well-funded operations.

ABC has always seen itself as a media company with interests in more than broadcasting. ABC has been a leader in magazine publishing for decades, particularly with trade magazines and special-interest consumer publications. The company has been periodically successful in the record industry (Impulse!, a jazz label, and Dunhill, home of the Mamas and the Papas), and has dabbled in the movie business (*Fort Apache: The Bronx*). ABC has also been active in cable, first as an investor in, and subsequently as the principal owner of, ESPN. It is also a partner with Hearst and NBC in the Lifetime and A&E cable channels. Other investments include a minority stake in several production companies outside the U.S.

ABC was the first of the three networks to change hands in the 1980s. The transition was a friendly one, prompted by a need to find a successor for Leonard Goldenson and a desire to expand the financial base. Capital Cities Communications merged with ABC in 1985; like ABC, Capital Cities owned television stations, and a wide range of publishing operations. In connection with the merger, stations were sold to comply with FCC regulations.

Fox Broadcasting Company (FBC)

In the 1950s, there were four networks: CBS, NBC, ABC, and DuMont. It is clear in retrospect that only two or three could survive, mainly because of the limited availability of VHF stations in major markets. DuMont lasted until 1955, largely because of the success of several major market stations, including New York's Channel 5 (then WNBD). After the national network folded, DuMont's station group was purchased in 1959 by John Kluge, who renamed the group Metromedia (flagship WNBD became WNEW, again the most important station in the group, still on Channel 5). In 1985, the Metromedia stations were sold to Rupert Murdoch, and became the Fox station group (WNEW became WNYW). This group reached approximately 20 percent of television households, and became the basis for the new Fox network.

Fox went on the air on October 9, 1986, with *The Late Show Starring Joan Rivers.* The show received much publicity, but it was not successful. Other low-cost programs followed as the network found its way. Seeking to attract young-adult viewers, the network had hits with *Married . . . With Children,* a sitcom that painted a cynical picture of

American family life, and *America's Most Wanted,* a reality-based show that encouraged viewers to call in with tips and help catch fugitive criminals. A later success was the animated series *The Simpsons.* By 1991, the Fox network had built up from a small block of Sunday-night programs to five nights of programming per week, plus a block of children's shows on weekday afternoons.

Fox Broadcasting Company is part of Twentieth Century-Fox, which is a division of Rupert Murdoch's international media conglomerate The News Corporation, Ltd. FBC does not own anything besides the network itself; sister companies operate the station group (Fox Television Stations), the movie studio (Twentieth Century-Fox), the television production operation (Twentieth Television) and other ventures (a home video label, Deluxe Laboratories).

Though Fox functions as a network and is commonly referred to as such, as of early 1991 the organization was not officially considered a network as defined by the FCC. From Fox's point of view, this is an advantageous situation: if Fox were a network under FCC rules, Twentieth Century-Fox might have to divest itself of its profitable syndication arm.

NETWORK STRUCTURE

ABC, CBS, and NBC are organized along similar lines, though specific policies, procedures, and reporting structures vary from one company to the next. Power has historically been shared between Los Angeles, where the programs are produced, and New York, where the advertising agencies and corporate headquarters are located. New York has lost considerable ground in the past two decades, and will probably continue to do so. Eventually, the networks may be headquartered in Los Angeles, with sales offices in New York.

Fox is a smaller organization, in part because it was created recently, and has not accumulated the large staff and wide variety of specialized departments that seem to grow with decades of operation. Also, Fox programs a limited schedule, without any news or sports. Fox is based in Los Angeles.

CBS Structure

CBS, Inc. is organized in nine divisions. Each of these is a part of the CBS Broadcast Group (the name is a holdover from the era when there was a CBS Records Group and a CBS Publishing Group). Ratings and research, network advertising and promotion, and program practices are handled at the group level; all other functions are decentralized.

CBS Entertainment is responsible for most (but not all) of the network's program schedule. This division supervises the development and production of original programs, acquires completed films, and schedules the programming. Departments include children's programming, comedy, drama, late-night, motion pictures for television, miniseries, and specials. A vice president oversees each area; he or she supervises a staff that includes one or more directors and managers who develop new programming and supervise current productions. The entertainment division operates as a self-contained organization, and includes a business-affairs group for negotiating agreements with producers, performers, and other key creative people. Casting and scheduling completes the department's list of responsibilities.

CBS News is responsible for several daily news programs, including the *CBS Evening News with Dan Rather, CBS This Morning,* and *CBS Morning News,* plus cut-ins (*CBS Newsbreak,* short newscasts seen between programs). The division also programs several prime time series (*60 Minutes, 48 Hours*) and provides special-event coverage (elections, crisis coverage).

CBS Sports, the other independent programming group, produces sports coverage (baseball, basketball, tennis, golf) and sports-information programs on weekends.

CBS Operations & Administration runs the technical and engineering side of the network, including all aspects of studio operations, union relations, and terrestrial and satellite distribution systems.

CBS Marketing is in charge of commercial advertising, setting rates, selling time, and devising special packages for sponsors. In an increasingly competitive advertising environment, more emphasis is now being placed on marketing tie-ins to other media and to consumer outreach programs.

CBS Affiliate Relations works directly with the 200-plus stations affiliated with the CBS Television Network. This division negotiates network compensation deals, develops promotions with affiliates, motivates affiliates to promote network programming, and encourages them to carry more of the network's total program schedule.

CBS Television Stations operates the five large stations owned by CBS (WCBS-New York, WCAU-Philadelphia, WBBM-Chicago, KCBS-Los Angeles, and WCIX-Miami). Each network-owned and -operated station ("network O&O") is managed locally, but certain key administrative, financial, personnel and programming issues are decided by, or with, the group's senior management.

CBS Radio operates 20 radio stations, plus several radio networks and a radio syndication business.

CBS Enterprises is responsible for international sales and licensing of programs owned by CBS, supervision of CBS's involvement in CBS/Fox Home Video, and co-ventures (including a studio lot in Los Angeles that CBS jointly owns with MTM).

ABC Structure

The structure of ABC is a variation on the same theme. The *ABC Television Network Group* is responsible at the group level for network advertising sales, affiliate relations, and public relations. In addition, the group oversees eight divisions.

ABC Entertainment programs prime time, and oversees daytime, children's, and late-night programming. An executive is in charge of these specialized genres, as well as of *ABC Early Morning Entertainment*, responsible for *Good Morning America*. Each subdivision is headed by a senior executive, with vice presidents, directors, managers, and supervisors responsible for the development of new programs and the guidance of those already on the air. ABC Entertainment also includes business affairs; broadcast standards and practices; and advertising and promotion.

ABC Sports, ABC News, and *Broadcast Operations and Engineering* parallel the CBS operations.

ABC Video Enterprises is more ambitious than its CBS counterpart; this group manages special-interest home video projects, as well as ABC's participation in Lifetime (33 percent ownership), A&E (38 percent), and ESPN (80 percent). Video Enterprises is also charged with finding opportunities in a changing technological and global marketplace. Investments in this vein include a 50 percent interest in Tele-Munchen GmbH, a production and distribution company in Germany, plus minority interests in production companies in France (Hamster Productions) and Spain (Tesauro S.A.).

Capital Cities/ABC-owned television stations, the radio stations, and radio networks are part of the *ABC Broadcast Group*. ABC's TV O&O's are WABC-New York, KABC-Los Angeles, WLS-Chicago, WPVI-Philadelphia, KGO-San Francisco, KTRK-Houston, WTVD-Durham-Raleigh, NC, and KFSN-Fresno.

Both Capital Cities and ABC, prior to their merger, were heavily involved in various publishing businesses; these operations continue within the Publishing Group. Fairchild Publications does trade newspapers and magazines (notably *Women's Wear Daily*), while ABC Publishing produces special-interest consumer magazines (Schwann catalogs, *Personal Publishing*, various *COMPUTE!* magazines) plus trade publications. Other ABC publishing ventures include *Institutional Investor* and *Practical Homemaker*.

NBC Structure

The National Broadcasting Company, Inc., includes *NBC Entertainment*, which is responsible for all programming other than news and sports; the *NBC Television Network*, whose responsibilities include both advertising sales and affiliate relations; *NBC News; NBC Sports; Operations and Technical Services; Personnel & Labor Relations; Corporate Communications* (which covers advertising and promotion for the programs and the corporation); *Business Affairs*; and *Television Stations*. Some of these are organized as distinct subsidiary companies, run by presidents, while others are divisions within NBC. The NBC station group includes

WNBC-New York, KNBC-Los Angeles, WMAQ-Chicago, WRC-Washington, DC, WKYC-Cleveland, and WTVJ-St. Petersburg, FL.

NBC Cable & Business Development includes the international sales group and supervises the network's involvement in Cablevision, CNBC, SportsChannel, and other ventures.

Fox Structure

The Fox Broadcasting Company (FBC) is structured to reflect the same basic list of responsibilities—the principal difference is one of scale. In fact, Fox is organized more like a cable network than ABC, CBS, or NBC. A senior executive is in charge of each aspect of the operation: programming, finance and administration, publicity and corporate creative services, on-air promotion, research, business affairs, and affiliate relations.

The Fox station group comprises WNYW-New York, KTTV-Los Angeles, WFLD-Chicago, KDAF-Dallas, WTTG-Washington, DC, KTSU-Salt Lake City, and KRIV-Houston.

HOW A PROGRAM GETS ON THE AIR

The networks provide programming only for certain parts of the day. Early-morning and sports programs are generally developed and produced inside the networks, though there are some exceptions in sports. News programs are also developed and produced internally.

Daytime, prime time, and children's programs are produced more often by independent production companies than by the networks themselves. A small number of established companies typically supply the network programmers in charge of each of these areas. For example, Mark Goodson Productions and Merv Griffin Enterprises dominate game shows; the television divisions of the motion picture studios, and a small number of unaffiliated suppliers, dominate action/adventure in prime time. The networks are also actively involved in daytime production; ABC, for example, produces all four of its daytime dramas (*All My Children, One Life to Live, General Hospital,* and *Loving*). The ways in which programs are developed, financed, and produced are discussed in detail in Part 4. The limitations on network production, due to the financial interest rules, are described in Chapter 14.

CHANGES IN NETWORK TELEVISION

From the late 1940s until the late 1970s, the three networks were essentially "the only game in town." Network programming dominated viewership, with public television and one or two independent stations only occasionally providing significant ratings competition.

The real product of the networks is not programs, but people: the networks earn money by delivering the largest possible audience of desireable viewers to advertisers. The greater the number of desireable viewers, the higher the advertising rate can be. For a prime time series, the average cost of a single network 30-second spot is $120,000 (in fact, spots are not sold singly; see Chapter 35 for a complete explanation of advertising on network television). One half-hour program is likely to include at least eight spots, for a total approaching $1,000,000. The daytime commercial load is even heavier. The production cost of a half-hour program in prime time is currently up to $600,000, but this cost can be divided in two because many prime time network programs are run twice. Therefore, the gross profit per half hour is likely to be roughly $700,000. Even after the deduction of network overhead and other expenses, selling advertising time on network television should be very profitable.

The total network share of national television advertising spending, however, has been dropping steadily since 1980. In 1979, the networks received 61.5 percent of national revenues; by 1987, the percentage had dropped to 51.2. At the same time, the networks' combined prime-time audience share has steadily dropped from 93 percent in 1977 to 89 percent in 1980, to 74 percent in 1985, to 71 percent in 1987, and to 65 percent in 1990.*

NBC, CBS, and ABC each earned more than $1 billion in 1971, which rose to over $2 billion in 1983. By 1985, however, the picture began to change. CBS lost money in the first quarter of 1987 (for the first time in the history of the company), and ABC came short of breaking even for the same year.

What happened?

The short answer given by network executives was increased program costs, and certainly this was a small part of the reason for the change. The long answer is more complex, and not yet understood completely. By the mid-1980s, independent stations, cable, and home video were drawing significant numbers of viewers away from network programs. The networks, scared by this trend and anxious about showing profitability, responded by moving and canceling series apparently at random, alarming producers and confusing viewers. Where commitments of more than a dozen episodes were once common for new series, one, two, three, or four episodes were now being ordered, and then aired in a manner which assured that viewers who enjoyed the program would have to search the schedule to find the same program again.

At about this time, each of the networks changed hands. The new owners, operating in a financial environment where short-term profits mattered more than long-term growth, have trimmed budgets wherever possible. At the same time, Fox and the cable networks have attracted talented producers, writers, and performers who might otherwise have appeared on network television.

---

* Source: Veronis, Suhler & Associates, *Communications Industry Forecast*, p.32.

To shore up their operations for the future, ABC and NBC have invested in other television operations. CBS is already in home video and, depending upon what happens with its ownership, the network may expand to other areas in the future.

Still, the fundamental question remains. In a fast-moving television business, how long will these dinosaurs survive? Already, in households that receive television through a cable system, the combined share of viewing for ABC, CBS, and NBC is roughly 46 percent, versus 70 percent for non-cable households. What will happen when most cable systems offer 100 channels or more?

It seems likely that network shares will not increase in any significant way in the future. The networks are fighting hard to change the financial interest and syndication rules (see Chapters 3 and 14)—to increase their ownership stake in programs that they finance—and to become more active in distribution. With the cable networks becoming more powerful, drawing an ever-increasing audience share from the networks, ABC, CBS, and NBC will receive a smaller portion of the available advertising dollars. Cutbacks and more efficient operation will only reduce operating costs so far. Ultimately, the networks may have to substantially change their ways of doing business if they are to survive against the newer services.

2 | Local Television

The traditional system for the delivery of broadcast television signals to U.S. households is the local TV station. Licensed by the FCC to operate on assigned frequencies, as of 1990, 677 stations operated on the VHF band (channels 2–13) and 792 on the UHF band (channels 14–83).* (Noncommercial public television stations are discussed in Chapter 4.) In addition, 779 low-power TV (LPTV) stations were in operation.

The number of VHF licenses issued has been relatively stable over the years: since 1960, only 100 have been added, mostly in outlying areas. In the same period, the number of commercial UHF stations has increased from an all-time low of 75 to 448 stations.

STATION OWNERSHIP AND AFFILIATION

The most valuable asset of a local television station is its operating license. The primary responsibility of each station's general manager, in fact, is to protect and preserve that license, keeping it free from legal entanglements and challenges from the public that the station serves.

The initial burst of licensing came in 1947 and 1948; from October 1948 until July 1952, the FCC did not approve any new licenses, using the period to develop a plan for "fair, efficient and equitable" allotments. Most VHF stations were licensed in the ten years following 1952. The majority were started by local businesspeople, or by companies that already had interests in other local media. Many VHF television stations were outgrowths of local radio stations, completing local media empires—the *Chicago Tribune*, for example, started WGN ("World's Greatest Newspaper") radio and, later, WGN television. Other stations were intended, from the start, to be building blocks for national networks: WNBC in New York, WRC in Washington, WMAQ in Chicago, WKYC in Cleveland, and KNBC in Los Angeles have been network-owned and -operated stations (O&O's) since the start of the NBC television network. Some companies, such as Westinghouse, owned and operated radio stations in various cities; when television came along, they duplicated the pattern wherever competition for licenses allowed.

Many television stations are now owned by groups, and local ownership has diminished greatly. Stations were bought and sold in the

---

* Source: FCC, November 30, 1990.

1980s with a regularity that would have seemed impossible fifteen or twenty years earlier. Television stations are glamorous media properties, and they appeared to avoid the risk inherent in other entertainment-industry ventures, such as motion-picture production. The FCC also eased its rules on license transfers, specifically, the amount of time an owner must hold a property prior to sale. In the past, the minimum ownership period was three years, but that rule has been eliminated.

The rules regarding media ownership have changed several times since the 1940s. Current FCC regulations limit ownership in two ways. First, no single entity may own more than 12 TV stations (plus up to 12 AM and 12 FM stations). Second, regardless of the number of stations owned, no entity can own television stations whose cumulative reach totals more than 25 percent of the total U.S. population (see Chapter 14).

There are nuances to these rules, however. A UHF station is assessed at half the value of VHF stations for the percentage limit, so a single company could theoretically own UHF stations reaching 50 percent of the U.S, and still comply with the rules. Companies that are more than half-owned by minority groups can own up to 14 TV stations, with a maximum reach of 30 percent of total U.S. households.

FCC rules also restrict cross-media ownership. The owner of a newspaper cannot purchase a television or radio station in the same market. When Rupert Murdoch was assembling Fox's station group, for example, his company was required to sell the *New York Post* and the *Boston Herald* in order to own television stations in these cities. Murdoch's situation was a complicated one, with more twists and turns than the usual deal, but it does provide an example of the wheeling-and-dealing in local television ownership. First, Murdoch bought all of the Metromedia stations, including WCVB in Boston; since he also owned the *Boston Herald,* he sold WCVB to Hearst. In the winter of 1986, Murdoch purchased Boston station WXNE (Channel 25) for $25 million, and renamed it WFXT. Since he still owned the *Herald,* he petitioned the FCC for a waiver that would permit ownership of both a newspaper and a UHF station; after two years of work with the FCC and Congress, the petition was denied. Since WFXT was not doing too well, Murdoch sold the station for $2 million and a $10 million note, payable in five to seven years, plus a percentage of revenues over a negotiated minimum. The buyer was a group of private investors that also owned the Boston Celtics. (As of this writing, Murdoch still owns the *Herald.*)

The owner of a television station cannot buy a cable system in the same market, though such combinations that existed prior to July 1, 1984, may remain in effect.

Station Groups

Group ownership has become the dominant form of station ownership in the U.S.—and an increasing number of stations are owned by companies with holdings in other media. Post-Newsweek, for example, owns cable systems, the *Washington Post, Newsweek*, and other newspapers and magazines; it also owns the television stations WFSB-Hartford, CT, WJXT-Jacksonville, FL, WPLG-Miami, and WDIV-Detroit. Allbritton owns small newspapers, as well as television stations WJLA-Washington, DC, KATV-Little Rock, KTUL-Tulsa, WCIV-Charleston, and WSET-Lynchburg, VA.

Viacom owns television stations, cable systems, cable networks, a program production and distribution company, and a library of programming. Act III Broadcasting owns television stations and magazines, producing motion pictures as well. Disney began a station division with its purchase of KHJ in Los Angeles (now KCAL); Paramount also owns stations.

Group W, a division of Westinghouse, is among the few powerful station groups that have used their major market stations (WBZ-Boston, KYW-Philadelphia, KDKA-Pittsburgh, KPIX-San Francisco, and WJZ-Belmont, NC) to launch national programming. *Evening Magazine* started as a creative collaboration between Group W stations that shared stories and other resources while producing each episode locally in their own markets. The system proved successful; the format, including rights to air stories produced by other stations, was syndicated to non-Westinghouse stations nationwide as *PM Magazine*. Support from Westinghouse stations also helped to launch and sustain *Hour Magazine, The Mike Douglas Show*, and other offerings from Group W Productions, a sister company.

Tribune Broadcasting owns stations, and is also in the syndication business.

The broadcast networks also own stations, assuring clearances for network programs in all time slots and in critical markets (see Chapter 1 for a more detailed explanation of network-owned and -operated stations, or network O&O's).

Station groups vary in the control and direction of their individual stations. For example, some central offices negotiate with syndicators on a group-wide basis; others encourage individual station management to make decisions based on local market conditions. In theory, general managers in station groups are encouraged to work together, sharing information about programming and personnel; in practice, this happens only on occasion.

Network Affiliation

The relationship between the networks and local television stations is based upon compatible needs. The networks must reach as many households as possible, and this is best accomplished with a network of affiliated stations in every television market. The local stations need programming, which the networks supply without a requirement for direct cash payment.

The *quid pro quo* between the network and its affiliate works as follows. The network provides a schedule of programs, with national or regional commercials included, as well as financial compensation for the airtime. The programs are offered to the affiliate, but if the affiliate chooses not to clear the time to run every program, then another station in the market may secure a clearance for that program (the transaction is often instigated by a competitive station; the network is obligated to do business with the station requesting the program). Affiliates may choose to schedule programs as they deem appropriate, though the network's affiliate-relations department usually encourages stations to run programs in accordance with the network schedule.

The networks theoretically buy airtime from their affiliates, but the formulas used to determine the rates are arcane, and sometimes blatantly unfair. In larger markets, what the network pays is only a fraction of an affiliate's overall revenues, while in smaller markets, network compensation contributes as much as 25–30 percent of revenues. For ABC, CBS, and NBC, a typical network compensation or "netcomp" formula takes the following factors into account: the number of commercial minutes in the hour, and the ratio of those sold nationally versus those sold locally; the *daypart* (programming time of day), which takes into account the size and demographic profile of the audience; the size of the market; the relative strength in the station, versus others in the market; and the amount of time that the program occupies. Some programs are not treated in the regular netcomp formula, but have their own special arrangements—on *The Today Show,* for example, NBC affiliates keep the revenues from the first and third half hours, and NBC keeps the money made from advertising in the second and fourth. In the ten largest television markets, the total annual netcomp to each affiliate is likely to be less than $2 million. In smaller markets, the figure will be some hundred thousands of dollars a year, or even less. NBC and CBS each paid approximately $130 million to affiliates in 1990; ABC paid $110 million.

Affiliates of ABC, CBS, and NBC depend upon their networks for a national news feed, or national material used in local newcasts (see page 189). Typically, the network feed is now one of several sources, such as CONUS and other news-feed services, and the networks also share coverage on an ad-hoc basis.

The relationship between affiliates and the network is controlled by FCC regulations. Networks may not control the rates, nor may they represent their affiliates, for the sale of non-network time; this provision excludes network O&O's, of course.

Until 1989, by FCC rule, network affiliation agreements were renewable every two years. At that time, the FCC eliminated the two-year rule; there is no longer a limitation on the term of these agreements. This was done in order to strengthen the hand of local stations.

Network affiliation dictates an overall programming strategy for local stations. News is a large part of every network affiliate operation.

Besides news, most network affiliates program only a limited number of hours locally: a few hours on weekday mornings, several more in the late afternoons, and, if viewers show an interest, overnight. The most important slot is the 6:00–7:00 P.M. period that is usually devoted to news.

Most network television affiliations were established in the 1950s and early 1960s, frequently as an extension of a radio affiliation. Stations only occasionally changed affiliations. In the aggressive business climate of the 1980s, however, more affiliates changed allegiance than ever before.

Most affiliation changes are the result of an increase in one network's strength, and the desire of a station with a solid news operation to build on that success. In the mid- and late 1970s, ABC, as the number one network, improved and expanded its affiliate lineup this way, stealing some affiliates away from NBC and CBS. When NBC became the number one network in the late 1980s, it, in turn, was able to entice some ABC affiliates to join. For example, in 1988, NBC dropped its UHF affiliate in Knoxville, Tennessee—WTVK—in favor of the CBS affiliate, the VHF station WBIR. The following year, NBC said goodbye to WROC-Rochester, NY (a 40-year affiliate of the network), to take on the area's CBS affiliate, WHEC.

Events that took place in Miami and West Palm Beach in the late 1980s provide an exaggerated example of the changes in affiliation patterns. The excitement began when Wometco sold its station group—including the CBS affiliate in Miami, WTVJ—to the investment firm of Kohlberg, Kravis, Roberts. Hoping to increase the coverage of its station group, CBS offered to buy WTVJ, but its $170-million offer was rejected, in large part because Lorimar-Telepictures had offered $405 million (that deal was not consumated). CBS then bought Miami's independent WCIX for $59 million; to assure coverage in Miami's northern suburbs, the network also convinced WPEC-Palm Beach, an ABC affiliate, to switch its affiliation to CBS. WTVX, the former CBS affiliate in Palm Beach, became an independent. NBC, in the meantime, purchased WTVJ, still the CBS affiliate, for $270 million. For several months, NBC was operating a CBS station until its agreement ran out. WSVN, the former NBC affiliate, in due course became the Fox station in Miami. WPBF, a new UHF station, became the new ABC affiliate in West Palm Beach. That station worked out a revolutionary arrangement with ABC: it waived its affiliate compensation and paid ABC for the right to carry the network's programming.*

Each network maintains approximately 200 affiliated stations. Fox is still building up; in 1989, there were 122 Fox affiliates, compared to ABC's 220, NBC's 207, and CBS's 193 stations.

---

* For more details, see "South Florida Merry-Go-Round" in Head and Sterling's *Broadcasting in America*, pp. 210-211.

Independent Stations

According to the 1990 INTV Census, there are 339 independent commercial stations currently on the air, although the figure includes Fox
affiliates (since the Fox network offers only a limited schedule, independent stations are generally grouped as "Fox indies" and "non-Fox
indies"). The total number has grown from 65 in 1970 and 115 in 1980
for two major reasons: the lower cost of equipment needed to start or to
improve a station, and an advertising base expanding by approximately
14 percent per year through the late 1980s. Strong cash flow attracted
significant investors to independent stations, particularly in the early
and mid-1980s. This created a larger, more vital market for syndicated
programming (see Chapter 3); syndicators were able to provide better
programs, which in turn attracted more viewers and fueled the expansion of independent stations nationwide.

Regardless of affiliation, independent stations have proven to be
an effective advertising and programming alternative to network affiliates. This is especially true in the late afternoon—when many indies
successfully program children's animation or sitcoms against high-
visibility talk shows and game shows on affiliates—and in late-night,
when many indies benefit from *The Arsenio Hall Show*. On weekends,
indies compete against the male-dominated network sports schedule
with movies.

Independent stations (Fox or non-Fox) do not command the advertising rates charged by network affiliates, but they operate on an entirely
different economic base. Indies build their schedules solely from syndicated product; Fox indies offer Fox's network schedule plus syndicated
product. A small number of independent stations produce their own
nightly news, but even in the largest markets, these undertakings are
usually limited to a single hour-long program per day. Many have long-
standing sports-coverage contracts with local teams. An independent
station can operate with a much smaller staff than can a network affiliate—particularly if it lacks a news department—and in most markets,
the indie's pay scale is lower than the scale at network affiliates (the
station's general manager may be an exception). As a result, an indie can
often make a profit even with low advertising revenues.

Spanish-Language Stations

Spanish-language stations generally operate as affiliates to a Spanish-
language network. There are three Spanish-language networks in the
U.S.: Univision, Telemundo, and Galavision. Local affiliates are predominantly cable channels, though most large Hispanic market support
at least one Spanish-language broadcast station.

Univision, the largest network, has over 500 affiliates—mostly cable systems and low-power television stations (see below)—and is headquartered in New York City. Univision's power is in its major-market

O&O's: WXTV-New York, KMEX-Los Angeles, WLTV-Miami, KUVN-Garland, TX (outside Dallas), KWEX-San Antonio, KLUZ-Albuquerque, KFTV-Fresno, KDTV-San Francisco, and KTVW-Phoenix. The combined reach of Univision's O&O's and affiliates is roughly 90 percent of Hispanic U.S. households.

Univision broadcasts 24 hours of programming each day from a Miami production center. Approximately half of this programming original, mostly produced in Miami; the other half is acquired from Venezuela, Argentina, and other Latin American countries. Local stations also produce their own programming. Univision is a subsidiary of Hallmark Cards, Inc.

Telemundo, the second largest Spanish-language network, is also based in New York City, and operates broadcast and production facilities in Hialeah (near Miami), Los Angeles, and Puerto Rico. Telemundo has six O&O's in the seven largest Hispanic markets: WNJU-New Jersey, KVEA-Los Angeles, WSCV-Ft. Lauderdale (reaching Miami), KVDA-San Antonio, KSTS-San Jose (reaching San Francisco), and KTMD-Galveston (reaching Houston). Telemundo also operates WKAQ-Puerto Rico, which is owned by Blair Television. In addition, the company owns K15CU, a low-powered station in Salinas-Monterrey which retransmits KSTS's signals. The Telemundo network's reach is approximately 80 percent of Hispanic U.S. households.

Telemundo broadcasts 65 hours per week; local stations fill in the rest with acquisitions from other Spanish-language sources, and sell block time to informercial ventures (see page 316) and other companies. Telemundo is seen on 21 broadcast affiliates and 10 cable-system affiliates, in addition to the network O&O's. Telemundo is owned by Reliance Holdings, led by investor Saul P. Steinberg.

Galavision is owned by Televisa, the Mexican television system (see page 390). Since the ownership is not American, the network is not allowed to own stations in the U.S. In operation as a cable television network since 1980, Galavision commenced broadcast operations with U.S.-owned Los Angeles and Houston affiliates in 1990.

Although advertisers are slowly discovering Spanish-language broadcasting as a means to reach an audience whose spending is on the rise, ratings do not provide especially detailed information on Hispanic viewing, so advertising rates are hard to set and enforce. Telemundo and Univision have invested $38 million in the development of a new Nielsen viewer-measurement system specifically for their target audience. The problem is complex: in most markets, Hispanic viewers regularly watch English-language shows, so their direct involvement with Spanish-language programming is vague and difficult to measure.

Other Types of Television Stations

A small number of stations operate as independents with non-traditional formats. In the 137 markets with fully independent stations, 29 stations broadcast predominantly religious programming, and 22 are home shopping channels.* The religious stations are self-supporting via contributions to a national service; effectively, they are direct-marketing tools for national or regional organizations. The Home Shopping Network (HSN) offers independent stations part-time and full-time affiliation, and pays a netcomp fee for the use of airtime. (For a detailed explanation of home shopping via television, see page 59.)

The FCC currently licenses approximately 800 low-power television (LPTV) stations, and has been adding 200 new ones each year. An LPTV station serves a very narrow geographic area. By definition, these operations are small in scale, with start-up costs in the $50,000–$100,000 range and a half-dozen people on staff. Most LPTV stations feed low-cost satellite networks to subscribers; programming consists mostly of religious shows, home shopping, music, and Spanish-language services. Local programs, if offered at all, are on the order of cable's public-access channels.

STATION OPERATIONS

Most television stations are organized along similar lines.

The General Manager, frequently a vice president of the company that owns the station, usually oversees day-to-day operations. The most important aspects of the job are guarding the station's valuable license and making revenues grow. The former requires positive relations with community instititutions and civic groups, and a judicious supervision of the station's news and other local programming. (Network programming is rarely inflammatory, whereas syndicated programs, notably talk shows, may require more attention.) The latter responsibility requires an understanding of the syndication marketplace as well as the ability to pick the right shows and schedule them in the proper time periods. This is most readily accomplished by supervising a skillful head of programming. The GM also works closely with the sales department (many GMs come up through the sales ranks) to set rates for the commercials and the time periods.

Most departments typically report to the GM. The *programming department* negotiates with syndicators, selecting and scheduling individual programs and series; it also develops and produces original programs. The *engineering* or *operations department* supervises the station's technical and maintenance staff; runs the studios, control rooms, master control (the control room responsible for assembling the air feed), and transmission facilities; and acquires new equipment. The *marketing* or *promotion department* handles on-air promotion, advertisements for the station's programming in other media, public relations, and special promotional tie-ins. At some stations, these functions are segregated into

---

* Source: 1990 INTV Census.

on-air and off-air departments. The *production department* —which is sometimes part of the programming department—may employ producers and directors, produce commercials for local advertisers, and schedule the non-news use of studio and editing facilities. The *sales department* manages the station's commercial inventory, sells local spots, and works with the station's rep firm (see page 23) to sell national spots. The sales department is often responsible for the *traffic department*, which prepares the commercial log; the log indicates to master control which commercials and programs to play and when to play them, and tells the billing department how to invoice advertisers. The *business* or *finance department* is responsible not only for traditional accounting functions, but for the overall financial operation of the station.

Each of these departments has its own manager, director, or vice president—titles are determined by the policies of the station group, or by local tradition.

Budget Overview

The following is a breakdown of how a typical network affiliate spends its money.

News is the biggest cost item, but is also the largest contributor of commercial revenues. In many of the top 50 markets, the cost of news is approximately 25 to 40 percent of the total operating budget. In "news-hungry" cities like New York and Washington, the figure may be higher; in 1989, stations in markets ranked 51 to 100 spent an average of 14.6 percent of their budgets on news.*

Upgrading technical equipment is an ongoing issue. New equipment becomes available every year, but most stations delay new purchases until they are essential. In the larger markets, stations upgrade their facilities to compete effectively against other stations. The network affiliate also needs non-technical equipment: cars for the sales staff, copying machines, and computers for the business, sales, and production departments. At a well-run station, capital costs should run approximately 5 to 20 percent of the annual budget, although these costs may be higher in the short run if the physical plant is seriously aging and in need of repairs or new equipment. An average of 7.5 percent of station expenses went for engineering costs in 1989.

Sales commissions and salaries cost a mature station about 10 percent of operating expenses.

As with the share of the budget that goes toward news, programming costs for network affiliates shrinks with market size. In the top 50 markets, the average is about 20 to 25 percent of operating expenses; in smaller markets, the average is in the teens. Programming costs cover payments for syndicated programs purchased for cash as well as original

---

* Source: National Association of Broadcasters.

non-news programming, though some stations include news costs in the budget category of programming.

The G&A (General and Adminstrative) budget pays the mortgage or rental of the physical plant; health and other insurance; salaries for the general manager and the business deparment staff; and other miscellaneous items. These outlays average 35 percent of total operating expenses.

The allocations are different for independent stations, mainly because the program hours are filled not with network programming (which is essentially provided at no charge), but with syndicated programs that must be acquired, either with cash or in exchange for commercial airtime. Although as much as half of an independent station's programming might be acquired by barter deals requiring little or no cash outlay (see Chapter 3), the typical balance is more like one-third barter, two-thirds cash acquisitions. The cash requirements for this type of operation are substantial: 55 to 60 percent of the total budget goes to program expense.

ADVERTISING SALES BY LOCAL STATIONS

A local station has one main source of income: the sale of commercial time, its advertising "inventory."

An independent station typically has the largest available inventory—up to about 8 minutes per half hour, or approximately 600 available 30-second spots (avails) every day. The cost of these spots is tied, in a general way, to ratings. The most popular shows generally command the highest rates, but this is not always the case. Sales managers exercise considerable flexibility over their inventory—they can price each spot according to market conditions, and they routinely change their prices.

The business of local television sales is not a matter of selling individual time slots to advertisers. Instead, it is a business of packaging large numbers of commercials in many time slots to allow sponsors to reach specific demographic groups—and/or to associate advertisers with specific types of programming. The objective is not simply to sell the current inventory, but to develop long-term client relationships with advertisers whose sales improve with television exposure.

Network affiliates operate in the same way, but overall, they have less time available for sale locally. Affiliates can sell only a minute or more per hour during those dayparts (such as early-morning) programmed by the networks. As a result, most of the affiliates' avails are in the dayparts that they program locally with syndicated programming or local news. A network affiliate's total weekday inventory is likely to be over 200 30-second spots.

A station's inventory is further reduced by barter transactions. In essence, a syndicator provides a program at no charge to the station, but trades for, or "holds back," some ad slots—say, 4½ of perhaps 6 or 6½ minutes of commercial time (the actual ratio may vary depending upon the program, and the deal). Many game shows and talk shows are offered by syndicators on a barter basis (see Chapter 3 for a more complete explanation of barter). Approximately 30 to 40 percent of an independent station's commercial inventory typically goes to pay for barter programming; for network affiliates, the number is lower, usually in the range of 15 to 25 percent.

The local sales manager takes charge of sales to local clients. Much of this activity is reactive: order-taking from established customers, presenting new packages based on well-known advertiser needs. Increasingly, stations are seeking out new business from customers who do not presently advertise on television at all. Local sales of commercial time accounts for 30 to 40 percent of a station's revenues, depending upon market size.

National Sales through Rep Firms

Regional or national advertisers who want to buy time in a local market work with a particular station's national sales representative, or "rep firm," to negotiate prices and time slots. Leading rep firms include Blair Television, Katz Communications, MMT Sales, Petry, Seltel, and Telerep. Reps work exclusively for one station in each market, and operate— in theory, at least—as extensions of the station's sales staff. The station's rep firm receives a call from an advertising agency whose client needs to buy time on a certain station. The rep firm then meets with the station's national sales manager to assemble a competitive package based on the dates, cost of the target audience, and dayparts that the agency wants to buy on its client's behalf. The agency and the rep firm negotiate, and the station receives an order.

Until the mid-1980s, rep firms and stations reacted to the national marketplace, and did not actively seek out new business. But nowadays, in an increasingly competitive advertising environment, national sales managers at local stations are taking a more active role with agencies and, in some cases, with clients. In a large market like Washington, D.C., roughly 30 to 50 percent of a station's sales of remaining inventory comes directly from national rep firms.

The rep firm typically charges a commission of 6 to 10 percent on each transaction; the advertising agency takes its cut of 15 percent from its client as well. The station receives its net after these deductions.

Rep firms do more than sell advertising time. They also advise their clients as to which syndicated programs are the most promising. For example, according to *Variety* (January 14, 1991), Katz Communications recommended that its clients 1) avoid new game shows, even if they allow viewers to play by phone; 2) be selective when choosing off-network sitcoms because of inflated prices and a flood of new shows in development; 3) stay with tried-and-true magazine shows and daytime talk shows; and 4) go with animation, the only promising new program area of the season.

Rates for Commercial Spots

Even within a single market, there is considerable variation in the cost of commercial spots. As a starting point, the cost is based on the number of people who see the show—or, more accurately, on a ratings service's estimate of viewership. In Washington, D.C. (a top-10 market), during slower times of the year, a spot on a daytime show may have cost under $100. But the cost of a spot on a Washington Redskins game aired in prime time might be as high as $10,000–$25,000. The price also depends upon the available inventory (and how anxious the sales manager is to sell off the time), the prices charged by the competition, the size of the overall package and its component parts, the anticipated ratings, and the skill of the sales staff.

Stations vary in their annual gross sales of commercial time, from year to year and from market to market. In a top 10 market like Washington, a network affiliate might gross about $40–$60 million, and an independent, about $15–$50 million. In a smaller market, like Nashville, a network affiliate might gross $20–$25 million, and an independent, $8–$10 million.

3 | Syndication

Since the network schedule provides affiliates with only about two-thirds of their program schedule, station programmers must produce or acquire programs to fill the remaining hours. Some of this time is filled with local programs, particularly news, but affiliates acquire three to five hours per day of programming from television syndication companies—or even more, if the station is on all night. Fox affiliates and independent stations have even more hours to fill. Syndicators distribute three types of programs to domestic television stations: movie packages, off-network programs, and original productions.

HISTORY AND EVOLUTION OF THE
SYNDICATION BUSINESS

Syndication began in the radio era, as producers and marketers realized that programs could be sold directly to stations, without a network distribution system. The basic structure was established in the 1930s: salespeople called on local program directors, who purchased their wares on a market-exclusive basis.

One of the more successful radio program syndicators was Ziv, a Cincinnati firm that marketed up to 37 radio series (*Easy Aces, Bold Venture*). Ziv started purchasing movie footage for television syndication in the 1940s, negotiating for television and radio rights to properties such as *The Cisco Kid*. Ziv-TV became an active supplier in the 1950s by concentrating on two time periods that were not yet fully exploited by the networks: 7:30 P.M. and 10:30 P.M. Programs produced on film (*Sea Hunt, Whirlybirds, Highway Patrol*) and the first color film series (*Cisco Kid*) were at first considered risky by the networks, but they soon followed Ziv's lead into these formats. Ziv was unusual because it produced as well as distributed programs. In 1957, Ziv even sold a series to ABC, *Tombstone Territory*. In the 1950s, most other syndicators distributed programs that were repackaged movie product (*Little Rascals, Laurel and Hardy*).

By 1963, Group W Productions was in production with *The Mike Douglas Show,* a daytime format produced at the station group's Cleveland facility. *The Mike Douglas Show* stayed on the air until the early 1970s (in the interim, the show moved from Cleveland to the Group W station in Philadelphia). The talk/variety format was successful for

Group W, which subsequently distributed *The Merv Griffin Show, The David Frost Show,* and other programs. With Douglas, Group W successfully experimented with a new form of financing called barter syndication (see page 32). *Hee-Haw, Wild Kingdom,* and *The Lawrence Welk Show* are examples of another phenomenon—former network shows that continued production, but changed their form of distribution to syndication.

The present-day syndication business began to take shape in the early 1970s, when the FCC required the networks to divest themselves of their syndication businesses (see page 28). Viacom, the CBS spin-off, was immediately successful, mining a library that included *I Love Lucy, The Andy Griffith Show, The Honeymooners, The Twilight Zone, The Dick Van Dyke Show, The Beverly Hillbillies, Hawaii Five-O, Perry Mason, Hogan's Heroes, Gunsmoke, My Three Sons,* and other classics. ABC's spin-off, Worldvision, worked from a library that included *The Streets of San Francisco, The Fugitive* and, in the main, other properties from Quinn Martin Productions. NBC's spin-off company, MTA Syndication, ceased operations in the early 1980s.

These *off-network programs* have been extremely successful over a remarkably long term, especially Viacom properties like *I Love Lucy, The Andy Griffith Show,* and *The Honeymooners.* Among more recent programs, off-network sitcoms and dramas distributed by the larger firms have dominated. Such offerings include *Golden Girls* from Buena Vista; *The Facts of Life* and *Who's the Boss* from Columbia Pictures Television; *Charles in Charge, Kate & Allie,* and *Quincy* from MCA-TV; *Cagney & Lacey* from Orion; *Cheers, Taxi,* and *Family Ties* from Paramount; *M*A*S*H** from Twentieth Television; *The Cosby Show* from Viacom; and *Perfect Strangers, Dallas, It's A Living, Night Court,* and *Head of the Class* from Warner Bros. Most of these programs are sold to stations for cash (see page 000). By the mid-1980s, cash prices in a single market for multiple runs of syndicated hour-long shows had escalated to as high as $1,625,000 per episode (paid to MCA-TV for *Magnum, P.I.*).* Local stations responded by turning away from "hours" for several years, which allowed cable networks like The USA Network and Lifetime to buy off-network hours (*The Equalizer* and *Miami Vice* on USA; *Moonlighting, L.A. Law,* and *Cagney & Lacey* on Lifetime) at more reasonable prices. Broadcast stations showed signs of returning to hours as prices dropped below previous levels. Columbia Pictures Television's *Hunter,* for example, cost up to $375,000 per episode in the larger markets in 1989.

Off-network half-hour sitcoms are often sold for cash, and sometimes for a cash/barter mix (see page 33). For desirable properties, stations seem willing to give up some commercial time in exchange for the competitive edge that the program should provide. Selling more marginal shows, however, can be difficult. For example, Turner Broadcasting

---

* Source: Paul Kagan Associates.

sold *The Wonder Years* to only 20 percent of the country's local stations in the first six months—largely because many stations were reluctant to surrender commercial time for a program whose performance was not proven.

The market for first-run syndicated product was established largely as a result of another FCC action, known as the Prime Time Access Rule (see page 29). This regulation effectively required the networks to leave the 7:00–8:00 P.M. time slot open six nights a week. The action created an opportunity for light entertainment programs, particularly game shows, as well as news and entertainment-magazine programs. In the 1970s, game shows dominated, with small distributors financing new versions of classic shows (*Name That Tune*), or creating new evening versions of programs that were already on the network schedule ($10,000 *Pyramid* [which became $25,000 *Pyramid*, then $100,000 *Pyramid*, in syndication], *Family Feud, The Price Is Right*).

King World, best-known from the 1950s until the 1970s as the distributor of *The Little Rascals*, was the most aggressive supplier of programming for this time slot. Realizing that the 7:00-8:00 P.M. slot could deliver a large audience to national advertisers, King World executives identified *Wheel of Fortune*, which debuted in syndication in 1983, as the type of game show that could be successful. The concept eventually extended beyond simply distributing a game show, to developing a package strong enough to anchor the evening schedule. With *Wheel* sold to well over 100 stations (a higher "clearance," or rate of sale, than most game shows achieve), King World started work on a second half-hour, and sold *Jeopardy!*—which first aired in the 1984–85 season—as a mate to *Wheel*. Then King World started working on early-fringe (late afternoon), and placed *Oprah Winfrey* (formerly a local talk show on Chicago's WLS) on many of the *Wheel of Fortune /Jeopardy!* stations.

Programs that anchor schedules are called *franchise shows*, and they are the most valuable syndicated properties. Multimedia Entertainment's *Donahue* became an important morning program, and held its key position for several years in the late 1970s and early 1980s until competition eventually encouraged stations to move it to the afternoon. In first-run syndication, talk shows developed a more outrageous edge, and since they attracted larger audiences than most local talk shows could muster, many local shows were driven off the air. Multimedia capitalized on the *Donahue* success with a more intimate show, *Sally Jessy Raphael*; Paramount competed with *Geraldo*, and added *The Joan Rivers Show*; King World is a market leader with *Oprah Winfrey*. Buena Vista's *Live! with Regis and Kathy Lee* is not controversial, but it does well with those affiliates that have a network morning show lead-in. Each year, new competition attempts to gain the high level of clearances enjoyed by these top-rated programs.

Syndication is a copycat business—when a format works, several syndicators try to develop a similar property. Although no company has duplicated the success of Paramount's *Entertainment Tonight*, the "tabloid magazine" format originated by Fox's *A Current Affair* has been adapted by Paramount's *Hard Copy*, King World's *Inside Edition*, and other programs.

Syndication also presents entrepreneurial opportunities for programs that might not be easily sold in other television formats. Wide-ranging examples include *Lifestyles of the Rich and Famous* and *Star Search* from Television Program Enterprises; *Siskel & Ebert* from Buena Vista (lifted from a successful PBS series); wrestling programs from World Wrestling Foundation; *Benny Hill*, from DLT; *Tales from the Darkside* and *Monsters* from Tribune Entertainment; and *People's Court* and *The Love Connection* from Warner Bros. Some ideas—such as Paramount's *Star Trek: The Next Generation*—are less risky than others.

Some syndication companies have been more venturesome in creating original syndication product, notably Paramount Television (*Entertainment Tonight, The Arsenio Hall Show, Star Trek: The Next Generation*). Buena Vista Television, Warner Brothers Television, and MCA-TV have historically been active in first-run product as well.

Children's programs are considered a relatively specialized form, and only a half-dozen syndicators are regular suppliers in this area. Such programs, especially cartoon series, can be valuable franchises. The successful Disney Afternoon package (including *DuckTales, Chip 'n' Dale's Rescue Rangers*, and *Talespin*) is one example; *Teenage Mutant Ninja Turtles* from Group W is another. Newer series are generally tied into successful merchandising programs involving toys, apparel, and other products. Many cartoon series are perennials: *The Woody Woodpecker Show* and *The Flintstones* from The Program Exchange; *The Yogi Bear Show, The Jetsons*, and other properties from Hanna-Barbera, distributed by Worldvision Enterprises. The various MGM and Warner Brothers cartoons distributed by Turner Program Services, as well as *Merrie Melodies* from Warner Brothers, are consistent and predictable performers. The children-oriented late-afternoon time slot, traditionally 3:00–5:00 P.M. on independent stations, is now widening to 2:30–5:30. While this block is generally dominated by Disney and Warner, some smaller companies have broken through: Zodiac Entertainment, for example, with *Widget*. First-run animation series are risky start-ups, but licensing characters already established in some other medium can help to limit the risk. First-run live-action shows aimed at children are also risky for syndicators, but several game and variety shows have occasionally been successful (*Fun House* from Warner Brothers, subsequently a weekly Fox network show).

THE FINANCIAL INTEREST AND SYNDICATION RULES

The financial interest and syndication ("fin-syn") rules were adopted by the FCC in 1970. Imposed to limit the financial involvement of the broadcast networks in the programming produced for them, these rules severely limited the networks' in-house production of prime time programming (see page 116). Although they were liberalized in 1991, the fin-syn rules will continue to shape the television business for years to come.

The fin-syn rules resulted from network practices that were commonplace in the 1960s. In that era, before cable television and the proliferation of independent stations, the networks and their affiliates were the only national markets for television programming. Producers would supply the networks with programs, charging license fees that would cover production costs and provide a profit margin. But that was often the end of the story. Network practices used to severely limit the producer's opportunity to exploit his or her creative properties beyond the initial broadcast—the network either owned the program or controlled its distribution. Producers were forced to negotiate with the network for their share of revenues from reruns; the network did not even permit domestic syndication of current programs. Furthermore, even when off the air, the best series often remained in warehouses because the network believed that supplying quality programming to independent stations—potentially, the competition—was not in the best interest of the network or its affiliates.

When the fin-syn rules went into effect in 1972, the networks divested their syndication rights. CBS sold its rights in off-network programs to a new company called Viacom, and ABC did the same to start Worldvision. The rules did not entirely eliminate prime time production, or co-production, by the networks; even at their most stringent, the rules allow a limited number of hours per week. CBS, for example, co-produces *Rescue 911* with the independent Arnold Shapiro Productions, and ABC co-produced *Moonlighting* with Picturemaker Productions (both were small production companies unaffiliated with studios).

The networks have not given up easily. Ongoing negotiations with the production community, the FCC, and Congress led to a 1980 consent decree allowing the production of five hours of programming by the networks. This decree has now expired, and in theory, the networks may produce as much prime time programming as they please. In addition, they can syndicate the programs they produce in-house domestically and internationally; see Chapter 14 for further discussion of recent changes in the fin-syn rules. Nonetheless, the expense of producing programs for prime time has resulted in only only a modest number of network projects. As might be expected, the networks have demonstrated some prejudice toward their own productions when selecting programs for their prime time schedules.

THE PRIME TIME ACCESS RULE

The Prime Time Access Rule (PTAR), enacted by the FCC in 1971, limits network affiliates in the top 50 markets to three hours of network prime time programming from Monday through Saturday night—thus creating the 8:00–11:00 P.M. block known as prime time. A new daypart called *prime access*—7:00–8:00 P.M. in the East and West, 6:00–7:00 P.M. Central and Mountain Time—also came into being. The FCC rule was intended

> to make available for competition among existing and potential program producers, both at the local and national levels, an arena of more adequate competition for the custom and favor of broadcasters and advertisers.

The FCC sought to limit the networks' grip on the best viewing hours, to introduce diversity of program forms and content in a time period with enough viewers, and to encourage new producers and distributors to enter the television business. By and large, the rule succeeded in these goals. In a typical market in 1990, one station schedules a pair of game shows (*Wheel of Fortune* and *Jeopardy!*); another pairs a magazine show (*Inside Edition*) with a game show (*Family Feud*); a third, an independent, pairs a sitcom (*The Cosby Show*) with a magazine (*Entertainment Tonight*); and the fourth, usually the Fox station or an indy, programs sitcoms for a younger audience (*Head of the Class, Perfect Strangers*). The missing component—and the one long-term failing of the PTAR—is locally-produced programming during prime access. For most of the 1980s, Group W's *Evening Magazine* and *PM Magazine* combined a syndicated package with some local production, but less costly programs have since replaced the format.

The PTAR has some special provisions and exceptions. Since part of the idea was to open valuable time slots to local and independent production, the rule specifically prohibits the scheduling of off-network syndicated programs on network affiliates. It does, however, allow for network news and runovers of network sports coverage.

METHODS OF FINANCING SYNDICATED PROGRAMS

There are three financing formats currently in use in domestic syndication: straight cash, barter, and cash-plus-barter.

Straight Cash Syndication

"Straight cash" or "cash syndication" is the traditional financing format for syndication. It is fairly straightforward: the syndicator wants to license the program in each market for the highest possible price. This format is most often used to sell successful off-network series and movie packages, whose ratings performances are (at least in theory) predictable. For an A-quality movie package, the cumulative national sale per film would be in the range of $1 to $1.5 million (this varies, of course, depending upon the title selection). Approximately $200,000 would come from New York, with a like amount from Los Angeles, and about $80,000 for Chicago. Smaller markets account for the rest, in parcels of tens of thousands of dollars.

The numbers are much higher for some episodic programs. *Roseanne*, distributed by Viacom, provides a good example of what a top-rated network series can make in syndication. KCOP-Los Angeles, an independent, paid $75,000–$80,000 per week; WWOR-New York paid $60,000 per week. A station in St. Louis—the 18th largest television market—paid $20,000 per episode. The standard term of these deals is four-and-a-half years.

Cash Syndication, Step-by-Step

The following section moves through the process of cash syndication, tracing the way in which the syndicator licenses a program in each market for as much money as possible.

1. The syndicator negotiates with a producer, studio, or network for the right to syndicate a series. The syndicator's estimate of the revenues that the program will earn during the entire term of the agreement (appropriately discounted for the time value of money) is frequently the starting point for negotiations. If the series is an original production, or additional episodes for an existing series, then the syndicator's payment will be used to pay the production costs. A co-financing arrangement with another distributor, sometimes involving the sale of international rights, for example, may also cover some production costs.

2. Based on the cost of the property, and the costs of marketing and selling the program (see Item 7 below), the syndicator targets the amounts to be extracted from each market. The value of a program in New York or Los Angeles, for example, will be much higher than in Baltimore or San Diego.

3. The syndicator gives the sales force marketing materials consistent with a unified sales strategy (suggested time slots, anticipated viewership demographics). The sales staff is also presented with the budget targets, and the numbers that it must meet in order to succeed.

4. The company's senior executives visit several important station groups, and individual stations in large markets, to muster support for the series. Armed with commitments from (at best) a few of these stations, the syndicator's sales force then visits other groups and stations. If the property is especially desirable, groups and stations bid against one another, and can drive the price up higher than the syndicator's original estimate. More often, the program will suit the plans of only one or two stations in the market, and the sales person will negotiate with a head of programming for a group, or with the station's general manager or program director. Some shows could clear 40 percent of the country and be profitable; a good movie package typically clears about 60 to 70 percent of the country. For a first-run entertainment or game show,

the range is typically 50 to 70 percent of U.S. markets. To break even, the syndicator must get its asking price in the majority of these markets.

5. Marketing generally begins in the fall, with much of the activity centered around December, January, and February (sometimes, if a pilot or completed episodes are available, marketing will start in the summer). INTV (Independent Television Stations) and NATPE (National Association of Television Program Executives) both hold conventions in December or January, the principal purpose of which is to connect syndicators with television station executives. Marketing continues through the spring and early summer.

6. When a station makes a commitment to a syndicator's program, the fee takes the form of a limited license, with payments due annually over the course of the agreement, regardless of how well the program performs. The station's advertising sales force sells commercial time in the program, hoping to make a profit on the program purchase; the station may schedule the program as it sees fit.

7. The syndicator deducts a sales commission, typically 35 percent of gross revenues. The syndicator usually collects an additional 10 to 15 percent to cover the cost of marketing and distributing the program, including advertising and promotion, convention expenses, editing, videotape and film transfer costs, satellite costs, and a percentage of the company's overhead.

8. The program's producer or studio receives revenues after the syndicator recoups the advance plus marketing and some overhead. These dollars may be used to cover a production deficit, or for other company projects, or taken as profits. These net revenues result only from this one distribution of the program; there may be subsequent or ongoing syndication deals (or cable sales) in addition.

Here's how the numbers work, for an offering of a reasonably well-known off-network half-hour sitcom with 65 episodes (three seasons' worth, generally considered the minimum number of episodes for the purposes of national syndication):

Gross cumulative package selling price (all U.S. markets):	$40,000,000*
Syndicator's expenses (15 percent):	($ 6,000,000)
Syndicator's sales commission (35 percent):	($14,000,000)
Return to producer/studio on this distribution:	$20,000,000

Barter Syndication

The second and third financing formats both involve a trade, or barter, of the station's commercial time in exchange for programming. With the

---

* Approximate package selling prices: New York, $5,000,000; Houston, $1,200,000; Indianapolis, $10,000; Tulsa, $900.

straight barter method, no cash is paid by either party; in a mixed form called "cash-plus-barter," the station provides some cash and some commercial time.

Barter syndication is the preferred format for once-a-week shows, children's shows, and some daily strips (a *strip* is a group of five shows per week, usually airing Monday through Friday in the same time slot). Although the actual number varies by type of program, time slot, and station policy, many half-hour programs include 6½ minutes of commercial time. The syndicator typically sells roughly 5 or 5½ of these minutes, and the station sells the remaining 1 or 1½ minutes. A barter program is generally targeted to break even or better with a clearance of above 75 percent of U.S. households, and an average rating for the time period. With a higher clearance, or a higher rating, a barter program can be a very significant money-maker. On the other hand, if the clearance or rating falls below expectations, the program can cost the syndicator money (see page 37).

Cash-plus-barter is the format most often used for popular game, news/magazine, and talk-show strips. (It was also used successfully by Viacom in the distribution of *The Cosby Show*). The price, and the number of spots that the syndicator holds back, is determined by the program's popularity.

Companies That Sell Barter Time

The barter industry has created a new type of advertising sales company, one that does nothing but sell available time in syndicated programs to advertisers. These companies are typically owned by one or more syndicators, and handle sales for their owners, and sometimes for one or more other syndication companies. Camelot Entertainment Sales, for example, is the barter advertising arm of King World, but also sells advertising time for Buena Vista Television, Jim Henson Associates, and Western International Syndication. Premier Advertising Sales is a joint venture between Paramount and MCA. Tribune Entertainment is one of several companies that sells commercial time only in its own products.

Barter and Cash-Plus-Barter Syndication, Step-by-Step

1. The syndicator reviews proposals for original productions, joint ventures, and acquisitions. Most proposals are turned down on the spot because they are inappropriate for the syndication marketplace (stations are unlikely to put the program on the air); because they will not compete effectively (an original game show, for example, is less likely to succeed than one with an established name); or because they require further development. For those projects that seem viable, the syndicator estimates income potential.

This estimate of income potential is based on two figures: the number of markets that the program is expected to clear, and the anticipated rating (a national average of local ratings, generally keyed to a specific and desirable demographic group, such as women 18–34; see Chapter 34). These two figures allow the syndicator to determine the price that national advertisers are likely to pay for each barter spot. The number of spots held back by the syndicator (five, for example) is then multiplied by the price per spot to determine the total estimated revenues for the program.

2. If the numbers look promising, and the program has a serious chance of succeeding in a marketplace where severe competition is the rule, the syndicator commissions a demonstration tape ("demo"), or, in some cases, a full-scale pilot. A demonstration tape usually costs roughly $25,000–$75,000; a pilot costs between $100,000 and $300,000, sometimes even more. The syndicator generally pays the production cost for the entire pilot or demo. In recent years, launching a new syndicated program has become especially difficult, largely because successful shows occupy the most important time slots. Massive sums of marketing and promotion dollars must be spent to tell viewers about a new show—and with so many options available via cable, viewers tend not to support new syndicated programs. Because syndication launches have become risky ventures, alliances have developed between syndicators and producers, sponsors, and foreign television companies to help cushion the risk and strengthen the property.

3. Two selling operations occur simultaneously. The barter advertising sales force presents the pilot or demo tape to advertising agencies, who can commit their client's advertising dollars to the venture. The program sales force presents the program to stations and station groups. Stations are encouraged not only to clear the series, but to schedule it in a time slot with a high HUT level (Homes Using Television, a measure of the number of households viewing television at a particular time).

The selling period begins in late fall, continues through the two programming conventions, and through the winter and spring. The process has become stressful for syndicators because many stations tentatively commit to several shows, not making final decisions until plans are announced by the other stations in the market. The situation is especially sensitive with regard to clearances in New York, Los Angeles, and Chicago; it is difficult, if not impossible, to succeed in barter syndication without clearances and good time slots in all three markets. By summer, the fog clears—the marketplace has determined which programs will be a "go" for fall, and production commences.

4. Advertisers sometimes pay for the commercial time in advance, but the syndicator often serves as the bank, providing the money up front for production and marketing. The program goes on the air, presumably in a flurry of on-air promotion and supported by some print and radio advertising. If the cumulative national rating is equal to the syndicator's estimate, no further action is required. If the rating falls below the estimate, however, then the syndicator is required to

reimburse the advertiser for the difference—to repay the difference in cost between the higher estimated rating and the lower actual one. If the rating proves to be higher, then the syndicator did not properly estimate its level of risk, and the company must wait until the following year to negotiate a better price with its clients (presuming, of course, that the program's ratings remain at the same level, or better!). A risky arrangement indeed.

Since the risk belongs to the syndicator, so does much of the reward. Prior to the distribution of any payments to producers, or other third parties (such as the those with profit participation in the property), the syndicator deducts a fee, typically 35 percent of gross, plus about 10 to 15 percent in expenses. In addition, the barter advertising company— which frequently belongs to the syndicator—receives 10 to 15 percent of the revenues. The advertising agencies also take a deduction; their traditional fee for any media buy is 15 percent of the cost of the advertising time (payable by the advertiser). The syndicator will recoup the costs of the production, typically with overhead deductions and interest added. After all of these costs are deducted, the net is shared among the syndicator, who typically receives the largest share, and any third-party participants.

5. If the deal is cash-plus-barter, then the syndicator also collects a cash license fee from stations who clear the show. The cash received is then subject to some of the syndicator-related expenses described above (but not those costs associated with advertising, which is relevant only to the barter aspect of the deal).

How Barter and Cash/Barter Syndication Make Money

Although the actual numbers are certain to vary, the following model— the launch of a first-run game show (195 episodes, or 39 weeks) that has succeeded in syndication before—illustrates how the cash/barter system generates profits. In this example, the syndicator's strategy emphasizes clearances in early-fringe and prime-access time slots, mainly on network affiliates. In order to get a high CPM (cost per thousand viewers) from advertisers (see page 305), the syndicator has guaranteed a high percentage of viewers in the women 18–49 group. The syndicator will sell one minute, or two 30-second spots, in each half-hour; for five shows a week, the syndicator would thus hold back ten 30-second spots. In addition, stations pay a cash license fee to the syndicator.

First, the net annual income is calculated by making certain assumptions about the marketplace, and the program's performance.

Estimated national clearance: 65–75 percent

Estimated national rating: 4.5 (or 4,140,000 households, based on a universe of 92,000,000 million)

VPS (Viewers Per Set) in the target demographic: 45 percent (since advertising is being sold based on a specific demographic group, the rates are based only on that group)

Estimated rating × VPS: 4.5 × 0.45 = 1,860,000 women 18–49

CPM for women 18–49: $8.50

Price per 30-second spot: 1,860 × $8.50 = $15,810

Minus ad agency's 15 percent commission = $13,500

Net revenue from 10 30-second spots, per week: $135,000

Cash license fees (paid by stations) per week: $100,000

Syndicator's net annual income: $135,000 (advertising revenues) + $100,000 (station license fees) = $235,000 × 52 weeks = $12,220,000

Next, the syndicator's first-year costs are calculated. Costs in subsequent years will be lower because the production cost of the pilot will already have been recouped, and ongoing marketing costs will be far lower.

Rights to series (upfront payment):	$ 500,000
Pilot production costs:	$ 300,000
First-year (39 weeks) production costs:	$3,900,000
Total rights and production costs:	$4,700,000

Finally, the syndicator must consider its costs of marketing and sales.

Marketing (first-class launch, including trade advertising, convention expenses, promotional money paid to local stations for local radio and print advertising): $2,000,000

Distribution fee (30 percent of net annual income, above): $12,200,000 × 0.30 = $3,666,667

Total marketing and sales costs: $5,666,667

The net profit, for the first year, is calculated as follows:

Net income:	$12,200,000
Rights and production costs:	($ 4,700,000)
Marketing/sales costs:	($ 5,666,667)
Net profit:	$ 1,833,333

After the syndicator deducts its hefty portion of the profits (usually 50 percent or more), it distributes the rest to the producer and any other "back-end" participants (see page 212).

In the real world, this system is riskier than it appears to be. If, for example, the actual VPS, as measured by Nielsen, turned out to be 36 percent and not 45 percent, then the net advertising revenues per week would drop to $117,045, which drops the net income (including station license fees) to $11,286,340, reducing the profit to $1,180,438. If, in addition, the program delivered only one less rating point, and came in at a 3.5, then income drops to $9,434,152, and the venture just about breaks even. A lower rating point, a problem with an advertiser, an inability to clear enough key time slots in key markets—each of these will erode income. Still, it may be worth losing money in the first year because the picture may appear to be more promising in the second, third, and so on.

The formula for a low-budget, once-a-week show, such as a music-countdown program, is less complicated. In the following model, production costs are low, the show has been on the air for several years, and it receives revenues from a foreign version.

National clearance: 65–70 percent
Rating: 1.2
CPM: $3.00
Price per 30-second spot: $2,800
Net advertising revenues for 6 30-second spots (after ad agency's 15 percent commission): $17,000
Income from British version: $7,500 gross – $1,500 production costs = $6,000

Net weekly revenues:	$23,000	($17,000 + $6,000)
Production costs/week:	($10,000)	
Marketing costs/week:	($ 2,000)	
Distribution costs/week:	($ 2,000)	
Net weekly profit:	$ 9,000	

CHANGES IN THE SYNDICATION BUSINESS

The syndication business experienced boom years in the 1970s and 1980s, when many new independent stations were going on the air, the prime access rule was new, and many time slots were available. In recent years, the number of choice time slots available for new programs has shrunken tremendously, particularly on network affiliates. This is due in part to the presence of established shows, in part to the expansion of local news programs, and in part to the popularity of hour-long talk shows (which occupy two half-hour slots, from the syndicator's perspective). Smaller syndicators have an especially difficult time competing because so few time slots are available. Larger ones, looking for growth, find that the time-slot issue is an impediment as well.

As the cable television networks have grown through the 1980s, they have attracted enough viewers to interest national advertisers. This additional income has allowed some cable networks to successfully compete against local-station syndicators for exclusive national licenses to an impressive variety of off-network series, including *L.A. Law, Spenser: For*

Hire, Cagney & Lacey, Moonlighting, The Tracey Ullman Show (Lifetime); *Frank's Place* (BET); *Beauty and the Beast* (CBN Family Channel); and *MacGyver, Murder, She Wrote, Miami Vice,* and *The Equalizer* (USA Network). Some programs, canceled by the networks, have continued production as cable series (*The Days and Nights of Molly Dodd,* on Lifetime). These ventures have been successful for the syndicators, the advertisers, and growing cable networks; in the second half of the 1980s, cable became a viable "first stop" for domestic syndication. Beyond the cash issue, cable is a single sale; for a syndicator to clear most of the country via broadcast stations, however, over 150 stations are generally required.

The international marketplace has also grown in the late 1980s and early 1990s, and has attracted the attention of the syndication companies. There are many new networks, and new opportunities for various types of programs. (The international marketplace is covered in detail in Chapters 39–42.)

4 | Public Television

Non-commercial broadcasting dates back to the 1920s, when colleges with an interest in broadcasting began licensed radio stations. Later realizing the value of these licenses, many colleges sold their properties to commercial ventures. In 1927, 98 non-commercial radio stations were on the air; in 1945, there were just 25. Relying on contributions and grants alone, most stations could barely support themselves—and no other means of support was generally available.

When the FCC issued its Sixth Report and Order in 1952, it ended a four-year freeze on new television channel licenses. After the freeze, the FCC licensed 80 VHF and 162 UHF non-commercial educational television stations. Later, the number was increased to a total of 600 allotments.

Non-commercial television began in 1953 when KUHT went on the air in Houston, Texas. For the next fifteen years, non-commercial stations started up in most of the nation's largest markets. Programming was predominantly educational, with some children's, cultural, and arts programming as well. Financial support was elusive; there was no uniform system for financing non-commercial broadcasting, so individual stations devised their own schemes for raising the necessary operating income.

Through the early 1960s, a political consensus emerged that something should be done to establish a viable alternative to commercial broadcasting, but determining the shape and direction of non-commercial broadcasting proved difficult. Different factions insisted on a system that would follow their own agendas—cultural, educational, local, national, politically involved, politically uninvolved, and so on.

The situation dramatically changed with a series of events in 1967. First, the Carnegie Commission on Educational Television (CCET) completed a two-year study recommending that Congress establish a non-commercial television system with a broader view than the old educational concept, a service that would be renamed "public" television. The new service would not be educational (the word "educational" was deemed "somber and static" in the report). Instead, public television would include an improved form of instructional or classroom television during the day, and high-quality general interest programs in the evening. CCET also recommended that the existing non-commercial stations be joined in a network that would be supported by federal funds.

Many of the commission's suggestions were made a part of the Public Broadcasting Act of 1967, which structured ongoing federal support for the new public broadcasting system.

THE CORPORATION FOR PUBLIC BROADCASTING (CPB)

The Public Broadcasting Act of 1967 established the Corporation for Public Broadcasting (CPB). Proposed by CCET, the CPB was supposed to serve as a buffer between the government and the new PBS (see below). It has served that purpose, although the original CCET concept of a board of directors composed of government appointees and private citizens was changed to a board composed entirely of government appointees. The result has been a closer tie between the federal government and public television than was originally intended. An example of the difficulties caused by this decision was the delay in providing long-term funding to CPB (the legislation finally passed in 1975). Some administrations have attempted to guide public television program policies by controlling funding to CPB—and by making ideological appointments to the CPB board—but these efforts have largely failed. In practice, the issue is no longer as significant as it once was; CPB now operates in its own fashion, relatively free of government interference. Still, because of the way that CPB is structured, increased government influence is always a possibility.

CPB's principal role is the distribution of an annual Congressional appropriation to public television stations and producers. In addition, according to the Public Broadcasting Act of 1967, CPB has the following responsibilities: encouraging the development of a wide range of program suppliers; maintaining high-quality program standards; assuring balanced reporting on controversial topics; interconnecting stations in a network that allows stations to program and schedule in accordance with local desires; nurturing new station development; conducting research and training; and operating a program archive. In reality, CPB is mainly an entity that finances new program development and production, pays for station activities, and funds National Public Radio.

The Public Broadcasting Service (PBS)

The Public Broadcasting Service, or PBS, was the network that the Public Broadcasting Act required CPB to create. PBS debuted in 1970, with 12 hours of programming per week as provided by National Educational Television (NET). The network concept did not last long; the Nixon administration, dismayed by a perceived liberal bias in news and information programs on public television, stymied the network's growth by vetoing a significant funding measure. To further limit the power of a potentially unfriendly network, the administration forced PBS to reorganize in 1973 with the bulk of the power going to individual stations. PBS became a membership organization, funded largely by dues paid by member stations. Under the 1973 Partnership Agreement, CPB was required to allocate a specific portion of its budget—roughly 50 percent—to local stations.

Although the ways in which money travels between CPB, PBS, and the PBS member stations is somewhat convoluted, member stations ultimately finance PBS by providing more than 85 percent of PBS's annual operating budget. The remaining 15 percent comes from ancillary sales—including the sale, rental, and licensing of PBS programs to institutions like schools and hospitals—and from a satellite-based data delivery system. Less than 2 percent of PBS's annual budget comes directly from CPB.

PBS is the foremost distributor of programming to public television stations (but not the only one; see below). The PBS National Program Service acquires the programs distributed by PBS and broadcast on the PBS network of member stations. PBS does not produce its own programming, but it does provide funds for others to do so. Programs are produced by member stations, other domestic and international broadcasters, film distributors, and independent producers.

PBS program operations are divided into three groups: Children's & Cultural, News & Public Affairs, and Acquisitions (which handles completed programs). Each group works closely with program suppliers in the development and financing of acquisitions and new production. There is a difference in approach between a program executive at PBS and one at a commercial network, however. Unlike their network counterparts, PBS program executives provide guidance of a general nature but are not deeply involved in production decisions. In addition, these executives generally muster support for the program within PBS and among member stations.

PBS is generally considered to be a bona fide television network by viewers, and is behaving more and more like one. More program decisions are being made by the PBS national office in Washington, D.C., and fewer by the stations themselves. The reason for this change is competition: the kinds of programs seen via PBS are now available from several national cable services, notably A&E and The Discovery Channel. For PBS to continue serving the largest possible number of viewers, centralization seems to be a reasonable strategy.

Other PBS Services

The Adult Learning Partnership, founded in 1981, provides adult learners with education via television. Courses are shown on public television stations, and anyone may watch for their own enjoyment. Approximately 250,000 students pay tuition to colleges and universities each year to participate in this coordinated effort between PBS, member stations, and area colleges.

The Elementary/Secondary Service provides daytime programming on public television stations for classroom use. Most stations supply schools with support materials, provided by program producers and community organizations. Many stations also transmit classroom programming after midnight so that schools can record the programs and replay them when needed.

PBS Enterprises develops goods and services, mainly related to new technologies. Its National Datacast, Inc., subsidiary uses an invisible portion of the broadcast signal to transmit data. PBS Video sells, rents, and licenses videocassettes to libraries, schools, hospitals and other institutions; in 1990, it began a consumer marketing operation. PBS Engineering is an R&D group that works on behalf of the system; its accomplishments include the nation's first satellite distribution system, and the development of closed captioning.

Other Public Television Program Distributors

PBS is not the only distributor of programs to public television stations. The Interregional Program Service—through the Boston-based Eastern Educational Network—distributes a large number of the programs seen on public television, including movie packages, series once seen on the commercial networks, and "Britcoms," the popular British situation comedies imported from Thames and other British broadcasters. The Southern Educational Communications Association (based in Columbia, South Carolina), the Pacific Mountain Network (in Lakewood, Colorado), and the Central Education Network (based in Des Plaines, Illinois) are among the other distributors of public television programming. Independent producers, unaffiliated with stations, often choose to distribute their programs through these companies.

PUBLIC TELEVISION STATIONS

In 1990, there were 121 VHF and 218 UHF non-commercial television stations on the air. These stations are owned by approximately 190 entities. Some of these entities own a single station, like WXXI in Rochester, New York; some own a large station and a smaller one, like WQED and its sister WQEX, both in Pittsburgh; and some are regional networks that operate multiple stations of various sizes throughout a geographic area, like a state (Kentucky Educational Television, New Hampshire Public Television, Maine Public Broadcasting Network, and Nebraska Educational Telecommunications Commission). Between 35 and 40 percent of public television stations are owned and operated by state or municipal institutions (many of these are small stations); 25 percent are owned and operated by educational insititutions, mostly by colleges and universities that operate the station for curricular reasons as well as public service; under 5 percent are operated by local school districts. The remaining 30 percent of the country's public television stations are owned by non-profit community groups, including local arts, cultural, educational, and civic organizations.

Each of the stations or station groups operates as a stand-alone non-profit company. Stations consider themselves to be independent television broadcasters who are members of PBS, and obtain programs from other sources as well. Most do not consider themselves to be PBS affiliates in anything like the commercial sense of the term, nor do they consider themselves to be "PBS stations." This attitude reflects the grass-roots individualism that developed during the Nixon years, and the fact that each station or group is responsible for its own financing and program decisions.

Financing for public television programming comes from several sources. Although each station differs in its approach, the following is a reasonably representative model. Approximately 40 to 50 percent of station revenues comes directly from "viewers like you," people who watch, and support, public television. Federal and state government allocations add approximately 15 percent. Contributions from area corporations and foundations, and from state organizations (such as a state council on the arts), add another 15 percent. Funding for specific program projects—from underwriters, PBS, CPB, the National Endowment for the Arts, the National Endowment for the Humanities, the National Science Foundation, and other sources—accounts for between 10 and 25 percent, depending upon the project budgets. The remainder comes from sweepstakes, auctions, special fund-raising events, subscription and advertising income from a monthly program guide, facilities leasing (renting television studios or editing rooms to outside producers), special funding grants for capital projects, local grant programs, and other miscellaneous sources.

Where does the money go? The biggest chunk—roughly 35 to 45 percent—pays for the acquisition and production of programming. Another 20 to 25 percent pays for marketing, including advertising, public relations, the preparation of program listings, and special events to promote the station and its programs. Between 15 and 20 percent goes to the station's day-to-day operations: salaries, office expenses, and the maintenance of the physical plant. The remaining 10 to 30 percent goes to capital additions, debt retirement, cash reserves, and miscellaneous items.

Each public television station builds its own program schedule. At many stations, the prime time schedule is taken intact from PBS, with occasional local variations. Some stations, including several in major markets, build their own schedules, placing PBS programs wherever they please. This is vexing for PBS producers and underwriters. The general feeling is that a larger audience might be reached if scheduling were more consistent nationwide.

PROGRAM PRODUCTION AND FINANCING

In commercial television, most entertainment programs are produced in Los Angeles; most news and talk shows are produced in New York; and some news programs are produced in Washington, D.C. In public television, programs of all kinds are produced all over the country.

Production by Public Television Stations

To a great extent, program production is controlled by individual public television stations. Some stations have become leading program suppliers: WGBH-Boston (*Frontline, NOVA*), WETA-Washington (*Washington Week in Review, The Civil War*), WNET-New York (*Great Performances, Nature, The MacNeil-Lehrer News Hour* [a co-production with WETA]), WQED-Pittsburgh (*Wonderworks, Infinite Voyage*), WTTW-Chicago (*The Frugal Gourmet*). The following stations are also involved in national program production, but less actively: KQED-San Francisco, WHYY-Philadelphia, WTCA-Minneapolis/St. Paul, and WPBT-Miami. Among the station groups, Maryland Public Television (*Wall Street Week*) and South Carolina Public Television are among the more prolific contributors of national programming.

Each of these stations operates as a kind of production company. Some projects are created in-house, either by full-time personnel or by specialists who are hired by the project; other programs are developed in association with outside producers or production companies. Stations that are active in national programming maintain a full-time staff to develop and nurture properties, and to arrange funding. Station executives pitch the project to CPB, PBS, corporate underwriters, foundations, and other sources. If the project is worthy (and fortunate), further development or production begins.

The project budget is likely to include more than the basic cost of production, however. Other costs include closed captioning, outreach marketing to schools or community groups, and promotional marketing. Because it is not really a network, PBS has no significant network promotion budget, and so each program must pay for its own advertising, public relations, and promotion. In order to fund its national program activities, the producing station takes a mark-up (usually called station overhead) of approximately 20 percent of the overall project cost. Taken as a group, these additional costs can add as much as one-third to the base program cost.

Production Companies

Children's Television Workshop (*Sesame Street, 3-2-1 Contact, Square One TV*) is the largest production company specializing in public television programming. Others include Varied Directions, Public Television, Inc. (Bill Moyers' company), Blackwell, Lancit Media, and Globalvision. As public television continues to evolve, an increasing number of production companies historically associated with commercial television are becoming suppliers to PBS.

Independent producers may work directly with PBS, CPB, or member stations in the development of new projects. The advantage to working with a station is clout: maneuvering through the sometimes byzantine process of garnering support among other member stations is nearly impossible for most producers to do without a station partner.

Producers of public television programming must also budget money for closed captioning, promotion, and outreach. The budget for an independent production may include a small packaging or overhead fee to cover some company expenses (even when produced by outside independents, public television shows are not made to earn a significant profit).

PROGRAM FINANCING

Finding money to produce and promote public television projects is a major challenge for member stations and for independent production companies alike. The process frequently involves scraping together financing from a variety of sources to make up the total. Funding sources for a typical program to be broadcast nationwide on public television break down as follows (with varying ratios depending upon the particular program): corporate grants, 15 percent of the annual production budget; PBS, 40 percent; CPB, 30 percent; the Challenge Fund, government grants, and endowments, 10 percent; and foundation grants, 5 percent. Programs with commercial value in other channels of distribution may be partially financed by motion picture companies—several *American Playhouse* productions, including *Stand and Deliver,* have been financed this way, and *Wonderworks* is another notable example. Such shows may also be funded by advances from home video companies, in exchange for cassette and disk rights. And as the international marketplace continues to grow, an increasing number of public television projects are being produced with international partners providing co-production financing.

Although the majority of productions funded by grants are initiated by the producer, some projects begin with a foundation or endowment seeking, for example, to establish a national forum (dance, arts for children, and so on).

CPB Program Fund

CPB provides funding for the development, research, and production of programs in three broad subject areas: news and public affairs, cultural and children's, and drama and arts. Frequently, CPB works closely with PBS to determine which programs are to be funded, and how much money will apportioned for each project. CPB's total annual budget is a Congressional appropriation; in fiscal year 1991, the appropriation totaled $242 million (excluding funding for satellite replacement), of which $47 million was earmarked for program development and production.

In addition, CPB administers a $150-million fund for the development and production of college-level educational materials, including instructional programs. The money is provided by the Annenberg School of Communications; the venture is called The Annenberg/CPB Project. Programs produced with money from this project include *The Brain*, an eight-part series from WNET; *The Planet Earth* (WQED); and *The Constitution: That Delicate Balance*, produced by the Media and Society Seminars of the Columbia University Graduate School of Journalism.

CPB also provides partial funding for the Challenge Fund, so named because CPB puts up half the money ($5 million) and challenges PBS member stations to match their investment. Stations pay into the fund based on their size and the population they serve. The fund was established in 1990 with $10 million.

Funding from Other Government Agencies

Some federal agencies contribute to specific public television projects. The National Endowment for the Arts, for example, helps to fund *Great Performances, American Playhouse,* and *Live from Lincoln Center;* the National Endowment for the Humanities granted production dollars to *Heritage: Civilization and the Jews;* the National Science Foundation provided funding for *The Brain,* as did the National Institutes of Health. Some of these grants must be matched by monies from other sources, frequently dollar for dollar.

Funding from Private Charities

Private foundations and trusts contribute a relatively small percentage of the overall public television production budget, but their contributions have been essential to financing such public television staples as *Sesame Street, Live from Lincoln Center,* and *Live from the Met,* as well as outstanding PBS presentations such as *The Civil War.* Leading contributors include the Arthur Vining Davis Foundation (which contributed to *The Civil War*), the MacArthur Fund (*The MacNeil-Lehrer News Hour, The Civil War,* and Bill Moyers projects), the Robert Wood Johnson Foundation (*The Health Quarterly*), the Lilly Foundation (*Eyes on the Prize*), and the Rockefeller Foundation (*Childhood in America*).

Corporate Funding

Corporations offer a significant amount of financing to public television productions, either for providing a service to the corporation's constituency or for public relations reasons. Some companies support programs because they believe in the program's point of view, or because they believe that the information is of value. Of course, corporate priorities or ownership can change, and funding may no longer be available for a specific project (Gulf Oil, for example, used to be a long-time supporter of the *National Geographic* specials). Oil companies have consistently been large-scale supporters: Mobil (*Firing Line, Masterpiece Theater, Mystery*), Exxon (*Great Performances, Live from Lincoln Center*), and Atlantic Richfield (*A Walk Through the 20th Century with Bill Moyers*). Other corporate contributors to public television programming include AT&T (*The MacNeil-Lehrer News Hour*), Pepsico (also *MacNeil-Lehrer*), GTE (*Scientific American Frontiers*), Digital Equipment (*The Infinite Voyage*), and IBM (*The Shape of the World*).

PBS Funding

From 1974 until 1990, each PBS member station also participated in the Station Program Cooperative (SPC). Individual stations committed funds from their own program budgets to help finance the most promising national projects. The SPC is defunct; PBS now funds national projects directly, without coordinating efforts from different stations.

Under PBS's new funding system, instituted in 1990, decision-making is centralized: the head of programming for the entire PBS system decides which programs will be funded by PBS. Working with a budget of approximately $80 million, PBS provides full or partial funding for ongoing programs (*NOVA, The MacNeil-Lehrer News Hour*) and for new shows (*Where in the World is Carmen Sandiego?*)

PBS RULES REGARDING PROGRAM FINANCING

PBS strictly limits the ways in which production financing can be arranged, and the ways that the financing sources may be credited. This may be an issue for any funding source, but it is especially important for corporate funders. The philosophy behind these rules is that public television must maintain its non-commercial image in the minds of viewers (and legislators), and that editorial control of the program cannot be surrendered in exchange for financing. In other words, airtime cannot be traded for any form of sponsorship or financing.

A comprehensive document, *PBS National Program Funding Standards and Practices,* is available from PBS. The following paraphrases many of its important rules:

• There can be no perception of a commercial relationship between the funder and the content of the program. This can be a judgment call, depending in part on the sensitivity of the issues involved. A major camera company can fund a photography how-to series, provided that its products are not prominently featured—but a major oil company funding a series on environmental conservation might not be acceptable.

• The funder may not affect the producer's decisions about script or topic selection, casting, or the choice of staff members—nor may the funder or its representatives attend editing sessions.

• The funder may not hold the copyright in the program. Furthermore, the funder cannot claim any future distribution rights, since a funder's plans for future exploitation of these rights might affect the content of the PBS program.

• Funding cannot be provided by the manufacturers or marketers of cigarettes or distilled spirits.

• On-air underwriting credits are "subject to the overall test of whether the credit is consistent with the non-commercial nature of public television, [and] consistent with the individual guidelines in credit elements."

How the underwriting credits should appear is outlined in some detail by the standards and practices document:

• The name of the funder must be preceded only by a generic and non-promotional phrase. Something akin to "the people of [company]" is acceptable, but "the experts at [company]" is not.

• A credit can include a brief audio or video clip, but only if it is not blatantly commercial. Well-known people (such as a company spokesperson) cannot be incorporated into credits, but general employee shots are allowable. A corporate mascot or logo like the Merill Lynch bull is acceptable, but not mascots or logos associated with specific products (Tony the Tiger for Kellogg's Frosted Flakes). One brand-name product can be shown and identified by audio, but it cannot be demonstrated or shown in operation. Up to three target markets can be mentioned ("makers of fine computers for home, office, and education").

• Funding credits may appear at the beginning of a program, *must* appear at the end, and should generally run 10 to 15 seconds long for each underwriter. A total of no more than 30 seconds can be allotted to underwriter credits.

• Credits given in exchange for services—"transportation provided by American Airlines"—may be incorporated into the normal production credits, and are not subject to the 30-second limitation. Producers are encouraged to minimize clutter and to keep these credits brief.

• A program producer or distributor's credit may appear in the traditional end-of-show position ("Children's Television Workshop").

There are many nuances, and occasional inconsistencies, so public-television program producers should check with PBS Program Business Affairs before making committments for underwriting credits. There are special rules regarding programs that will be seen by children—that is, programs shown during daytime hours—as well as rules regarding the print advertising and promotion of programs shown on PBS.

5 | Cable Systems

Cable television began as community antenna TV (CATV). In the early 1950s, some towns found that their reception was limited because of mountains and other obstructions that blocked incoming television broadcast signals. Local entrepreneurs constructed mountaintop antennas and charged a monthly subscription fee for access to the improved signals. Since these cable systems were not subject to the same technical limitations as broadcast television, each of the channels on the set could be filled. Slowly, CATV operators began filling their empty channels. A system in San Diego, for example, imported stations from nearby Los Angeles; some channels were filled with local productions (called "local origination" or "local O").

From the early 1950s until the mid-1970s, cable television was slow to grow. In most parts of the country, viewers were satisfied with their reception; the appeal of an independent station imported from a nearby city was limited because syndication was still in its early days, and program choices were generally undistinguished. In short, there was no real product for cable operators to sell beyond improved reception. The FCC limited cable's growth as well. In 1965—with 1,325 cable systems and 1.2 million subscribers in place—the FCC issued its First Report and Order, which held that

> if there is a signficant risk that CATV competition will destroy or seriously degrade the service offered by a television broadcaster, our statutory duties require us to seek means to prevent this result.

The report included a Notice of Inquiry and Notice of Proposed Rulemaking. Restrictive rules were soon adopted which effectively prevented operators in the top 100 markets from importing signals from other markets. In addition, the FCC required that any microwave facility bringing a distant signal into a market with four or more channels had to present "a clear and substantial showing that in the particular case a grant would not pose a substantial threat to UHF service in the area."

Cable operators and broadcasters were in and out of the courts through the 1960s and early 1970s, challenging these rules, their copyright implications, and the FCC's jurisdiction. The FCC modified and amended its regulations several times, gradually moving from a stance that favored broadcasters to one that encouraged the growth of cable.

(See Chapter 15 for a further discussion of the development of cable regulation.)

The mid-1970s brought a complete turnaround. With changes in FCC rules, cable systems were built in some large and medium-sized cities, and the number of national cable households began to grow. In the same period, RCA and Western Union launched satellites that could be used to distribute programming to cable television systems. Cable operators had an abundance of channel capacity, and as more systems were built, large companies and intrepid smaller ones began renting satellite time—to beam programming from cable networks to local systems equipped with receiving dishes.

HBO and WTCG (now WTBS) were among the first cable services to be distributed nationally, in 1976, via RCA's Satcom I. Five years later, more than a dozen satellite networks were available to cable operators and viewers, including CNN, Showtime, The Movie Channel, CBN, C-SPAN, Cinemax, ESPN, Nickelodeon, and many smaller part-time networks. By the mid-1980s, enough new networks had been added— MTV, VH-1, FNN, The Disney Channel, The Weather Channel—that new services were fighting for what was now a limited number of channels on most cable systems. Today, the trend is toward building or rebuilding systems with capacity for 100 channels or more. When systems with large capacity become the rule, there will be more room for more networks—but, most likely, fewer viewers per network, creating yet another growth issue for the cable business.

LOCAL CABLE TV

Although industry estimates vary slightly, approximately 55 million households in 25,000 commmunities now subscribe to cable television; this *cable penetration* is equal to slightly more than 55 percent of U.S. television households. Subscribers are served by approximately 10,700 cable systems nationwide. At least 2 million households have been added every year since 1980; in some years, as many as 6 million households have become new subscribers. Given continued growth at a rate of 2 million households per year—which is considered reasonable by most analysts—the percentage of U.S. television households subscribing to cable should exceed 70 percent by the end of the 1990s.

Cable Franchises

The technology of cable television requires a hard-wired connection between the transmitting facility ("headend") and each household. Cables must run through various terrains, and through various rights of way. For this reason, as well as the desire of local municipalities to assure their constituents the best possible cable service, the municipal government controls and regulates local cable television operation. One or more cable companies apply for the right to provide service to each community. Each submits a proposal which includes an explanation of the technical capabilities of the system, the channels that will be offered, the channel capacity of the system (at start-up and with future expansion), the rate schedule, the construction schedule, and background on the company and the individuals involved.

After a period of study (and lobbying by the cable operators), a franchise is awarded to one company, typically to provide service for a 15-year period. The franchise is a form of contract. If the cable company does not comply with the terms of the contract—does not, for example, lay cables in poorer areas, or offer the number of channels promised—the franchise may be challenged or, in rare cases, revoked. Cable franchises are generally awarded on a non-exclusive basis, but because of the expense involved, nearly all municipalities are served by cable companies that operate as monopolies. (See Chapter 15 for more details on cable franchises.)

Organization of a Local Cable System

Most cable systems are owned by large multiple system owners, or MSOs (see page 53), and operated locally by general managers. Decisions about which channels the system should carry are usually made by a national programming director, though such plans can be changed locally. Independently-owned cable systems are also run by a general manager, and make their own program decisions; all departments report to the GM.

The largest division of a local cable system is usually marketing, or sales/marketing. Cable requires an ongoing marketing relationship with each individual subscriber. The initial sell is done by direct marketing, either by mail, by phone, or, in many areas, door-to-door. Keeping subscribers, encouraging them to buy additional pay services or to install second sets, or convincing them to purchase pay-per-view programs are all done by the marketing department via bill stuffers, telemarketing, advertising on local media, and the monthly cable guide. Systems do not prepare their own cable guides; the task of assembling program information from each channel is too costly. Several companies publish national cable magazines that are customized for specific systems. *The Cable Guide* is one of several monthly publications that cable companies can purchase at bulk rate, adding a line on the cover to associate what is essentially a national magazine with their own local system. Guides are mailed by the publisher.

The quality of customer service also affects the percentage of subscribers who leave the system (this is called the "churn rate"). Customer service representatives respond to questions about programming, service, and billing.

The operation of the cable system's physical plant also requires a department. The headend is a master-control facility where incoming satellite signals are assigned to channels on the system, where local commercials play from racks of tape machines, and where locally-originated program sources are fed. Such sources may include an on-air guide to what's on, or a classified-ads channel. The installation and maintenance of the cable system itself—running cables to new locations, repairing line problems, and connecting individual households to the system—may be organized as a separate department in larger operations.

Two more departments are now commonplace, even among the smallest cable systems. The advertising-sales department sells commercial spots to local merchants, and frequently produces commercials for its clients. Rates are set locally, based on what the market will bear. A production department may employ several producers, directors, and studio crews to produce original programming, such as coverage of local sporting events.

Public access is also a part of some systems, frequently as a result of a promise made in the franchise proposal to dedicate one or more channels to this use. Typically, a local producer or entrepreneur purchases a block of time on a public access channel, sells time to commercial sponsors, and uses some or all of the proceeds to cover the cost of production. Additional money can be made by selling products to viewers. If the program is unsponsored (many public-access programs are non-commercial), production resources are generally supplied by a school, by the cable system (as part of the franchise agreement), or by an organization whose marketing interests are served by supporting specific types of public-access programs. Public-access programs and the financial practices associated with them are essentially unregulated, and there has been some controversy about the use of public-access channels for programs that feature nudity and break other taboos. Most cable systems self-regulate their public-access channels. Some claim freedom of speech as a defense for programs that may be offensive; local community groups or municipal government officials may take action in these situations, and seek to influence the cable operation's program policies.

How a Cable System Makes Money

The financial basis of a local cable franchise is essentially a wholesale/retail relationship. The operator of a cable system pays a cable network a monthly fee in the range of 5 to 40 cents per subscriber per month. The operator bundles together approximately 20 such services, adds the local broadcast stations (sometimes with improved reception), and sells the package to subscribers as "basic cable" for about $17, taking a mark-up of 100 percent or more. The cost of basic service may be considerably higher or lower, of course, depending on local company policy. Many cable networks offer channels to the operator in a barter arrangement that exchanges the program schedule for an increased number of viewers—viewers that will subsequently be sold to advertisers by the network. Pay services are even more profitable to the system operator: the wholesale price per subscriber per month is about $4 to $5, and the retail price to subscribers is usually $8 to $10.

Given a relatively small system with 10,000 subscribers, and with a pay channel like HBO in 25 percent of the households, the monthly revenues for a cable system after paying the per-subscriber charges to the basic network would be 10,000 x $10 for the basic service, or $100,000. HBO service, after deducting the HBO charge, would yield 10,000 × .25 × $4, for an additional $10,000 and a total of $110,000. From this amount, the cable system would cover operating costs and capital recovery. With a second and third pay channel (such as The Disney Channel and Showtime) in 15 percent of the households, the monthly revenues would increase by roughly 3,000 households × $8, yielding an additional $24,000.

Between one-third and one-half of a cable system's income goes to programming costs; up to one-third goes to payroll costs (including marketing and distribution); and up to the final third, to marketing, administration, operations, and profit.

Multiple System Operators (MSOs)

Some cable systems are locally-owned and -operated, but most are owned by larger companies that control dozens or even hundreds of systems. The top 50 Multiple System Owners (MSOs) serve more than 46 million households, over 90 percent of all cable subscribers.

The leading MSOs include TCI (Tele-Communications Inc.), with 8.5 million subscribers; Time Warner, with 6.1 million; UA Entertainment, with 2.6 million; and Continental Cablevision, with 2.6 million. Ten other companies have over 1 million subscribers each: Comcast Cable Communications, Cox Cable Communications, Storer Communications Cable Division, Cablevision Systems Corporation, Jones Spacelink, Newhouse Broadcasting (including Metrovision, NewChannels, and Vision), Times Mirror Cable, Heritage Communications, Viacom Cable, and Cablevision Industries.

As the larger MSOs have grown, they have exerted increasing control over the development of the programming services. At first, MSOs encouraged the growth of promising new services by making channels available even before the services were up and running. In time, MSOs also became investors in new services, sometimes using access to their subscriber bases as a negotiating point.

TCI, the country's largest MSO, has spun off Liberty Media Corporation to manage its part-ownership of cable networks like Turner Broadcasting Services (CNN, Headline News, TNT, and WTBS), The Discovery Channel, Black Entertainment Television (BET), QVC, Home Shopping Network, American Movie Classics, Showtime Networks (including The Movie Channel), and several regional sports services. ATC, the second largest MSO, is a Time Warner company; other Time Warner cable properties include HBO, Cinemax, and interests in E!, BET, and Turner Broadcasting Services. Cablevision Systems operates the nation's largest cable system (in Nassau and Suffolk counties outside New York City), and several others in large urban areas on the East Coast. It is also half-owner of American Movie Classics, Bravo, and the SportsChannel regional networks.

Historically, legislators, regulators, and the courts have not permitted distributors of radio, television, or motion picture product to own the companies which provide their "software." Two examples: the Supreme Court ordered the motion-picture studios to sell their theaters in 1948, and the television networks were required to sell off their syndication operations in 1970. With an eye to the future, TCI has set up a separate company to manage its programming assets; eventually, MSOs may be forced out of the programming business.

The Growing Strength of Local Cable Systems

Many cable systems now sell their own advertising time to local sponsors—in local breaks in the MTV and CNN schedules, for example. Since no dependable rating system exists to determine viewership of individual cable channels on individual cable systems (see Chapter 34), rates are largely negotiable, and the market is limited. When rating information becomes available, cable will probably become a competitive local advertising medium, taking business away from newspapers, billboards, and local radio and television stations. Cable also presents an unusual opportunity to advertise to a very specific geographic area at a relatively low cost. In a suburban town of 10,000 subscribers, a commercial on the cable system can be an extremely effective way to reach new customers for a car dealership, supermarket, or ice cream parlor.

While most cable companies are beginning to compete in the local-advertising marketplace, a small number are starting to compete in the television programming area—against local stations in the same market. Greater Rochester Cablevision is an ATC system with over 175,000 subscribers, serving all of the city of Rochester as well as 27 franchises in Rochester suburbs and outlying areas. Since this cable company transmits to most of the area already served by the television broadcasters, Greater Rochester Cablevision has started WGRC, which behaves like a local television station but which is received only by the company's subscribers. The "station" is programmed with syndicated shows; WGRC bids against the city's broadcast stations for available properties. WGRC operates at a disadvantage to broadcasters because it is not (yet) listed in ratings books, and because the television stations have roughly three times as many potential viewers. As cable penetration increases and ratings information become available, however, WGRC may become a serious competitor against the broadcast stations for programs, viewers, and advertising dollars.

In a related development, several cable systems petitioned the broadcast networks for status as affiliates in areas where there are not enough broadcast-station allocations to support ABC, CBS, NBC, PBS, and a Fox affiliate. Fox and TCI, for example, have been working together to develop cable systems as affiliates in small cities and towns that lack a fourth commercial station.

Basic Cable Networks

Cable services can be classified in one of three categories: superstations, basic (advertiser-supported) networks, and pay networks (the latter are discussed in Chapter 7). In addition, most cable systems carry at least one shopping network, as well as one regional sports network (see Chapter 8).

SUPERSTATIONS

A superstation is a broadcast station licensed to operate in a single market, and has its signal distributed nationally via satellite. The station itself is officially uninvolved in the national distribution; this is done by a *common carrier,* or a company that owns or leases time on a microwave and/or satellite.

WTBS-Atlanta—known nationally as TBS-Superstation—is the most successful superstation, with 31.7 million subscribers; its common carrier is Tempo Enterprises. TBS-Superstation is the only superstation with an entirely national orientation. Other superstations do not aggressively pursue a national audience, as a matter of choice. WGN-Chicago has 25 million subscribers; the common carrier is United Video. The following superstations each reach fewer than 12 million subs: WWOR-New York, WPIX-New York, KTLA-Los Angeles, KTVT-Dallas, and WSBK-Boston.* Eastern Microwave carries WWOR and WSBK, with United Video handling the others.

Superstations are a good deal for almost all parties concerned. The cable system buys the service for a few cents per subscriber, bundles it into the basic service package, and offers a rich assortment of movies, sports, children's shows, news, and other programming. The one major cost to the cable system comes from the copyright-licensing fees involved in carrying a distant signal (see page 123). And because it is carried across the country by cable systems, the superstation can attract national advertisers, and thus charge ad rates based on a national—not local—audience.

WTBS is one of four independent stations in Atlanta. The program schedule follows a traditional scheme used by most independent stations for decades: cartoons in the morning and after school, off-network

---

* All subscriber counts are from TBS Research.

series and a movie during the late morning and early afternoon, sitcoms around dinnertime, and either movies or sports in prime time. The formula works: besides ESPN and CNN, both more specialized services, TBS is the most successful general-interest cable network. TBS provides advertisers with a choice of two feeds: a local feed seen only in the Atlanta area, and a national feed that excludes Atlanta (TBS calls this double-feed method "commercial substitution"). Only about 10 percent of revenues comes from Atlanta; by contrast, WGN and WWOR depend upon local advertisers for most of their revenues.

Were it not for an FCC rule called "syndex" (see page 121), the losers in the superstation equation could be the syndicator who sells programs on a market-by-market basis—and the broadcaster who owns exclusive rights to a program in a market where viewers can see the same program on a cable channel. In fact, the loser is the viewer, who sees promos for a favorite show on, for example, WWOR, then finds that the common carrier has replaced the program with another program. TBS-Superstation provides a schedule free of exclusivity problems, paying two to ten times the local Atlanta rate when licensing programs from outsiders. The other superstations, being primarily local in their orientation, program for their home markets. In these cases, the common carrier must black out, or not carry, the program where there is likely to be a conflict, and may then replace the program with another—even selling commercial time in the replacement program.

BASIC CABLE NETWORKS

Although there are some variations, a basic cable network is a 24-hour advertiser-supported program service. The most successful cable networks reach more than half of the 92 million U.S. television households (as counted by Nielsen; see Chapter 34). The major cable networks are, in order of subscriber count: ESPN, CNN, The USA Network, Nickelodeon, MTV, The Nashville Network, The Discovery Channel, The Family Channel, and Lifetime.* Several other networks are close behind, and growing: TNT, A&E, The Weather Channel, and Headline News.

Programming

The real power of cable television—and the reason why cable networks have been so successful in drawing audiences away from broadcast networks—lies in the diversity of its programs, and the way in which those programs are scheduled.

CBN/Family Channel, for example, provides a full schedule of non-violent programming, with an emphasis on family values. Nickelodeon has positioned itself as the kids' network, with game shows, sitcoms, cartoons, and variety shows—all produced and marketed with

---

* Source: *NCTA Directory*, April 1990.

a style that school-aged children find enormously appealing. The Nashville Network (TNN) concentrates on the audience between the coasts, the large constituency of country music fans, with shows like *Crook & Chase* (an entertainment magazine), game shows, and talk/variety shows featuring country music. A&E appeals to somewhat older, more upscale viewers; its programs include vintage documentaries, a smattering of music, dance, and dramatic programs, sophisticated films, and—to draw in a younger audience—stand-up comedy. Lifetime's target audience, Monday through Saturday, is contemporary women 18–34; its schedule features talk shows, shows about parenting, game shows, movies, and off-network series that have a history of strong performance for this demographic group (*L.A. Law, Cagney & Lacey*). Like many basic cable networks, Lifetime is also producing movies for its viewers: six pictures were budgeted in 1990. On Sundays, the network becomes Lifetime Medical Television (LMT), which shows programs for the medical profession, providing an advertising environment for pharmaceutical firms and companies that need to reach medical professionals. Before being merged with the Consumer News and Business Channel (CNBC), the Financial News Network (FNN) was also a "split service." On weekdays, FNN was a financial news service, with talk, information, and news-magazine series in the evenings. But on weekends, FNN switched over to FNN:Score, a sports-news service (weekend sports viewers were often the same people that watched FNN during the week for financial news).

For viewers faced with more than 30 program choices, flipping from one channel to another has become common practice, much to the dismay of advertisers. Some cable channels are programmed with this type of viewing in mind. In at least some dayparts, The Weather Channel, CNN, Headline News, VH-1, and MTV are programmed in short bursts. These networks have learned that certain periods of the day require programs not in short forms, but in half-hour segments. MTV, for example, changed from an entire day of video disc jockeys (VJs) introducing song after song to a schedule that included some 30- and 60-minute shows (*Club MTV, Remote Control, Yo! MTV Raps*) as well.

Other cable networks have taken exactly the opposite approach. Faced with the need to broadcast 24 hours a day, 7 days a week, some networks schedule long-form programming like motion pictures and sporting events. The majority of programs on ESPN, TNT, and American Movie Classics run 90 minutes or more, and there are also 30- and 60-minute shows. Regardless of a movie's running time or a sporting event's duration, these networks wisely respect viewer's expectations, and begin programs on the hour or half-hour. When a program runs short, and does not end on the hour or half-hour, the time is filled with promos, and with short-form ("interstitial") programs. This strategy originated on pay TV networks, where it is still used.

Operations

Most basic cable and pay cable networks are owned by large media and entertainment companies. Hearst, ABC, and Viacom jointly own Lifetime and A&E; ABC owns most of ESPN, with a 20 percent stake held by Hearst; Turner Broadcasting jointly owns TBS-Superstation, TNT, CNN, and Headline News; The USA Network is jointly owned by Paramount, MCA, and HBO, a unit of Time Warner. Viacom, through its MTV Networks division, owns Nickelodeon, MTV, and VH-1, and co-owns Comedy Central with HBO. Viacom's Showtime Networks division operates the company's pay-TV networks: Showtime, The Movie Channel, and a pay-per-view operation. HBO's basic cable operations also include E! Entertainment Television, which HBO operates for joint owners Warner Communications, Warner Cable, ATC, and several other MSOs. Some cable networks operate as independent companies, though their investors may include large corporations: The Discovery Channel and BET (Black Entertainment Television) are examples.

A cable network is typically headed by a president, who is charged with daily operation and with growth (specifically, increasing the number of subscribers). Several senior executives, responsible for programming, advertising sales, marketing, operations, and legal affairs, report directly to the president. While the actual structure varies depending upon the network's needs and the people involved, every network includes these functions.

The programming department is responsible for the development and production of original programs, and for the acquisition of completed programs. This responsibility may be divided by program type or by daypart. At MTV, the programming department has subdivisions that oversee music (selection and scheduling of music videos), news (daily reports and long-form specials), development (series programs), on-air promotion, production (of studio segments and specials), and scheduling. At some networks, on-air promotion is a marketing function. MTV also shares some personnel and other functions, such as production management, with its sister networks.

The marketing department handles public relations and advertising—in print, on radio, and on other television networks. Ancillary product licensing—of the MTV or Nickelodeon logo, for example—may be part of marketing, or a separate department. Licensing of programming to ancillary television and home-video markets may be a marketing function, or may be the responsibility of the programming department.

The cable network's marketing department may also include affiliate relations and advertising sales. The affiliate-relations division sells the network service to cable systems, and works closely with the marketing department to develop and implement promotions locally.

The sales department sells commercial time. Prices are based on ratings information available from Nielsen, and sold on a CPM basis (see page 305). In order to compete effectively and increase advertising revenues, tie-ins to special promotions, like contests, are more common in cable than in broadcast television.

The network's operations functions may be organized into one or several departments. Engineering supervises the technical aspects of production, the master control facility, and the satellite transmissions. If the network does a lot of production with its own facilities, a full-scale engineering department may be required (this is the case at CNN, for example). At other networks, where technical requirements are not as complicated, the operations group may include financial and accounting departments, personnel, and general administrative functions.

The Economics of Basic Cable

Cable networks receive income from two principal sources: subscribers and advertisers. A top-end subscriber base of 50 million homes paying 8 cents per month generates $48 million per year (see page 52). For most services, advertising revenues are also significant. Although advertising rates can vary from several hundred dollars per 30-second spot during daytime to several thousand at night, a single hour-long program on a major cable network in the late afternoon should easily generate $500 per 30-second spot—more than $5,000 for the hour. By applying a similar formula to the entire day, allowing for highs and lows in viewing levels, a weekday's spots should be worth about $100,000, or up to $35 million per year.

In addition to subscription and advertising revenues, product licensing and international program sales can generate several million dollars per year. For an MTV, this will be more significant than for a Weather Channel.

TELEVISED SHOPPING SERVICES

Most cable systems offer at least one televised shopping network. These networks are unusual because every minute of airtime is used to sell products.

The business began in 1982, when the owner of WWQT-AM, a radio station in Clearwater, Florida, accepted merchandise in place of cash to settle an advertiser's debt. The station offered the merchandise for sale, over the air; listeners called in to order it, and even drove down to the station to pick up their purchases. Realizing that this might bigger than a local radio gimmick, entrepreneurs leased time on a local cable system, soon discovering that the idea worked in the local Tampa Bay market. After considering expansion to other Florida markets, the venture instead rented satellite time, and, in 1985, went national as the Home Shopping Network (HSN).

Within a year or so, there were 30 shopping services, including eight available nationwide via satellite. More were in the planning stages. QVC debuted in November 1986.

In 1987, the Home Shopping Network expanded beyond cable and began purchasing UHF stations. (Many of those UHF stations had previously been associated with religious programming or with unsuccessful pay-TV services.) In the same year, QVC made a deal for the exclusive right to represent Sears products. This was followed by JCPenney's entry into the field. JCPenney first bought an existing service called Value Television Network, then relaunched it as the Shop Television Network (STN), which was in turn revamped as JCPenney Shopping Network before ceasing operations.

By 1988, it was clear that the abundance of televised shopping networks could not be supported by the cable operators: there would have to be a shake-out. The Fashion Channel was purchased by Cable Value Network in 1988, which was itself taken over by QVC in 1989. Other networks were either bought by larger ones, or disbanded.

As of this writing, three networks remain. QVC is the industry leader, with 35.7 million cable subscribers, followed by HSN, with 21.1 million cable subscribers. The figures are misleading, however: HSN actually reaches over 50 million households by broadcasting on its eleven UHF stations. HSN operates three services. HSN 1 is distributed only to cable systems; HSN 2 is distributed to broadcast affiliates, HSN-owned and -operated television stations, and to some cable systems. HSN's Home Shopping Spree is offered both as a 24-hour service and in shorter increments for broadcast stations.

Merchandising

A televised shopping service is really a type of living catalog, with time slots rather than pages. QVC's program schedule, for example, devotes a single hour to one product category, such as porcelein figures, German beer steins, baseball collectibles, or kitchen accessories. HSN segments its schedule mainly for apparel items; otherwise, a variety of products is offered throughout the program day. Celebrities also play a part on televised shopping networks. Joan Rivers and Angie Dickinson, for example, have appeared presenting their own product lines on QVC; HSN works with Vanna White on a designer line sold exclusively on that station.

Each of the networks offers a wide range of merchandise. Generally, jewelry and fashion accessories are the best sellers. Kitchen items also move well—pots and pans coated with T-Fal, a non-stick cooking surface, have been consistently successful, mainly because they can be demonstrated so effectively. In some product categories, such as consumer electronics, brand names like Panasonic or Sharp can be important. In product categories where brands are not an issue, the networks work hard to find special values. QVC, for example, finds 18-karat gold to be a strong seller, for two reasons: the network's volume discount allows it to offer the gold at low prices, and 18-karat gold is not easily found in stores. HSN built its audience with close-outs and deeply discounted merchandise, cubic zirconium ("fake diamonds"), and Capidimonte. The latter is a brand of Italian-designer ceramic made by a company that liquidated its merchandise to the network; the manufacturer was subsequently commissioned to restart its business because of the demand generated by HSN and its viewers.

Program hosts are also an important part of the shopping network, because they demonstrate products, discuss features and benefits, and encourage viewers to pick up the telephone to order. Hosts are usually trained by the manufacturers, and may on occasion visit factories to gain greater insight into manufacturing, quality issues, and so forth.

Unit sales are difficult to estimate, but there are some dependable ranges for successful products. If a product is well-received and low-priced (say, $10), QVC might sell as many as 2,000 units; a reasonable sale for a $100 product would be about 300 units. While many of QVC's sales are made during the programmed hour, viewers can order at any time. HSN works differently: the product can be purchased only for the few minutes that it is on the air. At HSN, program producers and on-air hosts carefully monitor the number of viewers placing orders; if the item is not moving briskly, they move on to the next product.

Other than the fact that the principal marketing medium is television, each of the shopping channels operates as a traditional retailer. Dozens of buyers visit trade shows, factories, and other facilities, identify products appropriate for the distribution channel, and make quantity deals. In some cases, the product must pass a quality-assurance test before the deal is made final (QVC assays jewelry, for example). The merchandise is then shipped to the network's warehouse, and programmers schedule segments to sell the merchandise. If the product is an exclusive for a short period, it may go on the air within days. If the product requires the production of a special videotape to explain its unique features or operation, several weeks may pass before it is scheduled. Approximately 10 to 12 products are shown per hour.

Organization

The staff required to operate a shopping channel is large in comparison with other television channels, but is consistent with a firm that does national direct marketing. QVC and HSN each employ between 3,000 and 5,000 people—the higher figure is during the fourth quarter, for the holidays. Roughly two-thirds of the staff is employed in two areas: order entry (taking order by phone) and fulfillment (working in the warehouse or shipping). Customer service representatives answer consumer questions about products, handle credit issues, and follow up on lost merchandise and returns. Other departments include inventory control, MIS, finance, affiliate relations, merchandising, and broadcasting. Using QVC as a model (HSN is similar), the broadcasting department is headed by an executive vice president who also serves as executive producer. A vice president of talent supervises 18 performers working

3- to 4-hour shifts each day, 3 to 4 days each week. The TV chief engineer performs the traditional function. Several managers take care of specific production tasks—control room operations, post-production (production of promos for QVC, other cable channels, and for affiliates), and backstage operations (displaying products)—and there is also usually a coordinating producer. Including creative, supervisory, and technical staff, the production department consists of roughly 100 people—a small number, due to production efficiencies like robotic cameras.

The Economics of Televised Shopping

The financial relationship between cable operators and the televised shopping networks is unique, and unlike the relationship for any other program service. The cable operator receives approximately 5 percent of the gross collected revenues within the zip codes in their service area. Whereas another cable service might charge its cable operator a fee for each subscriber, the televised shopping network can be a small profit center for the operator.

In 1990, the combined gross sales of all televised shopping channels were approximately $2 billion. The growth of QVC from 1989 to 1990 is representative: as its total number of cable households increased from 16.1 to 35.8 million homes, the number of active customers increased from 871,000 to 2.6 million, and net sales increased from $193.2 million to $453.3 million. During the four-day Thanksgiving weekend in 1989, QVC grossed $25.6 million in sales.*

* Source: *TWICE Today,* June 4, 1990.

7 | Pay Cable Networks and Pay-Per-View

According to Walter Troy Spencer, "The concept of pay TV is almost as old as the practical technology of television itself. As early as 1938, viewers in England could watch prize fights telecast in theaters."*

Through the 1950s and 1960s, several entrepreneurs tried to build an over-the-air pay TV business. The best known was Subscription Television, Inc., headed by Pat Weaver—the NBC executive who started *Today* and *Tonight*. Weaver's plan was to bring pay television to Los Angeles and San Francisco, but the company failed mainly as a result of pressure from theater owners and local broadcasters. Weaver also proposed satellite-fed cultural pay TV programming in the mid-1960s. Other ventures, mostly experimental, enjoyed varying degrees of success, but none could truly be called the start of a business. Each was based on a similar principle: a program or program schedule is broadcast (or cablecast), but its signal is scrambled. Viewers pay a fee, and receive some sort of descrambling device in order to see the programming.

The FCC approved pay television service in December, 1968; an unsuccessful Supreme Court appeal by the National Association of Theater Owners and the Joint Committee Against Toll TV delayed any forward motion until September, 1969. In 1972, the FCC authorized several over-the-air pay TV stations on UHF. By 1983, 18 full-power UHF stations were broadcasting as pay television outlets—commonly called over-the-air subscription TV, subscription TV, or simply STV— serving nearly 1 million households. As cable, with its multiple pay services, became available and increased its penetration, the business eroded quickly. By the late 1980s, most STV stations had switched to over-the-air shopping channels (see Chapter 6).

During its brief heyday, STV offered HBO-style service on a UHF station in approximately a dozen major metropolitan areas that were not yet served by cable. ON TV, owned by Oak Media Development, was the industry leader. Subscribers paid a monthly fee, received a monthly program guide, and—via a descrambler—were able to see recent motion pictures, sporting events, Broadway productions like *Ain't Misbehavin'*, rock concerts featuring the Rolling Stones, and other special programs.

---

* Walter Troy Spencer, "Pay TV: An Alternative," in *TV Book: The Ultimate Television Book*, ed. Judy Fireman.

PAY CABLE

Pay cable began on November 8, 1972, with a Time-Life experiment. A new service called Home Box Office was cablecast to 365 Service Electric Cable TV subscribers in Wilkes-Barre, Pennsylvania. The first night's offering was an NHL game live from Madison Square Garden, followed by a recent film called *Sometimes a Great Notion.* In January 1973, HBO transmitted its first championship boxing match: Foreman *vs.* Frazier, from Kingston, Jamaica. In March, HBO showed its first pay TV special, the Pennsylvania Folk Festival. The basic pay TV scheduling format was set, but HBO remained a regional service until September 30, 1975, when it became the first cable service delivered via satellite.

Cable has proven the ideal medium for pay TV. Once a household becomes comfortable with the idea of paying a monthly bill for television service, the incremental addition of a pay service—or several pay services—is not a hard sell. Since cable households by and large require a "cable box" (more accurately, a "converter"), the installation of an enhanced model containing a pay TV descrambler is not a difficult barrier.

Pay cable penetration has always lagged behind basic cable penetration: at the end of 1980, there were 17.6 million cable households, but only 9.1 million subscribed to a pay service. At the end of 1989, the absolute numbers were higher and the ratio had narrowed: 52.6 million basic cable subs, and 40.5 million pay subs. As these figures show, roughly 80 to 85 percent of basic households subcribe to pay TV (many pay TV households subscribe to more than one pay service).*

Pay Cable Networks

According to the 1990 *National Cable Network Directory,* HBO is the largest pay cable network, with 17.3 million subs. HBO is followed by Showtime with 10 million, The Movie Channel, also with 10 million, Cinemax, with 6.4 million, and The Disney Channel, with 5 million. Special-interest pay networks have fewer subs: Bravo, an arts network, has 4 million, for example.

HBO and Cinemax are owned by Time Warner. Showtime, which debuted nationally in March 1978, is operated and half-owned by Viacom—more specifically, by the Showtime Networks group. Through the years, Viacom has had several partners; the latest is TCI. The Movie Channel began as The Star Channel in 1973, by bicycling (physically moving) tapes of motion pictures among eight Warner Cable systems. When American Express joined Warner Cable in a new venture called Warner Amex Satellite Entertainment Company (WASEC) in 1979, it was renamed The Movie Channel. After a period in which Viacom effectively replaced American Express as the partner, Viacom bought the channel.

---

* Source: Pay TV Subscriber History from *The Kagan Census of Cable and Pay TV* (1989) and *The Pay TV Newsletter,* April 24, 1990.

Each network has its own special appeal, though the similarites tend to outweigh the differences—The Disney Channel (see page 67) is the exception.

HBO has been the leading service from the start—the one whose muscular negotiations with Hollywood at one time helped Showtime to grow, largely as a result of studio resentment. For years, HBO has featured big-name boxing matches (now also a Showtime specialty) and coverage of the best Wimbledon matches. It also had sufficient foresight and clout to develop and produce its own motion pictures, thus assuring product flow (initially, through a series of investment packages called Silver Screen Partners). HBO established a high-class on-air look, using expensive animation packages to introduce features and even interstitial programs, advertising heavily, and attracting top names like Bette Midler, Diana Ross, Barbra Streisand, and the *Comic Relief* performers. HBO also innovated with the first stand-up comedy series and the first significant made-for-pay-cable motion pictures. Numerous award-winning documentaries (*How to Raise a Street-Smart Child, Down and Out in America*) have added a distinguished veneer to the network's original programming.

For its first few years, Showtime struggled to differentiate itself from HBO. Broadway shows (*Master Harold and the Boys, Sunday in the Park with George*), comedy series (*It's Gary Shandling's Show, Super Dave*), children's programs (*Shelley Duvall's Faerie Tale Theater*), and a broader variety of music programs have helped to give Showtime a distinctive identity. By 1983, it was clear that the best offensive tool was exclusive-rights deals with large motion picture studios; that year, Showtime signed the first 'output deal' for pay TV, with Paramount. This deal guaranteed a supply of Paramount movies that viewers could see at home only by subscribing to Showtime. The result of Showtime's move was that pay cable networks immediately started competing for studio product. By the mid-1980s, exclusive showings of particular feature films had become a key marketing issue for the pay cable networks.

Showtime grew through the 1980s with a series of output deals for pictures from small and large releasing companies (Cannon, Atlantic Releasing, Touchstone, MGM, Universal). Showtime has also placed more of an emphasis on regularly-scheduled programming, and on series television, than HBO.

The Movie Channel (TMC) is exclusively a movie network. There are no comedy specials, no music, no sports, no series—just movies. TMC has also invested in personalities and guest hosts, to introduce films and to fill in the time between them.

Cinemax began as an all-movie service (hence the name), but HBO has since repositioned the channel for slightly younger, more urban viewers. Music specials tend to feature fewer big stars, but more legendary players (Carl Perkins, Fats Domino, Sarah Vaughan, B.B. King, Roy Orbison, Chet Atkins), and non-rock genres (gospel, reggae, soul, country). Comedy specials have been more than simple stand-up; *Cinemax Comedy Experiment* featured full-scale productions from top and rising comedy stars (*Martin Mull Presents the History of White People in America*).

From a viewer's perspective, however, Showtime, HBO, Cinemax, and The Movie Channel are largely interchangeable—one may have certain movie titles that the other does not, but most of these can easily be seen by visiting the neighborhood video store.

Programming

Pay television services are, for the most part, in the business of exhibiting recent motion pictures. Viewers pay a fee to see the motion pictures about a year after they have appeared in theaters. The period when a motion picture is released for pay TV is called the "pay television window"; it frequently overlaps with windows for airline release and home-video release. Although the sequences of windows varies depending upon the deal, the following is roughly representative for a major studio release.

Theatrical release: January through April, 1992
Home video: Summer, 1992
Airline: Summer, 1992
Pay-per-view: Summer or fall, 1992
Hotel and related services: Summer or fall, 1992
Pay cable: Winter, 1992–3

Movies that do well on pay TV tend to be just as popular on home video.

Each film studio has a department responsible for the licensing of motion pictures to pay television. Independent production companies sell pay TV exhibition as one of several ancillary rights, and sometimes pre-sell home-video rights as well (though film studios, which have their own video labels, rarely do the latter). If a film has a reasonable budget (about $4 million or more), theatrical release, and name talent, the chances of selling it to pay cable are good to excellent.

In general, most major-studio movies are not sold to television by individual title. Instead, they are grouped as packages that usually contain top titles, mid-line entries, and marginal titles, frequently in batches of dozens of pictures. Unless there is an exclusive output deal, more than one pay service usually licenses each package. The services schedule the films from the package according to appeal; some of the films are never scheduled. After pay TV, the films are then licensed (or in the case of a studio, transferred internally) to a syndication company, which supplies first basic cable and possibly broadcast network, then local stations.

Some individual pictures, groups of pictures, or even complete packages are sold on an exclusive basis to a single pay TV company, usually for a limited period (one year, for example). The real value in an exclusive license is during the early weeks of the pay TV window, when there is excitement in the marketplace about viewing a hit title at home. This excitement helps to differentiate the service, and improves viewer satisfaction with pay TV as well. But as the hubbub dies down, the value of the exclusivity drops quickly.

A major motion picture release is typically sold by the studio's pay TV division directly to each pay network. The average sale is in the millions of dollars; obviously, the actual negotiated prices vary widely. To an independent company with a film that had a $4-million production budget and a domestic theatrical gross of $5 million, the pay TV licenses will probably be worth $250,000–$500,000.

The Economics of Pay Cable

Pay cable networks generate revenues almost exclusively from their subscribers; some additional revenues come from ancillary rights to programs and movies produced or owned by the networks. Growth in subscription revenues can be achieved only by increasing the wholesale cost per subscriber that the network charges the cable operator or by increasing the gross number of subs (which might be done by decreasing the wholesale cost). Since there is a finite universe of cable subscribers, and a relatively predictable percentage of cable households that will subscribe to pay services, most pay cable operations grew quickly through the mid-1980s, but have leveled off in the late 1980s and 1990s. Recognizing that pay cable is at a mature stage in its business cycle, the pay cable companies have expanded into pay-per-view, investments in other networks, and other ventures.

The Disney Channel

The Disney Channel is an unconventional pay TV network in terms of its business relationship with cable operators. Disney sells its service according to the number of *basic* cable, not pay cable, subscribers. This way, the cable operator has an incentive to increase the number of basic subscribers who opt for The Disney Channel. Showtime is also experimenting with this novel approach.

In the selection and scheduling of programming, The Disney Channel is also an anomaly compared to other pay TV networks; by using dayparts, it is closer to a conventional broadcast station. In 1991, the schedule began with programs for very young children in the morning (*Care Bears, Welcome to Pooh Corner, Dumbo's Circus*), for preschoolers in the midday (*Lunch Box, Music Box,* specials), then for elementary-school children after school (*Teen Win, Lose or Draw, The Mickey Mouse Club*). The dinner hour is usually occupied by a family movie with strong children's appeal (*The Shaggy Dog, Babar: The Movie*). Through the evening hours, The Disney Channel is programmed for grown-ups, usually with a classic or recent movie (though not one as recent as those on HBO or Showtime), an entertainment special, or a documentary. Disney's programming style is upbeat, supported by sophisticated, imaginative graphics and short-form interstitial programs selected from the massive Disney library.

As can be expected from Disney, there is more than just programming involved. The Disney Channel is used as a promotional outlet for other Disney activities, including new motion picture releases, new home-video releases, and theme park attractions. More than 5 million households with children watch The Disney Channel regularly, so the promotional benefits go beyond subscription revenues.

The Disney Channel is pigeonholed by many cable companies as a premium children's channel. Despite an impressive schedule of programming that appeals to adults, most cable subscribers think of it as a children's channel—no children, no Disney. Since Nickelodeon, another quality children's channel, is provided at no additional charge to basic cable subscribers, Disney can be a tough sell.

PAY-PER-VIEW

Pay-per-view (PPV) is a different form of pay television. The concept is simple: special programs and recently-released movies are shown on one or more channels used exclusively for PPV ("dedicated channels"). In order to watch the program, the viewer agrees to pay a separate charge—either by calling a special telephone number, or, on newer in-home hardware, by pressing a button on the cable console. PPV is a transaction-based, one-purchase-at-a-time business that depends upon impulse buys, and that requires a sophisticated marketing infrastructure. Viewers must be made aware of the PPV offerings in a variety of media, through a dedicated 24-hour "barker" channel (which features nothing but around-the-clock promos for PPV programs), direct mailings, advertisements, and bill stuffers. Then they must be encouraged to buy at the time that the product is actually available.

A pay-per-view operation requires special hardware at the head-end and in each household. At the headend, the cable operator must install a special computer that enables individual households to view each individual program. In each household, the cable converter must include an individual computer address that permits communication with the computer in the headend. In addition, a customer order-processing system is needed. Rudimentary systems simply post a telephone number for ordering; this is not ideal for impulse buys because it requires that the customer take an action outside of simply pressing a button to watch TV. Newer, more sophisticated systems include such a button—or, more often, the entry of a special ID code—but also require some form of verification to confirm that the person pressing the button will actually pay for the film (four-year-olds are notorious button-pushers). Newer computer systems not only take the order and enable (or activate) the addressable converter in the viewer's home, but take care of recordkeeping and billing as well. (An addressable converter is a cable box whose subscription code can be read by a central computer.)

Because of these special hardware requirements—and the continuous marketing effort required for a successful pay-per-view service—many cable operators have not made the service available. As of 1990, 16.2 million households were equipped to view at least one PPV channel.* The actual number who buy each individual PPV movie or event is, of course, much lower.

The most successful pay-per-view event to date was the boxing match between Evander Holyfield and George Forman, held in April, 1991. Approximately 8.5 percent of the cable subscribers who were equipped to receive PPV paid $39.95 to see the match; TVKO, the PPV arm of Time Warner, earned $55 million domestically. The most successful non-boxing PPV event was Wrestlemania VII, which earned $24 million at a $29.95 price. Concerts and other special events tend to be less lucrative: the biggest non-sports PPV event to date was 1989's New Kids on the Block concert, which grossed $5.5 million.

In a limited (but increasing) number of cases, a PPV window precedes the pay TV window for motion picture releases. For PPV programmers and marketers, finding movies and events that viewers will pay to see is an ongoing challenge. In many ways, PPV's most direct competition is home video: PPV's retail prices for motion pictures are generally competitive with the rental prices charged by neighborhood video stores.

An increasing number of systems have found that several PPV channels are preferable to one, provided that channels are available. The first two channels show first-run movies. When programmed properly, a new feature starts at the top of the hour on at least one of the channels. A third channel is used for action/adventure films, or special events. Some systems successfully operate a fourth channel with adult material (R-rated films and special programs), with virtually no marketing expense.

Movies can be a significant source of income for PPV services. On a successful four-channel system, two major movie channels can account for 40 to 50 percent of revenue. A month with one giant title will generally do better than a month with several name titles but no blockbuster. The cumulative monthly rate for a movie channel averages about 18 percent—that is, the total number of orders for a movie amounts to 18 percent of the number of households that receive the channel. The adult channel is a dependable contributor of up to 20 to 25 percent of monthly PPV income.

Events are less predictable. Ideally, an event should be a big-ticket item with lots of visibility, supported by a major national and local marketing campaign. As much as 40 percent of this market consists of

---

* Source: Paul Kagan Associates.

wrestling from WWF and Turner. Wrestlemania IV, considered to be a strong PPV event when it was broadcast in 1988, was purchased by 900,000 households, each paying $20 to $25 for a gross of approximately $20 million. Boxing can be strong, depending upon the match-ups, but it can also be unreliable. Buy rates in these categories, nationally, are 5 to 10 percent of the PPV households.

Concerts and other special events score buy rates well under 5 percent in most cases. Events account for up to 30 percent of PPV revenues, but this is an average; months with blockbusters help to pull up slower months.

Pay-Per-View Networks

Cable companies buy events and motion pictures from pay-per-view networks. The largest are Viewer's Choice I and Viewer's Choice II, owned by eight cable-system operators and two movie studios; they have 7 million and 2.3 million subscribers, respectively. Request Television and Request 2 from Group W Satellite Communications each have 3.4 million subs, and each one has two channels to accomodate staggered movie-start times, as described above. Playboy at Night serves 4 million subscribers.

Request 1, as an example, supplies an average of 10 first-run films per month, plus special events. Request 2 offers 15 titles, not necessarily all first-run.

It is customary for the cable company and the PPV network to equally share PPV revenues, although other deals may be negotiated.

Hotel and Institutional Systems

Several PPV services operate in hotels and other institutions; Spectravision is the industry leader. Films are released to hotel PPV prior to pay TV and home video, so the films are new and desirable. Up to eight films (often including one or two adult titles) are offered on as many channels. Ordering and billing are completely automated; the charges appear on the hotel bill. This automated system has also been used to offer expanded interactive services, such as automated check-out via the television screen and PPV keypad.

Rates are higher than typical PPV, usually $5 or more per movie. The split is usually 60 percent to Spectravision and 40 percent to the hotel or institution. Advances are in the tens of thousands for most films—over $100,000 for blockbusters. Films are licensed on a non-exclusive basis by a national programming office, and scheduled monthly.

8 Sports Programming

The business of television sports has been built on the unique ability of sports programs to deliver male viewers to advertisers.

Professional football is considered the ideal televised sport because it attracts large numbers of males in every age and economic group. Pro football's short schedule means that nearly every match-up can be promoted as a major event. Pro basketball has also become popular, but basketball delivers a narrower audience—mainly urban, and somewhat younger than football fans. Viewers of Major League Baseball are older, and the same is generally true of college basketball. Golf and tennis are special cases, reaching specific upscale target groups; tennis is the only sport that consistently attracts large numbers of female viewers. Auto racing is a successful advertising vehicle because it allows automotive companies (car manufacturers, oil and tire companies) to reach car buffs. Although hockey is popular in the North, Midwest, and Northwest, it is not as favored by national advertisers because the sport is not popular in the Sunbelt.

While these distinctions between types of sports are broad and somewhat stereotypical, they nonetheless reflect the preconceptions guiding advertising buyers toward one type of event and away from another.

NATIONAL SPORTS COVERAGE

Six networks dominate the national sports business: ABC, CBS, NBC, TNT, USA, and ESPN. Each of these networks regularly schedules large numbers of sporting events. HBO and Showtime also participate in sports coverage, but their coverage is generally limited to boxing (HBO also features tennis). HBO has several sports-information shows.

The networks negotiate with the leagues or other sports organizations for package deals that include multiple events. There are usually two packages of games that a league offers: one for broadcast networks, one for cable networks. Each sport has its own traditions, in terms of both organization and pricing policy.

Network and Cable Rights

The network package for Major League baseball now belongs to CBS. It includes 16 regular season games, plus the All-Star game, the league championship playoffs, and the World Series. The price: $260 million per year for four years. ESPN has baseball's cable deal—175 regular season games, usually seen on four weeknights each week. The price of that package is about $100 million per year.

The NFL has agreements with five entities for football games: NBC and CBS for Sunday afternoon games, ABC for Monday nights, TNT for the first half of the season on cable, ESPN for the second half. The total value of these five four-year agreements is approximately $3.6 billion. The richest package is owned by CBS—it cost more than $1.1 billion.

As for college football, the College Football Association (CFA) represents 63 member schools throughout the U.S.; PAC 10 and Big 10 negotiate as one, and thus account for 20 schools. Beginning in 1991, both the CFA and PAC/Big 10 games appeared on ABC. The CFA deal cost ABC $210 million over five years; the PAC/Big 10 package also runs five years, and cost $100 million. Notre Dame negotiated a separate deal with NBC for five to six games a year at $3 million per year, which the school shares with its opposing team.

The NBA holds the broadcasting rights for all national coverage of professional basketball. The network package—games played on Sunday afternoons from early January through the end of the championships in early June—includes roughly 35 games selected for television coverage by the NBA. In fact, the purchasing network expresses a preference for teams and match-ups, and the NBA schedules games accordingly. This package has been licensed on and off by CBS and by ABC for many years; in the early 1990s, NBC bought these rights for the first time, paying $150 million for four-year period. The NBA's cable package includes 50 regular season games plus 30 playoff games, scheduled in prime time and mainly on weeknights. That cable package is currently held by TNT; the contract totals $275 million, also for four years.

There is no single nationwide rights organization for college basketball—each conference negotiates its own deal. All three of the broadcast networks have packages for college basketball games. CBS has the largest one, a $1-billion NCAA deal that includes 16 games per year for seven years.

CBS is the leader in golf, with about 18 tournaments per year compared to ABC's 8 or 9 and NBC's 5 or 6. TNT does 3 tourneys a year, and ESPN does about 10. ESPN and USA cover only the early rounds of some tournaments; the later rounds are covered by the broadcast networks. Golf events vary in their value—the top tournaments such as the U.S. Open or the Masters Tournament reach large numbers of viewers in the target group, but the lesser ones do not.

CBS has the rights for U.S. Open tennis, at a cost of $20 million per year, but early rounds appear on USA Network ($9 million per year). There is a similar arrangement for Wimbledon and the French Open. NBC has the broadcast rights to the later rounds to both events; the earlier rounds of Wimbledon are shown on HBO, and the earlier rounds of the French Open appear on ESPN.

The cost of the package for each sport is typically based on its mid-term value, with the price of the early games skewed in favor of the sports organization, and the price of the later games balanced in favor of the network. For either a broadcast or cable network, the last year of one contract appears much cheaper than the first year of the next contract—the difference in advertising revenues from one year to the next is never as large. In general, the network either loses money or breaks even during the first two years of the contract, and makes more than enough to compensate during the succeeding two or three years.

The Olympics

The business of Olympics coverage is unusual for several reasons. First, the rights purchase requires a large upfront committment of dollars; if the deal is made five years in advance, as is common, 10 to 15 percent of the rights fee is paid to the various Olympic committees in each of the five years. Of this rights purchase, 66 percent goes to the local organizing committee hosting the games, 24 percent goes to the International Olympic Committee, and 10 percent goes to the U.S. Olympic Committee. Second, the production costs for Olympic coverage is high. Third, advertisers fund coverage through special budgets because their commitments are unusually intensive—a large number of commercials within a two- to three-week period.

The rights for the 1992 Winter Olympics cost $243 million; for the 1996 Winter games, it was $300 million. Since both are based in Europe, the production costs for U.S. companies will be high, in the range of $20 million. The Summer Olympics are more expensive because there are more events. In 1984, ABC spent about $225 million for rights; for the 1988 games in Seoul, NBC spent about $310 million for rights; and the same network paid $401 million for the 1992 games in Barcelona. Rights to the 1996 Summer Olympics in Atlanta will probably cost over $500 million (the Olympic Committee's budget estimates a total of $600 million in worldwide rights, and presumes that $100 million of that will come from other countries).

Production costs for locations outside the U.S. can be very high. An extraordinarily large staff for both planning and actual production, the complex logistics of transportation and staff housing, and the need to cover events in multiple locations can add up to $125 million or more for the summer games and about $75 million for the winter games. The host broadcaster—ABC for the Los Angeles games in 1984, for example—provides facilities and feeds for visiting countries for a fee, which does help allay some of the host broadcaster's own coverage costs.

The Structure of a Network Sports Division

The size of a network sports organization tends to vary over the course of the year, depending upon the number of events and the free-lance staff required to supplement the full-time employees. The staff size tends to range from 75 to 150 people, with roughly 100 full-time employees. One chief executive runs the operation, with two vice presidents—one in charge of production, and the other in charge of program acquisition, scheduling, and business affairs. Advertising sales are usually done by the network with the involvement of a liaison working in the sports department; publicity, on-air promotion, and print advertising may be handled by either the network's sports division or the network itself.

CABLE SPORTS: REGIONAL NETWORKS

In addition to the cable networks that carry sports events on a national basis, Prime Network and SportsChannel America own and operate cable channels that cover sports of local interest. SportsChannel New York, for example, shows games from the Mets and Yankees. These regional sports channels independently set rates for cable subscribers and for advertisers, negotiate the rights to local and regional events, and schedule games. Madison Square Garden Network (MSG) and Home Team Sports (HTS) are smaller cable services that feature regional sports programming.

Prime Network

Prime Network owns and operates six regional sports channels: Sunshine Network (Florida), Home Sports Entertainment (Texas region and bordering states), Prime Sports Network-Rocky Mountain, Prime Sports Network-Utah, Prime Sports Network-Upper Midwest (Dakotas, Minnesota, Iowa), and Prime Sports Network-Midwest (Illinois, Ohio, Indiana, Missouri, and bordering areas).

Jointly owned by TCI and cable-TV pioneer Bill Daniels, Prime Network in turn owns parts of other regional services, and shares its programming with several independent channels that are unaffiliated with Prime Network—notably, Madison Square Garden Network and Home Team Sports (see below).

With approximately 15 affiliates, Prime Network covers the country, and had 21 million basic-cable subscribers as of mid-1990. Affiliates contract with pro sports clubs, typically for rights only within the local territory—though the network negotiates on behalf of its affiliates for the rights to certain college games. Prime Network also represents its affiliates when purchasing national and international licenses.

Prime Ticket Network, wholly owned by Prime Network and located in Los Angeles, is the largest regional sports service in the country. Prime Ticket Network has an advantage over the area's SportsChannel outlet because it holds the rights to Lakers basketball and Kings hockey (both teams are owned by one of Prime Ticket's founders). In addition, Prime Ticket covers UCLA matches, USC athletics, and other events.

SportsChannel America

SportsChannel America is owned by Rainbow Program Holdings and NBC, and does more than carry sports events on a regional basis. SportsChannel America also offers a national feed to cable systems in much of the Northwest, Great Plains, and the South. Some of these national programs are carried on regional services like SportsChannel Florida (which competes directly with Prime Network's Sunshine Network.) SportsChannel Los Angeles and SportsChannel Bay Area (in San Francisco) draw from their own local events, and service all of California and Nevada, plus parts of Arizona and Oregon. Other network-owned and -operated facilities are located in Chicago, New York, New England, Philadelphia, Ohio, and Cincinnati. Each of these local services combines national programming from SportsChannel America with its own local coverage. The SportsChannel outlets are generally offered as pay services, but they also sell commercial time.

Madison Square Garden and Home Team Sports

Madison Square Garden Network (MSG)—owned by Paramount Communications—competes with SportsChannel New York and SportsChannel America in the New York area. The oldest cable network with all-sports programming, MSG covers Yankees baseball, Knicks basketball, Rangers hockey, and St. John's basketball; boxing and horse racing round out the MSG schedule. Home Team Sports (HTS), a basic service owned by Group W Satellite Communications, airs in Delaware, Maryland, Virginia, and North Carolina. HTS covers Baltimore Orioles baseball, Washington Bullets basketball, Washington Capitals hockey, and Atlantic Coast conference college sports to subscribers in the mid-Atlantic region.

Both Home Team Sports and Madison Square Garden share programming with Prime Network as well.

PAY-PER-VIEW SPORTS

As pay-per-view (see Chapter 7) matures, some national and regional sports events are likely to be sold on a per-game basis. Cablevision and NBC plan to offer the 1992 Summer Olympics Triplecast via PPV. The San Diego Padres already offer such a service to local cable subscribers—in 1991, prices were $6.95 per game, or $180 for a 50-game package. At present, PPV sports has been successful only in isolated instances, and with particular types of programs (such as wrestling and big-name boxing).

SYNDICATED SPORTS

Coverage rights to most sporting events are sold to either broadcast or cable networks, so syndication plays a relatively minor role in sports programming. Still, there are some exceptions.

The World Wrestling Federation produces and distributes several series, including WWF Superstars of Wrestling, WWF Wrestling Challenge, and WWF Wrestling Spotlight.

Raycom Sports and Entertainment is a leading distributor of sports-event programming. Raycom's 1990 offerings included 12 live games from the Southwest Conference; the Liberty Bowl; the Freedom Bowl; basketball games from the Big 10, PAC 10, and Big Eight, as well as other conferences; and game packages from Northwestern, Ohio State, Wisconsin, Michigin, Iowa, Indiana, Illinois, and other schools.

Some golf and racing events are also syndicated.

SPORTS COVERAGE ON LOCAL BROADCAST STATIONS

Local broadcast stations face increasing competition in their sports coverage from national and regional cable networks. In 1990, for example, WMAR-TV, Baltimore's NBC affiliate, broadcast 43 Orioles away games and 3 home games; HTS, the regional cable network for Baltimore, carried 85 games. This scenario has been repeated in most markets with hometown baseball. Viewers are forced to subscribe to cable (presuming that cable is available in their area), or to miss games; in any case, viewers must now pay for something that was previously provided at no charge. Since sports fans can be a vocal constituency, legislators count this as one of several reasons why cable television requires their scrutiny.

Pro football is sold to networks only on a national basis, so local coverage is not an issue. Basketball is sold nationally as well, but the NBA also sells rights for local sports coverage to individual stations and regional cable channels. Whenever there is a conflict, the network blacks out the game in the home city, or replaces it with an alternate game. The same is true for baseball. College football may air at one time of day for the network coverage, then later that same day for local coverage.

The cost of rights for local broadcast coverage depends upon the size of the market and the team's ability to draw a large audience (the latter is related to the team's won/lost record). A 50-game baseball package for a medium-sized market would probably cost a local station $5–10 million, or $100,000–$200,000 a game. In contrast, ESPN, a national cable network, pays an average of $570,000 a game; CBS, which pays $250 million a year primarily to air post-season games, pays considerably more for per-game rights.

Amateur Sports

Small-scale sporting events can be significant audience draws in their communities. Some cable television systems now regularly cover amateur sports on the high school and college levels. If audience interest is high, sale of commercial time in these programs can more than pay for the cost of covering the game. Since there is rarely competition for rights—and because showing the game generally increases local interest in the team—rights payments are uncommon.

SPORTS COVERAGE AS PROMOTION

Sports coverage is not television journalism—it is, in fact, more akin to show business. When covering a local game, for example, the director is frequently instructed to highlight the heroes, and to avoid showing the players after poorly-executed plays. The reasons are obvious: the renewal of the television contract is dependent in part upon the broadcaster or cablecaster's treatment of the team, and the more popular the team, the better the ratings for the broadcaster. Some broadcasters and production staffs are employed directly by the teams; in some instances, the team and the television company even work together on fan promotions.

TELEVISION AND SPORTS MARKETING

Television's widespread distribution of sports programming is also the core of the sports marketing business. Team logotypes are valuable merchandise-licensing properties. Corporate sponsorship of events like tennis and racing provides positive exposure above and beyond that afforded by mere advertising. Cigarette advertisers, for example, can gain television exposure by sponsoring race cars; these sponsors would otherwise be excluded from the medium. Stadium signage that is seen on television is also an effective type of advertising.

OLDER SPORTS PROGRAMMING

Sports coverage loses value immediately after it is broadcast. Even the most memorable World Series game or Super Bowl is of only minimal interest as a repeat program.

There is, however, a special marketplace for historical sports footage. Some programs have been successful in home video, particularly when sold as mail-order items. A small number of such shows have done well in syndication, and on cable services that specialize in historical programming. Still, broadcast and cable companies that do live sports programs tend to fill their schedules with more the same. Sports documentaries have met with a luke-warm reception.

Rights Issues

Each sport has its own management system for historical material. Major League Baseball claims ownership of all games—or at least, of the television coverage of all games since there has *been* television coverage. Older baseball footage may be hard to find, and rights are typically cleared by the library providing the footage. The NFL, the NHL, and the NBA operate in a similar fashion, though there may be some dealing with the individual teams as well. Golf and tennis footage is usually owned by either the production company, the network, or the association that granted the television rights. Use of college sports coverage must be cleared by either the appropriate conference that made the television deal, by the individual school, or sometimes both.

Often, simply finding old sports footage is as difficult as determining who owns the rights, and who has the right to clear the footage for use. Many games were never recorded; if they were, the material may have been destroyed or lost. Most stock-footage houses archive sports footage, but their libraries tend to be spotty.

When the rights are granted, they should include the right to show the players *and* the game. As for the fans—and anyone who was in or near the venue before, during, or after the game—releases may be necessary, particularly if the material will be used outside of its purely historical context (see Chapter 19).

9 Home Video

The term "television" implies the origination of a program at one location, and the transmission of that program over the air, or through cables, to a viewer at another location. Most television programs are simultaneously seen by more than one household. In addition, "television" suggests multiple channels. The term "video," on the other hand, refers to origination and playback devices that are located in one place, that operate on a single channel, and that have no transmission requirements. The term "video" is also used as a synonym for closed-circuit television (for example, to refer to a corporate video transmission system).

This chapter discusses home video: videogames, videocassettes, and videodiscs. The following chapters describe business video and music video.

As technologies evolve, the distinction between the terms "television" and "video" (as well as the lines that separate computers, videogames, and telephones) may become sufficiently blurred to call for an altogether new way of describing electronic communications.

HISTORY

The home video business began in the early 1970s with a series of consumer products. First came the videogame in 1972, a home version of a recently-introduced arcade pastime. Pong and Odyssey were the first devices that transformed the TV set into something other than a box that received broadcast television transmissions. Sony's Betamax arrived in 1975, followed in 1977 by the first VHS machines from Matsushita's JVC subsidiary. Several other home video formats, such as the Funai system marketed by Technicolor, never gained much popularity. In 1978, Magnavox sold its first laser videodisc system, followed in 1981 by RCA's CED videodisc, a system based on a traditional phonograph stylus. JVC announced plans for a third system called VHD that was never released in the U.S. During the same period, Apple, Atari, and Commodore introduced personal computers that used the TV set to display data and graphics. From this assortment of technical innovations, several significant product categories emerged under the banner of home video.

VIDEOGAMES

Videogames are more closely allied with computer software than traditional television programming, but because they are played on a television screen, they are treated briefly here.

Videogames have been a popular extension of television for two decades, with new systems—generally offering improved sounds and graphics—overtaking older ones every few years. Atari was an early leader, followed by Mattel (Intellivision), then Coleco (Colecovision), and, more recently, Nintendo. As of this writing, NEC TurboGrafx and Sega Genesis are technically superior systems beginning to erode the market share of the older Nintendo Entertainment System, but a new Nintendo system is expected to compete successfully.

A videogame system is a special purpose computer, roughly equal in power and capability to a mid-priced home computer. The hardware (Nintendo Entertainment System, for example) is priced to encourage deep market penetration; profit margins on game hardware are traditionally thin. The real money is made on sales of software cartridges.

Videogame software is generally developed by small and medium-sized companies that specialize in product for arcade videogames, home cartridges, and/or personal computer software. The game program may be licensed to a software publisher at any point during development, usually for an advance against royalties. In some cases, all rights are purchased on a one-time basis, but this is unusual. There is no fixed relationship between product development costs and the size of the advance from software publisher, though most deals cover a high percentage of the development budget with the advance.

If the software publisher is also the maker of the hardware (Nintendo, NEC, and Sega all publish software), the publisher/manufacturer may deduct a manufacturing fee or royalty from net proceeds. If the publisher is independent, it may be forced to manufacture the cartridge through the maker of the hardware. This had been the case with Nintendo, Sega, and NEC cartridges until 1990; limited exceptions are now being made. A hardware maker like Nintendo charges several dollars more per cartridge for basic manufacturing than an outside firm would charge. If the software publisher makes the cartridges by subcontracting manufacturing to a third party, then manufacturing costs may be lower—but Nintendo would require a fee for the right to its patent. Still, there may some advantages to working with an outside firm: faster delivery, better credit terms, and the elimination of the U.S. duties and customs charges that total about 8 percent of manufacturing costs.

Most software companies like Nintendo, Konami, and Acclaim sell product to toystores through a sales representative firm ("sales rep"). The sales rep often markets several videogame lines, but usually not more than one major brand. These reps service not only toystores, but also discount chains (Target, Wal-Mart, Sears, K-Mart). Record stores, video stores, and smaller chains like Long's Drug and Walgreen's are handled by record, computer-software, or toy distributors. Many software publishers supplement the reps' activity with telemarketing.

Most videogame cartridges sell for $25 to $50 at retail. On a cartridge that sells for $40, the wholesale price would be about $24. The sales rep usually receives about 5 percent, but the range of 3 to 8 percent of wholesale price is common; at a 5 percent rate, that commission would come to $1.20 for a $40 cartridge. The publisher spends about $1 or $2 on royalties, pays roughly $10 for manufacturing, and nets about $11.50 before overhead. The publisher and the retailer may work together on an advertising plan, using money that the publisher provides—up to about 3 percent of the total wholesale price. In order to collect their share of this "co-op advertising" fund, or Market Development Funds (MDF), the retailer must provide tearsheets of print ads or airchecks of radio commercials to the publisher.

The royalties that a software publisher will pay a company that develops videogames are based not on a percentage of sales, but on a flat rate per cartridge. A rate of 50 cents is considered low and $2 very high. Most royalty rates are clustered in the $1.00–$1.25 range, though higher rates may be paid to an especially skillful developer or to cover the costs of a large programming project. The rate may be on the lower side if the software publisher has to pay a licensing fee to use a well-known character, game format, or logo. These licensing fees usually range from 50 cents to $2, again, per cartridge. The publisher may also pay the videogame developer an advance against royalties to help fund project development and production—an average advance would be $75,000–$125,000. Much of this money pays the development staff: a director, a designer, a lead programmer, a second programmer, an artist and a composer. The term of the deal usually matches the life of the system, and the videogame developer may hold back certain rights in exchange for a lower royalty rate.

VIDEOCASSETTES

Introduced by Sony in 1975, the videocassette recorder (VCR) was first marketed as a machine that could record and play back television programs. Sony had the right idea with Betamax; that format was initially superior to VHS, a competitive system devised by JVC and released two years later. Ultimately, VHS became the dominant format, largely because a slower recording/playback speed and more tape per cassette meant that VHS tapes could record more programming than Betamax cassettes. In addition, Matsushita (which owned 51 percent of JVC) also aggressively licensed the VHS format to other manufacturers, which resulted in an large installed base of VHS machines and a demand for pre-recorded tapes in the VHS format. While the concept of "time-shift viewing" was initially the principal reason why consumers purchased

VCRs, the ability to play pre-recorded movies quickly became an equally compelling reason to buy a machine.

By 1977, several companies were selling pre-recorded videocassettes by mail (VidAmerica, now a small label, was renting by mail as well). As more VCRs were sold, an increasing number of film and television companies released product from their libraries on their own newly-founded labels, or else licensed films to independent labels—Magnetic Video, for example, licensed films from the Twentieth Century-Fox library in the years before CBS/Fox was formed. Most labels released films primarily for rental through a new type of retail outlet, the video store. Some companies, notably Vestron Video, also created videocassettes specifically for direct sale to consumers: "sell-through product."

With VCR penetration rapidly rising, and a new distribution system to reach the consumers now in place, each of the motion picture studios formed a home video label—first to release material from their libraries, then to aggressively market recent box office hits.

Distribution

The home video business employs a unique distribution system, a hybrid with roots in both record and book distribution. In a simple example, a major motion picture studio such as Warner Bros. produces a film for theatrical release. The film finishes its first theatrical run, then the studio's video division, Warner Home Video, releases the film on cassette (and, in some instances, on laserdisc). Independently-produced films are licensed to the label that makes the best offer.

The videocassette reaches the consumer in one of several different ways. Large retail accounts—record-store chains, drugstores, and mass merchants—are frequently serviced directly by the label via "one-step distribution." The label's sales force takes orders from a buyer at a large chain, and arranges for shipment of a specified number of titles at a price based on volume of units ordered and other factors. The majority of video retail accounts, however, are serviced with two-step distribution, which operates as follows. A video distributor like Commtron will take orders from video chains and some individual stores. It pre-orders the proper quantities of each title from the label before a "pre-book" or "order cut-off" date. The home video label then ships these tapes to Commtron, who sends them to a central warehouse (in the case of a chain) or to individual stores. The store decides whether to sell or to rent the cassette. Official release dates, called "street dates," are determined by the label.

Since barriers to entry and capital requirements are small, independent producers of special-interest programs release their own home video product. This is an especially viable method for titles that require distribution to a focused group of retail or direct-marketing outlets. For example, the producer of a baby-care tape would work with stores and marketers that specialize in related products.

Video Stores

The early years of video distribution at the local level were dominated by local "mom-and-pop" operations, storefronts staffed by members of the owner's family or by people living in the neighborhood. Working with limited inventories—and frequently offering sidelines like VCR repairs, candy, and popcorn—many of these stores were, and still are, successful.

Running a video store can be a complicated business, relying as it does on accurately tracking product that is repeatedly being rented and returned to the store. It also requires a sizeable capital investment to stock at least 3,000 titles for rental. Once, store owners favored membership fees to help them capitalize, and traded long-term discounts to customers for short-term cash. But now, with the proliferation of larger stores that do not charge a membership fee, neighborhood stores have eliminated fees and have dropped their prices to compete in a crowded marketplace. In addition, the store must invest in new titles regularly—and correctly estimate the number of copies of hit titles necessary to satisfy most customers, but not so many that the shelves are still full by 9:00 P.M. on a Saturday night. Stores must also order enough copies of smaller films to satisfy customers, but not so many that their shelves become cluttered with unwanted merchandise.

A small neighborhood video store stocks up to 3,000 titles; a medium-sized store, typically located in a strip shopping center, up to 5,000; a large chain store, like Blockbuster, carries up to 10,000. Like most retail operations, the success of a video store depends upon the product selection, the convenience of the location, and the quality of customer service.

The video store can be an ideal format for franchising. Several franchise systems have given the mom-and-pop outlets the benefits of regional advertising, superior signage, group purchasing, and inventory control.

Blockbuster, the number one video chain in the country with 1,500 stores, built its system in part by buying other chains. Blockbuster franchises pay about $70,000 in various fees to open a store, as well as the option to purchase their initial tape inventory, which can cost up to $600,000. Each franchisee pays the company $6,000 in annual computer fees, 7 percent of revenue as a royalty, and 2 percent of revenue for advertising expenses. Annual operating costs run about $460,000, with new tape purchases accounting for $160,000.*

West Coast Video, under the West Coast Video and National Video names, is the second largest U.S. chain with 600 stores, mostly franchised. West Coast Video charges a $50,000 franchise fee plus 7 percent of monthly revenues, including a 2 percent advertising allowance. In

---

* Source: Kidder, Peabody Equity Research.

addition, stores may purchase software from West Coast or from other vendors.

Franchising is subject to legal regulation, generally aimed at preventing fraud and excessive use of the franchise's power to strip away any economic benefits to the franchise value.

How a Video Store Makes Money

Video stores typically purchase cassettes for rental and for sale as sell-through product. Cassettes are purchased for a wholesale price based on number of units ordered, and resold for a retail price that is suggested by the label. Fair-trade laws generally require that the wholesale price offered to one buyer must be offered to all buyers purchasing the same number of units. The store (or chain) determines the number of cassettes that will be offered for rental, and the number that will be offered for sale. With an average price of $29.95 per cassette, and an average rental price of $2.50 for newer titles and $2.00 for older ones, the apparent break-even point is 12 rental transactions. In fact, the number is far higher, because of the cost of wages, rent, and other overhead items. Rental fees only provide 75 to 90 percent of the average store's revenues; the other 10 to 25 percent is made up by sales of cassettes and accessories, as well as other hardware (VCRs and camcorders) and software (videogame cartridges, CDs, and audiocassettes).

Operation of a Home Video Label

The supply side of the home video business is dominated by labels that operate as sister companies to motion picture studios—MCA Home Video, Warner Brothers Home Video, Walt Disney Home Video, and Orion Home Video are examples. Medium-sized companies find it difficult to license enough product to justify substantial overhead, though some independent companies have succeeded via aggressive management. Smaller labels generally require a special type of product profile, or a unique distribution system, in order to survive. Kultur, for example, offers only arts programming, such as opera, classical music, and ballet. Best Film & Video offers several lines of branded product, such as a Rand McNally travel series, and a series of health tapes produced with Prevention Magazine. Good Times specializes in mass-market tapes priced under $10 and sold to mass merchandisers (many of which also buy toys).

A home video label is organized very much like a book or record company. A senior executive, typically a president, oversees all aspects of the operation. A programming department is responsible for the acquisition of new titles and for original productions, if any. If the company is a large one, the programming department may be subdivided into groups for feature film acquisition, for non-movie product, and for original production. The operations department supervises duplication, packaging, warehousing, shipping, and inventory. The marketing department creates the package design, sales literature, and dealer promotions. The sales department sells certain accounts directly, and supervises the work of independent distributors and reps for other accounts. An accounting department takes care of billing and royalties, as well as traditional bookkeeping and reporting functions.

The economics of the home video label are based on a standard retail model. The following is an example of the costs involved for a title with a $19.95 list price and one-step distribution:

Rights and royalties	1.50
Cassette and duplication	1.00
Cover	1.00
Advertising and promotion	1.50
Label overhead and profit	8.00
Wholesale price	13.00
Dealer mark-up	6.95
Retail price	19.95

This model is applicable to high-visibility product like major motion picture releases, where sales exceeding 100,000 units are possible. Dealer mark-up may be lower if the emphasis is on selling a large number of copies to consumers.

Sometimes the mass-consumer market is sacrificed for higher profits from sales to smaller groups, such as the video stores. By pricing a film at $90 ($65 dealer cost), the label is saying that the film is intended not for sell-through, but for the rental pipeline. A true blockbuster title will sell about 400,000 units at this price point. The same title, priced at $24.95, would probably sell between 3 million and 6 million units; at $19.95, it would probably sell over 5 million units, maybe as many as 10 million units.

A home video label earns money only by selling cassettes. Although a cassette may be rented by dozens of customers, the label does not receive any further payment for these rentals.

Since many non-theatrical products are made for home video, or assembled from existing sources and repackaged for home video, the cost of production must be deducted from the label's net sales. A cooking tape that costs $100,000 to produce would have to sell about 20,000 units in order to break even—assuming that roughly $5 per unit is available to cover the cost of production.

For non-theatrical product, the International Tape/Disc Association awards gold certification for titles that sell 25,000 units, or $1 million at retail. For theatrical product, gold certification is awarded at sales of 125,000 units, or $9 million at retail.

Promotional Marketing, Commercials, and Home Video

There is now a VCR in two of every three television households. This installed base has reached advertiser "critical mass"—that is, there are now enough VCR households to make home video a viable advertising medium.

There is a fundamental problem, however, with home video as an advertising tool. Advertising requires a system of headcounts, and home video presently lacks a means to count its viewers. Nielsen is currently testing a system; others are in development.

Anxious to reach consumers in their own homes, many advertisers have nonetheless purchased commercial time on big box office films, correctly assuming that a successful theatrical film is typically rented or purchased by large number of viewers. The fees paid are based on anticipated sales, presently the only quantifiable aspect of the home video business. While it is possible to roughly estimate the number of tapes that have been sold, and the number of times that each rental tape has been screened, it is impossible to know how many viewers actually saw the commercial, and how many zapped (or fast-forwarded past) the commercial.

Some advertisers have successfully used home video as a medium for imaginative forms of promotional marketing. Downey Fabric Softener includes a commercial on the videocassette version of *The Wizard of Oz*. Downey pays several dollars to each viewer who sends them back a rebate coupon that comes with the tape. This permits Downey to count the number of viewers who purchased, and presumably screened, the tape. Downey is also involved in the video product's marketing, consumer and trade advertising, and public relations. This is just one of several promotional arrangements currently in use.

Direct Marketing of Videocassettes

Videocassettes are sold though several direct-marketing formats. The simplest format is the catalog sale, by which a catalog company buys wholesale price and sells retail. This system is used by a wide variety of catalog marketers, including L.L. Bean, whose video products are mainly private-label productions; Disney, whose video products are offered along with music boxes, records, clothing, toys, and other items; and specialty firms whose products appeal to viewers with a particular area of interest (such as fishing). Other catalogs offer primarily videocassettes, with hundreds of titles available, frequently at discount prices. The largest catalog operation is PCB (Publisher's Central Bureau), followed by Video Choice, owned by Playboy.

Video catalogs thrive on diversity. Big-name motion pictures do well, but so do classics and esoteric films that are not stocked with any consistency in video stores. Catalog companies generally buy from the labels at below-wholesale prices, since they order such large volumes.

Video clubs are now as common as record and book clubs, and follow the same procedures. A consumer signs up, receives one or more tapes for a very low price, and agrees to purchase a specified number of tapes in the future. Some clubs resemble catalog operations, using "positive option" sales—the consumer buys only what he or she wants.

Negative option clubs are more complicated. The club selects a title as its monthly selection; club members who want to buy the title do nothing, but members who do *not* want the title must notify the club within a specified period. The negative-option format has been successfully used for more than ten years by Columbia House and, more recently, by BMG Video Club and Time-Life Video Club.

Continuity or subscription clubs are used to sell certain product lines. Columbia House, for example, sells a series of *I Love Lucy* tapes; the consumer buys the first one for $4.95, then receives a new one every four to six weeks until they decide to cancel, paying $29.95 for each tape. Continuity distribution is best for series programming: examples include *World War II with Walter Cronkite*, *The World at War*, *Star Trek*, and James Bond movies. TV series, movies on the same topic, and military histories are among the best-sellers. Once again, the clubs buy at below-wholesale prices.

Columbia House operates a laserdisc direct-mail club as well.

Sales of Videocassettes in Non-Traditional Outlets

Video stores are ideally suited to the sale and rental of movie titles; consumers have developed patterns of visiting the local video store for an evening's entertainment. Due to the success of work-out tapes from Jane Fonda and others, the video store is also the outlet of choice for exercise video—though exercise tapes are routinely sold in book and record stores as well, in part because Fonda has developed books and records as ancillary products that are sold through these outlets. Many video stores include a rack of miscellaneous special-interest products that displays programs like *NOVA* and the *National Geographic* specials alongside other documentaries, how-to tapes, and similar non-movie product. Most stores stock only a limited number of these titles, updating the inventory on an irregular basis and using rack jobbers.

Many bookstores stock video titles for sale. Waldenbooks, the largest bookstore chain selling video, orders directly from the home video labels, or from book distributors who stock video product as well. Smaller bookstore chains order through wholesalers. Bookstores typically purchase product on a 100 percent returnable basis—any product can be returned to the label or distibutor if it does not sell within a specified period of time (usually 60 days). These returned videocassettes are generally good for invoice credit from the distibutor, credit that can be used to purchase other product. Bookstores tend to group all their tapes in one video section, which is stocked by a distributor or rack jobber. Movies and children's programs thus appear on the same shelves as cooking shows. In an ideal world, cooking videos would be placed alongside cookbooks, but this is not the way that the merchandising has evolved. As a result, most special-interest video programs have not sold particularly well in bookstores.

Record stores concentrate on music videos, but most of them sell videogame cartridges and movies as well. Chain record stores, and most independents, buy directly from the labels—or, more accurately, from large distribution systems like Polygram and WEA that operate as sister companies to record labels. Smaller stores buy from distributors known as rack jobbers. Rack jobbers also service mass merchandisers via a plan-o-gram system, in which each rack position is filled with a specific title. Plan-o-gram positions are determined by the type of store and customer base, the sales potential of each video title, and the ongoing success of titles aleady in position.

Specialty stores with video sidelines, such as sporting-goods stores, may order from their own distributors, from video distributors, or directly from the labels. Generally, the labels sell in accordance with each retail segment's customs and procedures.

VIDEODISCS

The consumer videodisc industry began in the 1970s. By the early 1980s, three incompatible systems were competing not only among themselves, but against several videocassette recording systems as well. LaserVision was the only system to survive the competition, and after an extraordinarily sluggish decade in the 1980s, the laserdisc system has found favor among videophiles, who appreciate the high-quality audio and video presentation.

As of this writing, more than 6,000 laserdisc titles are available in the U.S., with several hundred additional titles released annually. Laserdiscs are sold only in selected video stores. The business is a small one, so many studios and film distributors release discs through one of two large distributors, Image Entertainment or Pioneer LDC. (Warner, MGM/UA, and MCA home video divisions release their own laserdisc titles.) Most laserdiscs are sold to consumers for $25.95 to $34.95, but if the format continues to gain momentum, these prices may drop.

The economics of laserdiscs are similar to the videocassette model, but the manufacturing cost is slightly higher and the advertising costs are lower (the disc benefits from the promotional investment for the videocassette). A major laserdisc release will sell 10,000 to 50,000 units; a lesser title, 2,000 to 10,000 units.

10 Business Video

The term "business video" refers to a variety of unrelated forms: programs made by corporations to inform, train, or motivate employees, stockholders, or customers; customized programs for business use, made by outside vendors; and programs produced and marketed as off-the-shelf products, usually for training. This chapter deals with developing, producing, and distributing programs for business use.

Although music video is really a type of business video—in the sense that music videos are primarily promotional materials to sell records—the form is different enough to warrant a separate chapter.

DEVELOPMENT

Business-video projects are typically developed within companies, usually by a department or division with a specific communications need. Business video might be used to relay quarterly reports from the chairman of the company to employees or stockholders; to provide instruction for operating a new piece of equipment; to train salespeople on a new product line; or to teach proper interviewing techniques. An in-house production group is assigned to the project, and works closely with the department for which the project is being made. In some instances, the project is produced out of house. Projects are usually financed by departmental budgets, but may also be subsidized by a corporate video-department budget that is available to all departments.

IN-HOUSE PRODUCTION

Since the late 1970s, the cost of video hardware has been steadily dropping, allowing not only large corporations, but also many smaller organizations, to install and maintain production and editing facilities.

Most companies operate these facilities as audio/visual support services—akin to the company photographer, whose services are available by scheduling a date—and they are often set up as a subdivision of a creative-services unit. The audio/visual facilities are available to any department within the company, with development, production, and duplication costs allocated on a project basis.

The scope and capability of an in-house video group will vary depending upon the company's need and upon budget resources. Some groups employ a bare-bones staff, consisting of a studio manager and a producer or project manager, with free-lancers hired as needed for each project. Other video groups employ staff producers, directors, writers, editors, and technical crew. The most common situation is somewhere between the two, with in-house staff responsible for everyday projects—video news releases, point-of-purchase merchandising video, reports from executives to employees, and training tapes—and additional free-lancers added for larger projects such as video annual reports, materials for annual sales meetings, and major product introductions. With very few exceptions, these productions have no commercial value beyond internal and external company communications.

OUTSIDE PRODUCTION COMPANIES
AND BUSINESS VIDEO

Most company executives have the choice of either assigning a project to an in-house video unit or hiring an outside firm. An outside production company may be hired if it specializes in certain types of merchandising video, in interactive presentations that combine videodiscs and personal computers, or in large-scale company meetings. In some companies, the video department serves in an advisory role when outside vendors are hired, offering insights about production personnel and procedures, and occasionally providing facilities as well. In cases where an outside firm is used instead of an in-house group, there may be resentment on the part of the latter: an outside company has been hired to do something exciting and flashy, and the in-house staff has been deprived of the experience.

Every major metropolitan area supports several firms that specialize in video production for corporate clients. Most projects are produced on a work-for-hire (see page 138) basis—the production company is paid a fee for services rendered, and the client owns the master tapes and the copyright. In rare situations where the material may be valuable beyond its use by the company, production companies have arranged for an equity position, outright ownership after a period of exclusive in-company use, or distribution rights to sell the tapes to other companies.

Whenever a video project may have some commercial value, but neither marketing nor distribution plans are clear or well-defined, the production company and the client should each retain a percentage of ownership. The split should be based on the contribution of each party—creative, financial, or entrepreneurial. In situations where marketing and distribution plans are more clearly defined, and the production company will have an active role in the venture, the company may sometimes produce at cost, sacrificing mark-up for profit participation. Typically, the mark-up is in the range of 15 to 35 percent of the production budgets.

If the client distributes the program, then the production company is often required to do the job on a work-for-hire arrangement, at normal rates, and may negotiate for a royalty. A rate of 5 to 15 percent of distributor's net income, after deductions for marketing and manufacturing, is common.

OFF-THE-SHELF PRODUCT

For many years, specialty film-distribution companies supplied short films for sales training, motivation, and for specific topic areas, such as safety at building construction sites or the best way to run a meeting. Video has replaced film as the dominant medium, but the business is otherwise unchanged. A program is produced, most often by an independent company with a good idea and access to production money, then licensed to a distributor. The distributor either sells or rents the programs to clients; the producer shares in the revenues.

In this business, videocassette sales in the range of 100 to 500 units are common, with prices from $100 to $1,000, depending upon the length of the program, the topic, and the size of the market. Producers typically receive 10 to 20 percent of the distributor's gross revenues; the balance of the distributor's income pays sales commissions, direct-marketing costs, a percentage of convention expenses, and other operating costs, as well as profits.

11 Music Video

Despite its entertainment-industry roots, music video is a form of promotional video—the videos are made to sell records. Musical performances have been recorded on tape and film for decades, but it was not until 1981, and the debut of MTV, that creating visualizations of individual songs became an accepted marketing tool for records.

The record label usually decides which songs will be produced as music videos, and these choices usually correspond to whichever singles the record company will be servicing to radio stations. Most record companies employ a small staff responsible for producing and promoting music videos: the production coordinator selects and modifies idea treatments from independent music-video production companies, determines the schedule and budget, and approves the key hiring and creative decisions. In many cases, the recording artist suggests not only the concept, but a specific director and production company.

Production budgets for music videos usually start at $80,000 for well-known artists, and can reach as high as $500,000 or more for superstars. The artist, or the management company, may add to the production budget to pay for special personnel—such as a well-known motion picture director—or to finance special elements of the production—animation, for example, or an exotic shooting location. Some music videos, notably those produced for artists who are popular locally or regionally, have been produced for less than $5,000. In a low-budget production, the producer or director will usually beg or borrow necessary items that would have been purchased for cash if the budget were large enough to pay for them. Many low-budget productions are financed by the artist as a tool for self-promotion. The video may be shown in local clubs, and sent to MTV and other outlets on the outside chance that the video will be programmed and seen by a large audience. The artist's management may also show the video to record companies as an incentive to sign the artist.

Record companies typically finance the production of music videos, with 50 percent of the production costs charged back to the artist and recoupable against sales of albums (actually, of cassettes and compact discs). The advent of music-video sales complicates matters, however: should production costs be recoupable against album sales or video sales? The present policy favors album sales, since "long-form" videos (such as concert films) rarely break even.

EARNINGS FROM MUSIC VIDEO PRODUCTION

When the record company finances a video, it generally owns the copyright, and the right to exploit the video in all markets. The artist generally performs on the music video without receiving any additional fee; the artist may receive a small royalty from the sale of compilation videos, but only after recoupment of production costs. The production company and other creative contributors do not participate in these royalties—but as long-form videos are becoming profitable, these parties are starting to seek such participation.

When a record company releases a compilation of music-video clips, sales in the range of 20,000 to 40,000 units are common. With suggested list prices at $19.95 or less, royalties for the artists (at $4 per tape) can total roughly $120,000 for a single release. With ten songs on the tape, and a combined production cost exceeding $1 million, the artist may never see any home-video royalty income—since his or her deal with the record company usually allows the label to recoup production dollars *before* paying out royalties.

OUTLETS FOR MUSIC VIDEO

On cable television, MTV, VH-1, Black Entertainment Television (BET), The Jukebox Network, The Nashville Network, and Country Music Television are regarded as the most important showplaces for music video. On broadcast television, NBC's *Friday Night Videos*, TBS's *NightTracks*, several syndicated shows, and many local programs also feature music video.

The relationship between national music video networks and record companies is symbiotic. The networks need the videos as programming; the record companies need the networks to reach millions of viewers. MTV pays an annual fee to many record companies for the exclusive right to premiere a specified number of videos, which helps to defray the record company's production costs. In 1984, for example, MTV reportedly started paying CBS Records $8 million over a two-year period for exclusive rights to play roughly 40 videos per year. MTV's exclusive arrangements with record labels have angered other music channels, since some of them cannot play a certain video clip for up to six months after its initial release. Music video programs seen on local television do not pay fees to record companies.

PRODUCTION COMPANY ISSUES

A few dozen production companies, based mainly in Los Angeles and New York, produce most of the videos seen nationally. Unfortunately, this has contributed to a certain sameness in many music videos. Word-of-mouth recommendations, passed from one record company or artist to another, generates most of the work for production companies; it also helps when their videos are seen in clubs and on television.

A music video production company is typically an alliance between a producer and a director. In the best of circumstances, the producer and director collaborate to develop the initial creative concept, later refining it by working directly with the artist, the artist's management, and the record company (each may have a different degree of involvement). Then the producer attends to the usual details—hiring the crew, securing the locations, and keeping a close eye on the budget. The director works with the performers, choreographer (if there is to be any dance or specialized movement), the art director, and the wardrobe designer or supervisor. Most music videos are conceived, produced, and edited in about two to four weeks, from start to finish.

Rates and fees are negotiable. Mainstream production companies usually take 15 percent of each production budget for general overhead, plus 5 percent of the budget as the producer's fee, and 10 percent as the director's fee. A small, well-managed mainstream production company can produce between 15 and 20 music videos per year, with budgets in the $50,000–100,000 range. Many smaller companies supplement their music video work with corporate/industrial videos and other assignments; the larger outfits have a virtual army of producers and directors, and turn out dozens of videos each year. For larger companies, short-form music video is rarely the sole source of income—many of them also produce long-form programs, usually concert performances or music-video compilations with promotional clips added for home video release.

THE FUTURE OF MUSIC VIDEO

Compact discs are now being used to show song lyrics and relatively simple graphics in the CD+G format, and various interactive CD formats now offer video capability, albeit in a limited fashion (small images of short duration that move at less than 30 frames per second). Laser videodiscs are also gaining popularity. Eventually, a new kind of album format may emerge. Given these possibilities, and the ongoing popularity of MTV and other outlets, the commercial value of a music video is likely to increase in the future, especially if the video features an important artist.

12 New Distribution Technologies

Rapid technological development—particularly in distributing programs to households with only minimal intermediary activity by the network, station, or cable system—is likely dominate television and video through the 1990s. A new television standard known as high-definition television (HDTV) may also change a portion of the business.

SATELLITE DISTRIBUTION

The first communications satellite, Echo I, was launched by NASA in 1960, but it was not until the launch of Intelsat I (also called Early Bird) in 1965 that satellite transmission became a part of commercial broadcast technology. In the early years, satellites were used primarily by television networks to transmit live broadcasts from Europe. In 1974, RCA's Satcom I and Satcom II, and Western Union's Westar I and Westar II, made nationwide distribution of cable network programming possible. Through the 1970s and 1980s, several dozen satellites capable of retransmitting television programming were placed in orbit.

With satellite transmission, an uplink sends a television signal to the satellite. One of the satellite's transponders retransmits the signal back to earth, where the signal can be received by any downlink within a certain geographic region, or the satellite's "footprint." Most local television companies—and several million consumers—possess a downlink, more commonly called a satellite dish.

Most satellite services use the C band (3 to 4.2 Gigahertz). A total of 24 C-band satellites are presently in orbit over North America, with 5 to 9.5 watts of power on each transponder. In order to receive a transponder signal, the satellite dish must be 8 to 10 feet in diameter.

Ku band satellites use the 11.7–12.1 Ghz frequency range; this band is known as FSS (Fixed Satellite Service). There are 19 FSS satellites currently in orbit over North America, ranging in power from 20 to 45 watts per transponder; the FSS satellites require a 3-to 5-foot dish for clear reception. A second Ku band, from 12.2 to 12.7 Ghz, is known as the BSS (Broadcast Satellite Service) band. This band is for higher-powered satellites (with 100 to 200 watts); the required satellite antenna size is about 12 to 18 inches. The first BSS-band satellites covering the U.S. are planned for launch in 1993–94. Smaller-sized satellite dishes and satellite antennae, intended mainly for consumer use, are currently available to viewers in Japan and in several European countries.

Satellite Reception

Each C-band satellite contains 24 transponders. On Galaxy 1, a C-band satellite used by many cable services, the transponders have been leased as follows:

1. HBO (West Coast feed)
2. The Nashville Network
3. WGN
4. The Disney Channel (East Coast feed)
5. Showtime (East Coast feed)
6. Univision
7. CNN
8. CNN Headline News
9. ESPN
10. The Movie Channel (East Coast feed)
11. CBN Family Channel
12. A&E
13. Country Music TV
14. The Movie Channel (West Coast feed)
15. WWOR (New York)
16. Showtime (West Coast feed)
17. Inspirational Network
18. TBS-Superstation
19. Cinemax (East Coast feed)
20. Galavision
21. The USA Network (East Coast feed)
22. The Discovery Channel
23. HBO (East Coast feed)
24. The Disney Channel (West Coast feed)

Satcom 4, Galaxy 3, and Satcom 3R are also used mainly for cable networks. Other satellites are used for ABC, NBC, CBS, and PBS feeds; for college and professional sports feeds; by common carriers transmitting local television stations (KUSA-Denver, KCNC-Denver, WABC-New York, WXIA-Atlanta, and so on); and by a small number of other cable networks.

According to *Satellite TV Week,* a consumer magazine, there were 256 active channels during the summer of 1990 (including audio-only services). Approximately 55 of these channels were "scrambled."

For the first few years of satellite transmission, signals were intended mainly for retransmission by cable companies. But as more people bought satellite dishes, they could receive HBO for free, and this presented a threat to the pay services. The issue was resolved by scrambling the signal—and charging the subscriber a monthly fee for descrambling. All late-model satellite receivers now include a built-in descrambler that can be enabled, or activated, by paying a monthly fee to one of several companies offering packages of channels. Showtime Satellite Networks (owned by Viacom), for example, offers 18 popular channels for about $22 per month.

According to the Satellite Broadcasting and Communications Association of America, a non-profit industry group, a total of 3.1 million households owned satellite dishes by the summer of 1990, with 30,000 new dishes installed monthly.

Direct Broadcast Satellite (DBS)

With higher-powered satellites, and small, low-cost antennas planned for the near future, direct broadcast satellite (DBS) is becoming a more active area for entrepreneurs. SkyPix plans to offer 40 to 50 movie channels, all pay-per-view (showing 40 to 50 films simultaneously), plus 30 traditional channels showing children's programming, live events, superstations, and other programs. The DBS system uses higher-powered Ku band satellites, and requires a 2- to 3-foot dish as well as a special receiver. Primestar, whose investors include TCI and nine other large cable concerns, will offer three PPV channels plus seven superstations. Other such ventures are in the works.

FCC Rules Regarding Common Carriers and Satellite Transmission

Any company with the technical and financial capability to launch a satellite is eligible to do so. Keeping in mind agreements with other countries, particularly Canada and Mexico, the FCC then assigns an orbital position to the new satellite. Once the FCC authorizes a satellite, it works with the new licensee to clear International Telecommunications Union (ITU) issues. In 1979, the FCC deregulated the ownership of TV receive-only (TVRO) downlinks, so that any cable or broadcast system could own one or more dishes without any sort of license.

A company that transmits, or uplinks, signals to a satellite is classified as a *common carrier,* and can sell its transmission time and facilities to anyone willing to pay the price. But broadcasters and cable companies, by definition, control what is transmitted, so they cannot operate as common carriers. A new kind of company has evolved in the satellite industry: one which rents satellite transponder time and resells it to cable network services. Two such companies are Tempo and Eastern Microwave.

FIBER OPTICS

The cables that make cable television possible are made of copper or other conductive metal.* Copper wires have traditionally been used to interconnect households for cable service and for telephone service. During the past decade, the telephone companies have been rewiring most of their long-distance networks and many local systems with fiber optic cable. This has been done for three principal reasons: fiber optic cable maintains a high-quality signal; it is more dependable than copper wiring and less likely to deteroriate; and, most importantly, it can transmit thousands of times more information than copper cables, with a wider range of frequencies (or a wider 'bandwidth'). The telephone companies would like to rewire individual households, but they will do so only if they are permitted to provide additional services that cross the line between traditional telephone service and television.

The most important issue is bandwidth. Copper coaxial cable, currently in use in thousands of cable systems, can carry a few dozen television channels. A fiber optic cable, by comparison, can carry over 100 channels—with plenty of room left over for telephone conversations, data transmissions, and faxes.

With 90 million homes to be rewired, and an investment of more than $200 million at stake (a conservative estimate), the telephone companies are pressuring Congress to change the the Cable Act of 1984, which prohibits the transmission of visual images to television sets via telephone lines.

Ideally, and without regard to entrenched interests, the cable that provides telephone service could also carry signals for television service, plus access to home security, municipal services (fire, police, ambulance), and databases (public libraries, stock brokerage firms, banks). The phone company would probably operate the physical plant—the cables, line amplifiers, and switches that compose a telecommunications network. It would also provide many of the basic services, notably sending bills via E-Mail and collecting via electronic bank transfers. Because of the increased bandwidth, picturephone could be offered as well.

The increased number of channels would be used for traditional broadcast and cable services; in addition, several dozen could be used for pay-per-view services. With so many channels available, it would be possible to devote a pair of channels to the most popular new films, so that they begin every hour of the day and night. A channel might also be devoted entirely to *I Love Lucy,* so that viewers could watch their favorite episodes for a nominal fee.

---

* This section is adapted from an article written by Howard Blumenthal for *Video Review* magazine in 1990.

Interactive services should be possible as well, particularly with the telephone and the television connected into a single system. The potential for home shopping, home banking, home-based learning, and other such services could eventually be fulfilled by such a system.

HIGH-DEFINITION TELEVISION (HDTV)

The present U.S. television system, recommended by the National Television Standards Committee (NTSC) and approved by the FCC in the 1940s, presents images in a 3 × 4 ratio (3 units high, 4 wide). The horizontal resolution of the NTSC system is 525 lines. In the 1980s, more than a dozen companies worldwide began developing differing versions of a new television system. Most proposals for high-definition television (HDTV) offer two primary improvements over the current system: a wider screen, and increased resolution. Although the new proposed aspect ratios vary, most suggest a ratio that is closer to 3 × 5—roughly 20 percent wider than the present screen ratio. The increased resolution is usually proposed as 1125 lines—roughly double that of the present-day system, and roughly half the resolution available with 35mm motion picture film.

Present-day television equipment cannot accomodate the range of technical requirements demanded by HDTV. This means that video cameras, video switchers and other control equipment, video tape recorders and players, television transmitters, and cable television headends would all have to be replaced or substantially revamped in order to produce and broadcast in HDTV. Regardless of the HDTV standard that is ultimately approved by the FCC, additional bandwidth will be required. On broadcast, this additional bandwidth can be provided by assigning two traditional UHF broadcast channels to transmit a single HDTV broadcast channel. On cable, two channels can easily be assigned, though on systems with a small number of channels available, doing so may be at the expense of an existing service. By digitizing video, it may even be possible to compress the signals to a single channel.

HDTV reception on a standard NTSC television set is also at issue. The FCC will probably approve an HDTV standard only if its image can be seen on a standard TV set. This will mean either cropping the image, "letterboxing" it with black bands at the top and bottom of the screen, or electronically altering the image with technology that has yet to be invented.

There is another development route available, of course. HDTV can be offered as a standard outside the traditional broadcast domain. Households who want to see HDTV programming—which is likely to be dominated by major motion pictures—will buy either an HDTV VCR or, more likely, an HDTV laserdisc player, to show programs on an HDTV monitor in a home theater. HDTV signals might also be distributed via direct broadcast satellite.

The issue of a uniform television standard, however, remains. When the FCC approved the NTSC system, many other countries followed the U.S. lead, so that NTSC is the system used in Canada, Japan, and in other countries where our post-World War II influence was strong. Still, there are two other, incompatible television systems in use, one developed in Britain (PAL) and the other in France (SECAM). HDTV could be the first truly international television system, but will require the recommendation and approval of an international standards committee before it becomes a consumer product. This involves political questions as to which country's standard gets adopted; in addition, the free-market philosophy in the U.S. must change for the FCC to set any standard at all (see page 129).

HDTV may move ahead on another front: computer and multimedia data communications. HDTV programs are already being produced in the U.S. and abroad—sometimes as experiments, sometimes as a part of corporate marketing presentations, sometimes as a replacement for film. While this HDTV activity is likely to continue, it probably does not represent a meaningful step toward consumer acceptance of the new technology.

Part 2

REGULATION OF DISTRIBUTION

13 | FCC Basics

The Federal Communications Commission (FCC) is the principal government agency that regulates the television business. Its jurisdiction covers the means of mass television distribution: traditional broadcast, cable, satellite, and most emerging television technologies. Only home and business video—which do not use radio, wire, fiber, or other means of instantaneous mass distribution—currently escape FCC control. The FCC also regulates interstate telephone and telegraph service.

ORIGINS OF THE FCC

Television broadcasting involves sending signals on specific frequencies of radio waves. Radio waves are like light—there is a continuous spectrum of different waves, like the colors of the rainbow in the visible spectrum. Each small "color" gradation of the radio waves provides a different frequency, or broadcast channel. The spectrum of useful radio waves is broad, but not limitless. Some portions of the spectrum, like the FM band, travel limited distances, and can be reused in other parts of the country. Other frequencies, like the short wave bands, can travel great distances—particularly at night, when the reflective effect of the ionosphere is greater. If there are two stations broadcasting on the same frequency within range of each other, the signals will cross and interfere with each other, resulting in poor reception.

The first attempt at broadcast regulation in the U.S. was the Radio Act of 1912, which provided for the licensing of radio broadcasters by the Secretary of Commerce. Basically, this law allowed anyone who applied to get a license. Transmission was largely in Morse Code; as long as the airwaves were plentiful and the broadcasters few, there was no need to police who used what band. With the widespread introduction of sound reproduction via radio in the 1920s, however, the commercial potential of radio became clear, and the number of stations skyrocketed.

Faced with the need to bring some order to the use of a now-crowded spectrum, Congress passed the 1927 Radio Act, which set up the Federal Radio Commission. This Commission was empowered to pick and choose among potential broadcasters, assigning specific frequencies to particular licensees. The 1927 Act mandated that the standard for deciding who would qualify for a license was to be one of "public interest, convenience, and necessity." This phrase, the basis for regulating monopolies, had come into use in connection with the licensing of "natural monopolies": public utilities (such as water, gas, phone, and electric companies) and common carriers (such as railroads). When the 1927 Radio Act was drawn up, Congress thought that a "public interest, convenience, and necessity" approach should be used in dividing up the radio spectrum—even though the radio spectrum at that time provided enough diversity to prevent a true monopoly in most locations.

The 1927 Act was in effect until Congress adopted the Communications Act of 1934, which has remained the basis of communications law ever since. Although closely modeled on its 1927 predecessor, the 1934 Act created a new agency, the FCC, which took over the functions of the Radio Commission. The FCC also assumed, from the Interstate Commerce Commission, jurisdiction over interstate telephone and telegraph communications.

The FCC is a quasi-autonomous commission which has elements of each of the legislative, judicial, and executive branches of government. It is one of a group of independent regulatory agencies that provide expert oversight to various areas of commercial activity. Others include the Federal Aviation Agency (FAA), the Federal Trade Commission (FTC), the Securities and Exchange Commission (SEC), and the Interstate Commerce Commission (ICC). Each agency is established by acts of Congress, which set an overall framework of law and delegate the elaboration and implementation of that law to the agency.

ORGANIZATION OF THE FCC

The FCC consists of five Commissioners (seven before 1983), one of whom serves as Chairman. These Commissioners are nominated by the President for five-year terms. The President cannot appoint more than three of the five from one political party, and all appointments are subject to Senate approval. The Commissioners oversee a staff of about 1,800. The Chairman serves as the executive officer, with his actions subject to the approval of the majority of the Commission. Notwithstanding the President's role in naming the Commissioners, Congress has traditionally held the greatest power to influence the FCC, particularly since 1983. In that year, Congress dropped the FCC's permanent authorization, instead requiring reauthorization every two years. This reauthorization process provides a potent opportunity for Congressional "correction" of exercises of FCC independence.

The FCC includes the Commission itself and 14 major branches: the Office of the Inspector General, the Office of Legislative Affirs, the Office of Plans and Policy, the Office of the Managing Director, the Review Board, the Office of the Administrative Law Judges, the Office of Public Affairs, the Office of the General Counsel, the Office of Engineering and Technology, the Field Operations Bureau, the Common

Carrier Bureau, the Mass Media Bureau, the Private Radio Bureau, and the Office of International Communications. All of the branches report to the Managing Director, except for the Office of the Inspector General, which reports directly to the Commission. The Mass Media Bureau oversees broadcast and cable television, as well as radio stations and new mass-media video technologies.

The Commissioners set overall approaches; policy specifics are generally articulated at the staff level, then reviewed by the Commission before being adopted as official actions. The staff handles applications for licensing and renewal, again, with the Commission approving significant actions before they become official.

FUNCTIONING OF THE FCC

In its control of television, the FCC performs several distinct functions: rule-making, licensing and registration, adjudication, enforcement, and informal influence. Contacts with industry and public representatives during some activities must be "on the record" or documented to provide a public record and a fair opportunity for all sides to be heard. Other types of contacts, such as informal lobbying, go undocumented.

Rule-making is just what it sounds like: the process of issuing new rules and regulations, and amending or deleting existing ones. The largest area of rule-making centers around proposals to add new television and radio channels. Rule-making is governed by both internal FCC procedures and federal laws, including the Administrative Procedure Act and related regulations. Proposals for change may come from the public or regulated industries—or they may percolate within the FCC itself, often in response to less formal pressures from public and industry representatives, members of Congress, or the Administration. The formal procedure can begin with a notice of inquiry, which designates general interest. Once discussion has moved to the point where a specific change is contemplated, the FCC announces a notice of proposed rule-making and invites comments. If the proposed change is of sufficient importance or controversy, an oral hearing in front of the Commission may be scheduled, though this is unusual. Once all the comments have been reviewed, the staff prepares—and the Commission reviews and issues—a report and order. This document sets out the final rule or regulation, describing the rationale behind it. The final report and order, as with most FCC actions, can be appealed to the U.S. Court of Appeals for the District of Columbia for judicial review.

Licensing is the method by which the broadcast spectrum allocations controlled by the FCC are made and reviewed. It is described in detail on pages 108–9. Cable systems go through the simpler process of registration (see page 121).

Adjudication refers to the process by which the FCC settles disputes, either between private parties (as in a license challenge or the awarding of a new channel) or between the FCC and a private party (as in a disputed disciplinary action). In a formal adjudication, there will be a hearing, conducted in accordance with the Administrative Procedure Act and the general requirements of due process. The first hearing is usually before an administrative law judge, a specially-designated staff attorney. These hearings are modeled on traditional trials, with sworn testimony, opposing lawyers, and the like. The decisions of the administrative law judges are subject to appeal within the FCC, first to the Review Board, then to the full Commission. As usual, further appeals to the Court of Appeals, and thereafter the Supreme Court, are possible. If all appeals are pursued, adjudications can be time-consuming and expensive.

Enforcement involves action by the FCC to correct what it sees as lapses or wrong-doing by entities subject to its jurisdiction. Most commonly, this involves a broadcast licensee violating required practices. The worst penalty that can be imposed is the loss of a license, either through a failure to renew (rare) or an outright revocation (rarer still). This extreme penalty is usually imposed only if the licensee has a history of flagrant mismanagement, deception bordering on fraud, or gross negligence. For less serious transgressions, short-term or conditional renewals may be given, or fines assessed. The announced cause is seldom related to program content, since both the First Amendment and Section 326 of the 1934 Act prohibit censorship. Indecent or obscene programming, however, is an exception to this principle, and is treated differently under both the Constitution and the 1934 Act (see page 159).

Informal influence describes the FCC's ability—and willingness—to affect the television world without going through formal action. A concerned telephone call or letter from the FCC, for example, will certainly get the attention of a station manager. Public statements, articles, and Congressional testimony by Commission members and senior staff are also followed closely by the industry.

FCC PHILOSOPHY

Since its birth in 1934, the FCC has undergone an unusual number of changes in both its underlying philosophy and its rules and administrative actions. Some of this is inevitable in industries that have evolved as much as television and other communications businesses have over the years. Historically speaking, when faced with a change in the television business, the FCC has reacted in a predictable fashion. First, the agency ignores the change; then it tries to protect the status quo; and finally, with a certain degree of public and Congressional prodding, it incorporates the changes into a new status quo.

There is some justification, under the 1934 Act, for the FCC's protective tendency. The 1934 Act called on the FCC to regulate in the public interest, and from the beginning, the FCC has viewed this to mean strong, free broadcast service at the local level. This interpretation has made the health of the local broadcast station of particular concern to the FCC. Much of its conservatism has been motivated by this principle, rather than simply by knee-jerk protection of the establishment.

The FCC gave recognition to the new medium of television in 1941, approving the first attempts at commercial broadcasting. From 1948 to 1952, the licensing of television stations was suspended in order to allow the FCC to study potential interference problems and develop an orderly system of assigning portions of the broadcast spectrum to particular stations. In 1952, when licensing recommenced, the UHF channels were allocated as well. With the promulgation of color standards in 1953, the basic framework of broadcast television was complete.

The history of cable regulation, discussed more fully in Chapter 15, was marked by the FCC first ignoring the phenomenon of cable television, then trying to suppress it, and finally encouraging it within the FCC's sphere of control. The resulting Cable Communications Policy Act of 1984 clearly put cable operations under FCC authority—and clearly limited that authority in several respects.

Most recently, the 1980s saw a sizeable deregulation of the communications industry, sparked by the deregulatory spirit which climaxed in the Reagan presidency. But deregulation also gained impetus from a weakening in the argument that had led to the creation of the FCC in the first place. With cable, low-power broadcasting, and home video, many new programming sources became available to most Americans. The rationale behind the FCC's regulation of broadcasting, in contrast, was that since there were only so many channels in the broadcast spectrum, television had to be treated as a natural monopoly. Since viewers now have a wider range of options, the FCC has returned on many issues to the accepted verities of a free-market, laissez-faire approach. The patchwork of FCC control and permissiveness is described in the chapters that follow—Chapter 14 deals with the regulation of broadcast television, Chapter 15, with the regulation of cable, and Chapter 16, with new technologies.

The FCC and Broadcast Regulation

14

The FCC regulates broadcast television at both the local and network levels. The local control is the most pervasive—the very existence of local broadcast stations depends upon obtaining and renewing an FCC license. The control of the networks is far more indirect; nonetheless, the FCC's intervention at the network level has had a profound effect on shaping the structure of the television industry.

LOCAL REGULATION: LICENSING

The FCC decides who can use the broadcast airwaves, and exercises this authority by granting broadcast licenses to individuals and companies. Such a license is required for any significant broadcast activity, including all broadcast television. FCC licenses are quite specific as to the type of service permitted, the assigned frequency, the location of the transmitter, the applicable technical standards, and the signal strength. In television, the licensing process begins with the potential station identifying an available frequency and location. Ever since the early 1950s, the FCC has maintained a list of pre-determined allocations for television channels, and few standard VHF and UHF frequencies are unassigned. (There are somewhat more "low-power" allocations still available; see page 111.) Sometimes, new allocations are approved or are open for assignment; on rare occasions, an existing license may be revoked or abandoned, creating a new opening. A would-be entrant into the station business can also try to obtain a license by filing a competing application when an existing license comes up for renewal (see page 113).

Presuming that a frequency is available, the first step in seeking a license is filing an application for a construction permit. This permit, when issued, allows a period of time to build the specified broadcasting facilities and to get them running properly. For television stations, this interval is typically two years. Once the facilities are built, the FCC will review the technical and other pertinent data on their performance and, if satisfied, will issue the actual broadcast license to the station. Television licenses run for five years.

In order to obtain a license—or, for that matter, a construction permit—the licensee must meet a series of statutory requirements. First, the licensee must be a U.S. citizen, or a company owned principally by U.S. citizens. With corporate licenses, foreign ownership of more than 20 percent is prohibited; when Rupert Murdoch and his News Corporation acquired the stations that would consitute the Fox Network, he changed his citizenship from Australian to American. Second, the applicant must qualify as to character. Stations are supposed to be assigned to promote the public interest, so an owner with a serious criminal record or other major character defect would be undesirable. The third requirement is one of financial resources. This means not only the ability to build the facility, but also the ability to operate without revenues for some months when starting up broadcasting. The fourth requirement is meeting technical standards, such as protecting other stations from interference.

In granting a license, the FCC can consider other qualifications, such as minority involvement or local control. Additional criteria are particularly likely to be used if there are competing applications for the same openings, as is often the case with new applications.

RESTRICTIONS ON LICENSE HOLDING

In order to promote diversity of media ownership on the local level, the FCC adopted rules in 1975 that prohibit ownership of both broadcasting properties and newspapers in the same market. For instance, when a subsidiary of Murdoch's News Corporation acquired Channel 5 in New York City, the parent company had to sell the *New York Post*. Most newspaper/television ownership combinations that existed before the rule went into effect, however, did not require divestiture.

Locally, no entity is permitted to hold more than one license for television service in a given market. Since 1970, no entity can combine ownership of more than one radio service with a television service in a given market (pre-1970 combinations including AM, FM, and TV are "grandfathered," or permitted because they existed before the rule took effect). Exceptions to this only-two-to-a-market rule are possible for UHF stations that need the financial strength of a combination with both AM and FM stations.

To ensure diversity at the national level, the FCC has rules limiting the total number of broadcast stations that can be subject to common ownership: 12 stations in each of the TV, AM radio, and FM radio categories. Certain minority-owned groups, though, can own up to 14 stations in each category. In addition, no group can have stations that reach, in the aggregate, more than 25 percent of the total national TV audience. This figure can increase by 5 percent for minority-controlled stations, and the audience figures for UHF stations can be reduced by 50 percent in calculations for meeting this audience limit.

EQUAL EMPLOYMENT OPPORTUNITY

The FCC requires any licensee with five or more employees to establish and maintain an equal employment opportunity (EEO) program. The goal is to increase the employment of women and minorities in the broadcast industry. Since few television licensees can operate with fewer than five employees, most stations are subject to EEO rules.

Stations must submit a five-point EEO plan when applying for a new license or assigning/tranferring an existing one. Required information includes who in the proposed organization is responsible for implementing the program, the recruitment policies and methods to be employed, and the training available both on the job and from outside technical or professional schools. After obtaining a license to operate, each station is required to file an annual employment report detailing the number and percentage of employees by each job category, sex, and minority group. These reports describe the success or failure of the EEO plan, and must be available for review by the public. If a station is not meeting expected targets—both for the total number of women and minorities employed and for the number in management positions—the plan's failure will be reviewed by the FCC, usually in the context of license renewal.

The EEO targets are based on the availability of women and minorities in the civilian labor pool for the area covered by the broadcaster's license. All broadcasters must have targets for women; however, minority targets are required only if blacks, Hispanics, Asians/Pacific Islanders, and Native American/Alaskan Indians represent 5 percent or more of the area's labor pool.

Using a 50/50 guideline, the FCC keys the target for station employment at 50 percent of the group's ratio to the available labor force. For example, if Hispanics represent 20 percent of the local labor pool, employees of Hispanic origin would have to constitute 10 percent of the station's full-time staff. Further FCC requirements set targets for hiring, retention, and promotion of women and minorities in the "upper-four job categories" (officials/managers, professionals, technicians, and sales workers). At stations with 5 to 10 full-time employees, women and minorities should be represented in these positions at 25 percent of their availability in the labor force. This proportion jumps to 50 percent for stations with more than 11 full-time employees. Meeting these targets, while important, is not the end of the story; stations must meet additional EEO requirements.

When applying for renewal of a license, a broadcast station must give an even more detailed report on equal employment opportunity. This report indicates the actual number of women and minorities hired and promoted in the past 12 months as well as any complaints that have been filed with the EEO Commission. The station also supplies figures for the labor-force composition in its operating area, and the source of that data. While the breakdown of its current employees by race and sex is an undisputed number, the proportion of women and minorities in a local labor force is sometimes debatable. The FCC reporting form allows some flexibility, in that the station can use data other than the census-based Metropolitan Statistical Area (M.S.A.), city percentages, or county percentages—provided that the station can offer the usually-skeptical FCC a solid explanation for doing so. There are civil penalties for stations that fail to comply with EEO requirements. Adherence to an EEO plan is commonly scrutinized at license-renewal time.

Cable operators are also required to have an EEO plan and follow the same FCC guidelines for the percentage of women and minorities employed. Unlike broadcasters, however, cable operators do not have to file the EEO plan with the FCC as part of a certification request. Cable operators must file annual reports on their actual employment personnel practices; these reports, as well as the EEO plan, are reviewed in the recertification process. Cable companies have been fined for non-compliance—and in some cases, they have lost their certification to operate (see page 122).

Periodically, the FCC's EEO rules come under attack, with opponents charging that they constitute reverse discrimination, and proponents calling for the requirements to be based on parity, not 50 percent. When the FCC has tried to back off on the issue, however, Congress has made it clear that the rules are here to stay. EEO compliance is the one area of FCC activity in which the deregulatory fever of the 1980s has had almost no impact.

LOW-POWER STATIONS

When the original allocation structure was set up in 1952, the goal was to permit every community in the U.S. to receive at least one television station, and to offer as many communities as possible two channels. To prevent signal interference between broadcasters on the same channel or certain adjacent areas, a patchwork of assignments was made, particularly on the VHF band. This set-up left a number of frequency gaps that were too small to be filled by normal full-power stations.

In 1982, as part of the move to broaden viewer options, the FCC made available licenses for a new kind of television station that, because it would operate at considerably reduced power, could be slotted into such a gap. This development created a rush of applications that threatened to overwhelm the Commission's resources. In an unprecedented relaxation of the FCC's oversight responsibility, Congress amended the Communications Act to allow the FCC to hold a lottery among the potential applicants for each low-power opening. This arrangement would take the place of the FCC evaluating each applicant according to the "public interest, convenience, or necessity" standard. Once the lottery produces a winner, the winner's application is still studied by itself to ensure that it meets the necessary standards described on page 108–9. In the lotteries, the odds are weighted to favor applications showing minority and/or local control; the presence of each of these factors will double the winning chances of the applicant. The lottery system has greatly reduced—but not eliminated—the FCC's administrative burden in licensing low-power television (LPTV) stations.

There is no upper limit on the number of low-power stations that can be owned by a single group. While many low-power stations have been licensed, they have had only limited economic impact, and figure only marginally in the television industry as a whole.

MULTIPOINT DISTRIBUTION SERVICE

Another relatively new class of broadcast service is Multipoint Distribution. This resembles a cross between low-power television and cellular phones. A limited area at the top of the UHF band has been set aside for local transmissions reaching a relatively small area. A special converter receives the signals, feeding them to the television on an unused normal broadcast channel. Many of these small transmitters (the "multipoints") may be scattered around a service area. Multipoint services have also been licensed through a lottery approach. Because of the need for a converter and other technical limitations, the multipoint systems have been slow to catch on, particularly in areas already wired for cable, although systems offering multiple channels have had some success.

LICENSE RENEWALS

The Communications Act limits television licenses to a maximum of five years, at which time they come up for review and renewal. Up until 1981, this was a time-consuming ordeal, requiring reams of supporting material on how the station was serving the public interest, convenience, and necessity. As part of deregulation, the renewal application has now been shortened to "postcard" size. It is due four months before the license expires.

A "public-interest" review is still carried out, but it consists, at least at the FCC level, largely of looking into any complaints from the public or any record of non-compliance with FCC rules and procedures. If the record is clean, renewal is customarily granted at the staff level unless it is contested by some third party. Since the broadcaster must give notice of the upcoming renewal on its own airwaves, this act alone can occasionally spark disgruntled viewers to complain, or encourage would-be competitors to act. Any parties who do wish to contest the renewal can search the station's public inspection file (see below) for evidence of lapses and failures.

If the station has problems with its record, or if there is a contest from either a competing applicant or a concerned third party, there can be further FCC review on the matter, sometimes before an administrative law judge. That judge's decision is subject to appeal to the Commission and the courts.

A contested renewal is a rarity, and a successful challenge to a license renewal is even more unusual. This is because the licensee has a proven record, whereas the challenger presents promises of a speculative nature. Even so, challengers do sometimes prevail—and because a failure to renew is, in effect, a commercial death sentence, even the slim possibility that renewal might not happen encourages broadcasters to comply with the FCC's requirements.

PUBLIC INSPECTION FILE

Under FCC regulations, every television station has to maintain a public inspection file. This file must contain a wide variety of information, including 1) copies of the license renewal application, Ownership Report Forms, and Annual Employment Forms; 2) information on station ownership, network affiliation, management agreements, political broadcasts, and children's programming; 3) the FCC publication *The Public and Broadcasting—A Procedure Manual;* and 4) letters and other communications from the public and from citizen groups.

Certification that the public information file is complete is a necessary part of the renewal process. While the file must be kept available for public inspection, the public seldom looks at it, though potential challengers to a station's license renewal will.

LICENSE TRANSFERS

The FCC regulates the transfer of station licenses—not only when occasioned by the outright sale of the business or of the company holding the license, but also as part of any material change of ownership. Even the conversion of the owning company from corporate to partnership form, without any change of ultimate control, would have to be cleared with the FCC. As one would expect, minor adjustments in company structure, or in the make-up of minority ownership, can be reported on abbreviated forms and receive little, if any, scrutiny.

The transfer of control of a station, however, is a more serious matter. In theory, a TV broadcast license cannot be sold. Either the company holding the license is sold, or the facilities and goodwill of the station are sold to an entity that asks the FCC to reassign it the license. In either event, the FCC reviews the change to ensure that it is consistent with the public-interest standard. Prior to deregulation, this review process was rigorous, and the possibility of challenge an ever-present threat; more recently, however, this degree of scrutiny has been relaxed. The FCC has also eliminated the "anti-trafficking" rules that had previously prevented sales of stations within three years of a prior transfer.

The FCC's relaxations of these rules, its expansion of the maximum number of stations that can be owned by any one group, and the easy availability of mergers-and-acquisitions financing in the 1980s led to a major boom in station sales during the 1980s. The 1990s, though, have seen the return to a more conservative financial climate and the fall-off of advertising revenues. It is unlikely that there will be as much station-sale activity in the near future.

STATION OPERATIONS

In addition to overseeing the birth, life, and death of television stations, the FCC controls many of a station's operating procedures.

First of all, there are a number of technical and housekeeping rules for television broadcasters. Station identification messages must be broadcast at the beginning and end of each broadcast day, and hourly (as close to on-the-hour as is reasonably possible). Certain logs must be kept, although since deregulation, the number of logs has been greatly reduced, and such logs need cover only certain technical matters. Every station must also maintain the Emergency Broadcast System.

Some FCC rules govern advertising (see page 321). The FCC also requires a station to disclose commercial support of programming, and prohibits a station from receiving undisclosed compensation for the inclusion of material in a broadcast. These restrictions have their origin in the "payola" scandals of popular music on radio in the 1950s, when disc jockeys took bribes to play certain songs. Section 507 of the Communications Act prohibits a station, or any other entity connected with the production or broadcasting of a television program, from accepting or paying "valuable consideration" (which need not be cash) for the broadcast of any matter without disclosing the fact of that payment to the viewers. Section 507 is the reason for the "promotional consideration" announcements familiar to game-show viewers. It is typical for television employment contracts to contain a provision requiring the employee to obey Section 507.

POLITICAL BROADCASTING

Until it was dropped by the FCC in 1987, the "fairness doctrine" required that stations offer a reasonable opportunity for groups or individuals to express opposing points of view on controversial subjects of public importance. This requirement was a corollary to the "natural monopoly" view of television broadcasting; as that philosophy faded in the 1980s, so did support for the fairness doctrine.

There is, however, a vestige of the fairness-doctrine idea in the limited field of political broadcasts. Under Section 315 of the Communications Act, a television broadcaster that gives or sells air time to one candidate for a particular political office must provide an "equal opportunity" to other legally-qualified candidates for the same office. There are exceptions, though, for coverage of a candidate in bona fide newscasts, interviews, and documentaries. Thus, the appearance of a candidate who is legitimately in the news on *Meet the Press* or on local news does not mean that other candidates are entitled to an equal amount of airtime. Since televised debates are generally viewed as part of news coverage, they also fall outside Section 315. On the other hand, if a station does sell television advertising to one candidate, it must be willing to sell it to competitors for the same office on the same terms.

Broadcasters are limited in the rates that they can charge candidates for political ads. At no time may a station charge more for a political ad than for a "comparable use." During the 45 days before a primary and 60 days before a general or special election, the charges cannot exceed those offered to the station's most-favored commercial advertisers.

The final aspect of these politically-related rules is the "reasonable access" provision. This applies only to candidates for federal elective office: the President, the Vice President, and Congress. In short, broadcasters must sell (or give, a less likely option) candidates for these offices reasonable amounts of advertising time to get their messages across.

In each of these situations, there is a definition of the kind of "legally-qualified candidate for public office" who is entitled to benefit from these rules. These rules concerning political broadcasts have recently been the focus of active enforcement by the FCC.

NETWORK ISSUES

There are four principal areas in which the FCC governs the operations of network television: (1) affiliation agreements, (2) multiple-station ownership, 3) prime-time access, and 4) the financial interest and syndication ("fin-syn") rules.

Affiliation Agreements

The FCC protects the local affiliates in their relationships with the broadcast networks—most importantly, by preventing the network from forcing affiliates to take their programming. The affiliates may decline to take any given network offering for a host of reasons. In addition, the affiliation cannot be exclusive: the affiliate is allowed to take programs from any other source with which it can reach agreement, including another network. Other regulations prevent the network from controlling the affiliate's own advertising inventory, either by setting rates or by acting as a national sales representative for the station. The old rule that set a two-year maximum for the length of an affiliation agreement was dropped in 1989.

Multiple-Station Ownership

The FCC rules about multiple-station ownership have had the effect over the years of keeping most network affiliates under separate ownership from the networks themselves. Nonetheless, each of the networks—including Fox—has assembled a formidable group of network-owned and -operated stations (O&O's) in most of the key markets. The independent stations in these markets also tend to be owned by major station groups. And since these markets are critical to the success of syndicated program offerings, the networks (through their O&O's) and the major station groups are big players on the syndication scene. To this extent, the FCC's ownership restrictions have not achieved their objectives.

Prime-Time Access

The FCC helped those independent program suppliers facing a small number of broadcasters in the major markets by imposing the *prime-time access* rules (see page 29). Prime access requires that network affiliates in the top 50 markets take no more than three hours of network programming in the four-hour prime time block, including re-runs of a program that was formerly on the networks. There are exceptions to this rule, such as news and public-affairs programs, children's programs, sporting events, and special broadcasts like coverage of the Olympics. The effect of prime access has been to open up an hour of time—often 7:00–8:00 P.M.—that must be filled with independent programming. Although some lip service is given to the notion that the prime-time access rules will encourage the production of local and public affairs programs, the syndicators of shows like *Wheel of Fortune* and *Entertainment Tonight*—distributing these programs nationally—are the real beneficiaries.

The Financial Interest and Syndication Rules

The most important of the FCC's network restrictions are the financial interest and syndication ("fin-syn") rules. Until being modified in 1991, the fin-syn rules, adopted in 1970, completely barred the networks from acquiring any financial interest in the broadcast of outside-produced programs (those not solely produced by the network) other than the right to exhibit the programs on the network. The fin-syn rules also prevented the networks from engaging in the U.S. syndication business, although the networks could syndicate into the foreign market programs that they had solely produced or that had been produced by foreign entities. The networks had to sell off their post-broadcast U.S. rights to their own in-house productions for a lump-sum payment, and with no continuing financial stake. The definition of "network" was based on the amount of programming supplied per week (15 hours) in all time slots. (Although the Fox Network fits this definition, it was granted a waiver in 1990 that exempted it from the rules.)

The fin-syn rules were strengthened by Justice Department consent decrees—adopted from 1978 through 1980—which limited the amount of prime time programming that ABC, CBS, and NBC could produce in-house to five hours per week. Other dayparts were not affected. The consent decrees came to an end in 1990.

These restrictions were supposed to counter perceived excesses in the power of the networks over the suppliers of programming, and thus promote a diverse and vigorous independent-production community.

In response to the fin-syn rules, ABC, CBS, and NBC have licensed most of their prime time programming from producers for a limited number of showings (usually two). Those producers are then free to resell the program to syndicators, local stations, cable channels, and international companies. This custom of using outside producers in prime time has persisted even with the expiration of the consent decrees; indeed, the networks rarely programmed five hours' worth of in-house productions in prime time even when that limit was in effect. This reluctance to produce in-house has resulted partly from the networks' discovery that cost control is easier when using outside producers.

The fin-syn rules have largely kept the networks out of the direct production business, at least in prime-time entertainment programming. Perhaps more importantly, the rules have also kept the networks out of the pockets of those producers who have had successful off-network shows. This latter tendency has been somewhat undercut by the ever-growing deficits incurred by producers, which force them to "mortgage" potentially valuable rights to the syndication companies just to get the programs made (see page 203). Still, there is little question that the status of independent television producers—including the politically powerful major studios—would be very different had the fin-syn rules not been in effect.

1991 Changes to the Fin-Syn Rules

In 1991—after considerable pressure from both the networks and the production community—the FCC modified the fin-syn rules. The changes would apply to new series or programs first licensed after the effective date of the changes, which was 30 days after their publication. In the first place, the definition of "network" now focuses on the hours of prime time programming, not total programming, supplied (15 hours, or 5 nights at 3 hours per night), and on the number of households reached (75 percent).

The fin-syn rules will no longer apply to non-entertainment programming like news and sports, or to network programming outside of prime time. They do continue to cover prime-time network programs and the first-run syndication business. On outside-produced programs for prime time, the networks can acquire financial interests and both domestic and foreign syndication rights. They can do so, however, only if they separate the deal for these rights from the deal for the network license—waiting at least 30 days from the execution of the license before starting negotiations on the other rights, and certifying that the network license was not conditioned by the deal on the other rights.

Each network can now program 40 percent of its prime time schedule with in-house productions (including co-productions). Co-production arrangements are supposed to be initiated only by the outside party, and a 30-day "cooling-off" period is imposed before the deal becomes binding. The networks can have full financial interests and syndication rights, both domestic and foreign, in their in-house productions, although they are not supposed to play favorites or hold back product in the domestic marketplace. A network can even produce for the first-run syndication market, or for another network, with an ongoing financial interest—but, in these cases, the syndication must be handled at arm's length by an independent syndicator. The networks may not take an interest in independently-produced product for first-run syndication.

This new approach has not really satisfied anyone, nor is there agreement on how significant these changes to the fin-syn rules will be at the practical level. As of this writing, a legal battle is raging, with the studios, syndicators, and independent producers lined up on one side and the networks on the other. With the networks' share of the television audience shrinking and the number of alternative program sources (none of which are subject to similar restrictions) growing, the rationales that underlie the fin-syn rules are shifting significantly. It is possible that there will be further changes to the fin-syn rules in the near future.

15   The FCC and Cable Regulation

Cable television is subject to a regulatory structure that works on three levels: federal, state, and local.

FEDERAL CABLE REGULATION

At the federal level, the FCC now has clear authority, granted by the Cable Communications Policy Act of 1984, to regulate the operation of cable systems. This was not always the case. In the 1950s, when cable television was beginning, the FCC took a hands-off position. Cable operations tended to be small—and, to the extent that they had any impact on broadcasting, they merely extended the reach of established stations into areas where the stations would not otherwise have been received.

The FCC's hands-off attitude changed in the early 1960s, as more and more cable operators began to "import" signals from beyond the local area. These distant signals were picked up in their local broadcast area, then transmitted (usually by microwave relay) to a distant cable company, which in turn "cablecast" them as supplemental channels. This action provided both the grounds and the means for regulation by the FCC. For the first time, local stations started viewing cable as a competitor to their operations, rather than as merely an extension of those operations. The FCC shared this concern, and sought to protect established broadcasters. The microwave or other telecommunications link that usually brought the distant signal to the cable company was a common carrier or a radio transmission—and those forms were clearly subject to FCC jurisdiction.

In 1966, the FCC issued a series of rules on cable. The first was the "must-carry" rule, which required a cable system to carry the signals of all the local stations. A second rule called for blacking out distant signals when they duplicated programs offered by a local broadcaster. A third rule flatly prohibited the importation of distant signals into the biggest 100 markets, although cable systems could file with the FCC requesting permission and giving justification for why such service was necessary (permission was seldom granted). At about the same time, FCC regulations made it impractical for telephone companies to be involved as cable-service providers—thus barring one of the strongest potential cable operators from the business.

The FCC's right to maintain these and other restrictions was challenged both in the courts and in Congress. In 1968, the Supreme Court affirmed the FCC's jurisdiction over cable, to an extent "reasonably ancillary to the effective performance of the Commission's various responsibilities for the regulation of broadcasting." In 1970, the FCC imposed the "anti-siphoning" rule, which greatly restricted the showing of movies and sports events on cable services. In 1972, a compromise was worked out between the cable industry, the FCC, and the broadcasting interests; this agreement settled the issue of FCC control over cable and relaxed the distant-signal rules, so that wiring the top 100 television markets for cable could continue.

Two further developments spurred cable growth in the mid-1970's—one technical, the other legal. On the technical level, modern communications satellites suddenly made national signal transmission much less expensive. Until then, the major broadcast networks used much more costly cable and microwave networks to distribute their services around the country. In 1975, HBO used a satellite link to become the first cable-programming service available nationwide; HBO was followed by Ted Turner's WTCG, an independent station licensed to operate in Atlanta and later renamed WTBS. On the legal end, the FCC's anti-siphoning rules were struck down in the courts in 1977 for violating the First Amendment. In addition, in the deregulatory climate of the Reagan years, the FCC further loosened its distant-signal rules. In 1984, Congress adopted the Cable Communications Policy Act (the Cable Act) as an amendment to the Communications Act of 1934.

The 1984 Cable Act

The 1984 Cable Act (which became Title VI of the Communications Act of 1934) granted the FCC the express power to regulate cable television. In many instances, this power totally pre-empts the authority of state and local governments. Even in those areas where state and local action is permitted, the 1984 Act provides guidelines and parameters. The 1984 Act also makes clear the fact that cable services, like broadcast television, are not common carriers, and therefore do not have to provide general access to all comers.

Definition of a Cable System

The Cable Act provides a definition of a "cable system" covered by its provisions. If the cables utilize public rights-of-way of any kind, the installation is likely to be a cable system, subject to regulation. Small cable systems with under 1,000 subscribers, however, are exempt from some of the general rules. If the lines stay all within one continuous property, such as common antennae for an apartment complex, the system may not be covered by the 1984 Act.

Registration

All cable systems which carry any broadcast signals must be registered with the FCC. Registration takes the form of a filing that discloses information about the system—who its owners are, for example, and which services are to be carried on the system. In addition to FCC registration, the Cable Act requires that all cable systems be franchised by state or local authorities (see page 124).

Distant-Signal Rules

It is now permissible for a cable system to import signals broadcast from other communities, subject to the specific black-out provisions discussed below and subject to payment of the mandated copyright fees. Importation is generally done via microwave or satellite, using common carriers. Broadcast stations, by contrast, have no right to rebroadcast material from other stations without consent.

FCC rules still restrict importing material from distant channels that duplicates local transmissions. For instance, the law prevents carrying network programming from a distant source that duplicates network programming carried by a local station. In addition, there is a black-out provision that can apply to syndicated programming duplicated from a distant station. In order to avail itself of this protection, the local station running the syndicated programming must have an agreement with the syndicator which provides for local exclusivity, and must give notice of the request for this protection to both the FCC and the local cable company.

Sports Black-Outs

Cable companies cannot import a distant signal in order to circumvent the black-out of a sports event on a local channel. These black-outs are negotiated by teams so that a local broadcast of a game will not undercut fan interest in attending the game itself.

Original Programming and Technical Standards

The FCC does not require that a cable system carry any non-broadcast channels. If, however, the system produces its own programming, many general FCC rules apply. These rules pertain to obscene material (page 159); equal-opportunity advertising for political candidates (page 114); lotteries and gambling-related cablecasting (page 322); and sponsorship identification, sponsor lists, and payola prevention (page 114).

The FCC also has jurisdiction over technical standards for cable television. Since 1985, most of these requirements have softened to become simply guidelines that help promote standardization within the industry. The sole remaining technical requirement relates to testing and signal leakage.

Equal Employment Opportunity and Consumer Privacy

Cable systems employing five or more people full-time are subject to the equal employment opportunity requirements of the Communications Act of 1934 and the FCC, which are described in detail in Chapter 14. To reduce paperwork, cable systems are not required to file their EEO plan with the FCC in advance. However, all of the FCC guidelines and policies for broadcasters apply to cable systems as well. There are also extensive rules designed to prevent the improper use of private customer information by the cable system and third parties.

Cross-Ownership

The Cable Act and FCC rules restrict cross-ownership between broadcasting stations and cable operations: national broadcast networks cannot own any cable systems, and local broadcasters cannot own cable systems within their broadcast area. It is worth noting that these restrictions apply to ownership of cable *systems*, and not to program services or networks. The broadcast networks indeed have financial interests in cable networks (see Chapter 6). Finally, telephone companies are prohibited from owning cable systems within the areas for which they provide local telephone service. As of this writing, there are no rules governing multiple-system ownership or foreign ownership of cable systems, both of which are controlled in the case of broadcast stations.

Must-Carry Rule

The must-carry rule, requiring cable systems to carry all local broadcast signals, survived the enactment of the 1984 Cable Act, but has subsequently been thrown out by court order as violating the First Amendment. A subsequent effort by the FCC to redraft the must-carry rule to meet First Amendment scrutiny also failed, and it appears unlikely that it will be reinstated. It should be noted that cable systems still carry most local broadcast channels, perhaps because subscribers expect it.

Theft of Services

The Cable Act makes it expressly illegal to take signals from a cable system without authorization. This sets up punishment for the use of private taps and "black box" decoders, ranging from a relatively small fine and jail sentence for private users to up to $50,000 and two years in jail for repeat offenders engaging in signal theft for profit. The affected cable system can also sue for damages.

COPYRIGHT ASPECTS OF CABLE TELEVISION

All material carried by cable television—including programs, commercials, and music—must be cleared for copyright permission. In the case of original cable programming, such as provided by Showtime, MTV, and other basic and pay cable services, the cablecast itself is a public performance and requires a license from the copyright proprietor (see page 137). Under the old 1909 Copyright Act, the retransmission by cable of material broadcast by an over-the-air station was not a new performance or duplication. Therefore, the license obtained by the original broadcaster extended to subsequent cable distribution. This was changed by the 1976 Copyright Act.

The 1976 Copyright Act set up a *compulsory license* structure for cable companies re-transmitting broadcast signals. Under this arrangement, the cable system can transmit non-local broadcast signals, provided it pays the broadcaster an appropriate fee (which is collected by the Copyright Office and administered by the Copyright Royalty Tribunal). The basis on which these fees are calculated depends on the cable system's level of revenues. Systems with less than $75,000 in annual gross receipts pay a token amount for transmitting an unlimited number of imported signals. Systems with more than $75,000 but less than $292,000 in gross annual receipts pay 0.5 percent of their gross receipts up to $146,000 and 1 percent of gross receipts thereafter—again, with no limit on the number of imported signals. Finally, for systems with more than $292,000 in annual gross receipts, a complicated formula is used that is based on the kind and number of stations the cable system carries, and on whether the system is in a top 100 market or not. These formulas can make the first imported signal, if it is from an independent station, cost a cable system in a top 50 market royalties of almost 1.5 percent of gross receipts, with fees for additional signals trailing off from there. There is also a charge of 3.75 percent of gross receipts for carrying each distant signal in excess of the number that would have been permitted under the FCC's pre-1980 rules. Once received, the royalties are divided by the Tribunal among the copyright owners of the programs carried, who must file claims to share in the pot. The major beneficiaries have been the copyright owners of movies and sports programs.

STATE AND LOCAL CABLE REGULATION

At the state and local level, a patchwork of regulatory systems has evolved. Some states have set up quite active statewide regulatory boards for cable; other states leave regulation largely to the local communities. State and local control arises not only from the general legislative power, but also from the ability to govern the access of the cable company to the public rights-of-way. This access is necessary for maintaining and operating a system of any size, since cable can only run throughout a community if it follows the public roads, either above ground on poles or below ground in conduits. Access to these roads is in the hands of the state government or the municipalities.

State and local regulation is restricted, however, to those areas where the FCC has not asserted exclusive jurisdiction. While the states and localities can govern franchising and utility-pole attachments, subject to the requirements of the 1984 Act, they are largely prohibited from otherwise interfering in the operations of cable systems.

Franchising

The most important means by which states and local communities control cable is the franchising of cable systems. The power to franchise comes from control of the public rights-of-way. The 1984 Act sets only sketchy parameters for franchising, but it also makes holding a franchise a requirement for FCC registration. In most states, the franchising power has been delegated to the local level, where it is normally exercised by the city or town council.

The typical franchising process goes as follows. First, the local government may seek knowledgeable advisors to help it through the technical and legal considerations in awarding a cable franchise. The next step is usually a request for proposals, which announces to the cable television industry that the locality would like to award a franchise. Then comes the response from the interested cable companies, which submit proposals (often of great length) suggesting what they will provide and why each is the best candidate to provide the service requested. For better or worse, local political connections and concerns can sometimes influence the process, providing work for well-connected lawyers, lobbyists, and other local consultants with clout. The selection process continues with a review of the competing proposals. This review usually involves an investigation by the council and its advisors of the applicants and their proposals—an inspection of their finances, operating experience, and the feasibility of the various promises which have been made. In the process of this review, there should be a public hearing on the merits of each proposal, at which community members and other interested parties can air their views.

Once a potential franchise has been chosen, the town council negotiates an agreement with the company, based on the proposal and setting forth the terms of the franchise. The financial deal is subject to a Cable Act limitation: no more than 5 percent of gross revenues from the franchised service can be taken as the franchise fee. The agreement also includes the franchise term, technical and construction specifications, and requirements for certain levels of service, including the number of channels set aside for community access, local educational use, and other public-interest uses. Most franchises are awarded on a non-exclusive basis; in theory, another company can approach the municipality and propose the wiring of a further system within the service area. As a practical matter, given the high costs of entry, it is relatively rare for another service to come in and bid on a territory that has already been franchised. Franchise agreements are often challenged in court by disappointed claimants, who cite alleged flaws in the way the franchise was awarded.

When a franchise comes up for renewal, the Cable Act provides certain safeguards to protect the interests of the existing franchisee. For instance, at the franchisee's request—given within a six-month period starting three years before the renewal date—there is a public hearing at which the franchisee's service is reviewed. The hearing evaluates that level of service according to the following criteria, as specified in the Cable Act:

(A) The cable operator has substantially complied with the material terms of the existing franchise and with applicable law;

(B) The quality of the operator's service, including signal quality, response to consumer complaints, and billing practices, but without regard to the mix, or level of cable services or other services provided over the system, has been reasonable in light of community needs;

(C) The operator has the financial, legal, and technical ability to provide the services, facilities, and equipment as set forth in the operator's proposal; and

(D) The operator's proposal is reasonable to meet the future cable-related community needs and interests, taking into account the cost of meeting such needs and interests.

Although the franchising authority can theoretically deny a renewal to the existing operator, it can do so only if the franchisee has a documented record of poor performance or inability to meet one of these four criteria. The franchise authority may not consider a competing offer, except to help provide background for evaluating these criteria. This process acts to cut down the leverage of the municipality at renewal time, and helps protect the status quo. By now, the most desirable franchises in the country have been awarded, and franchises coming up for renewal are the main arena for competition between cable operators.

Utility-Pole Attachments

The states are permitted to control the attachment of cable lines to existing telephone and electric utility poles and conduits. In most circumstances, it is more sensible (and cheaper) for a cable company to add its cable lines to these poles and conduits than to set up new poles or dig new underground channels. This puts the cable company at the mercy of the owner of the existing poles and conduits. In order to prevent extortionate requests and to encourage the installation of cable, most states and localities have adopted rules that cap the rates which can be charged for such pole attachments. To the extent that states and localities have not adopted appropriate rules to govern this, the FCC retains jurisdiction.

Rate Regulation

Generally, state and local governments cannot regulate rates charged by cable companies, either for basic service or pay channels. In limited circumstances, basic-service rates may be regulated where there is a finding that the cable companies do not have any effective competition. The FCC has defined this situation as one in which there are not at least three free television signals that are receivable throughout a particular franchise area. This condition is under review by the FCC, however, and it is likely that the FCC's role in setting cable rates will expand.

Other Rules and Pre-emptions

The issue of cross-ownership of cable stations and other media outlets has largely been pre-empted by the Cable Act and the FCC, as have all aspects of satellite television. However, states and localities do retain their normal power to enact rules for reasons of public benefit and general safety. One example of such power would be restrictions on the size and placement of satellite dishes based on purely aesthetic or safety considerations. Such rules must be nondiscriminatory and cannot appear arbitrary.

FUTURE DEVELOPMENTS IN CABLE REGULATION

There is growing pressure at both the state and federal level to increase the regulation of cable television. As cable has established itself as a mainstream business, many systems have raised their rates faster than general inflation. In the spirit of free enterprise, they are seeking to charge what the market will bear. There are also complaints about substandard service in some areas. Since cable systems are generally not subject to direct competition from competing cable operators, the old arguments for regulating natural monopolies are attracting new adherents. Rate regulation of some kind stands a good chance of being enacted in the near future; the cross-ownership of cable services and cable operators is another issue which may soon come under regulation.

16 FCC Regulation of New Technologies

The FCC's regulation of television has carried over into the new distribution technologies; the only areas in which the FCC is not somehow involved are home and business video.

COMMUNICATIONS SATELLITES

From the beginning, the FCC has regulated the services of communication satellites under its authority to supervise radio transmissions and common carriers in the communications business. Although the FCC controls the rates and technical aspects of communication satellites, since 1972 it has maintained an "open-skies" policy, allowing almost any technically-competent and financially-qualified company to launch and operate a domestic communications satellite. The result of the open-skies policy has been an abundance of satellite communications channels available for U.S. television use. In addition, the FCC dropped its regulation of receive-only satellite antennae in 1979. These two developments have helped make satellite the carrier of choice for the national feeds of broadcast and cable networks alike—replacing the land lines and microwave systems of earlier eras.

Since there are stringent cross-ownership restrictions between common carriers on the one hand and broadcasters/cable systems on the other, the television companies do not own or lease their own satellite facilities. Instead, they contract with satellite companies for carrying the signals (these companies are "common carriers").

In the early days of satellite-transmitted television, most signals were open and unscrambled. Consequently, the business of supplying receiving dishes to private individuals became viable. While the initial investment was significant, many people, particularly in remote areas with no cable service, installed dishes and settled back to enjoy shows plucked out of the air, ostensibly free of charge. This led to two steps to prevent what the cable services (and especially the pay services) saw as a threat to their revenues: scrambling and legal restrictions.

Scrambling significantly decreases one's ability to intercept a viewable signal, although bootleg "black boxes" to descramble signals do exist. Such unauthorized intercepts have, however, been rendered illegal. By a balancing legal mandate, the scrambled signals must be licensed by services in areas where these signals are not otherwise available via cable. A legitimate business in issuing such licenses and their implementing decoders has evolved. Since the offerings available without paying for decoders have grown less interesting, the sale of dishes for picking up common-carrier satellite television feeds has stagnated.

DIRECT BROADCAST SATELLITES

The FCC regulates every direct broadcast satellite, under its general authority over the radio broadcast spectrum.

The first request for a DBS license came in 1980; by 1982, the FCC had established procedures and rules for granting them. These rules have some provisions similar to those for broadcast stations. For instance, foreign ownership and control of a DBS service is restricted, even at a minority level as low as 20 percent. There are also equal employment opportunity requirements, including one for filing an EEO plan (see Chapter 14) as part of the application for initiating a DBS service.

The FCC grants construction permits and DBS licenses—technically, interim licenses—to applicants once a public-comment period and a staff review determine that the proposed system is in the public interest. Once granted, the normal license term is five years. An unusually long (six-year) construction period is allowed, since DBS technology is still in an early stage. The technical specifications of a DBS service must agree with international standards.

FIBER OPTICS

Optical fiber is viewed by many as the delivery system of the future for the television industry. It has a huge capacity for data transmission, and could carry an unprecedented number of program options. In addition, it is a fully two-way medium, permitting instant pay-per-view ordering and other interactive services. With some exceptions, fiber-optic installation has been largely the province of the telephone companies, which have been shut out of ownership of broadcasting and of cable facilities in those areas where they provide phone service. The seemingly natural combination of audio and video systems under one fiber-optic network will not occur without a change of this basic restriction. The emergence of high-definition television, which is an extension of a fiber delivery system, may help provoke movement on this issue.

HIGH-DEFINITION TELEVISION (HDTV)

As a leader in the introduction of television service, the U.S. has been using a relatively primitive technical standard. The limited number of "lines" and restricted aspect ratio (the ratio of screen width to height) of the American standard result in poor detail resolution to the broadcast image, and a constricted view. Much of the rest of the world already enjoys a somewhat better system. High-definition television (see page 99) could lead to screens that are indistinguishable from movie screens for picture quality and width-to-height ratios. Many of the potential systems, however, require greater bandwidth than is currently used for broadcasting, which in turn might mean that the spectrum would have to be re-allocated.

The major impediment to HDTV is not technological: research teams here and abroad have invented a number of different approaches. The most promising involve digital video, which offers the clarity and signal economy that have helped digital recording revolutionize the audio industry. Rather, the principal difficulty is the lack of a unified standard, and at the center of this controversy is the FCC.

The FCC helped take the lead in deciding on the technical standard for U.S. television when it started up and when it switched over to color. The choices made may or may not have been the best available, but at least there *was* a standard—the decision to settle on a single approach led to quick implementation and consumer acceptance. In the deregulatory spirit of the 1980s, however, standard-setting acquired a bad name; far better, it was thought, to allow the marketplace to decide on the best approach. Unfortunately, the one example of this theory as applied on the mass-consumer level has not been a happy one: AM stereo. The determination of a standard for AM stereo broadcasting has been left to the marketplace. The result? The adoption by different AM stations of competing standards, which in turn has led to confusion among radio listeners and very slow acceptance of the new technology. There is no reason to think that a totally free-market approach to HDTV will fare any better.

The battle over HDTV is further complicated by the fact that several of the proposed technologies have originated not in the U.S., but in Europe and Japan. It has been suggested that FCC leadership could help to promote not only a more advanced standard, but a U.S.-based one as well. It will be interesting to see whether the FCC will choose to remain true to its free-market creed on this issue.

Part 3

REGULATION OF PROGRAMMING

Content Regulation

FREE SPEECH AND THE FIRST AMENDMENT

Early in the history of the United States, the founders of our federal government shared a thorough understanding of the need for governmental power—and a healthy fear of the abuses to which such power is prone. Therefore, between 1789 and 1791, shortly after the adoption of the Constitution, the States ratified the Bill of Rights, a series of 10 amendments to the Constitution. The purpose of these amendments was to limit the authority of the newly-established central power. The First Amendment established three fundamental aspects of liberty: freedom of speech, freedom of religion, and access to government. It reads as follows:

> Congress shall make no law respecting an establishment of religion, or prohibiting the free exercise thereof, or abridging the freedom of speech, or of the press; or the right of the people peaceably to assemble, and to petition the Government for a redress of grievances.

Television has repeatedly been recognized as a medium that is subject to First Amendment protection.

At first, these limits on governmental power applied only to Congress (that is, the federal government), although some states enacted similar measures in their own constitutions. After the Civil War, a series of additional constitutional amendments were adopted which did apply to the states. Perhaps chief among these was the Fourteenth Amendment:

> No State shall make or enforce any law which shall abridge the privileges or immunities of citizens of the United States; nor shall any State deprive any person of life, liberty, or property, without due process of law; nor deny to any person within its jurisdiction the equal protection of the law.

No specific reference was made in the Fourteenth Amendment to the Bill of Rights or to the First Amendment. In the first half of the 20th century, however, a series of judicial decisions confirmed that the Fourteenth Amendment concepts of due process and equal protection "incorporated" most, if not all, of the Bill of Rights' elements and made them applicable to the states. The applicability of the free-speech and free-press aspects of the First Amendment to state laws was recognized by the Supreme Court in decisions between 1925 and 1931.

The language of the First Amendment is extremely broad. Congress and, by incorporation, the states, "shall make no law . . . abridging the freedom of speech, or of the press." If taken literally, this wording would seem to imply that speech, the press, and (by extension) television are to be completely free of governmental regulation. Notwithstanding the plain language of the amendment, however, courts have always recognized exceptions and balanced the government's interest in various content restrictions against the free speech "interest" expressed in the First Amendment. The results of this process are rules that govern the content of television programming.

RULES THAT GOVERN CONTENT

The content of television production is subject to a series of laws and restrictions—most of them imposed by our legal system, some of them imposed by the television industry on itself as a matter of self-regulation. Some of these rules, such as those governing obscenity, are enforced directly by the government with criminal penalties. More prevalent are the laws enabling private individuals and companies to control the use of creative properties, the expression of certain kinds of hurtful falsehoods, or the invasion of rights of privacy and publicity.

These rules and restrictions can be viewed negatively—as handcuffs on the activities of program creators—because they conflict with the freedoms granted by the First Amendment. They can also be viewed positively, as rights that can be asserted to protect the economic and moral interests of individuals, businesses, and the community. However they are considered, these restrictions form the legal structure within which programming is created. Anyone participating in the production process will benefit from a working knowledge of them.

The three chapters that follow deal with these content rules. The level of detail in a general treatment such as this must be, by its very nature, somewhat superficial. Therefore, we have supplied in Appendix C1 a bibliography of articles, books, and other reference works for those who wish to research these issues in greater depth.

In addition, many content issues are governed by state law, and there are likely to be variations in the law from state to state, even when the laws recognize the same underlying principles. When we do cite specific state laws, we have paid particular attention to the laws of California and New York, since so much of the television industry is concentrated in these states. In cases for which an exact knowledge of the applicable state or federal law is important, it is advisable to consult a local attorney.

18 Copyright and the Protection of Creative Properties

There is one restriction on television content which itself has a constitutional basis. Article 1, Section 8 of the Constitution reads: "Congress shall have power . . . to promote the progress of science and useful arts by securing for limited times to authors and inventors the exclusive right to their respective writings and discoveries. . . ."

Following this lead, Congress has created a series of copyright laws, starting in 1790. The most recent general revision was enacted in 1976. Works created before January 1, 1978 (when the 1976 Act took effect) were subject to the provisions of the 1909 Copyright Act with respect to events prior to 1978. For events after December 31, 1977, these works are governed by the 1976 Act, modified by certain special provisions. All works created since January 1, 1978 are fully covered by the rules of the 1976 Act, which introduced several innovations discussed more fully below. The major development in copyright law since 1976 has been the changes made necessary by the U.S. joining the Berne Convention, which became effective March 1, 1989.

SCOPE OF FEDERAL LAW

Under the 1909 Act, most unpublished works were subject to state-law protection under theories of "common law copyright." With a few limited exceptions, such as plays, federal copyright only extended to *published* works. Under the 1976 Act, federal copyright has been extended to cover all unpublished works as well, and the role of state law has almost completely disappeared.

MATERIAL PROTECTED BY COPYRIGHT LAW

The Copyright Act of 1976 gives protection for "original works of authorship." Section 102 of the law states:

> (a) Copyright protection subsists, in accordance with this title, in original works of authorship fixed in any tangible medium of expression, now known or later developed, from which they can be perceived, reproduced, or otherwise communicated, either directly or with the aid of a machine or device. Works of authorship include the following categories:

(1) literary works;

(2) musical works, including any accompanying words;

(3) dramatic works, including any accompanying music;

(4) pantomimes and choreographic works;

(5) pictorial, graphic, and sculptural works;

(6) motion pictures and other audiovisual works; and

(7) sound recordings.

(b) In no case does copyright protection for an original work of authorship extend to any idea, procedure, process, system, method of operation, concept, principle, or discovery, regardless of the form in which it is described, explained, illustrated, or embodied in such work.

Television programs receive protection as "motion pictures or other audio-visual works." Scripts are protected as "literary works" or "dramatic works"; designs, as "pictorial, graphic, and sculptural works." Indeed, any creative work which is "fixed in a tangible medium of expression" (and thus satisfies the Constitutional requirement of a "writing") can potentially be covered by copyright protection—provided it is not simply an "idea," "concept," or "principle."

Courts have held that the *expression* of an idea is copyrightable, but that the underlying idea itself is not. Infringement occurs only if there is a "substantial similarity" between a protected element in the copyrighted work and some element of the new work. Of course, it is not always easy to tell where a raw idea leaves off and protectable expression begins. The point where an illegal rip-off occurs is a matter for judgment in each case, and a lawyer's advice may be helpful. There is also the "smell test": if the proposed use "stinks" to you, it probably will to a judge.

To prove an infringement of copyright, there must be evidence of copying. Proof of actual copying can also be inferred from access, which indicates the opportunity to copy. If the similar work was an independent creation, no infringement has taken place.

Although ideas are free from copyright protection, they can be subject to contractual protection (see page 146). Names of characters and names of shows, like ideas, are not subject to copyright protection. They can, however, receive protection under theories of unfair competition if the name is so strongly established that there could be public confusion over the new use (see page 323).

"Formats" fall into a gray area. For instance, the idea of a game show that awards prizes for answering questions cannot be copyrighted, nor can such aspects of a game show as a board listing the questions, a pretty female assistant, or a display which indicates the score. A near clone of the total look and overall feel of a particular game show would probably be found to be a copyright violation, but anything less should be permissible. On the other hand, a few clever lines of fiction or a few bars of music can constitute protectable expression.

Like ideas, facts, in and of themselves, are not copyrightable. Still, whether fact or fiction, a particular motion picture or video sequence, as shot and preserved on film or tape, is very likely to have enough expressive content for copyright protection, if only in the choices made in framing the shot. Therefore, one must be particularly careful in copying *verbatim* video clips or recorded audio segments. Courts have implied that video clips as short as seven or eight seconds can contain enough expression to merit protection, notwithstanding the doctrine of fair use (page 141).

RIGHTS PROTECTED BY COPYRIGHT LAW

United States copyright law gives the copyright owner(s) a particular set of exclusive rights in a work in the United States. The general rules are set forth in Section 106 of the 1976 Act:

> Subject to sections 107 through 120, the owner of copyright under this title has the exclusive rights to do and to authorize any of the following:
>
> (1) to reproduce the copyrighted work in copies or phonorecords;
>
> (2) to prepare derivative works based upon the copyrighted work;
>
> (3) to distribute copies or phonorecords of the copyrighted work to the public by sale or other transfer of ownership, or by rental, lease, or lending;
>
> (4) in the case of literary, musical, dramatic, and choreographic works, pantomimes, and motion pictures and other audiovisual works, to perform the copyrighted work publicly; and
>
> (5) in the case of literary, musical, dramatic, and choreographic works, pantomimes, and pictorial, graphic, or sculptural works, including the individual images of a motion picture or other audiovisual work, to display the copyrighted work publicly.

The copyright owner controls the making and distribution of reproductions of the work, including prints and videocassettes. In most cases, however, once an authorized copy has been sold, further dispositions of that copy are free from control. This is called the "first-sale doctrine." A special exception to this rule, however, prevents the rental of *sound* recordings. Rentals of authorized video copies are not restricted.

No one can create a derivative work without the owner's authorization. This includes the production and/or distribution of sequels, remakes, series, spin-offs, dubbed versions, novelizations, and any other work that embodies elements of protected expression from the original work.

The owner controls the public performance or display of a copyrighted work, but its private performance or display is not restricted. For example, a videocassette can legally be shown for free by its rightful owner in the home to family and normal guests. Charge admission, however, or change the venue to a public bar, and the showing probably becomes a public performance, subject to the control of the copyright holder.

AUTHORSHIP AND THE WORK FOR HIRE

Under the 1976 Copyright Act, the author or authors of the work own the copyright, from the moment of the work's creation. Joint authors share the ownership of their copyrighted work. Unless they agree otherwise, each joint owner can authorize the non-exclusive use of the work, subject to a responsibility to account for the other author's share of any earnings. Exclusive licenses require the consent of all authors.

The "author," however, is not always the living person who creates the product. Under the "work for hire" doctrine of the 1976 Act, an individual or company that employs the actual creator can be deemed the author. Employment generally means just that: showing up for work on a regular basis, having the necessary tax and social security payments drawn from one's paycheck (see page 343). These rules on *actual* employment are relaxed in the case of audiovisual works for film or television, where a consultant's or other independent contractor's work can be "for hire" if there is a signed written agreement confirming this fact. Collective works, translations, compilations, and instructional works can also be considered works for hire on this basis.

COPYRIGHT REGISTRATION

The formal requirements for obtaining copyright protection have been significantly loosened under the 1976 Act, and even further liberalized by the Berne Convention changes. Under the old (1909) act, publication with notice (see below) was necessary for federal protection, but copyright now attaches automatically at the moment of creation. Some protections of copyright can be lost by the failure to take certain registration steps. For a U.S.-origin work, which cannot claim all of the protections of the Berne Convention, registration is a prerequisite for bringing a copyright infringement case against a third party. Registration can be done at almost any time to make a suit possible, but should be done as soon as possible to avoid procedural delays. Early registration (within three months of publication) is also necessary in order to claim the statutory damages provided under the Copyright Act (see page 144) for infringement of a published work. The Berne Convention removes these incentives and penalties with respect to foreign-source works.

Copyright registration forms are included in Appendix A7. Original forms, along with information about current fees and procedures, can be obtained by writing to the Copyright Office, Library of Congress, Washington, D.C. 20559.

COPYRIGHT NOTICE

Until the Berne Convention took effect in the U.S. on March 1, 1989, giving *notice* of copyright, in a conspicuous place on the work itself, was still required to preserve protection for a published work. This notice combines three elements. The first element is a use of the word "copyright," the abbreviation "Copr.," or the symbol ©. For sound recordings, the symbol ℗ is used to indicate a copyright notice. The next element is the year of first publication of the work. Certain private circulations of a work do not constitute publication. The third element is the name of the entity—whether a real person or a business—that is claiming copyright. By custom, notices went on or near the title page of a written work, or in the head credits or final credits of a film or television program. Publication of a copyrighted work prior to March 1, 1989 without this type of notice could result in a loss of copyright protection. Provisions for correcting errors in notice are set out in the law.

Since March 1, 1989, the Berne Convention makes notice unnecessary for protection, even for U.S. authors. Notice is still necessary under the Uniform Copyright Convention, which continues in force for the U.S. and adds protection in a few additional countries, most notably the U.S.S.R. Notice is also useful in deterring potential infringers, in establishing the chain of title on the work itself, and in negating an "innocent infringement" defense. As a rule of thumb, if displaying or distributing the work makes one think that claiming copyright protection might be necessary, then notice is probably a good idea.

DEPOSIT OF COPYRIGHTED WORKS

In order to help build the collections of the Library of Congress, a prerequisite of registration was always the deposit of two complete copies of the best edition of the work. Even now, with registration voluntary, two copies of the best edition of any work *published* in the U.S. must be deposited with the Library of Congress within three months of publication. For certain classes of works, where deposit of the whole is difficult or impractical, special exceptions can be made. For sculptures or certain motion pictures, for instance, a deposit of photographs or other identifying material may suffice.

SUPPLEMENTS/SUBSTITUTES

In addition to the copyright law procedures, authors sometimes take additional steps to help prove their rights in the material they have written. For instance, the Writer's Guild of America maintains in both its New York and Los Angeles offices a registry for television and film scripts, treatments, and other material. Registration with the Guild does not provide any additional legal protection other than that normally provided by copyright, but it can serve as useful evidence that the author in question created the material. In fact, the registry is primarily used to establish that an idea or written material existed on a certain date. While registered works are rarely withdrawn as evidence for copyright or contractual disputes, written confirmation from the Writers Guild registry that a work was deposited on a given date is frequently requested as evidence. This service cannot be used to establish credit for a given work, however, and registration does not imply credit for authorship. Registration is open to members and non-members of the WGA alike.

As a similar evidentiary matter, authors sometimes mail copies of their work to themselves in a sealed envelope, hoping that the postmark will provide some proof as to the date of creation and the original authorship of the writer. This measure is of dubious value.

COMPULSORY LICENSES AND OTHER SPECIFIC EXCEPTIONS

There are certain exceptions in the copyright law to the exclusive rights normally enjoyed by a copyright holder. For instance, various compulsory licenses are granted under the Copyright Act. Section 111 grants cable systems a compulsory license to re-transmit any material going out over the air on a traditional U.S. television broadcast. For distant signals imported into the area, the cable system must make a required payment to the Copyright Office. The Copyright Royalty Tribunal then acts as a disbursing agent, distributing payments among the program copyright holders who file claim (see page 122).

The Copyright Royalty Tribunal also has jurisdiction over the licensing rates that public broadcasters pay for certain published non-dramatic musical works and published pictorial, graphic, and sculptural works (see Section 118 of the Copyright Act). Other television-related exceptions to the copyright holder's rights include the right of a transmitting organization, like a station or cable company, to make "ephemeral" copies of the work for help in duly-licensed transmissions (see Section 112 of the Copyright Act).

Section 110 permits the use of copyright materials "in the course of face-to-face teaching activities of a non-profit educational institution, in a classroom or similar place devoted to instruction"—provided, in the case of audio-visual works, that the copy being shown was lawfully made. Under Section 108, libraries and other archival institutions can also do limited copying to keep the items in their collection in good condition. Outside the scope of the television context, there are compulsory licenses for jukebox players and for the sound recording of a song or other musical work that has already been recorded and commercially released.

FAIR USE

The 1976 Copyright Act finally codified what used to be court-made law—that the "fair use" of copyrighted material does not represent an infringement of copyright. Section 107 of the 1976 Act provides that "the fair use of a copyrighted work . . . for purposes such as criticism, comment, news reporting, teaching (including multiple copies for classroom use), scholarship or research, is not an infringement of copyright." The statute goes on to specify four factors which are to be taken into account, non-exclusively, in determining whether fair use has been made:

(1) the purpose and character of the use, including whether such use is of a commercial nature or is for non-profit educational purposes;

(2) the nature of the copyrighted work;

(3) the amount and substantiality of the portion used in relation to the copyrighted work as a whole; and

(4) the effect of the use upon the potential market or value of the copyrighted work.

Fair use does not require the permission of the copyright holder. In the television context, fair use permits the use of short excerpts of films, television programs, and other copyrighted works for purposes such as news, information, reviewing, and teaching. Excerpts of a little over a minute or more from a feature film, however, have been held to be excessive and beyond the scope of fair use. Fair use is generally not permitted for material that has not been previously broadcast or otherwise published. The right to control the first broadcast or other publication of a copyrighted work has been held to be very important, and will frequently overcome the other arguments for fair use.

THE FIRST AMENDMENT AND NEWS ITEMS

In limited cases, the First Amendment also provides a means, analogous to fair use, for reproducing copyrighted works without permission. This exception to copyright law pertains to cases where the information in the copyrighted work—typically a film clip or still photograph—is so newsworthy in and of itself that, in the words of *Nimmer on Copyright,* "no amount of words describing the idea . . . could substitute for the public insight gained through the photographs." This rationale has been applied to photographs of the My Lai massacre and the Zapruder film of the Kennedy assassination.

TERM OF COPYRIGHT

The 1909 statute provided for an initial copyright term of 28 years from the date of publication, or 28 years from the date of registration in the case of unpublished works. The 1909 Act established a further renewal term, also of 28 years, available for the extension of the copyright. This renewal term was extended until the 1976 Act set it at 47 years, giving a total of 75 years of protection to works that have been properly copyrighted and renewed under the 1909 Act. Thus, any pre-1978 copyright, even if properly renewed, will go into the public domain in the United States 75 years after its copyright date. For instance, in 1991, anything copyrighted in the U.S. prior to 1916 should be in the public domain. It must be noted that the term of foreign copyright protection can vary, with some countries giving shorter protections and others longer.

Post-1978 works have a copyright period of the life of the author plus 50 years. In the case of works with multiple authors, the time runs from the death of the author who is the last to die. Works made for hire, and works published under pseudonyms, have a copyright term of a flat 75 years from the date of initial publication, or 100 years from the date of creation, whichever expires first.

TERMINATION

The copyright law permits authors and (after they are dead) certain specified individuals to terminate the licenses, assignments, and other transfers of copyrights after a relatively long period has passed. These termination windows reflect the intention that certain aspects of the renewal copyright were meant to benefit authors and not assignees. Section 203 of the Copyright Act provides a right of termination for post-1978 transfers of rights. This allows the copyright holder—or, if he or she is dead, designated family members—to terminate grants of copyright by notice to the grantee given within a five-year window that starts 35 years from the date of the grant, or, in the case of grants covering rights of publication in the work, that starts of 40 years from the grant or 35 years from publication, whichever is earlier. This termination will shut off new uses under the grant, but the continued use of derivative works prepared by the licensee prior to the termination is permitted. Thus, a television film made under a valid grant can still be shown after the termination. It may, however, have to face competition from a new version made under the grant of new rights.

There is also a provision allowing the termination of grants made prior to 1978. Under Section 304 of the Copyright Act, an author or the designated family members can terminate prior grants within a five-year window starting either on January 1, 1978 or 56 years from the date the copyright was originally secured, whichever is later. This allows the author or his or her heirs to enjoy the benefits of the extended renewal term given by the new Act. There is also an exception permitting the continued use of previously-created or derivative works.

In the case of each of these termination rights, no advance waiver will be effective. It should also be noted that in the case of a work for hire, the employer is actually considered the author, and so the paid creator would not have the benefit or these terminations.

There is one further termination right, which carries over from the 1909 Act. Under Section 304(a), the renewal procedures for pre-1978 copyrights still in their first term is preserved. Grants of the renewal term could be made by the author in advance. This grant, however, was not effective against the authorized family members who could exercise the renewal right—if the author had died before he or she could exercise the renewal right. This gives an unlimited termination right to the family members in this narrow circumstance, although it can be waived in advance by the family members. The statute holds no exception for derivative works, and a recent Supreme Court case has established that there is no automatic right to continue to exploit already-produced films or television programs based on such a terminated grant.

EXCLUSIVE LICENSES, ASSIGNMENTS, MORTGAGES

The copyright law requires that an *exclusive* assignment or license (including a mortgage or other security interest in the copyrighted work) be in a signed document in order to be effective between the parties. Indeed, in order to be effective against certain third parties, any such exclusive license or assignment should not only be executed as a signed agreement, but also be recorded with the Copyright Office. This gives legal notice to the world in general of the contents of the license or assignment.

COPYRIGHT INFRINGEMENT

A copyright is infringed when someone exercises one of the exclusive rights granted by the Copyright Act without the consent from the copyright holder, without approval from a licensee of the copyright holder, or without the excuse of a compulsory license, fair use, or other exception. In order to win a lawsuit over an infringement, the plaintiff must prove several key elements. It must be shown that there is a valid copyright in the material. The person suing must be either the copyright owner or the holder of an *exclusive* right which is being infringed. The exclusive-rights concept also applies to beneficial rights. For instance, an author who has assigned his or her original rights to someone else while retaining a royalty interest may still be able to sue as a beneficial-rights owner.

It must also be shown that a protected element of the original work has been used in some forbidden way. This involves establishing two points: first, that the infringing item or element is "substantially similar" to the protected work, and second, that the protected work was actually the basis for the infringing item or element. The former is determined by the judge or jury via straightforward comparison, without the testimony of experts. The latter can be proven directly or inferred so long as the plaintiff can prove that the alleged infringer had *access* to the original work. For example, if the original author had kept the original work in a trunk and never showed it to anyone, there could be no infringement because access was impossible.

Generally, an outraged copyright owner can sue not only the original infringer, but also anyone along the chain of publication. Lack of knowledge that a protected work is being infringed is not a defense, although it may reduce damage liability. For instance, if a scriptwriter plagiarizes a protected book in a teleplay and then sells it to a producer as an original piece, the producer, network, and individual stations can all, in theory, be sued as infringers.

E&O Insurance

This kind of exposure to liability makes Errors and Omissions (E&O) insurance a key part of any contract for distribution or telecasting. Most such contracts call for the producer to get and maintain E&O coverage for at least the first few years a program is shown; sometimes, the required coverage period is linked to the three-year statute of limitations on copyright claims. E&O insurance also covers claims for libel, slander, privacy, and publicity; it does not usually cover contract disputes. The typical limits on E&O coverage are $3 million for all occurrences and $1 million per single claim. Most distribution agreements call for the naming of the distributor as an additional insured on the policy.

E&O insurers generally require that certain clearance procedures be followed, and sometimes they print out a list on their application form of steps to take. This list is a useful reminder of good production practices; Appendix B10 is a typical application for E&O insurance.

Remedies for Infringement

The winning plaintiff in an infringement lawsuit has several possible remedies available. The first is an injunction against any further infringing use. The court can also force a recall of copies still in the channels of distribution or forbid further unauthorized showings.

In addition to putting a stop to the infringement, the aggrieved party can also recover damages and profits. The *damages* may be set to reflect actual harm suffered, such as lost sales; recovering *profits* involves compensating the plaintiff with the economic benefits of the infringement. Both approaches are inherently speculative, and may be inadequate to right the wrong. For instance, if a money-losing TV show is based without permission on a copyrighted film that also lost money, an amount of real damages and improper profits may be hard to prove. It is for such a situation that the Copyright Law has established "statutory damages." This is a set amount which a court can levy as damages—an award based simply on the infringement itself, which does not require proof of a particular level of actual harm. For most infringements, the range of these damages is currently $500 to $20,000 for all infringements of a given copyright; for willful infringements, the statutory damages can be up to $100,000. Awards of legal fees may also be given, which in some cases may exceed actual damages.

Criminal Penalties

In addition to the civil remedies discussed above, there are also criminal penalties for infringement done "willfully and for purposes of commercial advantage or private financial gain." For serious commercial piracy of motion pictures (including television programs) involving making or selling more than 65 copies within any six-month period, the penalty is a fee of up to $250,000 and up to five years in jail.

Taping and Piracy

Before the advent of home video, the unauthorized copying of an audiovisual program was expensive and difficult. Infringing uses of such a copy, even if made, were relatively easy to police. Home video machines, however, have changed this, creating both a simple mechanism for creating copies and a widespread and quite private market for their use. "Time shifting," the practice of recording shows off a broadcast station or cable service for later viewing, is probably the most benign (and the hardest to police) of these activities. When VCRs first came into use, the production community brought suit against Sony in an attempt either to stop the sale of VCRs, or to set up an extra charge on the sale of blank cassettes that would be deposited into a group fund. Producers would then collect a share of this fund, much as they do with compulsory cable-license fees. This scheme was squashed when the U.S. Supreme Court held that home recording for the purposes of time shifting constituted fair use, not copyright infringement.

Outright piracy—that is, the unauthorized copying of works not publicly disseminated by broadcast or cable, or the unauthorized copying of any program or film for commercial purposes—is punishable by the civil and criminal statutes of the Copyright Law. While the relatively harmless practice of copying tapes for friends and family is unlikely to come to anyone's notice, the potential penalties are stiff. Commercial piracy is a major concern of the production and distribution communities; they expend considerable resources in the U.S. on finding and closing down pirates.

INTERNATIONAL IMPLICATIONS OF COPYRIGHT LAW

The scope of the U.S. copyright law is essentially domestic. Although unpublished works by foreign authors are fully protected, that protection will cease on publication unless (1) one or more of the authors is a national, domiciliary, or governmental authority of a country that has a copyright treaty with the U.S.; (2) the work is first published in the U.S.

or in a country which is, at the time of publication, a member of the Universal Copyright Convention; (3) the work is first published by the United Nations or the Organization of American States; (4) the work is a Berne Convention work; or (5) the country of origin is covered by a special Presidential proclamation. The law of most foreign countries is similarly limited, and will not protect a U.S.-source work unless there are applicable international agreements in effect.

The U.S. has been a relative latecomer in joining the conventions (most notably the Berne Convention and the Universal Copyright Convention) that offer the major degree of international copyright protection. U.S. copyright law evolved with a variety of idiosyncracies which did not meet the requirements of the conventions, and which the U.S. was reluctant to give up. Therefore, up until 1955—when the U.S. joined the Universal Copyright Convention (UCC)—protection of a U.S. work abroad depended upon either the existence of an individually-negotiated treaty between the U.S. and the foreign country in question, or the simultaneous publication of the work in the U.S. and a country (frequently Canada) that was an adherent to one or more of the Conventions. The UCC was, in fact, tailored to permit such elements of the 1909 Act as the notice requirements, which were not permitted under the Berne Convention. The UCC gave protection throughout much of the world, but there were still gaps, some of which could be closed by joining the Berne Convention. With the adoption of the 1976 Copyright Act, many of the inconsistencies were eliminated, and the U.S. began to seriously consider joining Berne as well.

The principal stumbling block to the U.S. joining the Berne Convention was the Convention's requirement that moral rights (see page 155) be protected. With the determination that the U.S. gave enough protection to moral rights to qualify for Berne without changing existing law, Congress ratified the Berne Convention, which came into effect on March 1, 1989. Adherence to Berne did require some changes to U.S. law, particularly in the area of formalities (see page 138). Foreign works coming under Berne get even easier treatment on the registration point—copyright registration is not a prerequisite to bringing a lawsuit.

Under Berne, U.S. works will receive the same protection in another Berne country as applies to works originally copyrighted in that country. In some cases, this can include a copyright term in excess of that granted in the U.S. Whenever a question of foreign copyrights is raised, it is wise to consult with a knowledgeable expert.

PROTECTION OF IDEAS

Although it is not possible to copyright an idea, that does not mean that an idea is completely unprotectable. In most states, it is possible to obtain at least some protection under contract theories for an idea disclosed to another when the two parties have made a deal requiring compensation for the idea. For instance, a signed contract to pay for disclosing an idea will normally be enforced. A studio or producer may request a well-known author to submit raw ideas for programming, and can agree to pay for the ideas. The most notorious example of such an arrangement was the subject of a lawsuit which found that Art Buchwald had supplied the idea behind the film *Coming to America*. Buchwald had a signed contract with Paramount Pictures promising to pay him for ideas he supplied, with extra payments and net profits due if the ideas were actually used as a basis for a film. As of this writing, Buchwald and Paramount are still arguing over what net profits (if any) were generated by *Coming to America*.

Where there is a signed contract, the most frequently contested issue is whether or not the idea in question, or enough of it, was actually used. An idea, by its very nature, lacks those expressive elements which would give rise to copyright protection. Therefore, the standard of similarity necessary for an idea case is generally less stringent than that which would be required for a copyright-infringement case. Frequently, the contract will provide words such as "based on" to indicate the necessary relationship between the idea and the final product. In applying the "based on" concept, courts have used a variety of analyses, including a kind of mental paternity test. If it can be shown that the end product evolved naturally from the original idea, the final product will be held to be based upon the idea, even if many changes have been made and the number of actual elements in common has become relatively sparse. Any defendant in such an action will try to show a different source for the end product.

Even in the absence of a signed, written agreement, courts will sometimes still give protection to the provider of an idea. For instance, if there is a verbal understanding or if it is the accepted expectation in the industry that a payment would be made if the idea was disclosed and used, then an implied contract will sometimes be found.

Other theories for giving implied protection are "unjust enrichment," fraud, and the breach of a fiduciary relationship. For example, if an attorney (who has a fiduciary relationship to his client) uses for his own profit a television program idea disclosed by the client in confidence, it is likely that the client would be able to recover the fair value of the idea from the attorney.

In some states, such as New York, it must be shown that the idea was original and novel before any contract protection, whether express or implied, will be given. In such a state, an idea that was relatively obvious may not be given any legal protection.

Unsolicited Material

The desire of authors to impose implied contracts on producers, on the one hand, and the desire of producers, on the other hand, to avoid them, has led to a variety of strategies in the submission of unsolicited material. Some producers refuse to review any unsolicited material, returning such submissions to the sender either unopened or unread. Other producers will review such material, but will first send a letter to the person submitting the material seeking to counter any implication that a contract exists for its use. (A sample of such a letter appears in Appendix B2.) Some producers find that these actions are too time-consuming—they simply send rejections for material they don't wish to use, and negotiate agreements for material which they do wish to use.

Writers, when submitting unsolicited material, will sometimes seek to set up the implication that payment is to be made, even if non-copyrightable aspects of the material should be used. A writer may enclose with the material a letter which spells out, in some non-threatening manner, that the writer expects to be compensated if the material is used by the producer. While the efficacy of these one-sided letters is open to question, they are probably better than nothing.

In the end, the writer's greatest protection probably comes from the fact that it is usually relatively inexpensive, in the overall scheme of a production, for an established producer to pay a rights fee of some kind to the persons actually supplying ideas for the program. Indeed, such a license with one person can provide, under the paternity-test theory, protection against claims brought by other potential originators of the idea. Before bringing charges of theft for aspects of a project that was casually submitted, the aggrieved writer should consider that similar ideas may have been suggested to active production companies on more than one occasion.

19 Protection of Personal Rights

LIBEL AND SLANDER

Libel and slander are twin actions frequently linked under the word "defamation." Defamation has been defined as the publication or broadcast of false information, not otherwise privileged, which exposes the person (or other entity) described to hatred, contempt, or ridicule; which causes the person to be shunned or avoided; or which has the tendency to injure the person in his or her occupation. Liability attaches not only to the individual who writes or speaks the falsehood, but to any other entity "publishing" it as well. Broadcasting by a network, cable network, or local station will generally constitute such publishing. A cable system simply supplying an outside service may be free from challenge on the theory that it is a mere transmitter.

These are difficult and confused areas of the law. Indeed, one of the most respected legal treatises on the subject declares:

> It must be confessed at the beginning that there is a great deal of the law of defamation which makes no sense. It contains anomalies and absurdities for which no legal writer has ever had a kind word, and it is a curious compound of a strict liability imposed upon innocent defendants, as rigid in extremes anything found in the law, with a blind and almost perverse refusal to compensate the plaintiff for real and very serious harm.*

Libel involves written defamation and *slander* involves spoken defamation—the distinction is one of the anomalies mentioned above. In the case of slander, it is frequently necessary to prove actual specific damages, while in the case of libel, such damages can often be presumed from the nature of the defamatory writing. Although it is still open to some dispute among the various states, any form of recorded television production will generally be treated under the laws of libel, even though it is not in a written form. Purely live broadcast may constitute slander in some states.

---

* *Prosser and Keaton on the Law of Torts,* 5th Edition, 1984.

Requirements for Defamation

The first prerequisite for defamation is that the offensive statement in fact describe the person complaining of the falsehood. The actual name need not be used for the claim to succeed, so long as a reasonable person would think that the person complaining is the one to whom the defamatory statement in fact refers. Defamation claims have been upheld even when not only the name has been changed, but many of the personal characteristics, such as body shape, hair color, and age. If the claimant can show that there was sufficient identifying detail to lead reasonable people to believe that he or she was the one being talked about, then an action for defamation can be sustained. Ironically, the very act of changing names and some character traits can give rise to the kind of falsehood which is actionable. Therefore, if fictionalization of a real character is to take place in a program, the writer, producer, and director are advised to go to great lengths to clearly distance the fictionalized character from its original model. Coy references to a real person, made under a veil of fiction, can be dangerous. Defamation only applies to living persons, though, so the reputation of a dead individual receives no protection from libel and slander.

The second requirement for defamation is that the statement in question be false. Truth is, in and of itself, a complete defense against defamation. There is also a distinction between fact and opinion. The courts have held that an opinion in itself is not subject to being true or false; it merely represents the opinion of the speaker. The difference between opinion and fact, however, is not always possible or easy to discern. The statement that "Joe is a liar" on the one hand constitutes an opinion as to Joe's veracity; on the other hand, it can be taken as a statement of fact that Joe lies about things. Even though "opinions" are not absolutely safe from challenge, in practice, it is still generally helpful to couch controversial conclusions as matters of opinion. The talk-show host who begins every third sentence with "Well, in my opinion" is demonstrating the influence of somebody's legal department.

The third element of defamation is that the false statement must expose the person to some kind of harm to reputation. Thus, the statement that "Joe loves his country," even if false, would not generally be judged defamatory. False imputations of dishonesty, adultery, or venereal infections, however, are clearly within the danger zone.

Defamation and the First Amendment

Overlying these traditional aspects of defamation are requirements imposed by the First Amendment of the Constitution. In order to encourage robust reporting and a free exercise of the creative arts, the Supreme Court held in 1964—in the famous case of *New York Times v. Sullivan*—that the First Amendment prevents recovery for defamation against a public figure unless some kind of *fault* is demonstrated. A public official or other public figure who has been harmed must show that the author or publisher of a defamatory statement had "actual malice" in publishing of the falsehood in order to recover damages. Actual malice in this context does not mean hatred; rather, it has the technical meaning of either an actual knowledge that the statement in question was false, or a reckless disregard for the truth or falsehood of the statement. In the case of a private individual, the standard set by the Supreme Court is one of negligence in checking out the information that is published or broadcast, and requires that greater care be taken by the producer or reporter. As a practical matter, a finding of malice for statements made by the media about a public person is rare. The author and publisher of the supposedly libelous material will probably have exercised at least some care in their research. This includes checking sources, seeking confirmation, and asking for a response from the affected person. The negligence standard as applied to non-public figures is somewhat more stringent; therefore, the author and broadcaster of material relating to private people should exert themselves even more than normal to insure a truthful program. The distinction between a public and private person is sometimes a tricky one, and is frequently linked to context. A person who saves the President's life will be a public person within the context of that event, but may still be a private person in the context of his or her home life. In either case, a court will very seldom impose liability on a journalist, writer, or producer who can demonstrate that he or she has acted within normal journalistic standards of professional responsibility.

Prior Restraint and Damages

In enforcing the rules against libel and slander, a court will almost never prevent publication in advance. Such a prevention is called a "prior restraint" and, as an absolute exercise in information control, is repugnant for First Amendment reasons. The more usual remedy for a proven case of defamation is damages. As discussed above, in certain instances it may be necessary for a plaintiff to prove actual damages to reputation. In other cases, damages will be presumed from the statement itself. The chance of a plaintiff winning a suit and obtaining substantial damages is more likely for claims dealing with sexual matters or other general societal taboos than in the context of a political debate, where a certain level of robust charge and counter-charge is expected and tolerated.

PRIVACY AND PUBLICITY

The related rights of privacy and publicity are relative newcomers to American law. They have evolved considerably over the last 100 years, and they are still evolving. The *right of privacy* was first discussed in a *Harvard Law Review* article written in 1890 by Samuel Warren and the eventual Supreme Court Justice, Louis Brandeis. They suggested that a right to be "left alone" existed in the "common law"—that is, as a matter of judicial recognition, without ever having been enacted by a legislature. The first test of rights to privacy came in the State of New York in 1902. The case was brought by a young woman whose picture was used, without her permission, in a poster advertising baking flour. The New York Court of Appeals would not accept the common-law basis for the right of privacy, so she lost her case. This decision led to the passage by the New York State Legislature of a statute creating a "right of privacy." The successor to this statute, New York Civil Rights Law Section 50, now reads, in part:

> A person, firm or corporation that uses for advertising purposes, or for the purposes of trade, the name, portrait or picture of any living person without having first obtained the written consent of such person, or if a minor of his or her partner or guardian, is guilty of a misdemeanor.

A companion provision, Section 51, provides a civil damage remedy for violations of this right. Note that the items covered are "name, portrait or picture," and that the statute applies to "living persons" (see Appendix A9).

If the New York court was hesitant to create a new right based on a *Harvard Law Review* article, the courts in many other states were not. For instance, in 1905, the Georgia Supreme Court held that the right of privacy did exist even without a statute. California has also recognized a common-law privacy right. Over the years, most states have come down on one side or the other of this choice. Many states which did not recognize the right at common law subsequently adopted statutes, frequently based on the New York model.

Another law-review article—this time published in 1960 and written by the famous legal commentator, William Prosser—had a significant impact. Prosser suggested that the law of privacy had four parts: (1) a right against intrusion into a person's life and affairs, including by eavesdropping and spying; (2) a right against the public disclosure of embarrassing private facts; (3) a right against being put in a "false light"; and (4) a right against the appropriation of a person's identity by others, particularly for commercial purposes. The last of these four was an aspect of the right which is covered by the New York statute and its imitators. Although Prosser was writing as a private citizen and not as a judge or legislator, his analysis was adopted as the basis of the law in many states, particularly in those where the right of privacy was held to exist at common law.

The *right of publicity* is similar to New York's statutory privacy right and Prosser's fourth right of privacy. The two major distinctions that have come to be most frequently recognized are (1) that the right of publicity will be strongest in cases where the person in question actually exploits his or her persona, and (2) that the right of publicity can survive the death of the person whose identity is being exploited. The privacy right, as with defamation, was generally viewed to terminate on the death of the person in question. Thus, in 1985, California adopted a statutory publicity-right provision, supplementing its common-law and statutory rights of privacy. The new statute permits the heirs of a deceased celebrity to continue to exploit his or her identity in commercial products for a period of up to 50 years after the celebrity's death (see Appendix A10).

By 1991, most states had adopted, either by statute or as a matter of common law, some form of the rights of privacy and publicity. Most states, at a minimum, protect living people against commercial appropriation of their names and likenesses. There is, however, tremendous diversity between the laws of the different states, as to which further aspects of the rights they recognize. Given the confusion on these issues, it is important to know which state's rules will apply. In general, courts will apply the law of the domicile of the person seeking privacy or publicity protection. While this rule may help courts in reaching a decision, or a local programmer with only one or two states to worry about, it is less helpful to the producer or distributor of national programming.

Luckily, the free-speech provisions of the First Amendment of United States Constitution supply an overall national standard, at least with respect to factual statements on matters of general public interest.

The Supreme Court ruled on the problem in 1967, in the case of *Time, Inc. v. Hill.* This case involved a New York privacy lawsuit by members of a family who had been the victims of a crime some years before. *Life* magazine, a Time, Inc. publication, had run an article which set scenes from a play that was based loosely on this crime in the family's old house. The article implied inaccurate details about the family and the crime. (Richard Nixon represented the family in its appeal.) The Supreme Court held that privacy and publicity claims by public figures (including the family, in this case) would require a showing of the same element of "malice"—knowing falsehood or reckless disregard for truth—that had to be proved for a defamation claim.

Even without reference to the First Amendment, most privacy statutes and common-law formulations on the state level have been interpreted to hold that truthful biographical, informational, or news uses are "non-commercial" and therefore not a violation. This conclusion would apply even to a program broadcast on commercial television in a for-profit manner.

An extension of this logic allows, without consent, the name and likeness of an individual who appears in the program to be used in advertisements for the program itself—and, provided that the name and likeness are linked to the program in some way, they can even be used in ads for the service that runs the program.

DOCUDRAMAS

The laws—and exceptions—governing the rights of defamation, privacy, and publicity display themselves most vividly in the context of docudramas. This is because the application of the Constitutional aspects of libel, slander, privacy, and publicity law to docudramas must overcome an inherent contradiction. There is supposedly no First Amendment protection for a depiction that is knowingly false or deliberately fictionalized—the essence of the malice standard that applies to both defamation and privacy/publicity. Yet a docudrama is, of necessity, a fictionalized presentation of events based in truth. A print biographer can perhaps claim the goal of absolute accuracy, but a docudrama producer never can.

To begin with, the words spoken—unless they come directly from court transcripts or other *verbatim* sources—will always be, at best, reconstructions of past events. The characters will be played by actors, and not by the people themselves. The requirements of production will inevitably cause deletions and compressions of events and characters. Quite conscious fictionalization is a necessary part of the process—and the docudrama is a legally permissible art form.

The leading opinion as to the docudrama's blending of fact and fiction arose from the film *Missing.* In his opinion, the judge, Milton Pollack, stated:

> Self-evidently a docudrama partakes of author's license—it is a creative interpretation of reality—and if alterations of fact in scenes portrayed are not made with serious doubts of truth of the essence of the telescoped composite, such scenes do not ground a charge of actual malice.*

The *Missing* case and other docudrama cases suggest this simple guideline: a docudrama producer may use limited fictionalization, creating composite characters, incidents and dialogue, provided that the end result—with respect to any material questions—is representationally true, and provided that such representational truth has been arrived at responsibly.

Docudrama producers should stick to the following procedures in order to help keep their productions within legally permissible bounds:

Select a topic and characters of legitimate public interest. The First Amendment protections will be much less helpful in the examination of private events in the lives of private people.

Depict dead people. Death wipes out protection against defamation and the right of privacy (although not the right of publicity).

Get releases. If releases can be obtained, they provide the best line of defense. However, it may be better never to ask for a release than to ask and be refused.

---

* *Davis v. Costa-Gavras,* 654 F. Supp 653, 658 (S.D.N.Y. 1987)

Do voluminous research. The back-up work for a docudrama should be even more rigorous than the research for a hard news piece. Minor incidents and personality traits should also be noted. A wealth of accurate detail from numerous sources will give the scriptwriter the raw material from which to work, and will provide a higher level of protection. All research must be recorded and catalogued, so that it can be easily referenced as the review process goes forward.

Have a factual basis for every aspect of the script. Even with those scenes or characters that are fictionalized, there must be a factual basis for their "representational truth." Invented dialogue should reflect the opinions of the speaker. Although it is clear that excursions into "representational truth" are permitted, there is a point at which fictionalization goes too far. As a general matter, the more controversial or emotionally-charged the item, the more literal the depiction should be; sex and nudity are particularly dicey. The film should also respect chronology, and should not use composite characters to portray major figures.

Have a legal review of the script and film. A legal review will act as a useful check on the natural exuberance of producers and writers, and can prove helpful in demonstrating lack of negligence and malice.

Use disclaimers. An appropriate disclaimer, alerting the audience to the presence of fictionalized elements, should be placed in the credits. The greater the prominence of the disclaimer, the greater the protection it offers.

MORAL RIGHTS

The doctrine of moral rights developed in continental Europe. In addition to the "economic rights" Americans traditionally associate with copyright, European authors generally have a second set of "moral rights" in their work. In their classic form, these rights include (1) the right to control publication, (2) the right to withdraw the work, (3) the right to have authorship accurately attributed, and (4) the right to maintain the integrity of the work, by preventing desecration and unauthorized changes. These rights are typically held to be inalienable: they are not subject to a general waiver. In most countries, the rights are transmitted after death to the author's family or to a designated representative; in some countries, such as France, the rights are said to be perpetual.

In the context of audio-visual productions, which are by their nature collaborative works, the European jurisdictions typically recognize at least the scriptwriter and director as the "creators" of the work, with the power to exercise these rights. Some countries add the composer of the musical score and author of any underlying work to this list. The existence of these moral rights can significantly restrict the exploitation of an audio-visual production. For instance, French filmmakers have effectively barred the colorizing of their old black-and-white films for the French market, at least without specific consent. The re-editing of films for use on television, such as cutting for time purposes or inserting ad breaks, may also be restricted. In effect, the original version cannot be tampered with by the producers without the express approval of the designated creators.

In the U.S., there has been a general resistance to expressly recognizing the existence of any moral rights. Ironically, the U.S. copyright law, by giving the author control over publication and the preparation of derivative or otherwise infringing works, actually accords the author the power to control all of the usual moral rights as a matter of contract. Other laws, such as privacy, libel, and unfair competition, cover some of the same territory as moral rights. When the U.S. joined the Berne Convention on copyright, which requires moral-rights protection for authors, Congress pointed to these various rules in justifying going forward without changing U.S. law. The big difference between U.S. law and the provisions of most of the signatories to the Berne Convention is that classic moral rights cannot be contracted away on a general basis—the equivalent U.S. copyright protections and other legal rights, by contrast, can be, and usually are. The U.S. approach seems to be acceptable under the Berne Convention.

The American freedom to waive moral rights is both a blessing and a curse. On the one hand, it permits a freer commerce in film and television programming than is possible in Europe. In the case of a commissioned product with high commercial value and low artistic pretense—such as The Price is Right or All My Children—the ability to waive is probably no loss to society. On the other hand, some people consider colorizing the best black-and-white films as deplorable as painting a mustache on the Mona Lisa.

There is, however, a critical difference between television product and a painting such as the Mona Lisa. The painting is a one-of-a-kind object, and a mustache on it would be an irreparable act. A television film or other program, by contrast, is quite freely reproducible, and changes such as colorization or editing can be made without in any way damaging the existing copies of the original work. Congress, in acting on the colorization issue, recognized this by setting up a mechanism for the preservation of certain designated film masterpieces in their original form. It also required that colorized versions of these films disclose prominently that the colorization was done without the participation of the original creative team, if that is the case. As a practical matter, these disclaimers have been broadly adopted for application to most colorized films, whether or not required by law.

In the final analysis, the arguments for an unwaivable moral rights law depend on a view of the creative processes that is at heart a 19th-century one. In this view, the author/artist is a special being, with the power to pierce the veil of ordinary existence and bring us all, through art, into contact with the sublime. Under such a view, the artist must retain control over each particular use of his or her work. For most areas of television production, it makes more sense for the producer to be able to obtain general waivers of these rights, particularly when the creative person has been commissioned and well-compensated to exercise his or her craft.

UNFAIR COMPETITION

The laws of unfair competition protect the names and reputations of individuals or companies from being falsely involved in connection with goods or services. (See page 323 for a more detailed discussion of the law of unfair competition.) At the federal level, this law is embodied in the Lanham Act; there are also similar state principles. The laws of unfair competition can protect individuals and organizations against the use of their names or other indicia of identity in such a way as to falsely suggest the origin of a program. Thus, using a well-known title or making some other statement which implies that a program was authorized by—or originated with—someone who had not given his or her consent, would be actionable.

Protection of Society

Most of the issues relevant to the content of television programming, such as copyright, privacy, and publicity, are private rights that are exercised or waived by the private entities involved. There are, however, certain restrictions which are imposed and enforced as a matter of criminal and civil law by our government, on the theory that they protect society at large. In keeping with the principles of the First Amendment, these rules are neither very numerous, nor very broad in their applicability. Nonetheless, they can have quite powerful repercussions.

OBSCENITY

Notwithstanding the loosening of constraints over the past 30 years, the taboos against sex in the U.S. are very strong: so strong, indeed, that certain kinds of sexual speech are still held to be simply outside the coverage of the First Amendment. Since material labeled "obscene" is not protected by the First Amendment, it is subject to outright banning and criminal prosecution by the federal and state governments. The key question, therefore, is what constitutes obscene material. The Supreme Court, as the final arbiter on this matter, has wrestled with a definition of obscenity over the years, and has produced a series of pronouncements. Perhaps the most forthright, if the least specific, was the statement by one Supreme Court Justice that he knew pornography when he saw it.

The currently applicable test for obscenity was enunciated in the case of *Miller v. California* in 1973. Under this test, for material to be obscene, all three of the following factors must be proven: 1) the average person, applying contemporary community standards, would find that the work, taken as a whole, appeals to prurient interests; 2) the work, as measured by contemporary community standards, depicts or describes—in a patently offensive way—sexual conduct specifically defined by the applicable state law; and 3) the work taken as a whole lacks serious literary, artistic, political, or scientific value.

This standard, when reduced to its bare essence, is not too different from "I know it when I see it." In effect, if the material contains explicit sexual depictions which are likely to arouse and offend (in the opinion of the judge or jury) a sufficiently broad segment of the population, it will be deemed obscene—unless the work has some aspect of general merit that removes it from punishment. Because the strength of the sexual taboo has ebbed somewhat in most communities in the past 30 years, the community-standard aspect of this test has led to the permitting of fairly explicit sexual material, particularly in major urban centers.

The dissemination of overtly sexual material by television is generally limited to such media as home video or late-night, local cablecast; in either case, adults have a personal choice as to whether or not to view it. In fact, the Supreme Court has held that the private possession and perusal of obscene material in the home is not punishable. The consenting-adults argument, however, is no defense for transactions in obscene material: a private sale of an explicit videotape from one adult to another is still illegal. From a practical standpoint, though, few people are likely to complain about truly private transactions, and such sales are relatively unlikely to be punished.

Most states have anti-pornography statutes of one kind or another on their books. Some carry very serious criminal penalties. The enforcement of these statutes—or lack of enforcement—reflects the level of community concern. In conservative areas such as Cincinnati, Ohio, prosecutors and other enforcers of these laws may stand to gain more politically by bringing cases against supposedly obscene material than will prosecutors in more permissive places such as New York City and Los Angeles. There are also serious federal criminal laws forbidding the dissemination of obscene material. For instance, there are laws against shipping obscene material, including videos, in the mails or via interstate commerce.

OBSCENITY AND THE FCC

There are federal laws and FCC regulations governing the appearance of obscene and indecent material on broadcast television, and of obscene matter on cable television. Ironically, in its original formulation in the Communications Act, the prohibition against the use of indecent language via radio communication was paired with a provision forbidding the FCC to exercise any censorship over the content of broadcasts. The prohibition has since been moved out of the Communications Act and into the title on Crimes and Criminal Procedure. It reads, at 18 U.S.C. § 1464:

> Whoever utters any obscene, indecent, or profane language by means of radio communication shall be fined not more than $10,000 or imprisoned not more than two years, or both.

The distribution of obscene material via cable or subscription television is punishable under both Title 18 and the Cable Act. Title 18, § 1468, provides:

(a) Whoever knowingly utters any obscene language or distributes any obscene matter by means of cable television or subscription services on television, shall be punished by imprisonment for not more than two years or by fine in accordance with this title, or both.

(b) As used in this section, the term "distribute" means to send, transmit, retransmit, telecast, broadcast, or cablecast, including by wire, microwave, or satellite, or to produce or provide material for such distribution.

(c) Nothing in this chapter, or the Cable Communications Policy Act of 1984, or any other provision of Federal law, is intended to interfere with or preempt the power of the states, including political subdivisions thereof, to regulate the uttering of language that is obscene or otherwise unprotected by the Constitution or the distribution of matter that is obscene or otherwise unprotected by the Constitution, of any sort, by means of cable television or subscription services on television.

The Cable Act provides in Section 639 [47 U.S.C. § 559]:

Whoever transmits over any cable system any matter which is obscene or otherwise unprotected by the Constitution or the United States shall be fined not more than $10,000 or imprisoned not more than two years, or both.

There is an important difference between the FCC's approach to broadcast television and its approach to cable television.

The broadcast rules apply not only to "obscene" material, but also to material that is merely "indecent." Indecency includes the use of offensive words, even in contexts where no graphic sexual description is involved: thus the problem with George Carlin's famous seven words you can't use on the airwaves. Indecency probably also includes nonsexual nudity.

The laws governing cable services, however, provide only for the prohibition of obscene material. There has been a tradition of greater latitude in the cable area. This is partly due to the lesser legal control of cable—and also to the fact that the decision to receive cable is elective, and that in most cases, the more risqué channels can be switched off at the box in the home. Public-access services have been particularly active in showing non-obscene nudity, largely in a late-night time slot. Use of non-obscene sexual images and language is a matter for the programming policies of the cable system and network, exercised largely in light of commercial considerations. Hardcore material would still fall afoul of the obscenity standard.

NATIONAL SECURITY

In limited circumstances, the government can censor material that would endanger the national security. This authority has been quite narrowly defined, applying only when an immediate, specific threat from the publication or telecast of the material can be shown. For instance, it has been held that the government could prevent the publication of the sailing dates of transports, or the number and location of troops in time of war—and that the government can suppress a magazine article explaining in full detail how to build a hydrogen bomb. In the Pentagon Papers case, by contrast, the Supreme Court allowed the publication of an in-house Department of Defense study critical of the conduct of the Vietnam War. The government had simply not met the heavy burden of justification necessary to stop the information from flowing.

Even if information, once gathered, is hard to suppress on national-security grounds, the government and military can limit the access of reporters, including television newspeople, to sensitive material and locations. Furthermore, as a *quid pro quo* for obtaining access to military areas and missions, reporters will sometimes agree to limit certain aspects of their stories. This self-censorship, encouraged by the government, can be quite effective. Government officials sometimes sign contracts agreeing to keep certain information secret, and these contracts can be enforced.

PRE-TRIAL PUBLICITY

The First Amendment guarantees of free speech sometimes come into conflict with another constitutional guarantee: the right to a fair trial. It is sometimes claimed that pre-trial publicity of a particularly inflammatory nature can so prejudice public opinion about a criminal case that it becomes impossible for the defendant to receive a fair hearing by a jury. As a result, in certain very rare cases, there may be an injunction against publishing or televising a particular piece of information about the case. This remedy is only granted on proof that no other option, including moving the location of the trial to a city or town where the case is less well-known, will protect the rights of the accused.

"SON OF SAM" LAWS

The federal government and many states have adopted so-called "Son of Sam" Laws. These laws prevent a criminal from being able to profit from selling the rights to the story of his or her crimes to the media. In the late 1970s, New York City was the scene of a series of brutal attacks by a psychopathic killer who sent notes about his crimes signed with the name "Son of Sam." Enraged at the notion that this criminal might profit from a sale of the media rights to his crimes, New York State enacted a statute that confiscates any monies paid to the criminal (or to entities such as agents collecting on his behalf) for books, movies, magazine articles, or television shows in which the crime is reenacted or the criminal's "thoughts, feelings, opinions or emotions" about the crime are expressed. The funds so confiscated are given to a crime victims' compensation board, which then disburses them to victims of the crime. Similar laws have been enacted by the federal government and by many states.

The "Son of Sam" Laws have withstood the constitutional challenge that they violate free speech. The logic of the courts has been that the criminals are perfectly free to write or authorize a television story about their crimes; they just can't profit from them. The restriction is, in effect, a further monetary fine; free speech is unaffected. Whatever the validity of this argument, it is clear that the "Son of Sam" Laws are here to stay.

CHILDREN'S PROGRAMMING

After many years of false starts, canceled proceedings, and vetoed legislation, in 1990 Congress finally enacted legislation regulating children's television. The Children's Television Act of 1990 restricts the amount of advertising that can run in children's programming on both broadcast and cable television to 10.5 minutes per hour on weekends and 12 on weekdays (shorter periods are treated proportionately). The Act also requires the FCC to regulate program-length commercials, and calls on broadcast stations to serve "the educational and information needs of children through the licensee's overall programming, including programming specifically designed to serve such needs." The degree to which a broadcast station has met this standard is considered in connection with license renewal.

The FCC rules, finalized in August, 1991, define children's programming as being aimed at 12 years old and under. "Program-length commercials" are defined as "a program associated with a product, in which commercials for that product are aired." This continues to allow product driven shows to air, but if direct sales pitches for the product are contained within the program or in adjacent spots, then the entire program counts against the commercial time limits. The FCC did not narrowly define programs that would serve "the educational and informational needs of children," and recognized that this could include fictional programs.

These rules generally take effect on October 1, 1991, but implementation of the program-length commercial rules are delayed for most existing programs until January 1, 1992. License renewal review will start with licenses expiring June 1, 1992.

VIOLENCE ON TELEVISION

The level of violence on U.S. television often surprises visitors from other developed countries; for whatever reason, violent acts are a staple of U.S. programming. So far, efforts to mobilize legislative and regulatory controls have met with little success, and government involvement in this area would probably violate First Amendment principles. Some action has been started on the question of violence in children's programming. However, until the U.S. public loses its taste for violence-laced fantasy, violent programming will remain prevalent on television.

SELF-REGULATION BY THE TELEVISION INDUSTRY

The private side of the television business also regulates itself for the protection of society. Industry-wide self-regulation impinges on the antitrust rules, so industry-wide controls have largely fallen away. For instance, the National Association of Broadcasters code relating to program content was abandoned in 1982 as part of the settlement of an antitrust suit brought by the Justice Department, which saw the code as an example of impermissible coordination between supposedly competing businesses.

There is, however, considerable control exercised at the individual company level. Each of the networks maintains a standards and practices department, which reviews programming and advertisements in the light of company-wide standards. These departments issue and administer guidelines on a variety of issues. Many of their concerns reflect the need to conform with the FCC restrictions described in Chapter 14, the intellectual-property rules described in Chapter 18, and the personal-rights requirements described in Chapter 19. Other standards-and-practices recommendations reflect the twin goals of serving the good of society and preserving the image of the network (and, by association, of its advertisers). The areas of concern are predictable: alcohol, criminal activities, drugs, human relationships, obscenity, physical infirmities, race, religion, color, age, national origin, sex and sexuality, and violence. The list reads like a program guide for some of the more popular daytime talk shows, or an assignment board for a local news team during sweeps weeks: all of society's hot and tricky topics are there.

The stated requirements of the networks on these issues tend toward the general and platitudinous. One network, for instance, in setting guidelines for programming on "Human Relationships," declares: "The presentation of marriage, the family, interpersonal relationships, and other material dealing with sexuality shall not be treated exploitatively or irresponsibly, but with sensitivity." This pious injunction to be nice about things is at odds with the fact that nice is usually not as interesting to most of the audience as nasty, or at least mildly nasty. Applying standards that are worded this way is a matter of balancing the prospect of attracting a big audience with the consequences of offending some of it.

Outside of broadcast networks, there is much less institutionalized hand-wringing over program content. Most cable services, for instance, are aimed at specific target groups; the broadcast networks still seek to reach a broad cross-section of American society. The programming people at a cable network are generally quite in touch with what their audience wants to see, and if they get a little too aggressive, a memo from the advertising salespeople will usually correct the matter. There is no centralized politeness brigade to keep things within bounds.

Where they exist at networks, cable companies, or local stations, the standards and practices departments and their rules serve to institutionalize, on a private basis, the kind of community-standard approach that underlies the Supreme Court's rulings on obscenity. What is prohibited and what is permitted reflects general societal taboos. As usual, sex comes in for considerable regulation. Violence, which has been until recently subject to much less societal condemnation, is permitted to a far greater extent. Predictably, as the pressure to control some of this violence grows at a societal level, the violence level of television programming is coming under more and more scrutiny by both broadcast and cable companies. These companies have recently been granted a limited exemption from antitrust rules to permit them to collaborate in producing an industry-wide standard on violent content in programming. In light of society's fascination with violence, however, it is hard to predict whether or not private controls on television violence will increase in the future.

PUBLIC PRESSURE

In the end, the content of television programming in the U.S. is highly responsive to the desires of the public. Television production is so costly that unless there is a market for the resulting program, it will generally not be made. Furthermore, most programming depends upon commercial support, and few product manufacturers will want to antagonize public opinion by sponsoring programs that significant special-interest groups might protest as offensive. In fact, consumer campaigns can be quite effective in persuading sponsors and other program supporters to leave certain types of content without financial backing. The mass-distribution systems of broadcast television are much more susceptible to this type of boycott than is the essentially personal world of home video; cable lies somewhere in between. In sum, the content of programming reflects what the audience wants: society protects itself on the issues that truly arouse public opinion, and leaves the rest to find its market.

Part 4

PROGRAMMING AND PRODUCTION

21 Program Development: Overview/Prime-Time Fiction

The success of any television or video venture depends, in large part, upon the quality of its programs. There is no single path to follow in the development of a television show or series, but there are traditions that are common throughout the industry.

This chapter, the first of three on the process of program development, focuses on the development of properties for prime-time entertainment, mainly fiction. Chapter 22 looks at non-fiction entertainment programs; Chapter 23 covers news, talk, and information programs.

THE DEVELOPMENT OF PROGRAM IDEAS

Television programs grow from a fantastic variety of source ideas: news events, social issues, personalities, board games, family relationships, fads and trends, books, toys, or a writer's imagination.

In its raw and undeveloped form, an idea is not really useful. There are far more ideas than there are programs produced; only program development adds value to the idea. Eventually, after an investment of time (always) and money (frequently), the idea becomes a marketable property, gathering enough momentum to go into production.

Some ideas are created and developed within an organization, often by salaried personnel with no direct financial interest in the success or failure of the project. This is often the situation at local television stations, corporate and institutional facilities, and local cable companies—entities where in-house development and in-house production are common. The situation is different at cable and commercial networks, syndication companies, and most home video companies. There, ideas may be generated by either inside or outside personnel, but the development is most often carried through by outside production companies. A producer or production company may originate and develop an idea independently, or may be asked to develop an idea that originated within a network or syndication company.

DEVELOPMENT FUNDING

The funding of development varies considerably. The costs of rights acquisitions, writers, attorneys, budget preparation, travel, and other production elements can quickly add up to tens of thousands of dollars, if not more. The development cost of a true "in-house" project will be paid for from a dedicated budget, and there is some likelihood that the show will be produced and televised. An independent producer can also fund development from internal sources, but the odds of eventual production (and payback) are much lower. Some producers have a development deal with large companies, either end users or companies with a significant production/distribution business. Such a deal, sometimes called an "umbrella" arrangement, commits the company to giving the producer a set amount of money in exchange for the right to participate in the eventual production, should it occur. In the absence of such a relationship, at each step up in the development process, the producer tries to find someone to cover further development costs in return for a first right to participate later.

Frequently, the ultimate funder of development is the end user—for example, a broadcast network, a cable network, or a syndicator. The producer, writer, production company, or studio will present the partially-developed property to the end user at a *pitch meeting*. At this meeting, the creative/production team takes the end user's programming executives through the concept of the show, presenting written material as well. The programmer may make suggestions or counterproposals; if the pitch is successful, the end user will commit to funding further work on the project and may repay the development costs incurred to date.

Regardless of the arrangement, until the final decision to produce is made, the project can be killed off at any time and the development investment lost—unless another end user is interested (see "turnaround," page 172). Therefore, while the project is in development, there is a constant tension between spending money to add value to the idea and the desire to wager as little as possible on the gamble of eventual production.

If the idea for a television program or series is based on an existing property, then the appropriate rights to that property must be acquired, preferably before any significant development work begins. The acquisition of rights to a published work—in the illustration below, a book—represents the most common steps in the acquisition process. Many of the basic concepts in acquiring *any* property are outlined in this section.

ACQUIRING RIGHTS (TO A BOOK)

Books are often the source material for audio-visual productions, including programs for network and cable television, home video, and business video. The most lucrative market for published works is in the motion picture business, where audio-visual rights in properties are regularly licensed or purchased for subsequent use in theatrical features, most of which end up on television as well. The occasional blockbuster novel finds its way to an initial television production, most often via a mini-series; otherwise, programmers usually wind up with those properties not already tied up in film deals.

The most aggressive film and television producers compete for titles before the books are published. Studios and major Hollywood production companies maintain sources in the publishing community (authors, editors, and agents), so advance looks at promising manuscripts are common. *Kirkus Reviews, Publisher's Weekly,* and reviews in newspapers and magazines are also sources of information about new titles. Most major production companies hire readers who summarize new books and analyze their potential in the feature and television marketplace.

Once a desirable property has been identified, the production company (typically, through an assistant in the development department) contacts the publisher's subsidiary rights department to find out who holds the television rights to the property. In some cases, the publisher has been empowered to negotiate on the author's behalf; often, however, these rights are retained by the author, in which case a literary agent or personal attorney generally negotiates for the author.

Although a rights agreement between publisher or author and production company may be lengthy, two key issues guide the negotiation: money, and creative control of the property.

The Money

It is in the producer's interest to limit out-of-pocket expenses during the early stages of development, when matters are most speculative and there is often no guarantee of reimbursement. Rather than buying the property outright, producers usually negotiate the terms of the purchase (including the eventual purchase, or "exercise," price), then pay a fraction—typically 10 percent—of the exercise price for the exclusive option to purchase the property within a set period, such as one year from signing the agreement. This option money is sometimes credited against the exercise price. In many cases, up to two additional option periods, each six months long, may be initiated by the producer, for an additional 5 percent of the purchase price per option period. (These additional monies can be applied against the exercise price.) Sometimes the extensions are tied to the commitment of a writer, director, or star to the property, or are linked to some other type of progress in development.

Fiction Works

Successful fiction works command the highest price. Rights to a book as the basis for a network movie-of-the-week cost $20,000–$40,000, with major best-sellers topping $50,000. Pay television may pay even more, but rights fees for movies made for cable networks are likely to run $15,000–$25,000. Producers who buy rights for made-for-home-video productions pay roughly $10,000, sometimes less. In general, rates for made-for-TV and made-for-home-video productions are considerably lower than those paid for turning a book into a major motion picture, where hundreds of thousands of dollars—or even millions—is the norm. Mini-series are the one exception: since each segment is considered the equivalent of a movie-of-the-week, the rights fees are high.

Series deals are structured differently. For a network pilot, the rights payment for a book is likely to cost a producer $20,000–$35,000, plus a $1,000–$4,000 royalty payment per episode for half-hours, or $2,000–$8,000 for hours. These royalty payments entitle the producer to two showings ("plays") on a commercial network; each subsequent play costs the producer 20 percent of the original fee, up to a maximum of 100 percent after five reruns. Once 100 percent has been reached (for a total of 200 percent, including the original payment), the author does not normally receive further royalties for a given program. Pay cable rates are comparable to network ones; basic cable rates are typically 50 percent lower; syndication rates are comparable to basic cable rates, sometimes 10 to 20 percent lower.

Non-Fiction Works

Some non-fiction works, notably true-crime and relationship stories, are sold in the same way as fiction works. The rights to a non-fiction book may be meaningful or valuable because of a title's special franchise, or because of its authority in a particular field. If a title is particularly popular, the rights to a non-fiction book might be as expensive as those to a fictional work.

More often, however, non-fiction books will be purchased as the basis for a non-fiction series on the same subject. The author may be an expert, or the organization or depth of the information presented in the book may be unique or special. In these situations, the prices paid are usually much less than for fiction works: for a series, the up-front fee may run $500 to $5,000, sometimes as high as $10,000 if there is competition for the rights. The author might also receive a small per-episode royalty as a result of a strenuous negotiating, or as a "giveback" from a producer who is buying the rights for a relatively low price. This royalty may be as low as 1 or 2 percent of the producer's per-episode budget, though 5 percent is more common. The non-fiction author may also be paid a fee for ongoing consultation as the project progresses.

Life Stories

The life stories of real individuals are sometimes the basis for entertainment programming. It is not always necessary to secure the permission of an individual in order to base a program on his or her life (see page 154). Nonetheless, life-story rights are frequently acquired (and paid for) in order to forestall any legal problems and to obtain the person's cooperation in the process. The option/exercise fee approach is often used here as well. If the producer is acquiring rights from more than one individual for a single program, the total fees typically do not exceed the amounts that would be paid for a work of fiction. In addition, the inevitable surrender of control by the individual over the details of his or her life story can be a painful step.

Commissions and Other Deductions

The author rarely manages to keep all of the proceeds of the rights sale. In fact, the check usually goes first to the author's agent, who deducts a 10 or 15 percent commission and then writes the author a second check. A lawyer's compensation is based on either a flat fee, an hourly fee, or a monthly retainer. Since the lawyer receives the money shortly after the time of service, and gets paid even if the deal does not go through, the lawyer does not benefit directly from a windfall success, as an agent might. Some lawyers do receive a percentage of their clients' income in addition to, or in lieu of, standard fees (this practice is mostly limited to the Los Angeles community). Publishers usually insist on some involvement in television and movie deals: a 50/50 split with the author is typical. (In this case, the agent's commission and/or lawyer's fees are either deducted from the author's 50 percent or taken off the top.) If the author has some clout, or if the publisher lacks confidence in a property's television potential, then a different split—say, 75 (author)/25 (publisher)—is arranged.

Creative Control

Although many authors try to push the issue, producers tend to not even discuss sharing creative control with an author. There are several reasons for this. First, the producer himself surrenders this control to the financing source in exchange for the money to produce the series, so he cannot share what he does not have. Second, the author is stereotypically regarded as "difficult"; his or her frequent insistence on protecting a personal vision of the property can place the producer in conflict with the network or distributor. Third, many authors may develop an adversarial relationship with television and the medium's need for fast-moving entertainment. But the bottom line is that just as authors are protective of their creative efforts and insist upon control over the printed book, producers require control—and flexibility—over *their* audio-visual work.

Certainly there are exceptions: a top author may insist on writing the screenplay for the television adaptation, or at least the first draft; an author with special expertise may be retained as a technical consultant by the producer.

Playwrights are a different breed; they make their living writing stories for presentation by actors and directors. Their craft is similar to that of the television writer; in fact, many television writers started their careers in the theater. A playwright typically controls the media rights to his or her properties, with no need to involve the play's publisher or producer(s), other than financially. Most successful playwrights are represented by agents or lawyers.

TREATMENTS, SCRIPTS, AND DEALS

As development progresses, the idea—whether derived from an existing work or freshly invented—is written for audio-visual production. A treatment is a short (two to ten pages) outline for a script that traces the basic plot scene-by-scene; provides insight into the personalities and interactions of the characters; and offers enough information about the production's "look" so that a rough budget, including the costs of sets, locations, costumes, and special effects, can be made. The treatment (often called a "story") may also include some sample dialogue. The script itself is a more complete form, providing a scene-by-scene breakdown, stage instructions, and all of the dialogue. Treatments and scripts are the currency of writers working in "Hollywood," and are widely used throughout the television industry. This section will begin by explaining how treatments and scripts are commissioned and sold in connection with network, pay TV, and cable TV. A later section describes the traditions that have emerged in other parts of the business.

Step Deals and Turnaround

The treatment is a selling tool that the producer shows to potential sources of financing. Therefore, when a producer hires a writer to help with development, it may be to the producer's advantage to commit only to the writing of the story. If the property is a strong one—and the producer and writer have solid credentials—the financing source (a network, a studio, or a production company) will agree to go forward, usually through a *step deal*. (All of the "steps" described below are negotiated in advance.)

The step deal usually begins with commissioning a more detailed treatment that includes sample dialogue and character descriptions. If the concept is a series, then the treatment may include a long description of one sample episode (presumably the pilot), along with character sketches and brief outlines of a full season's programs. This stage may involve more than preparing a treatment—it may also require the producer to arrange commitments from key performers or from a director.

If the detailed treatment shows promise, the financier pays for the second step. For most network, pay, and cable programs, the writer or writing team is paid to produce a full script or teleplay, from first to final drafts. (The current Writers Guild of America [WGA] rate for a story for a 60-minute program is $7,839, and for a 60-minute teleplay, first draft, $12,926. When a producer commits to both at the same time, the rate is $19,647.) The producer usually owns the script as a work for hire, subject to the rights of the financing source and any retained rights of the author. Under the WGA agreement, when the program is produced, the writer can receive further residuals for reuse as well as royalties. If the writer originated the work and is entitled to a "separation of rights," then he or she will also have rights (see page 240) for additional programs in the series. If extra rewriting is required, the producer may choose any writer to do the work.

The financing source may decide not to proceed with the next step, and may cancel development at any point—for example, after one of the script drafts has been submitted. In this case, the project can be frozen with the financier, it can revert to the producer with no strings attached, or (most commonly) it can go into *turnaround*. In turnaround, the financier pulls out of the deal, so the producer once again owns the rights to the script and is free to seek an alternative source of financing. If the producer is successful in placing the project with another company, then he or she repays some of the development costs to the original financing party, which also receives some "back-end" participation (see page 212) in the form of 5 to 10 percent of the producer's net revenues.

The Importance of Writers

Writers—and their ideas—drive the network television business. Top writers are given producer's credits, sometimes as perks, more often as entitlements to control and shape the content of a series. A writer who creates a series receives a special credit and a per-episode royalty, and frequently writes several episodes each season. In addition, he or she may serve in a staff capacity—often as a story editor, supervising other writers and doing rewrites—and receive additional fees.

Development Deals

A studio or large production company may offer an independent producer or successful writer a *development deal*. In such a deal, the talent gets a guaranteed annual sum—hundreds of thousands a year, sometimes up to $1 million or $2 million—while the studio provides offices, a development fund, and other essential services. The dollars spent are deducted from the earnings of the talent from any property created under the arrangement. The studio gets a first look at anything the talent originates, typically on a step-deal basis, complete with turnaround. When a project goes into production, the talent earns fees as writer, director, producer, story editor, or whatever the talent's representative has negotiated and the realities of the guild agreements allow. Royalties and bonuses are also paid, and the talent's production company may be entitled to a significant portion of the project's "back end" (see page 212).

Packaging

The writer/producer team or hybrid may drive the development effort, but a project will not be approved for production until performers and other key participants are added. Many of the writers and producers who develop projects seek additional power to complete the "package"—and this power is supplied by agencies like the William Morris Agency, ICM, and CAA. Their client lists include many of the top performers, writers, directors, producers, music professionals, and designers in the entertainment business. These agencies cannot produce programming—to do so would be a conflict of interest, since they would be competing against their clients—so they work with producers and supply a full roster of performers and behind-the-scenes personnel in exchange for a hefty share of the producer's gross. This "cut" is often 5 percent of the production budget plus 5 percent from available revenues after recoupment (see page 210 for a discussion of recoupment).

Alternately, these agencies supply the same people to the production "à la carte" at a far lower commission—10 or 15 percent of the individual agency client's gross salary or fee. Some producers find agency packaging departments to be extremely helpful in selling programs to network buyers; other producers resent the agencies and their growing clout, regarding the packaging agency as an unwelcome co-producer.

PILOTS

Making a pilot is the most expensive and elaborate phase of development; it is also the last action before either full production is ordered or the project is dropped altogether. A pilot is a special program made as a kind of model or prototype, to demonstrate what the completed show (almost always a series) will look like. Sometimes the pilot is a truncated version of the show, in which case it may be called a "demo"; often it runs full-length, using full sets, locations, cast, and other production resources. The cost of the pilot is inevitably higher than the cost of a regular episode, because the economies of scale do not apply. Even though it is a one-off project, all of the business and legal arrangements for the full production must be finalized, sets built, and a production team assembled.

Pilots are necessary because it is nearly impossible to assess the impact that a program will have without actually making it. Scripts can be read, concepts discussed and embellished, designs reviewed, and casts auditioned—but so much depends upon the chemistry and how the elements work together that producing a sample show is the only way to gauge the program's chances. Therefore, before a broadcast network or other end user commits to ordering multiple episodes of a series, it almost always wants to see (and may be willing to pay for) a pilot. Sometimes, particularly in the depths of re-run season, a network will air some of its pilots, both as a means of measuring audience reaction and as a way of to "burn off" the pilot and recoup some financial value from it. Occasionally, a movie-of-the-week or other special is made that works as a "back-door pilot" but that also stands on its own.

The pilot is a valuable sales tool for the syndication and foreign markets, where lining up stations and markets before production begins in earnest is critical. Here, too, a completed pilot or demo gives the buyers a direct vision of what they are getting. Few game shows, talk shows, or other staples of the syndication market are launched these days without a pilot or demo being produced.

22 | Program Development: Other Entertainment Programs

The prime-time fiction community is extremely well-organized, with clear delineations between writers, producers, directors, and performers. Other types of programming may be the result of a single person's creative or journalistic vision, or the result of a team of specialists with overlapping talents. Many non-fiction programs, however, are created and developed in-house at the network—by a combination of existing staff, new hires, and part-time consultants. Non-fiction entertainment programming includes variety/comedy/music shows, game shows, and specials. Similar patterns apply to the fictional formats of daytime drama (soap operas) and children's programs.

VARIETY, COMEDY, AND MUSIC PROGRAMS

The development of a variety program is often an outgrowth of discussions between a network or syndicator and a celebrity performer (like a comedian or musician) or a producer who has a special vision or experience in a specific genre. If the program or series is to be based on the talents of a performer, he or she will generally work with a producer with a track record on similar programs.

Typically, the producer conceives the program format and assembles a creative team of writers, director, and other personnel to develop the program. The format is usually presented to the network programming executive(s) responsible for the project in a pitch meeting (see page 168) that is also attended by the producer's key creative contributors. At the meeting, the ideas are discussed in detail; the program executive raises issues and objections; and the producer responds to the best of his ability. If the program suits the network's or syndicator's needs, an exclusive option to the property is negotiated, and the producer is paid to develop the program further. This development money usually pays for one or more sample scripts.

The next step is the production of a pilot program, or a limited series (for example, a four-week run). If the program is successful, the network orders more episodes. And if, at any step during this process, the network decides to drop the project, the rights eventually revert back to the producer and/or performer (see page 173), who may sell it to another network or syndicator, sometimes after a prescribed period of time (or "holdback") has elapsed.

Some variety programs do not require extensive development. Awards programs, for example, are frequently expansions of trade or industry banquets. A producer, or a representative from an industry association (such as the Songwriter's Hall of Fame), pitches the network or syndicator. The basic concept may be altered or embellished—adding entertainment segments, off-premises interviews with big-name winners—but the process is straightforward. A producer is assigned to the project, and develops a format, a budget, and a list of celebrities who are likely to appear. If the network or syndicator believes the idea will be successful, the program is funded and produced. The network or syndicator typically retains the right to produce the program annually if it does succeed.

Programs featuring stand-up comedians are also developed in a straightforward fashion, and can be quite successful with the right comedians. A producer usually works closely with a comedy club or promoter to develop a roster, which is approved by the network or syndicator. A budget is created and approved, the comedians and the staff are hired, and the program is produced and edited.

Music programs generally require little creative development, though some with elaborate concepts call for as much development as a small motion picture. For music programs, once the act is selected, most of the development and pre-production time goes to choosing locations, lining up equipment, and arranging travel schedules. Specialized types of musical programs, like *Night Music* (in which several acts were carefully selected to complement one another), require more creative development—but much of the development time is devoted to arranging for appearances by performers.

GAME SHOWS

The development of game shows starts with a basic idea—like a game based on Hangman. Informal playtesting using game pieces roughed out on index cards and other inexpensive materials is the second step. The game is played over and over again, first with the office staff and then in more formal run-throughs. The latter are generally staged in a conference room with "civilian" contestants who are paid a nominal fee. This development process lasts at least a month, and sometimes as long as six months, until the game plays properly.

The producer pitches the game-show concept to networks or syndicators shortly after the informal run-throughs with the office staff. If the network or syndicator feels that the program is worthy of further development, the producer receives up to $10,000 (frequently closer to $2,000) to pay writers, a free-lance staff, and run-through contestants. After four to six weeks, the program executive is invited to a run-through. Changes are discussed, and another run-through, incorporating the suggestions, is typically scheduled for the following week. This process is usually repeated several times, and if the program continues to show merit, the program executive invites others from the network or syndication company to watch a run-through. Eventually, either a pilot is ordered or the project is dropped and moves to turnaround (see page 172).

A game-show pilot generally costs $150,000 to $300,000, and requires approximately two months for production. When the pilot is complete, it is tested (by a network), or used as a sales tool (by a syndicator). If the project tests well and fits into a network schedule slot—or if it clears a sufficient number of profitable time slots in large markets for syndication—a season's worth of shows is ordered.

Most game shows are developed by a small number of production companies that specialize in the genre, such as Mark Goodson Productions and Merv Griffin Enterprises. These production companies typically employ one or more development executives responsible for the creation of new properties; a combination of a bonus and an ongoing royalty is paid to those executives responsible for successful shows.

Original game ideas from outsiders may be licensed with the promise of an ongoing royalty, plus a small upfront payment, if necessary, to close the deal. If the outsider is essential to the concept or to the show's success, then he or she may be retained as a consultant or hired as a member of the program's staff.

An increasing number of game shows are based on successes from other media, or on vintage game shows that were successful in the past. *Scrabble* (NBC, syndication) and *Monopoly* (syndication) come from board games; *Where in the World is Carmen Sandiego?* (PBS) is based on a computer game. *The Price is Right* (CBS), *Classic Concentration* (NBC), *Family Feud* (syndication), *Jeopardy!* (syndication), and many of the programs seen on cable's USA Network are derived from earlier versions. (USA programs at least 10 half-hours of game shows daily, making it the largest U.S. market for game shows.) Some cable networks have developed successful franchises with games that fit neatly into their specialized niches: *Remote Control* (MTV), *Supermarket Sweep* and *Rodeo Drive* (Lifetime), and *Double Dare* and *Make the Grade* (Nickelodeon).

Many of the game shows seen on cable networks are developed and produced in-house. A staff producer takes charge of creating the show and presents the format to network executives, refining, budgeting, staffing, and ultimately delivering finished product. If the program is especially successful, those associated with the production may receive raises, bonuses, or new opportunities within their companies. Ownership of the show and its concept is retained by the network.

DAYTIME DRAMA (SOAP OPERAS)

In terms of development and production, daytime drama is an even more specialized form than the game show, and has a limited market.

Daytime drama—usually called "soap operas"—is a staple of the network daytime schedule. Research studies show that the audience for soap operas watches television much differently than do viewers of other programs. In short, daytime viewing patterns resemble a kind of addiction. Programmers and producers feed this addictive pattern by offering viewers a dose of romance and suspense, but they consciously structure scripts and storylines to leave the viewer wanting more. During the summer, programmers attempt to "hook" younger viewers on summer vacation. A successful soap commands phenomenal loyalty; even when the scripts or characters are uninspired, audience research shows that viewers will continue to watch, trusting that the situation will improve in time.

Daytime drama is seen almost exclusively on commercial network television, most often in the hour-long format. Each of the networks programs several soaps, generally with a particular audience in mind. On ABC, for example, *All My Children* has traditionally been issue-oriented; storylines have dealt with AIDS, teenage pregnancy, and other topical subjects. On the same network, *General Hospital*, because of its after-school time slot, is produced with storylines and characters that target high school and college students. ABC's *One Life to Live* began with a Western motif, but more general themes have broadened the program's appeal; similarly, ABC's *Loving* started by depicting life on a college campus, but this focus was later diffused. Several programs on these networks have been popular since radio days, with viewing habits passed from generation to generation; examples include *Guiding Light* and *As the World Turns* on CBS, and *Days of Our Lives* on NBC.

Although ABC, CBS, and NBC are constantly developing new daytime dramas, few new ones actually reach the air. The creative community is rather small; in fact, three people developed many of the soaps currently on the air. Agnes Nixon created *One Life to Live, All My Children,* and *Loving,* three of the four soaps currently on ABC. William J. Bell was responsible for *Another World* for NBC, as well as *The Young and the Restless* and its spin-off, *The Bold and the Beautiful,* for CBS. Both Nixon and Bell learned their craft from Irna Phillips, the leading creator and writer of radio soaps; the Phillips legacy includes *As the World Turns,* and substantial creative input into *Guiding Light*.

General network wisdom dictates that new soaps are best developed by experienced head writers of successful daytime series. Claire Labine and Paul Mayer jointly created *Ryan's Hope,* a program with a strong Irish orientation, for ABC. The network had confidence in the writers, and felt that their concept was unique and long-ranging; the series ran for more than a decade. Few writers and producers are as fortunate. Those without specific experience in the day-to-day head-writing of a successful soap face enormous odds, even with a spectacular idea. Still, given the right cast and the right idea, all of the networks will pay attention to a credible writer or producer.

A writer or producer typically pitches the idea for a daytime drama to the vice president or director of daytime development. Decisions are not made quickly. Several months will pass as network executives determine not only whether the idea has merit, but where and when the program could conceivably debut (years may pass before a time slot becomes available). Eventually, the writer may be offered $50,000–$75,000 to write a "bible"—the 150-page document with a description of each character—and a year's supply of storylines. Once the bible is accepted (it is likely to be revised several times along the way), the network will commission a sample week of stories. Then the wait for the time slot begins; the wait could take three to five years.

Pilots for daytime dramas are uncommon. If the network decides to go ahead, the series begins production, typically with six months of lead time prior to air. This period may be extended if the series is launched with a made-for-TV prime time movie, as is now frequent practice.

In keeping with the specialized nature of soap production, special AFTRA, WGA, and DGA rates and work rules apply (see Chapters 27 and 28).

Current weekly budgets for soaps are in the in the range of $400,000–$500,000 for a half-hour show, and $650,000–$700,000 per week for an hour-long one. Approximately half of each budget applies to "above-the-line" expenses, such as a large production staff, multiple writers, and the large cast. The biggest below-the-line items are set construction and decoration (a large number of sets are used), and studio time (long studio days are common). Although these figures are two to three times as high as the costs for game shows, soap operas are disproportionate contributors to each network's profitability. An hour-long soap typically earns up to $1 million per day, more than covering the costs of a full week's production.

Many cable networks have flirted with soaps, but none of them have successfully launched a full-fledged daytime drama series. This is largely due to the way in which people watch cable TV. The network daytime schedule benefits from a phenomenon known as "appointment viewing"—the viewer makes an appointment with himself to watch a specific program at a specific time of day. Cable does not work that way, so it is far more difficult to build up a following for a particular program. The production of 265 episodes per year is standard for broadcast networks, but is beyond the capacity of most cable networks.

Still, cable soaps should be possible once the cable networks develop daytime dramas that take advantage of the medium's unique viewership pattern.

CHILDREN'S PROGRAMS

Ideas for children's programs come from a variety of sources, but much of the development and production is done by production companies and networks that specialize in the form. Children's programming appears in several different configurations.

Saturday Morning Network Cartoons

The commercial networks schedule children's programs almost exclusively on Saturday mornings, with the exception of the occasional prime time special. Nearly all of this time is dominated by animated cartoon series, supplied by companies that specialize in animation: Hanna-Barbera, Ruby-Spears, Murikami Wolf Swenson, and Nelvana. Programming frequently starts with a network expressing interest in a particular license—a comic strip character (Garfield), a line of toys (Mario Brothers), a movie/TV/music spin-off (*Ghostbusters*, New Kids on the Block, *The Wizard of Oz*, Muppet Babies). Characters that are not supported in other media do appear, but these are now the exceptions.

The development of an animated series begins with the characters. Personalities are created, sample scripts are written, and—most important—characters are rendered, first on paper, then in sample animations. Characters are changed, eliminated, and combined, just as they are during the development of a motion picture script. Eventually, the network and the production company agree on a specific group of characters (usually subject to the approval of the licensor, if existing properties are used) and a particular style of production. A pilot is made, showing one or more sample cartoons and some transitional material, and the pilot is tested among sample viewers. Feedback from the research, the quality of the production, and the network's need for a particular program in a particular time slot will all determine whether the network will give the producer a series commitment.

Because animation is a highly-specialized form, networks tend to depend upon companies that have considerable experience in the field. Most animation is produced abroad; the Far East and Ireland are leading manufacturing centers.

Syndicated Cartoon Series

Nearly all successful syndicated series begin with licensing a known (and thus less risky) property. The development process for a syndicated cartoon series parallels the network process until the production of the pilot. For syndication, the pilot is created mainly as a sales tool to show stations; audience research may or may not be a part of the process. Since animation is costly, the pilot is likely to be brief, more like a demonstration or highlights tape than a completed program.

Timing

An animated series requires a long lead time: production of a pilot usually starts a year or more prior to the first airdate. Take, for example, a series that would start in September 1992. That would mean a delivery date to a network or syndicator of August 1992. Production should begin in January 1992, or even in the fall of 1991. Backing up from that date, a pilot must be completed by August 1991. The production company would require a "firm go" in January 1992—at the latest, within a few weeks of the National Association of Television Program Executives (NATPE) Convention, where syndicated properties are marketed to stations each January.

Other Children's Formats

Variety shows for children are largely dependent upon hosts (Dr. Fad, Pee-Wee Herman) and, frequently, upon gimmickry or puppetry (the anamorphic furniture and set pieces on *Pee-Wee's Playhouse*). These shows require a considerable allotment of time and resources for initial creative development, and for a pilot that shows the details of the creative approach. While each program's format is different, the key elements are the host and cast, the inclusion of special creative elements, and the substantial resources required to launch and sustain such a program.

Children's variety programs are typically scheduled once per week, usually on Saturday mornings. This is partly because of the availability of the proper audience at the time, partly to keep the creative elements fresh, and partly for budgetary reasons.

Pre-school programs usually involve a cast of specialty characters—*Sesame Street's* Muppets and human characters, *Zoobilee Zoo's* human animals, *Mister Rogers Neighborhood's* puppets, *Shining Time Station's* trains with expressive faces. These programs also feature brief segments that are usually developed and written in batches. All of the "Street" segments on *Sesame Street,* for example, are developed and produced from August until February; shows are then assembled by combining studio segments with non-studio material. Animated and/or puppet segments are also developed as a unit. The units may be knit together in the form of a storyline, or may be presented as a series of unrelated or semi-related features.

The development of a pre-school series frequently requires several "scratch tapes" and demos, followed by multiple pilot programs. Audience research is often part of the process as well. Most pre-school series are presented daily, with an annual batch of episodes repeated two or three times (individual segments may also be reused in later seasons). There are three markets for pre-school product: PBS and individual public television stations, Nickelodeon, and The Disney Channel.

SPECIALS

Specials tend to fall into two categories—entertainment and news—though the distinction between the two is sometimes blurry. Entertainment specials are based on the talents of a particular celebrity performer, a character license (*Peanuts*), or a special event (the Emmy Awards, the Miss America Pageant).

Celebrity Specials

By and large, celebrity specials are straightforward to develop. The project may begin with either the celebrity (and his or her management team), a network, or a production company. All three parties meet and agree upon a basic format that will showcase the celebrity's particular appeal. The production company works with the celebrity to develop the format in more detail, submits a budget, receives input from the network, redevelops the concept, reworks the budget, and makes a deal. There is no fixed format for a celebrity special—it can be a concert, a live performance, a magazine show, a variety show, or any other format that suits the performer's unique style.

In some cases, the special may be intended simply to target a specific audience segment. In other cases, the special is used to test the celebrity's appeal—in effect, as a form of market research—and may in fact be a pilot for a series.

Virtually all broadcast and cable networks program celebrity specials. Obviously, the appeal of the celebrity to the network's target audience is the most important part of the sale, but the track record of the creative team, and the creative concept for the special, are also important elements.

Special Events (Awards Shows, Pageants, Parades)

Most successful awards shows are television staples with histories that stretch back for decades: the Emmy Awards, the Academy Awards, the Tony Awards, the People's Choice Awards, the Golden Globe Awards, and the Grammy Awards. Launching a new awards program requires three essential elements: 1) a promise of major-celebrity presenters and award recipients; 2) a high level of national interest in the subject of the awards ceremony; and 3) a major national institution that does not stand to benefit directly from the airtime. (An awards ceremony presented by a magazine may be problematic, for example; most awards shows are presented by academies or associations.) Given this combination, a new awards show has a fighting chance, but without any one of these elements, the project may be doomed from the start. Few ideas are really new, and many awards ceremonies have been tried at least once—if it's not currently on the air, there's probably a reason why. Budgets are comparatively high for awards specials, and most programmers perceive a glut in this category. In sum, awards shows are a tough sell.

New pageants are also a tough sell. There are presently two pageant organizations with network exposure for their pageants: Miss America and Miss USA/Miss Universe. Each show is the pinnacle of a year-long search that begins at the local and state levels, and each one is as much a promotional machine for affiliated products and services as it is a television program.

The difficulty with launching a new pageant is, quite simply, convincing a programmer, a network, or an advertiser of the need for yet another pageant. The present group of network pageants is perceived as satisfactory; efforts at syndicated pageants (Miss Teen USA) have been hit-and-miss, mainly because of the inability to get clearances on top stations in good time slots.

Miss America is independently-owned and -operated; Miss USA and Miss Universe are owned and operated by a subsidiary of Paramount Communications.

Parades are a similar story. Those that have been established for decades remain on the air—The Rose Parade, Macy's Thanksgiving Day Parade—but most programmers consider new ventures to be risky. Parades seem to play best on holidays, since they run several hours long and require substantial breaks with the regular program schedule. Local parades and related events are sometimes covered by local television stations; in Philadelphia, for example, the popular Mummer's Parade is covered for many hours by a local network affiliate. This type of extensive local coverage becomes less common every year, as stations cut back on operations.

Truly special events, such as the anniversary of the Statue of Liberty's arrival, are judged on their ability to win viewers and secure sponsorship. Since they are enormously expensive to produce, big events must deliver extremely high ratings in order to be cost-effective. While every such event is risky, programmers try to limit their risk by working only with producers experienced in the form—and by having large celebrity rosters.

Specials Based on Character Licenses

Through the years, specific characters have gained enough popularity in other media to warrant television appearances. In some cases, these characters have become the basis for Saturday morning series (*Garfield*). *Peanuts* attracts an audience that is older and broader than the Saturday-morning crowd—and the license's long-term value has probably been enhanced by only occasional television appearances.

Most cartoon characters are simply not well-known enough to justify the risk involved in producing an animated special. Popularity among newspaper readers is not enough; a comic strip must achieve a kind of national notoriety before it becomes a viable television property. Some popular newspaper strips (*The Far Side* and *Ziggy*, for example) do not adapt especially well to television, because of appeal, content, or design.

23 Program Development: Information Programs

Most information programs seen on a network—news and magazine shows, talk shows, and documentaries—are produced in-house by the network's news division. The ideas for these programs may come from a news executive with responsibility for the overall success of the division; from a program-development executive working within the news department; or, often, from producers, executive producers, and reporters who handle news and information on a daily basis. The idea is generally an outgrowth of existing work, or a reaction to it: a desire to present information in a different way, or to present a different kind of information. An example of the first is *Nightline*, which provides long-form coverage and emphasizes conflict; an example of the second is *Jane Pauley's Real Life*, which looks at larger trends by focusing on smaller stories about real people.

The concept behind a particular information program begins as a theoretical discussion among working newspeople, who sketch out their ideas. After a few creative sessions, the ideas are written down and presented to a program executive who controls budgets and who can gain access to valuable airtime. The program executive garners internal support for the project, both within the news division and throughout the company. A production unit is assembled—frequently with the program's originators in key roles—and one or more shows are produced.

The process is similar at the local station level, though staff, technical, and financial resources are likely to be more limited.

NEWS AND MAGAZINE SHOWS IN SYNDICATION

News and magazine programs distributed to cable and local stations via syndication are frequently the work of a large production entity—Paramount, in the case of *Entertainment Tonight*, and Fox, for *A Current Affair*. One or more producers and writers are hired to develop an idea that was created internally or licensed from a creator, who generally receives a weekly royalty payment if the show goes into production ($500–$3,000 for a syndicated strip). The royalties are paid even if the creator is not directly involved in ongoing production. If the program is a special, the producer receives a flat fee, possibly a royalty, and a percentage of future revenues. The program is typically developed up to the point of a short-form pilot (about 15 minutes is common). The pilot is then shown to local stations and cable networks as a selling tool, and presented to advertising agencies and advertisers for the sale of barter time (see Chapter 3). If a sufficient number of clearances and a sufficient percentage of viewing households can be reached, the program begins production.

Because news and magazine shows can require large staffs and a web of correspondents throughout the country or the world, production units for these types of programs are usually set up under the aegis of a big company.

DOCUMENTARIES

The development and production of documentaries has always been challenging because the form only infrequently attracts large numbers of viewers. In the 1950s and 1960s, the networks and many local stations programmed documentaries in prime time, but an increasingly competitive marketplace eventually eliminated this practice.

Public television remains the strongest, most vibrant marketplace for documentary programs, yet even this is changing as public television reinvents itself. PBS has seen some of its greatest success with distinguished documentary programs and series, notably *The Civil War, NOVA,* and *Nature.*

Two cable networks regularly program documentaries: The Discovery Channel, whose schedule mostly consists of documentary programs of all sorts, and A&E, whose orientation is evolving from historical material to programs with wider appeal.

Program development for documentary production more or less follows these steps. First, the producer develops the creative concept based on his own personal interest, or on a programmer's interest in one or more shows about a particular subject (the environment, for example). Other idea sources include a popular book whose rights are available, or the work of an individual or institution that has attracted public notice. The producer then works out a budget; writes a proposal describing the project; and pitches it to programmers and other sources of financing (foundations, sponsors, endowment organizations, foreign broadcasters, and so on). Although some documentaries are funded quickly, these are the exceptions; one to three years is usually needed to gather production funds. Production is typically small-scale—single-camera with plenty of editing—and the staff is minimal. The schedule, though, can run almost a year.

Since documentaries are not widely regarded as big money-makers, a producer can usually raise the necessary funds without selling off either ownership interests or creative control.

TALK SHOWS

The success of a talk show is largely dependent upon the personality of the host, and upon the time of day that the program airs. For example, when David Letterman hosted a daytime talk show on NBC, it was a dismal failure. For many years, most local television markets supported one or more local talk shows: current syndication successes like *The Oprah Winfrey Show, Sally Jessy Raphael, Donahue,* and *Live! with Regis and Kathy Lee* all started on local stations. The principal difference between the syndicated versions of these programs and their earlier local versions is budget: the additional money pays for a better set and studio location, and for travel and accommodations for "better" guests. As fewer local stations run local talk shows, it seems unlikely that many more national talk programs will emerge from local television.

An alternate approach for syndicators involves identifying a celebrity as a potential talk-show host, producing a pilot, and putting considerable promotional muscle behind the show. *Geraldo* and *The Joan Rivers Show* are examples of syndicated programs hosted by celebrities, though this method of developing a talk show has generated mixed results.

The broadcast and cable networks have some involvement in talk shows, but new projects are relatively uncommon. The broadcast networks tend to program talk shows in late-night, either against *The Tonight Show* (*The Pat Sajak Show* was a recent example), or after midnight (*Later with Bob Costas*). Occasionally, a network will take a break from game shows and soaps during the day, but few daytime talk shows have appeared on commercial network television in recent years.

Some cable talk shows mimic commercial network formats, but add an unusual twist. TNN's *Nashville Now* is a country-music version of *The Tonight Show;* Lifetime's *Attitudes* offers a talk/service format for female viewers; CBN The Family Channel's *The 700 Club* is a religious talk show; *Larry King LIVE* features long interviews with guests who are well-known, associated with well-known causes, or controversial. Cable networks tend to be more open to potential talk show concepts than the broadcast networks, but high-visibility programs tailored to their specific audiences seem to be the only ones with a chance of success.

News Programming

For many viewers, television news programs are the primary source of information about world, national, and regional events, as well as weather and sports. News programming has itself become a popular program form, one that sustains more than one around-the-clock cable service, as well as numerous network and local programs.

NETWORK NEWS

ABC, CBS, and NBC each operate a news division; Fox is currently making plans for its own version of network news programming. Each news division is responsible for several hours of regularly-scheduled programs each day: some prime time programming, regularly-scheduled news breaks between shows, some weekend news and news analysis, and coverage of special events and breaking news stories. Each of the networks employs approximately a thousand employees in its news division. Network news is the largest programming activity that is based in New York, with considerable production in Washington, D.C., as well.

Programming

Each network news division produces a variety of program types, including regularly-scheduled broadcasts, news magazines, and news/talk shows. The news division is responsible for an early-morning news program (6:00-7:00 A.M.), several cut-ins through the day and night, a newscast during the dinner hour, and other prime time and Sunday-morning programs. NBC and CBS News also produce morning shows, *The Today Show* and *CBS This Morning*, respectively; ABC's *Good Morning America* is produced by the company's entertainment division. ABC News produces *Nightline*, the only regularly-scheduled late-night news/talk program. CBS News produces *Nightwatch*, which runs from 2:15 A.M. to 6:00 A.M.

The half-hour evening newscast is the signature program for each news division. Network news is fed live to affiliates at 6:00 P.M. Eastern Standard Time, though many stations air the program at 6:30 P.M. It is fed a second time for West Coast affiliates, either as a videotape of the original production, or, if stories have changed, as a new production.

In prime time, ABC's fixture is *20/20*, a weekly news magazine that attracts good ratings and costs less than other types of prime time programming. In addition, ABC News produces *Prime Time Live.* CBS's news magazine is *60 Minutes,* but the network also produces *48 Hours.* NBC has been unsuccessful in developing a viable prime time news magazine.

Each news division also produces weekly shows on Sunday mornings. CBS has *Sunday Morning* (a variation on the traditional newsmagazine format) and *Face the Nation;* NBC produces *Sunday Today* and *Meet the Press;* ABC has no morning magazine, but *Issues & Answers* and *This Week* are regular programs.

Special events are an important part of network news coverage. Some, like political conventions, are scheduled and planned well in advance; others, like the outbreak of war, may pre-empt regularly-scheduled programming. News executives have the option to pre-empt programming with breaking stories, but they must operate with considerable discretion. In theory, they consult closely with entertainment program executives (and sports entertainment executives) before pre-empting programs. For shorter reports and updates, pre-empting several minutes of a program is preferable to pre-empting commercials.

Operations

Each news division is headed by a president, the corporate executive responsible for the division's operation. At CBS News, vice presidents are in charge of the component parts of the division: news coverage, news services (see page 194), finance and administration, business affairs, CBS News Washington, and radio. At NBC News, an executive vice president and senior vice presidents run the day-to-day operations, and each SVP is responsible for several departments. At ABC News, one SVP is in charge of day-to-day operations; several vice presidents of news practices, finance, and the Washington bureau report to the SVP. In addition, each show unit at ABC News has an executive producer or program executive, also reporting to the SVP.

Network News Feeds

Each of the networks produces news reports for use on local stations. Correspondents, already on location to deliver stories for the nightly network news, tape second reports for use by local stations. This coverage is funded by affiliated stations, who pay for the cost of correspondents, production personnel, shooting and editing, and satellite time.

News on PBS

PBS itself does not maintain a news department. It does feed a nightly newscast, *The MacNeil-Lehrer News Hour,* which is produced by member stations WNET and WETA. In addition, other member stations produce news and public service programs. WGBH, for example, produces *Frontline;* Maryland Public Television produces *Wall Street Week.* Typically, these programs are funded in the same way that other PBS programs are funded. The productions operate as independent units, tied to the network for purposes of partial funding and distribution—to a certain extent, they are also linked to PBS by way of program practices permitted by public television's charter.

LOCAL BROADCAST NEWS

In most markets, the ABC, CBS, and NBC affiliates produce at least two daily newscasts, plus cut-ins throughout the day. In some markets, one or more independent stations also produces a daily newscast (either an early-evening or late-evening broadcast, but rarely both); and in some markets, a PBS station also produces a daily newscast.

Programming

For most news departments at major-market stations, the program day usually begins at about 4:00 A.M., in preparation for a half- or hour-long newscast at 6:00 A.M. or 6:30 A.M. (all times in this section, and throughout the book, are Eastern Standard Time unless otherwise noted). The audience for these newscasts has been growing over the years, as more viewers are waking up and starting their days earlier; this trend has not escaped the notice of advertisers.

The next task is the preparation of five-minute local cut-ins for the network morning program. These include not only local news, but some weather, sports, and—in some markets—commuter information.

A noon newscast has become increasingly common. At some stations, this newscast includes not only news, weather, and sports, but an interview or some community outreach activities as well. Local news is a profit center for many stations, and the mid-day spot presents a prime opportunity for the stations to increase the presence of their news franchise.

An evening newscast, usually scheduled at about 6:00 P.M., is standard. In most markets, the evening newscast has grown into an hour, 90 minutes, or longer. This newscast is the focus of the station's entire news operation, the one that reaches the largest number of viewers. The most prestigious anchor appears on the 6:00 news, along with the station's best reporters. Many stations also program a 5:00 P.M. newscast, which often features alternate anchors, and includes softer material like interviews and community-outreach coverage.

Some stations do live cut-ins during prime time; some do not.

The final local newscast is at 11:00 P.M., which is standard on all network affiliates and a growing number of independents (though some indies program 30 or 60 minutes of news at 10 P.M.). Stories seen on the 6:00 P.M. newscast are reworked, updated, and usually shortened for the late news. The 11:00 P.M. news has lost viewership in recent years—people seem to be going to sleep, and waking up, earlier, hence the trend toward early-morning newscasts.

The weekend schedule usually drops the noon news, limits the evening news to a half-hour or an hour, and limits the cut-ins throughout the day. This is because with a lower viewership on weekends, advertising revenues cannot support a full-scale production job.

On some local stations, the news department also produces a weekend news program, news magazine, news/talk show, or public affairs program; sometimes, these are produced by the station's program department. Occasional documentaries may be produced by the news or program department.

Operations

The success of a local news operation depends largely upon two factors: the quality/appeal of the "front four" (the two co-anchors, plus the weathercaster and sportscaster, who all appear on the 6:00 P.M. telecast) and the creative and managerial abilities of the news director. Certainly, much credit goes to producers, writers, reporters, and other contributors. Still, the solidly-crafted newscast as hosted by well-liked and well-respected on-camera talent is a crucial formula, albeit one that many experienced station managers overlook in the name of innovation.

The news department is usually the biggest department at a local television station; in a large market, it can include 80 people or more. Even in a smaller market, up to 40 people might be employed full-time.

The news director—occasionally titled the Vice President of News—is responsible for almost all aspects of staff selection and supervision. Major decisions, such as adding a new anchor or major reporter, are made with the approval of the station's general manager. The news director also oversees news coverage, budget preparation and management, community relations, and production.

An executive producer is assigned to each news program. At a large major-market station, one EP might be assigned to the morning news and noon news, another to the 5:00 P.M., another to the 6:00 P.M., and another to the 11:00 P.M.; at most stations, however, one or two EPs supervise all news programming. Early-morning and late-night newscasts may be broadcast without the executive producer actually present in the newsroom.

One step down from the executive producer is the producer, who takes charge of preparing the newscast and who works in the control room during the show. Consulting with the news director, the producer decides which stories will air, and in what order; which stories will be shortened or dropped because of breaking news or interviews that run longer than anticipated; and whether to pass late-breaking information to an on-camera newscaster via newly-written pages or by speaking directing into the newscaster's IFB (a clear plastic earphone).

A staff director, assigned by the station, directs the newscasts.

Most of the news staff is concerned with newsgathering, writing, and preparing stories. The assignment desk—the heart of the newsgathering operation—keeps in close contact with the police and fire departments, the mayor's office, the municipal government, local politicians, and community groups. Some information comes through in a well-organized manner: the mayor's public relations staff arranges a press conference, a movie-company publicist furnishes news about a visiting celebrity, a local community group announces a demonstration at a specific time and place. But most of the information comes from telephone tips, aggressive investigative research, and reports heard over the police radio. In a sense, the assignment desk is also a resource-management system, assigning a limited number of reporters, crews, and vans to cover the most important stories. Everyone keeps in close touch either by cellular phone or by private radio, since changes in assignment or location are common. In addition, the assignment desk determines how the newswriters and videotape editors will spend their time.

In a large market, eight or ten editors work the assignment desk. Resources at most stations include five to twenty reporters, five to ten crews (usually two people per crew, though one-person crews are becoming more common), and five to ten videotape editors.

The assignment desk is, in theory, an objective presenter of news. In practice, however, pressure from the station's management and from local political leaders may encourage the resources to be managed in a particular fashion.

News Coverage

News stories are covered in several different ways. A story coming in from a network or syndicated news feed usually includes a voice-over, sound recorded on location, and all of the necessary visuals. These stories can be aired without further editing, though many stories are edited for time or customized for a local market's approach to news coverage.

Most major stories are covered by a news reporter, working on location with a single-camera crew. The reporter prepares and researches the story while en route to the location; interviews the key players on camera; does some off-camera interviewing for background; determines the visual and audio elements that will be needed to tell the story; records a "stand-up" (the reporter standing in front of the location at the beginning and/or end of the story); and prepares a basic edit plan on the way back to the station. Some additional time may be taken upon arrival to screen the tapes and to refine the edit plan. The tapes and the written notes are passed to an editor. The reporter then writes a script, submits it to the producer for approval, records it, and gives it to the editor as well. On a more complicated story, the reporter may supervise the editor. Most stations employ between five and twenty reporters.

Some stories are not covered by reporters, only by crews. In such cases, a newswriter will draft the script. Sometimes, a reporter records a voice-over, and other times, the anchor narrates the story live.

Stories may also come from news feeds, purchased on a contract basis from syndication services like Group W Newsfeed and Conus. These services are described in detail on page 195.

Stations also subscribe to several news wire services, notably AP and UPI. Other specialized wires include the Dow Jones News Service, Reuters, and Sports Wire.

Anchors and Reporters

Most television stations have long-term contracts with anchors who are well-suited to the station's community image. Although local traditions vary, a certain amount of typecasting is common. The 6:00 P.M. newscast is anchored by a seasoned journalist (typically male, over 45 or 50) and co-anchored by a woman (typically under 45, and often a member of a minority group). The 5:00 P.M. newscast may be hosted by one of these anchors, and often by a third anchor who is newer to the market or lesser-known. That third anchor may do the 11:00 P.M. or the noon newscast. The morning and weekend newscasts are frequently hosted by a reporter gaining anchor experience. In the largest markets, where weekend newscast slots are more meaningful in terms of advertising revenues, regular weekend anchors may be employed.

In a major market, the lead anchor usually earns up to $500,000 per year (more in New York and Los Angeles), with the other anchors earning from $200,000 to $400,000 per year. There are local exceptions that are both higher and lower. Weekend anchors generally earn less than $100,000 per year, and their contracts usually call for three days of general-assignment reporting in addition to the weekend work.

Reporters may be hired and assigned in several ways. Most stations simply hire general-assignment reporters, and then allot a small number to specific beats (e.g., city government). Some will also hire a small number of specialty reporters (e.g., health and science), but these stories may also be covered by general-assignment reporters. A top reporter at a major-market station can earn over $100,000 per year (once again, more in New York and Los Angeles), but most reporters at major-market stations earn between $50,000 and $100,000. Outside of the top 10 markets, the maximum numbers drop below $75,000 or even below $50,000. In a non-union station outside the top 30 or 40 markets, reporter salaries drop below $30,000, even for a reporter with several years of experience.

Weather Reporting

Weather reporting is a self-contained function at just about every television station, supervised by the news director but requiring little ongoing staff or administrative support.

There are essentially two types of television weather reporters: those who are trained meteorologists and those who are not. Some stations insist upon trained scientists, but most are satisfied with a pleasant personality who attracts viewers (or at least, who does not repel them). One of the main reasons why people watch television news is to find out about the weather. While the weather reporter may seem like a minor player among the front four, he or she may be the program's principal draw—many people watch a particular newscast because they like, and trust, the weather reporter.

The weather reporter is generally supported by a fully-equipped weather station. This set-up includes not only the typical measurement instrumentation (barometer, hygrometer, thermometer, and so on), but also computer access to one or more national weather services. Accu-Weather provides not only raw weather data, but full-color video maps that can be used on the air for national, regional, or local forecasts. If the weather reporter is a trained meteorologist, he or she may use this information and construct a custom forecast. Some stations have also invested in sophisticated computer equipment that assists in forecasting, and in computer-graphics equipment adds color and movement to maps and other weather information.

A television station with early-morning, noon, evening, and late-night weather reports typically employs either two or three weather reporters. In a top 10 market, the job pays over $200,000 for an on-air personality who contributes to ratings, and between $150,000 and $200,000 for a team member. In a top 20 market, the scale is $75,000 to $150,000; in smaller markets, the job pays less than $50,000.

Sports Reporting

At a major-market station, one sports reporter will appear on the evening and late-night newscasts; a second sports reporter will appear on weekends, filing field reports several days each week. In the largest markets, a third field reporter and a sports producer may complete the team; in medium-sized and small markets, the entire sports department consists of two reporters.

Sports reporting is largely dependent upon game footage, which is widely available from a number of sources. Networks and their affiliates generally provide feeds to one another at no charge, as an accommodation. Major League Baseball and the NFL provide a daily feed during the season, on a contract basis. Group W Newsfeed (see below) also includes sports footage. Its services are provided—for a fee—on an exclusive basis to one station in each market.

Sports reporters may earn $150,000 per year, or even up to $200,000, if they are especially well-known—or if the contract includes game coverage or a weekend wrap-up show. Even in the top 10 markets, most sports reporters earn under $150,000, and in the top 20, well under $100,000.

News Services and Syndicated Packages

Conus, Group W NewsFeed, CNN Newsbeam, and other news services are available to stations on a market-exclusive basis. A series of complete news stories is prepared each day, and fed to stations in the afternoon, with enough time for the station to sort and edit the material for the evening newscast. Station fees vary depending upon market size, and are negotiable.

Conus is a news cooperative—member stations share their news coverage and their facilities. For example, if there is a plane crash near Boston, member station WCVB will package a Conus story that can be aired on any other member station as if it was their own. And if the mayor of Baltimore is visiting San Francisco, WBAL can use the facilities of KRON rather than sending its own crew. Conus satellite facilities will even take care of the transmission from San Francisco to Baltimore. Conus provides national coverage via a Washington bureau, and feeds stories to member stations six times daily. This news cooperative also does live coverage of events in Washington, D.C. Hubbard Broadcasting—a station group headquartered in Minneapolis/St. Paul and the owner of KSTP, a large station in that market—is the general partner in Conus, and its guiding force. Conus, in a joint venture with Viacom, runs the All News Channel (see page 196); some local stations use the All News Channel service to fill overnight program hours.

Westinghouse's Group W NewsFeed is also a news cooperative. In 1981, it became the first non-network satellite news service.

ABC, CBS, and NBC also operate news services in which their affiliates share coverage. As mentioned above, the networks can provide their affiliates with national and international coverage by using network correspondents.

News Consultants

Since many local stations share the same needs and challenges, they typically look for successful formulas used in other markets as models for their own formats and program features. Viable ideas are borrowed and adapted on a regular basis.

Many stations also employ a consulting firm to keep ahead of the competition. In theory, a news consultant represents the viewer's point of view, and brings a great deal of knowledge about the audience, and about successes from other markets, to the station. McHugh and Hoffman, Frank N. Magid Associates, and Audience Research & Development are three of the largest news-consulting firms. News consultants work on a confidential, exclusive basis with one station per market; contracts are annual.

Ideally, a news-consulting firm analyzes audience response to a station's news programming, and presents information about trends that may be taking shape. The firm does research to demonstrate how viewing habits and lifestyles are changing, and how to shape the programs, their scheduling, their content, and their presentation around the changes. Typically, a news-consulting firm will also work closely with newsroom personnel, offering specific suggestions to improve job performance, efficiency, and on-camera presentation. While this service may be critical, it may also be problematic: since the consultants emphasize presentation over news content, their very presence may be an annoyance to the news staff. Still, their input can be useful, provided that it is taken as useful advice that may improve ratings, and not as gospel truth. The consulting firm usually visits each client station roughly five or six times per year, staying two or three days each time.

CABLE NEWS

CNN operates two national cable-news channels: CNN and CNN Headline News. Conus operates the All News Channel. CNBC (Consumer News and Business Channel) features financial and consumer-oriented business news. The Weather Channel is a 24-hour news service devoted entirely to weather reporting and forecasting.

CNN is operated as a 24-hour network, offering a level of production quality and journalistic prowess that is competitive with commercial network news. There are three principal differences between CNN and network news operations. First, CNN operates with a staff of roughly 500 people, making it about one-half the size of a network news operation. Second, CNN does not emphasize personalities; although some CNN anchors and reporters are better known than others, CNN's programs do not depend on anchor-personalities in order to be successful. Third, CNN produces over 150 hours of programming per week (acquiring a small number of hours from other sources), compared with the 20 or 25 hours produced by the commercial networks. CNN also operates Headline News, a sister service that draws on the same newsgathering, but which offers a somewhat different look.

CNBC runs a financial wire all day long, while providing specialized news information. At night, CNBC programs talk and news magazine formats, produced in-house.

Conus and Viacom have a different strategy in mind for their All News Channel. The All News Channel is programmed in two ways. First, it can be used to fill hours on a program schedule (e.g., all night on a local broadcast station). Second, a cable operator or a group of cable systems can be use the All News Channel as the foundation for a local or regional cable news channel.

Some of the larger local cable systems operate a news channel. The model is News 12 Long Island, produced by Cablevision. It began in late 1986, with a straightforward premise: Long Island, a large market in the shadow of New York City, would support a local news service. The program schedule is essentially broken into four blocks: a live show from 6:00–9:00 A.M., a 9:00–10:00 A.M. show that is repeated hourly until 5:00 P.M., a 5:00–6:00 P.M. show that is repeated hourly until 10:00 P.M., and a 10:00–11:00 P.M. show that reruns all night. Each show is updated if there are major breaking stories that require further production. The channel is set up along the lines of a local news station, with approximately 150 people on staff.

News 12 is advertiser-supported and offered as a basic service to all of Cablevision's subscribers. In addition, the channel is seen on the one Long Island cable system that is not owned by Cablevision, and receives a per-sub fee from that system. Start-up costs were over $6 million; the channel costs approximately $10 million per year to operate, which is in line with the cost of news operations in most major markets. Similar services are planned in other suburban areas where Cablevision operates large systems.

The Orange County Newschannel provides a similar service in a large suburban area near Los Angeles. Operated by the successful local newspaper there, the channel debuted in 1990 with start-up costs in the $10 million range. In Chicago, TCI and the local Fox affiliate, WFLD, have announced plans for a 24-hour news service; others are in development.

Local broadcast stations have also begun relationships with local cable systems in their areas. KYW-Philadelphia, the NBC affiliate, provides special versions of its 11:00 P.M. news to cable stations in the area, newscasts that include several minutes of "neighborhood" coverage and stories of interest within the cable franchise area.

Many local cable systems also produce their own daily or weekly newscasts.

CONTENT CONSIDERATIONS

News programming depends, in large part, upon stories about people, and many of these stories involve negative information. While the function of news programming is telling stories accurately, fairly, and without bias, there are grey areas. Protection against defamation is covered in detail in Chapter 19, as are rights of privacy and publicity.

Some news stories involve information of a sensitive nature. And in some situations, sources of information ask to remain private, for fear of damage to personal reputation or injury.

NEWS SOURCES AND SOURCE PROTECTION

As a rule, television news, particularly on a local level, tries to be nonconfrontational. Facing the choice of digging deeply into a murky story or introducing the possibility of legal problems, most stations will try to convince the reporter that the legal hassles are not worth the trouble. Still, there are instances in which stations do air controversial stories, and reporters must protect sources. The rule of thumb here is corroboration: if the protected source's information can be verified by a second source, then the station will usually go with the story.

If a news source specifically asks to be protected, then it is generally accepted that the reporter has a moral responsibility to protect the source. Some stations will stand by their reporters' ethical judgment.

On the network level—where stories that have national impact more often require the protection of sources—each news department has guidelines regarding procedures. In general, the reporter must explain the situation to the news director, who generally involves the division's senior vice president or president in the decision to go with the story. Legal counsel is present at the meeting as well. Networks typically stand by their reporters, presenting a formidable united front to any parties that challenge the reporter's information or judgment.

25 Production Financing and Deal-Making

For most producers, the most challenging aspect of television production is obtaining financing. Even at the most basic level, production costs money. Figuring out how much—and where to get it from—is critical to the start-up of any project.

PREPARING A PRODUCTION BUDGET ESTIMATE

Since every production is different, the budgeting process begins with a blank spreadsheet, set up in columns in a format that has evolved over use in many productions. A cover sheet summarizes budget categories, followed by individual sheets that break out the detail. One useful system shows a reference code for each category and line item (for tracking actual costs), a description of the item ("producer," "telephone usage," "set storage"), the quantity needed, the unit cost or rate per item ($100/reel for the one-inch master videotapes, $500/week for a production assistant), and a column for calculation.

The most common categories for a videotape or live production are listed and described in the next sections. Note that this budgeting method offers just one of many possible category breakdowns, and that different production organizations use different formats. The budget format for a production shot on film differs in organization, though the basic concepts are similar; differences are largely due to personal style and company tradition.

Talent

AFTRA or SAG rates (see Chapter 28) should be used to calculate the performance budget; lower rates may apply, however, if the production is non-union. As in most categories, a daily or weekly fee is multiplied by the term of employment. For union performers, pension & welfare, plus various employment taxes, must be added. If any reuse payments (additional plays, ancillary markets, and so on) are to be made to the performer from the production budget, they should be listed as well.

Music

There are several types of costs associated with the use of music. Rights must be acquired to existing material, or else a composer, arranger, copyist, and other staff must be hired to create original material. The cost of original music should also include hiring the musicians; renting a recording studio; tape stock; and time spent editing, mixing, and mastering the music. Multiple-use payments may also be due. (See Chapter 33 for a detailed discussion of music and television.) Note that the American Federation of Musicians (AF of M) sets rates and rules for professional musicians.

Rights

Two types of rights are generally included in this part of the budget: rights to use still pictures and rights to use video clips or film clips. The costs of each can be estimated by contacting the libraries that are likely to supply these materials. Multiple purchases from a single source usually result in a volume discount. If an underlying property (such as a book) is being licensed, it can appear in this part of the budget as well.

Staff

The production staff typically accounts for a large part of the budget. This staff list should include the following people: producers, associate producers, production assistants, writers, researchers, secretaries, consultants, the director, and the director's staff (a control-room PA, associate director, and stage manager[s]). Technical or studio personnel should not be considered part of the production staff—they are more efficiently listed in the "studio" or "facilities" section. Once again, the spreadsheet lists the number of weeks (days) multiplied by the rate, plus benefits and taxes, if applicable. Rates for staff members hired under union agreements (DGA, WGA) are determined by the rules set forth in those agreements (see Chapter 27).

The challenge in developing the staff list is to accurately project the personnel needs for a project. It may be useful to create a grid showing scheduled days or weeks running along the top or bottom and the staff positions running up and down the side. A checkmark in each box shows who is working each week. By counting up the checkmarks, the producer can easily estimate the total staff budget (this grid is also useful for planning office space and related expenses).

Design and Staging

The "design and staging" category is usually more difficult to estimate, particularly if the program is not fully developed when the budget is being prepared. The biggest component of design/staging expenses is the cost of building—and, to a lesser extent, renting—set elements. The set designer, usually working for a flat fee, is listed in this category. Set items can include the costs of trucking the set from the shop to the studio, maintaining it over the course of a series, and storing it between seasons. Other elements that may be included in the design/staging section are prop construction and/or purchase, graphic artists and art materials, computer graphics, wardrobe, make-up, lighting design and direction, stagehands, grips, gaffers, carpenters, electricians, and prop specialists.

Location/Studio Facilities

Shooting locations are typically rented by the hour or by the day. The costs associated with a location may include more than simple rental, however. They may also include power generation (if a location does not have enough power on site), security personnel, crowd handling, trailers for use as offices or dressing rooms, transportation to and from the location, communications equipment (walkie talkies, cellular phone service, wired phone service), and so on. When a production location is in a public place, a permit from local authorities is required—and this permit also costs money. State and local film commissions can help the producer make the necessary arrangements.

Renting studio facilities is much easier to estimate. A studio is rented by the half-day, day, week, or month, at a negotiated rate. The published rate card is typically a starting point for discussions.

Technical and staging personnel should be included in the location or studio figure. Every crew member should be listed separately, with the number of hours/days to be worked and with overtime allotted as needed. Alternately, the supplier of the studio or mobile facility may package the equipment and crew for a single daily price (plus overtime).

Facilities Support

The production budget should also provide money for catering. On location, if dining facilities are not within minutes of the shooting site, the producer usually saves money by providing meals to cast and crew (since the cost of delays tends to be higher than the cost of food). Whether production is on location or in the studio, the budget should allot money for breakfast (rolls, bagels, danish, coffee)—and for lunch and dinner, for those production personnel who cannot leave the facility for a proper meal break. On a complicated production, it is always advisable to budget for staff and crew lunches and late dinners.

There are many other items related to shooting that fall under the catch-all category of "facilities support": lighting rentals, equipment rentals, petty cash, on-site office expenses, local transportation, audience/crowd handling, gifts/flowers for cast members, the end-of-shoot or "wrap" party (now quite common), and so on.

Office/Production

The costs of running an office must be calculated to include not only space rental, but office equipment, furniture, copying, supplies, shipping, phone usage, local transportation, and related items. The best way to estimate these items is to determine the average weekly or monthly cost of each one, then multiply by the time period.

Travel and Subsistence

Most productions involve some travel. Items like tickets (air, train), hotel/lodging, local travel (cabs, rental car), and per diem (meals, personal incidentals) should each be estimated per person, per day or per week. A complicated travel plan might require a separate grid altogether. Fare, lodging, local travel, and per diem run along the bottom; each week runs along the side, and within each week, each person who will travel is listed. With budgeting for the production staff, this system allows checkmarks to be placed, then counted.

Business Expenses

There are four principal types of business expenses. The first is insurance, including Errors & Omissions coverage (see page 144) as well as more general casualty/loss/liability coverage. The second business expense is accounting. If the production is complicated, an accountant or auditor should be paid by the week or month, as part of the staff; if the production is smaller, an outside accountant or auditor can be paid to review the invoices and checkbook, and to prepare a final accounting. The third is legal fees, best estimated by consulting in advance with an experienced attorney. There are usually two main types of legal costs: 1) those related to the financing and distribution deal, and 2) those related to clearing rights for music and photos, negotiating talent agreements, and so on. The fourth business expense is the relatively minor cost of copyright submission.

Special Expenses

Many productions require one or more additional categories to cover unique types of expenses. On a game show, for example, a "prizes" category is common. For a show that features a teleconference, a category might be devoted to satellite uplinking.

Completing the Budget

The total dollar amount for each category should be tallied and summarized on the cover page. Then, a contingency—typically 10 to 15 percent of some or all budget categories—should be added to the subtotal, to yield the grand total. On a weekly series, the grand total may then be divided into per-episode costs; on a strip series (a program seen five days a week), costs are usually indicated both per-episode and per week.

The producer's initial budget estimate is often much higher than the budget estimate that is ultimately approved, sometimes by as much as 50 percent. This may reflect the producer's desire to deliver the best possible show, to cover every possible eventuality, to have "fat" in areas that could be trimmed without affecting what it seen on the screen, or—most simply—to make as much money as possible.

The estimated budget should be a defining exercise for both producer and funder. Many projects are greeted with enthusiasm until the budget shows the financial realities. Some budgets are prepared by "backing into a number"—if a project can be delivered for a target figure, then it will be approved. Other budgets are prepared with a "zero-based" approach: the producer draws up a total figure, then attempts to protect the concept while adjusting the costs of line items.

A budget is usually revised several times prior to submission to the financing party, and several times after the grand total has been approved. In most production scenarios, the grand total is the most important number, and the producer will sometimes shift money from one category to another to compensate for the difference between the estimate and the actual numbers.

Once work begins on the program, budget reports, showing the amount of money spent in each category and for each line item, are prepared once or twice per week. This procedure helps pinpoint problems early in the life of the program. When a production is complete, a final budget accounting is prepared and submitted along with other delivery items (see page 273).

THE CHALLENGE OF PRODUCTION FINANCING

The producer or executive producer's most difficult task is finding the money to make the project. For independent productions, combining these sources to build up sufficient capital for the program is an art in itself. Even for programs produced in-house by a television station or corporation, raising money or gaining access to in-house resources can also be a difficult task.

The style of production financing has changed—particularly in the past ten years—from single-source to a system in which multiple sources participate. Producers of public-television programs are especially experienced in such multi-source financing (see Chapter 4), but the concept is becoming more familiar to producers who supply programming to the commercial networks.

GROWING PROGRAM DEFICITS

Until the early 1980s, ABC, CBS, and NBC bought the right to air a program twice in exchange for a license fee that more or less amount equaled the production cost. Producers earned their profits from syndication, an area in which the networks did not participate (see page 116). Since then, production costs have increased, but the networks have not raised their license fees in like fashion; instead, the networks have upheld the profitability of their program operations (in the face of shrinking market share) by holding the line on license fees to producers. The result is production deficits that must somehow be covered with money from other sources. For some properties (especially shows with the three or four years of production that made daily "stripping" possible), syndication was the answer. In other cases, sales to cable networks, foreign broadcasters, and other emerging markets created additional opportunities for producers of network programs.

Today, the network license fee rarely pays for the entire cost of production; in fact, it may only cover 80 percent of the total production budget at most. Given a production budget of $1 million or more (increasingly common for a network hour) and a license fee from the network of $800,000, the deficit per program equals $200,000. For 20 programs over the course of a single season, the total deficit is $4 million. With several seasons passing before the program plays either on cable or in syndication, the deficit can easily top $10 million—an unmanageable burden for a small company, and a serious one for a larger company. This is the reason why prime time network production is dominated by large studios. The studios either sell their own product to the networks, or finance, distribute, and co-produce projects from smaller companies—acting, in a sense, like banks for smaller companies.

When studios or larger production companies absorb the deficit, they view the dollars as an investment against future profits from syndication and other markets. But as the syndication marketplace has changed, this return has become more and more undependable, so the studios and large production companies have started looking to other financing sources for covering the deficits, leading to complicated multi-source deals. Instead of providing back-end revenues (money generated after the primary release of the program), formerly ancillary markets are now being asked to provide upfront production financing, often in exchange for profit participation and some distribution rights.

In cable and syndication, production deficits have become a fact of life, at least for the dramas and comedies that aspire to network production standards. Although there are usually more initial runs of programs in these markets, the ratings—and advertising revenues—are low, even when considered cumulatively. One solution has been to program less expensively, with sports, talk shows, game shows, and so on. The other option has been locating other markets and media to help cover production costs. For instance, in one scenario, the producer would receive 50 percent of the budget from a pay TV network, 15 percent from a home video label, 30 percent from a Canadian co-producer, and the final 5 percent from a pre-sale to a foreign broadcaster. In addition to the complexity of this kind of arrangement, there is the problem of a disappearing back end: with so many of the ancillary markets pre-sold, the producer is left with little opportunity for profit.

The arrangements are still evolving. Several commercial network shows have been co-produced with broadcasters in Canada, Australia, Italy, and other countries, mainly to share the burden of the production cost, and, undoubtedly, as a kind of experiment. Co-production with a Canadian broadcaster is now a fairly standard means of reducing costs for some syndicated programs (game shows, for example).

It is no longer enough for the producer to interest one licensee in a program—he or she must now appeal to several parties, each of which has its own peculiarities of taste and style. Even if the program's initial concept is acceptable to all concerned, each participant is likely to demand approval over key elements as production progresses, and a deadlock among the various parties is always a potential problem. Foreign investors and foreign co-producers can also complicate matters. They need projects that will satisfy local-content rules—rules that can dictate the nationalities of the production staff and talent, as well as the location of production and post-production activities. The program may start looking more and more foreign, which in turn may displease the U.S. participants.

The balance of this chapter will review the types of production financing that go into this mix; who usually provides them; the role of the distributor; the key ideas of recoupment and profit participation; and the nuts and bolts of how deals are put together.

TYPES AND SOURCES OF PRODUCTION FINANCING

The world of production financing can be broken down into six general categories: internal working capital, customers and clients, suppliers, inside and outside investors, banks and other lenders, and foreign partners.

Internal Working Capital

The early stages of a program's development are usually funded internally. Many production companies—and nearly all television stations and cable networks—budget a certain amount of money per year for developing new projects. Once the program is developed, it will often be "pitched" or "shopped" to other potential participants, and one component part of the deal will be funding for further development of the project.

If the production organization is a distributor or broadcaster/cablecaster, then all of the project's development, and some or all of its production, may be financed with internal capital. A home video company or cable network, for example, might employ a staff producer to develop and produce projects. Internal approvals at several stages may still be required in order to release the monies. Sometimes, money is approved only for each incremental step, and additional approval is needed to move the project to the next step.

In some cases, internal funds are used to produce a demonstration tape or a pilot, which then becomes a selling tool to attract additional investment from other companies.

Internal working capital can also be used to make up for the shortfalls that occur because of the delays in receiving funds from outside sources. Unless advances from customers or distributors are paid on time—and unless all suppliers are patient and understanding of the cash-flow crises that typify the production process—the schedule is likely to be affected until a certain check arrives and clears. A production company should have ready access to cash or a line of credit in order to smooth out the bumps in cash flow.

Internal capital is also used to close gaps in production funding. For example, if a production company gets a project 95 percent financed from other sources, it may decide to cover the remaining 5 percent itself from its own reserves in order to begin production. Sometimes, this is preferable to pre-selling rights that might be more valuable once the program is made.

Customers and Clients

Customers and clients are the most common source of production financing, particularly for independent producers. Television is a business in which end users like networks, cable companies, and video distributors will pay sizable sums—either in advance or on delivery—for the product they need. Since they have to buy programming regularly, they are quite accustomed to paying some or all of production costs. Customers and clients can take many forms, depending mainly on the type of distribution system. If the law permits, they can also buy rights in the program as part of the deal, or have their license fee treated in whole or in part as an investment.

Many programs are produced for private concerns. A corporation requiring a training video will typically pay the entire cost of development and production, for example.

In some cases, a combination of two or more customers furnish funding for a program. For example, a commercial broadcaster could account for partial financing, and a syndicator's advance, the remainder; or a cable network could provide some financing, with a European broadcaster making up the balance.

Suppliers

Suppliers, like television studios, location facilities (e.g., mobile vans and related personnel), and post-production facilities, may also provide a form of production financing. In exchange for a profit participation or partial ownership in a property, these facilities may offer reduced rates, or defer payment of bills until the project earns enough money to pay not only the initial amount, but a premium as well.

Supplier financing is most common for pilots, in which facilities and/or personnel may be traded for the promise of a locked-in production contract if the series is commissioned. If that occurs, the supplier will make back its money and then some.

Supplier financing is also common in the home video industry, particularly for independent producers who distribute their own product. In such a case, the tape duplicator may not only manufacture finished product on credit or without charge, but may also supply warehousing, shipping, and inventory control in exchange for profit participation or partial ownership.

Investors

Television and video are glamorous businesses that attract certain types of investors. Investors essentially come in two forms: those who are unaffiliated with the television and/or video industries (outside investors), and those who are in some aspect of the television business and who will buy into a project while acquiring certain distribution or telecasting rights (inside investors).

Outside Investors

For the pure-equity investor with no other means to benefit beyond a share of revenues, a television or video project is likely to be a difficult investment. There are at least two potential problem areas. First, television and video programs do not "earn out" in any predictable fashion. This can make investors nervous, especially if they are inexperienced in television/video. Second, if a producer is relying on outside investment money, he or she may be working outside the established production community, and may lack easy access to those production or distribution resources essential to a reasonable return and a predictable budget. Nor is it only the investor who may have problems. On a project that is running late and perhaps over budget, with one or more investors anxious to recoup their investments more rapidly than the marketplace will allow, the possibility of all-out panic may cause the producer to question the wisdom of working with outsiders.

That said, there are many isolated instances where outside investment has proven successful, sometimes with enormous returns for both investor and producer.

Wall Street investment firms, major insurance companies, and other traditional sources of investment capital generally invest in television through big production entities like studios, syndicators, and networks. This investment provides the television company with working capital to help with its self-funding efforts. In these situations, the investment in production and distribution is based on an assessment of the overall business of the company.

Inside Investors

Distributors and end users of programming often invest in production. Although the distinction between the distributor-as-investor and the purchaser-as-end-user is a blurred one, there is an important difference between the two.

The distributor usually gives a production company an advance to be used for production. This is deemed an investment (especially if it is not fully covered by pre-sales), since it depends on unpredictable market factors to generate a return on the capital supplied. In exchange for taking the risk, the distributor usually gets a share of profits. Of course, by controlling at least some aspect of distribution and revenues, the distributor is able to influence its own investment risk.

A purchaser/end user—for example, a network—is not trading an investment for a return. Instead, it is paying outright for particular rights or territories (in the form of license fees, for a network), and using the program in an active business of its own. Many purchasers, however, want to be treated like investors; they want the recoupment and profit positions that traditionally go to true risk-taking investors.

Because they are in a singularly powerful position, the major networks were seen as exerting this kind of pressure on the producers and distributors that supplied them with programming. In response, the FCC instituted the financial interest and syndication ("fin-syn") rules, which have forbidden the networks from having a financial interest in the independent productions that they carry on their prime time schedules. Other end users and distributors have not been so hampered, though a now-routine piece of negotiation between them and the producer is how much of a license fee or advance will count as an "investment," and with what results. As their power has ebbed, the networks have clamored for a relaxation of the fin-syn rules, and the FCC has recently acceded to some degree (see page 117).

Banks and Other Lenders

Banks and other lending institutions play a part in the production financing process, but only if the loan can be secured with property that can be readily valued and turned into cash. Unsold rights to specific program properties are difficult to present as collateral because of their inherently speculative nature. Besides, most lenders do not understand the intricacies of show business accounting. Therefore, most lending activity is either large-scale—multimillion dollar loans to studios, networks, syndicators, and technical facilities—or dependent upon the existence of a firm pre-sale.

For the independent producer or production company, a bank will only make a loan if there is a bona fide contract with a creditworthy distributor or end user that provides for set payments on a firm schedule. The bank is essentially covering cash flow—if there is a period in which the producer requires cash, but the distributor or end-user will not provide the necessary amount until a later point in production (such as delivery), a bank may provide a bridge loan. The risk of a failure to deliver is offset by a completion bond and other forms of insurance (see page 266).

Loans for project development, or for independent production without pre-sales, are almost impossible to obtain because of the risk involved.

In some cases, the contribution of an equity investor will take the form of a high-risk, non-recourse loan, generally with a substantial "kicker," such as a large share of net revenues. While this is technically a loan, it is actually treated like an investment.

Foreign Partners

With the trend toward globalization, many companies outside the U.S. have become sources of production capital for U.S. programs. Historically, foreign sales came after the fact, as part of the profit margin. More and more frequently, though, the foreign investment is arranged up-front to minimize production deficits.

Foreign investment in U.S. production is generally linked to a license of rights. In its simplest form, the deal is basically a pre-sale, with the additional kicker of profit participation and sometimes partial ownership. More often, however, investment from foreign sources is part of a co-production package. In a relationship that resembles a partnership (regardless of its strictly legal structure), the domestic producer and a foreign co-producer each provide certain elements in the production budget. The project may be shot overseas, for example, using facilities provided in whole or in part by the foreign co-producer. Co-production often involves cash from the foreign partner as well, supplementing the cash available to the U.S. producer from licenses to a domestic broadcaster, distributor, cablecaster, or home video company. Partners usually share the distribution rights—with each one usually retaining broadcast and cable rights in its home country—and split the revenues according to a negotiated formula. These deals are complicated, however, by the domestic-content requirements that commonly apply to broadcasters in their own countries (see pages 364 and 389), and by fluctuating foreign-exchange rates.

THE RELATIONSHIP BETWEEN PRODUCER AND DISTRIBUTOR

As in many industries, the producer manufactures the product, and the distributor takes care of sales and marketing. A successful product combines competent work by the producer with effective sales and marketing clout from the distributor.

Most independent producers license at least certain rights in their product to experienced distribution companies. This is especially true in markets that are difficult to sell without a specialized sales force, as in syndication and foreign. Syndication companies, for example, maintain relationships with stations, station groups, rep firms (who make recommendations to the stations that they represent), and sponsors (who buy barter advertising time); in addition, most syndication companies work regularly with the cable networks. Producers may act as their own distributors. In some cases, production companies have formed their own syndication companies or home video labels in an effort to retain more revenues and to pay closer attention to their product than an independent distributor might.

The Typical Distribution Deal

In most instances, the producer licenses a distributor to sell a program or series, in a particular territory or group of territories, for a specified period of time. The distributor then retains a negotiated percentage of revenues as a fee, frequently 30 to 35 percent (though this figure varies widely, depending upon the product, markets, and advances involved), plus reimbursement for certain distribution expenses (see page 215). The distributor will recoup any advance that it made to the producer and may retain a certain amount as profit participation, particularly if the advance was sizable. The distribution deal's definitions and limitations are negotiable, based on bargaining strength, industry tradition, and company policy, and there are many variations on the theme. A checklist for issues in distribution deals appears as Appendix B5; a model distribution agreement is reproduced as Appendix B7.

REVENUE STREAMS: RECOUPMENT

So far, the discussion in this chapter has centered on the spending side of deals. Of equal importance is the revenue side, where—with luck and clear contract language—investments are recouped and profits are earned and shared. When a party finances a commercial venture, it is almost always with the intention of recouping (recovering) the investment and realizing some profit. A television network recoups the investment in its programs by selling time slots to advertisers, usually earning a profit in the process. A home video label recoups by selling videocassettes to dealers and to consumers. Even the sponsor of a public television program hopes to recoup its investment, either in cash (from the proceeds of additional sales) or through the benefit of good community relations.

A true investment is not tied to a sale of particular rights, at least in theory; rather, an investment is recoupable in priority position from all sources of income generated by the property. However, end users may press to be treated as investors, at least for a portion of the fee, so the process of repaying investors can become quite complicated.

Recoupment Priorities

Recoupment usually occurs "in the first position," or from gross revenues received, before any profits or other revenue deductions are allowed. However simple this may sound, there are layers of activities and entities that are involved in the revenue stream of a television program.

At each layer, deductions are made, and the "net" at one level is the "gross" at the next layer down: for example, the distributor's net is usually the producer's gross. Where any particular investor's recoupment right "plugs in" is often a hotly-negotiated item. In most cases, distribution costs are recouped at a higher level than production costs.

Multiple Parties

With only one party eligible to recoup its investment at any given level, the formula is a relatively simple one. The investment is one of a list of items that are deducted from revenues at that level prior to determining the net. The situation becomes more complicated when several parties are entitled to recoupment, particularly when their investment contributions are not equal to one another. Two related issues must be considered: the relative *size* of each investor's share, and the *order* in which each investor may extract dollars.

The simplest formula is called *pari passu*, a Latin term meaning "by a like step." In pari passu recoupment, each party receives funds at the same time, but in proportion to its percentage investment at a particular point in time. The following example illustrates the pari passu formula. Party A has invested $2 million (50 percent) in a production, party B, $1,200,000 (30 percent), and party C, $800,000 (20 percent). When the first $100 arrives from any and all revenue sources, the parties receive $50, $30, and $20 respectively, at the same time. Pari passu recoupment is a fair means of sharing both risk and reward.

Recoupment by position is the opposite of pari passu recoupment. The party in the first position receives some or all of its investment, then the party in the second position recoups, then the party in the third position, and so on, down the line. Take the same $100 income, the same parties A, B, and C above, and an agreement for party A to recoup 100 percent of its $2-million investment in the first position. Party A would then receive the entire $100 and all additional dollars up to $2 million. Parties B and C would receive nothing until party A recouped.

There are several possible variations on the formulas. In order to provide the other parties with some income, party A might agree to accept less than 100 percent of the income, or to open "windows" for the others at various positions before its own complete recoupment.

In another variation, one or more of the parties might be entitled to recoup more than 100 percent of the original investment. Some deals offer, for example, 200 percent recoupment, but no future involvement in profits (or some lesser involvement in profits). From the perspective of the investor, a formula based on a multiple of the original investment is simple and easily managed. From the perspective of the producer, such a formula limits the long-term distribution of profits, and keeps the project's ultimate profitability unknown to the recoupment partners.

Separating and Combining Revenue Streams

A successful television program or series is likely to generate revenues from a variety of domestic and foreign sources. Sometimes the streams are split apart and treated as different "pots" for recoupment purposes. For example, the producer of a movie-of-the-week may get an advance from one distributor that will cover domestic syndication and cable sales, and another advance from a second distributor that will cover all foreign markets. Frequently, each of these two distributors will recoup its respective advance only from revenues from its own territories and markets. Given the fact that the distributor's efforts will help shape the success of the program in its own area, this is a reasonable arrangement. An outside investor, in contrast, will usually recoup from all revenue sources.

Revenue streams can also be tied together, with the proceeds from one market helping to cover the recoupment of costs or advances in another area. This technique is called "cross-collateralization," from a banking term that refers to mortgaging separate properties to support a single loan. Separate programs are sometimes cross-collateralized to cover the costs that each one runs up on its own; in that case, the programs would have to break even on an aggregated basis before a net would be earned on any one of them.

What Gets Recouped

The definition of what is recoupable is a critical point in negotiations. Since distribution costs, production costs, and advances are all subject to recoupment, these are prime areas for definitional license—here is where "Hollywood accounting" earns its reputation for legitimized theft. Every piece of overhead, interest, or other type of "indirect" costs added to the more truthfully labeled "direct" costs means a shifting of money from the net participants to the recoupment participants. This issue leads directly to the next topic: net profits and other "back-end" participation.

PROFIT PARTICIPATION AND OTHER
BACK-END FORMULAS

"Profits" is both a magical and a cursed word in television. Fortunes have been generated by the sale and resale of specials, series, and motion pictures to network, cable, syndication, home video, and foreign markets. Often, those fortunes are not shared by people who have a "net profit" participation or other formula for *back-end participation*. (The latter refers to money that comes out of revenues, as opposed to a *front-end* fee, which comes out of the production budget). As playwright David Mamet had one of his characters in *Speed the Plow* quip, "There is no net." There are two principal reasons behind this all-too-frequently accurate statement. The first is the convoluted and blatantly one-sided terms of participation agreements that are presented as take-it-or-leave-it propositions to back-end participants. The second is the "creative accounting" that shifts costs back and forth among various projects, with the most successful ones bearing the greatest burden of items allocated for recoupment. This section will examine both of these problems in detail, as well as several other obstacles to the profitability of any production.

The Problem of Labels

In theory, being a "gross" participant is better than being a "net" one. But in the end, labels mean very little—it is the details in the definition that truly matter.

"Gross revenues" should mean the total amount of money received, prior to any deductions. A network's gross, for example, should equal the total amount of money paid by the sponsors for advertising on the program. Even this simple explanation demands refinement, though: sponsors buy their commercial time through advertising agencies, who retain 15 percent of the sponsor's payment as a commission.

From the producer's perspective, gross might also be defined as the total monies received by the producer from the program's distributors (i.e., the "distributor's net").

A director or writer who negotiates to receive a percentage of the producer's gross is likely to have his own definition. This "gross" might well be offset by agency commissions, legal fees, or a stunning variety of incidentals—from the costs of shipping videocassettes to foreign countries for potential licensing to a full recoupment of basic production costs. The gross is now an "adjusted gross."

Although specific terms may vary, "adjusted gross" often functions as a synonym for what most people would call "net" or "net profits," though the adjusted gross will usually have fewer questionable deductions. The words "net," "profits," and "net profits" should be meaningful terms, but they have become so debased through misuse that they are now scorned, even as labels, by anyone with sufficient negotiating power. Other kinds of back-end payments involve flat fees or bonuses in place of, or in addition to, a percentage in a net or gross formula. "Points" are percentage points, and represent the percentage share of whatever is being divided ("net points," "gross points," and so on). Even the word "revenues" can be misleading. Many agreements only "recognize" revenue after it has come to rest in a particular account in a particular country, even though that may be months or even years after the check was cashed by the foreign subsidiary of the U.S.-based distributor.

In order to get to the root of a typical profit definition, one must ignore the customary meanings of certain terms and focus on the legalese of the profit-participation agreement itself. Hidden there will probably be many of the following issues concerning the recipient of the profit share ("Participant") and the payer of that share ("Company").

Revenue Adjustments

On the revenue side, there are many ways in which the Company can defer acknowledging funds that have actually been deposited into its bank accounts. International companies have particularly wide scope for this action. A common clause in profit definitions says that no funds shall count as being received until paid in dollars into the U.S. accounts of the Company. If the Company has foreign subsidiaries, they can collect foreign revenues in foreign currencies and leave them overseas indefinitely, as a kind of permanent loan from the Participants who are entitled to them. This can be avoided by insisting on a timeframe for the repatriation of funds held by the Company or its affiliates.

Some countries, however, have a "blocked currency" problem: they restrict the ability to take money out of the country. This can be circumvented by having an agreement allow the Participant to set up his or her own account in the country and take the appropriate share of blocked funds directly. The Participant may not be able to get the funds out of the country either, but at least they are available to spend over there.

Another method the Company can use for delaying recognition of monies received is the use of reserves and the related concept of "earned." The theory is that advances made are not really "earned" until the product is delivered, since they could conceivably be rescinded if something went wrong with the program. Therefore, the logic goes, all advances must be held in reserve until it is clear that there will be no problems. This line of thinking has been stretched to say that no license fee is earned until the contract has been completely performed. The license may run over several years—and even after the program has run several times with no problems, some or all of the licensing fee may be held in reserve and deemed not yet earned.

These delay tactics can be compounded, quite literally, when they are combined with clauses allowing the Company to earn interest on unrecouped amounts. If income which is actually on hand can be considered non-existent, then the Company will expect interest to be paid on these funds, piling on extra charges to be recouped (even on overhead costs and production fees). Another problem with interest is that the Company charges the prime rate plus some number, whereas it pays lenders several points less. All of these practices can be countered by limiting interest charges to amounts actually paid on amounts actually outstanding on expenses actually incurred.

Company delay can also be used to influence the exchange rate at which foreign receipts are converted into dollars. If the foreign distributor of the program is an affiliate of the Company, it will wait for the moment when the foreign currency is weak to report income, diminishing the dollar total. Similarly, any expenses or deductions will be converted and deducted when the foreign currency is strong. A fair contract will specify average exchange rates or key the rates to specific dates for evaluation.

Fees

Revenues to Participants are also reduced with double-charging of fees. The Company collects a fee for selling a program in a particular market, then turns around and sub-licenses it to another organization, which also deducts a percentage fee from its gross. It seems unfair that the Company keeps its full fee when someone else is being paid to do the work—especially when the "someone else" turns out to be an affiliate of the Company, or even a direct subsidiary. This kind of inside licensing for double fees, which is especially common with foreign sales and in other ancillary markets, can be prevented by capping the total amount of fees that can be charged by every party involved in selling into a particular market, and by forbidding the charging of additional fees for work done by an affiliate of the Company.

Exaggerated Deductions

Having taken steps to delay and minimize the receipt of income, the Company may try to increase the number of deductions that it can take. The first group of deductions are "adjustments" to the gross such as collection costs (legal actions for bad debts), agent fees, and applicable taxes. Tax deductions should cover taxes specifically withheld from the project's revenues, and not the general income taxes of the Company. If there is a benefit to the Company from an offset or tax credit, the fair share of this should be added back against the taxes deducted or even, if possible, passed along to the Participant.

The next set of deductions is usually the recoupment of distribution and marketing costs. One might think that these expenses are the cost of doing business, and should be covered by the Company out of its distribution fee; this is sometimes the negotiated result. But in the film business, these expenses are sometimes huge, given the prints and advertising necessary for a major release, and so they are recovered separately. The practice has been transferred over to television deals, even though the costs of distribution are actually much smaller.

Most Participants are willing to accept the deduction of direct, out-of-pocket costs of getting the programs on the air: tape stock, dubbing, shipping, customs, and so on. The trouble starts when these and other services are performed in-house and then charged against the program as a hefty fee. The Company may also tack an overhead allowance onto these charges, so that the program's earnings are being in effect charged twice for expenses that the fee should cover. Add an interest factor while these charges remain unrecouped, and the meaning of "Hollywood accounting" becomes clear.

Sales and marketing costs present additional opportunities for Company abuse. Television distribution may not involve massive media campaigns aimed at the general public, but there is quite extensive marketing targeted to potential end users: printing brochures, dubbing sales tapes, travel, phone, and attendance at conventions and sales markets (see page 220). Armies of television executives descend on Cannes, Las Vegas, and New Orleans every year to wheel and deal, trying to outdo one another with expensive display booths and celebrity appearances. Though many Participants grumble at the lavishness of these efforts, they at least acknowledge that "you have to spend money to make money." The problem comes when the expenses are allocated among the various properties that the Company represented at such functions. If the Company went to Cannes with a list of 20 properties, it may return with lucrative sales for only 5 of them. It is useless to allocate the expenses to the failures (since these properties may never make enough money to repay them), so the successes are made to bear the burden of the costs. While the successes probably do occupy a disproportionate amount of the Company staff's attention, the Participant does not expect its own program to carry most of the Company's overhead, especially in addition to the fee that is deducted. Some unscrupulous companies even allocate the same costs to more than one program, and end up making money on every expense they incur.

Some of these problems can be thwarted with language in the agreement between Participant and Company that requires deductions to be "directly related" to the program and to be "actual, out-of-pocket" expenditures. Another approach is to simply impose a cap, either as a percentage or (less commonly) as an absolute amount, which deductions for such items cannot exceed.

Double-counting is another deduction tactic. Residuals may turn up twice as deductible, as may insurance and other program-related costs. Sometimes an expenditure is calculated as both a distribution cost and a production cost; even worse, overhead and interest expenditures are added to both occurrences, even though overhead on distribution expenses is relatively rare.

After distribution fees and expenses have been deducted, the revenue stream—or what is left of it—is applied to recouping the production costs or the advance. If the Company is recouping the full production costs, these, too, are defined in a one-sided manner. For example, most production budgets include a general overhead factor, sometimes 20 percent or more. In theory, this factor is supposed to cover all of the small expenses of ongoing Company overhead that are attributable to the program but that do not appear in the official budget. In practice, though, many of the Company's profit calculations *already* account for a wide array of overhead costs, including telephone bills and the cost of parking spaces at the Company's main office. The Participant should keep the overhead factor, then, within reasonable bounds, and question the addition of interest to overhead and overhead to interest.

The Company's boilerplate definition of "penalties" may allow it to recoup 150 percent of the "normal" production cost if the program is over-budget. While the argument goes that this is an incentive to the talent to keep expenses under control, the Company may insist on penalties even when it has final approval on all artistic and business matters relating to the production.

Percentages of Percentages

Once the Company has taken all its deductions, the issue is just what the "points" promised to Participants are percentages of. Are they 10 percent of the "producer's share" of net profits? Because there is a customary 50/50 or 60/40 split between investor and producer, 10 percent of the producer's share will be no more than 5 percent of the "100 percent." In addition, if the promised percentage is 10 percent of the "producer's *retained* share" of net profits, any other grants which the producer has made will be taken off the top before the points are calculated, so the Participant's actual share shrinks even more.

General Defenses Against Profit-Participation Abuses

In addition to the specific remedies described above, there are some more general measures to protect a Participant from a Company's creative accounting methods. First, the long, standard-form profit definition in the profit-participation agreement is usually drafted to protect the Company as much as possible; a relatively short statement, with language limiting overhead and other general allocations, can tilt the agreement back in the Participant's favor. Second, the Participant should insist on a "most-favored-nation" clause. This item is derived from the laws of custom duties, where a "most favored nation" must have the benefit of any concession granted to any other country. In the world of profits, this means that the Participant cannot get a worse deal than anyone else in an agreed-upon class. If the class includes other recipients with some bargaining power, the entire deal may improve some; and if the deal includes the Company or its key executives, the deal might get better still.

Accounting Rights

One of the most effective means of monitoring a Company's questionable practices is the Participant's right to have an accounting done of the Company's financial books and records on a project. Most clauses will grant the Participant the right to audit the books within a certain time from receiving the statement, or the right have a "qualified representative" conduct the audit. The records will be made available at the Company's offices, during regular business hours. The right to audit may be limited to a single audit of any given period; any claims must be made shortly after the inspection. Sometimes the Company will hinder the right to an audit with so many restrictions and such short time intervals that the clauses become almost meaningless.

Auditors do turn up irregularities, even with a relatively honest Company; the problem is that such audits tend to be expensive, although a profit-participation agreement may provide for the Company to pick up the tab if serious shortfalls are discovered.

THE ALTERNATIVE TO PROFIT PARTICIPATION: FIXED PAYMENTS

For those who are skeptical of profit participation and its many blind alleyways, there are alternatives. The easiest way is to structure a bonus or royalty arrangement keyed to reaching easily-measurable targets—like the number of programs actually produced. For example, every time a week of shows is made, the participant could receive a flat dollar figure as a royalty or bonus: more shows, more money. If these shows air more than once, a further formula can be devised; if these shows air outside the U.S., then each show that airs in a specified list of countries triggers a specific payment. If the series reaches the three-or four-year mark, making syndication possible, then a bigger bonus is triggered.

Some producers receive bonuses when a program reaches, or exceeds, a specific rating point. Some receive bonuses when a pilot triggers a series order, or when a second, or third, or fourth year of programs is ordered. Bonuses may be used in combination with revenue-based profit participation. Bonuses may be paid "against" profit participation (that is, deducted from later earnings, if any), or they may be paid in addition to these monies.

In summary, there are no absolute rules regarding profit participation; every situation is different. For those few players with sufficient clout, the terms of profit participation are highly negotiable; for everyone else, David Mamet's words—"There is no net"—will probably ring true.

HOW DEALS GET DONE

How are deals actually made so that a production can be financed? The key to the process is experienced participants who know how to play the game, who can untangle complications and reconcile contradictions—at least enough to have some type of deal letter signed. (Sometimes the deal letter is all that gets signed; it is not uncommon, with a series several years into production, for the various lawyers to still be wrangling over the terms of the long-form agreement.)

The following section describes some of the essential elements involved in making a deal for production financing.

Who the Players Are

Certain television executives make programming decisions, and have the power to make financial commitments to a producer. Most end users and distributors have a programming or acquisitions department, which is where much of the initial action takes place. Typically, this department consists of the creative people, who evaluate and shape the artistic aspects of the program, and the business people, who judge the program in terms of its cost and its revenue potential. The inevitable tensions between creative vision and cost control play out daily between these factions; a successful project will meet the needs of both parties.

At the head of the programming or acquisitions department sits a chief or a committee of chiefs, who may or may not have the power to authorize development or production. This chief will take the distilled views of his or her department up to another level in the company for ratification, especially if the production seems controversial, particularly expensive, or otherwise out of the ordinary.

On the selling side are the production companies, independent producers, directors, writers, and anyone else with a good idea. The trick is getting the project in front of the right person on the buyer's side. Many projects that are submitted get shunted to low-paid readers (who may not have much experience) for a review, and a bad reader's report can doom a worthy project to obscurity. The project must be seen by someone actually empowered to make a commitment. Personal relationships can be essential here. One of the keys to a successful production career is a Rolodex full of senior program executives who will take your call, have lunch with you, or even share a weekend on your boat. For a newcomer, a well-connected agent, manager, or attorney can help open the doors. Nor are agents only for newcomers—many well-established producers and production companies still take their agents along when they pitch a project.

When the buyer is a broadcast or cable network, the pitching process stops with the network decision to take the program. If the production is meant for the syndication market, however, then the syndication company must turn around and sell it to the programmers at independent stations all across the country. Again, access is critical, though now the Rolodex should cover the whole country, not just a few production and distribution centers. Coverage in the top 10 or 15 international markets is becoming increasingly important as well.

Where the Players Meet

The players get together in formal meetings scheduled at their offices, in restaurants, or at other business venues. There are also short-notice meetings and impromptu appointments at conferences, sales markets, and conventions, and in quite informal settings like skiing in Aspen, sunbathing in the Hamptons, or sailing off St. Tropez. Even a haircut can give the barber the chance to make a pitch: hairdressers have risen to some of the most powerful positions in Hollywood.

Formal Meetings

Although a written submission is often required in advance, and some work can be done over the phone, there is no substitute for a face-to-face meeting in a formal setting. A good part of the art of the deal is the seller infecting the buyer with enthusiasm for a program. Selling projects in any television market—whether local, national, or international—also requires spending time in the city or cities where the principal buyers are located, setting up the necessary round of meetings and cultivating the connections and contacts that will put the person pitching the project into the system.

The Hubs

The premier deal-making location, both for national and international productions, is still the Los Angeles area; no place rivals L.A. for the concentration of television business people. The next most important center in the U.S. is New York City, trailed (at some distance) by central Florida, Chicago, Atlanta, and Nashville. In Canada, Toronto dominates the television business, although Vancouver and (to a lesser extent) Montreal are also important Canadian centers. Internationally, Tokyo, London, Paris, Munich, and Rome all have concentrations of power, with secondary hubs in Sydney, Mexico City, and Madrid/ Barcelona.

Before setting out to find fame and fortune in one of these hubs of the television business, an aspiring producer should consider using the resources of his or her local community to acquire basic experience, establish a reputation, and create a demonstration reel.

Conventions, Markets, and Social Occasions

There are a series of conventions and markets throughout the year, both domestically and internationally, where much television business gets done—or at least started—in a relatively short span of time. In the U.S., the key meetings are the syndication markets sponsored by the Association of Independent Television Stations (INTV) and the National Association of Television Program Executives (NATPE). INTV and NATPE are specifically designed for syndicators to show their programs to a wide range of buyers from around the country, and these meetings are central to the syndication sales business (see page 227). All kinds of business occur at these conventions, from finding a new advertising sales company to arranging a corporate merger. Provided the executives can take the time from the syndication business at hand, INTV and NATPE are opportunities to pitch, follow up on, and commit to new projects. Other important U.S. meetings include VSDA (Video Software Dealers Association) in Las Vegas and the International Film Market in Los Angeles.

Internationally, the most important conventions are the pair devoted to television and video which are held in Cannes every year. MIP-TV takes place in the spring, and focuses on sales to the traditional broadcast markets; MIPCOM is in the fall, and covers all aspects of the television and video business, including cable and satellite. Other events include the famous Cannes film festival (typically held in the late spring) and the lesser festivals held throughout the world. At these gatherings, the production, finance, distribution, and end-user communities from around the world forge alliances, initiate co-productions, and generally discuss deals. While few of these transactions are finalized in the hotel bars by the sea or on the chartered yachts by the pier, many deals are launched before the week of hectic meetings is finished.

Informal contacts in social situations are also a prime starting point for presenting and soliciting television projects. While it is bad form to let discussions centered on business dominate a dinner party, there is plenty of room for mentioning a possible project and setting up a formal meeting to talk further about it. This kind of networking is difficult for an outsider to do; it comes naturally, however, the longer one is in the business.

Negotiating the Deal

Television is often a rough-and-tumble world, full of strong characters who have gotten ahead by imposing their wills on others and making deals on their own terms. These people are likely to be adroit at all the manipulation, flattery, intimidation, and enticement that go into getting one's own way. Nowhere are these skills more evident than at the bargaining table. Countering these personalities is not always easy, especially when you are starting a career and have little leverage. Nonetheless, there are a few bits of preparation that can guide anyone through the negotiation process.

The first step is examining your own position, weighing its strengths and weaknesses. Identify what your minimum requirements are, and if you cannot have them met, it is best to walk away from the table. The next step is to put yourself in the other side's shoes: what are *their* strengths, weaknesses, and minimum requirements? This exercise will help you determine just where—and how far—you can push their positions. Do your homework about the deal as well. If you haven't read the fine print or don't know the industry custom on a particular point, you can be pushed around by someone who has and who does. Use your advisers—agents, managers, lawyers—wisely; don't defer all decision-making to them, but borrow their knowledge, experience, and skills in the manipulation game. If the other side insists on yelling and screaming, preserve your dignity by leaving the table or hanging up the phone—if they really want the deal, they will come back to you in a more civilized fashion.

Timing is also a factor. Insisting on the last drop of blood can draw out the deal process by weeks or months. Many deals have their ripe moment, when attentions are focused and the market ready. Missing that moment can do far more harm than missing the last triumph in the negotiations. In addition, the television community is small enough so that a reputation for gouging at the negotiating table can come back to haunt you. Be firm, but leave something for the other side to take home: there is considerable value in being "a pleasure to do business with."

26 Production Companies

Television programs are produced by an enormous variety of entities—from individuals working with little more than a camcorder and an editing rig in the basement, to large program factories with access to the biggest stars, the fattest budgets, and the latest in state-of-the-art equipment.

In general, productions can be classified as either "in-house" (done by a network, station, corporate video department, or distributor) or "out-of-house" (by free-lance producers and production companies). There is also a large grey area between the two, since productions are now financed and distributed by multiple parties, some or all of whom may be involved in the actual production of the program.

IN-HOUSE PRODUCTIONS

Programs are produced in-house for several reasons. Some types of productions, such as regularly-scheduled news programs, are the pride of the organization. They are also so complex and so closely linked to the network or station's image that outside packaging would be unfeasible. Morning news and information programs, like NBC's *The Today Show* and ABC's *Good Morning America,* are produced in-house so that the network can maintain control over a signature property. Under some circumstances, in-house productions can be done relatively cheaply. For example, the distributor may own or have access to a low-cost facility, or the producer may be able to hire staff on a long-term basis.

Local television stations were once the largest producers of in-house programming, turning out children's programs, talk and public affairs programs, magazine shows, documentaries, and remote coverage of all sorts. This is no longer the case, although some stations continue to provide locally-produced programs as a public service, or, in a small number of cases, because they continue to be financially successful. In Chicago, WGN's *Bozo the Clown* series, which debuted in the 1950s, still has a waiting list of several years for studio-audience tickets; in St. Paul, KSTP's *Good Company* remains popular; and so do Boston's *Good Day* on WCVB, Detroit's *Kelly & Company* on WXYZ, and Cleveland's *Morning Exchange* on WEWS. These are the exceptions, however. Most of the time slots once allotted to locally-produced daytime talk shows have been usurped by syndicated shows with bigger budgets and more star power; news magazine shows like Group W's *Evening Magazine* and *PM Magazine* have suffered a similar fate. In-house programming on most local television stations is now limited to the standard daily news programs and, if the station has the rights to cover a sports franchise, to sports coverage as well. (Local involvement in sports is rapidly shifting away from TV stations and toward regional cable sports networks, however.)

Basic cable and pay cable networks have depended heavily on in-house productions, frequently setting up entire studio and staff operations to take advantage of economies of scale. MTV produces its "VJ" segments in-house, Nickelodeon continues to produce its game shows in-house, and Lifetime produces many of its own talk and information programs. As cable matures, however, the role of outside production companies is growing. MTV and Nickelodeon, for example, both began with a schedule dominated by in-house productions and acquired programs; in time, each has commissioned outside production companies for programs.

In-house production is common in most major corporations, where taping regularly-scheduled information programs keeps a small to medium-sized staff of full-time employees busy. In some companies, this staff does every production, regardless of its size or importance. Most of these companies employ free-lancers or outside production companies to supplement the in-house staff, to handle workload overflow, and to work on productions that are beyond the capabilities of the in-house staff, facilities, or other company resources.

Even including the obvious fixed costs of staff and equipment, in-house productions appear to be low-cost ventures. A true evaluation, however, must take into account the project's hidden costs: use of part-time personnel employed by other departments, office space, supplies, equipment, telephone usage, insurance, and other items apparently provided at "no charge" to in-house production.

OUT-OF-HOUSE PRODUCTIONS

For a network or station, there are many advantages to producing out-of-house, the most obvious being the ability to produce many projects simultaneously. Typically, one program executive supervises several projects. Out-of-house productions provide programmers with a wide diversity of creative styles, and—particularly on the network level—with access to talented people who may be reluctant to commit themselves to any one organization.

Production Companies and Corporate Video

At the simplest level, doing out-of-house production involves hiring a producer and director, agreeing upon a production schedule and budget, and providing the necessary resources. This "one-shot" approach is appropriate for small-scale video productions (usually single-camera) like marketing tapes, video news releases, training materials, and speeches (for example, the company chairman's quarterly address to employees). The producer is usually paid a flat fee, with staggered payments: one-third on the first day of work, one-third on the first shoot day, and one-third on delivery of the finished product. A straight weekly fee is also common. On larger projects, the producer may be paid weekly, biweekly, or monthly for the run of the production schedule. Some producers own the equipment, but most of them rent what they need by the day, week, or month.

A larger project—a music video, a sophisticated marketing video, a full-scale training film, a corporate annual report, or a simple television series—requires more than one full-time person. Many small production companies specialize in these types of projects. Some full-service companies offer writing, producing, shooting, editing, and duplication; others concentrate on one or more aspects of production, and work closely with other vendors to complete the package. (These specialists may work directly with the client, or operate as subcontractors.)

Small production companies take many forms: a writer working with a producer/director, an editor working with a videographer, a team of producers or directors, or a collective of people who can do everything from write scripts to compose music to shoot and edit videotape. There is no fixed formula. Some companies consist of nothing more than two partners and a part-time secretary; others employ a half-dozen producers and regularly invest in the latest video equipment. Each of these companies, if successful, finds a niche and develops clients within it. One company, for example, specializes in videos for the automotive industries; another shoots news and news-magazine stories for syndicated television programs. Some companies combine computers and video for video walls, interactive kiosks, and touch-screens for museums, amusement parks, and point-of-purchase retail applications. Each niche has its own business cycle, so most specialized companies attempt to spread the workload over both busy and slow months. Specialty firms may also be unusually sensitive to fluctuations in the economy; if the computer business or the auto industry is having a rough year, then production companies in Silicon Valley or Detroit suffer the consequences.

Production Companies and Entertainment Programming

Entertainment programming is the magnet, the industry segment associated with fame and fortune. Small and medium-sized production companies find it difficult to compete with their larger-sized counterparts in the entertainment sector, but some of them succeed with more modest undertakings. They develop special types of projects (such as promotional campaigns or clip shows), or handle programs with unconventional marketing or financing schemes.

Most network and syndicated programs are produced by big production companies, many of them affiliated with motion picture studios. According to *Channels* Magazine's *1990 Field Guide*, the top companies each produce and/or distribute more than 500 hours of new programming each year. The largest suppliers are Walt Disney Productions, MCA TV, Warner Brothers Television (which includes Lorimar Television), and Paramount Television. These are followed by Columbia Pictures (including Merv Griffin Enterprises), Viacom, Twentieth Television, and New World Television, each supplying roughly 200 hours of programming per year. The output of Group W Productions, a Westinghouse Broadcasting Company, is slightly smaller. Hanna-Barbera and Cannell Distribution are successful production companies that have grown to the size of small studios. Smaller production companies include The Carsey-Werner Company (*The Cosby Show, Roseanne*), Witt-Thomas Productions (*The Golden Girls, Empty Nest*), and Dick Clark Productions (many specials, such as the American Music Awards).

Network, local, and (increasingly) basic cable schedules are filled with programs produced or co-produced by such companies. Besides the obvious clout that a large company brings to a deal, these companies provide something that few smaller entities can deliver: deficit financing. A network license fee rarely pays for the entire cost of production; on the contrary, it may only cover 50 percent of the total production budget. A successful program may play for two or three years before it generates significant profits from foreign markets, and it may take four years for the program to make money from domestic syndication. Only a production company with deep pockets can carry so sizable a deficit (see Chapter 25).

Deficits are not inevitable; some programs are made without them. Others are produced with foreign partners, or income from a pre-sale is used to cover production expenses. Still, the cash involved in producing any television series requires most smaller companies to secure a joint production agreement with a major production company, like a studio.

Although financial considerations are a significant factor, the television business is dominated by these larger players for other reasons as well. Warner, Paramount, Universal, and other studios have studio and post-production facilities; wardrobe, set, and casting departments; the marketing power needed to sell the programs; and the financial expertise to assure cash flow in spite of production deficits. They often have exclusive or "first look" arrangements with many of the top independent producers and production companies in L.A. No wonder the studios are sometimes called "program factories."

Each studio employs a team of executives who supervise the production of current programs and the development of new properties. Typically, a development executive will have strong ties to a network program department, often as a former employee. The development executive works closely with individual writers and producers in nurturing a property, and attends most or all of the network pitch meetings. A broadcast or cable network will either pass on the concept, or initiate a step development deal (see page 172). The deal itself is negotiated by an attorney working in the studio's business-affairs division. The writer and/or producer continues to work closely with the studio's development executive—through the rough scripts, polished drafts, and, if one is ordered, the pilot. When (and if) the network orders the series, the executive may become even more deeply involved with the project—joining the production staff, or working as the studio's production executive on the program—or else move on to another project. (In general, a large number of properties are in various stages of development at the major studios all at once.) This process is described in more detail in Chapter 21.

The Annual Cycles in Network, Syndicated, and Cable Programming

Although a new project can be pitched, piloted, and premiered at any time of the year, the networks have historically followed a seasonal cycle. A new property is pitched during the fall or winter; by spring, each network announces the programs that will be piloted. These pilots are produced in March and April, and tested with sample audiences. Series commitments are made by early summer, in time for production companies to supply the network with the first completed shows of the new season by early August. A complete season of programs is produced between August and March.

The syndication year is slightly different. Pitches are made during the spring and summer, with most pilots made in late summer or fall. Syndicators like to have their pilots ready for advance screenings to select station groups and advertisers before Thanksgiving. The first official showing of most programs planned for syndication is at the Association of Independent Television Stations (INTV) Convention in December; by the National Association of Television Program Executives (NATPE) Convention in January, many of the key deals are already signed. The next six months are spent clearing stations in as many markets as possible. Production usually begins in July or August, also for a September debut, with the shooting schedule completed sometime during the winter (depending upon the number of shows to be produced).

Public television is changing, having recently discarded the SPC system (see page 47). Under the new system, stations and producers present projects to PBS through the spring and summer, and financing decisions are made in the fall for programs that will air the following fall. Since public television programs almost always involve third-party funding (and, usually, interaction between an outside producer and a producing station), the development process actually begins at least a year prior to the PBS pitch. If PBS, and the closely-allied CPB, do not provide complete funding, then the producer must continue to seek funding from other sources, and the hunt for financing may even continue for some months into the year in which the production is scheduled to be seen.

Cable networks do not work on a strictly scheduled basis. Ideally, programmers like to start new shows in September, January, or March, but there is no hard and fast rule. As the cable networks continue to grow, however, they will probably focus on premiering new programs in September—in order to counter the considerable marketing thrust that the broadcast networks still mount at that time.

Production Staff

There are two types of staff on every television production. "Above-the-line" staff includes the creative and administrative people: the executives, producers, writers, director, cast, set designer, music composer, and so forth. "Below-the-line" refers to the facilities and technical people: engineers, construction crew, technical crew, camera operators, make-up artists, hair and wardrobe staff, editors, mixers, and so forth. The placement of musicians, graphic artists, and others who straddle the line is determined by the hiring company for its own convenience. The terms "above-the-line" and "below-the-line" date back to a style of accounting established during the Golden Age of Hollywood—"below-the-line" apparently refers to crew and facilities maintained as ongoing overhead items versus project-specific items that require special cash payment.

This chapter describes who does what in running a production. It is organized by titles, but titles can be misleading. Most of the titles described below can apply to several different functions, depending upon the type of program, the distribution channel, and tradition within the organization and the industry sector.

EXECUTIVE PRODUCER

Because the *executive producer* credit on a television production is the highest-ranking one, the title itself is the most overused—and misused—one in the industry. "Executive producer" refers to the business person most responsible for getting the series on the air—or arranging the majority of the production financing—or to the senior creative person on the project.

On a network series, the executive producer usually supervises all creative aspects of the program. The title is more often abused on a syndicated program, where marketing and financing schemes are often as important as (and sometimes more important than) the execution of the creative concept. It is not unusual to see a list of executive producers credited for a syndicated program, but it is unusual to find more than one or two of the people on that list who played an active role in actually producing the program. This situation occurs on occasion in cable television as well.

"Executive producer" is more clearly defined in local television. At a local station, the executive producer for entertainment programs reports to the program director, and supervises some or all original production. The executive producer in charge of news reports to the news director. The program director and news director are rarely the same person, except at small local stations.

In entrepreneurial ventures, like home video programs, the title of executive producer is taken by the person responsible for the financing and/or marketing, or is shared with a key creative person.

The duties of the executive producer generally include selection of senior staff members; approval of key performers; approval of script (and/or format); approval of technical facility; and approval of the business arrangements for all concerned. Since the executive producer is the senior manager, he or she devotes some percentage of time to people issues, though the day-to-day management of the staff is the responsibility of the producer. Some executive producers become more directly involved in one or more specific areas—such as casting, scripting, or deal-making—but the essence of the executive producer's job is supervision, not execution.

THE PRODUCER

The *producer* of a television program is the person responsible for the creative, logistic, budgetary, and technical aspects of a project or series. He or she reports to the executive producer, who effectively acts as the chairman of the board to the producer's president. The executive producer is concerned with the grand scheme, the producer, with day-to-day management. Some producers are concerned only with the creative aspects of production, and others are concerned only with logistics. These specialties are becoming quite common, not only on network series, but on programs intended for syndication and for other markets.

For a prime time network series, the producer may focus almost exclusively on the creative aspects of the production, with other staff members co-ordinating logistics. Many producers of prime time programs are also writers who shape the program's characters, storylines, and overall development through close supervision of other writers as well as direct involvement in casting decisions. In fact, a prime time series may have several producers, all working at different levels.

Senior producer is a means of elevating a producer to a higher level when the executive producer title is either inappropriate or unavailable.

Supervising producer is most often used on a network series, when an entire season's programs require large-scale coordination. A supervising producer is frequently concerned with logistics, schedules, and budgets, though the term may be applied to supervisors with primarily creative functions as well. The supervising producer takes charge of the series, while each episode may have its own producer(s).

A *line producer* is directly responsible for logistics, schedules, and budgets. Contributions to the creative effort are of secondary importance.

A *segment producer* is responsible for specific segments within a larger production.

Associate producer is another term that can be defined only within the context of a particular project or series. On a talk, game, or variety show, an associate producer may participate in the writing. On a talk show, an associate producer may be in charge of finding and scheduling ("booking") guests, and may supervise the resulting segments in the studio. On a magazine show, an associate producer may be a field producer—writing, directing, and editing stories. An associate producer on a network series is frequently in charge of post-production, but may also serve as the producer's point person in casting, working with writers, managing the budget and schedules, and so on. These duties are common for associate producers on variety shows, music and comedy specials, and information programs (such as home video how-to programs).

In its pure form, the job of associate producer entails assisting the producer, taking care of time-consuming details, and often supervising the other staff members. The associate producer is a liaison between senior and junior staff members, and between different departments (such as public relations and accounting).

The *production assistant* (PA) is a junior staff member. PA may be the first job for a newcomer, but many PAs are more experienced, and may be in line for associate producer jobs. A *production coordinator* is an upgraded production assistant, and may have some aspects of the associate producer's job. *Control room PA* is a more specialized job, and may be under the jurisdiction of the Director's Guild of America (DGA) in some situations. The control room PA logs tapes and time cues, and his or her duties may overlap with those of the associate director.

Agreements for Producers and Executive Producers

There are two key clusters of issues in every agreement for a producer or executive producer. The first is based on rendering services; the second is related to the creation of programs or program elements. Executive producer and producer agreements are typically two to ten pages long (more if a profit definition is involved), and tend to cover many details. Agreements with associate producers are briefer, detailing only the key points related to rights and services. Many production companies hire junior staff people without any written agreement at all, though a short memorandum detailing the key points of the business arrangement, and addressing the transfer of rights, is advisable.

The following items should be covered in all producing agreements. For the sake of convenience, the word "producer" will be used to include executive producer, producer, associate producer, and the other classifications listed above. The Appendix B11 checklist and the model agreement in Appendix B12 should also be consulted.

- The business relationship between the production company—or television station, or distribution company—and the producer. Is the producer an employee or an independent contractor? This distinction is important for purposes of tax liability, personal-injury insurance, unemployment insurance, workman's compensation, vesting in pension plans, and ownership of the proceeds of creative work. In short, an *employee* typically works on premises provided by the employer, under its direct supervision or control. An *independent contractor* works for himself or herself. Although he or she may work at an office or in a facility provided by the hiring company, this is usually a matter of convenience, not a condition of hiring. An independent contractor does not receive the typical employee benefits.

All of the creative efforts of an employee are considered to be a *work for hire*, whose copyright passes to the employer. In order for the creative work of an independent contractor to be considered a work for hire, it must be specifically described as such in a written work-for-hire agreement between the independent contractor and the hiring company.

The distinctions between employees and independent contractors are explained in greater detail in Chapter 38.

- A description of the services to be rendered by the producer. Such services may be stated in a general way, as in "the duties and obligations typically required of a producer of a major-market news program." The description can also be a long list of specific responsibilities followed by a catch-all phrase like "and all of the other duties typically required of a producer of a major-market news program." The best agreements provide a detailed list of the prospective employee's day-to-day responsibilities, but allow flexibility for personal growth.

- The degree of exclusivity. May the producer serve in a similar capacity on projects that are unrelated to the employer's programs? And may the producer serve in other capacities—as writer or director, for example—on other programs?

- Compensation—how much, and when it will be paid. Employees are usually paid weekly, biweekly, or twice a month; independent contractors are often paid semi-monthly or monthly. One popular alternative is linking partial payments to the project's schedule—an independent contractor might receive one-quarter of the total payment on signing the agreement, one-quarter on the first day of shooting, one-quarter on the start of editing, and one-quarter on delivery of the finished project. The formula varies, but the underlying philosophy is to pay the producer a reasonable wage while insuring his or her involvement through the end of the project. While it is clearly to the producer's advantage to front-load the payments, most agreements reflect a reasonable compromise.

- A description of the rights granted to the hiring company, not only with regard to the current project(s), but also projects in development. For example: if a producer begins development of a new project for a station while an employee of the station, the station will own all rights to the project unless some other arrangement is described in the agreement. Another example: if an associate producer develops a new idea while working on a one-shot, and the employer develops that idea into another project, then the producer will typically be guaranteed some involvement (like a combination of employment and profit participation) in the resulting project. Some hiring companies will not make commitments regarding future work, in effect dissuading employees and independent contractors from discussing new concepts with their employers.

- Who has the right of "final cut," or the right to declare a program complete. In some cases, a producer will have final artistic control; usually, though, the organization's management will retain this right. Related issues include control over marketing, distribution, and other business decisions.

- The on-screen credit to be received by the producer. This should be clearly described: not only the wording of the credit, but also the prominence and the placement of the credit (should it appear daily, weekly, on every episode, and so on).

- Representations, warranties, and indemnities. These parts of a producing agreement, often written in legalese, cover assurances that one party is giving to the other about originality and other legal issues. In the "Representations and Warranties" section, the producer states that he or she is free to enter the agreement, and that there are no agreements presently in effect that would affect his or her ability to perform the services described in the new agreement. The producer also confirms that any ideas brought to the project will be either original or in the public domain, and that any such ideas will not violate the rights of any other person or institution. The notion of rights here relates to copyrights and property rights as well as personal rights—the right to privacy, and protection from defamation, slander, and libel (see Chapters 18 and 19).

  Too many agreements are one-sided: the producer makes representations and warranties, but the hiring company does not. Ideally, both parties should present a comprehensive list of what they represent and warrant to one another. The concept of representations and warranties is discussed in greater detail on page 337.

  The "Indemnification" section that usually follows "Representations and Warranties" may include foreboding language; it provides both parties with clear financial remedies should any of the representations, warranties, or any other terms of the agreement be breached or proven untrue. This section is often quite technical and requires a lawyer's reading. In essence, "Indemnification" clauses detail who will pay the costs of defending against losses, and who will pay in the case of judgments that require damages. (For more about indemnities, see page 337.)

- Credits. Most agreements require the producer to allow the hiring company, and its licensees, to use the producer's name, biography, photograph, and so forth in the marketing of the program. In some instances, there is the right of the producer to remove his or her name from the program's credits, and from any related advertising or promotional materials.

- The right of the producer to be reimbursed for travel and entertainment expenses within a reasonable amount of time, usually up to 30 days after submission of an expense report. Such expenses may be limited by a process of pre-approval, or by budget parameters, or by company policies (employees may not be permitted to entertain one another, for example). Some companies will not reimburse items over $25 without a receipt.

THE DIRECTOR

A television director combines three essential assets: the ability to guide performers to their best work; the taste and discretion to compose and select the optimum visual presentation; and the technical know-how to supervise a crew of engineers and operators.

Although the specific responsibilities of the director's job vary depending upon the type of project, it is fair to say that most directors spend about half their time planning, and the other half either rehearsing, shooting, or editing.

The planning phase usually begins with a series of production meetings to determine technical requirements such as set and lighting design. The director will also interact with the cast and the performers.

On a situation comedy, the director typically works a five-day week. The first day is devoted to a script reading with cast members in the morning. In the afternoon, the director plans camera angles, frequently with the help of an associate director, and screens the edited version of the previous week's show. He or she spends the second day on the set, working with the performers. The third day is a camera rehearsal—most sitcoms are shot with three or four cameras—where performances and camera angles are integrated. The fourth day brings more rehearsal, and the recording of two (sometimes three) takes of the show. At this point, the director spends most of his or her time in the control room, offering performance comments only when necessary. The fifth day is devoted to screening and working with the editor to determine the best reading of each line in the script. Every director has his or her own style; some are more involved with editing than others.

A director of soap operas follows a substantially similar routine, though the amounts of time allotted to rehearsal and shooting are likely to be compressed in order to accommodate the need for five shows per week. (Several directors may be hired for a daily serial, each one preparing for two to seven days, then shooting for one.)

On a news program, the director's schedule is condensed to a single day, or, more accurately, a few hours prior to air plus the broadcast itself. The format of a news program is pre-determined, usually by the director working in concert with the producer, the news director, and a news consultant. Still, the director must review the entire script, screen as many of the edited videotape stories as possible, and prepare for any live interview segments.

Talk shows are generally recorded, or broadcast live, one per day, or, in a condensed schedule, perhaps two or even three per day. The director is typically paid a weekly salary through the season, or a fee per week of completed shows. If the job is under DGA jurisdiction (see below), then the director supervises the post-production as well; if the job is non-Guild, then the producer and director may work out their own agreements on this.

Game shows are usually recorded in batches of three to six half-hours per day, over a stretch of two to five days. The director may be hired per season or per week, or may be paid a flat rate per show or per working day.

Associate Director

Many television programs can be directed by one person. When direction involves more than three cameras and a small number of other cues (such as sound or lighting cues), the director is frequently assisted by an *associate director* (AD). The AD is responsible for all communication with videotape recording and playback facilities, and with departments that do not require the director's explicit creative attention, such as audio or videotape recorders/playback. The AD also times all segments, calls off countdowns to time cues, prepares logs of all audiotape and videotape recordings plus playback material, and maintains schedules.

Associate directors work on videotaped and live shows. Sometimes, when there is a great deal of real-time coordination, or when a production's tradition demands it, the AD is assisted by a control room production assistant.

"Assistant director" is a film term, and applies when a television program is shot on film. A film AD is in charge of the set; he or she issues call times for the cast and crew, prepares production reports (including actual time spent filming each scene, breaks, down-time due to equipment or personnel problems, and so on), and serves as the eyes of the production company on the set.

Director's Guild of America

The Director's Guild of America, or DGA, is a union for directors. The DGA has negotiated collective-bargaining agreements with the commercial networks and with those production companies that supply the networks with programming. A network or production company that is a signatory to a DGA agreement agrees to hire only DGA personnel to serve as directors, associate or assistant directors, control room production assistants, and stage managers. The DGA also has contracts with some suppliers to the syndication and cable markets, but there is no DGA agreement covering syndication in general, or basic cable. Production for these markets is frequently done by directors who are not members of the DGA.

A member of the DGA can only work for DGA signatories; to put it another way, union members can work only in union shops. Since there are many non-union opportunities in cable and home video, younger directors often choose to work there without becoming DGA members. (See page 344 for a general discussion of the role of unions in the television business.)

The following condenses the key points in the DGA Freelance Live and Tape Television Agreement. The DGA Basic Agreement that applies to motion picture production on film is similar in most spots.

- The director contributes to the overall creative effort, and should participate in the selection of key creative personnel. At the very least, the director should be informed of proposed decisions before they are finalized.
- The director shall receive minimum compensation as detailed in the agreement. A director of a network, prime time, hour-long dramatic program, for example, would receive a minimum of $21,542 for 15 days of work. A network, prime time variety hour series pays a minimum of $7,063 for 9 days; a prime time hour special pays $17,655 for 18 days. Similar rates are provided for other types of programs.
- When directing a pilot for a series, the director is entitled to additional compensation if the series is ordered.
- The director receives additional compensation for working on holidays and weekends.
- The director receives additional compensation for development services, for directing talent tests, for shooting underwater or in flight, and for other special situations.

- The director receives residuals for replays. For a network prime time program, the director receives 100 percent of the base rate. For plays on syndication, the first run pays 50 percent of the network base (or 40 percent of the non-network base if the program was originally produced for cable or syndication); the second run pays 40 percent of the network base (30 percent for non-network); and the scale works its way down to 5 percent for the thirteenth and each subsequent run. These numbers are provided only as rough figures; a detailed explanation of the current rates can be found in the DGA agreement.

- The production is required to pay fringe benefits on behalf of the director to the DGA. The amounts are as follows: $5^1/_2$ percent of gross salary for pension, plus 7 percent of gross salary for health and welfare. In addition, the director contributes $2^1/_2$ percent of gross compensation to the DGA.

- An insurance policy is required when the director works under dangerous conditions, such as underwater or in flight.

In theory, the standard DGA agreement should be sufficient as the contract between the hiring company and the director. In reality, a separate agreement is often advisable. The terms which must be addressed in a director's agreement are similar to the terms of a producer's agreement. The only significant difference, aside from the obvious description of services, is likely to be the DGA considerations outlined above—if the DGA agreement does apply.

PRODUCER-DIRECTOR HYPHENATES

A producer-director is one person who performs two jobs. From the perspective of the producer-director, the combination provides an unusual amount of control, and the flexibility to pursue the most enticing creative aspects of both jobs. The title, and the premium salary, are also appealing. From the perspective of the hiring company, a producer-director combination is a way to save money on two significant line items. The total paid to one individual is almost always less than the total that would be paid to two; sometimes, the combination can be hired for a premium of only 30 or 40 percent.

The *field producer*, one kind of producer-director hybrid, evolved with the use of portable video equipment. Single-camera production is more like simple filmmaking than traditional multi-camera television production—one person can produce, write, and direct a "field piece." In terms of hierarchy, a field producer is roughly equivalent to a segment producer, who in turn can be equal to or just above associate producer.

DGA rates and rules should be consulted when hiring producer-directors or field producers in Guild shops.

WRITER(S)

Chapter 21 describes the importance of the writer in the development of a television project. Most television programs require the services of at least one writer. When several writers are employed, a head writer often supervises the group.

The specific responsibilities of the television writer vary, depending upon the project and its requirements. A news writer may research a story, assemble and doublecheck the facts, and produce a work of journalistic substance; a news writer may also do little more than rewrite stories taken from wire services. Frequently, the job involves a little bit of both. A writer of variety programming—whether it's *Late Night with David Letterman* or *Sesame Street*—takes an active part in developing program segments and character interaction, then scripts the sequences with either finished dialogue or an outline. A writer of soaps is usually provided with a detailed storyline prepared by the producer, with the assignment to write dialogue for a particular episode or part of an episode. A writer of prime time comedy or drama usually submits a basic story outline, which is revised by the story editor and by the program producers; a first and second draft script follow, with a polishing typically included in the work agreement with the writer.

Some writers function as staff members, or employees; others work free-lance as independent contractors, providing works for hire. Even independent work is usually acquired by the production company.

The Writers Guild of America

The Writers Guild of America (WGA) is a union that represents approximately 10,000 professional writers working in motion pictures, television, and radio, but not commercial advertising. (See page 344 for a discussion of the role of unions in the television business.) The WGA negotiates agreements with the networks, syndication companies, and other entities involved in hiring writers to create television programming. When a company becomes a signatory to the WGA, it agrees to the terms of the Minimum Basic Agreement (MBA), which requires that all writers hired by the company are members of the WGA. When a writer becomes a member of the WGA, he or she cannot write for a company that is not a signatory to the MBA.

To become a signatory, a company simply contacts the WGA and requests an application. A new company may be required to post a bond prior to employing any writers. When a writer is hired, payments are made to the writer, with a pension and health contribution paid to the WGA's plans.

To become a member of the WGA, a writer must have an agreement with a signatory for work. (Broadcast companies tend to be signatories; basic cable, home video, and syndication companies are often not.) Upon signing the agreement, the writer then has 30 days to join the WGA. The initial dues are $1,000 for WGA/East and $1,500 for WGA/West, but identical services are provided to writers on both coasts. Members are required to pay $50 per year for dues, plus 1¾ percent of gross compensation related to WGA contracts (¼ percent is also placed in a strike fund, so that members may borrow interest-free in case of a strike).

The following are the key elements of the WGA agreement:

- Minimum rates for the writing of a story, first draft teleplay, and final draft teleplay. These rates are based on the length of the program, and whether it airs in prime time or on a network. Additional rates are quoted for rewrite and polish; for plot outline, back-up script, show format, and narration; and for a show bible (a complete explanation of the history and characters on a series). If the program is produced for pay TV or home video, and if it is in the style that normally airs in network prime time, then the network prime time rates apply.

- Rerun compensation. Calculating these payments can become complicated, and readers are advised to refer to the Writers Guild of America Basic Agreement, or the Schedule of Minimums, for a complete explanation and the latest information. In the 1988 agreement, compensation to a writer for each prime time network rerun (there are customarily two) was 100 percent of the original payment. Each rerun outside network prime time was payable based on a sliding scale: 50 percent of the applicable minimum if initially shown on a network, or 40 percent otherwise, for the first non-network rerun; 40/30 percent for the second run; 25 percent for the third; 25 percent for the fourth; and so on, down to 5 percent for the thirteenth and each subsequent run.

  Compensation for other types of programs are similar in approach, but different in numbers: check the current Basic Agreement for details. Residuals and re-use fees are also paid for replays on basic cable, for home video releases, and for foreign runs.

- Compensation for writers hired on a weekly basis, who work as staff members.

- The minimum rate at which a production company, network, or distributor may purchase an existing work from a professional writer (for example, a WGA member). The minimum for options is 5 percent for the first 180 days, and 10 percent for each period of 180 days thereafter.

- Additional compensation for a writer if a sequel is created based on his or her work—or if a character that first appeared in his or her work becomes the central character in a spin-off series or appears in other episodes.
- Payment rates, and a required number of writers, for variety shows—including rates for sketches.
- Payment rates for quiz and audience participation programs on both network and syndication; for serials other than prime time (for example, soap operas); and for religious programs, documentaries, and news programs.
- The requirement that the hiring company pay 6 percent of the writer's gross compensation to the WGA pension fund, plus 6 percent of the writer's gross compensation to the WGA health and welfare fund.
- Rules regarding working hours and conditions, travel, and notice prior to termination.
- Rules regarding appropriate credits. These rules are especially important, because they may trigger specific residual payments, or lead to a "separation of rights," whereby a writer who originates the project can hold back certain rights for himself or herself.

WRITER HYPHENATES

Since the writer is so critical to the creative development of a television project, many writers follow a natural inclination toward greater involvement in the production—as a producer, director, or, in some cases, performer.

The producer-writer is common in the Los Angeles prime time community, where good writers are highly valued, and where they are frequently given the opportunity to stretch their creative muscles. In the best of circumstances, a producer-writer molds a series and its characters with special insight; in the worst, the producer-writer can be a difficult hindrance to efficient production, power placed in the wrong hands. Some producer-writers concentrate on writing (and rewriting the work of others), wielding the producer's power only when needed to win a creative point. Others concentrate on rewrites, or supervise performers or a writing staff without generating original scripts on their own. Every situation is different.

The writer-director is doing two discrete jobs. In the office and through the planning stages, he or she concentrates on writing; in the studio or on the soundstage, directing requires total attention, and the writing is either delayed or scheduled for off-hours. As with the producer-director, two fees are paid, to the DGA and the WGA;

non-Guild hyphenates are paid a fee that is likely to be less than a full writing fee and a full directing fee combined.

The writer-performer is frequently found in comedy and in news. Many successful comedians have worked on the writing staff of comedy programs, making their first television appearances playing characters that they had written themselves. Similarly, many news writers have evolved into news reporters. A writer-performer is almost always paid a full fee for each service rendered—except in home and business video, and for other smaller-scale projects.

28 | Performers

Most television performers are members of one or both of AFTRA (the American Federation of Television and Radio Artists) and SAG (the Screen Actors Guild). AFTRA's jurisdiction is essentially videotape and live productions, as well as radio programs and commercials produced on videotape; SAG's jurisdiction is television programs produced on film, film commercials, and theatrical motion pictures. In short, AFTRA is the relevant union if the program is live or on tape, and SAG is the relevant union if the program is shot on film. AFTRA has local chapters in most of the top 30 television markets. SAG works out of about 25 regional offices, including New York, Los Angeles, Chicago, Boston, and Miami. (See page 344 for a general discussion of the role of unions in the television business.)

Nearly all commercial television productions are made with AFTRA or SAG members. The exceptions include productions made in the smallest broadcast markets; some programs on basic cable networks; some corporate video; some made-for-home-video productions; some music video; and most educational video. The vast majority of performers with the skill and talent required for successful on-camera performance are members of AFTRA, SAG, or both. Although producers are loathe to admit it, the rules of these unions are not too burdensome. What producers do tend to dispute, however, is how the payment of residuals is becoming more complex and expensive as distribution markets continue to evolve.

AFTRA AGREEMENT BASICS

It is difficult to discuss the provisions of a "basic" AFTRA agreement because there is no single agreement; instead, there are separate agreements between AFTRA and the commercial broadcast networks, public television, local television, and other entities. Copies of these agreements are generally available from AFTRA. There are some differences in work rules, but these separate agreements vary most in terms of minimums, residual schedules, and annual escalations. Each AFTRA agreement is quite complex.

For purposes of broad explanation, this section outlines the key points of the AFTRA network agreement. It should prove useful in understanding the mechanics of all AFTRA agreements.

- Each agreement includes wage tables for specific types of performers. Some of the charts simply list a minimum fee for a particular type of program and activity. Sportscasters, for example, receive $781 per event on network television (not including any pre-or post-game shows), or $1,984 per week; that payment includes up to seven events in the same sport, or one week's broadcasting of Olympic games. Other wage tables are more complicated. An off-camera announcer speaking more than ten lines, for example, receives fees based on the length of the program. If the program is 15 to 30 minutes long, the fee is $239, and pays for three rehearsal hours during one day, with a two-hour minimum session and a three-hour minimum daily call. Extra time costs $17 per hour. For multiple performances in the same calendar week, on the same show, the announcer receives between 25 percent and 200 percent extra. The numbers for other types of performers vary, but the basic structure is common for most of the wage tables.

- The producing company is required to contribute to AFTRA's pension and welfare fund. The contribution due is 10½ percent of the performer's gross compensation. ("Gross" includes the amount actually paid to the performer before deductions—plus overtime payments, commissions paid to third parties like agents, fees paid for the use of a performer's own wardrobe, and related subsidies.) There is no ceiling for pension and welfare payments in the AFTRA agreement.

- The performer must be given notice of the part to the played, the place of rehearsal, and the number of guaranteed days of performance (if any) not less than 24 hours in advance of the first reading or rehearsal session. Changes in the schedule must be provided 24 hours in advance as well.

- When work is completed, payment is due no later than the Thursday following the last working week. Specific rules apply for performers who are working for extended periods of time. Small penalties apply for late payments ($4 per day to a maximum of $120; weekends and holidays are not included).

- Residual compensation is due within 10 days of the first network re-broadcast, or within 60 days of a non-network re-broadcast. Compensation for foreign plays must be paid within 90 days of the first broadcast of the program.

- Performers receive a 5-minute rest period during each hour of rehearsal. There must be a 12-hour break between the end of work on one day and the start of work on the next (a penalty is charged if the break is less than 12 hours). Meal breaks are 70 minutes long (60 minutes, plus 5-five minute breaks at the start and finish). Performers working under hazardous conditions are paid an additional $100 per program.

- If a performer is paid over scale, he or she may agree to deduct overtime payments from the over-scale total—but only if this agreement is made at the time of the original contract.
- Understudies receive the same minimum scale rate as the performer for whom they are understudying.
- Performers are not usually paid for interviews and auditions of reasonable length, but they are entitled to payment for excessive time (e.g., over one hour). If the audition is a more formal affair, then the performer receives half the program rate.
- Performers are typically paid a wardrobe allowance when asked to appear in their own clothing. For regular wardrobe, the fee is $10 per outfit, and can go as high as $25 for formal evening wear.
- Singers and dancers are entitled to additional monies for "step-outs" (instances in which the performer steps out of the chorus line or group to sing and dance).
- Performers who double (play more than one role) may be entitled to additional compensation on certain types of programs.
- Performers must be advised of scenes involving nudity, and must approve such appearances in advance.
- A performer who warms up an audience is entitled to a percentage of the applicable program fee.
- If a performer's photograph is used on a program, but the performer does not appear in the program, he or she is entitled to $25 for each episode in which the photo appears.
- A performer who appears in remote telecasts may be entitled to a supplementary payment.
- A producer can require a performer's exclusive services only under certain conditions (e.g., a specific level of guaranteed compensation).
- For an ongoing series, a specific number of weeks' notice must be given if a program is canceled.
- If a program is canceled, the performers are entitled to payment for all hours spent rehearsing prior to the posting of the cancellation notice.
- Performers working on daytime serials or other ongoing series are entitled to two weeks of vacation time with pay if employed for less than five years, and three weeks, if employed longer. Performers who work on serials receive a premium for work on holidays.

- Performers are entitled to a per diem of $30 per day when working more than 20 miles from the "broadcast center" of New York, Chicago, Los Angeles, or Washington, D.C. Automobile travel is reimbursed in accordance with company policy; if there is no company policy, then the performer receives 30 cents per mile (at least $3 per day) for using his or her own car. The producer is required to provide a $200,000 accidental death and dismemberment travel-insurance policy for each performer.

- Travel time is considered work time—the hours spent traveling to or from a location are counted as rehearsal hours. If the performer's lodgings are more than 30 minutes from the location, then this travel time is also considered to be rehearsal time.

- A schedule of residual payments details payments due for reuses of the program in a variety of media. On network replays, the performers receive 75 percent of the applicable minimum plus 20 percent of rehearsal and doubling fees. All other replays are paid on a sliding scale (replays 1 and 2, 75 percent; 3, 4, and 5, 50 percent; 6, 10 percent; 7 and each subsequent play, 5 percent). Foreign residuals are based on regions of the world. Area 1, which essentially includes all of the U.K., is the most lucrative, at 25 percent of the original program fee; Area 2 (most of the rest of Europe) is 10 percent; Areas 3, 4, and 5 constitute the rest of the world (except the U.S. and Canada), and plays in these countries pay the performer 5 percent of his or her original fee.

- Performers receive 2.5 percent of producer's gross receipts for videocassettes and videodiscs on the first $1 million, and 3 percent thereafter. The monies are distributed pro-rata, with a 2-to-1 ratio between principal performers and other players.

- AFTRA will arbitrate conflicts with producing companies on behalf of its members.

SAG AGREEMENT BASICS

As with AFTRA, there are several types of SAG agreements—for commercials, for network programs, for motion pictures, and so forth. Once again, readers are encouraged to review an up-to-date version of the relevant agreement carefully, since there is a wide range of work rules and rate structures involved.

The SAG network agreement differs from the AFTRA network agreement in several ways:

- The pension and health benefit is based on $11\frac{1}{2}$ percent of gross compensation, including original earnings and residuals, but excluding meal fees and rest-period penalty fees. There is also a ceiling per program on these contributions.

- There are detailed provisions for optioning a performer's services.
- There is more detail than in the AFTRA agreement on hiring ongoing performers for episodic television, and the contract is arranged so that these details are easy to find. A section called "One Hour Programs," for example, sets forth the number of episodes that must be guaranteed, the overall time span in which these episodes can be produced without further payment, the number of weeks of work included without further payment, the minimum payment per episode, and the minimum layoff (a layoff is an interim when the performer's services are not required during the shooting period).
- Meal periods run 60 minutes; meals must be scheduled every 6 hours.
- The minimum per diem is $42, but the producer may deduct $12 when catering for each large lunch or dinner.
- When shooting on location, and under certain conditions, the 12-hour rest period may be reduced to 10 hours (but not every night).
- Penalties for rest-period violations are one day's salary, to a maximum of $950.
- In New York, the area considered "on location" is larger than the 20-mile radius in the AFTRA agreement. The SAG agreement defines "New York" as any area within 30 miles of Columbus Circle.
- For nude scenes, prior written consent of the performer is required. Also, the set must be closed, and no still pictures may be taken without the performer's prior written consent.

CASTING

There are several sources of performers for television productions.

Talent Agencies

A talent agency is a company that specializes in representing performers, although many agencies represent producers, writers, directors, and other key creative people as well. Most successful performers working on the national scene are represented by a large agency—the William Morris Agency, ICM, and CAA are the biggest. There are also smaller boutique agencies that either specialize in particular formats (game shows, daytime drama, sports, news) or offer a level of personal service that a larger agency rarely delivers to most of its clients.

Although the business arrangements vary with specific performers, an agency typically collects a 10 percent commission on gross earnings for every job within the entertainment industry—whether the agency arranges for the work or not. The performer's paycheck is sent to the agency, which deducts a commission and issues a new check to its client. If the job is not within the entertainment industry, and was not arranged by the agency—hosting a presentation at an automotive industry trade show, for example—the performer is normally paid directly, without agency involvement.

Contrary to the dreams of many performers, agencies do not usually seek out work for their clients. Instead, agencies are responsive to the needs of the marketplace. When producers, networks, or advertising agencies are casting for a program, they usually call the larger agencies as a matter of course. The smaller agencies do their best to keep up with what's happening, and to stay on the active list of various casting entities.

Some well-known performers work without an agent, instead employing an attorney to negotiate fees on their behalf. In most cases, the attorney earns an hourly rate for services. Some high-powered Los Angeles attorneys take a commission of 5 percent or more in addition to, or in lieu of, an hourly fee. (A more detailed discussion of the roles of agents, lawyers, and business managers appears in Chapter 29.)

Photographs, Resumes, and Videotapes

A photograph is a kind of calling card for a performer. The standard format for performer's photographs is a recent 8 × 10 inch glossy photo, with name printed below the photo. On the back is a printed resume or list of performance credits, union affiliations, and contact information (address and phone numbers for agency, for home, and for answering service).

Videotapes can be effective resume tools, if the casting person takes the time to screen them. It is simply faster to scan a pile of photographs; performers whose photos are promising may be evaluated on videotape, but more often, an in-person meeting or audition is the first step. Some types of productions (for example, local news shows) make extensive use of videotapes.

Interviews and Auditions

As a prerequisite to getting a job, performers expect to be interviewed and auditioned, sometimes several times.

An interview generally runs under 30 minutes (often, under 15 minutes), and offers the producer or casting director an opportunity to speak informally with the candidate. The session is useful in learning whether the candidate can ad-lib, how the candidate presents himself or herself, how he or she responds to others, and, to a certain extent, the candidate's personal interests and motivations. Under the showbusiness veneer, a casting interview is a job interview, and subject to the same restrictions and standards that rule all employment proceedings. Questions about age, religious affiliation, marital status, race, and color should not be asked; to do so may bring about a complaint and an investigation of company hiring practices.

An audition may be held in addition to, or in place of, an interview. The audition typically requires the performer to read lines, or to ad-lib within a structured situation. For example, a news reporter may be required to read a news report aloud (in an office, on videotape, or live on the air), or to prepare a sample story; a sportscaster might be recorded doing play-by-play at an event. Some auditions require the candidate to interact with other performers.

Often, the first round of auditions is casual, and does nothing more than eliminate the least likely candidates. It may conducted by an associate producer, who reports the most promising candidates to the producer, executive producer, and network executive(s). A director may be actively involved in the first round, or may join in as serious contenders are selected; this depends on the type of project and on personal style. A second round of auditions is usually more intensive, and yields between three and five finalists. A third round of auditions, now conducted with great attention to detail, allows the producer and others involved in the process to make a final decision. There may be more rounds, or fewer, depending upon the situation. If a substantial amount of work is required during the auditions, AFTRA or SAG may require that the performer(s) be paid.

Negotiating the Performance Agreement

Producers must balance two key issues when hiring talent: working with budget limitations, and attracting the best possible performers to the project. AFTRA and SAG prescribe minimum fees for performers working in productions within their jurisdictions. In non-union cases, market conditions unofficially dictate rates, subject to minimum wage regulations. Many performers, particularly those with experience, want to be paid more than the minimum fee. In many such cases, the performer sets a day rate for his or her services—this rate is usually negotiable, particularly if employment is for an extended period.

Before the producer tests anyone, or sits down to final auditions, it is important that a *pre-test option* is negotiated. A pre-test option fixes the basic terms of the agreement should the performer be successful in the audition. Without such an option, the network or distributor may "fall in love" with a particular performer, and insist that the producer deliver that performer regardless of price. That situation can place the performer in control, and a savvy agent can drive the price very high. A pre-test option that caps the performer's price is essential protection for the producer.

For well-known performers, or performers with strong agency or legal representation, the producer and the agent may spend hours, days, even weeks negotiating the fine points of daily/weekly/per-show salary, travel arrangements, profit participation, on-screen billing, use and appearance of the performer's name in advertising, and other such details.

A *letter agreement* is an appropriate form of contract for hiring the performer. This agreement should set forth the dates that the performer will be needed, the fees that will be paid, residuals, and so on. SAG and AFTRA have standard forms for certain kinds of hiring (see Appendixes B16 and B17).

A more formal agreement may be prepared for high-paid performers, or for anyone working on a project where lengthy contracts make good business sense. Appendix B12 is a typical short-form agreement for services, adaptable to the performer context.

Non-Union Employment

Most established television performers are members of AFTRA and SAG, and most major producing organizations are union signatories as well. However, many production companies, home video companies, business video companies, and cable networks are not signatories to agreements with the performance unions. The reason is basically the cost of benefit payments and residuals. Some of these companies are poorly-equipped, both financially and administratively, to pay on-going residuals, while others simply want a more favorable arrangement. A non-union shop can hire anyone it pleases because it is not beholden to an agreement that says otherwise. A union performer, however, is in violation of his or her agreement when working for a non-signatory within the union's jurisdiction, and may be subject to a penalty or, upon repeated offenses, the loss of union membership.

In certain situations, both AFTRA and SAG have negotiated "one-shot" short-term agreements covering particular projects, allowing a non-signatory company to hire union performers. AFTRA and SAG have been among the most reasonable unions in television, but even their flexibility has its limits.

The respective jurisdictions of AFTRA and SAG are limited only to American productions, resulting from deals made in the U.S. If the employment is purely foreign, then the producer may hire the performer outside the union agreement. There are grey areas defining the concept of "purely foreign"—if the production company is legitimately based abroad, and the project is produced abroad, then the production is probably foreign. Producers have been known to disguise a production as foreign in order to save on fees, withhold residuals, or avoid certain work rules.

WORKING WITH PERFORMERS

The performer is expected to do his or her job by following the instructions of the producer and director—who represent the production's management and owners—regardless of whether this expectation is explicitly worded in a contract. Most performers recognize this authority, take instructions, add their own creativity, and work hard to please their employers. The ideal situation is a lively give-and-take, with each party respectful of the other's role, but with a certain challenge and spice thrown in so that each does the best possible work. Ultimately, the performer should be comfortable with the words, the style, and the presentation.

Conversely, a strong performer matched with a needy director or production team can head off problems and present a polished product despite poor preparation, less-than-skillful direction, or troublesome production technique. To put this another way, experience counts for much in the television business, and a good performer can save a production.

Some performers, however, display a defiant attitude that can undermine the director's ability to complete the program or the producer's promises to a client.When there are problems, the performer can either (1) do the best he or she can under the circumstances, (2) fight the director and do what he or she believes is right, regardless of consequences, (3) complain to the powers-that-be, or 4) leave. In rare instances, he or she may attempt to have the offending producer or director fired, or try to take over. Both of these actions are predicated on the belief that the audience strongly associates the performer with the program, and that producers, directors, and writers are dispensable. The performer may win these battles, particularly if the producer feels that he or she has no choice—but will, in the process, acquire a reputation for "trouble."

Working with Celebrities

Celebrities live by special rules—even though being famous and being a talented television performer are not always synonymous, and even though celebrity alone does not guarantee that a given performer is well-suited for a particular role or project. Celebrities are typically paid considerably more than minimum union scale, and, depending on the project, may receive a profit participation as well. Many celebrities are accustomed to special treatment and perks as part of the deal.

With few exceptions, celebrities are represented by agents, lawyers, or managers, who negotiate on their clients' behalf. The negotiation usually begins with a producer's offer, typically countered by a statement of the performer's going rate. Once the basic price is set, the negotiation moves on to profit participation(s) (if relevant), perks, and working conditions. First-class airfare is required in the union agreements, but many celebrities request additional tickets for family members or other traveling companions. Hotel accommodations and per diems may be subject to the same sorts of requests; these are generally honored if the expense is not too great.

In the best of circumstances, working with a celebrity brings the staff and crew to its professional best. The presence of a celebrity on the set also forces an attentiveness to the schedule, since well-known performers are available only for brief time periods. Sometimes, working with a celebrity is a disappointment, especially when a huge ego is part of the package. In these cases, difficulties can be anticipated and minimized by speaking with other producers and directors who have worked with the performer in the past.

Working with Children

There are several key issues that must be considered when hiring young performers. To start with, every state has its own child-labor laws; these should be reviewed early in the planning of a production. The following are key provisions common to most child-labor laws.

- As a general matter, minors cannot be hired for any activity that may be hazardous or detrimental to the minor's moral development. This is an area open to interpretation; the state agency will not issue a work permit if it believes that there may be a problem.
- If the work interferes with ongoing school education, then a teacher must be hired, and hours must be allotted to classroom work. This is not a problem for infrequent short-term hires; the parent or guardian simply decides whether to take the child out of school to work.
- A parent or guardiar. must be present while the child is working. For instance, the California code requires that the parent or guardian be present within sight or sound for all minors under 16 years old.
- The work permit can be revoked if the commissioner or other supervising authority detects wrong-doing or abuse of rights or privileges.
- For each age group, there is usually a maximum amount of time allowed at the work place, a maximum number of working hours allowed, and a minimum number of rest, recreation, and education hours. Travel time may be considered part of the working day. In California, for instance, children aged 2 to 6 are allowed up to 6 hours at the work place with up to 3 hours of working time and not less than 3 hours of rest, recreation, and education. Children aged 9 to 16 can be at the workplace for up to 9 hours, and can work up to 5 hours on school days or 7 hours on days off, with 3 hours minimum of schooling and 1 hour minimum of rest and recreation.

Unless they are ratified by a court, most ongoing agreements for services are voidable by the minor at any time. In most (but not all) states, a parent or guardian can sign a sample release form on behalf of a minor (see below). Children are paid in amounts equal to what an adult would earn in comparable roles. Payments are made to a parent or guardian, who disburses monies to the benefit of the child. In some states, room and board can be deducted by the parent or guardian as are professional expenses such as travel, clothing, and legal and accounting fees. Essentially, the parent or guardian becomes the trustee for the child, and is held to standards common for fiduciary relationships.

Working with Unpaid Performers

Many of the people who appear on television are unpaid: they are interviewed, they appear in the background in entertainment and news footage, or they are the subjects of news reports.

Most people who appear on television do so of their own volition. The majority of these unpaid performers are willing to cooperate with the television establishment, and will generally agree to sign whatever documents are necessary to assure an appearance.

The Release Form

A release form (see Appendix B3) is a type of contract, and it deals with three types of rights, described briefly below, and in detail in Chapter 19.

Any creative expression is usually the property of the creator—in this case, the person signing the release form. In essence, this is a matter of copyright (see Chapter 18).

The rights of privacy and publicity are the rights to control the commercial use of a personal likeness or other identifying characteristics. If uses beyond the original program are contemplated, these rights should be specifically released.

The right against being libeled or slandered gives redress against someone making assertions that are untrue and harmful to the reputation of another person. Under the U.S. Constitution, anyone is allowed to be wrong in such assertions, provided that he or she did not act with negligence with respect to a private person, or with malice or reckless disregard of the truth with respect to a public person.

A typical release form always contains an affirmative grant of rights. It may also contain representations and warranties and a preventative grant.

The *affirmative grant* says that in exchange for good and valuable consideration, the unpaid performer grants the right to record and exploit his or her image, and to exploit his or her name and persona. Typically, the right is granted in perpetuity, for all uses and all media anywhere in the world—not only in the production itself, but also anything connected with advertising and publicity. With such a grant, the producer can exploit programs including the unpaid performer at its sole discretion.

The *representation and warranties* section, if present in the form, includes a promise that nothing said by the unpaid performer will be libelous or will otherwise violate the rights of any third party, and that the statements are free of claims.

The *preventative grant* or waiver says that the person who signs the agreement will not make any claims against the producer on issues of copyright, privacy, publicity, defamation, or for any other cause.

Release forms are advisable whenever any unpaid performer speaks on a television production, particularly outside of a news show or other factual context of public interest. For those who appear but do not speak, discretion and circumstances serve as a guide. Members of a studio audience should be ticketed; the use of the ticket is a transaction that shows the intent to participate on the part of every audience member, and a statement to this effect may even be printed on the ticket. People who are part of a crowd observing a public event, or the staging of an event for a television show, may be used in context in cut-away shots. But if anyone will be appearing prominently, it is advisable to secure a signed release form.

29 Agents, Attorneys, and Business Management

A substantial industry has been built by agents, lawyers, accountants, and other specialists who advise and act on behalf people of working in television. The governing notion is that many creative people are poor businesspeople, and that the business professional can help generate more money while untangling contractual problems.

AGENTS

By definition, an agent is someone authorized to act on behalf of someone else, the principal. The law of agency is a law of delegation of power. In television, and in the entertainment business at large, an agent is a representative who negotiates deals on behalf of clients, and, under the best of circumstances, finds work for these clients as well.

Agents are extremely common in some areas of the television business, and virtually non-existent in others. They are an important part of the commercial network production system, and agents actively participate in most important talent agreements for network, syndicated, pay cable, and local television productions. Agents are not part of the corporate or business video industries, except when high-priced talent (such as a well-known director, composer, or writer) is involved. The situation in home video and basic cable is similar. Agents tend to specialize, so a performer who appears on daytime drama may have one agent for that activity, and another—frequently, but not always, at the same agency—for voice-over work. This is often the case for writers and directors as well.

The largest agencies have offices in Los Angeles and New York, and, frequently, smaller ones in Chicago, London, and several other major cities around the world. The William Morris Agency, ICM, and CAA are among the most powerful agencies, representing performers of every description, as well as writers, directors, producers, scenic designers, and other creative personnel. Their domain is not limited to television—larger agencies maintain literary, motion picture, theatrical, and even corporate departments.

Smaller agencies may devote more attention to individual clients, particularly the lesser-knowns. Some agencies specialize in particular markets, such as news anchors and reporters, juvenile performers, or soap opera performers. Others offer full service, from book publishing to legitimate theater, usually with a concentration of power in one or two areas.

Agencies and creative people can work together for specific periods of time or on a per-project basis. For newcomers, an agreement to work together on a single project can sometimes be arranged; if the project is a success, the agency expects the creative person to sign up as a long-term client. Contracts generally run one to three years, and may be limited to only one type of representation—for performance but not for writing, for example. The agency receives the client's paychecks; deducts a commission of 10 or 15 percent of all income, including fees, royalties, and profit participation; and pays its client. If the client finds his or her own work, the agent is still entitled to the commission, under the terms of most agency agreements.

When an agency works closely with a producer—helping to sell the program to a distributor and supplying many of its own clients to the cast and staff—then the agency is said to be "packaging the project" (see page 173). For such packages, the agency receives 5 percent or more of the total project revenues, but does not deduct commissions from the clients' individual income.

An agency typically negotiates all terms and conditions of every agreement, from fees and profit participation to screen credit. After the basic terms have been hammered out by the individual agent, the agency's attorneys attend to the details.

Regulation of Agents and Other Representatives

Many states regulate the activities of agencies, either as a part of the regulation of employment agencies in general, or under rules specific to the entertainment business. Under such regulation, the agent must register and obtain a license. Failure to do so can lead to civil and even criminal penalties, including the cancellation of the agreements for representation and the refunding of fees previously taken. These laws also generally restrict the fees that the agent can charge to his or her client. Talent agents are not the only ones to whom these regulations apply; a manager or other representative who performs agent-like functions may be under the jurisdiction of the agent rules as well.

In New York, Article II of the General Business Law concerns licensing of all employment agencies, within which are special rules applicable to a "theatrical employment agency." A theatrical employment agency includes any person or company that procures, or attempts to procure, employment or engagements for motion pictures, radio, television, and other categories of the entertainment business. As for the manager-as-agent, the statute specifically excludes from its definition of a theatrical agency "the business of managing such entertainments, exhibitions or performances, or the artists or attractions constituting the same, where such business only incidentally involves the seeking of employment therefor." Although the words "only incidentally involves" are fairly restrictive, this provision at least recognizes that the activities of an agent and those of a manager inevitably overlap.

A New York theatrical agency must register with the state and file a great deal of information about itself, its personnel, and its business premises. It must post a $5,000 bond and file copies of its standard agreements. There is a limitation on the maximum fees that the agency can charge: 10 percent of the compensation payable to the talent (orchestra, concert, and opera fees can go up to 20 percent). Failure to comply is a misdemeanor punishable in some cases by up to a year in jail, and can lead to the return of fees.

In California, under Chapter 4 of the Labor Code, a "talent agent" is one who tries "to procure employment or engagements for an artist or artists." "Artists" include performers, writers, directors, cinematographers, composers, lyricists, arrangers, and other professionals in the entertainment industry, including specifically the television business. The manager problem is addressed in three ways. First of all, the regulations do not cover the activity of procuring recording contracts. Second, a manager can help an agent do his job, at the agent's initiative. Third, there is a one-year limit on bringing claims that a manager has acted as an unlicensed agent.

Other California requirements follow the normal pattern of registration and oversight. The law requires that a fee schedule be filed with the state and conspicuously posted, but there are no set maximums. Form contracts must be filed and approved, and a $10,000 bond is required. Civil penalties are available, but an agency's failure to obtain a license is not subject to criminal punishment.

Even when they do not have problems under the specific talent-agency laws, managers, attorneys, and other artist representatives generally share with agencies fiduciary duties in their relationships with their clients. Fiduciary duties require that the representative act with strict probity and avoid conflicts of interest. While the representative is allowed to earn an appropriate fee, it may not use its relationship with the client to obtain benefits for itself at the client's expense.

The various talent guilds, and performer unions like AFTRA and SAG, usually have their own restrictions on the activities of agents, including caps on the fees which can be charged. There is frequently a specific form of agency contract which the union requires to be used.

ATTORNEYS

Attorneys have two principal roles in television: to negotiate and document deals, and to "clean up messes."

Attorneys are usually paid by the hour, and most will be happy to allow the client to set the working parameters. Some clients are competent deal-makers, who consult the attorney as they plan the terms, and remain in contact as problems crop up during the negotiation. The lawyer may then draft the agreement from a basic memorandum of terms written by the client, or the lawyer may draft the entire agreement from information gathered at a meeting or telephone conversation. Alternatively, the lawyer may be asked to review an agreement drafted by the other party in the deal. In each of these situations, the client controls the amount of work done by the lawyer, thereby limiting the number of hours and the resulting legal bill.

Clients may also choose to assign the entire job to the attorney, from structuring the deal through negotiation, drafting, and reviewing the agreement. The lawyer works on his or her own schedule, contacting the client to review the key points of the deal. This is a more costly technique, but it frees up the client to do what he or she does best. Such work may be done on a flat-fee basis, but only under circumstances which suggest minimal risk for the attorney and the law firm.

The "messes" to which attorneys attend generally involve three areas: contracts, right clearances, and finance. Contracts are not only made, they are sometimes bent and broken—an attorney can offer strategies for dealing with breached promises, and usually works with the other party (or its lawyers) to reach a compromise solution.

Rights matters are best dealt with before the fact. Typical rights problems concern the depiction of people and their stories without a release, or the use of portions of other people's creative work, such as film clips or music excerpts. If an attorney has the chance to review the script or the program in advance, he or she can point out those instances where clearance is necessary. Such an advance review is usually required by the E&O insurer (see page 144). Sometimes the attorney does do the follow-up work. Routine matters can be handled by the production staff or by rights-clearance services specializing in particular areas, such as music or film clips. If items are missed before or during production and claims are made, the production company's attorney—together with the insurer—will assess the seriousness of the situation and take the lead in remedying it.

Finance problems are often more serious, and inevitably involve attorneys. Sometimes an agreed-upon payment schedule is not being followed by the financing entity, and the attorney is asked to cajole and threaten to obtain the money; perhaps the production company is at fault because it is running over budget or behind schedule. Asking for this type of legal help is expensive, and the attorney (since he or she is working for a client in financial distress) often asks for his or her fees upfront.

Most large and medium-sized production companies maintain several attorneys on staff. A general counsel usually attends to corporate affairs, and may become involved in the most important deals; a business affairs department handles the work related to programming and production. Most, if not all, of the deal-makers in the business affairs department are attorneys. A separate legal department drafts contacts and works to prevent and clean up messes.

In this litigious society, attorneys have become an integral part of the production operation. Lawyers should be consulted on any issues related to copyright, insurance, employment practices, government agencies, other producers or production companies, possible instances of libel or slander, music usage, the selection of a program title, and distribution agreements. In sum, almost any agreement signed by a network, station, production company, or individual should be reviewed by an attorney.

BUSINESS MANAGERS AND PERSONAL MANAGERS

A *business manager* helps to oversee the day-to-day financial aspects of a client's business life. The business manager typically receives all incoming checks, keeps the checkbook, makes sure that taxes are paid correctly and on time, deals with the banks, negotiates car leases and other such details, pays the credit card bills, keeps track of receipts for tax preparation, and works with the accountant to prepare taxes. For such services, a business manager may charge a flat monthly fee or, at most, a commission of 5 percent of the client's income.

A *personal manager* is more difficult to define. In theory, an agent is supposed to get jobs, but a personal manager, who is not legally an agent, is supposed to build a career. In fact, personal-management contracts frequently insist that the manager is not qualified to act as agent, and that he or she will not help the client to find work. Instead, the personal manager offers advice and guidance.

In the real world, successful personal managers sell access to powerful decision-makers and personal attention. Where an agent is likely to represent 50 clients, a personal manager handles only 5 or 10. A personal manager helps the client to make career decisions—about the way he or she looks, the company he or she keeps, the roles that should be accepted and rejected. All the while, the personal manager introduces the client to people who can make a difference.

The fee for a personal manager usually ranges from 15 to 25 percent of the client's entertainment income. Colonel Tom Parker, Elvis Presley's personal manager, reportedly charged 50 percent, and was probably worth every penny.

ACCOUNTANTS

Accountants serve as record-keepers and as advisers. The record-keeping function is required for management information and planning, for investors, for tax authorities, and, in the case of public companies, for the SEC. Even a sole practitioner, like a free-lance associate producer, should have an ongoing relationship with an accountant or accounting firm. Billing is based on hours worked, though flat rates for special projects, such as tax preparation, may be negotiated on a case-by-case basis.

The advising function is equally important. Accountants are excellent sources of information relating to tax rules and government regulations on, for example, unemployment insurance. The financial implications of a new project should be reviewed by an accountant while it is still in the planning stages.

Accountants, bookkeepers, and auditors also play a role in production—either as full-time or free-lance members of a production staff, or as outside contractors. Large productions require careful financial management, and a regular (often, daily) reckoning of expenditures. A production auditor provides detailed cost reports to a centralized production office on a regular basis, highlighting areas of potential difficulties. Some auditors play a broader role, keeping an eye on the entire production, and reporting any problems or potential problems to a production supervisor.

When the project is completed, the production accountant or production auditor works with the production manager to confirm that all invoices have been paid, that all deposits have been returned, and that there are no outstanding bills or expense reports lost in the towering piles of paper and files typically found in a production office. Submission of a final cost report is frequently specified in a production agreement; a final payment to a producer or production company may depend upon it.

The situation is less complex with ongoing production or programming ventures, such as a series. Staff, free-lance, or outside accountants prepare and/or review the books regularly—once a week or once a month, depending on the amount of work involved. They may also prepare the payroll, or keep track of royalties. The role of the accountant is an important one; sloppy accounting practices can cause serious problems for independent production companies, and may cause considerable embarrassment for the personnel in charge of expenditure control.

30 Location and Studio Production

Most television programs are produced either on location or in a television studio. Some programs are produced by assembling existing materials such as photographs, film, and videotape. This chapter covers location and studio production; the next chapter discusses post-production and the production of programs that involve assembling existing materials.

LOCATION PRODUCTION

Location production refers to a shoot done anywhere except a studio. Common locations include business offices, homes, sporting venues, city streets, and nightclubs.

For all types of production (with the exception of news coverage), it is necessary to secure permission from the owner of the location prior to setting up to shoot (see Appendix B29). This permission frequently requires negotiating a fee for use of the premises. An insurance policy may also be required; such a policy should cover the property owner for any liability due to personal injury in connection with the production, and should guarantee payment to the property owner in case of physical damage to the property. A negotiated arrangement is essential, whether the location is indoors or outdoors. Failure to arrange for use of a location usually results in costly production delays—as the producer or production manager negotiates on the spot—or in rescheduling.

If the location is outdoors in a public area, or if the shoot involves any public areas for set-up or vehicles, then the municipal or other local government should be contacted well in advance of the shoot. A municipal permit usually carries a fixed daily fee, and must be prominently posted on one of the vehicles during the production. In larger cities, and for large-scale productions in less-populated areas, the city or state film commission can help to make the necessary arrangements. When no such office is available, it is advisable to contact the mayor's office. Fees are generally fixed on the basis of the scale of production; under-the-table payments are uncommon.

If police protection is required, a flat fee is charged per man-hour or per man-day. It is considered poor style (and is also illegal) to "tip" officers, but it is generally acceptable to treat the officers as if they were members of the production team—to feed them while on location, to provide comfortable rest areas during breaks. Friendly relations go a long way toward smooth, problem-free operations. On some shoots, similar interaction with the fire department is required as well.

Single-Camera Location Crews

Most major cities support a small community of free-lance television technicians: camera operators, audio and video engineers, and so forth. Frequently trained in local television news and sports, these versatile crew members work either individually, or in small companies that offer not just engineering capability, but everything from production planning to shooting to editing to duplication of the finished tape.

Crews support themselves by working for a variety of clients. Corporate work (training video, video news releases, product demonstrations, point-of-purchase merchandising video) usually accounts for the bulk of the crew's work. Local, syndicated, and network programs may also hire these crews when their own staffs are overextended, or when a situation arises that favors free-lancers. An example of the latter is a story breaking in Portland: a Seattle-based free-lance crew might be able to reach the location faster than a network crew based in Los Angeles.

Crews are hired in two different ways. For most projects, the easiest way to hire an entire crew is to contact a production company that specializes in single-camera work. The company quotes a daily or weekly package price, not only for the crew members, but for all of the necessary equipment. Many of these crews offer resumé reels; it is also wise to check references with previous clients. One can also hire each crew member individually, and this may be the better choice if a particular videographer is a "must," or if the client company owns equipment. This method, however, is frequently more costly, because individual crew members may not own every piece of equipment needed for the job. The producer also accepts more technical responsibility, especially if the crew members are unaccustomed to working together.

The size of the crew depends upon the job, and is best determined by discussing the job in detail with the crew chief (usually the camera operator). For electronic news gathering (ENG) work, a two-person crew can move quickly and cover most stories: one person lights and operates the camera, the other is in charge of audio and video recording. For most productions, however, using a three- or four-person crew is preferable, and is more likely to result in flawless sound and picture quality. With this set-up, the camera operator works with a lighting assistant, one engineer handles audio, and another engineer does video.

Most crew-hiring deals are made by telephone, followed up with a letter (or a fax) that confirms the business arrangements: the dates, the number of working days, the rate (per day or per week, or the flat rate for the job), a promise to provide transportation and accommodations, confirmation of necessary insurance, and a payment schedule. A typical payment schedule is 50 percent upon hiring and 50 percent upon completion of the shoot. If the job includes editing, then 35 percent on hiring, 35 percent on completion of the shoot, and 30 percent on completion of editing is common. Many crews mark up the cost of tape stock, and for larger shoots, the producer can save money by buying his own stock ahead of time. If anything goes wrong with producer-supplied stock, the producer pays for the reshoot; if anything goes wrong with crew-supplied stock, then they will often reshoot at no charge, or at a dramatically reduced rate.

Multiple-Camera Crews and Truck Rentals

Single-camera coverage is ideal for news, interviews, magazine stories, and speeches. But additional cameras are necessary for most seminars, meetings, sporting events, and other productions where multiple speakers or simultaneous visual images must be captured in real time.

Many of the small production companies described above own small vans equipped with control-room facilities that can work with up to three cameras. These facilities are frequently modular, so they can be removed from the van and set up anywhere, provided that electrical power and shelter from weather is available.

Mobile facilities range from these minivans to full-scale control rooms on wheels that can handle a dozen or more cameras and seat just as many engineers and members of the production staff. Several "trucks" are available in most major cities, but the nature of the mobile video business is travel. It is not unusual to find a Pittsburgh-based truck accepting assignments throughout the East and Midwest; in fact, a good deal can be struck if the Pittsburgh-based truck is already in St. Louis, and is needed for a shoot in Kansas City or Chicago. Trucks are mainly used for sports coverage, and, to a lesser extent, for concerts and other special events.

A truck is usually rented with all of the necessary equipment and several key engineers and technicians. Additional crew members may be hired by the mobile video company—which is likely to be in contact with experienced personnel all over the country—or supplied by the producer. Payment terms for the truck are usually 50 percent on hiring and 50 percent on the completion of the shoot; the crew is paid after the job. Once again, the deal is made by phone (usually to a distant city) and confirmed in writing.

Specialized mobile facilities, for multiple-track audio recording or for the generation of on-site electrical power, are also available for rental.

STUDIO PRODUCTION

Nearly all television broadcasting stations own and operate at least one studio on the premises, and many operate two or more. These studios are used for daily production of the news, and, among more active producing stations, for original programming. In addition, studios are rented for the production of local commercials and, on occasion, to other clients, such as corporate video producers.

Each of the broadcast networks operates studios in New York, Los Angeles, Washington, D.C., and Chicago. In New York, these studios are used principally for news, morning programs (such as *Good Morning America*), sports coverage, and daytime dramas. In Los Angeles, the studios are used mainly for situation comedies, game shows, daytime dramas, and variety shows. Network studios in Washington and Chicago are used for news and public-affairs programs; ABC's *Nightline*, for example, is based in Washington, and so is NBC's *Meet the Press*. When a network and an O&O are housed in the same physical plant, studios, crews, and editing facilities are frequently shared by both organizations.

Many independent programs are not produced in television stations or network facilities, though. Los Angeles, New York, Chicago, and other cities support independently-owned and -operated television studios that are rented to producers. For example, Unitel, New York's largest studio rental company, supplies space to *Sesame Street*, MTV's 24-hour VJ operation, various King World projects (*Inside Edition, Arts & Entertainment Revue, Instant Replay*), and numerous corporate video projects. In Los Angeles, many of the old movie soundstages have been converted into television studios. Television studios are available for rental in the Disney/MGM and Universal complexes in Orlando, Florida. In Chicago, Oprah Winfrey's Harpo Studios is home to her own talk show and to outside projects; there are other independent studios in Chicago as well. There are fine studios in some out-of-the-way places: Nashville's Opryland (which includes one of the nation's largest studios, and which is home of the Grand Ole Opry, a huge theater-style studio), and the Osmond complex in Utah, for example. Many producers also rent studio space in Canada, where production costs tend to be low; Toronto is a leading center, with space available in Vancouver as well.

In other large cities, such as San Francisco and Philadelphia, some work is done at the television stations that have blocks of unbooked time to fill. WHYY-Philadelphia, for example, routinely rents its studios to producers. Some local markets also support a few independent facilities. Outside the top ten or fifteen markets, though, most studio production is done at television stations.

Studios rent their facilities by the day, usually with a half-day minimum. Since studio space is a perishable commodity, facilities are happy to package multiple days or weeks at a discount. The goal of nearly every studio owner is to keep the studio busy all of the time. This is best accomplished by signing a long-term cable company (like MTV, which produces studio segments daily), a corporation with ongoing communications needs (such as a teleconferencing center), or any type of series.

Short-term projects—home video productions, television specials, pilots, commercials, corporate video training tapes, and product demonstrations—usually pay higher day rates than long-term clients do.

A television studio is rented as a facility ready for production, complete with a control room, a lighting grid, power, a poured (flat) floor, and cable connections for lights, cameras, monitors, microphones, and other necessary equipment. Use of the control room, dressing rooms, a make-up area, and limited office space is always part of the deal. Additional charges, essential to customize the studio for specific production activities, mount up quickly: extra cameras, extra lighting equipment, painting and repainting the floor or walls, purchase of colored gels for the lights, and additional personnel. Some of these costs may be paid directly by the producer, but any costs not covered this way are subject to the studio's mark-up.

A film soundstage may be larger than a television studio. Many soundstages are used as studios, with lights and other equipment added as needed. In this instance, the control room is often a mobile production van, or a temporary set-up in a nearby office area. These temporary control-room facilities are called a "carry-in" (or, in Los Angeles, a "fly pack.")

Studio rentals are always negotiable. The price of the studio should be highest on "full facs" days, or days when the studio and all of its equipment are needed, and far lower—perhaps 75 to 80 percent less—on days when the studio is being used to set up or strike equipment and scenery. There is more flexibility with the costs of the studio, the equipment, and the facility's full-time personnel than there is with items that the studio must purchase on the client's behalf. It may be worth checking into the prices of those items purchased from outside, because the studio may not shop for the best possible prices on items it will buy for the client (since it passes the cost through), and the mark-up on these items—as well as on phone and copier usage—may be unacceptable.

A studio deal can be complicated, so it is advisable to arrange at least one in-person meeting. This meeting should include the producer or production manager (who actually makes the deal), the director, and—if the production is complicated—one or two key members of the technical staff. The facility's sales staff assesses the needs of the production, then submits a bid for the job. After soliciting bids from several studios, the producer or production manager starts negotiating. Upon agreement on key points, a one- or two-page letter agreement confirms the deal and the dates, listing the resources that will be provided by the studio, the price for the entire job (or the price of each day), plus the cost of overtime. It is wise to leave some room for modification; most television productions change during pre-production, and a deal that it too tightly structured may cost the producer more money than anticipated. Hard negotiating is not recommended, because if there is a breakdown of mutual goodwill, studios can easily add costs for items not included in the original bid. The studio bills some items at its discretion, and if the facility is treated fairly, there are usually fewer surprises when the final bill arrives.

Payment arrangements vary. A common deal is 10 percent to hold the studio dates—refundable if the production is canceled within 48 hours of the shoot—with 45 percent due on the first shooting day and 45 percent on completion. If the client rents the facility regularly, the final payment can be made as late as 30 days after completion.

TECHNICAL AND STAGING UNIONS

Three technical and staging unions dominate the television business: the International Alliance of Theatrical Stage Employees (IATSE), the National Association of Broadcast Employees and Technicians (NABET), and the International Brotherhood of Electrical Workers (IBEW). Each one negotiates rates and rules with employers on behalf of its members, assures fair working conditions, and operates a pension and welfare fund. The terms and conditions vary with each union's agreement, but there are some generally applicable rules. These concern the number of hours in a standard work day; the additional payments due for overtime hours; payments for work on weekends and holidays; notification of call times, changes, and cancellations; rest periods and turnarounds (the number of hours between working days); meal periods and penalties for missed meal periods; hazard pay; travel, food, and lodging; and the need for a payroll bond.

More than half of all television stations are unionized, most often by IATSE, IBEW, and NABET. The Teamsters represent employees at a few dozen stations, and the United Auto Workers at just one, in Flint, Michigan. (For a general discussion of the role of unions in the television business, see page 344.)

IATSE

The International Alliance of Theatrical Stage Employees, often "IATSE" or just "IA," was founded in 1893. IA members work in legitimate theater, motion picture production, motion picture exhibition (projectionists), and in network and local television production.

IATSE is represented by local chapters throughout the world. The organization of these locals, and the areas in which members may exclusively work, are guided by local traditions and by negotiated agreements. In San Francisco, for example, members of IATSE Local 16 are not involved in television production. In Los Angeles, 16 IATSE television and motion picture locals operate in a variety of production crafts and geographic regions. Local 44, Affiliated Property Craftsmen, supplies prop masters in the Los Angeles area. Local 695, International Sound, Cinetechnicians and TV Engineers, supplies audio engineers in the Los Angeles area. Local 706 is the chapter for Make-up Artists and

Hairstylists working throughout the U.S., its territories, and Canada (with the exception of 13 Eastern states). In New York, IATSE is the union for stagehands.

There are IATSE locals in more than 500 cities throughout the U.S. and Canada. The entire union has 60,000 members, more than one-third of whom work in television.

NABET

The National Association of Broadcast Employees and Technicians succeeded the Association of Technical Employees (ATE), which was organized in 1933 to represent employees of NBC Radio. When the NBC Blue network was spun off to form ABC, jurisdiction expanded to the new network as well. NABET represents most of the technical crew members who work at the network facilities, the radio stations, and the television stations owned by NBC and ABC; at many local radio and television stations not owned by NBC or ABC; and at some production companies. The word "employees" in the name of the union is accurate: half of the union's members are anchors, reporters, producers, directors, desk assistants, talent coordinators, graphic artists, and other non-technical personnel. In addition, NABET represents make-up artists, hairdressers, stagehands, script supervisors, and some film crews.

There are roughly 50 NABET locals in approximately 40 cities, with a total of 14,000 members working in television. In New York and Los Angeles, one local serves ABC, one serves NBC, and one serves film workers. In Washington, one local serves all members.

Until 1974, NABET operated in Canada as well as the U.S. NABET Canada is now autonomous.

NABET covers anyone employed in broadcasting, and competes with AFTRA, DGA, WGA, IATSE, and IBEW to represent employees.

IBEW

The International Brotherhood of Electrical Workers was formed in 1891 to represent telephone company employees. In 1931, IBEW started representing CBS radio engineers and technicians. Today, IBEW (sometimes called "IB") represents engineers and technicians at CBS network and local facilities, and at some local stations. IBEW also represents workers in the telephone industry.

INSURANCE

Whether working on location or in a studio, the producer uses several types of insurance to limit the risks involved in creating television productions.

An errors and omissions (E&O) policy—also called a producer's liability policy—insures against claims based on violation of copyright, personal rights, or property rights, including infringement of privacy. Although the range of coverage may vary depending upon the type of production and the risk involved, an E&O policy should protect the producer against suits for libel, slander, and privacy/publicity violations (see Chapter 19). In addition, an E&O policy protects against claims on the creative concepts used in the production: the originality of the concept, the script, the characters, the music, the production design, and so forth. The E&O package for most productions is a routine matter, but it may take on special importance when the risk is higher. For example, with a tabloid-type magazine program, a celebrity might claim libel, slander, or defamation of character. Another example is a basic storyline with a history of copyright problems and lawsuits.

There are several companies that supply E&O coverage. The application form from one of them appears in Appendix B10, with a typical list of questions to answer and procedures to follow.

The so-called "production package" typically protects the producer against losses due to property damage or personal injury. It contains some or all of the following coverages, depending, again, upon the producer's level of risk and the costs involved.

- Faulty Stock, Camera, and Processing Insurance pays for reshooting and other losses due to problems with the set's physical equipment, the raw materials used, or the editing facility.
- Negative Film Insurance covers physical damage to the master videotape(s) or film negative.
- Weather Insurance covers delays due to inclement or unusual weather.
- Aviation Accident Insurance, Marine Accident Insurance, and Animal Mortality Coverage are examples of special coverages, and are self-explanatory.
- Extra Expense Insurance reimburses the producer for the costs of any delays due to failure or loss of any equipment, wardrobe, and so on.
- Third Party Property Damage covers property that is donated, loaned, or rented to the producer.
- Cast Insurance pays the producer for any costs from delays related to key cast members who become ill during the course of shooting and editing. If a cast member dies, and material must be reshot or re-edited with a new performer, cast insurance covers this situation as well.
- Comprehensive General Liability covers damage to vehicles loaned to, rented, or donated to the production. Similar coverage is available for props, sets, and wardrobe, as well as for lighting, camera, and sound equipment.

- Worker's Compensation and Employer's Liability is not exclusively a production insurance; it provides coverage against claims for workers who are injured or disabled on the job. The cost and coverage varies on a state-by-state basis—high in California, lower in New York. There are some surprises in some states, so research is necessary.

As can be expected, there are limitations on coverage. Faulty Stock, Camera, and Processing Insurance, for example, does not cover errors in judgment made by the camera operator, such as the use of the wrong film, improper loading, or incorrect or inappropriate use of the camera. Similar limitations apply to most of the types of insurance listed above.

Insurance can be expensive, so coverages should be selected with a thorough understanding of the risks involved, the costs of correcting problems without insurance coverage, and the likelihood of mishaps. E&O and a basic production package are required in almost every contract for financing or distributing a program. Because the costs of coverage do vary, it is advisable to request bids from several companies that specialize in production insurance. Special cast insurance may be required if a key cast member is especially old or in poor health. Other types of specialty insurance may be required by contract if production conditions are unusual—for example, if dangerous animals will be used, or if shooting will take place in a rough inner-city neighborhood.

One further note. Deductibles are often high, so the producer should make some allowances for loss, damage, and theft in order to insure items valued in the hundreds or low thousands of dollars. This will cover the producer for small problems that do not warrant, or qualify for, a claim.

An accurate estimation of costs can only be made by an insurance agent. For budgeting purposes, it is normally safe to gauge insurance costs at roughly 3 to 5 percent of the total production budget. If the project is relatively small, then the proportion may be slightly higher. The cost of insuring a pilot will be, proportionately, far higher than the cost of insuring an entire series. Part of the reason may be minimum fees that are due regardless of the size and budget of the production. A blanket policy, held by a larger company, may help reduce costs; an independent producer or small production company will usually pay more than a larger company would for insurance.

31 Post-Production

Post-production is an umbrella term that covers editing, the addition of special effects, and sound mixing. There are several phases in the post-production process, and the complexity of each step is defined by the needs of the project.

First, the videotapes recorded on location or in the studio are logged—a list is made of each scene, and each acceptable take. The tapes are then screened by the person in charge of the edit (a producer or director, for example), who makes further notes and begins to visualize the completed production. Notes, logs, and ideas are used to prepare a written editing plan, sometimes with additional written material to be recorded as a voice-over.

The second step occurs in an editing room. If the project is relatively simple—a news story or a corporate speech that must be illustrated with footage, for example—the videotapes are edited into their final form in one step. If the project is more complicated—a situation comedy or a documentary, for example—then a rough cut is made from dubs of the master tapes as a basis for further discussion and criticism. A project may be rough-cut several times. Then the master tapes are edited to a final cut. Film editing proceeds in a similar fashion, though the physical processes may be more involved.

The third step is sound work. On a small-scale project, sound work is done in the editing room by adding voice, music, and sound effects. On larger projects, the soundtrack is dubbed onto 16- or 32-track tape; sound effects, music, and voices are recorded or rerecorded on individual tracks and mixed, in much the same way as a record is made. Finally, the tracks are "laid back" onto the master videotape or film negative, in synchronization with the video images.

A standardized time code system called SMPTE—pronounced *sim*-tee, and named for the Society of Motion Picture and Television Engineers—is used on all audio and videotapes so that the work can be organized and accessed by a computerized editing system.

EDITING FACILITIES

Compared with fully-equipped television studios, editing facilities are less costly to build and to maintain, so there are more of them. Networks and local stations typically build editing facilities for individual departments, such as news and on-air promotion. Productions that depend heavily upon editing, like magazine programs, frequently build editing suites in their production offices. Independent post-production houses are common in most cities—even a small independent facility may operate two or three editing suites.

The equipment, and the ability to maintain it, may vary from one editing facility to another—but the greatest difference lies in the skill and craftsmanship of the editor. For a creative endeavor in which a fraction of a second can make the difference between an effective presentation and a tedious one, in which unusual cutting can transform a mundane project into something that sparkles, the editor can be a significant contributor.

Networks do not normally rent out their editing facilities, usually because they lack excess capacity. Local stations do, when time is available. Independent editing houses handle most of the outside program and commercial work.

Editing facilities charge by the hour. Hourly charges depend upon the type of editing system used; a rough-cut (or off-line) system used for news stories and for rough-cutting high-budget projects costs about one-third as much as an on-line system used for fine cutting. Rates also depend upon the number of playback machines and the use of additional equipment, such as a title camera, animation stand, or digital special-effects devices. Dubs and window dubs—which show time code on the screen and make edit planning easier—cost extra, as do materials like blank tape stock.

Rate cards are published mainly for corporate clients and for agencies who pass costs on to clients. Most regular clients, including nearly all independent production companies, receive a 10 to 15 percent discount off the rate card amount. Clients with full-length programs, who buy large numbers of hours, may negotiate a deeper discount, up to 25 to 35 percent off. If editing is tied to a studio rental deal—as is often the case at larger facilities—then a package deal is common.

Every deal should be based on an hourly charge; even flat rates should reflect a maximum number of hours. This is because editing often takes longer than anticipated—it is difficult to estimate the job accurately, and clients and distributors may request unexpected changes.

Since post-production is the final step in the overall production process, editing facilities are often the last to get paid. For new clients, and for clients who have not established reputations for paying bills on time, most editing houses have strict rules regarding the removal of tapes from their premises prior to payment of invoices. The best way to minimize problems is to estimate the cost of the job, pay a portion as a down payment (20 percent is common), and cut a check for the estimated balance, to be held in reserve until it is due. If the final total is more or less, adjustments can be made. And if the project is exceeding the budget estimate, incremental payments are frequently requested by the editing facility. Unpaid bills, or unpaid portions of bills, are an unfortunate fact of life in the post-production business.

A lab letter (see Appendix B31) is an agreement between the 'lab' (more often, the post-production facility), the producer, and a financier or distributor. It says that the lab has tapes and/or films, and will not release the materials without permission of the authorized party (distributor or producer); that the distributor or producer may use the materials within the lab for duplication or further editing; and, finally, that the lab will not put a lien on the materials or hold them unavailable if the party has unpaid debts to the lab. Each party is allowed access, provided that they have paid their own bills to the facility.

USE OF EXISTING MATERIALS

Some television projects are put together in whole or in part by assembling existing materials, including photographs, illustrations, film, and videotape footage.

Strictly speaking, every piece of existing material that is protected by copyright should be cleared by the copyright holder for use—regardless of the amount of time that the sound or image is heard or seen, regardless of the size or character of the intended audience. This means that a producer must identify and contact the copyright holder for each item, then describe the production, how the material will be used within it, and where the program will be distributed. In many cases, the copyright holder will have already sold properties for use on television, so past experience may be the basis for either a fixed rate or negotiation. An agreement should be signed before the material is edited into the production. This agreement should detail the name of the program, its intended market and audience, the item to be used, limitations on its use, and the payments due.

In the real world, clearances are important, but in some cases, a producer will not obtain them. If, for example, a production is to be seen internally by a small number of company employees, or if the production is a rough demo made to secure future funding, a producer sometimes takes a chance and proceeds without the necessary clearances—but this action is *never* without an element of risk. If the material is seen for only a very short time, or it is distorted or manipulated to a point where recognition may be difficult, then once again the producer may choose to risk using the material without a clearance. The copyright holder is under no obligation to sell or license the material, of course, and many copyright holders routinely turn down requests for usage (for certain types of productions, or for any production at all).

If the copyright holder is difficult to reach, and the producer has made a conscientious effort to contact the party, then the producer can take the risk of using the material—with the understanding that the copyright holder may see the production. Once the copyright holder is aware that the material is being used, the producer may negotiate a reasonable fee. But the copyright holder may have little motivation to negotiate in a reasonable fashion—he or she may quote very high rates, demand that the material be removed from the program, or insist that the program be pulled from distribution as long as it contains the material. If the program has already aired with the material included, the copyright holder can stop the program from being shown or distributed until the material is removed, or charge a very high licensing fee.

Items that are in the public domain—material on which the copyright has not been renewed, for example—may be used without clearances. Sometimes, it is difficult to determine or to verify ownership; in these cases, the producer must make an honest, earnest effort to determine whether or not the item in question is in the public domain. Clearing music is especially tricky; a song or composition may be in the public domain, but its *performance* may be protected by copyright, thus requiring clearance. Short excerpts, particularly on news or information programs, may fall into the category of "fair use," which does not require permission. This is a limited exception, however, and should not be stretched beyond its proper bounds.

If a program is produced for distribution, the distributor must document all clearances. If something is not cleared, it is advisable for the producer to keep a history of contact (or attempted contact) with the copyright holder and advise the distributor of the potential for difficulties later on. (See Chapter 18 for more on copyright and the protection of creative properties.)

SCREEN CREDITS

Post-production on television programs also includes on-screen credits for people who worked on the production. The form and style of these credits is largely dependent upon tradition, negotiated agreements with individual staff and crew members, and rules set forth in union and guild agreements. On a network drama or situation comedy, for example, an individual full-frame or single-card credit (a credit that is the only one on-screen at a particular time) is shown at the start of the program for the producer(s), writer, and director, usually in that order; the other names appear at the end of the program. On most other programs, such as game, talk, news, magazine, and variety shows, all of the credits are shown at the end. These end credits begin with the producer(s), director, writer(s), production staff, and technical crew, then move on to music, design, business, and other departments.

The exact running order of credits, and the job titles, are usually determined by the producer, who is guided by contractual requirements, union requirements, and personal judgment. Sometimes, for example, the executive producers appear first on the credits, sometimes they appear last. The broadcast networks frequently have their own conventions and policies on what credits are allowed.

The name of the program, or its logo, does not need to appear on the credits. Some producers prefer to see it, others do not.

A television program may be produced without including credits of any kind. A copyright notice, however, must be included at some point in the program. It is most often shown either just before or just after the end credits. A proper form for the copyright notice is as follows:

Copyright © 1991, The Blumenthal and Goodenough Company

The name of the show need not be included in the copyright notice. Some producers include the words "all rights reserved" in addition to the copyright notice, but this is redundant. The notice should be large enough to be read clearly on any television set. For more on copyright notice and protection, see page 139; for instructions on the submission of a program to the copyright office, see Appendix A7.

COMPLETION MATERIALS ("DELIVERABLES")

When a program is complete, one of the staff members should arrange all of the important documents, neatly typed, in a production file or production book. Such materials are routinely required by distribution agreements in a section or schedule called Delivery Requirements, but they should be assembled upon completion of every television show, regardless of its intended market, and kept in a file that is cross-referenced to the master videotape. The following "deliverables" are likely to be required—along with the master tape (and sometimes work tapes)—before an independent producer or production company can receive final payment:

- *Agreements.* All cast, staff, crew, music, set-design, and other agreements. If the program is likely to have a commercial life beyond its initial showing, a memo outlining residuals should be included here as well.
- *Credit List.* The list of screen credits, as it appears on the final version of the program.
- *Release Forms.* Each form should be notated to identify it with the person appearing in the program.
- *Final Budget Accounting.* On a larger production, a final accounting may not be possible until 60 or 90 days after completion; still, the most accurate and up-to-date accounting possible should be included, sometimes accompanied by copies of all paid invoices.
- *Final Script.* A final script, if available, is especially useful if the production may be edited in the future. A show rundown, listing

each program element and its duration in minutes and seconds, should be included as well.

- *Music Cue Sheet.* This lists every piece of music, its composer, publishing, running time, and, preferably, time-code position in the program.
- *Insurance Forms.* A copy of the producer's E&O policy should be included in the file; for many productions, like those done by a local TV station, coverage will be part of a larger policy, and need not be included.

32 | Design

Television is a visual medium in which scenic and graphic design can contribute in a significant way to a project's success. Fortunately, the business of creating television stage settings, graphics, animation, and computer graphics is relatively straightforward and uncomplicated.

SCENIC DESIGN

Several titles are used to describe the person who designs the scenery. Production Designer is a term borrowed from the motion picture industry; when used in television, the title suggests active supervision of all graphic elements, as well as the design of the set and props. The role of the Art Director may include only set design, only graphics, or the entire production-design package. Scenic or Set Designer is the most common term in television; a designer is hired to visualize a concept for the scenery and to supervise its construction. Some producers and/or directors have very specific ideas, and the designer is asked to execute these ideas in a stylish fashion; other producers and/or directors meet with the designer with only a vague sense of what it is required. In that case, the designer not only visualizes the concept, but originates or develops it as well.

The process typically begins with several scenic designers attending creative meetings with the project's producer, director, or other production staff members. Each designer is told about the concept of the program, its style, and the functions that the set must fulfill. These may include, for example, a performance area for a rock band, a talk area to accommodate up to six guests, or a seating area for an on-camera audience of 200. Each designer is expected to contribute creative ideas to the discussion.

Promising candidates are then asked to draw a pencil sketch, or several sketches, showing ideas. These sketches may be prepared "on spec" (with the designer speculating time against the promise of future work) or for a small fee, usually less than a few hundred dollars. The schedule for submissions varies, but one week from first meeting to delivery is common. The sketches remain the property of the designer, but it is not unusual for a producer to incorporate some of the submitted ideas in the final design, even if another designer is hired. This is neither moral nor legal, particularly if the designer has been a principal contributor to the concept. In practice, however, such concepts are often developed as a result of group meetings, so that attribution of specific concepts may be difficult.

The sketches are a kind of audition: the designer with the best ideas is most likely to be awarded the work, although reputation and a history of on-time, on-budget delivery are also significant. The sketches do not usually come with construction bids, but designers are expected to provide a rough, non-binding estimate of construction costs.

The winning designer meets with the producer and his or her staff several times to revise the design. Throughout this process, large-sized pencil sketches are common. A color sketch is sometimes necessary, with paint and material swatches often used instead of, or in addition to, the color sketch. A white cardboard scale model is useful because it presents the set in a three-dimensional plan. A full-color scale model is uncommon because of the expense and the time involved in making one; still, for certain types of projects, a color model is essential for proper production planning. Color models usually require the designer to hire a model maker, for an additional fee.

Once the sketch or model has been approved, the designer prepares construction drawings—blueprints for the construction of each scenic element. The designer also requests bids from one or more scenic construction shops, recommends the best one for the job, and supervises the shop through construction, painting, and finishing. In theory, the designer must also be concerned with loading the set onto the trucks, and out to the studio; in practice, most designers try to leave these headaches to the shop and the studio stagehands. When the set arrives in the studio, the designer works closely with the stagehands, who place the pieces in the correct position in the studio and dress the set with props and small graphics.

After the set is seen on camera, some repainting or resurfacing is usually required. The designer assumes that minor changes will be necessary, and does not normally charge any additional design fees for fix-ups or for alterations. It is also common for a small number of set pieces to be redesigned or modified as a result of changes in the production—as the director starts blocking and rehearsing, unanticipated problems become evident and adjustments have to be made to the set. Major changes usually involve overtime payments to the carpenters, electricians, prop people, painters, stagehands, and other specialists who must physically transform the set, often on a tight schedule.

A designer may have an ongoing relationship with a program whose scenic needs keep changing: *The Tonight Show* and daytime dramas are the types of shows that keep staff designers busy. Once the basic set is completed, most programs require only maintenance of existing set pieces, or the occasional extra piece of scenery. At the networks, staff designers are typically assigned to this follow-through.

Design Agreements

Most designers routinely negotiate on their own behalf. Increasingly, top designers are working with agents or, in more limited cases, with attorneys.

Design agreements are often verbal, not written. This is because the job can take only a month, while the written agreement may take longer to draft, revise, redraft, and sign. Sometimes, the producer or designer requires a brief written agreement stating basic terms. Any agreement—written or verbal—with a scenic designer should cover the following elements:

- A list of responsibilities, including the conceptualization and rendering of a scenic design acceptable to the producer, with necessary revisions; supervision of construction and painting; supervision of load-in and strike(s); availability for revisions and new scenic elements.

- A payment schedule. The designer is typically paid half of the fee on acceptance of preliminary designs, and a portion when the set is physically in the studio (or when the program first airs). There may also be incremental payments pegged to acceptance of the completed design. But since the designer's involvement is typically two to eight weeks, and a corporate check often requires 30 days for processing, such interim payments may not be practicable.

- A negotiable weekly fee, if the designer is working on a series in network or syndicated television. The going rate is several hundred dollars per week, but it may be much higher or lower. This fee may also involve a promise to maintain ("babysit") the production.

- A credit for the designer, usually Production Designer, Art Director, or Scenic Designer. The use of this credit is largely negotiable.

- Ownership of the designs. Sometimes, all rights in the designs are transferred to the production company; increasingly, however, designers are seeking to keep the copyright themselves, subject to limits on re-use, and only license rights for the specific production to the producer.

The Scenic Artists' Union

One union for scenic artists is United Scenic Artists, Local 829. Local 829, which is part of the International Brotherhood of Painters and Allied Trades (IBPAT), has agreements with the three commercial networks and their stations in New York, and with their affiliated stations in Chicago. Technically, Local 829 has jurisdiction nationwide through three business offices, in New York, Chicago, and Los Angeles; in practice, though, its jurisdiction over the television industry is primarily in New York. Los Angeles art directors and related personnel usually work under the jurisdiction of the Art Directors' Guild, Local 876, an IATSE affiliate. If a union designer wants to work for a company that is not a union signatory, a project-specific agreement can usually be arranged.

The locals set minimum rates for television productions, commercials, and motion pictures, and require a pension and welfare payment of 10.5 percent of gross earnings, with a cap. As with other unions, there are rules regarding minimum call, meal periods, rest periods, penalties, and notification of calls and changes. Many designers do not strictly adhere to these rules, since they are trying to get the job done within limited studio hours, but the spirit of the rules is certainly respected on most productions.

Scenic Construction, Trucking, Load-In, Strikes, and Resets

Television scenery is usually built to the designer's specifications by shops that specialize in scenic construction. (Other types of construction shops can do the work, but the results are generally better with a shop that specializes in television). Work is done on a contract basis between the shop and the producing company: the shop submits a bid, with payment terms. Once the bid has been negotiated, and is acceptable to both parties, work begins in accordance with a delivery schedule. The shop is supervised by the designer—who visits several times during the construction and painting—but the shop actually contracts with, and is paid by, the producing company.

The scenery seen on network television, and on much of syndication and pay TV, is built in union shops, where union workers stamp each piece of scenery with a union symbol (called a "bug"). If the program is to be produced in a studio with union stagehands, it is important to coordinate the activities of the unions whose members construct, truck, and load the set into the studio. If all of these are workers are members of IATSE, as is often the case in New York and Los Angeles, then the coordination is routine. If a variety of unions are involved—or if one of the links in this chain is to be non-union—then arrangements must be made (and sometimes, negotiated) in advance. If the shop, the truckers, and the studio stagehands are all non-union, then there should be few coordination problems (non-union personnel may be less experienced than union personnel, however).

Television scenery is fragile, and should be moved only by companies and stagehands experienced in the trucking of scenery. The scenic construction shop usually makes arrangements for trucking.

Load-in is the process of removing scenery from the truck and assembling it in the studio. The trucking crew unloads, and stagehands hired for work in the studio set up. The crew chief follows the designer's floor plan for instructions as to placement, but the designer is available to answer questions. In some studios, under union rules, the designer is allowed to touch, but not move, scenery. (Some crews are more lenient than others, and some designers assume more responsibility than others do.)

Striking a set is the process of removing it from the studio, or, in some cases, taking it apart and setting it aside to make room for another show. The odds of damage are increased when the set is struck and reset often; in such cases, a long-term maintenance deal with the designer may be wise. Several stagehands who work on the show generally earn extra pay for working on strikes and resets; since these activities often take place before or after regular production hours, overtime pay scales are frequently involved.

GRAPHICS, COMPUTER ART, AND ANIMATION

Television graphics now encompass two-dimensional and three-dimensional still graphics, as well as animation. Some work is done in the "traditional" way: at an artist's table, with paint, ink, and other tangible media. But an increasing amount of graphics work is done using a computer-graphics system. In some cases, original material is first prepared using traditional methods, then modified or adapted for computer-graphic design.

The business of television graphics is handled in one of three ways. The first is setting up one or more staff members to operate as an in-house art department, taking care of the graphics (and sometimes, the scenic requirements) for programs, on-air promotion, and other activities. The second is hiring free-lancers to work on a project basis; an example would be the creation of a new graphic look for the local news. The third is working with a graphics firm, either on a long-term contract or per-project basis.

Regardless of the arrangement, the hiring process is similar to the one described above with regard to scenic design. The producer establishes a need for specific graphics, and meets with one or more graphic artists to discuss style, approach, schedule, and budget. The artist(s) work out some ideas and, within a few days, present(s) sketches to the producer (and/or the producer's staff). The sketches are revised and approved, with the finished work delivered in accordance with a schedule. If the work is done on a computer graphics system, the producer may attend the session.

Logo Design

A logotype is a graphic representation of the program's title. It may be straightforward—little more than a type treatment—or more complicated, involving illustrations, graphic work, and motion.

The design of logos for television is best handled by a graphic artist with experience in logo design. This may be a staff member or a free-lancer, or even a producer working with a paint-box artist who is paid by the hour. Logos are considered just one of many television graphics, so logo design should not necessarily command a supplementary fee.

Legal Considerations in Graphic Design

A graphic design is subject to the same legal considerations as of any other creative element in a production. Under copyright law, the use of a particular image requires the permission of the owner of that image. In addition, the work may not infringe on the rights of any third parties (see Chapter 18); this means that any photographs or graphic works that are owned by third parties must be cleared for use within the context of the program. Companies who sell old photographs and other vintage graphics set rates based on the type of production, its distribution, and the number of times that the program will be seen. These rates are flexible if the material will be seen by a very limited audience, or if the production leases multiple images. The producer should confirm that the rights fee covers *all* types of possible uses—otherwise, he or she will be held accountable for infringements. If a graphic element is owned by a third party who is not in the business of selling images, then the rate should be based on a fair-market price. Signed agreements must be completed prior to inclusion of the image in the production.

There is a grey area in the use of public images. The trade "dress" and trademarks of commercial products, such as packaged goods and their labels, are owned by their producers, and normally should not be used without permission. If the material itself is the subject of a legitimate public-interest program, however, the First Amendment will generally permit its use, provided that no false designation of origin is implied. Photos and video images of public figures can also be used in a news or public-affairs context; otherwise, the trademark, privacy, and publicity rules can prevent use without permission (see Chapter 19).

Digital Image Transformation

A generation of computer technology introduced in the mid-1980s now makes it possible to alter any image and transform it into a work of original art. There are no clear rules regarding the line of demarcation between truly original images and existing images that have been transformed to create new originals. The legal question is whether the new work is close enough to the old one to constitute a "derivative work." This is determined by a highly subjective test of "substantial similarity" (see page 143). As a practical matter, if the artist or rights-holder who owns the original image is likely to recognize the connection and demand money, deny permission to use the original image, or insist that the new work infringes on the work's copyright, then the new work is probably too similar to the original image to be used without permission. New images that satirize older ones are subject to greater latitude; satire is a recognized exception to usual copyright protections.

Animation

There are several forms of animation currently in use. The first is traditional cel animation, involving the painting and photographing of a gradually changing series of animation cels (hand-painted images on acetate sheets). The second form is a computerized system whereby images are drawn and manipulated without the use of any physical materials outside the computer domain. The third method is the less sophisticated kind of computer animation offered by electronic graphic systems like Quantel's Paint Box and Harry, or by a specially-equipped personal computer. The first two animation methods are usually handled by companies that specialize in animation, with the third used by in-house artists or free-lancers. Increasingly, Macintosh computers are used in computer animation; capabilities are limited, but the system is in use, and shows great promise for the future.

The animation process begins with the development of a basic storyline and the preparation of a storyboard that shows key frames in sketch form, usually with corresponding dialogue printed below the frame.

The designer is responsible for the visual development of the concept, and for revisions based on the client's suggestions and requests.

The client approves several key stages of the production process: the storyboards, a rough version of the animation, and then the finished work. Since animation projects proceed over the course of weeks, incremental reviews by the client are common, especially on larger or complicated projects. This process is essentially the same for both traditional film animation and for the newer computer-animation techniques. Normally, fees are paid in installments, in percentage payments keyed to the production schedule.

The Artist and Rights of Ownership

Most artists work either as employees or as independent contractors on a work-for-hire basis (see page 138). The proceeds of their work, therefore, belong to the employer or client who becomes the copyright holder. There are, however, two subtleties to be considered.

First, most artists—and most creative people, for that matter—are especially competent in certain styles and types of work. It is not unusual for an artist to rework an idea previously submitted to, or prepared for, another client. Since ideas are not subject to copyright protection (see page 146), the new work need not infringe on the rights of the former client, unless a great level of restrictiveness was specified in the first contract.

Second, a situation may arise in which the work of the artist is exploited beyond the parties' original intent. For example, an artist is hired to create an animated character for use in an industrial film, and that character proves to have value beyond its original use. The continuing ownership of the character (as opposed to its first appearance in the industrial film) may belong to the artist, or to the company that owns the industrial film, or to both parties. In the case of a true free-lance arrangement, if the producing company intended to purchase rights to the character beyond its original use in the industrial film, the rights should have been clearly specified—or included in a grant of all character uses in all markets in perpetuity. If the work was made "for hire," then the producing company, as a matter of law, owns the rights. Ideally, the contract should provide for continuing financial participation for the artist, even if the artist does not own part of the copyright. Even better (for the artist), the original contract should allocate only those rights that the producing company will actually exploit, reserving all other rights for the artist. Since situations like these are rarely simple, the reader may wish to consult an attorney who specializes in such matters.

33 | Music

The music business is a highly evolved one in its own right. Music on television is a complicated subject, involving issues that range from ownership of compositions and recordings to the creation of original music. Readers wishing additional detail should consult *This Business of Music* by Sidney Shemel and M. William Krasilovsky.

MUSIC AND COPYRIGHT LAW

Two aspects of copyright law apply specifically to the use of music on television: synchronization rights and performance rights.

Synchronization Rights

The copyright holder of a musical composition controls its reproduction in fixed, or recorded, form. The right to reproduce music on a record, tape, or compact disc is called a mechanical license (the term is left over from the days of player pianos and music boxes). A record company must acquire a mechanical license if a copyrighted composition is fixed or recorded in a way that can be read or replayed by a mechanical, electrical, electronic, or computer device.

A synchronization right, or "sync," right is, in effect, a kind of mechanical license. The sync right permits the music to be fixed to an audiovisual recording. The grant of the sync right permits the producer and/or distributor of a film or television program to affix a particular piece of music to the film, tape, videodisc, or other audio-visual embodiment. This license has traditionally been obtained by the television producer, either through direct negotiation with the composer or via the music publisher.

A synchronization license is not needed for a live show because the element of recording is absent; only a performance right is needed. If the "live" production is taped or filmed for later use, however, then a sync right is needed to cover the incorporation of the music in this physical form.

Performance Rights

The second aspect of copyright law that applies to television music comes into play when the program is shown to the public—the right to control public performances of the composition. When a television program, commercial, or other visual form is broadcast or cablecast, this constitutes a public performance of the music that the program contains. The performance right must be licensed from the copyright holder; this license has traditionally been secured on a blanket basis (see below) by the local station or cable network, usually from a performing rights society.

If the music is only incidental to the dramatic content of live action—for example, a radio is playing a particular song in the background of a television program—then the right is called a "small" performing right. If the music is an integral part of the program, as with a film musical or a televised opera, then the right is called a "grand" performing right. The "grand" and "small" rights are generally administered in very different fashions, as separate aspects of music publishing.

A private viewing of a videotape at home will generally not constitute a public performance requiring a license. However, if money is charged for the viewing, or if the viewing takes place in a commercial establishment (a bar, for example), then the viewing may be considered a public performance, and may require the acquisition of a performance license.

MUSIC PUBLISHING

The administration of both the sync and the performance rights falls under the general activity of music publishing. A composer and a music publisher enter into a business arrangement in which the publisher agrees to administer these and other rights on behalf of the composer, acting as a clearing/collecting agent for producers and others seeking to license the musical compositions. Music publishers vary greatly in their size, their clout, and their ability to make money for their client composers. Even composers of considerable stature license their songs to music publishing companies, though some artists own their publishing companies, in whole or in part. Grand performing rights are sometimes withheld by the composer and licensed through a different publishing company or agent.

A music publisher—like any other publisher—is responsible for the marketing of the property, the negotiation of licensing agreements, the collection of revenues, the issuing of royalty statements, and the payment of royalties.

The traditional split of performance and synchronization revenues between publisher and composer is 50/50. Sometimes, a publisher may yield to negotiating pressure and grant some of its usual share to the composer in what is called a co-publishing arrangement. The publisher, in turn, may deduct an administrative fee and/or charge for out-of-pocket expenses before revenues are distributed. In some cases, the publisher has pressured the composer to grant a portion of his or her 50 percent, but few publishers are successful in this effort (see discussion of performing rights organizations below).

Obtaining a Synchronization License

The television producer typically negotiates for the synchronization license prior to including the music in the production; if the rights are too costly, he or she can then move on to another composition. These rights can be obtained either directly from the composer (and lyricist, if there is one); by arrangement with the music publisher; or through an intermediary such as the Harry Fox Agency, which specializes in this activity. The cost of the sync license can be substantial for a well-known work. In most television productions, the producer commissions the music, keeping the cost of the sync license low as part of the overall deal for the composer's work. This is possible because the performance-license fees for a commissioned work—which the producer typically does not pay—can be extremely lucrative for the composer and for whoever is serving as the music publisher. Many producers own music-publishing companies specifically to cash in on a share of the music revenues. In an extreme case—such as a show with daily, weekly, or national exposure—the composer and publisher may absorb all of the recording costs just for the opportunity to collect their share of the performance-license fees.

Performance Licenses and Performing Rights Organizations

Music publishers normally do not collect small-performance revenues directly. Instead, monies are collected by performing rights organizations: ASCAP (American Society of Composers, Authors and Publishers), BMI (Broadcast Music Inc.), and—for European works, some religious, and gospel music—SESAC (Society of European Stage Authors and Composers). There has been some controversy and litigation regarding appropriate payments due to these organizations from the cable networks. Periodically, the commercial networks and broadcast stations also launch legal and business assaults on ASCAP and BMI in an effort to lower rates.

Performance fees can also be negotiated and paid directly to the composer or publisher. This is called "source licensing," and it is a relatively uncommon practice.

ASCAP and BMI grew out of a need for composers to band together to monitor the performance of music onstage, in live concerts, on radio, and later, on television. Neither the artist nor the publisher can possibly monitor every usage—a live band in North Dakota, a music video played on a local cable system in Oregon, a radio station in Florida, and so on. The performing rights organizations were formed to track usage, collect the appropriate license fees, and divide the income fairly among rights holders.

After the deduction of overhead, income from these sources is divided between the composer (and lyricist, if there are lyrics) and the publisher on a 50/50 basis. If no publishing company is listed on the cue sheet (see below), and the performing rights organization is unable to find the proper publisher, then the publisher's share goes uncollected. If there is no individual composer associated with the work, his or her share goes uncollected.

Blanket Licenses

Most performance-rights licensing takes place at the level of the broadcast station or cable network. Rather than negotiating deals for each individual use, stations and networks use *blanket licenses*. A blanket license allows the licensee to use any item in the performing rights organization's catalog for a specified period of time, without the need to negotiate for the performance right of each individual composition. Cue sheets provide the basis of allocating blanket license fees to ASCAP/BMI members.

Tracking Usage

In theory, ASCAP and BMI attempt to track the use of every piece of music used on every television program airing on every national, regional/local broadcast, cable, and satellite system. Indeed, when the stakes are high and the audiences are large—as on network television—tracking is extremely accurate. On local and other forms of television, the tracking may be somewhat less rigorous. The key to tracking is the music cue sheet.

A music cue sheet is a list of every piece of music used in a particular television program or film. The cue sheet lists the title and running time of each piece of music, as well as its composer, lyricist (if any), publisher, copyright owner, and performing arts institution (ASCAP, BMI). This list is generally delivered along with the master videotape; copies should be provided every time the videotape is publicly shown.

Whenever the program airs, ASCAP or BMI must be contacted and furnished with the information from the cue sheet. The performing arts organization feeds all of this information into its computers, and works out a formula which is used to determine the performance license fees due to the composer and publisher.

In those special cases where a grand license is required, ASCAP and BMI are not involved; instead, the license is sought directly from the publisher, or from the composer and lyricist.

THE AMERICAN FEDERATION OF MUSICIANS (AFM)

The American Federation of Musicians (AFM) is a performance union with 450 chapters throughout the U.S. and Canada. In these cities, the majority of working musicians are members of the union, and most television work is controlled by negotiated agreements between the AFM and producers, stations, networks, or distributors. The relevant agreements are the AFM Television Film Agreement (called the Television Agreement), which covers movies made for television, and the AFM Videotape Agreement, which covers other programs made for syndication and network television, regardless of whether the program is produced on film or videotape.

To understand the basic format of an AFM agreement, it is first necessary to understand the types of musicians covered by the agreement. A *recording musician* actually performs; his or her work is heard on the production. A *production musician* performs only during rehearsal. A *sideline musician* does not actually play an instrument, but pretends to do so, on camera; if the sideline musician has a speaking part, then he or she is entitled to an additional fee for that type of performance. A *contractor* is required if more than seven musicians are hired to play; he hires the musicians, and takes care of billing, collection, adherence to AFM work rules, and other paperwork. The *arranger* or orchestrator reworks the basic composition and assigns parts to individual musicians. A *copyist* provides a copy of the score to each musician. For larger projects, a *proofreader* is hired to check the score and the copies, and a *librarian* maintains the library of sheet music.

There are different minimum fees, and some variations in work rules, for each type of musician. In addition, the fees and rules vary depending upon the type of production and its intended market.

The rules in the basic Television Film Agreement are typical of most union agreements, but the many variations mentioned above make accurate computation tricky.

The current agreement lists scale payments per "sideman," a term that covers recording/performing and sideline musicians. These payments are based on hourly rates with a three-hour minimum, and overtime is broken down into 15-minute increments. For a single session, lasting 4 hours, the scale payment is roughly $180 for the three-hour base, plus $60 for four additional 15-minute overtime periods. These basic rates are subject to night and holiday premiums of 110 to 200 percent.

If a musician serves as a leader, or as the sole performer, then the minimum doubles. If a musician plays a second instrument, or "doubles," he or she is entitled to a 50 percent premium for the first double, and 20 percent for each additional double. Musicians are also entitled to a fee for "carting," the cost of transporting some of the larger instruments to and from the studio. Travel fees for work outside of designated geographic areas are, of course, reimbursed within a reasonable period. Musicians who appear on camera are also paid for time spent on wardrobe and make-up; rest periods, meal breaks, and notification of calls are all detailed in the Agreement as well.

The Television Videotape Agreement is similar, but some of the rates and rules differ slightly. On a weekly half-hour show, each player receives $186.40, plus an "air rate" of $76.40. These rates pay for two hours of rehearsal on the same day as the show is recorded. For a one-hour show, the rate is $315.95 plus an air rate of $95.35. Four rehearsal hours are included, in addition to the time spent actually recording the show. A 100 percent surcharge applies for reuse. There are specific limitations on the use of music in news and magazine programs. When music is heard in the background at a live event (such as a parade or a sporting event), no payments are made.

The most severe limitation in the Videotape Agreement is in the use of excerpts from other, usually older, programs. If a clip including music is used, every musician on the original production is entitled to receive between one and two hours' payment at the current Variety Show rate.

Theme music—music composed as the opening and/or closing theme (up to 3 minutes total), as opposed to music used in the body of the program—is also subject to special rules. Theme rates do not apply to a series, for example, unless musicians are employed for every episode within the series. Different rules apply for theme music to news, commentary, public-affairs, religious, and sports programs. Most AFM agreements are quite complex; when in doubt, the producer should request a written interpretation of any confusing clauses from the local AFM office.

Different rate scales apply for variety programs, including both specials and regularly-scheduled weekly programs, and for strip shows.

Night premiums and overtime rates as quoted in the Television Videotape Agreement differ from those given in the Television Film Agreement. Doubling costs 25 percent for the first double and 10 percent for each additional instance. Reuse rates are listed, ranging from 75 percent for the second and third run, down to 5 percent for the eighth and each subsequent run. Foreign reuse (outside the U.S. and Canada) fees can be bought out by paying 45 percent of the scale payment, or paid by area (Area 1 is the United Kingdom, at 15 percent of scale; Area 5, Middle and South America, is 5 percent of scale).

The Videotape Agreement also contains terms for basic cable and pay TV. These rates are somewhat lower than network and syndication rates, and offer the added advantage of easy accommodation for multiple plays. For example, with pay TV, the payment rate for 15 play dates within 18 months of the first exhibition is 150 percent of scale.

A third AFM agreement, for Documentary and Industrial Films, differs mainly in the minimum pay scales and the absence of reuse fees from the other two.

The pension rate for AFM is 9 percent of all payments. The contribution to the health and welfare fund is $6.50 per session per musician.

USE OF LIVE MUSIC

Earlier in the history of television, live music was an important part of variety shows and a surprising number of other types of programs, including talk and game shows. Some programs employed a large band; *The Tonight Show* is the only significant hold-over.

Today, the use of live musicians on television is generally limited to concert and performance programs, talk/variety shows employing relatively small bands (*Late Night with David Letterman*, *The Arsenio Hall Show*), large-scale variety specials, and the occasional musical game show.

The process of working with live musicians should begin with the selection of a music director, who supervises composition, arrangement, and copying, as well as the hiring of musicians. Each of these areas includes personnel who are guided by AFM rules, and paid according to AFM minimums. Some of these people are frequently paid over scale, notably the composer.

Rehearsals must be carefully scheduled to maximize the number of usable hours; this can be difficult when other elements of the production must be rehearsed as well. If the live show is scheduled at night, then additional payments may be due, and if the program is recorded and replayed, then reuse rates apply. Cartage, doubling, and leader rates must be considered as well.

The rates and rules regarding the use of star performers are similar, though overscale fees are common.

USE OF RECORDED MUSIC

Most of the music heard on television is pre-recorded by companies that specialize in creating and producing television music. Opens and closes for local news programs, show themes, music for promos and commercials—the list of customized music types is a long one.

Commissioned Music

Several music-production companies generally compete for a commission. Each is asked to bring samples of previous work. Some companies take the initiative and prepare a demo at their own expense, on spec, but the more successful ones only produce demos at the client's expense. The job is described in broad terms; the producer selects a company based on its previous experience and on the producer's instinct. Terms are negotiated, and the job is awarded.

In a typical arrangement, the music-production company is paid 50 percent to start work. Music is composed and presented to the client, who offers comments and criticism. After a few revisions, arrangements are written, players are hired, and the music is recorded. An additional

25 percent is usually due on the first day of recording. The music is mixed and edited, with the final 25 percent payable on delivery.

The music publishing rights in commissioned music are usually divided 50/50, as per the traditional split between publisher and composer. The television production company frequently has an affiliated music publishing company which administers publishing rights in its productions. Other arrangements may be negotiated, of course.

Rates may change over the years, but one leading music house suggested five pricing levels for the production of music for television. The low end is represented by a hungry newcomer using several synthesizers and recording all of the necessary work for a flat fee of roughly $1,500. One step up—$3,500 to $5,000—pays for a demo from a successful house, or a small-scale job (a "bed" for a series of on-air promos, a theme for a low-budget show). Generally, $6,000–$8,000 will pay for a small to medium-sized job, like a news theme for a station in a small market or the score for a basic cable, low-budget syndication, or medium-priced industrial project. Most of the well-known syndication and pay TV programs are in the next echelon: $15,000–$20,000. In the music-production business, the best jobs pay over $25,000.

Sync license fees are included in these prices, and so are recording costs. Performance royalties may be handled via a traditional ASCAP or BMI license, with the proceeds split between composer and publisher. Sometimes, a source licensing deal is negotiated, particularly for projects that the performing rights organization might not count when calculating license fees.

Lower-budget jobs are often done by non-AFM musicians, or sometimes by union members working secretly or under assumed names (see page 345).

If all rights are not transferred as part of the deal, music composed for one client may also be resold to another, non-competitive client. This is common practice, for example, when selling music to television news programs. A theme may be sold to no more than one station in each market, of course—but there is no reason why a station in Chicago cannot use the same music as a station in Denver, presuming that both station's creative needs can be satisfied.

Licensing Pre-Recorded Music

The use of existing recordings for television music requires several layers of rights and payments. First, there is the synchronization license for the use of the composition. Second, there is the payment to the musicians whose work is included in the recording. Third, there is a payment to a producer and/or record company, or to the artist who holds the rights to television use of the recording. The latter payment is often called a "needle-drop" right.

The synchronization license has already been discussed (see page 283).

The payment to the artist and musicians can be costly, and if the recording is an old one, some research may be necessary to find not only the names, but the addresses of the people involved (or their estates). Many older recordings were made on a flat-rate buyout contract, in which musicians exchanged their right to future earnings for a flat fee. This greatly simplifies matters. Also, prior to February 15, 1972, their recorded *performance* of music could not be copyrighted under federal law in the U.S., although the music itself might be. This is another advantage to using older recordings.

Most well-known recordings feature artists who are not only famous, but protected by lawyers and others who guard their interests. Securing permission to use a recording by Michael Jackson is likely to be difficult and costly, while the rights to a work by Emmylou Harris or The Band might be a more reasonable undertaking. Popular recording stars are likely to be unimpressed by typical television music fees, and, viewing the usage as a possible dilution of the music's value, they often refuse such offers.

The music publisher must also grant permission for the music's use and, if it is not handled by a performing rights society, a performance license. Determining who owns this right—and who may traffic in it—usually requires some patience. When negotiations do begin, the seller has the advantage of knowing the producer's specific interest. However, since this is "found money," the seller is also motivated to accept any reasonable figure.

In the real world, many smaller television productions incorporate well-known music without permission. This is especially true of programs produced for private use (an in-company training video, for example), and on local TV in the smallest markets, where the likelihood of any knowledgeable viewer questioning use is small. Still, this practice is technically a violation of copyright, and the consequences for the guilty can be severe. In larger markets, and on all forms of national television, producers are far more careful in securing the necessary permissions.

Music Libraries

Many television productions do not require original music or even the use of well-known recordings. A handful of companies specialize in the production and distribution of "pre-cleared" music that requires no additional sync or performance licenses and no permissions from performers or record companies. The library is paid a fee for its music (provided nowadays on compact disc), plus an annual renewal fee. A producer, production company, recording studio, television station, or other entity is then permitted unlimited use of the music.

Public-Domain Recordings

The use of recordings in the public domain can be a tricky business. Thorough research is required in order to determine that the recording, and all of its underlying rights, are in the public domain. Simply identifying the copyright of the recording itself is not sufficient to establish public-domain status.

If the musical composition is under copyright, then a sync license is required. This, too, can be complicated, particularly for an older song. Published sheet music, for example, may have a different copyright date from the copyright date of the composition itself.

Although, in the U.S., performances could not be copyrighted until 1972, arrangements have been copyrighted since early this century.

AFM payments and residuals may also be due via contract to musicians who played on the recording of a public-domain composition. The original record company, which may no longer be in operation, probably sold its master recordings—and the rights to use them—to a successor, and this entity should be tracked down as well.

Part 5

AUDIENCE MEASUREMENT AND ADVERTISING

34 Audience Measurement, Research, and Ratings

In the U.S., and in an increasing number of countries worldwide, broadcasting and advertising share a symbiotic relationship. Broadcasters provide the distribution of programs that include commercials; advertisers subsidize program production, acquisition, and other operations by paying for access to the broadcaster's (or cablecaster's) audience.

THE BASICS OF AUDIENCE MEASUREMENT

Effective advertising is a business of numbers. In print advertising, readership is measured by a formula that multiplies the number of copies printed and circulated by a certain number of readers per copy. Yet this method yields only a rough estimate of how many readers can later recall seeing an advertisement. With electronic media, it is equally, if not more, difficult to determine how many people are actually watching a commercial message at a given time. Television advertisers rely on estimates of audience size from independent market-research firms. Nielsen Media Research and the Arbitron Ratings Company are by far the largest such agencies in the U.S. Arbitron is owned by Control Data Corporation, and Nielsen, by Dun & Bradstreet; both parent companies own other companies specializing in research and data services.

Data Collection

Television audience size is not measured by counting the actual number of viewers tuned to a program. This type of counting would be prohibitively expensive and—according to the market-research firms—unnecessary.

Both Nielsen and Arbitron track the viewing patterns of smaller numbers of households; households are selected according to proven statistical research techniques, and serve as a representative sample of a far larger audience. A few hundred households represent a population of several million for local ratings, and a few thousand households represent over 90 million households for national ratings.

In a large market, Nielsen and Arbitron may each contact up to 5,000 households for participation in a single week's survey. Roughly two-thirds of the households contacted agree to make regular written entries in diaries—notations in a small schedule booklet each time any set in the house is turned on or off, and each time the channel is changed, always noting who is doing the viewing. (Both services report that approximately half the households do the job correctly, and half do not.) Nielsen and Arbitron collect four weeks' worth of diaries, tabulate the data, and enter the information into a database. Their findings are presented as a series of reports to advertising agencies, sponsors, networks, media buyers, rep firms, producers, distributors, and local stations, all of which pay a subscription fee for access to the information.

For national ratings, and for measurement in an increasing number of local markets, electronic metering systems have replaced the older diary format.

A Brief History of Audience Measurement

The need for measurement of radio audiences became clear by the late 1920s, as an experimental medium was changing into a viable advertising medium. Crossley ratings were first taken in 1930, via telephone polling: listeners were asked to recall what they had heard during the preceding hours. Hooperatings, introduced in 1935, improved upon the formula by collecting coincidental information—asking listeners not to recall what they had heard (which was likely to be inaccurate), but only what they were currently hearing. Trendex was among the early audience-measurement services; once again, polling was done via phone calls to viewers.

In the 1950s, Nielsen began inserting a record-keeping mechanism in television sets. By 1960, the American Research Bureau had introduced the Arbitron rating; the technical-sounding name came from an electronic box installed in sample homes that delivered viewership data every 90 seconds to a central computer. Although this method was a dramatic improvement over telephone polling, the same company's ARB ratings—which were based on telephone polling—remained dominant throughout the 1960s. Videodex, a diary-based ratings service, also appeared in the 1960s. In time, Nielsen and Arbitron became the only significant audience-measurement services.

Since the 1930s, two principal trends have guided the evolution of audience measurement. First, the information has become more and more accurate, as data-collection methodology and technology have improved. Second, the information has become available more quickly—where two weeks were once required for collecting and formatting diary data, the same information (and more) is now available overnight from electronic metering systems. Both trends are likely to continue, and to become more sophisticated in terms of tie-ins with other marketing-measurement systems. For example, in the future, a single household's viewing patterns might be correlated with their supermarket buying patterns to determine the true effectiveness of commercial advertising.

For television, Nielsen offers both national and local ratings;

Arbitron offers only local measurement, with a national service in development. Nielsen's system for measuring national audiences is somewhat similar to its system for measuring local audiences, but the two are different enough to warrant separate discussions.

MEASUREMENT OF NATIONAL AUDIENCES

The Nielsen Television Index (NTI) is Nielsen's national system for measuring network audiences. Four thousand households have their viewing habits monitored by electronic PeopleMeters. Households are paid $50 for the installation, remain in the sample for two years, and receive gifts for their participation from a merchandise catalog (most of the items are worth less than $20). Households are selected in accordance with statistical rules of sampling; according to Nielsen, the size and composition of the sample is representative of national viewership.

NTI data is reported in more than a dozen standard formats, generally published at least four times a year, and some as often as weekly. The best known report, called Pocketpiece (because the booklet is small enough to fit into the pocket of a suit jacket), is published weekly. Pocketpiece includes estimates of program viewership presented in three ways: alphabetically, by name of the program; in a color network schedule grid (see Figure 2); and chronologically, by time periods. The alphabetical listing shows the number of stations carrying the show, the percentage of the country that can see the show, the rating and share for the total audience, and viewers per thousand households, broken down by demographic groups. The schedule grid shows the HUT ("Homes Using Television") level, or the number of households watching TV at that time; average audience size in gross numbers (000) and in rating percentage; the share; and each quarter-hour's rating. The time period estimates show ratings by demographic groups. (See below for definitions of these terms.)

The PeopleMeter collects minute-by-minute viewing information. It also reports when the set is turned on or off, what channel is being watched, and how long the set has been tuned to that channel. Newer, more sophisticated systems allows viewer identification by pressing a button on a special remote control. National overnight ratings for prime time programs as determined by PeopleMeter households is available by 3:15 P.M. on the following day.

Nielsen's other NTI publications include more detailed reports on total U.S. household television usage, demographic breakdowns, and reports specifically written for advertisers, such as the Household & Cost Per Thousand Report.

Nielsen provides overnight ratings information from 25 major markets. This local information is collected by a simple electronic device (not the PeopleMeter); the data is limited to set on/off and channel being viewed. The data can be retrieved from Nielsen's computers by

6:00 A.M. on the following day, and is circulated in printed form once per week. Before Nielsen's PeopleMeters, audimeters were used to collect information for overnight ratings; these devices, located in only a few large metropolitan areas, provided local data that was then used to develop a national estimate.

Nielsen is developing a "smart" metering system for use in the late 1990s. New image-recognition technology will allow Nielsen to automatically identify every viewer, eliminating the need for diaries and pressing buttons. The technological challenge is a substantial one, since variables like room lighting, distance from the television, and viewers blocked by open newspapers might affect the system's reliability.

MEASUREMENT IN LOCAL MARKETS

Both Nielsen and Arbitron collect data with electronic meters in some local markets. The numbers are growing each year; as of this writing, Arbitron has over a dozen metered markets for local measurement, and Nielsen has over two dozen. Other local markets still use the diary format.

Sweeps

In February, May, July, and November, Arbitron measures 209 markets, and Nielsen, 211. Because these surveys sweep the country, these four-week periods are called *sweeps*. If there is client demand for additional surveys, as is often the case in the larger markets, then additional surveys are conducted, typically in January, March, and October. Individual households participate for only one week during the sweep.

The resulting ratings are used mainly by local stations (network affiliates and independents) to set advertising rates. Although past performance cannot forecast the future viewership, these ratings are, at least, a basis for negotiation.

Information Provided to Nielsen and Arbitron Subscribers

Local stations and other subscribers receive three basic types of information from Nielsen and Arbitron: a program's rating, its share, and the gross number of viewers watching a station each quarter-hour. A program's *rating* is the percentage of *total television households* in the sample area whose sets were tuned to that program; a program's *share* is the percentage of *total viewing households* whose sets were tuned to that program. The difference between these definitions is significant. Ratings indicate the absolute number of possible viewers, regardless of the time period. Shares, however, are based on the number of households whose television sets are actually turned on. The figure for these viewing households with sets actually turned on is often called the HUT (Homes Using Television). Share and rating information is provided for each station by quarter-hour, as are gross numbers of viewers watching that station every quarter-hour.

The different numbers vary in their significance among advertisers, programmers, and producers. For a local advertiser, the total number of households that saw the program—and its commercials—can be the most important figure. The ratings information is also useful because it shows the relative strength, or value, of each station and program as an advertising medium. To a network programmer or producer, the program's share—its drawing power against competitors in the time slot—may be critical. Programmers and producers are also extremely interested in ratings; after all, a local program with a low rating may not be able to attract or sustain sponsorship, regardless of its share relative to other programs in the time slot. A syndicated program with poor ratings will either be rescheduled to another time slot where it may perform better (or do less damage to the schedule), or it may be canceled.

The "Ratings Book"

Both Nielsen and Arbitron publish their viewership statistics in several formats. The most common is the market ratings book, which Nielsen calls Viewers in Profile, and Arbitron, the Arbitron Local Market Television Report. The Nielsen book begins with a profile of the market and the research sample: the total number of households; the number of television households; the percentage of households with multiple sets, with UHF, and with cable; the relative sizes of the counties within the market; and the demographic breakdown of households in the sample. In addition, there is statistical data about the sample (the standard errors, the measurement schedule) as well as information about the stations (pre-emptions of network schedules, operating hours).

The "Daypart Summary" (see Figure 3) provides share information, and detailed rating information, by times of day: 7:00–9:00 A.M., 9:00 A.M.–12:00 P.M., 12:00–4:00 P.M., 4:00–6:00 P.M., 6:00–8:00 P.M., 8:00–11:00 P.M., 11:00–11:30 P.M., and 11:30 P.M.–1:00 A.M. There are other configurations shown as well, such as 3:00–5:00 P.M., and 4:00–7:30 P.M. This information is useful for sponsors who purchase rotation schedules, rather than spots on individual programs. It also shows trends that are difficult to detect on more detailed reports. For each station, in each daypart, these charts show the ratings and shares in the central metropolitan area ("Metro") and in the DMA (Designated Market Area; see below). The charts show share history over the past four rating periods, with the DMA ratings broken down by demographic group (women, for example, are classified as 18+, 12–24, 18–34, 18–49, 21–49, 25–49, 25–54, and "working"). The Daypart Summary also shows distribution of viewers over adjacent DMAs, the gross numbers of viewers (in thousands), and other information relating to the percentage of Metro and DMA households who sampled the station during the daypart.

The "Program Averages" section of Nielsen's Viewers in Profile book provides information about the performance of entire individual programs. Each program is listed with its rating and share, for each of the four weeks of the measurement period. The share trend shows the program's share during the past four measurement periods (16 weeks). A HUT figure represents the total number of homes using television during the time period. As in the dayparts summary, the ratings statistics for each program are broken down by demographic groups (there are some additional breakdowns in this section), plus gross viewership numbers, again broken down by group.

The longest section in the book, "Time Period," shows viewership by time period (typically, half-hours). This section provides many of the same statistics as the Program Averages section, but the presentation makes it easier to see program performance within individual time periods.

The "Persons Shares" section shows the viewing habits of individual demographic groups (e.g., Men 18–49, Children 6–11, Persons 12–24).

As the complex organization of the ratings book suggests, viewer-related data can be processed in a variety of meaningful ways. Most large clients use the books for reference, but access the database via desktop computer, a set-up that allows subscribers to request and compare specific pieces of information. For example, in considering an anchor candidate, a station in Baltimore might review the ratings history of his news show in Milwaukee. A station in Boston might determine whether to move a popular syndicated prime access (7:00–8:00 P.M.) series into early fringe (3:00/3:30–5:00/5:30 P.M.) by examining the history of similar strategies in Albany, Columbus, and Providence. These sophisticated computations are now commonplace in local television, and although they can be done by hand using printed ratings books from each of the markets, the database provides a far more flexible system for research. Syndicators, for example, use this information to show stations how specific properties can attract larger audiences within specific time slots.

Definition of Market Sizes

ADI, or Area of Dominant Influence, is the Arbitron term that defines a particular market area. An ADI covers all the counties whose viewing is dominated by signals from a particular city, and every county belongs to one (and only one) ADI. The top ten ADIs, as of 1990, are New York, Los Angeles, Chicago, Philadelphia, San Francisco, Boston, Dallas/Fort Worth, Detroit, Washington, D.C., and Houston.

Nielsen's DMA (Designated Market Area) is a similar concept—every county is assigned to one DMA, though Nielsen will split a county into two DMAs if viewing patterns within the county vary due to unusual terrain or the reception of peripheral signals. Differences in

Nielsen's and Arbitron's respective methodologies result in some significant disparities in definitions of market size. Dallas/Fort Worth, market number seven among ADIs, is number nine among DMAs; Washington, D.C., ADI number nine, is DMA number seven. Houston is a top ten market among ADIs, but not DMAs; Cleveland is number ten among DMAs, but not among ADIs (the distinction may be significant if the advertising plan calls for buying commercial time in the top ten markets). For the most part, however, a market's ADI and DMA designation are identical, or within a few positions up or down. Among the top 50 markets, there are few significant differences. But in markets 51 to 100, differences of three or four positions are common, and above 101, the variations are larger. (Springfield, MA is the 98th ADI and the 109th DMA; this is one of the largest spreads.) Both Nielsen and Arbitron measure over 200 market areas—there are 209 ADIs and 211 DMAs. Arbitron does not measure Alaska and Hawaii (among DMAs, Honolulu is 71).

SYNDICATION AND CABLE RATINGS

Nielsen also uses its NTI data from PeopleMeters to prepare the NSS Pocketpiece, a weekly report of the Nielsen Syndication Service. The format follows that of the NTI Pocketpiece. All three sections list the programs alphabetically, but there is no information provided about the time that programs air, because in syndication programming, a program's time slot varies from one market to the next. Program-audience estimates are presented in three series of charts. The first lists each syndicated program, the number of stations carrying the program, the percentage of television households that can receive the program, and ratings broken down by demographic segments. The second chart shows viewership in thousands for a program, again by demographic group; the third chart shows viewers per thousand households. Coverage-area ratings measure the audience in markets where the program can actually be seen, and are particularly useful for syndicated shows, which may not be seen in 100 percent of the country. The national rating for a program not seen in all markets will be lower than its coverage-area rating.

Cassandra, an analysis system acquired by Nielsen in 1980, provides data on individual syndicated programs. In addition to household and demographic data, Cassandra reports comparative information regarding lead-ins, as well as competitive history. (A "lead-in" is a program that precedes another program, and that presumably brings some of its viewers to the subsequent show.) Cassandra statistics are developed on a market-by-market basis, but their cumulative (nationwide) results are frequently used to compare the relative ratings success of syndicated programs. At the end of every sweep period, Cassandra provides rankings of syndicated shows.

Cable Ratings

Both Nielsen and Arbitron collect data relating to cable television viewership. Diary households are encouraged to write down the cable channel number and the name of the program; with electronically-measured households, cable viewership is automatically reported, and People-Meters are also used. Neither Nielsen nor Arbitron provides detailed viewership information about cable viewing in their regular reports, but both services offer special cable television reports on a regular basis, in print and via computer-accessible database.

On an average weekday night, the cumulative rating earned by *all* cable networks is generally equal to the rating earned by the number two or number three broadcast network.

CHALLENGES CREATED BY CHANGING MEDIA

The popularity of cable television and home video has complicated the audience-measurement process. Many viewers armed with remote controls bounce back and forth between numerous broadcast and cable channels within limited periods. In just one minute, a viewer armed with a remote control can easily sample a dozen or more channels. Were this easily measured and reported, the value of the information would be dubious at best. For example, a viewer who is more or less simultaneously viewing three or four programs would be difficult to count for advertising purposes; indeed, it is often the ads that are skipped.

Home video presents a special challenge for audience measurement. Normally, broadcast and cable data is collected by noting the channel number—and this is done either by having the viewer fill out a diary or by connecting a meter to the television's tuner. As for time-shifting (recording broadcast or cable programs for viewing at a later date), PeopleMeter systems can measure the program as it is being recorded, but cannot determine whether is actually seen, or how many times it has been seen. In order to collect data on other aspects of home video, it is necessary to know the name of the software being played— be it a videogame, a videocassette, or a laserdisc—and how it is being used. Manual identification of video is relatively simple—a viewer need only write down a title—but this information cannot be verified. More reliable electronic identification would require an encoded signal on every piece of software, and a reader connected to the videogame, VCR, or laserdisc player. Identification is only part of the issue, though. If a videocassette contains a commercial, a sponsor needs to know if the commercial was viewed, whether it was viewed at standard speed, and how many times the tape, and the commercial, was viewed. The same is true of a laserdisc. These variations become even more complicated with regard to a videogame, and with newer devices like interactive compact-disc software.

Nielsen is working on a system of home-video tracking, which would operate as follows. A video software label contracts with Nielsen to track a specific title. Nielsen assigns a code and a continuous time stamp that is recorded onto the Vertical Blanking Interval (VBI) on every copy of the videocassette title. The cassettes are placed in general distribution, and when a PeopleMeter household rents or buys the tape, the PeopleMeter not only recognizes the tape as an encoded title, but tracks which portions of the tape were played, and how often. Such a method of tracking home-video usage could measure a program's viewership down to the second.

35 Advertising

Advertising provides nearly all of the financing for commercial domestic broadcast television, and approximately half of the financing for domestic cable television (the other half is provided by subscriber revenues). This chapter explains how television advertising works.

ADVERTISING AGENCIES

A full-service advertising agency provides its clients with consumer and market research, as well as the development, implementation, and evaluation of advertising strategies and campaigns. Specifically, the agency works with the client to determine the target customer(s), identify one or more marketing objectives, and recommend a message and a style of presentation. The agency produces the physical materials—such as print advertisements and television commercials—then selects and purchases the space (print media) and time (electronic media) for these advertisements.

The largest agencies are huge corporations offering not only advertising, but related services, including public relations, direct marketing, and sales promotion. Some agencies will even produce specialized programming for a client. According to *Advertising Age*, the top ten advertising agencies in 1990, in terms of U.S. network television placements, were: Leo Burnett, Saatchi & Saatchi, D'Arcy Masius Benton & Bowles, Grey Advertising, Young & Rubicam, Backer Spielvogel Bates, J. Walter Thompson, BBDO, Ogilvy & Mather, and McCann-Erickson. Smaller agencies that have established distinguished reputations for television advertising include Chiat/Day/Mojo and Hal Riney & Partners.

Organization

An advertising agency is typically organized in three basic groups. *Creative Services* develops the advertising concepts, refines them as required by the account team and the client, then produces the commercials and other materials. A creative director is the senior person on the creative team; one creative director may be responsible for several accounts. *Media Services* negotiates for airtime and other media buys on the client's behalf. Finally, *Account Services* is responsible for client relations. This group works with Creative Services to assure that the client's needs are met; that the storyboards and the commercials are consistent with the marketing strategy; and that production is proceeding in accordance with the client's requirements and budget limitations. The account executive is the senior person on the account team; one account supervisor usually manages several accounts.

Agency Billing

The advertising agency makes money in three ways.

First, the agency receives a commission on every media buy, sometimes as much as 15 percent. If, for example, a 30-second spot costs $1,000, the agency actually buys the spot for $850, bills the client for $1,000, and retains $150 as a commission. If client billings total $1 million for a year, the agency retains $150,000 in commissions. The agency's commission or fee structure can be negotiated as part of the client-agency agreement.

Second, the agency may receive a fee for its services, often a monthly retainer that the client will pay over and above, in lieu of, or in combination with, the agency's commissions. The monthly retainer generally reflects the number of hours spent by members of the account and creative teams working on the assignment. For example, an art director earning $1,000 per week might be spending half of his or her time on a certain account, or 20 hours per week. This time is billed at approximately three times the labor cost (which covers taxes, benefits, office, overhead, supervisory management, and other related expenses, plus a profit). The client is billed $1,500 for the artist's 20 hours of work per week. Unlike legal charges, these billings are based not on the time logged by any one or two people, but on a reasonable estimate of the hours spent by the team assembled for, or assigned to, a given project.

Third, the agency receives a reimbursement for production costs. When the agency arranges for the production of a commercial, or a series of commercials, the agency bills the client for the cost of production. In addition, the agency usually (but not always) receives a mark-up on production costs, typically in the range of 10 percent.

Media Decisions

Television is only one of many media available to the media buyer. It can be the most effective medium when the goal is mass coverage at a relatively low CPM (cost per thousand people who will see the commercial); when the advertiser needs to reach a broad demographic segment of the audience; and when the impact of sound, picture, and movement can help to deliver the message to potential customers.* Television advertising also works well for products or services that lend themselves to an empathic relationship between viewers and on-screen characters or situations.

---

* Courtland L. Bovée and William F. Arens, *Contemporary Advertising*.

Television advertising has its drawbacks as well. The cost of producing a television commercial is almost always higher than the cost of producing advertising materials for radio, print, billboards, or other media. Although the CPM can be lower than with other media, the larger number of viewers can drive the gross cost far higher than it would be with other media. This is especially true of network television; local television and cable, however, can be surprisingly affordable.

Network television is a true mass medium, in the sense that it reaches all kinds of demographic groups. Regional networks, local syndication, and cable channels can be better choices if the goal is to reach more specific demographic or psychographic groups, such as country-music lovers or young teens.

Through the late 1960s, television advertisements were 60 seconds long; now, they are mostly 30 seconds and, more and more often, 15 seconds long. As a result, commercials with complicated messages may not be effective. Clutter is a growing problem as well—too many messages barraging the viewer. Unlike print advertisements, which may only interrupt the reader every few minutes, television commercials work in a dynamic environment where messages can speed by too quickly to register an impact on first, second, or even third viewing. Zapping via remote control further aggravates the situation.

ADVERTISING ON NETWORK TELEVISION

There are several methods by which advertisers buy time on network programs: sponsorship, spot buying, and upfront buying.

Sponsorship

The most involved form of television advertising is sponsorship of an individual program. Two types of sponsorship are available on network television.

The first is *full-program sponsorship* (a classic example is *Hallmark Hall of Fame*). In this format, a single sponsor buys most or all of the commercial time within a program. Full sponsorship can provide enhanced visibility amidst a cluttered programming and commercial environment. If there is a synergy between the program and the advertiser or its message, a full sponsorship can provide viewers with the image of corporate importance. The advertiser's involvement frequently goes beyond buying commercial time; the production may be promoted by a public-relations and print-advertising campaign. Full sponsorship was more prevalent in the 1950s than it is today; examples from that period include *Armstrong Circle Theater, General Electric Theater, Camel News Caravan, U.S. Steel Hour, The Lux Show with Rosemary Clooney,* and *GE College Bowl*. Full-program sponsorship is uncommon on commercial television, since skyrocketing productions costs have made many advertisers wary of putting all their eggs in one basket. Still, a form of exclusive participation is evident on public television. Several large corporations have successfully identified themselves with high-visibility public television programs—Mobil with *Masterpiece Theatre*, for example.

With a *participating sponsorship*, several sponsors share a form of exclusive sponsorship within a program or series. For a premium fee, and a commitment to an ongoing position within the program or series, each participating sponsor is assured exclusivity within its product category. If, for example, Bud Lite helps sponsor the World Series, then no other light-beer brand can advertise (a non-light beer may be allowed, depending upon the arrangement). The participating sponsor may also receive a "billboard," or an on-screen logo with a voice-over advertising slogan, such as "brought to you by . . ."; the billboard usually appears at the beginning of a program. Participating sponsorships may be sold either for entire programs or events, or for parts of events, such as the first and second halves of a football game.

Spot Buying

Most network advertising is not sold on the basis of a sponsor affiliation with program content. Instead, commercial time is sold on a *spot* or *scatter* basis. In a relatively recent development, advertisers buy time in groups of programs whose *cumulative* viewership offers the desired demographics, psychographics, and geographic skew.

In the 1950s and 1960s, a company that wanted to advertise on network television would select a program that seemed compatible with its advertising message, and buy one 60-second commercial in the program each week. At that time, there were 39 weeks of original shows, with 13 weeks of reruns; now, there are 20 to 22 weeks of original shows. By the mid-1970s, the networks changed their scheduling practices, largely as a result of intramural competition. They began to drift away from programming the same shows in the same time slots week after week. Instead, they started debuting new shows at times other than September (and other than January, which once marked the "second season"), canceling programs in mid-season and moving shows around on the schedules. The old buying practices were no longer viable, so each advertiser had its agency's media department buy television time as a package (of commercials) whose cumulative impact would, hopefully, equal the impact of the old system. The immediate benefit to the networks was the ability to place advertisers in less desirable shows. Given the possibility of a less desirable audience, or a smaller one, the networks began to guarantee a specific number of viewers (within specific demographic and geographic groups)—but on the basis of the entire package, not on the performance of any particular program.

Upfront Buying

This "package guarantee" method of selling advertising time on network shows evolved into the tradition known as *upfront buying*. In upfront buying, the networks offer advertisers "avails" (time slots) at a discount months before the season begins.

Upfront Buying: Network Prime Time

Immediately after each network's program department announces the prime time schedule for the fall season (in May), the network sales departments start selling commercial time on those programs. They offer advertisers approximately 65 to 75 percent of prime time avails at a 15 percent discount. The prime time upfront buying season generally begins in May and goes through early July (the upfront buying season begins as early as March for Saturday morning children's programming and for other dayparts).

During the upfront buying season, advertising agencies register each client's budget with the network, along with a request for a package of shows that reach the client's target audience. The network sales department responds with a proposal detailing the number of spots, the programs, and their air dates. After negotiation, agreement is reached on the CPM (which may actually be cost per thousand *households*, if only one viewer in each household is in the proper demographic category). The network and advertiser also work out the list of shows, the dates on which the spots will appear, and the probable rating. The advertiser commits to the time, but the degree of commitment can vary. If the client commits to 52 weeks, the deal is likely to be more flexible than a deal for a smaller commitment. A deal might include the option to cancel up to 25 percent of the order for first quarter, for example. Rates are likely to be lower if the advertiser buys more time overall, or more time in less desirable shows.

For a client with $10 million to spend in prime time, the advertising agency's media-planning department devises a plan. The media planners work closely with the client, in conjunction with the account group and media buyers, and eventually make recommendations as to the best way to reach the target audience. Based on estimates of how the package will perform, the network and the agency negotiate a CPM. Working from estimated ratings, the network guarantees to deliver a certain number of viewers in each demographic group. If the ratings turn out to be lower than the network promised, the advertiser is entitled to *make-goods*, or additional commercials in prime time programs. The new shows and dates, however, may not be desirable ones, or may not meet the client's needs. The agency, therefore, tries to avoid make-goods by buying time in programs for which the anticipated ratings and the actual ratings are most likely to be similar.

Negotiations are staged on several fronts. First, the agency may want more units within specific programs—"Can you give me one more *Wonder Years* and take out a *Roseanne?*"—or may require a lower CPM to compensate for potentially low ratings (which translate into a missed opportunity to reach some viewers). A provisional deal is made; the time is reserved, and the network will not sell that inventory within a specified number of days. In the interim, the agency presents the package to the client for approval. The client usually approves, but only after discussing problems with the deal: the cost is higher than it should be, the program mix is not right. As a rule, a hold on network time is a commitment, and is rarely released.

A client with a $10-million network prime time budget might assign $3–$4 million to each network. The average cost of a spot works out to about $125,000, so the client's budget would probably buy 80 prime time spots. A spot on a top-rated show costs roughly $300,000–$400,000; a spot on a lower-rated show with comparatively weak performance, about $50,000.

For the networks, the benefit of the upfront buy is that the money is on the books; the downside is the 15 percent discount offered, and the need to make good on programs that did not perform as hoped or planned. For the agency and client, the upfront buy assures the best possible commercial positions, and saves money; but the prospect of make-goods can put the client in the position of having commercials run on the wrong shows.

In recent seasons, there has been a great deal of brinkmanship on the upfront market. With the shrinking network audience share and a general slump in advertising spending, many advertisers have balked at the networks' high prices. The spot market has been weak, and some major advertisers—unimpressed by the so-called "discount" being offered for an upfront buy—have been holding out for better rates. The risk to the network is that with fewer upfront sales, already low spot prices will drop even further; the risk to advertisers is that if spot buying increases, the market will tighten up so that spot rates end up higher than upfront rates. Basically, upfront buying only works well so long as the market for commercial time slots is predictable.

Upfront Buying: Network Daytime

There is an upfront buying season for daytime programs as well, which begins after the prime time buying season ends in July. Daytime revenue has been stagnating recently. As the population of women outside the home increases, and more household chores are handled by teenagers, husbands, and other family members, the traditional daytime audience—adult, female—is changing.

Compared with the cost of prime time, advertising on daytime is inexpensive. The CPM for women under 50 during daytime (about $5, on average) is roughly 25 percent of the CPM for the same group during prime time ($20, on average). Daytime television still delivers a relatively "pure" audience of women under 50. While maintaining traditional ties with household, food, and other long-time daytime advertisers, networks have been wooing new types of sponsors, like automotive companies, into daytime—with only limited success.

The average price of a network daytime 30-second spot can be as low as $12,000 during the upfront buying season.

Upfront Buying: Network News

The upfront buying season for network news usually takes place during the summer. The average price per 30-second spot is $55,000, with network news usually attracting an older audience than other dayparts. Most advertisers buy time on the news because it is the best way to reach the 25–54 group, or 55+ men and women.

Advertising on Network Sports Programs

From the perspective of large national advertisers, the key concept for sports programs is exclusivity. Spots in major national events are sold on an exclusive basis within product categories. In automotive, one of the larger categories for sports advertising, the general rule is one domestic and one foreign automotive sponsor. Beer, soft drinks, and fast food may also be subject to exclusive buys. Many exclusivity agreements are negotiated well in advance, and run for more than one year. Because of the pervasiveness of exclusivity, the idea of an upfront buying "season" is not as strict here as in other parts of network television. The sales department gets to work selling time shortly after rights to sports events are purchased. Many sports programs are sold on a series basis: some or all of the baseball or football season, for example. A sponsor with one or more spots in each game is called a "strip sponsor"; a "spot participant" buys time in individual events.

Of network events, the weekly NFL broadcasts are the highest performers; the cost of a spot on a regular telecast is over $100,000 per 30-second spot (a 30-second spot on the Super Bowl costs $800,000 or more). In contrast, baseball on CBS brings the network approximately $40,000 per 30-second spot (based on a 5 rating, and an $8.00–$8.50 CPM). An event with somewhat less appeal, such as a weekend bowling match, would cost about $20,000 per spot. All of this is dependent upon the competitive market environment; in a very soft market, these rates drop by as much as 50 percent.

Locally, baseball brings in about $10,000 per 30-second spot in the largest markets, and $1,000 or less in the smaller ones. If the local team is a winner of the most recent World Series, then the rates might be up to twice as high as in other years, because of increased viewership.

LOCAL TELEVISION ADVERTISING

Two types of advertising buys are available on local stations: 1) time slots that the network leaves open for affiliates during and between its own programs, and 2) slots that are available on non-network shows, mainly during non-prime time hours.

The process of putting national advertising onto local stations begins with a media plan, a strategic breakout for the entire year. The advertiser determines the plan's broad requirements; the agency refines the strategy, produces the commercials, and buys the time.

Once the list of target markets is determined by agency and client, the agency contacts some or all of the stations in each market (often through a "rep firm"; see page 23) and makes an avail request. Specifically, this might be a buy for first quarter, favoring men 18–49, based on a specific number of 700 gross rating points (GRPs) per week, distributed 30 percent in prime time, 15 percent in early fringe (before evening news), 15 percent in late fringe (after late news), and 40 percent in daytime. The avail request also specifies the amount of money that the advertiser is willing to pay: $200 per rating point in early fringe and $350 in prime time, for example.

In trying to reach all of the viewers in a given market, the agency purchases time on most or all of the stations. Each station responds to the avail request, then the negotiations begin, often with the involvement of a national rep firm (see page 23). Stations agree to sell some spots, but hold back others in anticipation of higher rates from other advertisers. For example, an advertiser who needs to reach teens may be willing to pay a premium for a spot in *The Simpsons.* An advertiser with more general needs might also buy *The Simpsons,* but not at a premium price. The station's sales manager makes decisions not only on price, however. Advertising time is perishable, so it may be wiser to sell for 75 percent of the desired rate than to wait and see the time unsold. There is no highest or lowest available rate; rates are based entirely on supply and demand.

Although some stations publish rate cards, the consensus is that rates are generally negotiable. Many agencies refer to rates published in the *Media Market Guide* (Bethlehem Publishing, Bethlehem, NH, 603-869-2418) or a similar seasonal directory. Rates in these directories are based on polls of media buyers nationwide; they can be a useful starting point for negotiations. This marketplace changes rapidly, however, so rates are likely to be out of date soon after publication.

Stations are expected to "post" (report) results. If the station sold commercial time based on an average 4 rating, and the program only gets a 2 rating, then the station arranges a make-good for the advertiser in the form of additional advertising time. Stations do not refund money paid for advertising, and a good sales manager insures important clients' success on his or her station by filling open commercial slots with additional client spots, at no charge. This is generally preferable to using the commercial time for per-inquiry advertising (see page 315) or for direct-response advertising.

Direct-response advertising, used mainly for the sale of magazine subscriptions, books, and records, allows stations to fill unsold time. Direct-response advertisers pay reduced rates for standby positions within a "wide rotator"—a large chunk of the schedule. If the station is sold out, the spots don't run.

Many stations do not run direct-response or per-inquiry advertising. Instead, they fill open time with promos, to encourage viewers to watch other shows on the schedule, or with public service announcements that fulfill FCC public service mandates.

In many markets, the concept of value-added selling is becoming popular. Stations sell not only airtime, but involvement in station promotions as well. This technique is common in local radio.

The mix of local versus national advertising varies with each station. Some stations prefer the relative stability of national advertisers, whose large advertising budgets do not change as often as local advertiser's budgets. Large national clients can be faceless, though—and when times get rough, local advertisers are more likely to support broadcasters with whom they have worked successfully during the good times.

NEWER ADVERTISING MEDIA

Cable television has changed the television advertising marketplace in several significant ways. Cable has spread the television audience over 30 or more channels, more than five times the number of broadcast channels available in most markets. Although many of these channels are watched by relatively small numbers of viewers, or watched for only limited periods of time by larger numbers of viewers, they have contributed to a steady decline in viewership of ABC, CBS, and NBC. Home video has also contributed to this decline. Households with VCRs rent, on average, three to five tapes per month, which means less time spent watching broadcast television. Videogame use also cuts into broadcast-television viewing. Household viewing activity as measured by Nielsen—which does not include VCR playback or videogames— peaked in the mid-1980s at 7 hours 10 minutes per day, but dropped by the 1989–1990 season to 6 hours 55 minutes.

Cable Networks

As the cable networks have matured, they have become more like the commercial broadcast networks in their style of doing business. The cable networks announce their fall schedules in the spring, and an up-front buying season follows. Audience research techniques for cable have been steadily improving, so advertising agencies are now confident that a system based on ratings guarantees will provide the appropriate level of coverage for their clients. Cable buys on the largest networks, such as CNN and MTV, are considered to be very solid investments; the smaller networks are not regarded quite as highly.

Since cable does not reach all U.S. television households, cable buys are evaluated against other cable buys. And unlike network-audience research, cable-audience research is not provided by day, but only by month. Any given daily rating is not as meaningful as the average daily performance over the course of a week or more.

Cable television has increased the supply side of the economic equation for television sports. With cable, sports programming is now available all day, every day. Since sports programs appeal to a particular audience segment—mainly male 18-49 (though most events are viewed by other audience segments as well)—advertisers tend to reach the same audience with commercials on cable sports programs as they do with commercials on network programs. In general, CPMs are in the $4–$7 range, but if the market is soft, the rates are lower.

Home Video as an Advertising Medium

The progress of home video as an advertising medium has been sluggish because of the lack of dependable audience measurement (see page 000). There are ongoing attempts toward such statistics, however. Alexander & Associates does telephone research on a weekly basis; Nielsen has been working with the home video labels to encode videocassettes so that their PeopleMeters will read them. Within the current Nielsen system, there is one wrinkle—the PeopleMeter only counts home video when the viewer *records* a program for later viewing, and not when the program is played back.

To date, the most popular use of home video has been as a promotional marketing medium. In one promotion for a cereal brand, the video label exchanged commercial time on the tape for what amounted to advertising space on the back of a cereal box. No cash changed hands, but the cross-promotion was probably worthwhile. Research shows that people do watch commercials included on pre-recorded cassettes, and home video may eventually become a promising advertising medium (for a more detailed discussion, see Chapter 9).

PRODUCING TELEVISION COMMERCIALS

The advertising agency starts development on a commercial by meeting with the client and identifying the client's marketing objective: increased market share, new product launch, or product differentiation, for example. The creative department works closely with the account department to define and shape an advertising strategy that supports the client's marketing goals. This strategy includes developing creative concepts for print and television advertising, including an overall style and look for the campaign; choosing a slogan, or a spokesperson (if appropriate); preparing scripts and storyboards; suggesting casting ideas; and considering other creative elements like computer animation and special effects.

These sketches, scripts, and storyboards are presented to the client—or, more specifically, to a team consisting of the advertising manager, the product manager, and the marketing manager. This team reviews everything to be sure that the commercial's message and style are consistent with the marketing objective and strategy, and that the commercials do not conflict with company policy.

The approved storyboard is shown to several (usually three) independent production companies, who submit cost estimates for production and post-production of the spot(s). At the same time, these companies offer suggestions to improve the commercials. Some commercials are bid to a single entity—for example, a director who has worked successfully with the client in the past, or one who has a special style that is the basis for the storyboard. The choice of director is almost always based on reputation—and on the quality/style of the commercials on the director's sample "reel" (a cassette filled with the director's work). Many directors are associated with production companies, working as a principal or partner.

The director works with the agency on casting, scripting, and the choice of crew and locations. A national spot generally requires several weeks of pre-production: designing and building sets, choosing locations, composing/arranging/recording music, and attending to the many small details that are part of any television shoot. The shoot itself usually lasts between one and three days for one or more commercials, though some spots take longer. Budgets vary depending upon the campaign and the client's needs; the average cost of a spot shown nationally in 1990 was $174,000.*

The production is completed in the editing room (where scenes are assembled and graphics added) and in the sound-editing room (where the voice-over, sound effects, and music are added, and where the soundtrack is mixed and equalized). Most national commercials are shot on 35mm film; many local spots are produced on videotape.

For most campaigns, several different commercials are produced and tested. The commercials are shown to various groups of people who buy similar products. Commercials are analyzed on the basis of their appeal to specific demographic, psychographic, and geographic groups. While a network spot must appeal to the widest possible audience within a specific target category (such as children), many spots are produced with narrower national audiences in mind—urban black viewers, for example. Other spots are produced for specific regions where certain product preferences are already strong, or need

---

* Source: American Association of Advertising Agencies.

strengthening. A commercial should test successfully before it is placed on the air. While remakes can be quite expensive, the long-term cost of the commercial time—and the potential effect of a successful campaign on a product's market penetration and market share—can more than justify the additional expenditure.

PER-INQUIRY ADVERTISING

Per-inquiry (P.I.) advertising provides suppliers with a low-cost means of marketing their products, at the same time allowing stations to transform unsold commercial time into revenues.

The deal begins with a supplier, typically a manufacturer or distributor, who identifies a product suitable for this specialized form of direct marketing. The product should be priced in the $20–$50 range or higher, and it should appear special or unique, the sort of product that might not easily be found elsewhere (the Ginzu Knife, for example). The supplier produces a commercial, hiring a broker to place the commercial on cable networks and local broadcast stations. The broker typically receives about 5 percent of the product's selling price.

The cable network or local station does not receive a cash payment in exchange for the airtime. Instead, the commercial is shown, and the network or station receives a percentage of each sale attributable to its activities, usually 25 to 35 percent of the selling price.

When a viewer calls the 800 number on the screen, he or she reaches a telemarketing clearinghouse, a firm hired by the supplier to take orders. This firm charges the supplier one fee for each call for information, a higher fee for each call resulting in a sale, and a still higher fee for each call that can be transformed into an "upsale"—a sale of multiple or additional products. The price per call is typically $1 to $3, though these figures vary depending upon the size of the firm, the time spent per call, the number of orders, and so on.

The supplier receives customer payments and an accounting from the telemarketing firm, then passes the payments and records to the broker. The broker deducts the agreed-upon percentage, then pays the station or cable network. Stations and networks are dependent upon accurate, honest recordkeeping for their income, so they are likely to require approval of the telemarketing company, or, in some cases, insist upon using a particular company for this purpose. Since the station owns the airtime, it is in a position to force this decision.

P.I. marketing generally requires some testing. Several commercials may be produced, for example, before one proves to be successful; several venues may be tried before finding the one or two cable networks most suitable for a particular product. Television stations, whose audiences are broader and less segmented than cable networks, usually start new P.I. spots during the overnight period, then schedule the most profitable ones in late-evening and early-morning time slots. Stations are under no obligation to schedule the spots at all, and may program them in any manner that seems reasonable.

INFOMERCIALS AND PROGRAM-LENGTH COMMERCIALS

Although the terms "infomercial" and "program-length commercial" have become associated with a very contemporary approach to marketing, the concept dates back to radio and early television. With these formats, the advertiser can deliver the message for a longer period than a traditional commercial spot allows. In the early days, demonstrations, frequently by the program host, often lasted longer than the allotted 60-seconds. Recently, specialty firms have expanded the infomercial into a direct-marketing format that is rapidly growing in popularity, and that may eventually become a mainstream marketing medium.

The term "infomercial" was probably coined in the mid-1970s to describe the extended-length commercial formats then being tried on cable television. At that time, the term suggested a commercial with a two- to five-minute running time; the extra minutes were offered as an incentive for advertisers who were wary of cable and the new medium's lack of audience research. By the late 1980s, the term "infomercial" also referred to a program-length commercial—that is, a program whose *only* purpose is marketing a product or service.

Program-length commercials run mainly on independent stations and cable networks, though network affiliates run them as well. A direct-marketing firm, typically one that specializes in this format, purchases half-hour program blocks, usually at relatively undesirable times (early weekend mornings, weekday overnight). The cost of the commercial time is low. Even on a top-rated basic cable network, the cost per 30-second spot is only a few hundred dollars. The direct marketer buys all of the spots in the half hour, and provides the program as well. The total cost for the airtime, on a top-rated cable network, is not much more than $2,000–$3,000 (that figure also applies that time period in most major markets).

The direct marketer uses the entire half hour to sell one, or several, products. The product is demonstrated, frequently in a traditional talk-show format; viewers are then told how to order. This sequence may be repeated several times within the half hour. With a $50 gadget that costs the marketer perhaps $10, the cost of show production, overhead, and airtime can usually be recouped by selling more than a 100 units. (The cost of production is amortized over a long period because individual videotapes are used many times, in many markets.)

Television can be a potent direct-marketing medium. According to *Philadelphia* Magazine (December 1990), one firm at its peak sold 10,000 real estate courses per week at $300 per course, for weekly revenues of $3 million. Another firm sold enough $99 kitchen gadgets to gross $48 million in a year. While these figures are on the high side, they show the potential of a unique approach.

Normally, neither the station nor the cable network participates in the direct marketer's revenues. This may change, particularly as the marketers' public image improves. Many of them are considered charlatans because of dubious business practices, exaggerated advertising claims, and aggressive sales pitches. Eventually, the relationship between the station/cable network and the direct marketer may come to resemble the one between the station/cable network and the P.I. advertiser (see page 315).

It seems likely that infomercials will become more prevalent. Local stations, particularly independent ones, have replaced some of their paid religious programming with infomercial programs (up to 10 percent of some independent stations' revenues come from paid programming). Cable networks find the programs to be useful as filler, particularly during the less desirable time slots. The format is working—sales of most well-managed firms specializing in program-length commercials are impressive—so new marketers are likely to join the mix. A trade organization, the National Infomercial Marketing Association, is even forming to develop industry standards. As the business matures, some traditional advertisers may find that a full half-hour program is ideally suited to their marketing needs. A car manufacturer, for example, can do far more in a half hour than in a 30-second spot. The same is true for a computer maker, and for many other types of companies. Paid programs may also go beyond product demonstrations, into topics that sponsors believe to be good for business—or a good match for their own public relations objectives.

36 Regulation of Advertising

Television advertising is subject to rules and regulations at a number of different levels. Content is closely scrutinized and controlled, principally by the Federal Trade Commission at the federal level and by a variety of governmental authorities at the state and local levels. There are also some rules, enforced by the FCC, on the amounts and types of advertising carried on broadcast stations, cable, and the other FCC-regulated media. Finally, there is regulation by the industry itself: stations, networks, and cable companies all have their own standards on what they will accept. In addition, there are industry groups, made up of advertising agencies and their clients, that suggest codes of practices.

THE FTC AND THE CONTROL OF ADVERTISING

The Federal Trade Commission (FTC) is the government's principal overseer of the content and methods of advertising; in fact, it regulates advertising across all fields of publication, not just television. The FTC is an independent agency, like the FCC, with Commissioners nominated by the President and confirmed by Congress (see page 104 for further discussion of agencies). When the FTC was set up in 1912, its principal intended purpose was to regulate in the area of antitrust law. The legislation that established the FTC, however, included the power to regulate unfair business practices, and from the beginning, this jurisdiction was held to cover false advertising. The FTC's power to control false advertising has been confirmed and expanded by Congressional action in the years since, most importantly by the Wheeler-Lea Act in 1938. Section 5(a)(1) of the Federal Trade Commission Act now prohibits both "unfair methods of competition in commerce" and "unfair or deceptive acts or practices in commerce," and the Act gives the FTC the power to intervene and prevent them. These phrases have been interpreted to include false, misleading, or deceptive advertising. The "commerce" referred to in the Act is interstate commerce or international commerce; a finding of interstate commerce will generally be made in the case of an advertisement on a television station or cable service.

The Federal Trade Commission Improvement Act of 1975 gave the FTC authorization to establish industry-wide trade rules over and above the prevention of deceptive advertising. One consequence of the 1975 act was the FTC's proposing extensive restrictions on children's advertising on television. The proposal was not only controversial at the time, but also became an oft-cited example of burdensome over-regulation. Continuing concern in children's television has led Congress to enact, in 1990, a set of laws governing many aspects of children's television (see page 322).

The backlash against regulation that characterized the 1980s affected the FTC, and the Commission's power to set industry-wide trade rules on advertising fairness was restricted. The FTC is still empowered, however, to investigate and resolve individual cases of advertising deception. Complaints can be filed with the FTC by a consumer, a competitor, Congress, or any local, state, or federal agency.

"Deceptive": The Standard

"Deceptive" advertising was defined in 1983 by a three-member majority of the Commission as occurring if there is a "representation, omission or practice that is likely to mislead the consumer acting reasonably in the circumstances to the consumer's detriment." An alternative formulation, suggested by the other members of the Commission, states that an act is deceptive if it has a tendency or capacity to mislead a substantial number of consumers in a material way. Is there a difference between these definitions? Some interpretations say yes: the first approach might require proof of actual injury, while the second requires only that the advertising have the *capacity* to mislead. In practice, it has been held that regardless of which standard is applied, no actual injury need have taken place.

In determining whether or not an advertisement is deceptive, the FTC asks whether the *average* purchaser—not necessarily the least sophisticated or least intelligent possible buyer—would be deceived. Specially-targeted ads, however, are examined in light of the target audiences. Advertising directed at children, for instance, may be judged by a standard reflecting the lessened sophistication of the younger audience.

The context of the entire ad is considered in deciding whether or not the advertisement is deceptive. Thus, the "Joe Isuzu" ads, which combine blatant lies with the statement that lies are being told, would not be deemed deceptive.

The false information can be visual as well as verbal or written. A depiction of a product may be touched up in such a way as to make the picture itself a misleading item. In one commercial which caused difficulty, a knife was shown cutting through a nail, which it could indeed do. When the cutting edge was shown later in the commercial, however, a different knife was substituted, which looked fresh and perfect. This was a deceptive practice. Similarly, in one demonstration comparing shaving creams, the advertiser added foreign substances to the creams to make his own cream look superior. Time-compression photographs can be deceptive, in that they present a distorted picture of a product's characteristics; the use of an actor in a white doctors' coat can give the false impression that the product is endorsed by doctors. As much care should be taken in avoiding misrepresentation through images as through words.

Whether written, verbal, or visual, the misrepresentation need not be an affirmative one. Leaving *out* important details can be as much a source of deception as is putting in affirmative lies.

For advertisers seeking to avoid false or misleading ads, the first line of defense should be common sense: be truthful in fact and in spirit. In making statements about a product, the advertiser and the creative people at the advertising agency should stick closely to substantiated facts. From the FTC standpoint, the key element is to have adequate back-up—gathered in advance—for product claims. If the advertiser does not have proof that the product will do what he says it will do, the statement simply should not be made.

As any observer of American advertising will surely understand, however, advertising statements are not limited to dry facts. A certain level of exaggeration and hyperbole is par for the course in the advertising world, and is permitted as "puffing." Generalizations like "it's great," "amazing," or "wonderful" make no specific claim which can deceive or mislead, and the average buyer will know to discount them. Claims that a toothpaste will "beautify the smile" or that a sewing machine is "almost human" have been permitted under this standard. Unfortunately, the line between permitted puffing and punishable deception is not always clear.

Most large advertising agencies have in-house legal counsel that reviews all advertising copy with an eye towards avoiding deceptive claims; smaller firms frequently retain outside counsel to examine the material. It is strongly recommended that any advertising involving claims of performance or superiority over other brands should be vetted by an attorney.

FTC Guides

The FTC has issued a series of guides concerning particular products and practices. They are available in loose, individually bound form from the FTC, and are also reprinted in standard reference works on the FTC.

Some of the guides focus on specific methods of advertising, including bait advertising, debt collection, endorsements and testimonials, the use of the word "free," guarantees, and statements about prices. Others guides are directed at specific products, claims or industries: automobile fuel economy, beauty schools, pet foods, film and film processing, vocational schools.

Consumer Protection Trade Rules

In addition to the guides that concern deceptive advertising, the FTC has issued rules on a variety of commercial practices. Most of these rules focus on consumer-protection issues that do not affect the television industry (for example, funeral-industry practices). One rule, though, concerns advertising about the size of television picture tubes. There are also rules on advertising consumer-credit and leasing arrangements. The most important of the FTC's consumer-protection rules related to television—those governing advertising aimed at children (see page 162)—were never adopted. Congress has recently taken steps to rectify this through the FCC (see page 322).

The FTC and Complaints Against Advertisers

Complaints against advertisers can come from competitors, consumers, and the FTC's own internal monitoring staff. After investigating, the FTC takes one of several courses of action. Most often, it simply requests that the advertiser change the offending commercial or remove it from the air, and the advertiser complies or works out a compromise with the FTC. If that doesn't work, a cease-and-desist order from the FTC will insist that the offending ad be removed; in the case of knowing violations, the FTC can impose a $10,000 fine. The advertiser may also agree to sign a consent decree in which the company does not admit guilt, but agrees to stop running the commercials and to refrain from similar practices in future advertisements. In severe situations involving food, drugs, medical devices, and cosmetics—where the FTC has broader authority—the FTC may ask the Department of Justice to try the advertiser on a misdemeanor charge.

Advertisers are given 30 days to respond to FTC requests, and may contest any decision. They can eventually appeal FTC decisions in the federal court system.

THE FCC AND ADVERTISING CONTENT

The FCC has largely given up its role as a regulator of the content of advertising. The 1934 Communications Act does allow the FCC to suspend the license of any broadcaster transmitting false or deceptive signals or communications. Nonetheless, as early as the 1970s, the FCC recognized the greater expertise of the FTC on these matters, and by 1985, the FCC had dropped most of its specific policies on false and misleading advertising. The FTC will generally not move against a broadcast licensee that carries a deceptive ad. However, the FCC makes broadcasters generally responsible for controlling any false, misleading, or deceptive matter over the air, by virtue of the public-interest standard.

FCC Prohibitions on Television Advertising

The FCC prohibits subliminal advertising (messages that are so brief or so inconspicuous that they work only at a subconscious level), holding this technique to be against the public interest. Specific federal legislation also bars advertising cigarettes and small cigars on the electronic media under the jurisdiction of the FCC, including cable television and satellite transmissions. The mention of a cigarette producer that sponsors a sports contest or other reported event is acceptable, however, provided that the references are not so exaggerated that they become, in effect, commercial messages.

There are also statutory and FCC prohibitions against television advertising of lotteries and gambling activities. By definition, a lottery has 1) a prize which is 2) awarded by chance, and 3) involves entrants who have paid money or supplied some other valuable consideration (which can include the purchase of a product). A "contest" that lacks one of these elements is exempt, and can be advertised on television. For instance, if "no purchase is necessary to enter and win," the element of consideration is missing. If the prizes are awarded on the basis of some bona fide measure of skill, the element of chance is not there. However, since the interpretation of these rules can get quite technical, consulting with legal counsel is advisable before advertising a lottery on television. These rules also prohibit the advertisement of gambling activities in general.

State lotteries can be broadcast and advertised, provided that the broadcast licensee is located in a lottery state, and provided that the state lottery that the station covers is conducted either by that state or by an adjacent one. Because of the skill involved in picking a winner and because you can attend without betting, advertising horse racing does not come under these bans. Casino gambling is covered by the ban, and so ads for casinos have adopted such coy euphemisms as "action" in advertising their activities on television.

The FCC has dropped many of its old rules banning particular kinds of advertising. These discarded prohibitions include rules on ads for alcoholic beverages and astrology. There are still minor limitations on beer ads (for example, advertisers cannot list the alcohol content of beers in most states). States may control liquor commercials, and many broadcasters and cable systems impose their own restrictions on them.

Children's Television

After many false starts at the regulatory level, Congress enacted the Children's Television Act of 1990. This law mandated the FCC to impose limits on the amount of advertising that can be included in children's programs. It also directed the FCC to review compliance with these restrictions in connection with license renewals, as well as to evaluate the licensee's attention to the educational and informational needs of children in its programming. Finally, the Act calls on the FCC to tackle the issues of program-length commercials and the general commercialization of children's television. As described on page 162, the FCC has adopted new rules that would limit advertising time during children's programs to no more than 10.5 minutes per hour on weekends and 12 minutes on weekdays. The FCC has also defined program-length commercials as programs linked to a product in which commercials for that product are aired.

AMOUNTS OF ADVERTISING

As a general matter, television stations and cable operators are not obligated to accept commercials at all. Those that do accept commercials may turn down particular ones they do not wish to run, provided the reason doesn't invoke some other general principle of the law. Stations and cable operators are not "common carriers" in this respect, and there are no minimums. The main exception to this principle is the equal opportunity and reasonable-access rules for political advertising (see page 114).

The broadcast networks, most cable companies, and most individual broadcast stations do set limits on the number of ads that they carry on their programs. These amounts vary, depending on the time period and the particular medium involved. For instance, the major networks generally restrict advertising on prime time programs to 8 to 10 minutes per hour; for their daytime programming, the maximum is typically 12 to 15 minutes. Ad time on cable and local stations may run in the range of 12 to 15 minutes per hour.

Until 1984, the FCC set its own limits on the total amount of commercial time that could be included in television programming. As a general matter, ad time was restricted to 16 commercial minutes per programming hour. In June of 1984, however, these rules were repealed, as part of a general deregulation of television broadcasting. The new policy was to allow the balance between ads and programming to be set by the marketplace and factors of public acceptance. The private sector used to have its own rules on the maximum number of commercials, and the National Association of Broadcasters suggested time limits in its Television Code. The Code and its limits, however, were effectively abolished in 1982 in connection with the settlement of antitrust litigation. Recently, at Congress's direction, the FCC has proposed a limit on the amount of advertising on children's television.

Public broadcast stations are prohibited from airing advertisements to promote any for-profit product or service, and from carrying ads for or against any political candidates. Public broadcasters may include limited mentions of program funders (see page 47).

UNFAIR COMPETITION AND THE LANHAM ACT

Certain federal and state laws permit companies and individuals to take private legal action to prevent certain kinds of false advertising, under the theory that it constitutes unfair competition to misdescribe one's own product or to lie about a competitor's. The most important of these laws is Section 43(a) of the Federal Lanham Act (see Appendix A13).

In the context of advertising, Section 43(a) prohibits statements about goods or services that imply a false origin. The Lanham Act applies to direct trademark violations—for example, the use of the words "Coca-Cola" on a product not manufactured by the Coca-Cola company. It also forbids advertising a product as made by a certain company or as endorsed by an individual when that simply is not the case. Nor need the claims be made explicitly: false involvement or endorsement can also be implied. The Lanham Act can affect certain kinds of comparative ads, if there is the implication that the manufacturer of the other product is in some way endorsing the advertisement or the statements in it.

The Lanham Act does not provide for private action against all false advertising, however. Most courts have held that false claims which have nothing to do with the origin of the goods are simply not covered; a few courts, and certain commentators, have construed the Lanham Act a bit more broadly. In addition, the right to sue is limited to competitors or to the person or company whose involvement is being impermissibly suggested. The Lanham Act does not give the general public a right to sue for these misrepresentations.

STATE LAWS

Many states have adopted unfair competition laws which provide protections similar to those given under the Lanham Act. As a general matter, it must be proved that the advertising is confusing the buying public as to the origin of the goods and services being advertised. Some states allow claims for other kinds of deceptions, not necessarily limited to those about origin.

The states frequently have their own laws prohibiting false advertising in general. One form of these are generically called the 'Printer's Ink" laws; another, less common model is the Uniform Deceptive Trade Practice Act. Whatever the approach, enforcement will vary widely, depending on the priority that the state regulatory and prosecuting authorities give deceptive advertising. (The Association of Attorneys General has encouraged its members to actively pursue false advertising claims.) There are even some local rules, administered by bodies such as a municipal consumer-protection commission or bureau, that concern local advertisers.

CONSUMER CLAIMS

It is possible for consumers to bring claims against false advertising, either singly or as part of a class action. The legal theories for such actions include fraud, misrepresentation, breach of contract, and breach of warranties, express and implied. Since, in many cases of misleading advertising, the harm to any one individual is likely to be small in comparison to the legal costs, almost every such suit is brought on a class-action basis—and even here, the rules on class actions can be fairly restrictive. Although they have been successfully maintained in some instances, and have produced significant recoveries, consumer suits for false advertising are uncommon.

INDUSTRY REVIEW OF ADVERTISING CONTENT

The first step in checking the content of a commercial occurs between the client and the advertising agency. As the ad is scripted and story-boarded, it is often reviewed by the ad agency's counsel and, in many instances, the client's counsel as well; advertising that makes affirmative claims will be subject to particular scrutiny. Back-up is assembled for any claims made, and general attention is given to the legal issues—not only pertaining to advertising itself, but also to matters of copyright clearance, privacy and publicity, and those content restrictions that apply to all television programs.

The broadcast networks are quite active in reviewing the content of the advertisements that they run, insisting that they have some input at the storyboard level. The networks' review involves not only the substantive questions of legal compliance, but also the advertising's adherence to network standards and practices. Areas of particular sensitivity to the networks include beer and wine, toys, over-the-counter drugs, and sanitary protection. None of the big three networks will yet run birth control ads, although condoms can be mentioned in public-service spots. All in all, such standards are fairly predictable for mass-market distributors concerned with their image and accustomed to avoiding controversy.

Cable is, by and large, much more permissive about advertising than broadcast (with the exception of the Family Channel and other consciously wholesome companies), and local stations vary greatly. Cable companies are more lenient in their review of commercials.

Various trade groups of advertising agencies and their clients have issued guidelines for their members to follow in making ads. These relatively platitudinous and commonsensical codes have helped shape the attitudes of the industry, in turn influencing the type of ads that appear on television. Some groups have even set up review committees with the power to review potentially offensive ads and recommend (but not force) their change or withdrawal. The American Association of Advertising Agencies has been active both in promoting a creative code (adopted in 1962) and in setting up a review system. In 1971, the AAAA joined with the Council of Better Business Bureaus, the Association of National Advertisers, and the American Advertising Federation to establish the National Advertising Division, which reviews ads for misleading or deceptive content, and the National Advertising Review Board, which hears appeals.

Compliance with NAD and NARB rulings is voluntary, but remarkably uniform. This is either because of the adverse publicity that non-compliance would bring to an advertiser, or because non-compliance can be reported to the appropriate governmental agency for action.

Part 6

LEGAL AND BUSINESS AFFAIRS

37 | Contracts

Contract law is one of the great developments of Western mercantile culture. Under contract law, courts will grant the force of law to an arrangement agreed upon by private parties. But courts will not enforce every statement or promise—for instance, a gratuitous or frivolous offer. What courts enforce is a serious transaction between two or more parties in exchange for value on all sides. This value is sometimes called "consideration," and it is a necessity for a binding agreement. In some instances, however, "consideration" can be supplied by the known reliance of one party on the promise of the other, even if nothing of material value is being exchanged.

VERBAL AND WRITTEN AGREEMENTS

Notwithstanding the old truism that "an oral agreement isn't worth the paper its written on," until 1677, verbal deals were generally enforceable under common law. The change came with the adoption in England of the "statute of frauds," a measure intended to prevent the frauds that may occur whenever there is no signed, written agreement. Although England has since dropped its statute of frauds, most U.S. states have adopted some form of it. Typically, sales agreements for goods over $500, contracts requiring performance over a significant amount of time (commonly a year), the sale or transfer of real estate, contracts for marriage, and contracts of guaranty and surety must all be in writing, and signed, to be enforced. In television, verbal agreements are often used for short-term employments, particularly if there are no rights in intellectual property or privacy being transferred. Whenever rights are being transferred, or whenever any future service or right is contemplated, a written agreement should be used.

The signed agreement need not be a single piece of paper. If a distributor writes a signed letter offering to license a program to a station and the station sends back a signed letter saying it accepts the deal, the requirements of the statute of frauds will be met. Informal documents such job orders, booking sheets, and deal memos (see page 330) can also constitute a sufficient writing.

In most states, it is also necessary for one party to deliver the contract to the other party, or to the other party's representatives, for a contract to be formed. If you sign the deal but keep the signed copy to yourself, delivery has not occurred.

As discussed on page 143, federal copyright law requires that *exclusive* assignment or license take the form of a signed document in order to be effective. Similarly, some privacy-law statutes require that any waiver of privacy rights be done in writing.

In the television business, sometimes a *deal memo* is sent that confirms a deal without any provision for signature. In other cases, correspondence and contract drafts may go back and forth for months without a final agreement getting signed. In some cases, the money may be paid, the services may be provided, the program may be broadcast on national television—and still no signatures.

In cases in which a contract is not signed but performance has gone forward, the courts are at least aware that some kind of agreement existed between the parties. The courts will seek to determine what the deal was and enforce it—even though the technical requirements of the statute of frauds have not been met. Then there is the concept of reliance. If one party makes a verbal promise to another party, and this other party relies on it with the knowledge of the party that made the promise, then the promise can often be enforced even in the absence of any signed contract.

Since the television industry is somewhat casual about signing agreements before work begins on projects, term sheets, confirming letters, or deal memos—even if unsigned by the other side—are sometimes used to guide a court once performance has begun, particularly if these items go uncontroverted. The ultimate weapon, short of a signed contract, is the reliance letter. It gives notice to the other side that actual reliance is being put on the submitted terms, even though there is nothing yet signed. Of course, the other side can send back a "don't rely" letter, or even a "don't rely but we are relying" letter. If performance continues and a dispute breaks out, the courts may have a hard time untangling the record.

CONTRACT FORMATS

The signed document constituting a contract need not be in any particular form, but it must include adequate evidence of the necessary terms of the agreement, and must indicate the intent of the persons signing it to be bound by it.

In effect, anything that says "this is a contract, these are the parties, and these are the terms" should do the job. Over time, a series of generally-accepted forms have evolved. The oldest and most formal is the *indenture form*. The wording is derived from the forms used for contracts in the late Middle Ages. The indenture form looks something like this:

AGREEMENT

This agreement made as of this 1st day of January, 1992 by and between the Smith Corporation, a Delaware corporation, and John Doe, an individual,

WITNESSETH

WHEREAS, the Smith Corporation wishes undertake a transaction with Doe and Doe wishes to undertake a transaction with the Smith Corporation;

NOW, THEREFORE, the parties hereto agree as follows:

Buried within the arcane language of this form is a simple statement: the document is a contract between Smith Corporation and Doe, the reasons for the contract are that Doe and Smith Corporation want to do a deal, the deal is as follows. Such a contract might close:

IN WITNESS WHEREOF, the parties hereto have executed this Agreement as of the date first above written.

_____
John Doe

SMITH CORPORATION

By: _____
Lisa Smith, President

A more modern but equally enforceable form of contract is the *letter agreement*. The letter agreement begins by stating who the parties are, and that the letter is a contract. A typical starting clause might read:

John Doe
[address]

January 1, 1992

Smith Corporation
[address]

Dear Ms. Smith:

When the enclosed copy of this letter is signed on behalf of the Smith Corporation and returned to me, this letter will set forth the terms of our agreement concerning the deal to be done between us on the following terms:

Such a contract might close with:

> Please confirm that the foregoing accurately represents the agreement between us by executing the enclosed copy on the indicated line and returning it to me.

Yours sincerely,
John Doe

ACCEPTED AND AGREED:

SMITH CORPORATION

By: _____
    Lisa Smith, President

Similarly, a *memorandum* form may be used to set forth an agreement:

> From: Smith Corporation
> To: Doe
> Re: Deal
> Date: January 1, 1992
>
>   This memorandum will set forth the terms of our deal and, when signed on the indicated lines below, will constitute our binding agreement.

The memorandum form usually closes with some type of signature lines.

None of these forms has any special advantage as a matter of law, although particular industry segments may have their preferences or traditions. They are all equally binding as contracts. By and large, the indenture form is considered more formal than the letter agreement, and the letter more formal than the memo. As a matter of style, the formality of the agreement should match the complexity of the transaction. For instance, the memo form is fine for a deal that can be adequately described within a page or two. If the agreement requires several pages, the letter agreement is better; if dozens of pages are necessary, the indenture form may be the most appropriate format.

FORM AGREEMENTS

People in the television business frequently use pre-printed form agreements, which can be real timesavers—with two provisos. First, the contract must fit the deal and vice versa. Although using a form agreement helps save on legal costs, this can be a false economy if the form simply isn't the right one, or if the deal has a complication not covered by a standard form. Second, the forms must be fair enough to both sides to actually get signed. Although there is always the temptation, when using a form agreement, to make it as favorable as possible to the drafter, the contract cannot be so one-sided that no one will sign it.

STYLE

As a matter of law, a contract does not require any particular style of writing; it need only state, in language that is specific and clear, the principal terms of the deal. A certain style of writing known as "legalese" has developed over the years, but to the extent that it confuses the untrained reader, legalese is not recommended. In certain instances, time-honored legal formulas may save space or provide a shorthand for complicated concepts. In general, though, if the use of legalese might lead to a misunderstanding, the contract should be worded in plain language.

NECESSARY TERMS

To be enforceable, a contract must contain certain critical, basic terms. If the price, dates, or items to be sold or licensed are left out or are left to future negotiations, the entire contract will probably not be considered binding by a court. In such cases, there just isn't enough actually agreed upon to constitute a real deal. The common television-industry practice of leaving terms for later good-faith negotiation runs the danger of rendering at least the provision—and perhaps even the entire agreement—unenforceable. To prevent this possibility, negotiation clauses should never be for basic terms, and when they are used, they should outline a detailed procedure, with specific dates, parameters, and other objective criteria on how negotiations are to proceed.

SIGNATURES

Any signature that identifies the signing party and its intent to be bound is adequate for a contract. Thus, the use of a first name or initials, if effective on these points, can constitute a signature. Although it is the custom in this country that signatures should appear at the end of a document, there is no requirement for this in most states, provided the signatures appear at a place in the document where they demonstrate the necessary intent to be bound. The agreement is generally signed at an indicated space, frequently on a line over the printed or typed name of the person signing. In order to make clear whether the person is signing individually, as an officer of a corporation, or as a partner, agent, or trustee, the signature line should specify the capacity in which this person is signing. Also, if the person is signing on behalf of another entity, the signature line should be proceeded by the word "by." This designates that the person is signing on behalf of the entity, such as a corporation or partnership, and not on his or her own behalf.

WITNESSES, NOTARIES AND SEALS

Corporate and personal seals are generally not a necessity for agreements. In most instances, the signatures on a contract do not have to be authenticated by witnesses, and the contract does not have to be signed in front of a Notary Public (although these steps can be useful as evidentiary matters should be signature ever be disputed.) For land transactions and other circumstances in which the contract is to be filed as a matter of public record, witnesses or notarial authentication may be required, but this is seldom the case for a television contract. In some instances, a corporate seal may be used as an additional piece of formal evidence to authenticate that a corporate action was properly taken.

ORIGINALS

Original signed copies are clearly preferred by a court called upon to enforce an agreement. If an original signed copy is not available, however, the best available copy will have to be presented to the court. A conformed copy, a photocopy, or even a telefaxed copy of the signed original is usually considered acceptable—as long as there is sufficient evidence establishing that the signed original existed and that the offered copy is a true copy of it.

INITIALING

Initials next to a change in the contract indicate that the parties were aware of it at the time of the signing and that it was not inserted after the fact by one of the parties. In the case of changes added, whether by hand or in print, to an otherwise clean agreement, it is advisable to initial the changes to minimize the potential for future disagreements. Likewise, initials at the bottom of a contract page indicate that it is one of the original pages and that substitute pages have not been inserted. Unless a conflict between the parties is likely, the level of trust is exceedingly low, or a high degree of formality is desired, the individual pages of an agreement do not have to be initialed—particularly if each side will have a fully-signed copy.

SIGNING AUTHORITY AND POWERS OF ATTORNEY

Real people can sign for themselves; business entities, being artificial creations, cannot. Therefore, people must sign on behalf of business entities. The ability to sign on behalf of an entity hinges on the person having either general or specific authorization to do so. In the case of a corporation, one can generally presume that the chairman, president, or a senior vice president can execute most customary business contracts for a company. For a contract involving large amounts of money, however, specific board approval may be required to grant the authority. The other party to such a deal may request to see a certified copy of this board action, together with certified specimens of the signatures of the officers who are signing. In the case of a partnership, any general partner can usually sign on behalf of the partnership and bind it.

A person acting under a power of attorney can also bind a business entity—or an individual—within the scope of the granted power. Talent agents will sometimes sign on behalf of their clients and, if properly authorized as agents, will have the power of an attorney-in-fact for entering contracts within the scope of the agent's authority. If this is not so, it may be grounds for the agent's client to disown the contract, particularly if it was not reasonable to think that the agent had the power to sign.

In the final analysis, the ability of a party to bind another entity is usually evaluated on the basis of apparent authority. If the entity in question has apparently authorized the agent to sign—and this authority is relied upon by a person who could not have possibly known that the agent actually had no such power—then the entity will be bound by the signature. For better or worse, in most television deals, the parties rely on the apparent authority of an appropriate corporate officer to bind the corporation to the contract, without requiring the inspection of the corporate resolution granting the power.

DATES

Every contract should have a date to indicate when it was signed, when it is to be effective, or both. Certain widely-understood codes apply in giving a date. For instance, if an agreement is to be effective on a date that is specified, but which is not necessarily the date of signature, this date should be expressed with the words "as of." A contract that reads "This agreement, dated *as of* the 1st day of January 1992" could have actually been signed weeks before or after January 1, 1992. By contrast, if the contract date is to indicate the date of actual signing, then "as of" should not be used. The words "This contract, made this 1st day of January, 1992" imply that the signatures were affixed on the date given. Sometimes a date is put next to the signature line to indicate the date of signature. This practice can be used in conjunction with an "as of" date for the entire contract, showing both the effective date for the agreement and the actual dates of execution.

STATIONERY AND LETTERHEAD

There is no magic to the use of stationery or letterhead in connection with an agreement, although in some situations there may be some evidentiary value in the use of original letterhead. If the letter agreement form is to be used, it is logical that it appear on the customary letterhead of the party that is writing the letter.

ORDER OF TERMS

The order in which terms of an agreement are set forth do not effect its binding nature; as a practical matter, however, a good agreement should read easily and logically. Thus, it is customary to begin with the terms of greatest importance and proceed to the more minor details as the contract progresses. In drafting a contract, one should begin as if telling an uninitiated person about the contents of the deal. A program license agreement, for instance, might well start by saying that a license is being granted and move on to describe the programs and the term or territories involved. The next topic might be the compensation for the license; further topics would include representations and warranties of the parties (see below); and the final provisions might cover choice of law and other technical matters.

CHOICE OF LAW

Contract law is basically state law, and there are the inevitable variations between the states on specific points. The choice of which state's law is to apply to the contract is too frequently neglected by contracting parties. Sometimes, the variations in contract law between different states can have significant implications.

Parties cannot simply choose any law, however, to govern their agreements. There must be some relation of a logical and substantial nature between the law which is chosen to govern the agreement and the subject matter of the agreement, the location of the parties in general, or the location of the parties at the time of signing. In the absence of an affirmative choice of law, the applicable state law will be chosen by the court seeking to enforce the contract (as a starting point, most courts will prefer their own local law). A court will consider other factors as well, such as the respective domiciles of the parties, the state in which performance is to take place, and the state in which the contract was signed.

MINORS

Minors—children under the age at which they become independently responsible adults (in most states, at 18)—receive many protections under traditional common-law principles. At common law, most contracts with a minor could be voided by the minor at any time until he or she became an adult, and for a reasonable time thereafter. Some states, recognizing that such a blanket rule would not be appropriate for a contract with a minor that was not abusive, have made provision for a court to review such a contract; if the court approves it, the contract would be binding and not voidable. In California, for instance, the court has discretion to approve a wide range of agreements with minors, including contracts for acting services, management and agency agreements, and grants of rights in creative properties and life stories. No time limit is set on the duration of service contracts, beyond the seven-year limit generally applicable in California.

New York law is more stringent about the scope of agreements with minors that the court can approve. Although the court can permit service contracts, management agreements, and agency agreements, these documents cannot have terms of greater than three years (certain negative covenants [see page 342] and participation agreements may extend beyond the three-year limit). In addition, New York law does not empower courts to approve grants of rights in intellectual property, although the "work for hire" doctrine may take care of much of this at the copyright level. By contrast, a parent is specifically authorized to waive privacy rights under the New York statute without a court proceeding.

REPRESENTATIONS AND WARRANTIES

Many contracts contain items which are called *representations and warranties* —fancy words for promises about statements of fact. Thus, if a party represents and warrants that the contract is signed on Tuesday, he is stating that it is a fact: Tuesday is the date when the contract is signed. If this fact turns out to be wrong and damages result, this is grounds for a suit by the other party for a breach of the contract. Representations and warranties are frequently linked in the television world to statements about rights clearances and the authority to enter into agreements. As a general matter, parties only make representations and warranties about matters with which they are personally acquainted, or over which they have personal control. In some instances, a representation and warranty can be softened by the insertion of "to the best of the party's knowledge" or similar words. In this case, a breach will not occur if the statement proves wrong—but it will occur if the representing and warranting party *knew* before signing that the statement was wrong. Claims under a "to the best of knowledge" representation and warranty can bog down in arguments over what constitutes knowledge.

INDEMNITIES

An *indemnity,* frequently paired with representations and warranties, is a promise by one party to pay specified costs and losses of another party. In the contract context, an indemnity clause generally says that if Party A suffers a loss because of Party B—for example, because one of the reps and warranties proves to be untrue—then Party B will make Party A's losses good, and will cover any expenses. An indemnity should be given only for matters which the giver agreed to do, as to which the giver has provided a representation and warranty, or which are otherwise within the indemnifying party's knowledge, control, and legitimate risk.

Indemnities can have important wrinkles. One is whether the indemnity covers only breaches (actual defaults) or whether it also covers "alleged breaches," or defaults which someone else asserts. With an alleged breach, if someone wrongfully sues Party B, claiming that certain rights were not cleared, and if that claim is then defeated in court, Party A, as the indemnifier, would still have to reimburse Party B for the costs of the lawsuit. If it were an indemnity limited to actual breaches, the indemnifying party (Party A) would not be called upon to pay the costs of Party B. Unless specifically mentioned, indemnities may not include legal fees, and so a provision for reasonable attorney's fees is frequently inserted. Indemnities sometimes give the indemnifying party a right to be involved in directing any litigation for which he or she is financially responsible. Likewise, the indemnifying party sometimes has the right to approve any settlements for which it will have to reimburse the other party.

LENGTH OF YEARS

Although in most instances the term, or duration, of an agreement is up to the parties to decide between themselves, there are some general limitations which can apply. Most courts will impose some time limit on service contracts, if only as a matter of public policy to prevent endless employment commitments. In New York, factors such as the level of compensation and the customs of the industry are considered. In California, the legislature has set a statutory limit of seven years for any contract for personal services.

There are also limitations on the duration of certain grants of rights. Under the Copyright Act, there are reversions permitted of copyright transfers and licenses (see page 142). Options, including those for turnaround (see page 172), may be subject to the arcane "rule against perpetuities." This rule prohibits property (including creative works) from being tied up with contingent rights for endless periods. As a rule of thumb, options that are open for more than 21 years may be subject to cancellation.

TERMS CONTRARY TO LAW OR PUBLIC POLICY

A court will refuse to enforce individual terms—or, indeed, whole contracts—which it deems to be contrary to public policy. For instance, contracts for murder or theft will not be enforced. Also, laws on certain points may take precedence over the agreement of the parties. The

California limit of seven years for employment agreements is one example of this.

FORCE MAJEURE

Force majeure describes a circumstance where performance of the contract is rendered impossible or unreasonably difficult by the intervention of a force beyond the control of the affected party. In television productions, this might include earthquakes, labor disputes, fires, wars, or other natural and man-made disasters. In such a case, the contract can be suspended, or even terminated, with consequences less than for full breach of contract. Television contracts frequently describe in detail those events that constitute force majeure, and the consequences—including suspension and termination of the contract.

INCAPACITY

Television contracts, particularly those for talent services, frequently have clauses dealing with the incapacity of the talent. In most cases, after a short waiting period, the producer can choose to either suspend the contract and start it up again when the talent recovers, or terminate the contract without further obligation.

BREACHES

What happens when one or both parties to a contract fail to live up to the deal they have made? This failure, often called a breach or a default, can occur in several ways. One party can fail to carry out an *affirmative obligation* (making a payment or delivering a finished program), or can breach a *negative obligation* (by failing to adhere to an exclusivity provision). If a representation and warranty turns out to be false, this can also cause a default.

Default or breach may be grounds for action if they are "material." Technical lapses which have no real consequences for the aggrieved party are generally shrugged off as being non-material by a court brought in to settle the dispute. If seemingly trivial points are indeed of importance, a party can strengthen his or her hand by providing that full performance of them is "of the essence" (see page 341—"time is of the essence"). Even then, if the default is truly trivial, a court may still disregard it.

Contracts will sometimes provide time periods for remedying certain kinds of lapses, generally running from when the failing party gets notice of its default. This allows accidental failures to be fixed without the whole contract going into default.

Sometimes a party declares that he or she is not going to be bound by the contract. Even though there may not yet be any actual failure to perform, such a statement can constitute an anticipatory breach, particularly if it is not disclaimed after a request for confirmation by the other side.

REMEDIES

If a contract is in material breach, the injured party has a number of possible responses. As a starting point, there are certain measures of "self-help." For instance, the aggrieved party can suspend his or her own performance under the contract. If a producer has failed to make payments as per the contract, an actor may stop showing up at the set. If there is a dispute over who is in breach, however, suspension of performance can be a dangerous step. If money is due for a print, for a soundtrack, or for other production elements, the lab or sound mixer may be able to hold onto the material under a "mechanic's lien" until the debt is paid.

While the dispute is pending, the aggrieved party should seek to mitigate his or her damages, taking whatever steps are reasonably available to minimize the losses coming from the breach. Thus, if contracts with suppliers can be canceled, this should be done; if another purchaser for the project is waiting in the wings, he or she should be considered. A failure to mitigate can be held against the aggrieved party when it comes time for a court to make good his or her losses.

Beyond the self-help steps, the aggrieved party may have to go to court—or, if the contract so provides, to arbitration—to get satisfaction for the breach. A court or arbitration panel normally starts by awarding damages, that is, payments that will rectify the losses incurred. In deciding how much to award, the first consideration is restitution, or reimbursing the aggrieved party for any out-of-pocket losses that the failure of the contract has caused. An additional consideration will be lost profits, some or all of which a court may force the breaching party to pay. If the defaulting party made profits through breaking the deal ("unjust enrichment"), a court can force some or all of these profits to be turned over to the aggrieved party. There is also the possibility of an award of punitive damages, although this is unlikely in a contract case, absent some elements of especially willful misbehavior. If the case involves a copyright claim, the statutory damages provided by the Copyright Act may apply (see page 144).

In addition to damages, a court may grant equitable remedies (the term refers to the old-fashioned "courts of equity" in which these remedies evolved). Equitable remedies are given only when money damages are inadequate in some fashion. These remedies include "specific performance," that is, the ordering by the court that the contract be carried out. Specific performance is appropriate if the contract is for the sale of some existing tangible item, like a motion-picture negative; it is untenable in the case of a contract to perform some kind of skilled service, like writing, acting, or directing. Recision, or the undoing of the entire contract, may be appropriate if there has been a sale of rights in a program for which no payment has ever been made. A third equitable remedy is injunction, a court order that forbids some act—for example, the telecast of a show for which the rights were improperly cleared.

Equitable remedies tend to be more powerful contractual medicine than simple damages; therefore, courts tend to use them only if it is shown that damages will not do the job. In addition, the parties themselves may have agreed in the contract to waive equitable remedies. Producers and distributors particularly dread the possibility of an injunction on the entire program because of a payment dispute in the talent contest. This waiver often occurs when rights are being transferred or credits being given.

LAWYER WORDS IN REAL LANGUAGE

Contracts frequently use terms and expressions that have very specific legal meanings. However, these meanings may not be obvious to the layman who reads them in a contract—or, even worse, who includes them without consulting a lawyer. This section will address some of these words and phrases, and explain the perils and pitfalls they involve.

Time is of the essence: This phrase means that the actions specified in the contract *must* be taken on or by a particular date. There is no extension, no grace period, no time to remedy. If the event does not happen on the date specified, there is potentially a serious breach of the agreement.

Best efforts: More than just a good try. Some states will interpret this phrase to mean the very best effort of which the person is capable—including, if necessary, making a significant financial sacrifice or employing the utmost effort. A better formulation for giving something a good try is "endeavor in good faith."

Consultation vs. approval: Consultation on a matter means just that—the other party must consult you. It does not mean that they have to agree with you. After fair consultation they may tell you "I appreciate your ideas, but I don't want to use any of them." A right of "review" is similarly limited. A right of *approval*, by contrast, permits the party to say no and make it stick. A requirement for *written* approval is essentially an evidentiary matter, to avoid swearing matches between parties over what was said verbally.

Reasonable and *sole discretion*: There is an implied duty to act reasonably and in good faith under a contract. Nonetheless, it is frequently written in television contracts that certain actions can only be taken if they are "reasonable," or if there is a "reasonable basis," or if they are taken "reasonably." Such a provision is often linked to a circumstance in which one of the parties is empowered to take a discretionary action, such as exercise an approval. If approval is "not to be unreasonably withheld," or "is to be given on a reasonable basis," this puts some limit on the discretion of the approving party. Should the approving party fail to approve something, the other party can claim that this failure is unreasonable and then proceed anyway, with some possibility of not being found in breach of the contract. By contrast, a phrase like "in her sole discretion," when linked to an approval right, makes it probable that a whim of the approving party will be enforceable—and that any action taken by the other party in disregard of that whim is risky.

Covenants: "Covenant" is a fancy word for an agreement or promise. Covenants are sometimes divided between "affirmative covenants" and "negative covenants." Affirmative covenants are promises to actually do things; negative covenants are promises to refrain from doing things. A contract will usually be binding without ever mentioning the word "covenant."

38 Work Relationships, Unions, Legal Entities, and Tax Issues

Several types of working relationships and business entities are commonplace in television program development and production, station and network ownership, and distribution. These forms are also common to other industries.

EMPLOYEES AND INDEPENDENT CONTRACTORS

An *employee* is an individual who works directly for a business entity. Typically, an employee works under the direction and supervision of an employer, usually in accordance with a fixed schedule, in facilities provided by the employer. The employer pays the employee a salary, with deductions taken for federal, state, and local taxes, and makes contributions to a workman's compensation fund and social security in the name of the employee. The employer may also provide health insurance and benefits such as a pension fund, profit-sharing, and a company car. An employee does not hire other employees, except as a representative of the employer.

An *independent contractor* (IC) is an individual who is self-employed; an independent contractor may also be a company, partnership, or corporation. Unlike an employee, an individual who is an IC works without direct supervision of the employer, sets his or her own hours, and frequently works at his or her own location rather than company facilities. An IC is normally paid a gross fee for services rendered, and is responsible for the payment of all taxes, insurance, and other monies due to government agencies.

An IC costs the hiring company less to maintain than an employee; with an IC, the employer does not have responsibility for all of the related costs discussed above. An employer may, in effect, hire an employee, but seek to save money (illegally) by calling the employee an IC. In this scenario, the employer may, in the short-term, avoid some liability in taxation, social security, unemployment insurance, and workman's compensation. But the penalties can be severe—the employer may be liable for taxes not paid by the employee, and for additional penalties. Rules regarding deductions for home office and other business expenses are generally in favor of the IC (see page 352); employees have a tougher time justifying the use of a home when a traditional office is provided.

The employee/contractor distinction can be of considerable importance under copyright law when determining the owner of a work for hire. Unless alternate contractual arrangements are made, the courts will usually judge the proceeds of employment as a work for hire, whereas the ownership of an independent contractor's creations must be specifically transferred by written agreement (see page 138).

An independent contractor may hire other independent contractors or even employees on his or her own account.

UNIONS

Most productions made for the mainstream television marketplace involve unions that represent on- or off-screen talent or crew. Several of these unions are discussed in Part 4. Unions and employers are now regulated by federal law, particularly the National Labor Relations Act (NLRA); state law, once very active in this area, has been largely preempted by the federal rules.

Voluntary Union Production

Because the television unions have attracted a substantial number of high-quality professionals, many broadcasters and production companies voluntarily choose to use union labor. In effect, using union labor is like buying brand-name goods: although they cost more than no-name products, by and large, one knows the quality one is getting. The union choice may also reflect a desire to avoid the difficulties that can plague a production if there should be a dispute over representation or jurisdiction.

If a company has decided to use union labor in one or more job categories, it can either hire members directly by becoming a union signatory, or in most cases it can arrange for a service company that is already a signatory to provide the workers. If the company will be the direct employer, then it contacts the appropriate union about signing a union agreement. This agreement establishes the minimum terms and conditions for employing union members. For small independent companies, bonds or personal guarantees by the owners may be required, to ensure payment of wages and benefits in the case of a budget shortfall or other financial problem.

The union agreement typically requires the employer to only use union labor in the agreed-upon category, either on the project in question or in all the company's activities. The NLRA imposes limits on this kind of hiring agreement, however. The most a union contract can legally require is that any employee hired in a unionized job pay initiation fees and dues; the employee need not agree to other union membership provisions, such as exclusivity (that is, the rule that he or she can only work for a union signatory). In "right-to-work" states, even this provision is dropped, and the union signatory can hire non-union workers, who must nonetheless be treated the same as union employees.

Even outside the right-to-work states, organizations can often use both union and non-union employees. The affiliation agreement with a union typically has effect moving down a chain of corporate subsidiaries, not upward. Therefore, the company should investigate having a subsidiary company become the union signatory. That way, while one branch of the corporate tree will be union-only in the specified job categories, other branches can operate union-free. In addition, becoming a union signatory in one job area does not necessarily mean across-the-board affiliation; many companies are signatories with some of the television unions and not with others.

A union can sometimes compel an employer to recognize its role in bargaining. If enough employees (30 percent) in an appropriate bargaining unit—usually, a particular job category—get together and request a union election, the employer must comply. If the election is in favor of the union, it will then have the right to negotiate a contract with management; if the union loses, it is barred from trying again for 12 months. Should any company find itself facing a union-organization campaign, it should seek advice from professionals experienced in labor relations.

While most of the talent unions do not have overlapping jurisdictions (for example, the film/videotape split of SAG and AFTRA), some of the craft and technical areas are potentially represented by different unions. This is sometimes an accident of history: who organized what union when. If a company without an established union tie is contemplating using union labor where there are alternative choices, it is somewhat possible to pick the more attractive union in advance, based on rates, skills, work rules, and so on.

Non-Union Production

If the budget permits, union production is usually the easiest choice. Non-union personnel may be hired when the budget is tight; when some aspect of the union work rules or residual structures would be a burden on the production; or when the production is being done for a company whose tradition is non-union in certain categories. Sometimes the unions will cooperate with a producer, cutting special deals to reflect unusual circumstances. Some of the unions even have special codes for low-budget or non-commercial productions. It can be worth talking to the union if the hardship is real, and the concessions sought are not too major. In other cases, the employer may have the money, but may still opt for non-union personnel to avoid irksome restrictions, or simply to help the bottom line.

Using non-union labor can be a plus, particularly where there is a reservoir of solid independent talent from which to draw. Often, young people starting in the television business are not yet signed to a union, and will be willing to work for less money to get the experience and a credit. Even experienced workers may choose to remain non-union, enjoying the freedom to seek jobs on their own terms. However, especially when undercapitalized and independent operators are involved, the old problems of exploitation and non-payment which led to the founding of unions in the first place may recur; employees should approach these jobs with their eyes open.

Having unionized labor working for a company that is not a union signatory can be risky for all concerned, especially if it lasts for any significant length of time. Assumed names are often used, which renders the credit largely useless for resumé purposes. If the union finds out, it can fine or even expel the offending members. On the other hand, the union members can also turn around, once hired, and seek union representation for the entire production (particularly if they have been found out by the union). This can put the producer in a box, because it is illegal under the NLRA to fire an employee for union activity. The last thing most producers need is a representation battle in the middle of production.

Foreign Productions and Unions

The jurisdiction of U.S. unions over foreign employment is limited. If the employer is U.S.-based, then union jurisdiction may apply, even to shooting abroad. Even if the employer is truly foreign-based, and the employment (typically shooting and post-production) takes place abroad, the unions sometimes try to assert authority if the deal was made in the U.S., or if the union member leaves the U.S. specifically to negotiate the agreement. The validity of this "location of the deal" approach is questionable, but some prospective employees—particularly those with savvy agents—have been known to "just happen to run into" a foreign producer while "coincidentally" traveling to Canada, Mexico, or St. Barts.

SOLE PROPRIETORSHIP

The sole proprietorship is an individual doing business on his or her own behalf. In most states, a sole proprietor using a fictitious business name must be identified and registered by filing a "doing business as" (DBA) certificate, with a designated authority (e.g., a county clerk). A sole proprietorship may hire employees, and the individual in charge must personally comply with tax, social security, insurance, and other employee-related government requirements. A sole proprietor is also subject to unlimited personal liability for all debts, claims, and obligations of the business. A sole proprietor pays personal income tax on the profits from the business; for larger businesses, this can become rather complicated, and retaining the services of a good accountant throughout the year is recommended.

Outsiders can make investments in the form of a loan, or by contractual arrangements that set a rate of return. If profits and losses are shared, however, the law may deem the entity to be a partnership.

PARTNERSHIP

There are two types of partnerships: general and limited. A general partnership is an association of two or more persons who jointly own and operate a business, typically sharing profits and losses. A limited partnership has two kinds of partners: general partner and limited partner. The general partner is responsible for the operation of the business and is liable for its financial obligations; the limited partners, who are not involved in the operation of the business, are passive investors liable only up to their stated capital contributions.

Partnerships do not pay federal taxes on their income. Instead, profits and losses are passed on to the partners, who pay taxes as individuals. Profits and losses from the partnership can be offset by the performance of other ventures, but limited partners and other passive investors face restrictions, which often limit the offset to other so-called "passive" investments. The partnership must file an information return with the IRS and with applicable state and city agencies. It may also be subject to sales, property, and other non-income taxes.

General Partnerships

A general partnership is usually formed by negotiating and signing a partnership agreement which defines the duties and rights of the partners. In most states, the partners can be any recognizable independent entity: individuals, agencies, corporations, trusts, even other partnerships. The agreement normally specifies the amount of capital or the kind of services that each partner is to contribute to the partnership, and it specifies how profits and losses are allocated to the partners (profits may be treated differently than losses). The agreement may also detail how the partnership is to be operated: who is to work full-time, and in what capacity; whether unanimous agreement is needed to admit new partners; how partnership decisions are to be made; and how and when the partnership is to be dissolved. If particular conditions are not specified, or no formal agreement has been signed, the relevant state law will apply and will usually provide answers to these and other questions. As to third parties, each general partner is individually liable for all of the debts, claims, and other obligations of the partnership.

In most states, a partnership using an assumed name must file an assumed-name certificate with the county clerk or some other designated official. It must also comply with employment rules and other laws applicable to any business structure.

Joint Ventures

A joint venture is a general partnership formed for a specific, limited purpose, such as the production of a particular television program or series. Joint ventures are governed by the agreements founding them and by normal partnership rules.

Limited Partnerships

A limited partnership is similar to a general partnership except that it has two kinds of partners: general and limited. A limited partner is akin to a shareholder in a corporation—a passive investor who is not individually liable for the debts of the company. In fact, a limited partner may not, by law, participate in the day-to-day management of a limited partnership without risking the loss of limited partner status. Because it resembles both a partnership and a corporation, the limited partnership is appealing to a partner who wants to supply capital but not be involved in management.

Limited partnerships are frequently governed by the rules made for general partnerships, with some key differences. For instance, statutes authorizing limited partnerships go to considerable length to insure that third parties are not led to believe that the full credit of limited partners is standing behind the debts of the limited partnership.

In order to form a limited partnership, the general partner(s) must file a certificate of limited partnership in the office of the appropriate state official (e.g., secretary of state, county clerk). This certificate generally states the name, address, and class of business of the partnership, as well as the name of each partner, his or her address, and his or her status as a general or limited partner. Usually, the certificate also details each limited partner's contribution to the partnership (in cash or property), to what extent any additional contribution may be required, and the right of each limited partner to compensation (a share of income, for example). Because the certificate is available for public inspection, the information is made available to creditors, who have a right to know whose credit is backing the debts of the partnership. The certificate must be amended whenever the information changes. A general or limited partner may be an individual, a general partnership, a limited partnership, or a corporation. Many states also require the publication of this information in a local newspaper.

If a limited partner's name is used in the name of the limited partnership, or if he or she takes part in the management of the business, then he or she is likely to be considered a general partner, no matter what the agreements say. Still, a limited partner usually has the right to give general advice concerning the operation of the business, to inspect the books periodically, to receive a formal accounting on a regular basis, and to seek dissolution of the business by court order. A limited partner may also do business with the limited partnership; for example, a limited partner may loan money to the limited partnership.

The partnership agreement may authorize or restrict the admission of additional limited partners. The agreement may provide an order of priority among the limited partners with respect to profits or return of their contribution. In the absence of such an agreement, all limited partners are equal, usually on a pari passu basis.

Typically, a limited partner may not withdraw his, her, or its money unless (1) the other partners consent, (2) the certificate is canceled or amended to reflect the reduced capital of the partnership, or (3) the assets of the partnership exceed its liabilities (excluding the liabilities of the partnership to the general and limited partners for their respective contributions). If the partnership is being dissolved, then procedures are detailed by either state guidelines or the partnership agreement. If a limited partner withdraws, that partner still remains liable for the amount of money withdrawn (plus interest) if that money is needed to pay debts incurred before the withdrawal.

In the past, there were many tax advantages to investing through limited partnerships, and they were frequently used for tax shelters. As with other partnerships, losses can be passed through directly to partners, including the limited partners, but profits are not subject to double taxation. Tax reform severely limited the benefits by making limited partnership income and loss "passive." Passive losses can only be offset against passive income, which does not include wages and fees. This has put an end to most limited-partnership investments motivated by tax loss.

CORPORATIONS

In Latin, the root word "corpus" means "body." As this suggests, the corporation is viewed by law as a separate legal entity, a body distinct from any other entities which may own interests in it.

Most U.S. corporations are established under state laws. A corporation is formed by filing a certificate of incorporation, sometimes called "articles of incorporation," with the appropriate state official (usually the secretary of state). This certificate first states the name of the corporation, which must usually include the words Incorporated, Corporation, or Limited (or an abbreviation of any of these terms) to indicate corporate status—specific terms vary from state to state. The certificate also indicates the business location; its purpose; the number, type, and stated value of shares, along with a description of the rights or restrictions applicable to any type of stock; and the duration of the corporation (usually it is perpetual). Amending the corporate certificate normally requires special majority approval of the stockholders, and there may be other requirements in addition. Further rules regarding the operation of the corporation (usually called the "by-laws") may be written and used, but they do not need to be filed. The by-laws provide specifics on how the company is to be operated; if neither they nor the certificate cover a particular matter, then standard rules under the governing state law apply.

Those who have invested in the corporation become stockholders, but the class of their shares, and the rights that go along with them, may vary. "Common shares" normally carry some form of unlimited profit participation and some form of voting power. "Preferred shares" normally carry a first right to profits (though frequently with a limit) and may entitle the shareholder to limited voting rights. Various hybrid types of shares may be created for specific purposes. Shares of stock are normally transferable; they can be bought or sold at any time, subject to certain state, SEC, and in-company restrictions. Profits are paid as dividends in accordance with the rules regarding types of shares, or are held for corporate expansion. Shareholders may inspect the books and records of the corporation, and if they believe that the directors or officers are behaving improperly, they may take legal action to stop the wrong-doing and seek damages.

The business of a corporation is overseen by a board of directors, which generally consists of three members or more, elected yearly by the shareholders. If there are fewer than three shareholders, then there usually can be fewer than three seats on the board of directors. The board is responsible for setting corporate policy, for approving corporate actions (like large expenditures), and for electing the principal corporate officers.

In a small corporation, only a president and a secretary are required in most states, although treasurer and vice president are other common officers. Further creativity with titles is possible, within the limits of the by-laws and the cleverness of the board of directors.

Since corporations are treated as separate legal entities, they file income tax returns and pay taxes on income. Profits are taxed at the corporate level, and dividends to shareholders are taxed as individual income. The exception is the S corporation, described below.

S Corporations

The S corporations, formed in accordance with Sub-Chapter S of the IRS Code, is a special type of corporation for tax purposes. (The regular corporation is called a C corporation, a term rarely used.) An S corporation has the same basic organizational structure as a regular corporation, but has some of the tax advantages of a partnership. S corporation status is obtained by filing an election within two-and-a-half months of formation, or, with respect to succeeding years for established companies, within two-and-a-half months of the start of the year that precedes the year that the election is to take place.

An S corporation must file an information return with the IRS, but it pays no federal income tax. Instead, profits and losses are passed on to shareholders, and monies are treated as personal income. This helps to avoid double taxation on profits and allows losses to be deducted (up to the shareholder's investment in the S corporation). Excess losses may be carried over from previous years on personal returns—subject to limitations that are best described by an accountant familiar with current IRS regulations.

An S corporation may have up to 35 stockholders, none of whom can be foreign or corporate entities. In addition, an S corporation cannot be a subsidiary of another corporation. Other rules are equally stringent. Some states do not recognize S corporations as distinct from regular corporations for purposes of state income tax.

Loan-Out Corporations

Individuals active in the television business have often used "loan-out corporations" as a vehicle for providing their services. The theory of the loan-out corporation is simple enough. The individual forms a corporation which he or she controls. This corporation hires the individual who formed it, with the salary to be set from time to time to reflect the activity of the corporation and its other financial needs. Then the individual gets a job—either short-term (a writing, directing, or acting assignment) or long-term (becoming executive producer on a series). Instead of the individual being hired directly, the deal is made with the loan-out company, which in turn lends the services of its employee. In order to give the hiring company legal comfort that the individual will be committed to doing the work, the individual invariably signs an "inducement letter," which confirms that he or she will do the work and will look only to the loan-out corporation for compensation.

The original reason why many people in the television business set up loan-out companies was to take advantage of favorable tax breaks that were available to corporations but not to self-employed individuals. In particular, there were considerable advantages in the amount of pension monies that could be saved on a pre-tax basis. Over the years, most of the benefits have been eroded by reforms to the tax laws; furthermore, the IRS has taken a dim view of loan-out arrangements, and has challenged their use in some cases. Nonetheless, many people who have loan-out corporations have kept them in place, in part to preserve old benefits, in part because they provide some centralization to a fragmented set of employment relationships, and in part because certain kinds of deductions—like those for a business car or a personal assistant—may be less scrutinized by the IRS if taken by a corporation versus an individual.

One group for which loan-out corporations are still potentially advantageous is highly-paid writers. Here, the loan-out continues to offer access to pension and health-insurance benefits, and the possibility of a changed fiscal year.

Setting up and maintaining a loan-out corporation does involve some trouble and expense, so anyone who is considering forming one should consult with a tax advisor over the potential costs and benefits.

FOREIGN ENTITIES

With the increased globalization of television, video, and other media, many foreign entities are now doing business in the U.S. These entities will have their own names, rules and forms, governed by the law of the country in which they are established. Any entity (a corporation or an individual) not resident in the U.S. that is judged to be "doing business" in the U.S. may be liable for U.S. income taxation, and subject to state corporate qualification. If U.S. taxes apply, then the company must fill out a tax return covering all worldwide income allocable to the U.S., and must pay at the applicable standard rate (for example, personal or corporate). Cross-border co-production deals can be deemed to be partnerships doing business in the U.S., and potential foreign-production partners should structure the arrangement to avoid U.S. tax involvement. A non-resident foreign entity which is not judged to be doing business in the U.S. may receive income earned from business dealings with U.S. companies or from passive investments in the U.S. without filing a U.S. return—although a withholding tax of up to 30 percent will often be deducted at the source of payment. This approach can be varied by tax treaties, which frequently exist between the countries in question.

TAX ISSUES

Business Deductions

Many persons in the television business are self-employed, or work free-lance, without a permanent business affiliation. For tax purposes, these people will need to deduct a variety of expenses related to their work. Unfortunately, the IRS has made the deduction of many of these expenses more and more difficult. For instance, free-lancers often work out of their homes, and would like to deduct the expense of a home office. This is now possible only if the home office is fully dedicated (100 percent) to work purposes: a desk in the corner of what is otherwise a bedroom, living room, or family study will not qualify. In addition, home-office expenses can only be deducted from the income which the business conducted from that office actually produces.

　　Home workers are often writers. The IRS has required writers to hold off on deducting some kinds of writing expenses on projects until the project is completed. The IRS also generally forces a writer to treat advances as taxable income when the advances are actually received, as opposed to delaying until delivery of the finished work.

Production Advances, Expenses, and Costs

The tax treatment of production advances, expenses, and costs can be a source of potential problems to a production company. On the expense side, a television project is a capital asset, and the expenses associated with its development and production should be capitalized by the producing entity until such time as the project is put into distribution, sold off, or abandoned. If it is sold or abandoned, all of the costs then become deductible. If the project is put into distribution, or the producer otherwise retains an ongoing participation, the costs are deductible over a period of time. This period is usually the anticipated economic life of the program as calculated using the "income forecast method," which ties the deductibility to the rate at which the anticipated revenues are received.

In most instances, however, the producer will have received advances over the course of the production to help finance the program. In a worst-case scenario, the IRS could characterize these advances as income that is taxable when received—yet not allow any deduction of the related expenses until the program is delivered or shown. If these two events—the receipt of the advance, and the showing or delivery of the project—fall in different tax years, it is conceivable that there could be a distorted amount of income recognized. Most production companies avoid this by claiming that they are not in receipt of the advance until the program is delivered, and that until that point, the advance is really just a non-taxable loan. They also point out that if the advance is income, then the show has in effect gone into service already, so that they should deduct its expenses. Unfortunately, the theoretical underpinnings of these arguments may be open to question. Any production company that is likely to be receiving substantial production advances should consult with tax advisors to help structure ways to avoid unrealistic bulges in taxable income.

Part 7

INTERNATIONAL TELEVISION

Overview of World Markets

In the U.S., television programming is largely a domestic affair: aside from occasional British programs shown on public television, the vast majority of programs seen on U.S. television are produced in the U.S. In most other countries, however, domestic productions share the schedule with imports, predominantly U.S. network programs.

In countries around the world, large numbers of new broadcast and cable channels are being launched. Programming for these channels consists of not only U.S. productions, but imports from companies based in France, the U.K., Mexico, Japan, and elsewhere.

FOREIGN DISTRIBUTION OF U.S. PROGRAMS

Network shows are usually distributed by the international distribution arm of the producing studio, or, if the program was independently produced, through the international arm of a domestic syndication company.

Programs produced for pay or basic cable TV may be handled by the international sales arm of the network, or may be licensed to another distributor.

Shows produced for first-run domestic syndication are sold when completed by the syndicator's own international department. Larger syndication companies operate offices in key television markets world-wide, and work with commissioned sales representatives that specialize in smaller markets. The sale of *format rights* is common for game shows and some other non-fiction programs. *The Price is Right,* for example, is currently in production in the U.K., France (*Le Just Prix*), Italy (*OK! Il Prezzo e Guisto*), the Netherlands (*Prijzenslag*), Germany (*Der Preiss Ist Heist*), and elsewhere.

Joint ventures have become increasingly common as well. Programs are co-produced, for example, by a U.S. producer and Canada's CTV, or by an Italian or British broadcast network and its counterpart in the U.S. These combinations come about for several reasons, including shared production requirements, investment, and a desire to widen the area of business opportunities for future ventures. Foreign cable networks have developed as joint ventures between companies with successful formats and local partners: this arrangement has been the key to the international growth of services such as MTV and France's Canal Plus.

OVERVIEW OF WORLD TELEVISION MARKETS

Many U.S. companies see the world in two discrete halves: our country, and the other countries. Since the individual markets outside the U.S. can be difficult to comprehend, the natural—and invalid—assumption is that each country's system is in some way based upon a U.S. model. Indeed, some systems were originally based upon a U.S. model, but they have since evolved in very different directions. Some countries have broadcast services that are owned and operated by the government, plus other services that are privately held. And although it may be convenient to refer to "Japanese television" as if all of Japan's networks function as a single entity, more precise language is needed.

Canada is the largest market for programs produced in the U.S.; programs from the U.K. and Australia are seen about as often in Canada as they are in the U.S. Most French-language programs seen on Canadian television are produced domestically. In order to protect Canada's national identity from U.S. influence, a quota system for domestic programs is in effect.

Germany, the U.K., France, Spain, and Italy are the most active buyers and sellers of television programming in Western Europe. The Scandinavian and Benelux countries are medium-sized markets. Eastern Europe is still a mystery; in terms of sheer population and growth potential, the market may someday become enormous, but present-day commercial ventures remain risky. Pan-European networks, generally specializing in a particular type of programming, are seen throughout the Western part of the continent via DBS and cable systems.

Japan and Australia are only slightly smaller than the largest European markets. Japanese companies occasionally co-produce with European broadcasters, and now own, either jointly or wholly, worldwide entertainment companies. Australia supplies some English-language programming seen in the U.S., the U.K., and elsewhere. Taiwan, Hong Kong, the Philippines, Thailand, India, China, and South Korea are all considered to be smaller markets due to a combination of factors, including language and translation problems, local cultures and traditions, and (in some cases) limited numbers of television households.

In Latin America, Mexico and Brazil are medium-sized markets dominated by large, powerful networks. Mexico is a leading supplier of Spanish-language programs seen in the U.S. and throughout Latin America; Venezuela is also a vital player in South America. The smaller countries, and the islands, buy programming, but their populations are generally small, so license fees are low.

The Middle Eastern countries are minor markets, often with tough censorship rules. African nations are not considered vital television markets (although France's Canal Plus is involved in a joint venture in French-speaking Africa). South Africa is an important market, but most U.S. companies refuse to do business there. In most cases, the combination of a television system that has been slow in developing, linguistic/cultural differences from the West, and a general lack of involvement in the global business marketplace makes these nations marginal players in terms of television.

Rapid changes in technology, politics, and economics are certain to alter the pecking order overseas. (See Figure 4 for a list of the largest world television markets.) The importance of Asian countries is likely to grow, and some countries in Latin America, Africa, and the Middle East are likely to mature into robust markets as new media develop and systems of distribution become more sophisticated. Newer channels—via DBS, via cable, and via broadcast—should emerge in many of these regions within the next decade.

The following chapters discuss broadcasting, cable, and home video in the major world markets.

TELEVISION STANDARDS

Three different systems are used throughout the world to record, play back, transmit, and receive television signals.

NTSC is a system that transmits the television image at 525 lines per second. This system is the standard used in the U.S., Canada, Japan, and the Far East. It was developed in the U.S. and became the standard in 1954.

PAL, a 625-line system, was developed in Germany. PAL is used in the U.K., Western Europe (except France), and much of South America.

SECAM, developed by the French, is the standard for France; like PAL, it uses 625 lines. SECAM is also the system predominant in Africa, because of French political involvement on that continent during the period when television standards were adopted. SECAM is the system used throughout the Middle East; a modified version is the standard in Eastern Europe and the USSR.

Because both PAL and SECAM were first adopted in 1967, more than 15 years after the NTSC standard was adopted, both systems are superior to NTSC, offering greater image clarity.

Tapes recorded in one system cannot be played on a video player from another—an NTSC tape, for example, cannot be played on a PAL or SECAM videotape machine. Multi-standard VCRs and TV sets are becoming available, though, at reasonable prices for consumers. Its also possible to hire a facility to convert tapes from one standard to another, with generally acceptable results.

40 | Canada

Since its inception in the 1930s, broadcasting in Canada has been a mix of public and private endeavors. Adopting the most appealing aspects of the U.S. and the U.K. systems, Canada developed its own model, with one additional twist. Because Canada is home to two different cultures—each with its own language—there are both English-language and French-language broadcasters.

THE CANADIAN BROADCASTING CORPORATION (CBC)

Founded in 1936 as Canada's version of the BBC, the government-owned Canadian Broadcasting Corporation (CBC) operates radio and television networks and other services in English and in French. The television operations are supported by tax revenues and by commercial revenues. The CBC owns and operates 30 television stations (English plus French) in the provincial capitals and other large cities. In smaller cities and outlying regions, CBC programming is carried by privately-owned affiliates.

Approximately 75 percent of CBC operations are financed by Parliamentary allocation; the remaining 25 percent comes from commercial revenues and activities in the enterprises group, such as foreign sales of CBC productions.

CBC radio services are non-commercial. The CBC operates a pair of domestic radio networks plus Radio Canada International, an international radio service. The CBC's main headquarters are in Ottawa; the English-speaking networks are based in Toronto, and the French-Speaking networks, in Montreal.

ENGLISH-LANGUAGE NETWORKS AND STATIONS

CBC English Television Network

Based in Toronto, the CBC English Television Network offers a wide range of entertainment, sports, children's, news, and other types of programming. The following schedule is for Monday, October 29, 1990, on CBLT, the CBC-owned and -operated station in Toronto. The program mix makes CBLT resemble a combination of a traditional U.S. independent station, commercial network affiliate, and public television station (note that the U.S. sitcoms are programmed by the network, not by the local station). CBLT signs on just before 8:30 A.M., 2½ hours after privately-owned stations in the Toronto area.

8:30 A.M.—*Newfoundland Outdoors* (Canadian magazine)
9:00 A.M.—*F.I.T.* (Canadian fitness)
9:30 A.M.—*Wok with Yan* (Canadian-produced, Chinese cooking)
10:00 A.M.—*Fred Penner's Place* (Canadian pre-school series)
10:15 A.M.—*Under the Umbrella Tree* (Canadian pre-school)
10:30 A.M.—*Mr. Dressup* (Canadian pre-school)
11:00 A.M.—*Sesame Street* (Canadian version)
Noon—*Midday* (Canadian news)
1:00 P.M.—*All My Children* (U.S. daytime drama)
2:00 P.M.—*Coronation Street* (U.K. daytime drama)
2:30 P.M.—*Alice* (U.S. sitcom)
3:00 P.M.—*Welcome Back, Kotter* (U.S. sitcom)
3:30 P.M.—*Facts of Life* (U.S. sitcom)
4:00 P.M.—*WKRP in Cincinnati* (U.S. sitcom)
4:30 P.M.—*Danger Bay* (Canadian action-adventure, produced with U.S.'s Disney Channel)
5:00 P.M.—*Video Hits* (Canadian music video)
5:30 P.M.—*Golden Girls* (U.S. sitcom)
6:00 P.M.—Local news
7:00 P.M.—*Monitor* (Canadian news magazine)
7:30 P.M.—*Mom P.I.* (Canadian detective series)
8:00 P.M.—*Fresh Prince of Bel Air* (U.S. sitcom)
9:00 P.M.—*Newhart* (U.S. sitcom)
9:30 P.M.—*Designing Women* (U.S. sitcom)
10:00 P.M.—*The National–Journal* (Canadian nightly news and news magazine)
11:00 P.M.—Local news
11:30 P.M.—*Newhart* (U.S. sitcom)
Midnight—*Kate & Allie* (U.S. sitcom)
1:00 A.M.—Movie: *The General Died at Dawn,* starring Gary Cooper
2:45 A.M.—Off the air

CBLT's evening schedule for the rest of the week combines Canadian and U.S. programming. Tuesday night features *the fifth estate* (an investigative news magazine), *Market Place* (consumer news), and *Man Alive* (personality-oriented news magazine), all Canadian shows. On Wednesday night, the schedule includes *The Wonder Years* (simulcast to maximize advertising revenues); *The Fanelli Boys* (sitcom), another U.S.

import; and *The Nature of Things* (a Canadian series about the environment). Thursday's shows are the U.S. import *Empty Nest* and three Canadian series: *Adrienne Clarkson Presents, CODCO,* and *Kids in the Hall.* Friday night's line-up has *Street Legal* (Canadian-produced legal series) and *Dallas* (U.S. series).

Prime time schedules tend to be the same on every CBC station. Daytime schedules vary, but the program types, and sources, are essentially similar. CBC provides regular coverage of hockey and baseball, the two most popular sports in Canada.

CBC programming is managed by program type, with a senior program executive responsible for each schedule. Individual program departments include children's, current affairs, dramatic series, movies and mini-series, sitcoms, sports, variety, and film shorts.

Local CBC stations provide additional news, public affairs, and children's programming. Private CBC affiliates buy their own programming to supplement the CBC schedule. Channel 3, located outside Toronto, features reruns of *Leave It to Beaver, The Andy Griffith Show,* and other imports on its daytime schedule.

In recent years, the CBC has encouraged its privately-held affiliates to become independent stations.

CTV Television Network

The English-speaking CTV network was formed in the early 1960s by privately-owned commercial stations operating in several large Canadian cities. Sixteen stations actually own the network; in addition, a handful of supplemental affiliates, mainly in smaller cities, carry its shows. The network supplies about 40 hours a week of programming, including national news and most prime time entertainment. Stations produce some local programs, then fill in the rest of the schedule with acquisitions, largely from the U.S. CTV supports itself through advertising revenues.

CTV is Canada's mass-appeal network. After an exercise show, CTV airs *A.M. Canada* from 6:30 until 9:00 A.M. daily. Then the network mixes syndicated talk shows (*The Joan Rivers Show*), Canadian talk shows (*Dini Petty*), news, and syndicated programs. In the evenings, CTV's schedule is dominated by U.S. network fare—*Matlock, Unsolved Mysteries, Jake & the Fatman, The Cosby Show, Knot's Landing, Full House, Night Court*—with only occasional Canadian programming, such as *Katts & Dogg,* a Miss Canada pageant, or figure skating. Like CBC's English television network, CTV also provides regular hockey and baseball coverage.

Global Television

Global Television is licensed as a regional station for Toronto, but its signal is seen outside the city via retransmissions and cable, so it is considered a network. The Global schedule offers cartoon series in the morning (*Police Academy, Inspector Gadget, Tiny Toon Adventures*), with game shows (*Bumper Stumpers, Chain Reaction, Liar's Club, Last Word,* all co-productions with U.S. companies), soaps (the Canadian series *100 Huntley Street,* as well as *Days of Our Lives, Santa Barbara, The Bold and the Beautiful, The Young and the Restless*), and news at noon and in the early evening. Global's evening programming is similar to CTV's: *Major Dad, MacGyver, 21 Jump Street, Who's the Boss?, Growing Pains, In the Heat of the Night, The Simpsons, Cheers,* and *Dear John.* Only a few of the shows carried on Global are produced in Canada: *T and T, Good Grief, Diamonds,* and *Super Dave* (a co-production with Showtime) were the only Canadian-produced shows on Global's prime time schedule during the week of October 27, 1990. *The Sportsline,* which appears after the evening news, is a Canadian production, but is followed by *Late Night with David Letterman.* It is generally believed that action will be taken to hold Global to its mandate—to act like a purely Canadian network and not just as an outlet for U.S. programs.

Independent English-Language Stations

Early in the 1970s, the Canadian Radio-Television Commission licensed independent stations for the first time. City TV, based in Toronto, is a unique alternative to traditional broadcasting. Operating on a "small is beautiful" principle, City TV started with a young staff, portable video equipment, and innovative, inexpensive, and highly-localized programming. In time, City TV has evolved into a hip urban station with three specialties: news, music, and movies. City TV programs on fashion and lifestyle are regularly exported to other countries.

Independent stations have flourished in Canada through the late 1980s, largely by appealing to specific audience segments. Several aggressive players are moving toward the formation of new networks. CanWest, which owns Global, also owns five independent stations in Western Canada. Western International Communication (WIC) started with BCTV, an independent in British Columbia; plans to buy two more independents in Western Canada; and has expressed an interest in CHCH-Hamilton, near Toronto. Baton Broadcasting, which began as the owner of CFTO (CTV's Toronto affiliate), owns CTV and CBC affiliates throughout Ontario and in Saskatchewan.

Regional English-Language Networks and Stations

TVOntario (TVO), operated by the Ontario Educational Communications Authority, is a regional public broadcaster. TVO provides English-language programming throughout the province; it also broadcasts with an alternative French soundtrack. TVO participates in the international marketplace, principally in children's programming. Other examples of regional public-television networks include Access Alberta (operated by the Alberta Educational Communications Corporations) and Knowledge Network in Vancouver, B.C.

FRENCH-LANGUAGE NETWORKS AND STATIONS

French-language television is parallel in structure to the English-language system. The CBC's French network is Société de Radio Canada (SRC, or simply Radio Canada). Headquartered in Montreal, SRC owns and operates stations in Quebec City and in other French-speaking city centers, broadcasting throughout the country. Every provincial capital has a CBC French-language channel that offers a combination of distinctly French-Canadian programming—some network, some local.

TVA is a network of privately-owned stations. TeleMetropole, located in Montreal, is the name of the network's principal station, but TVA has affiliates throughout the province of Quebec. Reseau de Television Quatre Saisons (TQS) is another network of privately-owned stations throughout Quebec. Both networks offer a commercial program schedule of children's, news, comedy, drama, and variety shows.

Radio Quebec, funded by Quebec's provincial government, is an educational station. Because it is more commercial in orientation than its English-language equivalents, Radio Quebec is more popular (some funding is received via sale of commercial time during specific dayparts). The daytime schedule is educational. In prime time, Radio Quebec competes with a select group of dramas, some original productions, some produced in France, and some independent productions.

As a rule, French-language broadcasters show a far higher percentage of Canadian-made programming than their English-language counterparts. Remarkably little is imported from France because the cultural differences are too pronounced; tolerance for dubbed or subtitled programming is also low. As a result, a vibrant French-language production community has grown up in and around Montreal.

CANADIAN RADIO-TELEVISION AND TELECOMMUNICATIONS COMMISSION (CRTC)

Canada's regulatory body for broadcast and cable communications is the Canadian Radio-Television and Telecommunications Commission (CRTC). Based in Ottawa, the CRTC supervises broadcasting and cable-casting, as well as telecommunications and telephone service.

The CRTC is staffed by a chairman and eight full-time commissioners. The chairman serves for seven years, the commissioners, for five-year terms. In addition, part-time commissioners from different regions participate in specific areas, largely to add regional balance to the commission. The CRTC houses two distinct bodies: one regulates broadcasting, the other regulates telecommunications. On the broadcasting side, there are three subdivisions: radio, television, and cable. Within each subdivision, there is a policy group and an operations group.

The commission takes a more active role in controlling Canadian broadcast programming than, for example, the FCC does in the U.S.

In order to keep Canadian culture distinct from U.S. culture, the CRTC requires that the government-owned CBC stations carry at least 60 percent "Canadian content" in prime time. A particular program's "Canadian content" is determined by a formula that considers such factors as storyline, setting, casting, and production personnel. For privately-owned broadcasters, the quota is 50 percent.

The CRTC imposes many restrictions and limitations on the use of the public airwaves. Hard liquor is one of several product categories that cannot be advertised on Canadian television (this type of restriction exists in most countries). In addition, scripts for food products are subject to approval. Abusive language is not permitted, on the grounds that society must be protected.

The commission licenses stations, renews licenses, and issues sanctions when a problem exists. Occasionally, it will attach conditions to a station's broadcast license or license renewal. For example, if better work in children's programming is desired (or demanded) by the public, this will be stipulated in the license grant. If complaints have come to the attention of the CRTC regarding cultural stereotyping, violence, or other objectionables, the CRTC may act on these matters as well. The CRTC's highest priority, though, is ensuring that broadcasters provide a substantial quantity of high-quality Canadian programming. If a broadcaster has been financially successful, the CRTC may increase the quota of Canadian content required, or the amount of money spent on Canadian productions. This is quite different from the way that the FCC, and most other regulatory bodies, operate. Much of the reason for this unusual relationship between regulators and broadcasters is Canada's population distribution (the population is concentrated in a small number of cities, with vast open spaces and a large gap between the east and west coasts) as well as the view that Canadian broadcasters must be protected from the vast influence of the U.S. At the core of the CRTC philosophy is what is often called "the old Canadian schizophrenia"—a belief that unfettered free enterprise alone will not allow success without some government involvement.

Still, the CRTC does not act as a censor. In fact, the CRTC does not intervene with regard to specific programs, only to general programming direction.

A new Broadcasting Act was passed in 1991, granting the CRTC jurisdiction over cable television, satellite delivery, fiber optics, and other new technologies. The CRTC does not regulate home video.

CABLE TELEVISION

The CRTC has awarded licenses for exclusive service to approximately 800 cable systems. In smaller communities, one cable company serves the entire population; in larger communities, the CRTC divides the city into zones, and several companies provide exclusive service. Cable companies are owned locally; multiple-system ownership is not as prevalent in Canada as it is in the U.S., but it is growing.

Cable television is extremely popular in Canada—with 69 percent *cable penetration*, Canada ranks third in the world (behind Belgium and the Netherlands). The main reason for cable's popularity is direct access to U.S. television channels. Cable systems must adhere to the "3-plus-1 Policy"—all Canadian channels in the service area must be carried if the system is to carry ABC, CBS, NBC (3), plus PBS (1). In some areas, cable's popularity is also due to improved reception.

In order to protect Canadian broadcasters, who depend upon Canadian advertisers for income, the rule of *simultaneous substitution* applies to cable systems. If the CBC and CBS both carry *Dallas*, for example, the cable operator must substitute the CBC signal (with CBC commercials intact) in place of the CBS signal. The reasoning is that since the CBS affiliate in Buffalo, New York (for example), is not licensed to operate in Toronto, it should not profit from Toronto's viewership.

The CRTC also regulates cable rates. When the cable system is first set up, the CRTC approves fees and small increases; from that point on, the CRTC must also approve large fee increases. The costs for basic cable service and for pay channels are roughly comparable to the rates charged in the U.S.

Cable Networks

Canada's basic cable services—called specialty services—earn revenue via both commercials and per-subscriber fees. Between conventional broadcast stations and specialty services, basic cable comprises approximately 25 to 30 channels on most Canadian cable systems.

MuchMusic, a 24-hour music-video channel, features short video clips hosted by a VJ as well as longer daily programs and specials. MuchMusic plays predominantly rock music, but other forms of Canadian music, such as country, are featured as well; Musique Plus is the French-language equivalent. CBC Newsworld, which resembles CNN (with more 30- and 60-minute programs), often features regional information programs, CBC news programs, and CBS and public affairs programs. YTV is a children's and youth service; the CRTC discourages YTV from scheduling programs that are similar to the offerings on adult program services. Vision TV, a family service with some religious and ethical programming, buys programs from the U.K. and elsewhere, carries many projects financed by the National Film Board of Canada, and reruns CBC programs. Other basic cable services include a shopping channel, a weather channel, and a pair of Parliamentary channels (one English, one French) similar to C-SPAN.

Among discretionary (or pay) services, First Choice is the movie channel serving the eastern half of Canada; its western equivalent is called SuperChannel. The Family Channel shows Disney programming plus a healthy portion of Canadian children's product. TSN is Canada's pay-sports network. Since the CBC and CTV have the most valuable sports licenses for hockey, baseball, and football, TSN uses secondary sports events and fill-ins to fill its 24-hour schedule.

Many of Canada's cable services have French-language equivalents, but for the most part, these French services are not doing well.

HOME VIDEO

Roughly 65 percent of Canadian households own VCRs. The system is set up much as it is in the U.S., with about 5,000 stores selling and renting videocassettes at prices comparable to U.S. prices. Neighborhood video stores are feeling the pinch as large chains (Jumbo Video, West Coast Video) increase market share. The dominant releasing companies are Video One Canada, Ltd. and Bellevue Home Entertainment, which have established joint ventures with U.S. companies for videocassette distribution in Canada.

41 Europe

This chapter concentrates on television and video in the United Kingdom, Germany, France, Italy, and Spain. A section at the end of the chapter discusses some smaller European markets.

THE UNITED KINGDOM

Broadcasting began in the United Kingdom in 1922 as a private collaboration of radio manufacturers operating their own stations. Five years later, the British Broadcasting Corporation (BBC) was established by Royal Charter. In 1954, Parliament passed a bill authorizing a second government-owned broadcasting corporation, the Independent Television Authority, later renamed the Independent Broadcasting Authority (IBA). In 1991, the IBA was succeeded by the Independent Television Commission (ITC). The ITC currently regulates privately-operated broadcast and cable companies. Plans to change the entire independent/private TV business in the U.K. are currently under way, with 1993 as a target date for the new system to take effect. The BBC is also scheduled for a complete reorganization before 1995.

The BBC

The BBC operates five domestic radio networks: BBC Radio 1 (pop music), BBC Radio 2 (middle-of-the road/easy listening), BBC Radio 3 (classical), BBC Radio 4 (news, drama, general interest), and BBC Radio 5 (sports, news, talk, some music). In addition, the BBC runs a group of local radio stations throughout the U.K. BBC External Services broadcasts in 35 languages to nations throughout the world; BBC World Service broadcasts worldwide in English via short-wave.

The BBC has two television networks seen throughout the U.K.: BBC 1 and BBC 2. Both services develop and produce their own programs, produce projects with international partners, and purchase completed programs from a wide variety of sources. Each channel employs its own program staff.

The BBC also runs a Pan-European satellite television service, with programming from BBC 1 and BBC 2, called BBC Europe. The BBC plans to expand this service to become BBC World Television.

BBC 1, the more popular of the two networks, is generally considered to be the mainstream service. There are six program categories, each supervised by a head of programming. Light Entertainment includes variety shows (*Royal Variety Performance, Top of the Pops*) and situation comedy (*'Allo 'Allo, Steptoe & Son*). Drama comprises long- and short-term series (*EastEnders, Neighbours*). Sports Programming features tennis, soccer, cricket, golf, snooker, horse racing, and other sports. General Interest offers programs such as *Antiques Roadshow* (the highest-rated general-interest program in the U.K.) and *Crimewatch UK*. News and Current Affairs is responsible for the *Six O'Clock News* and *Nine O'Clock News, Breakfast Time* (which resembles *The Today Show* or *Good Morning America*), and some documentary/magazine shows. Programmes for Children and Family covers a wide range of shows, from *Jim'll Fix It* to the fantasy/science fiction series *Chronicles of Narnia*.

BBC 2 features programs for narrower audiences; it is more of a highbrow service compared to BBC 1, and usually attracts less than a third of BBC 1's ratings. BBC 2 is responsible for some of the popular dramatic shows seen in the U.S. and worldwide, as well as specialties like the Chelsea Flower Show, *The Nature of Australia*, and the World Snooker Final. BBC 2 allots time for programming of interest to specific ethnic groups.

The BBC television operations are funded by a mandatory license fee, essentially a user tax on television sets (roughly £80 per year per household), plus a government subsidy. This subsidy arrangement may soon be challenged in the courts.

Commercial Broadcasting

Despite a substantial faction of lawmakers who were originally opposed to the idea of commercially-supported broadcasting (Lord Reith of the House of Lords likened it to the bubonic plague), regional commercial television stations now operate throughout the U.K. Fifteen regional licenses are available, and as of this writing, all but two were subject to a fierce bidding competition for ten-year licenses set to begin in 1993.

Under the old system, Thames Television and London Weekend Television (LWT) shared the license for the London region—Thames on weekdays, LWT on weekends. Granada Television, known to U.S. audiences for *Brideshead Revisited* and *The Jewel in the Crown*, served the northwest of England (around Manchester). Broadcasting companies such as LWT, Thames, Central, Granada, and Yorkshire produced most of the programming for ITV, a network of regional stations. Under the new system, the ITV network will become a national service to be renamed Channel Three in 1993.

The commercial independents remain squarely in the entertainment business, producing and purchasing programs that are likely to garner the largest possible audiences for their advertisers. In real terms, this means game shows, situation comedies, popular motion pictures, soap operas, sports, news, and other mass-audience formats. The regional independents, as a whole, receive 90 percent of their income from advertising.

With grand intentions of offering a true programming alternative and a "nursery for new forms and new methods of presenting ideas,"* the IBA launched Channel Four in 1981. As a result of the changes in U.K. television, Channel Four now operates as a separate corporation administered by the IBA's successor, the ITC. Channel Four does not create its own programming; instead, it finances (or co-finances) productions and purchases completed work. Channel Four broadcasts on a limited schedule.

In 1994, another commercially-supported broadcast service, Channel Five, will go on the air. Because of technical limitations, only about 70 percent of the U.K. will be able to receive Channel Five; some population centers in the South and East will not be able to receive the signal, nor will those in the northern reaches of Scotland. In any case, a special aerial will probably be required to receive Channel Five, and there is some concern about signal interference with VCRs. One company will be awarded the franchise to operate Channel Five; the ITC will begin accepting proposals in 1992.

Cable Television

High costs of physical installation, strong broadcast-signal quality, and a scarcity of programming until the late 1980s are the primary reasons why cable penetration in the U.K. is under 2 percent. As of early 1990, only 16 cable franchises were operating, but an additional 45 were awarded, so the industry is likely to grow through the 1990s. Satellite delivery is also gaining in popularity, providing cable with direct competition.

From 1984 until it was replaced by the ITC at the end of 1990, the Cable Authority granted local cable franchises to companies within the U.K. and, with some restrictions, to foreign companies operating in the U.K. Under British law, franchises cannot be granted to any company that owns a television, radio, or newspaper operation in the franchise area; local authorities, religious groups, and political organizations are also prohibited from owning a franchise. The Cable Authority also supervised programming and advertising practices. Under the new Broadcasting Bill, the responsibilities of the Cable Authority will be transferred to the new ITC.

Viewers in the U.K. enjoy a limited number of cable channel choices, but they do receive BBC 1 and BBC 2, ITV, and Channel Four. Sky One is a satellite network also seen on some cable systems; it offers U.S. comedy and drama, as well as British game shows, sitcoms, dramas, talk shows, documentaries, and so on, and some programming from other countries. British Sky News is a 24-hour service, largely local in character. British Sky Galaxy offers children's programs by day and

---

* The Annan Committee, quoted in *World Broadcasting Systems: A Comparative Analysis* by Sydney W. Head, p. 82.

general entertainment, game shows, drama, and comedy at night. Sky News and Sky Galaxy are also transmitted by direct broadcast satellite (see below).

Many of the following cable channels are carried on only selected U.K. cable systems; some are available in other countries as well. SuperChannel, owned by the Marucci family of Italy, is an advertiser-supported channel offering low-budget programming, music videos, and old movies. The Children's Channel—owned by DC Thomson, Thames, BT, and Central—shows cartoons and educational programming throughout the day. MTV Europe is a 24-hour service owned by Viacom and the Mirror Group, and is also seen in 27 countries. The Discovery Channel, owned by United Cable (a major MSO in the U.K.) and United Artists, features documentaries and other non-fiction programming. Some cable systems also import CNN.

Cable subscribers in the U.K. pay roughly £10 per month for basic cable service.

Satellite Broadcasting

The delivery of programming via direct broadcast satellite (DBS) is growing more rapidly in the U.K. than cable television.

In the early 1990s, two DBS companies competed for a foothold in a small but potentially lucrative market. Within two years, British Satellite Broadcasting (BSB) was absorbed by Rupert Murdoch's New International. The new company, called British Sky Broadcasting, operates two sets of services, each on a separate satellite.

To satisfy viewers in the U.K. who invested in the original BSB, five channels are offered on the high-powered Marco Polo satellite: British Sky News, British Sky Galaxy (both described above), a sports channel, British Sky Movie Channel 1, and British Sky Movie 2. The movie channels require a decoder.

On the ASTRA satellite, DBS subscribers can receive a different set of services (based on the original Murdoch offering): Sky One, a general interest network; Sky News, which is similar to CNN, and offers newscasts from ABC and NBC News; Sky Movies; and the Movie Channel. The latter two are encoded pay TV services.

Home Video

The U.K. is one of the world's largest home video markets: VCR penetration is 70 percent, and there is strong rental and sell-through activity. Overnight rentals cost about £1.5, and many tapes sell for about £10. Rental and sell-through product consists mainly of U.S. films, and U.S. video labels dominate the market. Warner, Columbia, Fox, Disney/Touchstone, and CIC (which distributes Universal and Paramount product) are the biggest labels; other successful ones include Guild, EV, MCEG/Virgin, VCI (Video Collection), Polygram, Tempo, and Medusa. There are 25,000 video outlets in the U.K., but many of them are corner candy stores and news agents who stock only the top titles. The largest video chain in the U.K. is Ritz, which has grown to over 800 outlets since the late 1980s; the U.S.-based Blockbuster Video has opened over a dozen stores there as well.

GERMANY

Although Germany is once again a single nation, the former West Germany dominates the broadcasting field. Broadcast, cable, and home video in this part of Germany represent one of the world's most vital markets.

ARD

In an effort to limit the power of a central German government after World War II, the Allies placed the development of cultural matters (broadcasting included) in the hands of the states, or *länder.* Broadcasting stations developed in the *länder,* and in several cases, *länder* combined resources; the result is a total of nine regional broadcasters in eleven states, plus two more owned by the federal government. Each of the regional broadcasters is owned by its regional government. All of these are part of a network cooperative known as ARD, short for Arbeitsgemeinschaft der Offentlich-rechtlichen Rundfunkstalten der Bundesrepublik Deutschland (rough translation: the Federation of Public Broadcasting Corporations of the Federal Republic of Germany). ARD is also called Das Erste (Channel One).

ARD, Germany's highest-rated network, broadcasts from early morning until late night, with a mix of sports, news, drama, and cultural programming with highbrow appeal. Regional member WDR (Westdeutscher Rundfunk), located in Cologne, serves the West; NDR (Norddeutscher Rundfunk), in Hamburg, serves the North; and BR (Bayerischer Rundfunk), in Munich, serves the Southeast. Together, these three entities provide approximately 60 percent of ARD's network programming.

The network programs most of the day; the regional stations program from the early evening onward. All ARD members are active locally, and all contribute at least some programming to the network. ARD members work with independent production companies, acquire completed programs, and produce some of their own programming (such as sports).

Co-production deals are made at the member level, not by the national headquarters (which moves each year to a different regional broadcast facility). WDR International is very active in co-producing internationally. Studio Hamburg and NDR International are both international program operations within NDR; NDR International is charged with reviewing proposals for new projects. BR is smaller, but an ambitious co-producer, particularly in the motion picture area. WDR and

NDR also distribute programs outside the network, and other regional members have followed suit. The commercial arm of ARD, Degeto Films, buys and sells programming for the national network and for regional stations.

ARD is a non-profit commercial service, with advertising limited to 20 minutes per day (none on Sunday), shown in four 5-minute blocks. Restrictions are being lifted, however, so that more time can be sold at higher unit prices. ARD is also planning to start a satellite program service called 1Plus.

ZDF

Zweites Deutsches Fersehen (ZDF), or Second German Television, was launched in 1961 as a national network, but not without a fight from the *länder*, who believed that they alone had the right to establish broadcast stations. ZDF is owned by the eleven *länder*, but decision-making is centralized in the head offices in Mainz. As with ARD, the programming is sophisticated; but unlike ARD, ZDF is a national service without local affiliates or local producing entities. Of the two, ZDF is more aggressive, both in ratings competition at home and in international ventures. ZDF initiated the formation of the European Co-Production Agreement (ECA), which has been responsible for more than 200 hours of new programming. The agreement also includes Channel Four (U.K.), RAI (Italy), ORF (Austria), RTVE (Spain), SRG/SSR (Switzerland), and A2 (France).

ZDF's operating hours are similar to those of ARD, and so are the advertising restrictions imposed on the network. ZDF is launching a new satellite service called 3Sat.

Third Channels

In addition to ARD and ZDF, the broadcast organizations in the *länder* operate independent channels. WDR3 and BR3, two of the biggest of these independents, are available on cable throughout most of Germany.

RTL-Plus

RTL-Plus—previously known as Radio-Television Luxembourg—is owned by CLT (Compagnie Luxembourgeoise de Télédiffusion) and UFA (a Bertelsmann subsidiary). The network, based in Cologne, can be seen only in parts of Germany: it reaches approximately 5 million households by over-the-air transmission, plus another 6 million by cable.

When it began in 1984, RTL-Plus programmed low-cost studio-based productions. By 1987, it was building strength by acquiring series produced in the U.S. and by featuring programming with wide audience appeal. Since then, RTL-Plus's entertainment focus has shifted "downmarket"—to some soft-core pornography, and plenty of B-movies. RTL-Plus is also acquiring a reputation for sports coverage, having bought the rights to German football and Wimbledon.

Sat 1

Sat 1 is owned in large part by Germany's Springer-Verlag publishing group, APF (a combination of 140 publishers), and PKS (a joint venture between the German Co-operative Bank and Germany's Kirch Group). The Sat 1 network reaches less than half of Germany's viewers. When it debuted in 1985, Sat 1 spent lavish sums on programming in its early days, but has since scaled down its expenditures. Broadcast ratings do not accurately reflect Sat 1's success with general-interest entertainment: game shows, televised shopping, morning talk, inexpensive U.S. reruns, and soft-core erotica. Among cable viewers, Sat 1 is as popular with these programs as ARD or ZDF. The network is moving toward an increased amount of original productions.

Tele5

Jointly owned by Tele-Munchen (Germany), CLT (Luxembourg), Fininvest (Italy), Wolfgang Fisher (Germany), and ABC (U.S.), Tele5 is a small network currently seen in about half of Germany. Programming is general-interest, based upon a formula that has been successful for the Fininvest organization in other countries: a strong emphasis on sports and music, with soaps, talk, and plenty of acquired series.

PRO7

After an ill-fated launch as a service called Eureka, this channel changed its name and its programming in 1989. With its vintage U.S. TV series, popular among the target 20–40-year-old market, and its feature films (largely from the Kirch library), PRO7 has gained a substantial following. The network is owned by Gerhard Ackermans and Thomas Kirch.

Regulation of German Television

Each of the *länder* has its own rules and regulations for broadcasting and cablecasting; these are based upon a national standard. The Federal Office of Post and Communications (Deutsche Bundespost) controls the technical side of television broadcasting and cablecasting for all of Germany.

Neither ARD nor ZDF is permitted to run advertisements after 8:00 P.M.; a small percentage of other airtime may be devoted to commercials.

Cable Television

Nearly 40 percent of German households subscribe to cable. Homegrown cable services are few; instead, the cable networks are conduits for broadcasters from Germany and from neighboring countries, including Austria, France, the U.K., and Switzerland. German viewers receive Sky Channel and Pan-European services like MTV, SuperChannel, and

EuroSport. In addition, households are offered a pay service called Premiere, a German version of France's Canal Plus (see page 377). Premiere is owned by Bertelsmann's UFA film/television subsidiary, Canal Plus, and the Kirch Group. Like other Canal Plus operations, this one offers mostly feature films and sports (notably soccer), with a flashy on-air look.

Home Video

Roughly half of the households in western Germany own VCRs. VCR owners are served by neighborhood "videotiques" that rent and sell videocassettes, by supermarkets, and by department stores that concentrate on sell-through. Recent films rent for DM10 for top titles; older films rent for about DM7. In addition to U.S. and U.K. home video labels, many German film companies operate labels. Top video labels include Fox, CIC, Euro Video, Columbia, Beta-Taurus, VCL/Carol, Starlight, Markeling, VPS, and Warner.

One rather unusual aspect of German home video is its rating system. Many films intended for adult viewers are "indexed"—that is, they are classified in the same category as pornography. *Rambo* is an example of such a film—intended for adult viewers, but hardly pornographic by most standards. Stores that sell films indexed for the 18+ age group are not permitted to advertise the films, to display the boxes face-out (only "spine-out"), or to put up posters for the film. In order to be rented in the mainstream home video market, a film needs a "16-certificate," certifying that it is suitable for younger viewers. Indexing has slowed the growth of the German home video market, particularly in the rental area.

Television in East Germany

Because of unification, television in the former East Germany will be changed by television in the former West Germany. Two television networks, DDR 1 and DDR 2, no longer operate.

The five *länder* in the former East Germany are starting regional services. ZDF plans to spread its signal to the new areas. A new regional network called Landerkette has begun showing many of the programs previously seen on DDR1 and DDR2.

Cable penetration in the former East Germany is under 5 percent, but satellite dishes are common in some regions. VCR ownership is about 20 percent, with home video seen as a tremendous growth market.

FRANCE

The organization of French television is complicated. Originally, radio broadcasting in France was private, but because some French broadcasters sided with the German occupation forces following World War II, the system was nationalized. A series of political changes have further altered the system. The result is a group of state-owned organizations, an unrelated group of privately-owned companies, and one large network that was once public and is now private. With many new companies and combinations of older players in a new format, plus public subsidies and quotas, the mix of old and new can be confounding for outsiders.

State-Owned Services

TDF, Télédiffusion de France, is responsible for the transmission facilities used by all government-owned French broadcasters.

Société Française de Production et de Creation Audiovisuelles (SFP) is an enormous production operation. It employs 2,500 people, and operates studios throughout the country (including 15 in Paris) plus mobile units. SFP sells programs to all of the French networks (including the private ones), co-produces with companies outside France, and commissions work from companies inside and outside France. SFP is not, itself, a network or broadcaster.

Antenne-2 (A2) is based in Paris. This is a government-owned network supported roughly half by advertising, half by a user tax. A2 programming includes game shows, news, variety, drama, magazine, children's, and films. The broadcast schedule runs from early morning until late at night, daily except Sunday. To eliminate unproductive competition between A2 and FR3 (see below), a single management team is taking charge of both networks.

France Regions 3 (FR3) is also based in Paris. Programming is similar to A2's, but the schedule runs only from late afternoon until just past midnight. The first few hours, typically from about 5:00 P.M. until 7:30 P.M., are programmed locally by each of the 12 provincial affiliates. Afterwards, FR3 operates as a traditional nationwide network. Programming focuses on information and culture; it is a mix of original product and acquisitions, many of which come from the U.S.

Le Sept, which debuted in 1989, is a cultural service available mainly on cable during the week (mid-afternoon until late night) and over the air, via national broadcasting facilities, on Saturdays (early afternoon through late night). The plan is for Le Sept to become a Pan-European service; it is presently seen in Germany, Switzerland, Luxembourg, and Denmark. Le Sept is a relatively small network with limited financial resources.

The French government also operates Radio France (three radio networks) and RFO (Radio Télévision Française d'Outre Mer), which broadcasts French programming overseas.

Privately-Owned Services

The private television business in France is dominated by Television Français 1 (TF1), a network that overshadows most other French broadcast networks.

Television Français 1 (TF1)

The top-rated Television Français 1 was a government-owned network until it was sold to Bouygues, a large French construction concern, and Maxwell, a British communications conglomerate. (These companies own 50 percent of TF1; the other 50 percent is owned by smaller shareholders). Much of TF1's programming is produced in-house, including game shows, news, sports, and cultural shows. Sitcoms and dramas are produced both in-house and by outside producers. The company is restricted in feature film production, and must work with a partners on such ventures.

TF1 attracts more than 50 percent of the total advertising revenues for French television, and 92 percent of its revenues come from advertising. There is a limit on how much time can be allotted to advertising—12 minutes per hour.

To assure a flow of high-profile programming, TF1 has formed STARCOM, a production company, with Berlusconi (of Italy) and Beta (of Germany). TF1 recently purchased, and now operates, Eurosport, a Pan-European sports channel.

Canal Plus

Canal Plus is a broadcast pay channel that requires a decoder to be received during certain hours (during other hours, no decoder is needed). Over 3 million viewers pay 160 francs per month to see recent movies and a healthy dose of sports coverage (bicycling, soccer, tennis, boxing, wrestling). In addition, Canal Plus transmits commercially-sponsored programming between 12:30 and 1:30 P.M. and again between 6:30 and 8:30 P.M. daily; no decoder is needed to receive these telecasts.

Canal Plus has one major advantage over other pay services: it collects directly from subscribers, with no middleman. With this system, Canal Plus's net revenue per subscriber is far higher than, for example, the net revenue collected by HBO.

The Paris-based company began in 1984, and after a rough start-up, it is now the world's second largest pay TV service (HBO is first). Canal Plus's growth has been possible largely because it is not shackled by broadcast regulation; instead, the operation is largely considered to be a kind of cable service. Owned by Havas, Compagnie Generale des Eaux, and stockholders like banks and insurance companies, Canal Plus has also launched pay TV operations, frequently with local partners, in Spain, Belgium, French-speaking Africa, and Italy. Plans are being made for pay channels in Scandinavia and in the U.K., and for a children's channel as well.

La Cinq (La 5)

La Cinq (La 5) is owned by Reteitalia, TVES, the Vernes Group, and Hachette. La Cinq's program schedule depends heavily upon imports, especially U.S. imports (in fact, the company has been fined for exceeding French content guidelines). When the network went private, La

Cinq's intent was to compete against TF1 for the mass audience. After heavy spending on celebrities and other attempts at upscale programming, La Cinq revised its approach.

Metropole 6 (M6)

Metropole 6 (M6), seen in about half of French households, is largely dependent upon music video and inexpensive U.S. imports. M6 is owned by Compagnie Luxembourgeoise de Télédiffusion, Lyonnaise des Eaux Dumez, Union D'Etudes et D'Investissements (Crédit Agricole), and several other investors.

M6 is generally regarded as a niche service, reasonably well-managed with comparatively low overhead. Programming focusing on music, and a prime-time schedule dominated by U.S. sitcoms (previously considered unsuitable for French viewers), has proven successful in attracting a youthful viewership.

Regulation of French Television

The Conseil Superieur de l'Audiovisuel (CSA), or National Audiovisual Communications Council, is France's third such regulatory body in less than a decade. The CSA took control in 1989, replacing the Haute Autorité (1982–1986) and the CNCL (1986–1988). Charged with the allocation of radio and television frequencies, as well as the assignment of transponders and the awarding of cable franchises, the CSA supervises program practices (limits on sex and violence, and the quota system described below). It also appoints the heads of A2, FR3, La Sept, Radio France, and TDF.

CSA regulations prohibit commercial interruptions on A2 and FR3, France's public-service channels. The private networks, notably TF1, are restricted to 12 minutes of advertising per hour; TF1 is allowed one four-minute break during movie presentations (for La Cinq and Le Sept, the breaks may be slightly longer).

The CSA enforces quota laws. During prime time—defined as 6:00–11:00 P.M. each day plus Wednesday afternoons, when schools let out early—networks may choose from one of two possible strategies. They can produce up to 15 percent of their own programs, and broadcast not less than 120 hours of these original programs during prime time. Or, they may devote 65 percent of their schedule to programs produced by EEC countries, and at least 15 percent of their schedule to original French programs.

The difficulty with original French programming regards financing: programs must have English-language soundtracks to succeed in the international marketplace (whose monies are needed to supplement most original French productions). These soundtracks add an average of 20 percent to the cost of the production. The situation is made more difficult by the limited availability of public subsidies.

Cable Television

Cable penetration in France is under 10 percent: 500,000 subscribers in just over 20 million households. The average cable household receives

30 channels. These include five German channels, two or three Swiss, four from the U.K., the domestic French channels, plus some Pan-European services such as SuperChannel and MTV Europe. The complement is similar to cable offerings throughout Europe. A French pay service called Cine Cinema offers 16 hours per day of old films for 30 francs per subscriber.

Home Video

VCR penetration in France is over 40 percent; rental prices are 25–35 francs per film. Per-capita sales are considerably higher than in other countries, because an efficient distribution system has driven video-cassette prices down considerably.

Major video labels in the French sell-through market include WEA and Polygram, Prosperine (almost exclusively French product), GCR (Gaumont, Columbia, and RCA Home Video in a joint venture), Film Office (which owns the Disney catalog for France), Fox, CIC, and Fil à Film. GCR, CIC, Fox, Warner, and Delta are the big rental operations; TF1, Delta, Hachette Video, UGC, MGM, and Insep are also significant players.

ITALY

Two organizations dominate Italian television: Radiotelevisione Italiana (RAI), owned by a corporation that is in turn owned by the government, and Fininvest, a private concern owned by Silvio Berlusconi, a large media company. Italian television is frequently called a "duopoly."

RAI, which originated in the 1950s, has long been linked with Italian politics, and this has been the cause of many problems—for example, Italy did not receive color TV until 1977, long after the rest of Europe. The RAI monopoly began losing ground in 1971, when a small, privately-operated cable system started up in a northern Italian town. After three years of fighting, Tele Biella won the legal right to serve a region, paving the way for other local cable companies and local broadcasters. The courts continue to uphold the RAI monopoly for national broadcasting, but unofficial networks—called "soft" networks or para-networks—evolved as independent local stations throughout Italy, and connected with each other. More recent developments will eventually eliminate approximately half of the hundreds of unlicensed stations presently in operation.

RAI

RAI operates three networks: RAI-1, RAI-2, and RAI-3. Each network is managed independently, but all three share the same chairman. RAI-1 is Italy's highest-rated network; light entertainment (situation comedies, big-name variety shows, major series from the U.S. and elsewhere) is the strong suit. RAI-2 does not compete as aggressively, either as a counter-programmer to the commercial networks, or within the international programming marketplace. RAI-3, emphasizing news and culture, is the more traditional public channel; it relies heavily on non-fiction and factual programs, and has a distinctly Italian flavor. One popular program, *La Macchina della Verita*, puts contemporary people in the news to a lie-detector test. *Una Giornata in Pretura (A Day in Court)* offers real-life trials—particulary the scandalous ones. More traditional documentary and information programming is also common, and RAI-3 participates in international ventures in these program formats.

News programming on the RAI networks is party-controlled: RAI-1, by the Christian Democrats, RAI-2, by the Socialists, and RAI-3, by the Communists. These factions are involved in the details of news operations—including selecting the news-programming staff and the on-air talent.

RAI has a significant advantage over the Reteitalia networks (see below) because it has a legal monopoly on the right to show live programming. This means that viewers turn to RAI for news and for sports coverage.

RAI is supported by a combination of license fees and advertising; advertising is limited to 5 percent of total airtime.

SACIS is the RAI subsidiary that buys and sells programming for all three networks in the international marketplace.

Fininvest/Reteitalia

The Fininvest networks operate under an international broadcasting company called Reteitalia. All of the Reteitalia networks began in the 1980s. Based in Milan, they are almost entirely devoted to light entertainment (movies fill almost half of their schedules). The Reteitalia channels were built by scheduling U.S. imports, spiced with strip-tease programs not seen on the government services. While the networks have matured—and while most of the Reteitalia shows have become more sophisticated—bawdy, fun-loving sex-play remains an important part of the programming formula in Italy.

As of this writing, Reteitalia had begun building a stronghold in non-prime time sectors, such as daytime and late-night—periods in which RAI has traditionally "dumped" programs of lesser appeal in order to meet quota requirements.

Reteitalia's Canale-5 is its highest-rated service, just behind RAI-1 and RAI-2, but very competitive with them. The other two Reteitalia networks are Italia 1 and Rete 4 (also called Retequattro).

Other Networks and Stations

Odeon TV, owned by Pathé and other investors, is a private television network that reaches two-thirds of Italian households. Nine other smaller networks, notably TeleMonteCarlo and RETE A, also broadcast in Italy. Hundreds of regional stations are also in operation, many of them unlicensed.

Regulation of Italian Television

Italy's Ministry of Post and Telecommunications provides RAI with its operating authority, but the Ministry of Finance controls and regulates RAI's expenditures, collecting the license fees that fund a large percentage of its operation. Regulation of television in Italy, particularly among the commercial services, is not strong. The marketplace dictates rules regarding international co-productions, where personal relationships are especially important.

Cable Television

Despite the significance of Tele Biella's bout with RAI, cable television is a minor factor in the Italian television industry. For the most part, systems are small and serve only as retransmission services in mountainous areas.

Pay television channels include Telepiu, which debuted in June 1991, and Capo Distra, a sports channel.

Home Video

VCR penetration in Italy is approximately 38 percent. Nothing much was happening in Italy until the late 1980s. The home video market has high piracy rates—currently 40 percent, compared with a Continental low of just 2 percent in the Scandinavian countries. Sell-through prices range from 20,000 to 40,000 lire. Most of the lucrative domestic home video catalogs are controlled by entrepreneurial companies that started early—the Cepparo family, for example, owns several labels, including Starlight, Cine Hollywood, Education Video, and Airone Video, as well as the rights to National Geographic, BBC, Anglia, and others. RAI product is distributed through its record company, Fonit-Cetra. Fininvest holds a surprisingly small number of rights to programs that were created either for the network or as co-productions, so its backlist is weak. The market leader among video labels in Italy is Disney, followed by RCA Columbia and Vivideo. Other large labels include Cecu Gori, Domovideo, Panarecord, CIC, Fox, and Warner. Mondadori, an Italian publisher, owns a substantial label as well. The key to Mondadori's success is a door-to-door sales force of more than 1,000 people, one of many unusual means of videocassette distribution that exist in Italy.

Low-priced video titles (archive film compilations, travelogues, and cult movies) are for sale on some 40,000 street kiosks and newstands, at prices in the $10–$20 US range. (Videos are sold on newstands because they are exempt from a 19 percent sales tax when sold in the same package as print matter.) Video magazines, video encyclopedias on a wide variety of topics, and even amateur videos packaged for commercial sale have become popular through this distribution channel. Successful publishers in this format include Editori, Curcio, Mondadori, and RCS Video.

SPAIN

Spanish television has historically been dominated by a government broadcaster, the RTVE (Radio Television España), which replaced SNR in 1973. There is no set license fee or tax in Spain; the RTVE networks support themselves through advertising and, to a far lesser extent, through exploiting ancillary rights. Essentially, RTVE operates like a private company, but it is owned by the government. Advertising is restricted to no more than eight minutes per hour (and an average of no more than six minutes per hour).

RTVE-1, which debuted in 1955, is the light entertainment network. RTVE-2 began in 1964, and emphasizes cultural, news, and information shows, as well as programs of regional interest. RTVE-2 also has roughly 20 percent as much advertising as RTVE-1. Both networks follow the tradition of in-house production, though about one-third of their programming is currently acquired or jointly produced. Old habits die hard, though: RTVE wants extremely long license periods for the programs it carries, and insists upon buy-outs. RTVE-1 and RTVE-2 have become more flexible in recent years, partly in response to changing political climate, but largely in order to protect themselves against the impending threat of private television. Still, these networks are by far the most powerful television forces in Spain.

Spain's regional channels, called *autonomas*, are publicly owned, and funded largely by local governments. Advertising is proving to be a productive form of financing as well; Televisio de Catalunya (TV3), the largest *autonoma*, is funded exclusively through advertising revenues. Based in Barcelona, TV3 reaches roughly one-sixth of the Spanish population. TV 33 is a sister station owned by the same company, and shares TV3's programming department. Euskal Telebisa in the Basque region operates two channels, one in the Basque language and one in Castilian. Televisia de Galaicia (TVG), Television de Andalucia (Tele-Sur), Television de Valencia, and Television Autonoma de Madrid (Telemadrid) are regional channels that reach small portions of the overall population. Telemadrid serves a young, affluent, urban audience, and because of its sophisticated programming needs, it is becoming an increasingly significant player in the world marketplace. Many *autonomas* went on the air in mid-1980s or later; all of them are affiliated as members of the Federation of Autonomous Channels, and they may eventually form a network. These channels do work together in some acquisitions and co-productions with companies outside Spain, but the process requires patience on the part of the producer.

Private channels did not appear on the Spanish television scene until the early 1990s. Socialist Premier Felipe Gonzales took the better part of a decade to pass a private television bill and to assign network franchises. The apparent reason: 80 percent of the Spanish public depends upon television as its primary source of information, so Gonzales was reluctant to weaken the government's power to control information.

Each of the new private networks is headquartered in or near Madrid. Antena 3-TV, owned by Tisa (publisher of *Lan Vanguardia*), began with a mix of prime time sports, situation comedies, and game shows, concentrating on "balanced" (i.e. not government-controlled) news and current affairs programming. Telecinco (Tele 5), owned by Berlusconi and a wealthy charity for the blind called ONCE, features entertainment, sports, and a minimum of news. Canal Plus is a Spanish version of the popular French service, owned with the French by Prisa, a Spanish media group. Limited in its access to Spanish films because the majority of them are owned by RTVE, the Canal Plus network plans to program imports, while fighting for rights to Spanish-language features. Basic subscription fees are 3000 pesetas for the use of a descrambler and a schedule of 15 hours of programming per week; an additional six hours are provided at no charge (unscrambled) to all viewers.

Regulation of Spanish Television

Spain's private networks are owned by multiple partners because government regulations stipulate that only 25 percent of a broadcasting company can be owned by non-Spanish money. Also, no single entity can own a percentage of more than one channel.

Spanish content regulations are also restrictive: nearly half of the programs seen on Spanish television must be of Spanish origin. Also, 15 percent of programming must be original, produced by the licenseholder.

Cable Television

Cable penetration in Spain is a rather low 6 percent. With rough and rocky terrain, cables are difficult to install; high installation costs, coupled with Spain's economic position and inadequate cooperation at the local government level, have slowed cable's growth.

Home Video

In the late 1980s, VCR penetration in Spain topped 44 percent. The Spanish home video market was regarded as the model of a good retailing operation, with low piracy rates. Since then, however, the Spanish home video market has plummeted, mainly because of the introduction of new television channels. Video retailers are scrambling to stay alive, which has pushed up piracy rates: many retailers make unauthorized copies of their tapes, since they can no longer afford to invest in multiple copies. "Community video" has also played a role in the decline of the home video market. With community video, every apartment in a building is wired to a kind of mini-cable system, so one rented videocassette can be played throughout the building. There is some legal question as to the future of this system.

Sell-through began in the late 1980s; prices are currently in the range of 2,000–3,000 pesetas. Top American titles (dubbed into Spanish) are especially popular, and U.S. video labels dominate the market. Feature films are by far the most popular titles, with music and pornography consistent but relatively minor sellers. Leading Spanish video labels include Warner, CBS/Fox, CIC-Columbia, MGM, Polygram, and Spanish companies like Filmayer (which distributes Disney product), Videoman, Lauren Films, Recordvision, and CB Films.

OTHER EUROPEAN COUNTRIES

The following European countries are medium-sized television markets.

Belgium

Belgians speak either Flemish or French, so there are two distinct television industries.

RTBF Belgian Television operates two channels for French-speaking viewers: RTBF1 (general-interest programs) and Tele-21 (sports and special events). RTBF has accepted commercial advertising since 1989, though it is a government-owned broadcaster. Due to its small budget, RTBF fills much of its schedule with lower-priced programming, or with programs bulk-purchased from suppliers.

Canal Plus Belgique, part-owned by RTBF, was launched in 1989. After a difficult start-up (and the addition of essential soccer coverage), the network has thrived.

There are no private advertiser-supported stations in Belgium's French community. However, RTL-TVi, based in nearby Luxembourg, serves the area. This commercial French-language station is so well-entrenched that it raised objections when the RTBF began to accept advertising.

Flemish viewers are served by both public and private channels. Belgium's BRT1 is a general-entertainment and news service for Flemish-speaking viewers; TV2 is a sports and specials service for the same audience. Both are government-owned, and are operated by Belgishe Radio en Televisia. BRT1 and TV2 feature mostly local programming, and neither service accepts advertising. Vlaamse TV Maatschappi (VTM) is a private service in operation since 1989. 40 percent of VTM's programming is imported (*Raad van Fortuin*, a local *Wheel of Fortune* production, is especially popular; most VTM programs are not original productions, however, but dubbed versions of an original show from another culture). VTM is supported by advertising, and has been granted a monopoly for commercial broadcasting in Belgium. The company is small, but is carefully managed.

With 92 percent cable penetration, Belgium leads the world. Most channel offerings are broadcast imports from other countries, or cable services originating abroad.

The Netherlands

Broadcasting in the Netherlands is quite complicated; for example, individual networks, owned by the government, are each programmed by multiple companies, with each company representing a special-interest group. The special-interest organizations include many dues-paying members, who pay for subscription magazines with program listings. Each company has a social, political, or religious outlook that is, at least in theory, reflected in the programming that it schedules on the network during the company's own program block.

NOS (Nederlandse Omroeprogramma Stichting), the public broadcast network service, offers three channels. Netherlands 1 carries shows from a variety of religious and social groups, including Catholic KRO, Protestant NCRV, Socialist VARA, and Evangelical EO. Netherlands 2's airtime is programmed by three different companies: AVRO, TROS, and Veronica, each one a public broadcaster whose schedule combines local and imported (mostly U.S.) programming, primarily family-oriented shows. Established in 1988, the Netherlands 3 network is programmed by special-interest groups like IKON (an ecumenical group), RVU (an open university), Humanistisch Verbond (humanists), and various political parties. Netherlands 3 offers sports and cultural shows, and uses advertising to generate half of its revenues, with the government making up the balance.

Veronique, a commercial television channel broadcasting to the Dutch from Luxembourg, is also popular. It is owned by Compagnie Luxembourgeoise de Télédiffusion.

Canal Plus is setting up operations in the Netherlands, and a private news channel is also in development.

The Netherlands is the second most cabled country in the world, with 91 percent penetration. As with Belgium, channel offerings come from all over Europe.

Sweden

Swedish television is financed entirely by receiver license fees; television advertising is not permitted in Sweden. This is the practice in Norway and Denmark as well.

State-run Sveriges Television operates two channels. Stockholm-based SVT1 has a national emphasis, while SVT2 has more of a regional focus. Programming is general-interest, with the Swedish Educational Broadcasting Company supplying much of the daytime schedule.

Commercial services operating outside Scandinavia are also beamed into Sweden from the U.K. and from Norway. Offering programs from the U.S. and elsewhere, ScanSat's TV3 (from the U.K.) is available in Sweden, but it has received the official disapproval of the Swedish government. TV Norge (from Norway) offers predominantly British programming.

42 The Pacific Rim and Latin America

This chapter focuses on television in two regions: the Pacific Rim and Latin America. Among countries in the Pacific, Japan and Australia are the most significant markets. In Latin America, Mexico, Brazil, and Venezuela are viable outlets for television productions.

JAPAN

Japan is rapidly becoming a major player on the international television scene through a combination of joint ventures, investments, and acquisitions. Sony, for example, owns Columbia Pictures' television division, which includes Merv Griffin Enterprises properties like *Wheel of Fortune* and *Jeopardy!*; Matsushita owns MCA; and Gaga has a stake in U.S. distributor Fox-Lorber.

At home, more than 35 million Japanese households are served by seven networks. NHK General Network and NHK Educational Network are both government-owned; Fuji TV, Tokyo Broadcasting System (TBS), Nippon Television (NTV), TV Asahi, and TV Twelve are commercial networks.

Non-Commercial Networks

NHK (Nippon Hoso Kyokai, or Japanese Broadcasting Corporation) was originally based on the BBC model. It was set up in the radio era as a public-service system financed by license fees. These voluntary payments come from thousands of fee collectors who appeal to the Japanese sense of honor and civic duty as they go door-to-door throughout Japan. NHK sets its own fees, subject to government approval; presently, the fee is US $95 per household for one or more color set. Based in Tokyo, with seven additional regional headquarters, NHK operates more than 50 telecasting stations plus a Children's Channel.

NHK General's program mix is dominated by news, commentary, cultural shows, and educational programming. For many years, NHK was Japan's ratings leader, but because of competition from the commercial stations, NHK has dropped from first place to last place in the ratings.

MICO, a consortium of Japanese banks and trading companies, was formed by NHK to extend its enterprises beyond regulations that would otherwise encumber NHK's activities. Officially, NHK is a large client of MICO; in effect, MICO is the international co-production arm of NHK.

Commercial Networks

Japan's five commercial networks grew from local stations operating in the Tokyo area. In theory, commercial networks are not permitted to operate in Japan. In practice, the more powerful Tokyo stations began transmitting their programs to affiliated stations elsewhere in Japan; because the Tokyo stations were owned by newspapers with nationwide advertising capabilities, it wasn't long before the newspapers were selling national advertising for their television operations as well. NTV, Fuji TV, TBS, and TV Asahi focus on Japanese-made programming. In general, Japan is a strong market for U.S. films—but not for U.S.-made entertainment programs, which have traditionally performed badly in the ratings.

Nippon Television (NTV), the largest private network, went on the air in 1952. It currently has 33 affiliated stations. NTV's programming strengths include sports (especially baseball coverage), talk shows, and the popular period dramas depicting old Japan.

The Fuji Telecasting Company's Fuji TV has been Japan's ratings leader for the past decade. Fuji TV is a general-interest network that features game shows, sitcoms, and variety shows. The network has not shown much interest in the international market, though an affiliated company, Fujisankei Communications Group, is becoming involved in Hollywood film projects. (The Communications Group's production credits include *Memphis Belle* and other lesser-known films.)

The Tokyo Broadcasting System's TBS, which started up in 1959, is a light-entertainment network with general interest offerings in all categories.

The Asahi National Broadcasting Company's TV Asahi also began in 1959. The TV Asahi network has been especially successful with its news and talk shows.

TV Tokyo—also known as Twelve TV—is a comparatively small network, and is owned by Japan's Nikkei Newspaper Group.

Regulation of Japanese Television

Japanese television is regulated by the Ministry of Posts and Telecommunications in Tokyo. The National Association of Commercial Broadcasters also has a regulatory code, but compliance with it is voluntary.

It may come as a surprise to Western viewers that Japanese television permits nudity on late-night television—and that soft-core pornography is a regular feature of several late-night programs.

Cable Television and Direct Broadcast Satellite

Cable penetration in Japan is under 20 percent, and even then, cable is available mainly in expensive apartment houses, hotels, and some outlying areas. Cable is expected to expand as more channels are offered; many are in the planning stages. Because of the crowded condition of Japan's cities, and the resulting installation challenge, much of the attention is on satellite delivery via DBS and small-sized dishes. NHK operates a DBS service that reaches more than 2 million households.

Japan Satellite Broadcasting (JBS) offers direct competition to NHK in the DBS area. Owned by a consortium of 100 companies (including the Seibu Group, the Tokyo Group, and Mitsubishi), JSB's The Wowow Channel features sports, news, movies, and home shopping.

Home Video

Roughly 70 percent of Japanese households own at least one VCR, so both sales and rental of pre-recorded product is a strong business. Laserdiscs also account for a considerable number of home video sales. Foreign-made motion pictures are by far the most popular products, followed by Japanese motion pictures, Japanese music video, and soft-core pornography. Approximately 12,000–15,000 retail shops sell or rent videocassettes; rentals cost between $2 and $3 per night, and a typical sell-through price is $25. Significant home video labels include Bandai, CIC-Victor (for Paramount and Universal films), Toei, Bandai, Gaga, and Seiyu.

AUSTRALIA

As in the U.K., the Australian television system is a combination of public and private services. The government-owned network, the Australian Broadcasting Commission (ABC), began in 1932 as a public radio service. ABC covers 98 percent of the country via 86 broadcast facilities. The programming is upscale—classical music, high-quality films, sophisticated drama, and so forth.

Special Broadcasting Service (SBS), established as a public broadcaster in the early 1980s on UHF stations, serves Australia's ethnic minorities. Currently available on 22 channels throughout Australia, SBS carries programs from Greece, Italy, Yugoslavia, France, Germany, and elsewhere.

Australia's three commercial networks are newer than ABC, and formed in the 1980s by assembling key local stations in Australia's large cities: Sydney, Melbourne, Brisbane, Adelaide, and Perth. Australian Television Network, Network Ten Australia, and Nine Network have each experienced severe financial difficulties. In 1989, Rupert Murdoch, a former owner of one of the networks, blamed the problems on "the entry of three relative amateurs"; Australian media consultant Peter Cox declared that "Ego and greed was the motivating factor for the current owners to buy the television stations, and they have nearly destroyed the industry in the process."* Two of the commercial channels

* *TV World*, November/December 1989.

are currently in receivership. The trouble apparently began as each of these large-scale commercial enterprises competed for high-visibility U.S. programming. Each network tried to outbid the other, raising prices beyond the level that could be supported by advertising alone. Ironically, Australian viewers ultimately demonstrated a preference for programs of Australian origin—nine of the ten highest-rated programs are Australian.

Each of the networks programs a combination of game shows, sit-coms, dramatic series, soaps, news, sports, and variety. Australian Television Network's specialty is prime time comedy. Nine Network's strong suit is news; the colorful series *A Current Affair* originated here, prior to its U.S. run. Network Ten features movies and sports; its best-known export is a series often seen on U.S. public television, *Neighbours.*. Many U.S. programs are seen in Australian prime time, and the formats for numerous U.S. game shows have been adapted for production in Australia.

Regulation of Australian Television

The Australian Broadcasting Tribunal (ABT) has the power to license stations and regulate all aspects of broadcasting. The ABT requires that 50 percent of the network schedules from 6:00 A.M. to midnight feature programs of Australian origin (the quota rises to 60 percent in 1994). The percentage is calculated according to a point system known as the Australian Content for Commercial Television Program Standard. Points are awarded for the program's content, its "Australian look," the scale of the production, the types and numbers of Australians involved in the making of the production, the target audience (children's and educational shows score higher than mass entertainment), and other criteria.

Cable Television

There is no cable television in Australia, for two reasons. First, there are no reception problems with the existing television system—everyone in the cities receives strong, clean signals. Second, the outback regions are too sparsely settled for cable to be economically viable. DBS systems, which are in the planning stages for a mid-1990s start-up, may include pay-per-view service.

Home Video

Australia's home video business is healthy, due in large part to nearly 70 percent VCR penetration. Rental prices are comparable to those in the U.S. Sell-though is on the rise, mostly because of reduced pricing. Action and adventure titles are popular, with sexually-explicit videocassettes accounting for approximately 15 percent of sales.

LATIN AMERICA

New channels are starting up throughout Latin America. CNN, ESPN, Galavision, Visnews (an international news service), and a part-time transmission from the Italian RAI networks are among the offerings that can be seen throughout Latin America.

Nonetheless, television's development in many Latin American nations has been slower than in much of the world. In Mexico, for example, the population is over 80 million, but only 27 million TV sets are in use, and only about 6 million of these are color sets.

Mexico

Mexican television consists of one group of broadcast channels that are operated by the government, and a second group that are operated under government concession by Televisa, a large private company.

Instituto Mexicana de Television (also known as Imevision) operates three government networks. Channel 7 is a national network, and Channel 13 covers most of Mexico's populated regions. Channel 11 is operated by the Instituto Politecnico Nacional; Channel 22 broadcasts only in the afternoons. All of these channels offer entertainment, information, and a wide variety of program formats.

Televisa operates four commercial channels, all of which are headquartered in Mexico City. Channel 2 was the first network to serve all of Mexico; programming is nearly all Mexican, consisting of both Mexican film product and shows produced in Televisa's large studio complex. Channel 4, which broadcasts to the Mexico City area (where nearly half of Mexico's television viewers live), offers a similar range of programming. Channel 5, which covers a somewhat wider geographical area around Mexico City, offers mainly imported programs, largely from the U.S. Channel 9 serves a similar territory, principally with programs produced in Europe.

Televisa is active in the U.S. market—as a major source of Spanish-language programs, and as part-owner of the Galavision Spanish-language network. Cablevision, a cable system that Televisa owns, offers six networks from the U.S.

Regulation of Mexican Television

The Mexican government maintains close control over broadcasting. Even private stations must provide the government with 30 minutes per day for "social advertising"—promoting good health, for example. Network facilities must be made available to the President on his request, and emergencies must be broadcast. Then there is the concept of *fiscal time.* Private stations almost had to surrender 49 percent ownership in their companies to the government, or to pay a 25 percent tax on revenues. Instead, fiscal time became the form of payment—the government uses 12.5 percent of the each private network's daily schedule for its own programming (which is usually cultural or educational).

Mexican television is regulated by the Communication and Transportation Ministry, which handles frequency allocations and other technical matters, and the Interior Ministry, which supervises program and operational practices. All private networks must belong to the National Chamber of the Radio and Television Industry, a liaison body that works to maintain a good relationship between the government and the broadcasters.

Cable Television and Home Video

Cable is not a significant factor in Mexican television, but is steadily growing. Roughly 60,000 households subscribe to cable; this figure is expected to double or triple in the next few years. Multivision, one of Mexico's largest suppliers of cable programming, offers eight channels on about 100 cable systems. On most cable systems, programming includes both Mexican and U.S. channels.

With VCR penetration under 10 percent, home video is a minor industry in Mexico. Videovisa, affiliated with the Televisa broadcast operation, dominates the video market. The entrepreneurial Videomaximo distributes many independent labels, and because it is not limited to Televisa-owned stores, it seems to be flourishing.

Brazil

The Brazilian government operates 17 regional stations, but does not run a network as such. Funteve is the controlling body for many, but not all, of these stations. The private networks operate as government concessions, and are extremely careful about breaching their relationship by airing politically or morally sensitive programming.

TV Globo, part of the Brazilian media conglomerate Rede Globo, is the country's most successful private network. It began in 1967, and covers the nation via 61 affiliated stations. Globo, an aggressive player in the international television marketplace, is the fifth largest television network in the world. Roughly 25 percent of Globo's daytime schedule comes from the U.S. (mainly films), with local productions accounting for the rest of the program schedule. SBT is Brazil's second biggest private network; it started up in 1981, and is led by a popular TV host and politician, Silvio Santo. Bandeirantes and Manchete—which debuted in 1967 and 1983, respectively—vie for third place. Other broadcast networks in Brazil include TV Gazeta and TV Record.

Specialty broadcast channels have begun to emerge in Brazil. Abril TV has had some success with a Brazilian version of MTV on its UHF station in São Paulo; four stations are now affiliated with the service. TV Jovem Pan, another UHF station in São Paulo, programs hard news.

One technical note: Brazil's television standard, a variation on PAL called PAL-M, is a 525-line system that is compatible with NTSC but not with traditional PAL. Therefore, videocassettes for the Brazilian market appear in the NTSC format.

Private networks and television stations in Brazil must be owned by Brazilian nationals, so international involvement in Brazilian television is limited to co-productions. Also, all foreign films must be dubbed into Portuguese before they are shown on the air.

Cable television is insignificant in Brazil, though SuperChannel, the country's largest cable operator, has 20,000 subscribers in São Paulo. VCR penetration is relatively low, but the home video industry is growing rapidly. The business is primarily rental-driven, with prices for overnight rental at about $1. Sell-through prices can still exceed $75 per tape. Twenty thousand copies sold in Brazil is considered a huge success—in 1988, the top-selling film, *E.T. The Extra Terrestrial,* sold 13,000 units. Leading Brazilian video labels include CIC/Universal, CIC/Paramount, Globo Video, Transvideo, Warner Home Video, and Abril Video/Disney.

Venezuela

There are five broadcast networks in Venezuela: Canal 5, Canena Venezolana de Television (CVTV), Radio Caracas TV (RCTV), Venevision, and TELEVEN Canal 10 (the first two are government-owned, the other three are private). Venezuelan programs—especially the soap operas called *novellas*—are popular throughout the Spanish-speaking U.S. and Latin America. Omnivision, a satellite-delivered pay-cable service based in Venezuela and serving nine cities, recently began a joint venture with HBO (HBO Olé) for Latin-American markets. Cable plays a small role in Venezuelan television, though VCR penetration, at 22 percent, is on the rise.

Appendix A

LEGAL DOCUMENTS AND FORMS

Appendix A1
Communications Act of 1934: Excerpts

[As amended through Dec. 31, 1990. The Cable Act of 1984 is included as Title VI of the Communications Act of 1934.]

Title VI—Cable Communications

Section

COMMUNICATIONS ACT OF 1934, AS AMENDED

AN ACT To provide for the regulation of interstate and foreign communication by
wire or radio, and for other purposes.

*Be it enacted by the Senate and House of Representatives of the United States of America in Congress
assembled,*

TITLE I—GENERAL PROVISIONS

DEFINITIONS

Sec. 3. [47 U.S.C. 153] For the purposes of this Act, unless the context otherwise requires—

(a) "Wire communication" or "communication by wire" means the transmission of writing, signs, signals, pictures, and sounds of all kinds by aid of wire, cable, or other like connection between the points of origin and reception of such transmission, including all instrumentalities, facilities, apparatus, and services (among other things, the receipt, forwarding, and delivery of communications) incidental to such transmission.

(b) "Radio communication" or "communication by radio" means the transmission by radio of writing, signs, signals, pictures, and sounds of all kinds, including all instrumentalities, facilities, apparatus, and services (among other things, the receipt, forwarding, and delivery of communications) incidental to such transmission.

(c) "Licensee" means the holder of a radio station license granted or continued in force under authority of this Act.

(d) "Transmission of energy by radio" or "radio transmission of energy" includes both such transmission and all instrumentalities, facilities, and services incidental to such transmission.

(e) "Interstate communication" or "interstate transmission" means communication or transmission (1) from any State, Territory, or possession of the United States (other than the Canal Zone), or the District of Columbia, to any other State, Territory, or possession of the United States (other than the Canal Zone), or the District of Columbia, (2) from or to the United States to or from the Canal Zone, insofar as such communication or transmission takes place within the United States, or (3) between points within the United States but through a foreign country; but shall not, with respect to the provisions of title II of this Act (other than section 223 thereof), include wire or radio communication between points in the same State, Territory, or possession of the United States, or the District of Columbia, through any place outside thereof, if such communication is regulated by a State commission.

(f) "Foreign communication" or "foreign transmission" means communication or transmission from or to any place in the United States to or from a foreign country, or between a station in the United States and a mobile station located outside the United States.

(g) "United States" means the several States and Territories, the District of Columbia, and the possessions of the United States, but does not include the Canal Zone.

(h) "Common carrier" or "carrier" means any person engaged as a common carrier for hire, in interstate or foreign communication by wire or radio or in interstate or foreign radio transmission of energy, except where reference is made to common carriers not subject to this Act; but a person engaged in radio broadcasting shall not, insofar as such person is so engaged, be deemed a common carrier.

(i) "Person" includes an individual, partnership, association, joint-stock company, trust, or corporation.

(j) "Corporation" includes any corporation, joint-stock company, or association.

(k) "Radio station" or "station" means a station equipped to engage in radio communication or radio transmission of energy.

[(l)–(m) deleted]

(n) "Mobile service" means a radio communication service carried on between mobile stations or receivers and land stations, and by mobile stations communicating among themselves, and includes both one-way and two-way radio communication services.

(o) "Broadcasting" means the dissemination of radio communications intended to be received by the public, directly or by the intermediary of relay stations.

(p) "Chain broadcasting" means simultaneous broadcasting of an identical program by two or more connected stations.

[(q)–(z)(2)(bb) deleted]

(cc) "Station license," "radio station license," or "license" means that instrument of authorization required by this Act or the rules and regulations of the Commission made pursuant to this Act, for the use or operation of apparatus for transmission of energy, or communications, or signals by radio by whatever name the instrument may be designated by the Commission.

(dd) "Broadcast station," "broadcasting station," or "radio broadcast station" means a radio station equipped to engage in broadcasting as herein defined.

(ee) "Construction permit" or "permit for construction" means that instrument of authorization required by this Act or the rules and regulations of the Commission made pursuant to this Act for the construction of a station, or the installation of apparatus, for the transmission of energy, or communications, or signals by radio, by whatever name the instrument may be designated by the Commission.

[(z)(2)(ff)–(z)(2)(gg) deleted]

NEW TECHNOLOGIES AND SERVICES

SEC. 7. [47 U.S.C. 157]

(a) It shall be the policy of the United States to encourage the provision of new technologies and services to the public. Any person or party (other than the Commission) who opposes a new technology or service proposed to be permitted under this chapter shall have the burden to demonstrate that such proposal is inconsistent with the public interest.

(b) The Commission shall determine whether any new technology or service proposed in a petition or application is in the public interest within one year after such petition or application is filed or twelve months after December 8, 1983, if later. If the Commission initiates its own proceeding for a new technology or service, such proceeding shall be completed within 12 months after it is initiated or twelve months after December 8, 1983, if later.

TITLE III—PROVISIONS RELATING TO RADIO

PART I—GENERAL PROVISIONS

STANDARDS FOR CHILDREN'S TELEVISION PROGRAMMING

SEC. 303A. [47 U.S.C. 303a] (a) The Commission shall, within 30 days after October 18, 1990, initiate a rulemaking proceeding to prescribe standards applicable to commercial television broadcast licensees with respect to the time devoted to commercial matter in conjunction with children's television programming. The Commission shall, within 180 days after October 18, 1990, complete the rulemaking proceeding and prescribe final standards that meet the requirements of subsection (b) of this section.

(b) Except as provided in subsection (c) of this section, the standards prescribed under subsection (a) of this section shall include the requirement that each commercial television broadcast licensee shall limit the duration of advertising in children's television programming to not more than 10.5 minutes per hour on weekends and not more than 12 minutes per hour on weekdays.

(c) After January 1, 1993, the Commission—

(1) may review and evaluate the advertising duration limitations required by subsection (b) of this section; and

(2) may, after notice and public comment and a demonstration of the need for modification of such limitations, modify such limitations in accordance with the public interest.

(d) As used in this section, the term 'commercial television broadcast licensee' includes a cable operator, as defined in section 522 of this title.

CONSIDERATION OF CHILDREN'S TELEVISION SERVICE IN BROADCAST LICENSE RENEWAL

SEC. 303B. [47 U.S.C. 303b] (a) After the standards required by section 303a of this title are in effect, the Commission shall, in its review of any application for renewal of a television broadcast license, consider the extent to which the licensee—

(1) has complied with such standards; and

(2) has served the educational and informational needs of children through the licensee's overall programming, including programming specifically designed to serve such needs.

(b) In addition to consideration of the licensee's programming as required under subsection (a) of this section, the Commission may consider—

(1) any special nonbroadcast efforts by the licensee which enhance the educational and informational value of such programming to children; and

(2) any special efforts by the licensee to produce or support programming broadcast by another station in the licensee's marketplace which is specifically designed to serve the educational and informational needs of children.

TELEVISION PROGRAM IMPROVEMENT

SEC. 303C. [47 U.S.C. 303c] (a) This section may be cited as the 'Television Program Improvement Act of 1990'.

(b) For purposes of this section—

(1) the term 'antitrust laws' has the meaning given it in subsection (a) of the first section of the Clayton Act (15 U.S.C. 12(a)), except that such term includes section 5 of the Federal Trade Commission Act (15 U.S.C. 45) to the extent that such section 5 applies to unfair methods of competition;

(2) the term 'person in the television industry' means a television network, any entity which produces programming (including theatrical motion pictures) for telecasting or telecasts programming, the National Cable Television Association, the Association of Independent Television Stations, Incorporated, the National Association of Broadcasters, the Motion

Picture Association of America, the Community Antenna Television Association, and each of the networks' affiliate organizations, and shall include any individual acting on behalf of such person; and

    (3) the term 'telecast' means—

        (A) to broadcast by a television broadcast station; or

        (B) to transmit by a cable television system or a satellite television distribution service.

    (c) The antitrust laws shall not apply to any joint discussion, consideration, review, action, or agreement by or among persons in the television industry for the purpose of, and limited to, developing and disseminating voluntary guidelines designed to alleviate the negative impact of violence in telecast material.

    (d) (1) The exemption provided in subsection (c) of this section shall not apply to any joint discussion, consideration, review, action, or agreement which results in a boycott of any person.

    (2) The exemption provided in subsection (c) of this section shall apply only to any joint discussion, consideration, review, action, or agreement engaged in only during the 3-year period beginning on December 1, 1990.

WAIVER BY LICENSEE

SEC. 304. [47 U.S.C. 304] No station license shall be granted by the Commission until the applicant therefore shall have signed a waiver of any claim to the use of any particular frequency or of the electromagnetic spectrum as against the regulatory power of the United States because of the previous use of the same, whether by license or otherwise.

ALLOCATION OF FACILITIES; TERM OF LICENSES

SEC. 307. [47 U.S.C. 307] (a) The Commission, if public convenience, interest or necessity will be served thereby, subject to the limitations of this Act, shall grant to any applicant therefor a station license provided for by this Act.

[(b)–(e) omitted]

FACILITIES FOR CANDIDATES FOR PUBLIC OFFICE

SEC. 315. [47 U.S.C. 315] (a) If any licensee shall permit any person who is a legally qualified candidate for any public office to use a broadcasting station, he shall afford equal opportunities to all other such candidates for that office in the use of such broadcasting station: *Provided,* That such licensee shall have no power of censorship over the material broadcast under the provision of this section. No obligation is hereby imposed under this subsection upon any licensee to allow the use of its station by any such candidate. Appearance by a legally qualified candidate on any—

    (1) bona fide newscast,

    (2) bona fide news interview,

    (3) bona fide news documentary (if the appearance of the candidate is incidental to the presentation of the subject or subjects covered by the news documentary), or

    (4) on-the-spot coverage of bona fide news events (including but not limited to political conventions and activities incidental thereto),

shall not be deemed to be use of a broadcasting station within the meaning of this subsection. Nothing in the foregoing sentence shall be construed as relieving broadcasters, in connection with the presentation of newscasts, news interviews, news documentaries, and on-the-spot coverage of news events, from the obligation imposed upon them under this Act to operate in the public interest and to afford reasonable opportunity for the discussion of conflicting views on issues of public importance.

    (b) The charges made for the use of any broadcasting station by any person who is a legally qualified candidate for any public office in connection with his campaign for nomination for election, or election, to such office shall not exceed—

    (1) during the forty-five days preceding the date of a primary or primary runoff election and during the sixty days preceding the date of a general or special election in which such

person is a candidate, the lowest unit charge of the station for the same class and amount of time for the same period; and

(2) at any other time, the charges made for comparable use of such station by other users thereof.

(c) For purposes of this section—

(1) the term "broadcasting station" includes a community antenna television system; and

(2) the term "licensee" and "station licensee" when used with respect to a community antenna television system mean the operator of such system.

(d) The Commission shall prescribe appropriate rules and regulations to carry out the provisions of this section.

ANNOUNCEMENT WITH RESPECT TO CERTAIN MATTER BROADCAST

SEC. 317. [47 U.S.C. 317] (a)(1) All matter broadcast by any radio station for which any money, service or other valuable consideration is directly or indirectly paid, or promised to or charged or accepted by, the station so broadcasting, from any person, shall, at the time the same is so broadcast, be announced as paid for or furnished, as the case may be, by such person: *Provided,* That "service or other valuable consideration" shall not include any service or property furnished without charge or at a nominal charge for use on, or in connection with, a broadcast unless it is so furnished in consideration for an identification in a broadcast of any person, product, service, trademark, or brand name beyond an identification which is reasonably related to the use of such service or property on the broadcast.

(2) Nothing in this section shall preclude the Commission from requiring that an appropriate announcement shall be made at the time of the broadcast in the case of any political program or any program involving the discussion of any controversial issue for which any films, records, transcriptions, talent, scripts, or other material or service of any kind have been furnished, without charge or at a nominal charge, directly or indirectly, as an inducement to the broadcast of such program.

(b) In any case where a report has been made to a radio station, as required by section 507 of this Act, of circumstances which would have required an announcement under this section had the consideration been received by such radio station, an appropriate announcement shall be made by such radio station.

(c) The licensee of each radio station shall exercise reasonable diligence to obtain from its employees, and from other persons with whom it deals directly in connection with any program or program matter for broadcast, information to enable such licensee to make the announcement required by this section.

(d) The Commission may waive the requirement of an announcement as provided in this section in any case or class of cases with respect to which it determines that the public interest, convenience, or necessity does not require the broadcasting of such announcement.

(e) The Commission shall prescribe appropriate rules and regulations to carry out the provisions of this section.

CENSORSHIP; INDECENT LANGUAGE

SEC. 326. [47 U.S.C. 326] Nothing in this Act shall be understood or construed to give the Commission the power of censorship over the radio communications or signals transmitted by any radio station, and no regulation or condition shall be promulgated or fixed by the Commission which shall interfere with the right of free speech by means of radio communication.

VERY HIGH FREQUENCY STATIONS

SEC. 331. [47 U.S.C. 331] It shall be the policy of the Federal Communications Commission to allocate channels for very high frequency commercial television broadcasting in a manner which ensures that not less than one such channel shall be allocated to each State, if technically feasible. In any case in which licensee of a very high frequency commercial television broadcast station notifies the Commission to the effect that such licensee will agree to the reallocation of its channel to a community within a State in which there is allocated no very high frequency commercial television broadcast channel at the time such notification, the Commission shall, not withstanding any other provision of law, order such reallocation and issue a license to such licensee for that purpose pursuant to such notification for a term of not to exceed 5 years as provided in section 307(d) of the Communications Act of 1934.

DEFINITIONS

SEC. 397. [47 U.S.C. 397] For the purposes of this part—

[(1) deleted]

(2) The term "Corporation" means the Corporation for Public Broadcasting authorized to be established in subpart D.

[(3)–(5) deleted]

(6) The terms "noncommercial educational broadcast station" and "public broadcast station" mean a television or radio broadcast station which—

(A) under the rules and regulations of the Commission in effect on the effective date of this paragraph, is eligible to be licensed by the Commission as a noncommercial educational radio or television broadcast station and which is owned and operated by a public agency or nonprofit private foundation, corporation, or association; or

(B) is owned and operated by a municipality and which transmits only noncommercial programs for education purposes.

(7) The term "noncommercial telecommunications entity" means any enterprise which—

(A) is owned and operated by a State, a political or special purpose subdivision of a State, a public agency, or a nonprofit private foundation, corporation, or association; and

(B) has been organized primarily for the purpose of disseminating audio or video noncommercial educational and cultural programs to the public by means other than a primary television or radio broadcast station, including, but not limited to, coaxial cable, optical fiber, broadcast translators, cassettes, discs, microwave, or laser transmission through the atmosphere.

(8) The term "nonprofit" (as applied to any foundation, corporation, or association) means a foundation, corporation, or association, no part of the net earnings of which inures, or may lawfully inure, to the benefit of any private shareholder or individual.

[(9)–(10) deleted]

(11) The term "Public broadcasting entity" means the Corporation, any licensee or permittee of a public broadcast station, or any nonprofit institution engaged primarily in the production, acquisition, distribution, or dissemination of educational and cultural television or radio programs.

(12) The term "public telecommunications entity" means any enterprise which—

(A) is a public broadcast station or a noncommercial telecommunications entity; and

(B) disseminates public telecommunications services to the public.

[(13)–(17) deleted]

SUPPORT OF POLITICAL CANDIDATES PROHIBITED

SEC. 399. [47 U.S.C. 399] No noncommercial educational broadcasting station may support or oppose any candidate for political office.

USE OF BUSINESS OR INSTITUTIONAL LOGOGRAMS

SEC. 399A. [47 U.S.C. 399a] (a) For purposes of this section, the term "business or institutional logogram" means any aural or visual letters or words, or any symbol or sign, which is used for the exclusive purpose of identifying any corporation, company, or other organization, and which is not used for the purpose of promoting the products, services, or facilities of such corporation, company, or other organization.

(b) Each public television station and each public radio station shall be authorized to broadcast announcements which include the use of any business or institutional logogram and which include a reference to the location of the corporation, company, or other organization involved, except that such announcements may not interrupt regular programming.

(c) The provisions of this section shall not be construed to limit the authority of the Commission to prescribe regulations relating to the manner in which logograms may be used to identify corporations, companies, or other organizations.

OFFERING OF CERTAIN SERVICES, FACILITIES, OR PRODUCTS BY PUBLIC BROADCAST STATIONS

SEC. 399B. [47 U.S.C. 399b] (a) For purposes of this section, the term "advertisement" means any message or other programming material which is broadcast or otherwise transmitted in exchange for any remuneration, and which is intended—

(1) to promote any service, facility, or product offered by any person who is engaged in such offering for profit;

(2) to express the views of any person with respect to any matter of public importance or interest; or

(3) to support or oppose any candidate for political office.

(b)(1) Except as provided in paragraph (2), each public broadcast station shall be authorized to engage in the offering of services, facilities, or products in exchange for remuneration.

(2) No public broadcast station may make its facilities available to any person for the broadcasting of any advertisement.

(c) Any public broadcast station which engages in any offering specified in subsection (b)(1) may not use any funds distributed by the Corporation under section 396(k) to defray any costs associated with such offering. Any such offering by a public broadcast station shall not interfere with the provision of public telecommunications services by such station.

(d) Each public broadcast station which engages in the activity specified in subsection (b)(1) shall, in consultation with the Corporation, develop an accounting system which is designed to identify any amounts received as remuneration for, or costs related to, such activities under this section, and to account for such amounts separately from any other amounts received by such station from any source.

TITLE V—PENAL PROVISIONS—FORFEITURES

DISCLOSURE OF CERTAIN PAYMENTS

SEC. 507. [47 U.S.C. 508] (a) Subject to subsection (d), any employee of a radio station who accepts or agrees to accept from any person (other than such station), or any person (other than such station) who pays or agrees to pay such employee, any money, service or other valuable consideration for the broadcast of any matter over such station shall, in advance of such broadcast, disclose the fact of such acceptance or agreement to such station.

(b) Subject to subsection (d), any person who, in connection with the production or preparation of any program or program matter which is intended for broadcasting over any radio station, accepts or agrees to accept, or pays or agrees to pay, any money, service or other valuable consideration for the inclusion of any matter as a part of such program or program matter, shall, in advance of such broadcast, disclose the fact of such acceptance or payment or agreement to the payee's employer, or to the person for which such program or program matter is being produced, or to the licensee of such station over which such program is broadcast.

(c) Subject to subsection (d), any person who supplies to any other person any program or program matter which is intended for broadcasting over any radio station shall, in advance of such broadcast, disclose to such other person any information of which he has knowledge, or which has been disclosed to him, as to any money, service or other valuable consideration which any person has paid or accepted, or has agreed to pay or accept, for the inclusion of any matter as a part of such program or program matter.

(d) The provisions of this section requiring the disclosure of information shall not apply in any case where, because of a waiver made by the Commission under section 317(d), an announcement is not required to be made under section 317.

(e) The inclusion in the program of the announcement required by section 317 shall constitute the disclosure required by this section.

(f) The term "service or other valuable consideration" as used in this section shall not include any service or property furnished without charge or at a nominal charge for use on, or in connection with, a broadcast, or for use on a program which is intended for broadcasting over any radio station, unless it is so furnished in consideration for an identification in such broadcast or in such program of any person, product, service, trademark, or brand name beyond an identification which is reasonably related to the use of such service or property in such broadcast or such program.

(g) Any person who violates any provision of this section shall, for each such violation, be fined not more than $10,000 or imprisoned not more than one year, or both.

PROHIBITED PRACTICES IN CASE OF CONTESTS OF INTELLECTUAL
KNOWLEDGE, INTELLECTUAL SKILL, OR CHANCE

SEC. 508. [47 U.S.C. 509] (a) It shall be unlawful for any person, with intent to deceive the listening or viewing public—

(1) To supply to any contestant in a purportedly bona fide contest of intellectual knowledge or intellectual skill any special and secret assistance whereby the outcome of such contest will be in whole or in part prearranged or predetermined.

(2) By means of persuasion, bribery, intimidation, or otherwise, to induce or cause any contestant in a purportedly bona fide contest of intellectual knowledge or intellectual skill to refrain in any manner from using or displaying his knowledge or skill in such contest, whereby the outcome thereof will be in whole or in part prearranged or predetermined.

(3) To engage in any artifice or scheme for the purpose of prearranging or predetermining in whole or in part the outcome of a purportedly bona fide contest of intellectual knowledge, intellectual skill, or chance.

(4) To produce or participate in the production for broadcasting of, to broadcast or participate in the broadcasting of, to offer to a licensee for broadcasting, or to sponsor, any radio program, knowing or having reasonable ground for believing that, in connection with a purportedly bona fide contest of intellectual knowledge, intellectual skill, or chance constituting any part of such program, any person has done or is going to do any act or thing referred to in paragraph (1), (2), or (3) of this subsection.

(5) To conspire with any other person or persons to do any act or thing prohibited by paragraph (1), (2), (3), or (4) of this subsection, if one or more of such persons do any act to effect the object of such conspiracy.

(b) For the purpose of this section—

(1) The term "contest" means any contest broadcast by a radio station in connection with which any money or any other thing of value is offered as a prize or prizes to be paid or presented by the program sponsor or by any other person or persons, as announced in the course of the broadcast.

(2) The term "the listening or viewing public" means those members of the public who, with the aid of radio receiving sets, listen to or view programs broadcast by radio stations.

(c) Whoever violates subsection (a) shall be fined not more than $10,000 or imprisoned not more than one year, or both.

TITLE VI—CABLE COMMUNICATIONS

PART I—GENERAL PROVISIONS

PURPOSES

SEC. 601. [47 U.S.C. 521] The purposes of this title are to—

(1) establish a national policy concerning cable communications;

(2) establish franchise procedures and standards which encourage the growth and development of cable systems and which assure that cable systems are responsive to the needs and interests of the local community;

(3) establish guidelines for the exercise of Federal, State, and local authority with respect to the regulation of cable systems;

(4) assure that cable communications provide and are encouraged to provide the widest possible diversity of information sources and services to the public;

(5) establish an orderly process for franchise renewal which protects cable operators against unfair denials of renewal where the operator's past performance and proposal for future performance meet the standards established by this title; and

(6) promote competition in cable communications and minimize unnecessary regulation that would impose an undue economic burden on cable systems.

DEFINITIONS

SEC. 602. [47 U.S.C. 522] For purposes of this title—

(1) the term 'affiliate', when used in relation to any person, means another person who owns or controls, is owned or controlled by, or is under common ownership or control with, such person;

(2) the term 'basic cable service' means any service tier which includes the retransmission of local television broadcast signals;

(3) the terms 'cable channel' or 'channel' means a portion of the electromagnetic frequency spectrum which is used in a cable system and which is capable of delivering a television channel (as television channel is defined by the Commission by regulation);

(4) the term 'cable operator' means any person or group of persons (A) who provides cable service over a cable system and directly or through one or more affiliates owns a significant interest in such cable system, or (B) who otherwise controls or is responsible for, through any arrangement, the management and operation of such a cable system;

(5) the term 'cable service' means—

(A) the one-way transmission to subscribers of (i) video programming, or (ii) other programming service, and

(B) subscriber interaction, if any, which is required for the selection of such video programming or other programming service;

(6) the term 'cable system' means a facility, consisting of a set of closed transmission paths and associated signal generation, reception, and control equipment that is designed to provide cable service which includes video programming and which is provided to multiple subscribers within a community, but such term does not include (A) a facility that serves only to retransmit the television signals of 1 or more television broadcast stations; (B) a facility that serves only subscribers in 1 or more multiple unit dwellings under common ownership, control, or management, unless such facility or facilities uses any public right-of-way; (C) a facility of a common carrier which is subject, in whole or in part, to the provisions of title II of this Act, except that such facility shall be considered a cable system (other than for purposes of section 621(c)) to the extent such facility is used in the transmission of video programming directly to subscribers; or (D) any facilities of any electric utility used solely for operating its electric utility systems;

(7) the term 'Federal agency' means any agency of the United States, including the Commission;

(8) the term 'franchise' means an initial authorization, or renewal thereof (including a renewal of an authorization which has been granted subject to section 626), issued by a franchising authority, whether such authorization is designated as a franchise, permit, license, resolution, contract, certificate, agreement, or otherwise, which authorizes the construction or operation of a cable system;

(9) the term 'franchising authority' means any governmental entity empowered by Federal, State, or local law to grant a franchise;

(10) the term 'grade B contour' means the field strength of a television broadcast station computed in accordance with regulations promulgated by the Commission;

(11) the term "other programming service" means information that a cable operator makes available to all subscribers generally;

(12) the term "person" means an individual, partnership, association, joint stock company, trust, corporation, or governmental entity;

(13) the term "public, educational, or governmental access facilities" means—

(A) channel capacity designated for public, educational, or governmental use; and

(B) facilities and equipment for the use of such channel capacity;

(14) the term "service tier" means a category of cable service or other services provided by a cable operator and for which a separate rate is charged by the cable operator;

(15) the term "State" means any State, or political subdivision, or agency thereof; and

(16) the term "video programming" means programming provided by, or generally considered comparable to programming provided by, a television broadcast station.

PART II—USE OF CABLE CHANNELS AND CABLE OWNERSHIP RESTRICTIONS

CABLE CHANNELS FOR PUBLIC, EDUCATIONAL, OR GOVERNMENTAL USE

SEC. 611. [47 U.S.C. 531] (a) A franchising authority may establish requirements in a franchise with respect to the designation or use of channel capacity for public, educational, or governmental use only to the extent provided in this section.

(b) A franchising authority may in its request for proposals require as part of a franchise, and may require as part of a cable operator's proposal for a franchise renewal, subject to section 626, that channel capacity be designated for public, educational, or governmental use, and channel capacity on institutional networks be designated for educational or governmental use, and may require rules and procedures for the use of the channel capacity designated pursuant to this section.

(c) A franchising authority may enforce any requirement in any franchise regarding the providing or use of such channel capacity. Such enforcement authority includes the authority to enforce any provisions of the franchise for services, facilities, or equipment proposed by the cable operator which relate to public, educational, or governmental use of channel capacity, whether or not required by the franchising authority pursuant to subsection (b).

(d) In the case of any franchise under which channel capacity is designated under subsection (b), the franchising authority shall prescribe—

(1) rules and procedures under which the cable operator is permitted to use such channel capacity for the provision of other services if such channel capacity is not being used for the purposes designated, and

(2) rules and procedures under which such permitted use shall cease.

(e) Subject to section 624(d), a cable operator shall not exercise any editorial control over any public, educational, or governmental use of channel capacity provided pursuant to this section.

(f) For purposes of this section, the term "institutional network" means a communication network which is constructed or operated by the cable operator and which is generally available only to subscribers who are not residential subscribers.

CABLE CHANNELS FOR COMMERCIAL USE

SEC. 612. [47 U.S.C. 532] (a) The purpose of this section is to assure that the widest possible diversity of information sources are made available to the public from cable systems in a manner consistent with growth and development of cable systems.

(b)(1) A cable operator shall designate channel capacity for commercial use by persons unaffiliated with the operator in accordance with the following requirements:

(A) An operator of any cable system with 36 or more (but not more than 54) activated channels shall designate 10 percent of such channels which are not otherwise required for use (or the use of which is not prohibited) by Federal law or regulation.

(B) An operator of any cable system with 55 or more (but not more than 100) activated channels shall designate 15 percent of such channels which are not otherwise required for use (or the use of which is not prohibited) by Federal law or regulation.

(C)   An operator of any cable system with more than 100 activated channels shall designate 15 percent of all such channels.

(D)   An operator of any cable system with fewer than 36 activated channels shall not be required to designate channel capacity for commercial use by persons unaffiliated with the operator, unless the cable system is required to provide such channel capacity under the terms of a franchise in effect on the date of the enactment of this title.

(E)   An operator of any cable system in operation on the date of the enactment of this title shall not be required to remove any service actually being provided on July 1, 1984, in order to comply with this section, but shall make channel capacity available for commercial use as such capacity becomes available until such time as the cable operator is in full compliance with this section.

(2) Any Federal agency, State, or franchising authority may not require any cable system to designate channel capacity for commercial use by unaffiliated persons in excess of the capacity specified in paragraph (1), except as otherwise provided in this section.

(3) A cable operator may not be required, as part of a request for proposals or as part of a proposal for renewal, subject to section 626, to designate channel capacity for any use (other than commercial use by unaffiliated persons under this section) except as provided in sections 611 and 637, but a cable operator may offer in a franchise, or proposal for renewal thereof, to provide, consistent with applicable law, such capacity for other than commercial use by such persons.

(4) A cable operator may use any unused channel capacity designated pursuant to this section until the use of such channel capacity is obtained, pursuant to a written agreement, by a person unaffiliated with the operator.

(5) For the purposes of this section—

(A)   the term "activated channels" means those channels engineered at the headend of the cable system for the provision of services generally available to residential subscribers of the cable system, regardless of whether such services actually are provided, including any channel designated for public, educational, or governmental use; and

(B)   the term "commercial use" means the provision of video programming, whether or not for profit.

(6) Any channel capacity which has been designated for public, educational, or governmental use may not be considered as designated under this section for commercial use for purpose of this section.

(c)(1) If a person unaffiliated with the cable operator seeks to use channel capacity designated pursuant to subsection (b) for commercial use, the cable operator shall establish, consistent with the purpose of this section, the price, terms, and conditions of such use which are at least sufficient to assure that such use will not adversely affect the operation, financial condition, or market development of the cable system.

(2) A cable operator shall not exercise any editorial control over any video programming provided pursuant to this section, or in any other way consider the content of such programming, except that an operator may consider such content to the minimum extent necessary to establish a reasonable price for the commercial use of designated channel capacity by an unaffiliated person.

(3) Any cable system channel designated in accordance with this section shall not be used to provide a cable service that is being provided over such system on the date of the enactment of this title, if the provision of such programming is intended to avoid the purpose of this section.

(d) Any person aggrieved by the failure or refusal of a cable operator to make channel capacity available for use pursuant to this section may bring an action in the district court of the United States for the judicial district in which the cable system is located to compel that such capacity be made available. If the court finds that the channel capacity sought by such person has not been made available in accordance with this section, or finds that the price, terms, or conditions established by the cable operator are unreasonable, the court may order such system to make available to such person the channel capacity sought, and further determine the appropriate price, terms, or conditions for such use consistent with subsection (c), and may award actual damages if it deems such relief appropriate. In any such action, the court shall not consider any price, term, or condition established between an operator and an affiliate for comparable services.

(e)(1) Any person aggrieved by the failure or refusal of a cable operator to make channel capacity available pursuant to this section may petition the Commission for relief under this subsection upon a showing of prior adjudicated violations of this section. Records of previous adjudications resulting in a court determination that the operator has violated this section shall be considered as sufficient for the showing necessary under this subsection. If the Commission finds that the channel capacity sought by such person has not been made available in accordance with this section, or that the price, terms, or conditions established by such system are unreasonable under subsection (c), the Commission shall, by rule or order, require such operator to make available such channel capacity under price, terms, and conditions consistent with subsection (c).

(2) In any case in which the Commission finds that the prior adjudicated violations of this section constitute a pattern or practice of violations by an operator, the Commission may also establish any further rule or order necessary to assure that the operator provides the diversity of information sources required by this section.

(3) In any case in which the Commission finds that the prior adjudicated violations of this section constitute a pattern or practice of violations by any person who is an operator of more than one cable system, the Commission may also establish any further rule or order necessary to assure that such person provides the diversity of information sources required by this section.

(f) In any action brought under this section in any Federal district court or before the Commission, there shall be a presumption that the price, terms, and conditions for use of channel capacity designated pursuant to subsection (b) are reasonable and in good faith unless shown by clear and convincing evidence to the contrary.

(g) Notwithstanding sections 621(c) and 623(a), at such time as cable systems with 36 or more activated channels are available to 70 percent of households within the United States and are subscribed to by 70 percent of the households to which such systems are available, the Commission may promulgate any additional rules necessary to provide diversity of information sources. Any rules promulgated by the Commission pursuant to this subsection shall not preempt authority expressly granted to franchising authorities under this title.

(h) Any cable service offered pursuant to this section shall not be provided, or shall be provided subject to conditions, if such cable service in the judgment of the franchising authority is obscene, or is in conflict with community standards in that it is lewd, lascivious, filthy, or indecent or is otherwise unprotected by the Constitution of the United States.

OWNERSHIP RESTRICTIONS

SEC. 613. [47 U.S.C. 533] (a) It shall be unlawful for any person to be a cable operator if such person, directly or through 1 or more affiliates, owns or controls, the licensee of a television broadcast station and the predicted grade B contour of such station covers any portion of the community served by such operator's cable system.

(b)(1) It shall be unlawful for any common carrier, subject in whole or in part to title II of this Act, to provide video programming directly to subscribers in its telephone service area, either directly or indirectly through an affiliate owned by, operated by, controlled by, or under common control with the common carrier.

(2) It shall be unlawful for any common carrier, subject in whole or in part to title II of this Act, to provide channels of communications or pole line conduit space, or other rental arrangements, to any entity which is directly or indirectly owned by, operated by, controlled by, or under common control with such common carrier, if such facilities or arrangements are to be used for, or in connection with, the provision of video programming directly to subscribers in the telephone service area of the common carrier.

(3) This subsection shall not apply to any common carrier to the extent such carrier provides telephone exchange service in any rural area (as defined by the Commission).

(4) In those areas where the provision of video programming directly to subscribers through a cable system demonstrably could not exist except through a cable system owned by, operated by, controlled by, or affiliated with the common carrier involved, or upon other showing of good cause, the Commission may, on petition for waiver, waive the applicability of paragraphs (1) and (2) of this subsection. Any such waiver shall be made in accordance with

section 63.56 of title 47, Code of Federal Regulations (as in effect September 20, 1984) and shall be granted by the Commission upon a finding that the issuance of such waiver is justified by the particular circumstances demonstrated by the petitioner, taking into account the policy of this subsection.

(c) The Commission may prescribe rules with respect to the ownership or control of cable systems by persons who own or control other media of mass communications which serve the same community served by a cable system.

(d) Any State or franchising authority may not prohibit the ownership or control of a cable system by any person because of such person's ownership or control of any media of mass communications or other media interests.

(e)(1) Subject to paragraph (2), a State or franchising authority may hold any ownership interest in any cable system.

(2) Any State or franchising authority shall not exercise any editorial control regarding the content of any cable service on a cable system in which such governmental entity holds ownership interest (other than programming on any channel designated for educational or governmental use), unless such control is exercised through an entity separate from the franchising authority.

(f) This section shall not apply to prohibit any combination of any interests held by any person on July 1, 1984, to the extent of the interests so held as of such date, if the holding of such interests was not inconsistent with any applicable Federal or State law or regulations in effect on that date.

(g) For purposes of this section, the term "media of mass communications" shall have the meaning given such term under section 309(i)(3)(C)(i) of this Act.

PART III—FRANCHISING AND REGULATION

GENERAL FRANCHISE REQUIREMENTS

Sec. 621. [47 U.S.C. 541] (a)(1) A franchising authority may award, in accordance with the provisions of this title 1 or more franchises within its jurisdiction.

(2) Any franchise shall be construed to authorize the construction of a cable system over public rights-of-way, and through easements, which is within the area to be served by the cable system and which have been dedicated for compatible uses, except that in using such easements the cable operator shall ensure—

(A) that the safety, functioning, and appearance of the property and the convenience and the safety of other persons not be adversely affected by the installation or construction of facilities necessary for a cable system;

(B) that the cost of the installation, construction, operation, or removal of such facilities be borne by the cable operator or subscriber, or a combination of both; and

(C) that the owner of the property be justly compensated by the cable operator for any damages caused by the installation, construction, operation, or removal of such facilities by the cable operator.

(3) In awarding a franchise or franchises, a franchising authority shall assure that access to cable service is not denied to any group of potential residential cable subscribers because of the income of the residents of the local area in which such group resides.

(b)(1) Except to the extent provided in paragraph (2), a cable operator may not provide cable service without a franchise.

(2) Paragraph (1) shall not require any person lawfully providing cable service without a franchise on July 1, 1984, to obtain a franchise unless the franchising authority so requires.

(c) Any cable system shall not be subject to regulation as a common carrier or utility by reason of providing any cable service.

(d)(1) A State or the Commission may require the filing of informational tariffs for any intrastate communications service provided by a cable system, other than cable service, that would be subject to regulation by the Commission or any State if offered by a common carrier subject in whole or in part, to title II of this Act. Such informational tariffs shall specify the rates, terms, and conditions for the provision of such service, including whether it is made available to all subscribers generally, and shall take effect on the date specified therein.

(2) Nothing in this title shall be construed to affect the authority of any State to regulate any cable operator to the extent that such operator provides any communication service other than cable service, whether offered on a common carrier or private contract basis.

(3) For purposes of this subsection, the term "State" has the meaning given it in section 3(v).

(e) Nothing in this title shall be construed to affect the authority of any State to license or otherwise regulate any facility or combination of facilities which serves only subscribers in one or more multiple unit dwellings under common ownership, control, or management and which does not use any public right-of-way.

FRANCHISE FEES

SEC. 622. [47 U.S.C. 542] (a) Subject to the limitation of subsection (b), any cable operator may be required under the terms of any franchise to pay a franchise fee.

(b) For any twelve-month period, the franchise fees paid by a cable operator with respect to any cable system shall not exceed 5 percent of such cable operator's gross revenues derived in such period from the operation of the cable system. For purposes of this section, the 12-month period shall be the 12-month period applicable under the franchise for accounting purposes. Nothing in this subsection shall prohibit a franchising authority and a cable operator from agreeing that franchise fees which lawfully could be collected for any such 12-month period shall be paid on a prepaid or deferred basis; except that the sum of the fees paid during the term of the franchise may not exceed the amount, including the time value of money, which would have lawfully been collected if such fees had been paid per annum.

(c) A cable operator may pass through to subscribers the amount of any increase in a franchise fee, unless the franchising authority demonstrates that the rate structure specified in the franchise reflects all costs of franchise fees and so notifies the cable operator in writing.

(d) In any court action under subsection (c), the franchising authority shall demonstrate that the rate structure reflects all costs of the franchise fees.

(e) Any cable operator shall pass through to subscribers the amount of any decrease in a franchise fee.

(f) A cable operator may designate that portion of a subscriber's bill attributable to the franchise fee as a separate item on the bill.

(g) For the purposes of this section—

(1) the term "franchise fee" includes any tax, fee, or assessment of any kind imposed by a franchising authority or other governmental entity on a cable operator or cable subscriber, or both, solely because of their status as such;

(2) the term "franchise fee" does not include—

(A) any tax, fee, or assessment of general applicability (including any such tax, fee, or assessment imposed on both utilities and cable operators or their services but not including a tax, fee, or assessment which is unduly discriminatory against cable operators or cable subscribers);

(B) in the case of any franchise in effect on the date of the enactment of this title, payments which are required by the franchise to be made by the cable operator during the term of such franchise for, or in support of the use of, public, educational, or governmental access facilities;

(C) in the case of any franchise granted after such date of enactment, capital costs which are required by the franchise to be incurred by the cable operator for public, educational, or governmental access facilities;

(D) requirements or charges incidental to the awarding or enforcing of the franchise, including payments for bonds, security funds, letters of credit, insurance, indemnification, penalties, or liquidated damages; or

(E) any fee imposed under title 17, United States Code.

(h)(1) Nothing in this Act shall be construed to limit any authority of a franchising authority to impose a tax, fee, or other assessment of any kind on any person (other than a cable operator) with respect to cable service or other communications service provided by such person over a cable system for which charges are assessed to subscribers but not received by the cable operator.

(2) For any 12-month period, the fees paid by such person with respect to any such cable service or other communications service shall not exceed 5 percent of such person's gross revenues derived in such period from the provision of such service over the cable system.

(i) Any Federal agency may not regulate the amount of the franchise fees paid by a cable operator, or regulate the use of funds derived from such fees, except as provided in this section.

REGULATION OF RATES

SEC. 623. [47 U.S.C. 543] (a) Any Federal agency or State may not regulate the rates for the provision of cable service except to the extent provided under this section. Any franchising authority may regulate the rates for the provision of cable service, or any other communications service provided over a cable system to cable subscribers, but only to the extent provided under this section.

(b)(1) Within 180 days after the date of the enactment of this title, the Commission shall prescribe and make effective regulations which authorize a franchising authority to regulate rates for the provision of basic cable service in circumstances in which a cable system is not subject to effective competition. Such regulations may apply to any franchise granted after the effective date of such regulations. Such regulations shall not apply to any rate while such rate is subject to the provisions of subsection 9(c).

(2) For purposes of rate regulation under this subsection, such regulations shall—

(A) define the circumstances in which a cable system is not subject to effective competition; and

(B) establish standards for such rate regulation.

(3) The Commission shall periodically review such regulations, taking into account developments in technology, and may amend such regulations, consistent with paragraphs (1) and (2), to the extent the Commission determines necessary.

(c) In the case of any cable system for which a franchise has been granted on or before the effective date of this title, until the end of the 2-year period beginning on such effective date, the franchising authority may, to the extent provided in a franchise—

(1) regulate the rates for the provision of basic cable service, including multiple tiers of basic cable service;

(2) require the provision of any service tier provided without charge (disregarding any installation or rental charge for equipment necessary for receipt of such tier); or

(3) regulate rates for the initial installation or the rental of 1 set of the minimum equipment which is necessary for the subscriber's receipt of basic cable service.

(d) Any request for an increase in any rate regulated pursuant to subsection (b) or (c) for which final action is not taken within 180 days after receipt of such request by the franchising authority shall be deemed to be granted, unless the 180-day period is extended by mutual agreement of the cable operator and the franchising authority.

(e)(1) In addition to any other rate increase which is subject to the approval of a franchising authority, any rate subject to regulation pursuant to this section may be increased after the effective date of this title at the discretion of the cable operator by an amount not to exceed 5 percent per year if the franchise (as in effect on the effective date of this title) does not specify a fixed rate or rates for basic cable service for a specified period or periods which would be exceeded if such increase took effect.

(2) Nothing in this section shall be construed to limit provisions of a franchise which permits a cable operator to increase any rate at the operator's discretion; however, the aggregate increases per year allowed under paragraph (1) shall be reduced by the amount of any increase taken such year under such franchise provisions.

(f) Nothing in this title shall be construed as prohibiting any Federal agency, State, or a franchising authority, from—

(1) prohibiting discrimination among customers of basic cable service, or

(2) requiring and regulating the installation or rental of equipment which facilitates the reception of basic cable service by hearing impaired individuals.

(g) Any State law in existence on the effective date of this title which provides for any limitation or preemption of regulation by any franchising authority (or the State or any political subdivision or agency thereof) of rates for cable service shall remain in effect during the 2-year period beginning on such effective date, to the extent such law provides for such limitation or preemption. As used in this section, the term "State" has the meaning given it in section 3(v).

(h) Not later than 6 years after the date of the enactment of this title, the Commission shall prepare and submit to the Congress a report regarding rate regulation of cable services, including such legislative recommendations as the Commission considers appropriate. Such report and recommendations shall be based on a study of such regulation which the Commission shall conduct regarding the effect of competition in the marketplace.

REGULATION OF SERVICES, FACILITIES, AND EQUIPMENT

SEC. 624. [47 U.S.C. 544] (a) Any franchising authority may not regulate the services, facilities, and equipment provided by a cable operator except to the extent consistent with this title.

(b) In the case of any franchise granted after the effective date of this title, the franchising authority, to the extent related to the establishment or operation of a cable system—

(1) in its request for proposals for a franchise (including requests for renewal proposals, subject to section 626), may establish requirements for facilities and equipment, but may not establish requirements for video programming or other information services; and

(2) subject to section 625, may enforce any requirements contained within the franchise—

(A) for facilities and equipment; and

(B) for broad categories of video programming or other services.

(c) In the case of any franchise in effect on the effective date of this title, the franchising authority may, subject to section 625, enforce requirements contained within the franchise for the provision of services, facilities, and equipment, whether or not related to the establishment or operation of a cable system.

(d)(1) Nothing in this title shall be construed as prohibiting a franchising authority and a cable operator from specifying, in a franchise or renewal thereof, that certain cable services shall not be provided or shall be provided subject to conditions, if such cable services are obscene or are otherwise unprotected by the Constitution of the United States.

(2)(A) In order to restrict the viewing programming which is obscene or indecent, upon the request of a subscriber, a cable operator shall provide (by sale or lease) a device by which the subscriber can prohibit viewing of a particular cable service during periods selected by that subscriber.

(B) Subparagraph (A) shall take effect 180 days after the effective date of this title.

(e) The Commission may establish technical standards relating to the facilities and equipment of cable systems which a franchising authority may require in the franchise.

(f)(1) Any Federal agency, State, or franchising authority may not impose requirements regarding the provision or content of cable services, except as expressly provided in this title.

(2) Paragraph (1) shall not apply to—

(A) any rule, regulation, or order issued under any Federal law, as such rule, regulation, or order (i) was in effect on September 21, 1983, or (ii) may be amended after such date if the rule, regulation, or order as amended is not inconsistent with the express provisions of this title; and

(B) any rule, regulation, or order under title 17, United States Code.

MODIFICATION OF FRANCHISE OBLIGATIONS

SEC. 625. [47 U.S.C. 545] (a)(1) During the period a franchise is in effect, the cable operator may obtain from the franchising authority modifications of the requirements in such franchise—

(A) in the case of any such requirement for facilities or equipment, including public, educational, or governmental access facilities or equipment, if the cable operator demonstrates that (i) it is commercially impracticable for the operator to comply with such requirement, and (ii) the proposal by the cable operator for modification of such requirement is appropriate because of commercial impracticability; or

(B) in the case of any such requirement for services, if the cable operator demonstrates that the mix, quality, and level of services required by the franchise at the time it was granted will be maintained after such modification.

(2) Any final decision by a franchising authority under this subsection shall be made in a public proceeding. Such decision shall be made within 120 days after receipt of such request by the franchising authority, unless such 120-day period is extended by mutual agreement of the cable operator and the franchising authority.

(b)(1) Any cable operator whose request for modification under subsection (a) has been denied by a final decision of a franchising authority may obtain modification of such franchise requirements pursuant to the provisions of section 635.

(2) In the case of any proposed modification of a requirement for facilities or equipment, the court shall grant such modification only if the cable operator demonstrates to the court that—

(A) it is commercially impracticable for the operator to comply with such requirement; and

(B) the terms of the modification requested are appropriate because of commercial impracticability.

(3) In the case of any proposed modification of a requirement for services, the court shall grant such modification only if the cable operator demonstrates to the court that the mix, quality, and level of services required by the franchise at the time it was granted will be maintained after such modification.

(c) Notwithstanding subsections (a) and (b), a cable operator may, upon 30 days' advance notice to the franchising authority, rearrange, replace, or remove a particular cable service required by the franchise if—

(1) such service is no longer available to the operator; or

(2) such service is available to the operator only upon the payment of a royalty required under section 801(b)(2) of title 17, United States Code, which the cable operator can document—

(A) is substantially in excess of the amount of such payment required on the date of the operator's offer to provide such service, and

(B) has not been specifically compensated for through a rate increase or other adjustment.

(d) Notwithstanding subsections (a) and (b), a cable operator may take such actions to rearrange a particular service from one service tier to another, or otherwise offer the service, if the rates for all of the service tiers involved in such actions are not subject to regulation under section 623.

(e) A cable operator may not obtain modification under this section of any requirement for services relating to public, educational, or governmental access.

(f) For purposes of this section, the term 'commercially impracticable' means, with respect to any requirement applicable to a cable operator, that it is commercially impracticable for the operator to comply with such requirement as a result of a change in conditions which is beyond the control of the operator and the nonoccurrence of which was a basic assumption on which the requirement was based.

RENEWAL

SEC. 626. [47 U.S.C. 546] (a) During the 6-month period which begins with the 36th month before the franchise expiration, the franchising authority may on its own initiative, and shall at the request of the cable operator, commence proceedings which afford the public in the franchise area appropriate notice and participation for the purpose of—

(1) identifying the future cable-related community needs and interests; and

(2) reviewing the performance of the cable operator under the franchise during the then current franchise term.

(b)(1) Upon completion of a proceeding under subsection (a), a cable operator seeking renewal of a franchise may, on its own initiative or at the request of a franchising authority, submit a proposal for renewal.

(2) Subject to section 624, any such proposal shall contain such material as the franchising authority may require, including proposals for an upgrade of the cable system.

(3) The franchising authority may establish a date by which such proposal shall be submitted.

(c)(1) Upon submittal by a cable operator of a proposal to the franchising authority for the renewal of a franchise, the franchising authority shall provide prompt public notice of such proposal and, during the 4-month period which begins on the completion of any proceedings under subsection (a), renew the franchise or, issue a preliminary assessment that the franchise should not be renewed and, at the request of the operator or on its own initiative, commence an administrative proceeding, after providing prompt public notice of such proceeding, in accordance with paragraph (2) to consider whether—

(A) the cable operator has substantially complied with the material terms of the existing franchise and with applicable law;

(B) the quality of the operator's service, including signal quality, response to consumer complaints, and billing practices, but without regard to the mix, quality, or level of cable services or other services provided over the system, has been reasonable in light of community needs;

(C) the operator has the financial, legal, and technical ability to provide the services, facilities, and equipment as set forth in the operator's proposal; and

(D) the operator's proposal is reasonable to meet the future cable-related community needs and interests, taking into account the cost of meeting such needs and interests.

(2) In any proceeding under paragraph (1), the cable operator shall be afforded adequate notice and the cable operator and the franchise authority, or its designee, shall be afforded fair opportunity for full participation, including the right to introduce evidence (including evidence related to issues raised in the proceeding under subsection (a)), to require the production of evidence, and to question witnesses. A transcript shall be made of any such proceeding.

(3) At the completion of a proceeding under this subsection, the franchising authority shall issue a written decision granting or denying the proposal for renewal based upon the record of such proceeding, and transmit a copy of such decision to the cable operator. Such decision shall state the reasons therefor.

(d) Any denial of a proposal for renewal shall be based on one or more adverse findings made with respect to the factors described in subparagraphs (A) through (D) of subsection (c)(1), pursuant to the record of the proceeding under subsection (c). A franchising authority may not base a denial of renewal on a failure to substantially comply with the material terms of the franchise under subsection (c)(1)(A) or on events considered under subsection (c)(1)(B) in any case in which a violation of the franchise or the events considered under subsection (c)(1)(B) occur after the effective date of this title unless the franchising authority has provided the operator with notice and the opportunity to cure, or in any case in which it is documented that the franchising authority has waived its right to object, or has effectively acquiesced.

(e)(1) Any cable operator whose proposal for renewal has been denied by a final decision of a franchising authority made pursuant to this section, or has been adversely affected by a failure of the franchising authority to act in accordance with the procedural requirements of this section, may appeal such final decision or failure pursuant to the provisions of section 635.

(2) The court shall grant appropriate relief if the court finds that—

(A) any action of the franchising authority is not in compliance with the procedural requirements of this section; or

(B) in the event of a final decision of the franchising authority denying the renewal proposal, the operator has demonstrated that the adverse finding of the franchising authority with respect to each of the factors described in subparagraphs (A) through (D) of subsection (c)(1)on which the denial is based is not supported by a preponderance of the evidence, based on the record of the proceeding conducted under subsection (c).

(f) Any decision of a franchising authority on a proposal for renewal shall not be considered final unless all administrative review by the State has occurred or the opportunity therefor has lapsed.

(g) For purposes of this section, the term "franchise expiration" means the date of the expiration of the term of the franchise, as provided under the franchise, as it was in effect on the date of the enactment of this title.

(h) Notwithstanding the provisions of subsections (a) through (g) of this section, a cable operator may submit a proposal for the renewal of a franchise pursuant to this subsection at any time, and a franchising authority may, after affording the public adequate notice and opportunity for comment, grant or deny such proposal at any time (including after proceedings pursuant to this section have commenced). The provisions of subsections (a) through (g) of this section shall not apply to a decision to grant or deny a proposal under this subsection. The denial of a renewal pursuant to this subsection shall not affect action on a renewal proposal that is submitted in accordance with subsections (a) through (g).

CONDITIONS OF SALE

SEC. 627. [47 U.S.C. 547] (a) If a renewal of a franchise held by a cable operator is denied and the franchising authority acquires ownership of the cable system or effects a transfer of ownership of the system to another person, any such acquisition or transfer shall be—

(1) at fair market value, determined on the basis of the cable system valued as a going concern but with no value allocated to the franchise itself, or

(2) in the case of any franchise existing on the effective date of this title, at a price determined in accordance with the franchise if such franchise contains provisions applicable to such an acquisition or transfer.

(b) If a franchise held by a cable operator is revoked for cause and the franchising authority acquires ownership of the cable system or effects a transfer of ownership of the system to another person, any such acquisition or transfer shall be—

(1) at an equitable price, or

(2) in the case of any franchise existing on the effective date of this title, at a price determined in accordance with the franchise if such franchise contains provisions applicable to such an acquisition or transfer.

PART IV—MISCELLANEOUS PROVISIONS

CONSUMER PROTECTION

SEC. 632. [47 U.S.C. 552] (a) A franchising authority may require, as part of a franchise (including a franchise renewal, subject to section 626), provisions for enforcement of—

(1) customer service requirements of the cable operator; and

(2) construction schedules and other construction-related requirements of the cable operator.

(b) A franchising authority may enforce any provision, contained in any franchise, relating to requirements described in paragraph (1) or (2) of subsection (a), to the extent not inconsistent with this title.

(c) Nothing in this title shall be construed to prohibit any State or any franchising authority from enacting or enforcing any consumer protection law, to the extent not inconsistent with this title.

UNAUTHORIZED RECEPTION OF CABLE SERVICE

SEC. 633. [47 U.S.C. 553] (a)(1) No person shall intercept or receive or assist in intercepting or receiving any communications service offered over a cable system, unless specifically authorized to do so by a cable operator or as may otherwise be specifically authorized by law.

(2) For the purpose of this section, the term "assist in intercepting or receiving" shall include the manufacture or distribution of equipment intended by the manufacturer or distributor (as the

case may be) for unauthorized reception of any communications service offered over a cable system in violation of subparagraph (1).

(b)(1) Any person who willfully violates subsection (a)(1) shall be fined not more than $1,000 or imprisoned for not more than 6 months, or both.

(2) Any person who violates subsection (a)(1) willfully and for purposes of commercial advantage or private financial gain shall be fined not more than $25,000 or imprisoned for not more than 1 year, or both, for the first such offense and shall be fined not more than $50,000 or imprisoned for not more than 2 years, or both, for any subsequent offense.

(c)(1) Any person aggrieved by any violation of subsection (a)(1) may bring a civil action in a United States district court or in any other court of competent jurisdiction.

(2) The court may—

(A)   grant temporary and final injunctions on such terms as it may deem reasonable to prevent or restrain violations of subsection (a)(1);

(B) award damages as described in paragraph (3); and

(C) direct the recovery of full costs, including awarding reasonable attorneys' fees to an aggrieved party who prevails.

(3)(A) Damages awarded by any court under this section shall be computed in accordance with either of the following clauses:

(i)   the party aggrieved may recover the actual damages suffered by him as a result of the violation and any profits of the violator that are attributable to the violation which are not taken into account in computing the actual damages; in determining the violator's profits, the party aggrieved shall be required to prove only the violator's gross revenue, and the violator shall be required to prove his deductible expenses and the elements of profit attributable to factors other than the violation; or

(ii)   the party aggrieved may recover an award of statutory damages for all violations involved in the action, in a sum of not less than $250 or more than $10,000 as the court considers just.

(B) In any case in which the court finds that the violation was committed willfully and for purposes of commercial advantage or private financial gain, the court in its discretion may increase the award of damages, whether actual or statutory under subparagraph (A), by an amount of not more than $50,000.

(C) In any case where the court finds that the violator was not aware and had no reason to believe that his acts constituted a violation of this section, the court in its discretion may reduce the award of damages to a sum of not less than $100.

(D) Nothing in this title shall prevent any State or franchising authority from enacting or enforcing laws, consistent with this section, regarding the unauthorized interception or reception of any cable service or other communications service.

EXISTING FRANCHISES

SEC. 637. [47 U.S.C. 557] (a) The provisions of—

(1) any franchise in effect on the effective date of this title, including any such provisions which relate to the designation, use, or support for the use of channel capacity for public, educational, or governmental use, and

(2) any law of any State (as defined in section 3(v)) in effect on the date of the enactment of this section, or any regulation promulgated pursuant to such law, which relates to such designation, use or support of such channel capacity,

shall remain in effect, subject to the express provisions of this title, and for not longer than the then current remaining term of the franchise as such franchise existed on such effective date.

(b) For purposes of subsection (a) and other provisions of this title, a franchise shall be considered in effect on the effective date of this title if such franchise was granted on or before such effective date.

CRIMINAL AND CIVIL LIABILITY

SEC. 638. [47 U.S.C. 558] Nothing in this title shall be deemed to affect the criminal or civil liability of cable programmers or cable operators pursuant to the Federal, State, or local law of libel, slander, obscenity, incitement, invasions of privacy, false or misleading advertising, or other similar laws, except that cable operators shall not incur any such liability for any program carried on any channel designated for public, educational, governmental use or on any other channel obtained under section 612 or under similar arrangements.

OBSCENE PROGRAMMING

SEC. 639. [47 U.S.C. 559] Whoever transmits over any cable system any matter which is obscene or otherwise unprotected by the Constitution of the United States shall be fined not more than $10,000 or imprisoned not more than 2 years, or both.

Appendix A2

Other Federal Laws Affecting Broadcasting and Cable Operations

FEDERAL CIGARETTE LABELING AND ADVERTISING ACT

UNLAWFUL ADVERTISEMENTS

SEC. 6. [15 U.S.C. 1335] After January 1, 1971, it shall be unlawful to advertise cigarettes and little cigars on any medium of electronic communication subject to the jurisdiction of the Federal Communications Commission.

TITLE 18—CRIMES AND CRIMINAL PROCEDURE

PART I—CRIMES

CHAPTER 61—LOTTERIES

(§§ 1301–1307)

*　　*　　*　　*　　*　　*　　*

SEC.
1304. Broadcasting lottery information.
1307. Exceptions relating to certain advertisements and other information and to State-conducted lotteries.

§ 1304. Broadcast lottery information

Whoever broadcasts by means of any radio or television station for which a license is required by any law of the United States, or whoever, operating any such station, knowingly permits the broadcasting of, any advertisement of or information concerning any lottery, gift, enterprise, or similar scheme, offering prizes dependent in whole or in part upon lot or chance, or any list of the prizes drawn or awarded by means of any such lottery, gift, enterprise, or scheme, whether said list contains any part or all of such prizes, shall be fined not more than $1,000 or imprisoned not more than one year, or both.

Each day's broadcasting shall constitute a separate offense.

*　　*　　*　　*　　*　　*　　*

§ 1307. Exceptions relating to certain advertisements and other information and to State-conducted lotteries

(a) The provisions of sections 1301, 1302, 1303, and 1304 shall not apply to—

(1) an advertisement, list of prizes, or other information concerning a lottery conducted by a State acting under the authority of State law which is—

(A) contained in a publication published in that State or in a State which conducts such a lottery; or

(B) broadcast by a radio or television station licensed to a location in that State or a State which conducts such a lottery; or

(2) an advertisement, list of prizes, or other information concerning a lottery, gift enterprise, or similar scheme, other than one described in paragraph (1), that is authorized or not otherwise prohibited by the State in which it is conducted and which is—

(A) conducted by a not-for-profit organization or a governmental organization; or

(B) conducted as a promotional activity by a commercial organization and is clearly occasional and ancillary to the primary business of that organization.

(b) The provisions of section 1301, 1302, and 1303 shall not apply to the transportation or mailing—

(1) to addresses within a State of equipment, tickets, or material concerning a lottery which is conducted by that State acting under the authority of State law; or

(2) to an addressee within a foreign country of equipment, tickets, or material designed to be used within that foreign country in a lottery which is authorized by the law of that foreign country.

(c) For the purposes of this section (1) "State" means a State of the United States, the District of Columbia, the Commonwealth of Puerto Rico, or any territory or possession of the United States; and (2) "foreign country" means any empire, country, dominion, colony, or protectorate, or any subdivision thereof (other than the United States, its territories or possession).

(d) For the purposes of subsection (b) of this section "lottery" means the pooling of proceeds derived from the sale of tickets or chances and allotting those proceeds or parts thereof by chance to one or more chance takers or tickets purchasers. "Lottery" does not include the placing or accepting of bets or wagers on sporting events or contests. For purposes of this section, the term a "not-for-profit organization" means any organization that would qualify as tax exempt under section 501(c)(3) of the Internal Revenue Code of 1986.

CHAPTER 63—MAIL FRAUD

(§§ 1341–1343)

Sec.
1343. Fraud by wire, radio, or television.
1367. Interference with the operation of a satellite.

§ 1343. Fraud by wire, radio, or television

Whoever, having devised or intending to devise any scheme or artifice to defraud, or for obtaining money or property by means of false or fraudulent pretenses, representations, or promises, transmits or causes to be transmitted by means of wire, radio, or television communication in interstate or foreign commerce, any writings, signs, signals, pictures, or sounds for the purpose of executing such scheme or artifice, shall be fined not more than $1,000 or imprisoned not more than five years, or both.

*   *   *   *   *   *   *

§ 1367. Interference with the operation of a satellite

(a) Whoever, without the authority of the satellite operator, intentionally or maliciously interferes with the authorized operation of a communications or weather satellite or obstructs or hinders any satellite transmission shall be fined in accordance with this title or imprisoned not more than ten years or both.

(b) This section does not prohibit any lawfully authorized investigative, protective, or intelligence activity of a law enforcement agency or of an intelligence agency of the United States."

CHAPTER 71—OBSCENITY

(§§ 1461–1468)

SEC.
1464.   Broadcast obscene language.
1468.   Distributing obscene material by cable or subscription television

§ 1464. Broadcasting obscene language

Whoever utters any obscene, indecent, or profane language by means of radio communication shall be fined not more than $10,000 or imprisoned not more than two years, or both.

*   *   *   *   *   *   *

§ 1468. Distributing obscene material by cable or subscription television

(a) Whoever knowingly utters any obscene language or distributes any obscene matter by means of cable television or subscription services on television, shall be punished by imprisonment for not more than 2 years or by a fine in accordance with this title, or both.

(b) As used in this section, the term "distribute" means to send, transmit, retransmit, telecast, broadcast, or cablecast, including by wire, microwave, or satellite, or to produce or provide material for such distribution.

(c) Nothing in this chapter, or the Cable Communications Policy Act of 1984, or any other provision of Federal law, is intended to interfere with or preempt the power of the States, including political subdivisions thereof, to regulate the uttering of language that is obscene or otherwise unprotected by the Constitution or the distribution of matter that is obscene or otherwise unprotected by the Constitution, of any sort, by means of cable television or subscription services on television.

Appendix A3
FCC Regulations: Excerpts

[47 C.F.R., as issued October 1990, but including the addition of Sections 73.658–73.662]

PART 73—RADIO BROADCAST SERVICES

Subpart E—Television Broadcast Stations

§ 73.621   Noncommercial educational TV stations.

In addition to the other provisions of this subpart, the following shall be applicable to noncommercial educational television broadcast stations:

(a) Except as provided in paragraph (b) of this section, noncommercial educational broadcast stations will be licensed only to nonprofit educational organizations upon a showing that the proposed stations will be used primarily to serve the educational needs of the community; for the advancement of educational programs; and to furnish a nonprofit and noncommercial television broadcast service.

(1) In determining the eligibility of publicly supported educational organizations, the accreditation of their respective state departments of education shall be taken into consideration.

(2) In determining the eligibility of privately controlled educational organizations, the accreditation of state departments of education or recognized regional and national educational accrediting organizations shall be taken into consideration.

(b) Where a municipality or other political subdivision has no independently constituted educational organization such as, for example, a board of education having autonomy with respect to carrying out the municipality's educational program, such municipality shall be eligible for a noncommercial educational television broadcast station. In such circumstances, a full and detailed showing must be made that a grant of the application will be consistent with the intent and purpose of the Commission's rules and regulations relating to such stations.

(c) Noncommercial educational television broadcast stations may transmit educational, cultural and entertainment programs, and programs designed for use by schools and school systems in connection with regular school courses, as well as routine and administrative material pertaining thereto.

(d) A noncommercial educational television station may broadcast programs produced by or at the expense of, or furnished by persons other than the licensee, if no other consideration than the furnishing of the program and the costs incidental to its production and broadcast are received by the licensee. The payment of line charges by another station, network, or someone other than the licensee of a noncommercial educational television station, or general contributions to the operating costs of a station, shall not be considered as being prohibited by this paragraph.

(e) Each station shall furnish a nonprofit and noncommercial broadcast service. Noncommercial educational television stations shall be subject to the provisions of § 73.1212 to the extent that they are applicable to the broadcast of programs produced by, or at the expense of, or furnished by others. No *promotional* announcements *on behalf of for profit entities* shall be broadcast at any time in exchange for the receipt, in whole or in part, of consideration to the licensee, its principals, or employees. However, acknowledgements of contributions can be made. *The scheduling of any announcements and acknowledgements may not interrupt regular programming.*

[(f)–(g) deleted]

§ 73.658 Affiliation agreements and network program practices; territorial exclusivity in non-network program arrangements.

(a) *Exclusive affiliation of station.* No license shall be granted to a television broadcast station having any contract, arrangement, or understanding, express or implied, with a network organization under which the station is prevented or hindered from, or penalized for, broadcasting the programs of any other network organization. (The term "network organization" as used in this section includes national and regional network organizations. See ch. VII, J, of Report on Chain Broadcasting.)

(b) *Territorial exclusively.* No license shall be granted to a television broadcast station having any contract, arrangement, or understanding, express or implied, with a network organization which prevents or hinders another broadcast station located in the same community from broadcasting the network's programs not taken by the former station, or which prevents or hinders another broadcast station located in a different community from broadcasting any program of the network organization. This section shall not be construed to prohibit any contract, arrangement, or understanding between a station and a network organization pursuant to which the station is granted the first call in its community upon the programs of the network organization. As employed in this paragraph, the term "community" is defined as the community specified in the instrument of authorization as the location of the station.

(c) [Reserved]

(d) *Station commitment of broadcast time.* No license shall be granted to a television broadcast station having any contract, arrangement, or understanding, express or implied, with any network organization, which provides for optioning of the station's time to the network organization, or which has the same restraining effect as time optioning. As used in this section, time optioning is any contract, arrangement, or understanding, express or implied, between a station and a network organization which prevents or hinders the station from scheduling programs before the network agrees to utilize the time during which such programs are scheduled, or which requires the station to clear time already scheduled when the network organization seeks to utilize the time.

(e) *Right to reject programs.* No license shall be granted to a television broadcast station having any contract, arrangement, or understanding, express or implied, with a network organization which, with respect to programs offered or already contracted for pursuant to an affiliation contract, prevents or hinders the station from:

(1) Rejecting or refusing network programs which the station reasonably believes to be unsatisfactory or unsuitable or contrary to the public interest, or

(2) Substituting a program which, in the station's opinion, is of greater local or national importance.

(f) *Network ownership of stations.* No license shall be granted to a network organization, or to any person directly or indirectly controlled by or under common control of a network organization for a television broadcast station in any locality where the existing television broadcast stations are so few or of such unequal desirability (in terms of coverage, power, frequency, or other related matters) that competition would be substantially restrained by such licensing. (The work "control" as used in this section, is not limited to full control but includes such a measure of control as would substantially affect the availability of the station to other networks.)

(g) *Dual network operation.* No license shall be issued to a television broadcast station affiliated with a network organization which maintains more than one network of television broadcast stations: *Provided,* That this section shall not be applicable if such networks are not operated simultaneously, or if there is no substantial overlap in the territory served by the group of stations comprising each such network.

(h) *Control by networks of station rates.* No license shall be granted to a television broadcast station having any contract, arrangement, or understanding, express or implied, with a network organization under which the station is prevented or hindered from, or penalized for, fixing or altering its rates for the sale of broadcast time for other than the network's programs.

(i) No license shall be granted to a television broadcast station which is represented for the sale of non-network time by a network organization or by an organization directly or indirectly controlled by or under common control with a network organization, if the station has any contract, arrangement or understanding, express or implied, which provides for the affiliation of the station with such network organization: *Provided, however,* That this rule shall not be applicable to stations licensed to a network organization or to a subsidiary of a network organization.

(j) *Network syndication and program practices.* (1) Except as provided in paragraph (j)(3) of this section, no television network shall:

(i) After June 1, 1973, sell, license, or distribute television programs to television station licensees within the United States for non-network television exhibition or otherwise engage in the business commonly known as "syndication" within the United States; or sell, license, or distribute television programs of which it is not the sole producer for exhibition outside the United States; or reserve any option or right to share in revenues or profits in connection with such domestic and/or foreign sale, license, or distribution; or

(ii) After August 1, 1972, acquire any financial or proprietary right or interest in the exhibition, distribution, or other commercial use of any television program produced wholly or in part by a person other than such television network, except the license or other exclusive right to network exhibition within the United States and on foreign stations regularly included within such television network: *Provided,* That if such network does not timely avail itself of such license or other exclusive right to network exhibition within the United States, the grantor of such license or right to network exhibition may, upon making a timely offer reasonably to compensate the network, reacquire such license or other exclusive right to exhibition of the program.

(2) Nothing contained in paragraphs (j)(1) and (2) of this section shall prevent any television network from selling or distributing programs of which it is the sole producer for television exhibition outside the United States, or from selling or otherwise disposing of any program rights not acquired from another person, including the right to distribute programs for non-network exhibition (as in syndication) within the United States as long as it does not itself engage in such distribution within the United States or retain the right to share the revenues or profits therefrom.

(3) Nothing contained in this paragraph shall be construed to include any television network formed for the purpose of producing, distributing, or syndicating program materials for educational, noncommercial, or public broadcasting exhibition or uses.

(4) For the purposes of this paragraph and paragraph (k) of this section the term network means any person, entity, or corporation which offers an interconnected program service on a regular basis for 15 or more hours per week to at least 25 affiliated television licensees in 10 or more States; and/or any person, entity, or corporation controlling, controlled by, or under common control with such person, entity, or corporation.

[As of June 28, 1991, paragraph (j) is deleted, and replaced by new Sections 73.659 through 73.662, the text of which appears below]

Section 73.659   Television network financial interests and syndication rights in programs.

(a) No television network may hold or acquire continuing financial interests or syndication rights in any prime time entertainment program or series exhibited on its network unless such interests or rights are held or acquired under one of the following circumstances:

(1) The program or series is solely produced by the network;

(2) The program or series is a co-production between the network and a foreign production entity;

(3) The program or series is a co-production between the network and a domestic production entity where such co-production arrangement (i) was initiated, in writing, by the outside production entity and (ii) does not become binding on the outside production entity until thirty (30) days after it is executed;

(4) The interests or rights in a program or series are acquired from an outside producer through negotiations commencing no earlier than thirty (30) days subsequent to the execution of any network license fee agreement for that program or series.

(b) No television network may hold or acquire continuing financial interests or syndication rights in any first-run non-network program or series distributed in the United States unless the network has solely produced that program or series.

(c) No more than forty (40) percent of a television network's total prime time entertainment programming schedule during a programming year shall consist of programming in which the network holds or acquires continuing financial interests or syndication rights pursuant to paragraphs (a)(1), (a)(2), or (a)(3) above.

Section 73.660   Television network participation in program syndication.

(a) No television network may syndicate any prime time entertainment program to television stations within the United States: 1) the syndication rights to which have been acquired pursuant to the provisions of Section 73.659(a)(4); or 2) that has not previously been aired on its network. Such programs shall be syndicated domestically through an independent syndicator.

(b) No television network may syndicate prime time entertainment programs to any station with which it is affiliated on terms or conditions that are more favorable than those offered to other nonaffiliated stations. Favoritism shall be rebuttably presumed if productions in which a network has an interest are syndicated to network owned or affiliated stations in more than thirty (30) percent of the markets where the program has been sold.

(c) Where a television network has syndication rights in prime time entertainment programming, such programming shall be made available for non-network broadcast exhibition within the United States no later than the earlier of: 1) the end of the fourth year after network exhibition of such a series has commenced, or the subsequent anniversary of that date as to all programs in that series aired after the fourth year, or 2) one hundred eighty (180) days after network exhibition of such a series or program is completed.

Section 73.661 Network television program ownership and syndication reports.

(a) A television network shall maintain reports identifying prime time television entertainment programming exhibited on any television network in which the network holds or acquires financial interests or syndication rights. Any agreements containing such rights shall be made available to the Commission upon its request.

(b) Each television network shall maintain reports identifying all programs that the network has syndicated, and shall list therein all stations within the United States to which syndicated program sales have been made by the network. Any agreements entered into in connection with such syndication sales shall be made available to the Commission upon its request.

(c) Each television network shall, with respect to each program or series in which rights have been obtained pursuant to Section 73.659(a), certify in writing on the specified form that no financial interests or syndication rights were obtained as a condition of network licensing or airing of the programs, and verify compliance with the provisions of Section 73.659.

(d) The records maintained pursuant to paragraphs (a), (b), and (c) above shall be placed in the public file of each station owned by the network before the first regular business day of September and March of each year. These records shall be maintained in the public file for a period of five years and made available to the Commission upon its request.

Section 73.662 Definitions for television network financial interest, syndication, and prime time access rules.

For purposes of Sections 73.658(k), 73.659, 73.660, and 73.661:

(a) a "continuing financial interest" is a right to receive revenue from the non-network broadcast or syndicated use of a television program by a network.

(b) a "co-production" is a program in which copyright ownership, financial responsibility, and business and production control are shared.

(c) an "domestic production entity" is a production entity registered to do business in the United States that is not owned or controlled, in full or in part, by the television network with which it seeks to co-produce.

(d) "entertainment programs" include series, made-for-television movies, mini-series, and entertainment specials, and do not include sports, public affairs, or news programs.

(e) a "foreign production entity" is a production entity that is registered to do business and is located outside of the United States.

(f) an "independent syndicator" is one not owned or controlled, in full or in part, by a television network.

(g) a "prime time" program is one that has network exhibition during the hours of 7–11 P.M. eastern and pacific time or 6–10 P.M. central and mountain time.

(h) a program "solely produced by a network" is a program in which the network is the sole copyright owner, has full financial responsibility, and full business and production control.

(i) a "television network" is any person, entity, or corporation providing on a regular basis more than fifteen (15) hours of prime time programming per week (exclusive of live coverage of bona fide news events of national importance) to interconnected affiliates that reach, in aggregate, at least seventy-five (75) percent of television households nationwide; and/or any person, entity, or corporation controlling, controlled by, or under common control with such person, entity, or corporation. Not included within this definition is any television network formed for the purpose of producing, distributing, or syndicating program material for educational, non-commercial, or public broadcasting exhibition, or for non-English language exhibition, or that predominately distributes programming involving the direct sale of products or services.

Note: "National audience reach" for purposes of this definition is the total number of United States television households in the Arbitron Area of Dominant Influence (ADI) markets in which the stations or regular television station affiliates of the network are located, divided by the total national television households as measured by the most current ADI data publicly available at the start of each television season. "Regular basis" means providing, on average for the prior six months, more than the specified number of hours of programming per week.

(j) a "television programming year" commences on the first day of September and ends on the last day of August the subsequent year.

(k) Effective September 8, 1975, commercial television stations owned by or affiliated with a national television network in the 50 largest television markets (see Note 1 to this paragraph) shall devote, during the four hours of prime time (7–11 P.M. e.t. and p.t., 6–10 P.M. c.t. and m.t.), no more than three hours to the presentation of programs from a national network, programs formerly on a national network (off-network programs) other than feature films, or, on Saturdays, feature films: *Provided, However,* That the following categories of programs need not be counted toward the three-hour limitation:

(1) On nights other than Saturdays, network or off-network programs designed for children, public affairs programs or documentary programs (see Note 2 to this paragraph for definitions).

(2) Special news programs dealing with fast-breaking news events, on-the-spot coverage of news events or other material related to such coverage, and political broadcasts by or on behalf of legally qualified candidates for public office.

(3) Regular network news broadcasts up to a half hour, when immediately adjacent to a full hour of continuous locally produced news or locally produced public affairs programming.

(4) Runovers of live network broadcasts of sporting events, where the event has been reasonably scheduled to conclude before prime time or occupy only a certain amount of prime time, but the event has gone beyond its expected duration due to circumstances not reasonably foreseeable by the networks or under their control. This exemption does not apply to post-game material.

(5) In the case of stations in the Mountain and Pacific time zones, on evenings when network prime-time programming consists of a sports event or other program broadcast live and simultaneously throughout the contiguous 48 states, such stations may assume that the network's schedule that evening occupies no more of prime time in these time zones than it does in the Eastern and Central time zones.

(6) Network broadcasts of an international sports event (such as the Olympic Games), New Year's Day college football games, or any other network programming of a special nature other than motion pictures or other sports events, when the network devotes all of its time on the same evening to the same programming, except brief incidental fill material.

NOTE 1: The top 50 markets to which this paragraph applies are the 50 largest markets in terms of average prime time audience for all stations in the market. For broadcast years before fall 1980, the 50 markets are the largest 50 as listed in the Arbitron publication "Television Markets and Rankings Guide," generally published in November, which will apply for the broadcast year starting the following fall, except that, for 1978–79, "Syracuse-Elmira" will not be included and the Salt Lake City market will be included. For broadcast years starting in the fall of 1980 and thereafter, the 50 largest markets to which this paragraph applies will be determined at 3-year intervals, on the basis of the average of two Arbitron February–March audience surveys occurring roughly $2^{1}/_{2}$ years and roughly $3^{1}/_{2}$ years before the start of the 3-year period. The 50 markets to which this paragraph will apply for 3 years from fall 1980 to fall 1983 will be determined by an average of the prime time audience figures (all market stations combined) contained in the reports of Arbitron February/March 1977 and February/March 1978 audience surveys. Shortly after the results of the 1978 survey are available the Commission will issue a list of the 50 largest markets to which this paragraph will apply from fall 1980 to fall 1983. The same procedure will take place, on the basis of February/March 1980 and 1981 surveys, for the 3-year period from fall 1983 to fall 1986.

NOTE 2: As used in this paragraph, the term "programs designed for children" means programs primarily designed for children aged 2 through 12. The term "documentary programs" means programs which are nonfictional and educational or informational, but not including programs where the information is used as part of a contest among participants in the program, and not including programs relating to the visual entertainment arts (stage, motion pictures or television) where more than 50% of the program is devoted to the presentation of entertainment material itself. The term "public affairs programs" means talks, commentaries, discussions, speeches, editorials, political programs, documentaries, forums, panels, roundtables, and similar programs primarily concerning local, national, and international public affairs.

[The following Notes 3 and 4 are added effective June 28, 1991:]

NOTE 3: Programming distributed by an entity prior to becoming a network, and subsequently produced episodes of a series first exhibited by that entity prior to becoming a network, are not network programming for purposes of this paragraph or Sections 73.659–73.662 of these rules.

NOTE 4: For thirty-six (36) months after an entity becomes a network, stations owned by or affiliated with that network are exempt from compliance with the requirements of this paragraph with respect to programming already under contract at the time the entity became a network.

[(a)–(1) deleted]

(m) *Territorial exclusivity in non-network arrangements.* (1) No television station shall enter into any contract, arrangement, or understanding, expressed or implied; with a non-network program producer, distributor, or supplier, or other person; which prevents or hinders another television station located in a community over 56.3 kilometers (35 miles) away, as determined by the reference points contained in § 76.53 of this chapter, (if reference points for a community are not listed in § 76.53, the location of the main post office will be used) from broadcasting any program purchased by the former station from such non-network program producer, distributor, supplier, or other person, except that a television station may secure exclusivity against a television station licensed to another designated community in a hyphenated market specified in the market listing as contained in § 76.51 of this chapter for those 100 markets listed, and for markets not listed in § 76.51 of this chapter, the listing as contained in the ARB Television Market Analysis for the most recent year at the time that the exclusivity contract, arrangement or understanding is complete under practices of the industry. As used in this paragraph, the term "community" is defined as the community specified in the instrument of authorization as the location of the station.

(2) Notwithstanding paragraph (m)(1) of this section, a television station may enter into a contract, arrangement, or understanding with a producer, supplier, or distributor of a non-network program if that contract, arrangement, or understanding provides that the broadcast station has exclusive national rights such that no other television station in the United States may broadcast the program.

PART 74—EXPERIMENTAL, AUXILIARY, AND SPECIAL BROADCAST AND OTHER PROGRAM DISTRIBUTIONAL SERVICES

Subpart G—Low Power TV, TV Translator, and TV Booster Stations

§ 74.701 Definitions

(a) *Television broadcast translator station.* A station in the broadcast service operated for the purpose of retransmitting the programs and signals of a television broadcast station, without significantly altering any characteristic of the original signal other than its frequency and amplitude, for the purpose of providing television reception to the general public.

(b) *Primary station.* The television broadcast station which provides the programs and signals being retransmitted by a television broadcast translator station.

(c) *VHF translator.* A television broadcast translator station operating on a VHF television broadcast channel.

(d) *UHF translator.* A television broadcast translator station operating on a UHF television broadcast channel.

(e) *UHF translator signal booster.* A station in the broadcasting service operated for the sole purpose of retransmitting the signals of the UHF translator station by amplifying and reradiating such signals which have been received directly through space, without significantly altering any characteristic of the incoming signal other than its amplitude.

(f) *Low power TV station.* A station authorized under the provisions of this subpart that may retransmit the programs and signals of a TV broadcast station and that may originate programming in any amount greater than 30 seconds per hour and/or operates a subscription service. (See § 73.641 of part 73 of this chapter.)

(g) *Program origination.* For purposes of this part, program origination shall be any transmissions other than the simultaneous retransmission of the programs and signals of a TV broadcast station. Origination shall include locally generated television program signals and program signals obtained via video recordings (tapes and discs), microwave, common carrier circuits, or other sources.

(h) *Local origination.* Program origination if the parameters of the program source signal, as it reaches the transmitter site, are under the control of the low power TV station licensee. Transmission of TV program signals generated at the transmitter site constitutes local origination. Local origination also includes transmission of programs reaching the transmitter site via TV STL stations, but does not include transmission of signals obtained from either terrestrial or satellite microwave feeds or low power TV stations.

(i) *Television broadcast booster station.* A station in the broadcast service operated by the licensee or permittee of a full service television broadcast station for the purpose of retransmitting the programs and signals of such primary station without significantly altering any characteristic of the original signal other than its amplitude. A television broadcast booster station may only be located such that its entire service area is located within the protected contour of the primary station it retransmits. For purposes of this paragraph, the service area of the booster and the protected contour of the primary station will be determined by the methods prescribed in § 74.705(c).

§ 74.702   Channel assignments.

(a) An applicant for a new low power TV or TV translator station or for changes in the facilities of an authorized station shall endeavor to select a channel on which its operation is not likely to cause interference. The applications must be specific with regard to the channel requested. Only one channel will be assigned to each station.

(1) Any one of the 12 standard VHF Channels (2 to 13 inclusive) may be assigned to a VHF low power TV or TV translator station. Channels 5 and 6 assigned in Alaska shall not cause harmful interference to and must accept interference from non-Government fixed operation authorized prior to January 1, 1982.

(2) Any one of the UHF Channels from 14 to 69, inclusive, may be assigned to a UHF low power TV or TV translator station. In accordance with § 73.603(c) of part 73, Channel 37 will not be assigned to such stations.

(3) Application for new low power TV or TV translator stations or for changes in existing stations, specifying operation above 806 MHz will not be accepted for filing. License renewals for existing TV translator stations operating on channels 70 (806–812 MHz) through 83 (884–890 MHz) will be granted only on a secondary basis to land mobile radio operations.

(b) Changes in the TV Table of Allotments (§ 73.606(b) of Part 73 of this chapter), authorizations to construct new TV broadcast stations or to change facilities of existing ones, may be made without regard to existing or proposed low power TV or TV translator stations. Where such a change results in a low power TV or TV translator station causing actual interference to reception of the TV broadcast station, the licensee or permittee of the low power TV or TV translator station shall eliminate the interference or file an application for a change in channel assignment pursuant to § 73.3572 of part 73 of this chapter.

(c) A television broadcast booster station will be authorized on the channel assigned to its primary station.

§ 74.703   Interference.

(a) An application for a new low power TV, TV translator, or TV booster station or for a change in the facilities of such an authorized station will not be granted when it is apparent that interference will be caused. The licensee of a new low power TV, TV translator, or TV booster shall protect existing low power TV and TV translator stations from interference within the protected contour defined in § 74.707.

(b) It shall be the responsibility of the licensee of a low power TV, TV translator, or TV booster station to correct at its expense any condition of interference to the direct reception of the signal of any other TV broadcast station operating on the same channel as that used by the low power TV, TV translator, or TV booster station or an adjacent channel which occurs as a result of the operation of the low power TV, TV translator, or TV booster station. Interference will be considered to occur whenever reception of a regularly used signal is impaired by the signals radiated by the low power TV, TV translator, or TV booster station, regardless of the quality of the reception or the strength of the signal so used. If the interference cannot be promptly eliminated by the application of suitable techniques, operation of the offending low power TV, TV translator, or TV booster station shall be suspended and shall not be resumed until the interference has been eliminated. If the complainant refuses to permit the low power TV, TV translator, or TV booster station to apply remedial techniques that demonstrably will eliminate the interference without impairment of the original reception, the licensee of the low power TV, TV translator, or TV booster station is absolved of further responsibility. TV booster stations will be exempt from the provisions of this paragraph to the extent that they may cause limited interference to their primary stations' signal subject to the conditions of paragraph (g) of this section.

(c) It shall be the responsibility of the licensee of a low power TV, TV translator, or TV booster station to correct any condition of interference which results from the radiation of radio frequency energy outside its assigned channel. Upon notice by the FCC to the station licensee or operator that such interference is caused by spurious omissions of the station, operation of the station shall be immediately suspended and not resumed until the interference has been eliminated. However, short test transmissions may be made during the period of suspended operation to check the efficacy of remedial measures.

(d) When a low power TV or TV translator station causes interference to a CATV system by radiations within its assigned channel at the cable headend or on the output channel of any system converter located at a receiver, the earlier user, whether cable system or low power TV or TV translator station, will be given priority on the channel, and the later user will be responsible for correction of the interference. When a low power TV or TV translator station causes interference to an MDS of ITFS system by radiations within its assigned channel on the output channel of any system converter located at a receiver, the earlier user, whether MDS system or low power TV or TV translator station, will be given priority on the channel, and the later user will be responsible for correction of the interference.

(e) Low power TV and TV translator stations are being authorized on a secondary basis to existing land mobile uses and must correct whatever interference they cause to land mobile stations or cease operation.

(f) In each instance where suspension of operation is required, the licensee shall submit a full report to the FCC in Washington, D.C., after operation is resumed, containing details of the nature of the interference, the source of the interfering signals, and the remedial steps taken to eliminate the interference.

(g) A TV booster station may not disrupt the existing service of its primary station nor may it cause interference to the signal provided by the primary station within the principal community to be served.

§ 74.731 Purpose and permissible service.

(a) Television broadcast translator stations and television broadcast booster stations provide a means whereby the signals of television broadcast stations may be retransmitted to areas in which direct reception of such television broadcast stations is unsatisfactory due to distance or intervening terrain barriers.

(b) Except as provided in paragraph (f) of this section, a television broadcast translator station or television broadcast booster station may be used only to receive the signals of a television broadcast station, another television broadcast translator station, a television translator relay station, a television intercity relay station, a television STL station, or other suitable source such as a CARS or common carrier microwave station, for the simultaneous retransmission of the programs and signals of a television broadcast station. Such retransmissions may be accomplished by either:

(1) Reception of the television programs and signals of a television broadcast station directly through space, conversion to a different channel by simple heterodyne frequency conversion and suitable amplification; or,

(2) Modulation and amplification of a video and audio feed, in which case modulating equipment meeting the requirements of § 74.750(d) shall be used.

(c) The transmissions of each television broadcast translator station shall be intended for direct reception by the general public and any other use shall be incidental thereto. A television broadcast translator station shall not be operated solely for the purpose of relaying signals to one or more fixed receiving points for retransmission, distribution, or further relaying.

(d) The technical characteristics of the retransmitted signals shall not be deliberately altered so as to hinder reception on conventional television broadcast receivers.

(e) A television broadcast translator station shall not deliberately retransmit the signals of any station other than the station it is authorized by license to retransmit. Precautions shall be taken to avoid unintentional retransmission of such other signals.

(f) A locally generated radio frequency signal similar to that of a TV broadcast station and modulated with visual and aural information may be connected to the input terminals of a television broadcast translator or low power station for the purposes of transmitting still photographs, slides and voice announcements. The radio frequency signals shall be on the same channel as the normally used off-the-air signal being rebroadcast. When transmitting originations concerning financial support or public service announcements, connection of the locally generated signals shall be made automatically either by means of a time switch or upon receipt of a control signal from the TV station being rebroadcast designed to actuate the switching circuit. The switching circuit will be so designed that the input circuit will be returned to the off-the-air signal within 30 seconds. The connection for emergency transmissions may be made manually. The apparatus used to generate the local signal which is used to modulate the translator or low power station must be capable of producing a visual or aural signal or both which will provide acceptable reception on television receivers designed for the transmission standards employed by TV broadcast stations. The visual and aural materials so transmitted shall be limited to emergency warnings of imminent danger, to local public service announcements and to seeking or acknowledging financial support deemed necessary to the continued operation of the station. Accordingly, the originations concerning financial support and PSAs are limited to 30 seconds each, no more than once per hour. Acknowledgements of financial support may include identification of the contributors, the size and nature of the contribution and advertising messages of contributors. Emergency transmissions shall be no longer or more frequent than necessary to protect life and property.

(g) Low power TV stations may operate under the following modes of service:

(1) As a TV translator station, subject to the requirements of this part;

(2) For origination of programming and commercial matter as defined in § 74.701(f);

(3) For the transmission of subscription television broadcast (STV) programs, intended to be received in intelligible form by members of the public for a fee or charge subject to the provisions of §§ 73.642(e) and 73.644.

(h) A low power TV station may not be operated solely for the purpose of relaying signals to one or more fixed receiving points for retransmission, distribution or relaying.

(i) Low power TV stations are subject to no minimum required hours of operation and may operate in any of the 3 modes described in paragraph (g) of this section for any number of hours.

(j) Television broadcast booster stations provide a means whereby the licensee of a television broadcast station may provide service to areas of low signal strength in any region within the primary station's Grade B contour. The booster station may not be located outside the predicted Grade B of its primary station nor may the predicted Grade B signal of the television booster station extend beyond the predicted Grade B contour of the primary station. A television broadcast booster station is authorized to retransmit only the signals of its primary station; it shall not retransmit the signals of any other stations nor make independent transmissions. However, locally generated signals may be used to excite the booster apparatus for the purpose of conducting tests and measurements essential to the proper installation and maintenance of the apparatus.

(k) The transmissions of a television broadcast booster station shall be intended for direct reception by the general public. Such stations will not be permitted to establish a point-to-point television relay system.

§ 74.732 Eligibility and licensing requirements.

(a) A license for a low power TV or TV translator station may be issued to any qualified individual, organized group of individuals, broadcast station licensee, or local civil governmental body.

(b) More than one low power TV or TV translator station may be licensed to the same applicant whether or not such stations serve substantially the same area. Low power TV and TV translator stations are not counted for purposes of § 73.3555, concerning multiple ownership.

(c) Only one channel will be assigned to each low power TV or TV translator station. Additional low power or translator stations may be authorized to provide additional reception. A separate application is required for each station and each application must be complete in all respects.

(d) The FCC will not act on applications for new low power TV or TV translator stations, for changes in facilities of existing stations, or for changes in output channel tendered by displaced stations pursuant to § 73.3572(a)(1), when such changes will result in a major change until the applicable time for filing a petition to deny has passed pursuant to § 73.3584(c).

(e) A proposal to change the primary TV station being retransmitted or an application of a licensed translator station to include low power TV station operation, i.e., program origination or subscription service will be subject only to a notification requirement.

(f) Applications for transfer of ownership or control of a low power TV or TV translator station will be subject to petitions to deny.

(g) A television broadcast booster station will be authorized only to the licensee or permittee of the television station whose signals the booster will rebroadcast, to areas within the Grade B contour of the primary station.

(h) No numerical limit is placed on the number of booster stations that may be licensed to a single licensee. A separate license is required for each television broadcast booster station.

PART 76—CABLE TELEVISION SERVICE

Subpart A—General

§ 76.1 Purpose.

The rules and regulations set forth in this part provide for the certification of cable television systems and for their operation in conformity with standards for carriage of television broadcast signals, program exclusivity, cablecasting, access channels, and related matters.

§ 76.5 Definitions.

(a) *Cable system or cable television system.* A facility consisting of a set of closed transmission paths and associated signal generation, reception, and control equipment that is designed to provide cable service which includes video programming and which is provided to multiple subscribers within a community, but such term does not include (1) a facility that services only to retransmit the television signals of one or more television broadcast stations; (2) a facility that serves only subscribers in one or more multiple unit dwellings under common ownership, control or management, unless such facility or facilities uses any public right-of-way; (3) a facility of a common carrier which is subject, in whole or in part, to the provisions of Title II of the Communications Act of 1934, as amended, except that such facility shall be considered a cable system to the extent such facility is used in the transmission of video programming directly to subscribers; or (4) any facilities of any electric utility used solely for operating its electric utility systems.

NOTE: The provisions of subparts D and F of this part shall also apply to all facilities defined previously as cable systems on or before April 28, 1985.

(b) *Television station; television broadcast station.* Any television broadcast station operating on a channel regularly assigned to its community by § 73.606 of this chapter, and any television broadcast station licensed by a foreign government: *Provided, however,* That a television broadcast station licensed by a foreign government shall not be entitled to assert a claim to carriage or program exclusivity, pursuant to subpart D or F of this part, but may otherwise be carried if consistent with the rules.

(c) *Television translator station.* A television broadcast translator station as defined in § 74.701 of this chapter.

(d) *Grade A and Grade B contours.* The field intensity contours defined in § 73.683(a) of this chapter.

(e) *Specified zone of a television broadcast station.* The area extending 35 air miles from the reference point in the community to which that station is licensed or authorized by the Commission. A list of reference points is contained in § 76.53. A television broadcast station that is authorized but not operating has a specified zone that terminates eighteen (18) months after the initial grant of its construction permit.

(f) *Major television market.* The specified zone of a commercial television station licensed to a community listed in § 76.51, or a combination of such specified zones where more than one community is listed.

(g) *Designated community in a major television market.* A community listed in § 76.51.

(h) *Smaller television market.* The specified zone of a commercial television station licensed to a community that is not listed in § 76.51.

(i) *Significantly viewed.* Viewed in other than cable television households as follows: (1) For a full or partial network station—a share of viewing hours of at least 3 percent (total week hours), and a net weekly circulation of at least 25 percent; and (2) for an independent station—a share of viewing hours of at least 2 percent (total week hours), and a net weekly circulation of at least 5 percent. See § 76.54.

NOTE: As used in this paragraph, "share of viewing hours" means the total hours that noncable television households viewed the subject station during the week, expressed as a percentage of the total hours these households viewed all stations during the period, and "net weekly circulation" means the number of noncable television households that viewed the station for 5 minutes or more during the entire week, expressed as a percentage of the total noncable television households in the survey area.

(j) *Full network station.* A commercial television broadcast station that generally carries in weekly prime time hours 85 percent of the hours of programming offered by one of the three major national television networks with which it has a primary affiliation (i.e., right of first refusal or first call).

(k) *Partial network station.* A commercial television broadcast station that generally carries in prime time more than 10 hours of programming per week offered by the three major national television networks, but less than the amount specified in paragraph (j) of this section.

(l) *Independent station.* A commercial television broadcast station that generally carries in prime time not more than 10 hours of programming per week offered by the three major national television networks.

(m) A network program is any program delivered simultaneously to more than one broadcast station regional or national, commercial or noncommercial.

(n) *Prime time.* The 5-hour period from 6 to 11 P.M., local time, except that in the central time zone the relevant period shall be between the hours of 5 and 10 P.M., and in the mountain time zone each station shall elect whether the period shall be 6 to 11 P.M. or 5 to 10 P.M.

NOTE: Unless the Commission is notified to the contrary, a station in the mountain time zone shall be presumed to have elected the 6 to 11 P.M. period.

(o) *Cablecasting.* Programming (exclusive of broadcast signals) carried on a cable television system. See paragraphs (y), (z) and (aa) (Classes II, III, and IV cable television channels) of this section.

(p) *Origination cablecasting.* Programming (exclusive of broadcast signals) carried on a cable television system over one or more channels and subject to the exclusive control of the cable operator.

(q) *Legally qualified candidate.* (1) Any person who:

(i) Has publicly announced his or her intention to run for nomination or office;

(ii) Is qualified under the applicable local, State or Federal law to hold the office for which he or she is a candidate; and

(iii) Has met the qualifications set forth in either paragraphs (q)(2), (3) or (4) of this section.

(2) A person seeking election to any public office including that of President or Vice President of the United States, or nomination for any public office except that of President or Vice President, by means of a primary, general or special election, shall be considered a legally qualified

candidate if, in addition to meeting the criteria set forth in paragraph (q)(1) of this section, that person:

(i) Has qualified for a place on the ballot, or

(ii) Has publicly committed himself or herself to seeking election by the write-in method and is eligible under applicable law to be voted for by sticker, by writing in his or her name on the ballot or by other method, and makes a substantial showing that he or she is a bona fide candidate for nomination or office.

Persons seeking election to the office of President or Vice President of the United States shall, for the purposes of the Communications Act and the rules thereunder, be considered legally qualified candidates only in those States or territories (or the District of Columbia) in which they have met the requirements set forth in paragraphs (q)(1) and (2) of this rule; except that any such person who has met the requirements set forth in paragraphs (q)(1) and (2) in at least 10 States (or nine and the District of Columbia) shall be considered a legally qualified candidate for election in all States, territories and the District of Columbia for purposes of this Act.

(3) A person seeking nomination to any public office except that of President or Vice President of the United States, by means of a convention, caucus or similar procedure, shall be considered a legally qualified candidate if, in addition to meeting the requirements set forth in paragraph (q)(1) of this section, that person makes a substantial showing that he or she is a bona fide candidate for such nomination; except that no person shall be considered a legally qualified candidate for nomination by the means set forth in this paragraph prior to 90 days before the beginning of the convention, caucus or similar procedure in which he or she seeks nomination.

(4) A person seeking nomination for the office of President or Vice President of the United States shall, for the purposes of the Communications Act and the rules thereunder, be considered a legally qualified candidate only in those States or territories (or the District of Columbia) in which, in addition meeting the requirements set forth in paragraph (q)(1) of this section.

(i) He or she, or proposed delegates on his or her behalf, have qualified for the primary of Presidential preference ballot in that State, territory or the District of Columbia, or

(ii) He or she has made a substantial showing of bona fide candidacy for such nomination in that State, territory of the District of Columbia; except that such person meeting the requirements set forth in paragraph (q)(1) and (4) in at least 10 States (or nine and the District of Columbia) shall be considered a legally qualified candidate for nomination in all States, territories and the District of Columbia for purposes of the Act.

(5) The term "substantial showing" of bona fide candidacy as used in paragraph (q)(2), (3) and (4) of this section means evidence that the person claiming to be a candidate has engaged to a substantial degree in activities commonly associated with political campaigning. Such activities normally would include making campaign speeches, distributing campaign literature, issuing press releases, maintaining a campaign headquarters (even though the headquarters in some instances might be the residence of the candidate or his campaign manager). Not all of the listed activities are necessarily required in each case to demonstrate a substantial showing, and there may be activities not listed herein which would contribute to such a showing.

(r) *Class I cable television channel.* A signaling path provided by a cable television system to relay to subscriber terminals television broadcast programs that are received off-the-air or are obtained by microwave or by direct connection to a television broadcast station.

(s) *Class II cable television channel.* A signaling path provided by a cable television system to deliver to subscriber terminals television signals that are intended for reception by a television broadcast receiver without the use of an auxiliary decoding device and which signals are not involved in a broadcast transmission path.

(t) *Class III cable television channel.* A signaling path provided by a cable television system to deliver to subscriber terminals signals that are intended for reception by equipment other than a television broadcast receiver or by a television broadcast receiver only when used with auxiliary decoding equipment.

(u) *Class IV cable television channel.* A signaling path provided by a cable television system to transmit signals of any type from a subscriber terminal to another point in the cable television system.

(v) *Subscriber terminal.* The cable television system terminal to which a subscriber's equipment is connected. Separate terminals may be provided for delivery of signals of various classes.

NOTE: Terminal devices interconnected to subscriber terminals of a cable system shall comply with subpart H of part 15.

(w) *System noise.* That combination of undesired and fluctuating disturbances within a cable television channel that degrades the transmission of the desired signal and that is due to modulation processes or thermal or other noise-producing effects, but does not include hum and other undesired signals of discrete frequency. System noise is specified in terms of its rms voltage or its mean power level as measured in the 4 MHz bandwidth between 1.25 and 5.25 MHz above the lower channel boundary of a cable television channel.

(x) *Terminal isolation.* The attenuation, at any subscriber terminal, between that terminal and any other subscriber terminal in the cable television system.

(y) *Visual signal level.* The rms voltage produced by the visual signal during the transmission of synchronizing pulses.

(z) *Affiliate.* When used in relation to any person, another person who owns or controls, is owned or controlled by, or is under common ownership or control with, such person.

(aa) *Person.* An individual, partnership, association, joint stock company, trust, corporation, or governmental entity.

(bb) *Significant interest.* A cognizable interest for attributing interests in broadcast, cable, and newspaper properties pursuant to §§ 73.3555, 73.3615, and 76.501.

(cc) *Cable system operator.* Any person or group of persons (1) who provides cable service over a cable system and directly or through one or more affiliates owns a significant interest in such cable system; or (2) who otherwise controls or is responsible for, through any arrangement, the management and operation of such a cable system.

(dd) *System community unit: Community unit.* A cable television system, or portion of a cable television system, that operates or will operate within a separate and distinct community or municipal entity (including unincorporated communities within unincorporated areas and including single, discrete unincorporated areas).

(ee) *Subscribers.* A member of the general public who receives broadcast programming distributed by a cable television system and does not further distribute it.

(ff) *Cable service.* The one-way transmission to subscribers of video programming, or other programming service; and, subscriber interaction, if any, which is required for the selection of such video programming or other programming service. For the purposes of this definition, "video programming" is programming provided by, or generally considered comparable to programming provided by, a television broadcast station; and, "other programming service" is information that a cable operator makes available to all subscribers generally.

(gg) *Basic cable service.* For purposes of regulating the rates for the provision of basic cable service in circumstances in which a cable system is not subject to effective competition, basic cable service is any service tier which includes the retransmission of any broadcast television signals in the following categories:

(1) For communities located outside all major and smaller television markets (as defined in this section):

(i) Television broadcast stations within whose Grade B contours the community of the community unit is located, in whole or in part;

(ii) Television translator stations with 100 watts or higher power serving the community of the community unit and for community units that commence operations or expand channel capacity after March 30, 1972, noncommercial educational translator stations with 5 watts or higher power serving the community of the community unit;

(iii) Noncommercial educational television broadcast stations within whose specified zone the community of the community unit is located, in whole or in part;

(iv) Commercial television broadcast stations that are significantly viewed in the community of the community unit. See § 76.54.

(2) For communities in smaller television markets (as defined in this section):

(i) Television broadcast stations within whose specified zone the community of the community unit is located, in whole or in part;

(ii) Noncommercial educational television broadcast stations within whose Grade B contours the community of the community unit is located, in whole or in part;

(iii) Commercial television broadcast stations licensed to communities in other smaller television markets, within whose Grade B contours the community of the community unit is located, in whole or in part;

(iv) Television broadcast stations licensed to other communities which are generally considered to be part of the same smaller television market (Example: Burlington, VT-Plattsburgh, NY, television market);

(v) Television translator stations with 100 watts or higher power serving the community of the community unit and, for community units that commence operations or expand channel capacity after March 30, 1972, noncommercial educational translator stations with 5 watts or higher power serving the community of the community unit;

(vi) Commercial television broadcast stations that are significantly viewed in the community unit. See § 76.54.

(3) For communities in major television markets (as defined in this section) and in communities located both wholly or partially within both major and smaller television markets:

(i) Television broadcast stations within whose specified zone the community of the community unit is located, in whole or in part;

(ii) Noncommercial educational television broadcast stations within whose Grade B contours the community of the community unit is located, in whole or in part;

(iii) Television translator stations with 100 watts or higher power serving the community of the community unit and, for those community units that commence operations or expand channel capacity after March 30, 1972, noncommercial educational translator stations with 5 watts or higher power serving the community of the community unit;

(iv) Television broadcast stations licensed to other designated communities of the same major television market (Example: Cincinnati, Ohio-Newport, Ky., television market);

(v) Commercial television broadcast stations that are significantly viewed in the community of the community unit. See § 76.54.

(4) In the absence of at least three signals in one of the above categories, any unaltered broadcast television signals.

(hh) *Input selector switch.* Any device that enables a viewer to select between cable service and off-the-air television signals. Such a device may be more sophisticated than a mere two-sided switch, may utilize other cable interface equipment, and may be built into consumer television receivers.

(ii) A *"syndicated program"* is any program sold, licensed, distributed or offered to television station licensees in more than one market within the United States other than as network programming as defined in § 76.5(o).

Subpart C—Federal-State/Local Regulatory Relationships

§ 76.33   Standards for rate regulation.

(a) Effective October 29, 1988, a franchising authority may regulate the rates of a cable system subject to the following conditions (cable systems that were subject to rate regulation prior to this date will remain subject to that regulation pending demonstration that they may not be regulated pursuant to this section):

(1) Only basic cable service as defined in § 76.5(gg) may be regulated;

(2) Only cable systems that are not subject to effective competition may be rate regulated. A cable system will be determined to be subject to effective competition whenever 100 percent of the cable community receives service from at least three unduplicated broadcast television signals. It is not necessary that the same three signals provide service to the entire community. Signals shall be counted on the basis of their predicted Grade B contour (as defined in § 73.683 of the rules) or whether they are significantly viewed within the cable community, as defined in

§ 76.54(b) and (c) of the rules. A signal that is significantly viewed shall be considered to be available to 100 percent of the cable community. A translator station authorized to serve the cable community is to be counted in the same manner as a full-service station, except that its coverage area shall be based on its protected contour as specified in § 74.707 of the rules, provided that the translator is not used to retransmit a station already providing a Grade B contour or significantly viewed signal within the cable community.

(3) The Commission may grant waivers of this standard where the filing party demonstrates with engineering studies in accordance with § 73.686 of the Commission's rules or by other showings that such Grade B level signals are (or are not) in fact available within the community. In performing the engineering studies noted above, cluster measurements, as provided in § 73.686(b)(2)(viii), may be taken in place of mobile runs as provided in § 73.686(b)(2)(v). Responsibility for the cost of engineering studies undertaken to refute the predicted availability of Grade B service will fall on the party that loses in the waiver proceeding. Any party intending to obtain this study must first inform the other party and provide it an opportunity to negotiate a resolution. Parties not taking this first step will be assigned full responsibility for the study costs.

(4) A cable system, once determined to be subject to effective competition after the effective date of this section, shall not be subject to regulation for one year after any change in market conditions which would cause it to be determined not to be subject to effective competition.

(b) In establishing any rate for the provision of basic cable service by cable systems subject to paragraph (a) of this section, the franchising authority shall:

(1) Give formal notice to the public;

(2) Provide an opportunity for interested parties to make their views known, at least through written submissions; and,

(3) Make a formal statement (including summary explanation) when a decision on a rate matter is made.

(c) Any party may petition the Commission for relief of the provisions in this section in accordance with the provisions and procedures set forth in § 76.7 for petitions for special relief.

Subpart D—Carriage of Television Broadcast Signals

§ 76.60 Carriage of other television signals.

A cable system may carry the signals of any television station including low power television stations, television translator stations, foreign television stations, subscription television broadcasts, satellite distributed program services, direct broadcast satellite stations and programming from any other source. A cable system may also carry any ancillary service transmission on the vertical blanking interval or the aural baseband of any television broadcast signal including, but not limited to, multichannel television sound and teletext.

§ 76.67 Sports broadcasts.

(a) No community unit located in whole or in part within the specified zone of a television broadcast station licensed to a community in which a sports event is taking place, shall, on request of the holder of the broadcast rights to that event, or its agent, carry the live television broadcast of that event if the event is not available live on a television broadcast signal carried by the community unit meeting the criteria specified in §§ 76.5(gg)(1) through 76.5(gg)(3) of this part. For purposes of this section, if there is no television station licensed to the community in which the sports event is taking place, the applicable specified zone shall be that of the television station licensed to the community with which the sports event or team is identified, or, if the event or local team is not identified with any particular community, the nearest community to which a television station is licensed.

(b) Notification of the programming to be deleted pursuant to this section shall include the following information:

(1) As to programming to be deleted from television broadcast signals regularly carried by the community unit:

(i) The name and address of the party requesting the program deletion;

(ii) The date, time and expected duration of the sports event the television broadcast of which is to be deleted;

(iii) The call letters of the television broadcast station(s) from which the deletion is to be made.

(2) As to programming to be deleted from television broadcast signals not regularly carried by the community unit:

(i) The name and address of the party requesting the program deletion;

(ii) The date, time and expected duration of the sports event the television broadcast of which is to be deleted.

(c) Notifications given pursuant to this section must be received, as to regularly scheduled events, no later than the Monday preceding the calendar week (Sunday–Saturday) during which the program deletion is to be made. Notifications as to events not regularly scheduled and revisions of notices previously submitted, must be received within twenty-four (24) hours after the time of the telecast to be deleted is known, but in any event no later than twenty-four (24) hours from the time the subject telecast is to take place.

(d) Whenever, pursuant to this section, a community unit is required to delete a television program on a signal regularly carried by the community unit, such community unit may, consistent with the rules contained in Subpart F of this part, substitute a program from any other television broadcast station. A program substituted may be carried to its completion, and the community unit need not return to its regularly carried signal until it can do so without interrupting a program already in progress.

(e) The provisions of this section shall not be deemed to require the deletion of any portion of a television signal which a community unit was lawfully carrying prior to March 31, 1972.

(f) The provisions of this section shall not apply to any community unit having fewer than 1,000 subscribers.

Subpart F—Nonduplication Protection and Syndicated Exclusivity

SOURCE: 53 FR 27171, July 19, 1988, unless otherwise noted.

§ 76.92   Network non-duplication; extent of protection.

(a) Upon receiving notification pursuant to § 76.94, a cable community unit located in whole or in part within the geographic zone for a network program, the network non-duplication rights to which are held by a commercial television station licensed by the Commission, shall not carry that program as broadcast by any other television signal, except as otherwise provided below.

(b) For purposes of this section, the order of nonduplication priority of television signals carried by a community unit is as follows:

(1) First, all television broadcast stations within whose specified zone the community of the community unit is located, in whole or in part;

(2) Second, all smaller market television broadcast stations within whose secondary zone the community of the community unit is located, in whole or in part.

(c) For purposes of this section, all noncommercial educational television broadcast stations licensed to a community located in whole or in part within a major television market as specified in § 76.51 shall be treated in the same manner as a major market commercial television broadcast station, and all noncommercial educational television broadcast stations not licensed to a community located in whole or in part within a major television market shall be treated in the same manner as a smaller market television broadcast station.

(d) Any community unit operating in a community to which a 100-watt or higher power translator is located within the predicted Grade B signal contour of the television broadcast station that the translator station retransmits, and which translator is carried by the community unit shall, upon request of such translator station licensee or permittee, delete the duplicating network programming of any television broadcast station whose reference point (See Section 76.53) is more than 55 miles from the community of the community unit.

(e) Any community unit which operates in a community located in whole or in part within the secondary zone of a smaller market television broadcast station is not required to delete the duplicating network programming of any major market television broadcast station whose reference point (See § 76.53) is also within 55 miles of the community of the community unit.

(f) A community unit is not required to delete the duplicating network programming of any television broadcast station which is significantly viewed in the cable television community pursuant to § 76.54.

NOTE: With respect to network programming, the geographic zone within which the television station is entitled to enforce network non-duplication protection and priority of shall be that geographic area agreed upon between the network and the television station. In no event shall such rights exceed the area within which the television station may acquire broadcast territorial exclusivity rights as defined in § 73.658(m), except that small market television stations shall be entitled to a secondary protection zone of 20 additional miles. To the extent rights are obtained for any hyphenated market named in § 76.51, such rights shall not exceed those permitted under § 73.658(m) for each named community in that market.

§ 76.93   Parties entitled to network non-duplication protection.

Television broadcast station licensees shall be entitled to exercise non-duplication rights pursuant to § 76.92 in accordance with the contractual provisions of the network-affiliate agreement.

§ 76.94   Notification.

(a) In order to exercise non-duplication rights pursuant to § 76.92, television stations shall notify each cable television system operator of the non-duplication sought in accordance with the requirements of this Section. Except as otherwise provided in paragraph (b) of this section, non-duplication protection notices shall include the following information:

(1) The name and address of the party requesting non-duplication protection and the television broadcast station holding the non-duplication right;

(2) The name of the program or series (including specific episodes where necessary) for which protection is sought; and

(3) The dates on which protection is to begin and end.

(b) Broadcasters entering into contracts providing for network non-duplication protection shall notify affected cable systems within 60 calendar days of the signing of such a contract; provided, however, that for such contracts signed before May 5, 1989, a broadcaster may provide notice on or before June 19, 1989. In the event the broadcaster is unable based on the information contained in the contract, to furnish all the information required by paragraph (a) of this section at that time, the broadcaster must provide modified notices that contain the following information:

(1) The name of the network (or networks) which has (or have) extended non-duplication protection to the broadcaster;

(2) The time periods by time of day (local time) and by network (if more than one) for each day of the week that the broadcaster will be broadcasting programs from that network (or networks) and for which non-duplication protection is requested; and

(3) The duration and extent (e.g., simultaneous, same-day, seven-day, etc.) of the non-duplication protection which has been agreed upon by the network (or networks) and the broadcaster.

(c) Except as otherwise provided in paragraph (d) of this section, a broadcaster shall be entitled to non-duplication protection beginning on the later of:

(1) The date specified in its notice (as described in paragraphs (a) or (b) of this section, whichever is applicable) to the cable television system; or

(2) The first day of the calendar week (Sunday–Saturday) that begins 60 days after the cable television system receives from the broadcaster.

(d) A broadcaster shall provide the following information to the cable television system under the following circumstances:

(1) In the event the protection specified in the notices described in paragraphs (a) or (b) of this section has been limited or ended prior to the time specified in the notice, or in the event a time

period, as identified to the cable system in a notice pursuant to paragraph (b) of this section, for which a broadcaster has obtained protection is shifted to another time of day or another day (but not expanded), the broadcaster shall, as soon as possible, inform each cable television system operator that has previously received the notice of all changes from the original notice. Notice to be furnished "as soon as possible" under this subsection shall be furnished by telephone, telegraph, facsimile, overnight mail or other similar expedient means.

(2) In the event the protection specified in the modified notices described in paragraph (b) of this section has been expanded, the broadcaster shall, at least 60 calendar days prior to broadcast of a protected program entitled to such expanded protection, notify each cable system operator that has previously received notice of all changes from the original notice.

(e) In determining which programs must be deleted from a television signal, a cable television system operator may rely on information from any of the following sources published or otherwise made available:

(1) Newspapers or magazines of general circulation.

(2) A television station whose programs may be subject to deletion. If a cable television system asks a television station for information about its program schedule, the television station shall answer the request:

(i) Within ten business days following the television station's receipt of the request; or

(ii) Sixty days before the program or programs mentioned in the request for information will be broadcast; whichever comes later.

(3) The broadcaster requesting exclusivity.

(f) A broadcaster exercising exclusivity pursuant to § 76.92 shall provide to the cable system, upon request, an exact copy of those portions of the contracts, such portions to be signed by both the network and the broadcaster, setting forth in full the provisions pertinent to the duration, nature, and extent of the non-duplication terms concerning broadcast signal exhibition to which the parties have agreed.

§ 76.95 Exceptions.

(a) The provisions of §§ 76.92–76.94 shall not apply to a cable system serving fewer than 1,000 subscribers. Within 60 days following the provision of service to 1,000 subscribers, the operator of each such system shall file a notice to that effect with the Commission, and serve a copy of that notice on every television station that would be entitled to exercise network non-duplication protection against it.

(b) Network non-duplication protection need not be extended to a higher priority station for one hour following the scheduled time of completion of the broadcast of a live sports event by that station or by a lower priority station against which a cable community unit would otherwise be required to provide non-duplication protection following the scheduled time of completion.

§ 76.97 Effective dates.

The network non-duplication protection and exceptions thereto outlined in §§ 76.92 through 76.95 shall become enforceable on January 1, 1990. The rules in effect on May 18, 1988, will remain operative until January 1, 1990.

§ 76.151 Syndicated program exclusivity: extent of protection.

Upon receiving notification pursuant to § 76.155, a cable community unit located in whole or in part within the geographic zone for a syndicated program, the syndicated exclusivity rights to which are held by a commercial television station licensed by the Commission, shall not carry that program as broadcast by any other television signal, except as otherwise provided below.

NOTE: With respect to each syndicated program, the geographic zone within which the television station is entitled to enforce syndicated exclusivity rights shall be that geographic area agreed upon between the non-network program supplier, producer or distributor and the television station. In no event shall such zone exceed the area within which the television station has acquired broadcast territorial exclusivity rights as defined in § 73.658(m). To the extent rights are obtained for any hyphenated market named in § 76.51, such rights shall not exceed those permitted under § 73.658(m) for each named community in that market.

§ 76.153   Parties entitled to syndicated exclusivity.

(a) Television broadcast station licensees shall be entitled to exercise exclusivity rights pursuant to § 76.151 in accordance with the contractual provisions of their syndicated program license agreements, consistent with § 76.159.

(b) Distributors of syndicated programming shall be entitled to exercise exclusive rights pursuant to § 76.151 for a period of one year from the initial broadcast syndication licensing of such programming anywhere in the United States; provided, however, that distributors shall not be entitled to exercise such rights in areas in which the programming has already been licensed.

§ 76.155   Notification.

(a) In order to exercise exclusivity rights pursuant to § 76.151, distributors or television stations shall notify each cable television system operator of the exclusivity sought in accordance with the requirements of this section. Syndicated program exclusivity notices shall include the following information:

(1) The name and address of the party requesting exclusivity and the television broadcast station or other party holding the exclusive right;

(2) The name of the program or series (including specific episodes where necessary) for which exclusivity is sought;

(3) The dates on which exclusivity is to begin and end.

(b) Broadcasters entering into contracts on or after August 18, 1988, which contain syndicated exclusivity protection shall notify affected cable systems within sixty calendar days of the signing of such a contract. Broadcasters who have entered into contracts prior to August 18, 1988, and who comply with the requirements specified in § 76.159 shall notify affected cable systems on or before June 19, 1989; provided, however, that with respect to such pre-August 18, 1988, contracts that require amendment in order to invoke the provisions of these rules, notification may be given within sixty calendar days of the signing of such amendment. A broadcaster shall be entitled to exclusivity protection beginning on the later of:

(1) The date specified in its notice to the cable television system; or

(2) The first day of the calendar week (Sunday–Saturday) that begins 60 days after the cable television system receives notice from the broadcaster;

(c) In determining which programs must be deleted from a television broadcast signal, a cable television system operator may rely on information from any of the following sources published or otherwise made available.

(1) Newspapers or magazines of general circulation;

(2) A television station whose programs may be subject to deletion. If a cable television system asks a television station for information about its program schedule, the television station shall answer the request:

(i) Within ten business days following the television station's receipt of the request; or

(ii) Sixty days before the program or programs mentioned in the request for information will be broadcast; whichever comes later.

(3) The distributor or television station requesting exclusivity.

(d) In the event the exclusivity specified in paragraph (a) of this section has been limited or has ended prior to the time specified in the notice, the distributor or broadcaster who has supplied the original notice shall, as soon as possible, inform each cable television system operator that has previously received the notice of all changes from the original notice. In the event the original notice specified contingent dates on which exclusivity is to begin and/or end, the distributor or broadcaster shall, as soon as possible, notify the cable television system operator of the occurrence of the relevant contingency. Notice to be furnished "as soon as possible" under this subsection shall be furnished by telephone, telegraph, facsimile, overnight mail or other similar expedient means.

§ 76.156   Exceptions.

(a) Notwithstanding the requirements of §§ 76.151–76.155, a broadcast signal is not required to be deleted from a cable community unit when that cable community unit falls, in whole or in part, within that signal's grade B contour, or when the signal is significantly viewed pursuant to § 76.54 in the cable community.

(b) The provisions of §§ 76.151–76.155 shall not apply to a cable system serving fewer than 1,000 subscribers. Within 60 days following the provision of service to 1,000 subscribers, the operator of each such system shall file a notice to that effect with the Commission, and serve a copy of that notice on every television station that would be entitled to exercise syndicated exclusivity protection against it.

§ 76.157   Exclusivity contracts.

A distributor or television station exercising exclusivity pursuant to § 76.151 shall provide to the cable system, upon request, an exact copy of those portions of the exclusivity contracts, such portions to be signed by both the distributor and the television station, setting forth in full the provisions pertinent to the duration, nature, and extent of the exclusivity terms concerning broadcast signal exhibition to which the parties have agreed.

§ 76.158   Indemnification contracts.

No licensee shall enter into any contract to indemnify a cable system for liability resulting from failure to delete programming in accordance with the provisions of this subpart unless the licensee has a reasonable basis for concluding that such program deletion is not required by this subpart.

§ 76.159   Requirements for invocation of protection.

For a station licensee to be eligible to invoke the provisions of this subpart, it must have a contract or other written indicia that it holds syndicated exclusivity rights for the exhibition of the program in question. Contracts entered on or after August 18, 1988, must contain the following words: "the licensee [or substitute name] shall, by the terms of this contract, be entitled to invoke the protection against duplication of programming imported under the Compulsory Copyright License, as provided in § 76.151 of the FCC rules [or 'as provided in the FCC's syndicated exclusivity rules']." Contracts entered into prior to August 18, 1988, must contain either the foregoing language or a clear and specific reference to the licensee's authority to exercise exclusivity rights as to the specific programming against cable television broadcast signal carriage by the cable system in question upon the contingency that the government re-imposed syndicated exclusivity protection. In the absence of such a specific reference in contracts entered into prior to August 18, 1988, the provisions of these rules may be invoked only if (a) the contract is amended to include the specific language referenced above or (b) a specific written acknowledgment is obtained from the party from whom the broadcast exhibition rights were obtained that the existing contract was intended, or should now be construed by agreement of the parties, to include such rights. A general acknowledgment by a supplier of exhibition rights that specific contract language was intended to convey rights under these rules will be accepted with respect to all contracts containing that specific language. Nothing in this Section shall be construed as a grant of exclusive rights to a broadcaster where such rights are not agreed to by the parties.

§ 76.161   Substitutions.

Whenever, pursuant to the requirements of the syndicated exclusivity rules, a community unit is required to delete a television program on a broadcast signal that is permitted to be carried under the Commission's rules, such community unit may, consistent with these rules and the sports blackout rules at 47 CFR 76.67, substitute a program from any other television broadcast station. Programs substituted pursuant to this section may be carried to their completion.

§ 76.163   Effective dates.

No cable system shall be required to delete programming pursuant to the provisions of §§ 76.151 through 76.159 prior to January 1, 1990.

Subpart J—Diversification of Control

§ 76.501   Cross-ownership.

(a) No cable television system (including all parties under common control) shall carry the signal of any television broadcast station if such system directly or indirectly owns, operates, controls, or has an interest in:

(1) A national television network (such as ABC, CBS, or NBC); or

(2) A TV broadcast station whose predicted Grade B contour, computed in accordance with § 73.684 of Part 73 of this chapter, overlaps in whole or in part the service area of such system (i.e., the area within which the system is serving subscribers).

[Notes deleted]

(b) *Effective date.* (1) The provisions of paragraphs (a)(1) and (3) of this section are not effective until August 10, 1975, as to ownership interests proscribed herein if such interests were in existence on or before July 1, 1970 (*e.g.,* if a franchise were in existence on or before July 1, 1970): *Provided, however,* That the provisions of paragraph (a) of this section are effective on August 10, 1970, as to such interests acquired after July 1, 1970.

(2) The provisions of paragraph (a)(2) of this section are not effective until November 8, 1987, as to ownership interests proscribed herein if such interests were in existence on or before July 1, 1970 (e.g., if franchise were in existence on or before July 1970), and will be applied to cause divestiture as to ownership interests proscribed herein only where the cable system is directly or indirectly, owned, operated, controlled by, or has an interest in a non-satellite television broadcast station which places a principal community contour encompassing the entire community and there is no other commercial non-satellite television broadcast station placing a principal community contour encompassing the entire community.

PART 100—DIRECT BROADCAST SATELLITE SERVICE

Subpart A—General Information

§ 100.1   Basis and purpose.

(a) The rules following in this part are promulgated pursuant to the provisions of Title III of the Communications Act of 1934, as amended, which vests authority in the Federal Communications Commission to regulate radio transmissions and to issue licenses for radio stations.

(b) The purpose of this part is to prescribe the manner in which parts of the radio frequency spectrum may be made available for the development of interim direct broadcast satellite service. Interim direct broadcast satellite systems shall be granted licenses pursuant to these interim rules during the period prior to the adoption of permanent rules. The Direct Broadcast Satellite Service shall operate in the frequency band 12.2–12.7 GHz.

§ 100.3   Definitions.

Direct Broadcast Satellite Service. A radiocommunication service in which signals transmitted or retransmitted by space stations are intended for direct reception by the general public. In the Direct Broadcast Satellite Service the term *direct reception* shall encompass both individual reception and community reception.

Subpart B—Administrative Procedures

§ 100.11   Eligibility.

An authorization for operation of a station in the Direct Broadcast Satellite Service shall not be granted to or held by:

(a) Any alien or the representative of any alien;

(b) Any foreign government or the representative thereof;

(c) Any corporation organized under the laws of any foreign government;

(d) Any corporation of which any officer or director is an alien;

(e) Any corporation of which more than one-fifth of the capital stock is owned of record or voted by aliens or their representatives or by a foreign government or representative thereof, or by any corporation organized under the laws of a foreign country;

(f) Any corporation directly or indirectly controlled by any other corporation of which any officer or more than one-fourth of the directors are aliens, if the Commission finds that the public interest will be served by the refusal or revocation of such license; or

(g) Any corporation directly or indirectly controlled by any other corporation of which more than one-fourth of the capital stock is owned of record or voted by aliens, their representatives, or by a foreign government or representatives thereof, or by any corporation organized under the laws of a foreign country, if the Commission finds that the public interest will be served by the refusal or revocation of such license.

§ 100.13   Application requirements.

(a) Each application for an interim direct broadcast satellite system shall include a showing describing the type of service that will be provided, the technology that will be employed, and all other pertinent information. The application may be presented in narrative format.

(b) Applicants may request specific frequencies and orbital positions. However, frequencies and orbital positions shall not be assigned until completion of the 1983 Region 2 Administrative Radio Conference for the Broadcasting-Satellite Service. The Commission shall generally consider all frequencies and orbital positions to be of equal value, and conflicting requests for frequencies and orbital positions will not necessarily give rise to comparative hearing rights as long as unassigned frequencies and orbital slots remain.

§ 100.15   Licensing procedures.

(a) Each application for an interim direct broadcast satellite system shall be placed on public notice for 45 days, during which time interested parties may file comments and petitions related to the application.

(b) A 45 day cut-off period shall also be established for the filing of applications to be considered in conjunction with the original application. Additional applications filed before the cut-off date shall be considered to have equal priority with the original application and shall be considered together in the assignment of frequencies and orbital positions. If applications have included requests for particular frequencies or orbital positions, the cut-off date shall be considered in establishing the priority of such requests.

(c) Each application for an interim direct broadcast satellite system, after the public comment period and staff review, shall be acted upon by the Commission to determine if authorization of the proposed system is in the public interest.

§ 100.17   License term.

All authorizations for interim direct broadcast satellite systems shall be granted for a period of five years.

§ 100.19   License conditions.

(a) All authorizations for interim direct broadcast satellite systems shall be subject to the policies set forth in the *Report and Order* in General Docket 80-603 and with any policies and rules the Commission may adopt at a later date. It is the intention of the Commission, however, that in most circumstances the regulatory policies in force at the time of authorization to construct a satellite shall remain in force for that satellite throughout its operating lifetime.

(b) Parties granted authorizations shall proceed with diligence in constructing interim direct broadcast satellite systems. Permittees of interim direct broadcast satellite systems shall be required to begin construction or complete contracting for construction of the satellite station within one year of the grant of the construction permit. The satellite station shall also be required to be in operation within six years of the construction permit grant, unless otherwise determined by the Commission upon proper showing in any particular case. Transfer of control of the construction permit shall not be considered to justify extension of these deadlines.

Subpart C—Technical Requirements

§ 100.21   Technical requirements.

Prior to the 1983 Regional Administrative Radio Conference for the Broadcasting-Satellite Service, interim direct broadcast satellite systems shall be operated in accordance with the sharing criteria and technical characteristics contained in Annexes 8 and 9 of the Final Acts of the World Administrative Radio Conference for the Planning of the Broadcasting-Satellite Service in Frequency Bands 11.7–12.2 GHz (in Regions 2 and 3) and 11.7–12.5 GHz (in Region 1), Geneva, 1977; *Provided, however,* That upon adequate showing systems may be implemented that use values for the technical characteristics different from those specified in the Final Acts if such action does not result in interference to other operational or planned systems in excess of that determined in accordance with Annex 9 of the Final Acts.

Subpart D—Operating Requirements

§ 100.51   Equal employment opportunities.

(a) *General policy.* Equal opportunity in employment shall be afforded all licensees or permittees of direct broadcast satellite stations licensed as broadcasters to all qualified persons, and no person shall be discriminated against in employment because of race, color, religion, national origin, or sex.

(b) *Equal employment opportunity program.* Each station shall establish, maintain, and carry out a positive continuing program of specific practices designed to assure equal opportunity in every aspect of station employment policy and practice. Under the terms of its program, a station shall:

(1) Define the responsibility of each level of management to ensure a positive application and vigorous enforcement of the policy of equal opportunity, and establish a procedure to review and control managerial and supervisory performance.

(2) Inform its employees and recognized employee organizations of the positive equal employment opportunity policy and program and enlist their cooperation.

(3) Communicate the station's equal employment opportunity policy and program and its employment needs to sources of qualified applicants without regard to race, color, religion, national origin, or sex, and solicit their recruitment assistance on a continuing basis.

(4) Conduct a continuing campaign to exclude every form of prejudice or discrimination based upon race, color, religion, national origin, or sex from the station's personnel policies and practices and working conditions.

(5) Conduct continuing review of job structure and employment practices and adopt positive recruitment, training, job design and other measures needed in order to ensure genuine equality of opportunity to participate fully in all organizational units, occupations and levels of responsibility in the station.

(c) Applicants for a construction permit for a new facility, for authority to obtain assignment of the construction permit or license of such a station, for authority to acquire control of an entity holding such construction permit or license, (other than pro forma or involuntary assignments of transfers) and for renewal of license, shall file with the FCC programs designed to provide equal employment opportunities for American Indians and Alaskan Natives; Asians and Pacific Islanders; Blacks, not of Hispanic origin; Hispanics; and women, or amendments to such programs. Guidelines for the preparation of such programs are set forth in Forms 396 and 396A. A program need not be filed by an applicant who employs or proposes to employ less than five full-time employees. Additionally, a program for minority group members need not be filed if minorities constitute less than five percent, in the aggregate, of the labor force in the applicant's labor recruitment area. Applicants exempt from the filing requirement should submit a statement of explanation with their applications.

(d) Each licensee or permittee with five or more full-time employees shall file an annual employment report with the FCC on or before May 31 of each year on FCC Form 395.

Appendix A4

Address for FCC Forms and Information

Consumer Assistance and Small Business Offices
Federal Communications Commission
1919 M Street N.W.
Washington, D.C. 20554
202-632-7000 or
202-632-7260

The FCC can provide information on application filing and reporting requirements, check status of pending applications, and explain rules and regulations. The FCC cannot and will not comment or assist you with any information on matters pending before the Review Board or any administrative law judge.

Appendix A5
Copyright Law of 1976: Excerpts

[U.S. Code Title 17, as amended through
Dec. 31, 1990]

[These Copyright Law excerpts include provisions relating to Section 106A which become effective 6 months after December, 1991.]

TABLE OF CONTENTS [Omitted sections not listed]

CHAPTER 1—SUBJECT MATTER & SCOPE OF COPYRIGHT

§ 101. Definitions

As used in this title, the following terms and their variant forms mean the following:

An "anonymous work" is a work on the copies or phonorecords of which no natural person is identified as author.

"Audiovisual works" are works that consist of a series of related images which are intrinsically intended to be shown by the use of machines, or devices such as projectors, viewers, or electronic equipment, together with accompanying sounds, if any, regardless of the nature of the material objects, such as films or tapes, in which the works are embodied.

The "Berne Convention" is the Convention for the Protection of Literary and Artistic Works, signed at Berne, Switzerland, on September 9, 1886, and all acts, protocols, and revisions thereto.

A work is a "Berne Convention work" if—

(1) in the case of an unpublished work, one or more of the authors is a national of a nation adhering to the Berne Convention, or in the case of a published work, one or more of the authors is a national of a nation adhering to the Berne Convention on the date of first publication;

(2) the work was first published in a nation adhering to the Berne Convention, or was simultaneously first published in a nation adhering to the Berne Convention and in a foreign nation that does not adhere to the Berne Convention;

(3) in the case of an audiovisual work—

(A) if one or more of the authors is a legal entity, that author has its headquarters in a nation adhering to the Berne Convention; or

(B) if one or more of the authors is an individual, that author is domiciled, or has his or her habitual residence in, a nation adhering to the Berne Convention; or

(4) in the case of a pictorial, graphic, or sculptural work that is incorporated in a building or other structure, the building or structure that is located in a nation adhering to the Berne Convention.

For purposes of paragraph (1), an author who is domiciled in or has his or her habitual residence in, a nation adhering to the Berne Convention is considered to be a national of that nation. For purposes of paragraph (2), a work is considered to have been simultaneously published in two or more nations if its dates of publication are within 30 days of one another.

The "best edition" of a work is the edition, published in the United States at any time before the date of deposit, that the Library of Congress determines to be most suitable for its purposes.

A person's "children" are that person's immediate offspring, whether legitimate or not, and any children legally adopted by that person.

A "collective work" is a work, such as a periodical issue, anthology, or encyclopedia, in which a number of contributions, constituting separate and independent works in themselves, are assembled into a collective whole.

A "compilation" is a work formed by the collection and assembling of preexisting materials or of data that are selected, coordinated, or arranged in such a way that the resulting work as a whole constitutes an original work of authorship. The term "compilation" includes collective works.

"Copies" are material objects, other than phonorecords, in which a work is fixed by any method now known or later developed, and from which the work can be perceived, reproduced, or otherwise communicated, either directly or with the aid of a machine or device. The term "copies" includes the material object, other than a phonorecord, in which the work is first fixed.

"Copyright owner", with respect to any one of the exclusive rights comprised in a copyright, refers to the owner of that particular right.

The "country of origin" of a Berne Convention work, for purposes of section 411, is the United States if—

(1) in the case of a published work, the work is first published—

(A) in the United States;

(B) simultaneously in the United States and another nation or nations adhering to the Berne Convention, whose law grants a term of copyright protection that is the same as or longer than the term provided in the United States;

(C) simultaneously in the United States and a foreign nation that does not adhere to the Berne Convention; or

(D) in a foreign nation that does not adhere to the Berne Convention, and all of the authors of the work are nationals, domiciliaries, or habitual residents of, or in the case of an audiovisual work legal entities with headquarters in, the United States;

(2) in the case of an unpublished work, all the authors of the work are nationals, domiciliaries, or habitual residents of the United States, or, in the case of an unpublished audiovisual work, all the authors are legal entities with headquarters in the United States; or

(3) in the case of a pictorial, graphic, or sculptural work incorporated in a building or structure, the building or structure is located in the United States.

For the purposes of section 411, the "country of origin" of any other Berne Convention work is not the United States.

A work is "created" when it is fixed in a copy or phonorecord for the first time; where a work is prepared over a period of time, the portion of it that has been fixed at any particular time constitutes the work as of that time, and where the work has been prepared in different versions, each version constitutes a separate work.

A "derivative work" is a work based upon one or more preexisting works, such as a translation, musical arrangement, dramatization, fictionalization, motion picture version, sound recording, art reproduction, abridgment, condensation, or any other form in which a work may be recast, transformed, or adapted. A work consisting of editorial revisions, annotations, elaborations, or other modifications which, as a whole, represent an original work of authorship, is a "derivative work".

A "device", "machine", or "process" is one now known or later developed.

To "display" a work means to show a copy of it, either directly or by means of a film, slide, television image, or any other device or process or, in the case of a motion picture or other audiovisual work, to show individual images nonsequentially.

A work is "fixed" in a tangible medium of expression when its embodiment in a copy or phonorecord, by or under the authority of the author, is sufficiently permanent or stable to permit it to be perceived, reproduced, or otherwise communicated for a period of more than transitory duration. A work consisting of sounds, images, or both, that are being transmitted, is "fixed" for purposes of this title if a fixation of the work is being made simultaneously with its transmission.

The terms "including" and "such as" are illustrative and not limitative.

A "joint work" is a work prepared by two or more authors with the intention that their contributions be merged into inseparable or interdependent parts of a unitary whole.

"Literary works" are works, other than audiovisual works, expressed in words, numbers, or other verbal or numerical symbols or indicia, regardless of the nature of the material objects, such as books, periodicals, manuscripts, phonorecords, film, tapes, disks, or cards, in which they are embodied.

"Motion pictures" are audiovisual works consisting of a series of related images which, when shown in succession, impart an impression of motion, together with accompanying sounds, if any.

To "perform" a work means to recite, render, play, dance, or act it, either directly or by means of any device or process or, in the case of a motion picture or other audiovisual work, to show its images in any sequence or to make the sounds accompanying it audible.

"Phonorecords" are material objects in which sounds, other than those accompanying a motion picture or other audiovisual work, are fixed by any method now known or later developed, and from which the sounds can be perceived, reproduced, or otherwise communicated, either directly or with the aid of a machine or device. The term "phonorecords" incudes the material object in which the sounds are first fixed.

"Pictorial, graphic, and sculptural works" include two-dimensional and three-dimensional works of fine, graphic, and applied art, photographs, prints and art reproductions, maps, globes, charts, diagrams, models, and technical drawings, including architectural plans. Such works shall include works of artistic craftsmanship insofar as their form but not their mechanical or utilitarian aspects are concerned; the design of a useful article, as defined in this section, shall be considered a pictorial, graphic, or sculptural work only if, and only to the extent that, such design incorporates pictorial, graphic, or sculptural features that can be identified separately from, and are capable of existing independently of, the utilitarian aspects of the article.

A "pseudonymous work" is a work on the copies or phonorecords of which the author is identified under a fictitious name.

"Publication" is the distribution of copies or phonorecords of a work to the public by sale or other transfer of ownership, or by rental, lease, or lending. The offering to distribute copies or phonorecords to a group of persons for purposes of further distribution, public performance, or public display, constitutes publication. A public performance or display of a work does not of itself constitute publication.

To perform or display a work "publicly" means—

(1) to perform or display it at a place open to the public or at any place where a substantial number of persons outside of a normal circle of a family and its social acquaintances is gathered; or

(2) to transmit or otherwise communicate a performance or display of the work to a place specified by clause (1) or to the public, by means of any device or process, whether the members of the public capable of receiving the performance or display receive it in the same place or in separate places and at the same time or at different times.

"Sound recordings" are works that result from the fixation of a series of musical, spoken, or other sounds, but not including the sounds accompanying a motion picture or other audiovisual work, regardless of the nature of the material objects, such as disks, tapes, or other phonorecords, in which they are embodied.

"State" includes the District of Columbia and the Commonwealth of Puerto Rico, and any territories to which this title is made applicable by an Act of Congress.

A "transfer of copyright ownership" is an assignment, mortgage, exclusive license, or any other conveyance, alienation, or hypothecation of a copyright or of any of the exclusive rights comprised in a copyright, whether or not it is limited in time or place of effect, but not including a nonexclusive license.

A "transmission program" is a body of material that, as an aggregate, has been produced for the sole purpose of transmission to the public in sequence and as a unit.

To "transmit" a performance or display is to communicate it by any device or process whereby images or sounds are received beyond the place from which they are sent.

The "United States", when used in a geographical sense, comprises the several States, the District of Columbia and the Commonwealth of Puerto Rico, and the organized territories under the jurisdiction of the United States Government.

A "useful article" is an article having an intrinsic utilitarian function that is not merely to portray the appearance of the article or to convey information. An article that is normally a part of a useful article is considered a "useful article".

The author's "widow" or "widower" is the author's surviving spouse under the law of the author's domicile at the time of his or her death, whether or not the spouse has later remarried.

A 'work of visual art' is—

(1) a painting, drawing, print, or sculpture, existing in a single copy, in a limited edition of 200 copies or fewer that are signed and consecutively numbered by the author, or, in the case of a sculpture, in multiple cast, carved, or fabricated sculptures of 200 or fewer that are consecutively numbered by the author and bear the signature or other identifying mark of the author; or

(2) a still photographic image produced for exhibition purposes only, existing in a single copy that is signed by the author, or in a limited edition of 200 copies or fewer that are signed and consecutively numbered by the author.

A work of visual art does not include—

(A)(i) any poster, map, globe, chart, technical drawing, diagram, model, applied art, motion picture or other audio-visual work, book, magazine, newspaper, periodical, data base, electronic information service, electronic publication, or similar publication;

(ii) any merchandising item or advertising, promotional, descriptive, covering, or packaging material, or container;

(iii) any portion or part of any item described in clause (i) or (ii);

(B) any work made for hire; or

(C) any work not subject to copyright protection under this title.

A "work of the United States Government" is a work prepared by an officer or employee of the United States Government as part of that person's official duties.

A "work made for hire" is—

(1) a work prepared by an employee within the scope of his or her employment; or

(2) a work specially ordered or commissioned for use as a contribution to a collective work, as a part of a motion picture or other audiovisual work, as a translation, as a supplementary work, as a compilation, as an instructional text, as a test, as answer material for a test, or as an atlas, if the parties expressly agree in a written instrument signed by them that the work shall be considered a work made for hire. For the purpose of the foregoing sentence, a "supplementary work" is a work prepared for publication as a secondary adjunct to a work by another author for the purpose of introducing, concluding, illustrating, explaining, revising, commenting upon, or assisting in the use of the other work, such as forewords, afterwords, pictorial illustrations, maps, charts, tables, editorial notes, musical arrangements, answer material for tests, bibliographies, appendixes, and indexes, and an "instructional text" is a literary, pictorial, or graphic work prepared for publication and with the purpose of use in systematic instructional activities.

A "computer program" is a set of statements or instructions to be used directly or indirectly in a computer in order to bring about a certain result.

§ 102. Subject matter of copyright: In general

(a) Copyright protection subsists, in accordance with this title, in original works of authorship fixed in any tangible medium of expression, now known or later developed, from which they can be perceived, reproduced, or otherwise communicated, either directly or with the aid of a machine or device. Works of authorship include the following categories:

(1) literary works;
(2) musical works, including any accompanying words;
(3) dramatic works, including any accompanying music;
(4) pantomimes and choreographic works;
(5) pictorial, graphic, and sculptural works;
(6) motion pictures and other audiovisual works; and
(7) sound recordings.

(b) In no case does copyright protection for an original work of authorship extend to any idea, procedure, process, system, method of operation, concept, principle, or discovery, regardless of the form in which it is described, explained, illustrated, or embodied in such work.

§ 103. Subject matter of copyright: Compilations and derivative works

(a) The subject matter of copyright as specified by section 102 includes compilations and derivative works, but protection for a work employing preexisting material in which copyright subsists does not extend to any part of the work in which such material has been used unlawfully.

(b) The copyright in a compilation or derivative work extends only to the material contributed by the author of such work, as distinguished from the preexisting material employed in the work, and does not imply any exclusive right in the preexisting material. The copyright in such work is independent of, and does not affect or enlarge the scope, duration, ownership, or subsistence of, any copyright protection in the preexisting material.

§ 104. Subject matter of copyright: National origin

(a) UNPUBLISHED WORKS.—The works specified by sections 102 and 103, while unpublished, are subject to protection under this title without regard to the nationality or domicile of the author.

(b) PUBLISHED WORKS.—The works specified by sections 102 and 103, when published, are subject to protection under this title if—

(1) on the date of first publication, one or more of the authors is a national or domiciliary of the United States, or is a national, domiciliary, or sovereign authority of a foreign nation that is a party to a copyright treaty to which the United States is also a party, or is a stateless person, wherever that person may be domiciled; or

(2) the work is first published in the United States or in a foreign nation that, on the date of first publication, is a party to the Universal Copyright Convention; or

(3) the work is first published by the United Nations or any of its specialized agencies, or by the Organization of American States; or

(4) the work is a Berne Convention work; or

(5) the work comes within the scope of a Presidential proclamation. Whenever the President finds that a particular foreign nation extends, to works by authors who are nationals or domiciliaries of the United States or to works that are first published in the United States, copyright protection on substantially the same basis as that on which the foreign nation extends protection to works of its own nationals and domiciliaries and works first published in that nation, the President may by proclamation extend protection under this title to works of which one or more of the authors is, on the date of first publication, a national, domiciliary, or sovereign authority of that nation, or which was first published in that nation. The President may revise, suspend, or revoke any such proclamation or impose any conditions or limitations on protection under a proclamation.

(c) EFFECT OF BERNE CONVENTION.—No right or interest in a work eligible for protection under this title may be claimed by virtue of, or in reliance upon, the provisions of the Berne Convention, or the adherence of the United States thereto. Any rights in a work eligible for protection under this title that derive from this title, other Federal or State statutes, or the common law, shall not be expanded or reduced by virtue of, or in reliance upon, the provisions of the Berne Convention, or the adherence of the United States thereto.

§ 105. Subject matter of copyright: United States Government works

Copyright protection under this title is not available for any work of the United States Government, but the United States Government is not precluded from receiving and holding copyrights transferred to it by assignment, bequest, or otherwise.

§ 106. Exclusive rights in copyrighted works

Subject to sections 107 through 120, the owner of copyright under this title has the exclusive rights to do and to authorize any of the following:

(1) to reproduce the copyrighted work in copies or phonorecords;

(2) to prepare derivative works based upon the copyrighted work;

(3) to distribute copies or phonorecords of the copyrighted work to the public by sale or other transfer of ownership, or by rental, lease, or lending;

(4) in the case of literary, musical, dramatic, and choreographic works, pantomimes, and motion pictures and other audiovisual works, to perform the copyrighted work publicly; and

(5) in the case of literary, musical, dramatic, and choreographic works, pantomimes, and pictorial, graphic, or sculptural works, including the individual images of a motion picture or other audiovisual work, to display the copyrighted work publicly.

§ 106A. Rights of certain authors to attribution and integrity

(a) RIGHTS OF ATTRIBUTION AND INTEGRITY.—Subject to section 107 and independent of the exclusive rights provided in section 106, the author of a work of visual art—

(1) shall have the right—

(A) to claim authorship of that work, and

(B) to prevent the use of his or her name as the author of any work of visual art which he or she did not create;

(2) shall have the right to prevent the use of his or her name as the author of the work of visual art in the event of a distortion, mutilation, or other modification of the work which would be prejudicial to his or her honor or reputation; and

(3) subject to the limitations set forth in section 113(d), shall have the right—

(A) to prevent any intentional distortion, mutilation, or other modification of that work which would be prejudicial to his or her honor or reputation, and any intentional distortion, mutilation, or modification of that work is a violation of that right, and

(B) to prevent any destruction of a work of recognized stature, and any intentional or grossly negligent destruction of that work is a violation of that right.

(b) SCOPE AND EXERCISE OF RIGHTS.—Only the author of a work of visual art has the rights conferred by subsection (a) in that work, whether or not the author is the copyright owner. The authors of a joint work of visual art are coowners of the rights conferred by subsection (a) in that work.

(c) EXCEPTIONS.—(1) The modification of a work of visual art which is a result of the passage of time or the inherent nature of the materials is not a distortion, mutilation, or other modification described in subsection (a)(3)(A).

(2) The modification of a work of visual art which is the result of conservation, or of the public presentation, including lighting and placement, of the work is not a destruction, distortion, mutilation, or other modification described in subsection (a)(3) unless the modification is caused by gross negligence.

(3) The rights described in paragraphs (1) and (2) of subsection (a) shall not apply to any reproduction, depiction, portrayal, or other use of a work in, upon, or in any connection with any item described in subparagraph (A) or (B) of the definition of "work of visual art" in section 101, and any such reproduction, depiction, portrayal, or other use of a work is not a destruction, distortion, mutilation, or other modification described in paragraph (3) of subsection (a).

(d) DURATION OF RIGHTS.—(1) With respect to works of visual art created on or after the effective date set forth in section 610(a) of the Visual Artists Rights Act of 1990, the rights conferred by subsection (a) shall endure for a term consisting of the life of the author.

(2) With respect to works of visual art created before the effective date set forth in section 610(a) of the Visual Artists Rights Act of 1990, but title to which has not, as of such effective date, been transferred from the author, the rights conferred by subsection (a) shall be coextensive with, and shall expire at the same time as, the rights conferred by section 106.

(3) In the case of a joint work prepared by two or more authors, the rights conferred by subsection (a) shall endure for a term consisting of the life of the last surviving author.

(4) All terms of the rights conferred by subsection (a) run to the end of the calendar year in which they would otherwise expire.

(e) TRANSFER AND WAIVER.—(1) The rights conferred by subsection (a) may not be transferred, but those rights may be waived if the author expressly agrees to such waiver in a written instrument signed by the author. Such instrument shall specifically identify the work, and uses of that work, to which the waiver applies, and the waiver shall apply only to the work and uses so identified. In the case of a joint work prepared by two or more authors, a waiver of rights under this paragraph made by one such author waives such rights for all such authors.

(2) Ownership of the rights conferred by subsection (a) with respect to a work of visual art is distinct from ownership of any copy of that work, or of a copyright or any exclusive right under a copyright in that work. Transfer of ownership of any copy of a work of visual art, or of a copyright or any exclusive right under a copyright, shall not constitute a waiver of the rights conferred by subsection (a). Except as may otherwise be agreed by the author in a written instrument signed by the author, a waiver of the rights conferred by subsection (a) with respect to a work of visual art shall not constitute a transfer of ownership of any copy of that work, or of ownership of a copyright or of any exclusive right under a copyright in that work.

§ 107. Limitations on exclusive rights: Fair use

Notwithstanding the provisions of sections 106 and 106A, the fair use of a copyrighted work, including such use by reproduction in copies or phonorecords or by any other means specified by that section, for purposes such as criticism, comment, news reporting, teaching (including multiple copies for classroom use), scholarship, or research, is not an infringement of copyright. In determining whether the use made of a work in any particular case is a fair use the factors to be considered shall include—

(1) the purpose and character of the use, including whether such use is of a commercial nature or is for nonprofit educational purposes;

(2) the nature of the copyrighted work;

(3) the amount and substantiality of the portion used in relation to the copyrighted work as a whole; and

(4) the effect of the use upon the potential market for or value of the copyrighted work.

§ 111.   Limitations on exclusive rights: Secondary transmissions

(a) CERTAIN SECONDARY TRANSMISSIONS EXEMPTED.—The secondary transmission of a primary transmission embodying a performance or display of a work is not an infringement of copyright if—

(1) the secondary transmission is not made by a cable system, and consists entirely of the relaying, by the management of a hotel, apartment house, or similar establishment, or signals transmitted by a broadcast station licensed by the Federal Communications Commission, within the local service area of such station, to the private lodgings of guests or residents of such establishment, and no direct charge is made to see or hear the secondary transmission; or

(2) the secondary transmission is made solely for the purpose and under the conditions specified by clause (2) of section 110; or

(3) the secondary transmission is made by any carrier who has no direct or indirect control over the content or selection of the primary transmission or over the particular recipients of the secondary transmission, and whose activities with respect to the secondary transmission consist solely of providing wires, cables, or other communications channels for the use of others: *Provided,* That the provisions of this clause extend only to the activities of said carrier with respect to secondary transmissions and do not exempt from liability the activities of others with respect to their own primary or secondary transmissions;

(4) the secondary transmission is made by a satellite carrier for private home viewing pursuant to a statutory license under section 119; or

(5) the secondary transmission is not made by a cable system but is made by a governmental body, or other nonprofit organization, without any purpose of direct or indirect commercial advantage, and without charge to the recipients of the secondary transmission other than assessments necessary to defray the actual and reasonable costs of maintaining and operating the secondary transmission service.

(b) SECONDARY TRANSMISSION OF PRIMARY TRANSMISSION TO CONTROLLED GROUP.— Notwithstanding the provisions of subsections (a) and (c), the secondary transmission to the public of a primary transmission embodying a performance or display of a work is actionable as an act of infringement under section 501, and is fully subject to the remedies provided by sections 502 through 506 and 509, if the primary transmission is not made for reception by the public at large but is controlled and limited to reception by particular members of the public: *Provided, however,* That such secondary transmission is not actionable as an act of infringement if—

(1) the primary transmission is made by a broadcast station licensed by the Federal Communications Commission; and

(2) the carriage of the signals comprising the secondary transmission is required under the rules, regulations, or authorizations of the Federal Communications Commission; and

(3) the signal of the primary transmitter is not altered or changed in any way by the secondary transmitter.

(c) SECONDARY TRANSMISSIONS BY CABLE SYSTEMS.—

(1) Subject to the provisions of clauses (2), (3), and (4) of this subsection, secondary transmissions to the public by a cable system of a primary transmission made by a broadcast station licensed by the Federal Communications Commission or by an appropriate governmental authority of Canada or Mexico and embodying a performance of Canada or Mexico and embodying a performance or display of a work shall be subject to compulsory licensing upon compliance with the requirements of subsection (d) where the carriage of the signals comprising the secondary transmission is permissible under the rules, regulations, or authorizations of the Federal Communications Commission.

(2) Notwithstanding the provisions of clause (1) of this subsection, the willful or repeated secondary transmission to the public by a cable system of a primary transmission made by a broadcast station licensed by the Federal Communications Commission or by an appropriate governmental authority of Canada or Mexico and embodying a performance or display of a work is actionable as an act of infringement under section 501, and is fully subject to the remedies provided by sections 502 through 506 and 509, in the following cases:

(A) where the carriage of the signals comprising the secondary transmission is not permissible under the rules, regulations, or authorizations of the Federal Communications Commission; or

(B) where the cable system has not deposited the statement of account and royalty fee required by subsection (d).

(3) Notwithstanding the provisions of clause (1) of this subsection and subject to the provisions of subsection (e) of this section, the secondary transmission to the public by a cable system of a primary transmission made by a broadcast station licensed by the Federal Communications Commission or by an appropriate governmental authority of Canada or Mexico and embodying a performance or display of a work is actionable as an act of infringement under section 501, and is fully subject to the remedies provided by sections 502 through 506 and sections 509 and 510, if the content of the particular program in which the performance or display is embodied, or any commercial advertising or station announcements transmitted by the primary transmitter during, or immediately before or after, the transmission of such program, is in any way willfully altered by the cable system through changes, deletions, or additions, except for the alteration, deletion, or substitution of commercial advertisements performed by those engaged in television commercial advertising market research: *Provided,* That the research company has obtained the prior consent of the advertiser who has purchased the original commercial advertisement, the television station broadcasting that commercial advertisement, and the cable system performing the secondary transmission: *And provided further,* That such commercial alteration, deletion, or substitution is not performed for the purpose of deriving income from the sale of that commercial time.

(4) Notwithstanding the provisions of clause (1) of this subsection, the secondary transmission to the public by a cable system of a primary transmission made by a broadcast station licensed by an appropriate governmental authority of Canada or Mexico and embodying a performance or display of a work is actionable as an act of infringement under section 501, and is fully subject to the remedies provided by sections 502 through 506 and section 509, if (A) with respect to Canadian signals, the community of the cable system is located more than 150 miles from the United States-Canadian border and is also located south of the forty-second parallel of latitude, or (B) with respect to Mexican signals, the secondary transmission is made by a cable system which received the primary transmission by means other than direct interception of a free space radio wave emitted by such broadcast television station, unless prior to April 15, 1976, such cable system was actually carrying, or was specifically authorized to carry, the signal of such foreign station on the system pursuant to the rules, regulations, or authorizations of the Federal Communications Commission.

(d) COMPULSORY LICENSE FOR SECONDARY TRANSMISSIONS BY CABLE SYSTEMS.—

(1) A cable system whose secondary transmissions have been subject to compulsory licensing under subsection (c) shall, on a semiannual basis, deposit with the Register of Copyrights, in accordance with requirements that the Register shall, after consultation with the Copyright Royalty Tribunal (if and when the Tribunal has been constituted), prescribe by regulation—

(A) a statement of account, covering the six months next preceding, specifying the number of channels on which the cable system made secondary transmissions to its subscribers, the names and locations of all primary transmitters whose transmissions were further transmitted by the cable system, the total number of subscribers, the gross amounts paid to the cable system for the basic service of providing secondary transmissions of primary broadcast transmitters, and such other data as the Register of Copyrights may, after consultation with the Copyright Royalty Tribunal (if and when the Tribunal has been constituted), from time to time prescribe by regulation. In determining the total number of subscribers and the gross amounts paid to the cable system for the basic service of providing secondary transmissions of primary broadcast transmitters, the system shall not include subscribers and amounts collected from subscribers receiving secondary transmissions for private home viewing pursuant to section 119. Such statement shall also include a special statement of account covering any nonnetwork television programming that was carried by the cable system in whole or in part beyond the local service area of the primary transmitter, under rules, regulations, or authorizations of the Federal Communications Commission permitting the substitution or addition of signals under certain circumstances, together with logs showing the times, dates, stations, and programs involved in such substituted or added carriage; and

(B) except in the case of a cable system whose royalty is specified in subclause (C) or (D), a total royalty fee for the period covered by the statement, computed on the basis of specified percentages of the gross receipts from subscribers to the cable service during said period for the basic service of providing secondary transmissions of primary broadcast transmitters, as follows:

(i) 0.675 of 1 per centum of such gross receipts for the privilege of further transmitting any nonnetwork programming of a primary transmitter in whole or in part beyond the local service area of such primary transmitter, such amount to be applied against the fee, if any, payable pursuant to paragraphs (ii) through (iv);

(ii) 0.675 of 1 per centum of such gross receipts for the first distant signal equivalent;

(iii) 0.425 of 1 per centum of such gross receipts for each of the second, third, and fourth distant signal equivalents;

(iv) 0.2 of 1 per centum of such gross receipts for the fifth distant signal equivalent and each additional distant signal equivalent thereafter; and

in computing the amounts payable under paragraphs (ii) through (iv), above, any fraction of a distant signal equivalent shall be computed at its fractional value and, in the case of any cable system located partly within and partly without the local service area of a primary transmitter, gross receipts shall be limited to those gross receipts derived from subscribers located without the local service area of such primary transmitter; and

(C) if the actual gross receipts paid by subscribers to a cable system for the period covered by the statement for the basic service of providing secondary transmissions of primary broadcast transmitters total $80,000 or less, gross receipts of the cable system for the purpose of this subclause shall be computed by subtracting from such actual gross receipts the amount by which $80,000 exceeds such actual gross receipts, except that in no case shall a cable system's gross receipts be reduced to less than $3,000. The royalty fee payable under this subclause shall be 0.5 of 1 per centum, regardless of the number of distant signal equivalents, if any; and

(D) if the actual gross receipts paid by subscribers to a cable system for the period covered by the statement, for the basic service of providing secondary transmissions of primary broadcast transmitters, are more than $80,000 but less than $160,000, the royalty fee payable under this subclause shall be (i) 0.5 of 1 per centum of any gross receipts up to $80,000; and (ii) 1 per centum of any gross receipts in excess of $80,000 but less than $160,000, regardless of the number of distant signal equivalents, if any.

(2) The Register of Copyrights shall receive all fees deposited under this section and, after deducting the reasonable costs incurred by the Copyright Office under this section, shall deposit the balance in the Treasury of the United States, in such manner as the Secretary of the Treasury directs. All funds held by the Secretary of the Treasury shall be invested in interest-bearing United States securities for later distribution with interest by the Copyright Royalty Tribunal as provided by this title. The Register shall submit to the Copyright Royalty Tribunal, on a semiannual basis, a compilation of all statements of account covering the relevant six-month period provided by clause (1) of this subsection.

(3) The royalty fees thus deposited shall, in accordance with the procedures provided by paragraph (4), be distributed to those among the following copyright owners who claim that their works were the subject of secondary transmissions by cable systems during the relevant semiannual period:

(A) any such owner whose work was included in a secondary transmission made by a cable system of a nonnetwork television program in whole or in part beyond the local service area of the primary transmitter; and

(B) any such owner whose work was included in a secondary transmission identified in a special statement of account deposited under clause (1)(A); and

(C) any such owner whose work was included in nonnetwork programming consisting exclusively of aural signals carried by a cable system in whole or in part beyond the local service area of the primary transmitter of such programs.

(4) The royalty fees thus deposited shall be distributed in accordance with the following procedures:

(A) During the month of July in each year, every person claiming to be entitled to compulsory license fees for secondary transmissions shall file a claim with the Copyright Royalty Tribunal, in accordance with requirements that the Tribunal shall prescribe by regulation. Notwithstanding any provisions of the antitrust laws, for purposes of this clause any claimants may agree among themselves as to the proportionate division of compulsory licensing fees among them, may lump their claims together and file them jointly or as a single claim, or may designate a common agent to receive payment on their behalf.

(B) After the first day of August of each year, the Copyright Royalty Tribunal shall determine whether there exists a controversy concerning the distribution of royalty fees. If the Tribunal determines that no such controversy exists, it shall, after deducting its reasonable administrative costs under this section, distribute such fees to the copyright owners entitled, or to their designated agents. If the Tribunal finds the existence of a controversy, it shall, pursuant to chapter 8 of this title, conduct a proceeding to determine the distribution of royalty fees.

(C) During the pendency of any proceeding under this subsection, the Copyright Royalty Tribunal shall withhold from distribution an amount sufficient to satisfy all claims with respect to which a controversy exists, but shall have discretion to proceed to distribute any amounts that are not in controversy.

(e) NONSIMULTANEOUS SECONDARY TRANSMISSIONS BY CABLE SYSTEMS.—

(1) Notwithstanding those provisions of the second paragraph of subsection (f) relating to nonsimultaneous secondary transmissions by a cable system, any such transmissions are actionable as an act of infringement under section 501, and are fully subject to the remedies provided by sections 502 through 506 and sections 509 and 510, unless—

(A) the program on the videotape is transmitted no more than one time to the cable system's subscribers; and

(B) the copyrighted program, episode, or motion picture videotape, including the commercials contained within such program, episode, or picture, is transmitted without deletion or editing; and

(C) an owner or officer of the cable system (i) prevents the duplication of the videotape while in the possession of the system, (ii) prevents unauthorized duplication while in the possession of the facility making the videotape for the system if the system owns or controls the facility, or takes reasonable precautions to prevent such duplication if it does not own or control the facility, (iii) takes adequate precautions to prevent duplication while the tape is being transported, and (iv) subject to clause (2), erases or destroys, or causes the erasure or destruction of, the videotape; and

(D) within forty-five days after the end of each calendar quarter, an owner or officer of the cable system executes an affidavit attesting (i) to the steps and precautions taken to prevent duplication of the videotape, and (ii) subject to clause (2), to the erasure or destruction of all videotapes made or used during such quarter; and

(E) such owner or officer places or causes each such affidavit, and affidavits received pursuant to clause (2)(C), to be placed in a file, open to public inspection, at such system's main office in the community where the transmission is made or in the nearest community where such system maintains an office; and

(F) the nonsimultaneous transmission is one that the cable system would be authorized to transmit under the rules, regulations, and authorizations of the Federal Communications Commission in effect at the time of the nonsimultaneous transmission if the transmission had been made simultaneously, except that this subclause shall not apply to inadvertent or accidental transmissions.

(2) If a cable system transfers to any person a videotape of a program nonsimultaneously transmitted by it, such transfer is actionable as an act of infringement under section 501, and is fully subject to the remedies provided by sections 502 through 506 and 509, except that, pursuant to a written, nonprofit contract providing for the equitable sharing of the costs of such videotape and its transfer, a videotape nonsimultaneously transmitted by

in accordance with clause (1), may be transferred by one cable system in Alaska to another system in Alaska, by one cable system in Hawaii permitted to make such nonsimultaneous transmissions to another such cable system in Hawaii, or by one cable system in Guam, the Northern Mariana Islands, or the Trust Territory of the Pacific Islands, to another cable system in any of those three territories, if—

(A) each such contract is available for public inspection in the offices of the cable systems involved, and a copy of such contract is filed, within thirty days after such contract is entered into, with the Copyright Office (which Office shall make each such contract available for public inspection); and

(B) the cable system to which the videotape is transferred complies with clause (1)(A), (B), (C)(i), (iii), and (iv), and (D) through (F); and

(C) such system provides a copy of the affidavit required to be made in accordance with clause (1)(D) to each cable system making a previous nonsimultaneous transmission of the same videotape.

(3) This subsection shall not be construed to supersede the exclusivity protection provisions of any existing agreement, or any such agreement hereafter entered into, between a cable system and a television broadcast station in the area in which the cable system is located, or a network with which such station is affiliated.

(4) As used in this subsection, the term "videotape", and each of its variant forms, means the reproduction of the images and sounds of a program or programs broadcast by a television broadcast station licensed by the Federal Communications Commission, regardless of the nature of the material objects, such as tapes or films, in which the reproduction is embodied.

(f) DEFINITIONS.—As used in this section, the following terms and their variant forms mean the following:

A "primary transmission" is a transmission made to the public by the transmitting facility whose signals are being received and further transmitted by the secondary transmission service, regardless of where or when the performance or display was first transmitted.

A "secondary transmission" is the further transmitting of a primary transmission simultaneously with the primary transmission, or nonsimultaneously with the primary transmission if by a "cable system" not located in whole or in part within the boundary of the forty-eight contiguous States, Hawaii, or Puerto Rico: *Provided, however,* That a nonsimultaneous further transmission by a cable system located in Hawaii of a primary transmission shall be deemed to be a secondary transmission if the carriage of the television broadcast signal comprising such further transmission is permissible under the rules, regulations, or authorizations of the Federal Communications Commission.

A "cable system" is a facility, located in any State, Territory, Trust Territory, or Possession, that in whole or in part receives signals transmitted or programs broadcast by one or more television broadcast stations licensed by the Federal Communications Commission, and makes secondary transmissions of such signals or programs by wires, cables, or other communications channels to subscribing members of the public who pay for such service. For purposes of determining the royalty fee under subsection (d)(1), two or more cable systems in contiguous communities under common ownership or control or operating from one headend shall be considered as one system.

The "local service area of a primary transmitter", in the case of a television broadcast station, comprises the area in which such station is entitled to insist upon its signal being retransmitted by a cable system pursuant to the rules, regulations, and authorizations of the Federal Communications Commission in effect on April 15, 1976, or in the case of a television broadcast station licensed by an appropriate governmental authority of Canada or Mexico, the area in which it would be entitled to insist upon its signal being retransmitted if it were a television broadcast station subject to such rules, regulations, and authorizations. In the case of a low power television station, as defined by the rules and regulations of the Federal Communications Commission, the "local service area of a primary transmitter" comprises the area within 35 miles of the transmitter site, except that in the case of such a station located in a standard metropolitan statistical area which has one of the 50 largest populations of all standard metropolitan statistical areas (based on the 1980 decennial census of population taken by the Secretary of Commerce), the number of miles shall be 20 miles. The "local service area of a primary transmitter", in the case of a radio broadcast station, comprises the primary service area of such station, pursuant to the rules and regulations of the Federal Communications Commission.

A "distant signal equivalent" is the value assigned to the secondary transmission of any nonnetwork television programming carried by a cable system in whole or in part beyond the local service area of the primary transmitter of such programing. It is computed by assigning a value of one to each independent station and a value of one-quarter to each network station and noncommercial educational station for the nonnetwork programing so carried pursuant to the rules, regulations, and authorizations of the Federal Communications Commission. The foregoing values for independent, network, and noncommercial educational stations are subject, however, to the following exceptions and limitations. Where the rules and regulations of the Federal Communications Commission require a cable system to omit the further transmission of a particular program and such rules and regulations also permit the substitution of another program embodying a performance or display of a work in place of the omitted transmission, or where such rules and regulations in effect on the date of enactment of this Act permit a cable system, at its election, to effect such deletion and substitution of a nonlive program or to carry additional programs not transmitted by primary transmitters within whose local service area the cable system is located, no value shall be assigned for the substituted or additional program; where the rules, regulations, or authorizations of the Federal Communications Commission in effect on the date of enactment of this Act permit a cable system, at its election, to omit the further transmission of a particular program and such rules, regulations, or authorizations also permit the substitution of another program embodying a performance or display of a work in place of the omitted transmission, the value assigned for the substituted or additional program shall be, in the case of a live program, the value of one full distant signal equivalent multiplied by a fraction that has as its numerator the number of days in the year in which such substitution occurs and as its denominator the number of days in the year. In the case of a station carried pursuant to the late-night or specialty programming rules of the Federal Communications Commission, or a station carried on a part-time basis where full-time carriage is not possible because the cable system lacks the activated channel capacity to retransmit on a full-time basis all signals which it is authorized to carry, the values for independent, network, and noncommercial educational stations set forth above, as the case may be, shall be multiplied by a fraction which is equal to the ratio of the broadcast hours of such station carried by the cable system to the total broadcast hours of the station.

A "network station" is a television broadcast station that is owned or operated by, or affiliated with, one or more of the television networks in the United States providing nationwide transmissions, and that transmits a substantial part of the programing supplied by such networks for a substantial part of that station's typical broadcast day.

An "independent station" is a commercial television broadcast station other than a network station.

A "noncommercial educational station" is a television station that is a noncommercial educational broadcast station as defined in section 397 of title 47.

§ 118. Scope of exclusive rights: Use of certain works in connection with noncommercial broadcasting

(a) The exclusive rights provided by section 106 shall, with respect to the works specified by subsection (b) and the activities specified by subsection (d), be subject to the conditions and limitations prescribed by this section.

(b) Not later than thirty days after the Copyright Royalty Tribunal has been constituted in accordance with section 802, the Chairman of the Tribunal shall cause notice to be published in the Federal Register of the initiation of proceedings for the purpose of determining reasonable terms and rates of royalty payments for the activities specified by subsection (d) with respect to published nondramatic musical works and published pictorial, graphic, and sculptural works during a period beginning as provided in clause (3) of this subsection and ending on December 31, 1982. Copyright owners and public broadcasting entitles shall negotiate in good faith and cooperate fully with the Tribunal in an effort to reach reasonable and expeditious results. Notwithstanding any provision of the antitrust laws, any owners of copyright in works specified by this subsection and any public broadcasting entities, respectively, may negotiate and agree upon the terms and rates of royalty payments and the proportionate division of fees paid among various copyright owners, and may designate common agents to negotiate, agree to, pay, or receive payments.

(1) Any owner of copyright in a work specified in this subsection or any public broadcasting entity may, within one hundred and twenty days after publication of the notice specified in this subsection, submit to the Copyright Royalty Tribunal proposed licenses covering such activities with respect to such works. The Copyright Royalty Tribunal shall proceed on the basis of the proposals submitted to it as well as any other relevant information. The Copyright Royalty Tribunal shall permit any interested party to submit information relevant to such proceedings.

(2) License agreements, voluntarily negotiated at any time between one or more copyright owners and one or more public broadcasting entities shall be given effect in lieu of any determination by the Tribunal: *Provided,* That copies of such agreements are filed in the Copyright Office within thirty days of execution in accordance with regulations that the Register of Copyrights shall prescribe.

(3) Within six months, but not earlier than one hundred and twenty days, from the date of publication of the notice specified in this subsection of Copyright Royalty Tribunal shall make a determination and publish in the Federal Register a schedule of rates and terms which, subject to clause (2) of this subsection, shall be binding on all owners of copyright in works specified by this subsection and public broadcasting entities, regardless of whether or not such copyright owners and public broadcasting entities have submitted proposals to the Tribunal. In establishing such rates and terms the Copyright Royalty Tribunal may consider the rates for comparable circumstances under voluntary license agreements negotiated as provided in clause (2) of this subsection. The Copyright Royalty Tribunal shall also establish requirements by which copyright owners may receive reasonable notice of the use of their works under this section, and under which records of such use shall be kept by public broadcasting entities.

(4) With respect to the period beginning on the effective date of this title and ending on the date of publication of such rates and terms, this title shall not afford to owners of copyright or public broadcasting entities any greater or lesser rights with respect to the activities specified in subsection (d) as applied to works specified in this subsection than those afforded under the law in effect on December 31, 1977, as held applicable and construed by a court in an action brought under this title.

(c) The initial procedure specified in subsection (b) shall be repeated and concluded between June 30 and December 31, 1982, and at five-year intervals thereafter, in accordance with regulations that the Copyright Royalty Tribunal shall prescribe.

(d) Subject to the transitional provisions of subsection (b)(4), and to the terms of any voluntary license agreements that have been negotiated as provided by subsection (b)(2), a public broadcasting entity may, upon compliance with the provisions of this section, including the rates and terms established by the Copyright Royalty Tribunal under subsection (b)(3), engage in the following activities with respect to published nondramatic musical works and published pictorial, graphic, and sculptural works:

(1) performance or display of a work by or in the course of a transmission made by a noncommercial educational broadcast station referred to in subsection (g); and

(2) production of a transmission program, reproduction of copies or phonorecords of such a transmission program, and distribution of such copies or phonorecords, where such production, reproduction, or distribution is made by a nonprofit institution or organization solely for the purpose of transmissions specified in clause (1); and

(3) the making of reproductions by a governmental body or a nonprofit institution of a transmission program simultaneously with its transmission as specified in clause (1), and the performance or display of the contents of such program under the conditions specified by clause (1) of section 110, but only if the reproductions are used for performances or displays

for a period of no more than seven days from the date of the transmission specified in clause (1), and are destroyed before or at the end of such period. No person supplying, in accordance with clause (2), a reproduction of a transmission program to governmental bodies or nonprofit institutions under this clause shall have any liability as a result of failure of such body or institution to destroy such reproduction: *Provided*, That it shall have notified such body or institution of the requirement for such destruction pursuant to this clause: *And provided further*, That if such body or institution itself fails to destroy such reproduction it shall be deemed to have infringed.

(e) Except as expressly provided in this subsection, this section shall have no applicability to works other than those specified in subsection (b).

(1) Owners of copyright in nondramatic literary works and public broadcasting entities may, during the course of voluntary negotiations, agree among themselves, respectively, as to the terms and rates of royalty payments without liability under the antitrust laws. Any such terms and rates of royalty payments shall be effective upon filing in the Copyright Office, in accordance with regulations that the Register of Copyrights shall prescribe.

(2) On January 3, 1980, the Register of Copyrights, after consulting with authors and other owners of copyright in nondramatic literary works and their representatives, and with public broadcasting entities and their representatives, shall submit to the Congress a report setting forth the extent to which voluntary licensing arrangements have been reached with respect to the use of nondramatic literary works by such broadcast stations. The report should also describe any problems that may have arisen, and present legislative or other recommendations, if warranted.

(f) Nothing in this section shall be construed to permit, beyond the limits of fair use as provided by section 107, the unauthorized dramatization of a nondramatic musical work, the production of a transmission program drawn to any substantial extent from a published compilation of pictorial, graphic, or sculptural works, or the unauthorized use of any portion of an audiovisual work.

(g) As used in this section, the term "public broadcasting entity" means a noncommercial educational broadcast station as defined in section 397 of title 47 and any nonprofit institution or organization engaged in the activities described in clause (2) of subsection (d).

§ 119. Limitations on exclusive rights: Secondary transmissions of superstations and network stations for private home viewing

[Note: Unless extended, this section will cease to be effective December 31, 1994.]

(a) SECONDARY TRANSMISSIONS BY SATELLITE CARRIERS.—

(1) SUPERSTATIONS.—Subject to the provisions of paragraphs (3), (4), and (6) of this subsection, secondary transmissions of a primary transmission made by a superstation and embodying a performance or display of a work shall be subject to statutory licensing under this section if the secondary transmission is made by a satellite carrier to the public for private home viewing, and the carrier makes a direct or indirect charge for each retransmission service to each household receiving the secondary transmission or to a distributor that has contracted with the carrier for direct or indirect delivery of the secondary transmission to the public for private home viewing.

(2) NETWORK STATIONS.—

(A) IN GENERAL.—Subject to the provisions of subparagraphs (B) and (C) of this paragraph and paragraphs (3), (4), (5), and (6) of this subsection, secondary transmissions of programming contained in a primary transmission made by a network station and embodying a performance or display of a work shall be subject to statutory licensing under this section if the secondary transmission is made by a satellite carrier to the public for private home viewing, and the carrier makes a direct or indirect charge for such retransmission service to each subscriber receiving the secondary transmission.

(B) SECONDARY TRANSMISSIONS TO UNSERVED HOUSEHOLDS.—The statutory license provided for in subparagraph (A) shall be limited to secondary transmissions to persons who reside in unserved households.

(C) SUBMISSION OF SUBSCRIBER LISTS TO NETWORKS.—A satellite carrier that makes secondary transmissions of a primary transmission made by a network station pursuant to subparagraph (A) shall, 90 days after the effective date of the Satellite Home Viewer Act of 1988, or 90 days after commencing such secondary transmissions, whichever is later, submit to the network that owns or is affiliated with the network station a list identifying (by street address, including county and zip code) all subscribers to which the satellite carrier currently makes secondary transmissions of that primary transmission. Thereafter, on the 15th of each month, the satellite carrier shall submit to the network a list identifying (by street address, including county and zip code) any persons who have been added or dropped as such subscribers since the last submission under this subparagraph. Such subscriber information submitted by a satellite carrier may be used only for purposes of monitoring compliance by the satellite carrier with this subsection. The submission requirements of this subparagraph shall apply to a satellite carrier only if the network to whom the submissions are to be made places on file with the Register of Copyrights, on or after the effective date of the Satellite Home Viewer Act of 1988, a document identifying the name and address of the person to whom such submissions are to be made. The Register shall maintain for public inspection a file of all such documents.

(3) NONCOMPLIANCE WITH REPORTING AND PAYMENT REQUIREMENTS.—Notwithstanding the provisions of paragraphs (1) and (2), the willful or repeated secondary transmission to the public by a satellite carrier of a primary transmission made by a superstation or a network station and embodying a performance or display of a work is actionable as an act of infringement under section 501, and is fully subject to the remedies provided by sections 502 through 506 and 509, where the satellite carrier has not deposited the statement of account and royalty fee required by subsection (b), or has failed to make the submissions to networks required by paragraph (2)(C).

(4) WILLFUL ALTERATIONS.—Notwithstanding the provisions of paragraphs (1) and (2), the secondary transmission to the public by a satellite carrier of a primary transmission made by a superstation or a network station and embodying a performance or display of a work is actionable as an act of infringement under section 501, and is fully subject to the remedies provided by sections 502 through 506 and sections 509 and 510, if the content of the particular program in which the performance or display is embodied, or any commercial advertising or station announcement transmitted by the primary transmitter during, or immediately before or after, the transmission of such program, is in any way willfully altered by the satellite carrier through changes, deletions, or additions, or is combined with programming from any other broadcast signal.

(5) VIOLATION OF TERRITORIAL RESTRICTIONS ON STATUTORY LICENSE FOR NETWORK STATIONS.—

(A) INDIVIDUAL VIOLATIONS.—The willful or repeated secondary transmission by a satellite carrier of a primary transmission made by a network station and embodying a performance or display of a work to a subscriber who does not reside in an unserved household is actionable as an act of infringement under section 501 and is fully subject to the remedies provided by sections 502 through 506 and 509, except that—

(i) no damages shall be awarded for such act of infringement if the satellite carrier took corrective action by promptly withdrawing service from the ineligible subscriber, and

(ii) any statutory damages shall not exceed $5 for such subscriber for each month during which the violation occurred.

(B) PATTERN OF VIOLATIONS.—If a satellite carrier engages in a willful or repeated pattern or practice of delivering a primary transmission made by a network station and embodying a performance or display of a work to subscribers who do not reside in unserved households, then in addition to the remedies set forth in subparagraph (A)—

(i) if the pattern or practice has been carried out on a substantially nationwide basis, the court shall order a permanent injunction barring the secondary transmission by the satellite carrier, for private home viewing, of the primary transmissions of any primary network station affiliated with the same network, and the court may order statutory damages of not to exceed $250,000 for each 6-month period during which the pattern or practice was carried out; and

(ii) if the pattern or practice has been carried out on a local or regional basis, the court shall order a permanent injunction barring the secondary transmission, for private home viewing in that locality or region, by the satellite carrier of the primary transmissions of any primary network station affiliated with the same network, and the court may order statutory damages of not to exceed $250,000 for each 6-month period during which the pattern or practice was carried out.

(C) PREVIOUS SUBSCRIBERS EXCLUDED.—Subparagraphs (A) and (B) do not apply to secondary transmissions by a satellite carrier to persons who subscribed to receive such secondary transmissions from the satellite carrier or a distributor before the date of the enactment of the Satellite Home Viewer Act of 1988.

(6) DISCRIMINATION BY A SATELLITE CARRIER.—Notwithstanding the provisions of paragraph (1), the willful or repeated secondary transmission to the public by a satellite carrier of a primary transmission made by a superstation or a network station and embodying a performance or display of a work is actionable as an act of infringement under section 501, and is fully subject to the remedies provided by sections 502 through 506 and 509, if the satellite carrier unlawfully discriminates against a distributor.

(7) GEOGRAPHIC LIMITATION ON SECONDARY TRANSMISSIONS.—The statutory license created by this section shall apply only to secondary transmissions to households located in the United States.

(b) STATUTORY LICENSE FOR SECONDARY TRANSMISSIONS FOR PRIVATE HOME VIEWING.—

(1) DEPOSITS WITH THE REGISTER OF COPYRIGHTS.—A satellite carrier whose secondary transmissions are subject to statutory licensing under subsection (a) shall, on a semiannual basis, deposit with the Register of Copyrights, in accordance with requirements that the Register shall, after consultation with the Copyright Royalty Tribunal, prescribe by regulation—

(A) a statement of account, covering the preceding 6-month period, specifying the names and locations of all superstations and network stations whose signals were transmitted, at any time during that period, to subscribers for private home viewing as described in subsections (a)(1) and (a)(2), the total number of subscribers that received such transmissions, and such other data as the Register of Copyrights may, after consultation with the Copyright Royalty Tribunal, from time to time prescribe by regulation; and

(B) a royalty fee for that 6-month period, computed by—

(i) multiplying the total number of subscribers receiving each secondary transmission of a superstation during each calendar month by 12 cents;

(ii) multiplying the number of subscribers receiving each secondary transmission of a network station during each calendar month by 3 cents; and

(iii) adding together the totals computed under clauses (i) and (ii).

(2) INVESTMENT OF FEES.—The Register of Copyrights shall receive all fees deposited under this section and, after deducting the reasonable costs incurred by the Copyright Office under this section (other than the costs deducted under paragraph (4)), shall deposit the balance in the Treasury of the United States, in such manner as the Secretary of the Treasury directs. All funds held by the Secretary of the Treasury shall be invested in interest-bearing securities of the United States for later distribution with interest by the Copyright Royalty Tribunal as provided by this title.

(3) PERSONS TO WHOM FEES ARE DISTRIBUTED.—The royalty fees deposited under paragraph (2) shall, in accordance with the procedures provided by paragraph (4), be distributed to those copyright owners whose works were included in a secondary transmission for private home viewing made by a satellite carrier during the applicable 6-month accounting period and who file a claim with the Copyright Royalty Tribunal under paragraph (4).

(4) PROCEDURES FOR DISTRIBUTION.—The royalty fees deposited under paragraph (2) shall be distributed in accordance with the following procedures:

(A) FILING OF CLAIMS FOR FEES.—During the month of July in each year, each person claiming to be entitled to statutory license fees for secondary transmissions for private home viewing shall file a claim with the Copyright Royalty Tribunal, in accordance with requirements that the Tribunal shall prescribe by regulation. For purposes of this paragraph, any claimants may agree among themselves as to the proportionate division of statutory license fees among them, may lump their claims together and file them jointly or as a single claim, or may designate a common agent to receive payment on their behalf.

(B) DETERMINATION OF CONTROVERSY; DISTRIBUTIONS.—After the first day of August of each year, the Copyright Royalty Tribunal shall determine whether there exists a controversy concerning the distribution of royalty fees. If the Tribunal determines that no such controversy exists, the Tribunal shall, after deducting reasonable administrative costs under this paragraph, distribute such fees to the copyright owners entitled to receive them, or to their designated agents. If the Tribunal finds the existence of a controversy, the Tribunal shall, pursuant to chapter 8 of this title, conduct a proceeding to determine the distribution of royalty fees.

(C) WITHHOLDING OF FEES DURING CONTROVERSY.—During the pendency of any proceeding under this subsection, the Copyright Royalty Tribunal shall withhold from distribution an amount sufficient to satisfy all claims with respect to which a controversy exists, but shall have discretion to proceed to distribute any amounts that are not in controversy.

(c) DETERMINATION OF ROYALTY FEES.—

(1) APPLICABILITY AND DETERMINATION OF ROYALTY FEES.—The rate of the royalty fee payable under subsection (b)(1)(B) shall be effective until December 31, 1992, unless a royalty fee is established under paragraph (2), (3), (4) of this subsection. After that date, the fee shall be determined either in accordance with the voluntary negotiation procedure specified in paragraph (2) or in accordance with the compulsory arbitration procedure specified in paragraphs (3) and (4).

(2) FEE SET BY VOLUNTARY NEGOTIATION.—

(A) NOTICE OF INITIATION OF PROCEEDINGS.—On or before July 1, 1991, the Copyright Royalty Tribunal shall cause notice to be published in the Federal Register of the initiation of voluntary negotiation proceedings for the purpose of determining the royalty fee to be paid by satellite carriers under subsection (b)(1)(B).

(B) NEGOTIATIONS.—Satellite carriers, distributors, and copyright owners entitled to royalty fees under this section shall negotiate in good faith in an effort to reach a voluntary agreement or voluntary agreements for the payment of royalty fees. Any such satellite carriers, distributors, and copyright owners may at any time negotiate and agree to the royalty fee, and may designate common agents to negotiate, agree to, or pay such fees. If the parties fail to identify common agents, the Copyright Royalty Tribunal shall do so, after requesting recommendations from the parties to the negotiation proceeding. The parties to each negotiation proceeding shall bear the entire cost thereof.

(C) AGREEMENTS BINDING ON PARTIES; FILING OF AGREEMENTS.—Voluntary agreements negotiated at any time in accordance with this paragraph shall be binding upon all satellite carriers, distributors, and copyright owners that are parties thereto. Copies of such agreements shall be filed with the Copyright Office within 30 days after execution in accordance with regulations that the Register of Copyrights shall prescribe.

(D) PERIOD AGREEMENT IS IN EFFECT.—The obligation to pay the royalty fees established under a voluntary agreement which has been filed with the Copyright Office in accordance with this paragraph shall become effective on the date specified in the agreement, and shall remain in effect until December 31, 1994.

(3) FEE SET BY COMPULSORY ARBITRATION.—

(A) NOTICE OF INITIATION OF PROCEEDINGS.—On or before December 31, 1991, the Copyright Royalty Tribunal shall cause notice to be published in the Federal Register of the initiation of arbitration proceedings for the purpose of determining a reasonable royalty fee to be paid under subsection (b)(1)(B) by satellite carriers who are not parties to a voluntary agreement filed with the Copyright Office in accordance with paragraph (2). Such notice shall include the names and qualifications of potential arbitrators chosen by the Tribunal from a list of available arbitrators obtained from the American Arbitration Association or such similar organization as the Tribunal shall select.

(B) SELECTION OF ARBITRATION PANEL.—Not later than 10 days after publication of the notice initiating an arbitration proceeding, and in accordance with procedures to be specified by the Copyright Royalty Tribunal, one arbitrator shall be selected from the published list by copyright owners who claim to be entitled to royalty fees under subsection (b)(4) and who are not party to a voluntary agreement filed with the Copyright Office in accordance with paragraph (2), and one arbitrator shall be selected from the published list by satellite carriers and distributors who are not parties to such a voluntary agreement. The two arbitrators so selected shall, within 10 days after their selection, choose a third arbitrator from the same list, who shall serve as chairperson of the arbitrators. If either group fail to agree upon the selection of an arbitrator, or if the arbitrators selected by such groups fail to agree upon the selection of a chairperson, the Copyright Royalty Tribunal shall promptly select the arbitrator or chairperson, respectively. The arbitrators selected under this subparagraph shall constitute an Arbitration Panel.

(C) ARBITRATION PROCEEDING.—The Arbitration Panel shall conduct an arbitration proceeding in accordance with such procedures as it may adopt. The Panel shall act on the basis of a fully documented written record. Any copyright owner who claims to be entitled to royalty fees under subsection (b)(4), any satellite carrier, and any distributor, who is not party to a voluntary agreement filed with the Copyright Office in accordance with paragraph (2), may submit relevant information and proposals to the Panel. The parties to the proceeding shall bear the entire cost thereof in such manner and proportion as the Panel shall direct.

(D) FACTORS FOR DETERMINING ROYALTY FEES.—In determining royalty fees under this paragraph, the Arbitration Panel shall consider the approximate average cost to a cable system for the right to secondarily transmit to the public a primary transmission by a broadcast station, the fee established under any voluntary agreement filed with the Copyright Office in accordance with paragraph (2), and the last fee proposed by the parties, before proceedings under this paragraph, for the secondary transmission of superstations or network stations for private home viewing. The fee shall also be calculated to achieve the following objectives:

(i) To maximize the availability of creative works to the public.

(ii) To afford the copyright owner a fair return for his or her creative work and the copyright user a fair income under existing economic conditions.

(iii) To reflect the relative roles of the copyright owner and the copyright user in the product made available to the public with respect to relative creative contribution, technological contribution, capital investment, cost, risk, and contribution to the opening of new markets for creative expression and media for their communication.

(iv) To minimize any disruptive impact on the structure of the industries involved and on generally prevailing industry practices.

(E) REPORT TO COPYRIGHT ROYALTY TRIBUNAL.—Not later than 60 days after publication of the notice initiating an arbitration proceeding, the Arbitration Panel shall report to the Copyright Royalty Tribunal its determination concerning the royalty fee. Such report shall be accompanied by the written record, and shall set forth the facts that the Panel found relevant to its determination and the reasons why its determination is consistent with the criteria set forth in subparagraph (D).

(F) ACTION BY COPYRIGHT ROYALTY TRIBUNAL.—Within 60 days after receiving the report of the Arbitration Panel under subparagraph (E), the Copyright Royalty Tribunal shall adopt or reject the determination of the Panel. The Tribunal shall adopt the determination of the Panel unless the Tribunal finds that the determination is clearly inconsistent with the criteria set forth in subparagraph (D). If the Tribunal rejects the determination of the Panel, the Tribunal shall, before the end of that 60-day period, and after full examination of the record created in the arbitration proceeding, issue an order, consistent with the criteria set forth in subparagraph (D), setting the royalty fee under this paragraph. The Tribunal shall cause to be published in the Federal Register the determination of the Panel, and the decision of the Tribunal with respect to the determination (including any order issued under the preceding sentence). The Tribunal shall also publicize such determination and decision in such other manner as the Tribunal considers appropriate. The Tribunal shall also make the report of the Arbitration Panel and the accompanying record available for public inspection and copying.

(G) PERIOD DURING WHICH DECISION OF PANEL OR ORDER OF TRIBUNAL EFFECTIVE.—The obligation to pay the royalty fee established under a determination of the Arbitration Panel which is confirmed by the Copyright Royalty Tribunal in accordance with this paragraph, or established by any order issued under subparagraph (F), shall become effective on the date when the decision of the Tribunal is published in the Federal Register under subparagraph (F), and shall remain in effect until modified in accordance with paragraph (4), or until December 3, 1994.

(H) PERSONS SUBJECT TO ROYALTY FEE.—The royalty fee adopted or ordered under subparagraph (F) shall be binding on all satellite carriers, distributors, and copyright owners, who are not party to a voluntary agreement filed with the Copyright Office under paragraph (2).

(4) JUDICIAL REVIEW.—Any decision of the Copyright Royalty Tribunal under paragraph (3) with respect to a determination of the Arbitration Panel may be appealed, by any aggrieved party who would be bound by the determination, to the United States Court of Appeals for the District of Columbia Circuit, within 30 days after the publication of the decision in the Federal Register. The pendency of an appeal under this paragraph shall not relieve satellite carriers of the obligation under subsection (b)(1) to deposit the statement of account and royalty fees specified in that subsection. The court shall have jurisdiction to modify or vacate a decision of the Tribunal only if it finds, on the basis of the record before the Tribunal and the statutory criteria set forth in paragraph (3)(D), that the Arbitration Panel or the Tribunal acted in an arbitrary manner. If the court modifies the decision of the Tribunal, the court shall have jurisdiction to enter its own determination with respect to royalty fees, to order the repayment of any excess fees deposited under subsection (b)(1)(B), and to order the payment of any underpaid fees, and the interest pertaining respectively thereto, in accordance with its final judgment. The court may further vacate the decision of the Tribunal and remand the case for arbitration proceedings in accordance with paragraph (3).

(d) DEFINITIONS.—As used in this section—

(1) DISTRIBUTOR.—The term "distributor" means an entity which contracts to distribute secondary transmissions from a satellite carrier and, either as a single channel or in a package with other programming, provides the secondary transmission either directly to individual subscribers for private home viewing or indirectly through other program distribution entities.

(2) NETWORK STATION.—The term "network station" has the meaning given that term in section 111(f) of this title, and includes any translator station or terrestrial satellite station that rebroadcasts all or substantially all of the programming broadcast by a network station.

(3) PRIMARY NETWORK STATION.—The term "primary network station" means a network station that broadcasts or rebroadcasts the basic programming service of a particular national network.

(4) PRIMARY TRANSMISSION.—The term "primary transmission" has the meaning given that term in section 111(f) of this title.

(5) PRIVATE HOME VIEWING.—The term "private home viewing" means the viewing, for private use in a household by means of satellite reception equipment which is operated by an individual in that household and which serves only such household, of a secondary transmission delivered by a satellite carrier of a primary transmission of a television station licensed by the Federal Communications Commission.

(6) SATELLITE CARRIER.—The term "satellite carrier" means an entity that uses the facilities of a satellite or satellite service licensed by the Federal Communications Commission, to establish and operate a channel of communications for point-to-multipoint distribution of television station signals, and that owns or leases a capacity or service on a satellite in order to provide such point-to-multipoint distribution, except to the extent that such entity provides such distribution pursuant to tariff under the Communications Act of 1934, other than for private home viewing.

(7) SECONDARY TRANSMISSION.—The term "secondary transmission" has the meaning given that term in section 111(f) of this title.

(8) SUBSCRIBER.—The term "subscriber" means an individual who receives a secondary transmission service for private home viewing by means of a secondary transmission from a satellite carrier and pays a fee for the service, directly or indirectly, to the satellite carrier or to a distributor.

(9) SUPERSTATION.—The term "superstation" means a television broadcast station, other than a network station, licensed by the Federal Communications Commission that is secondarily transmitted by a satellite carrier.

(10) UNSERVED HOUSEHOLD.—The term "unserved household", with respect to a particular television network, means a household that—

(A) cannot receive, through the use of a conventional outdoor rooftop receiving antenna, an over-the-air signal of grade B intensity (as defined by the Federal Communications Commission) of a primary network station affiliated with that network, and

(B) has not, within 90 days before the date on which that household subscribes, either initially or on renewal, to receive secondary transmissions by a satellite carrier of a network station affiliated with that network, subscribed to a cable system that provides the signal of a primary network station affiliated with that network.

(e) EXCLUSIVITY OF THIS SECTION WITH RESPECT TO SECONDARY TRANSMISSIONS OF BROADCAST STATIONS BY SATELLITE TO MEMBERS OF THE PUBLIC.—No provision of section 111 of this title or any other law (other than this section) shall be construed to contain any authorization, exemption, or license through which secondary transmissions by satellite carrier for private home viewing of programming contained in a primary transmission made by a superstation or a network station may be made without obtaining the consent of the copyright owner.

CHAPTER 2—COPYRIGHT OWNERSHIP AND TRANSFER

§ 201. Ownership of copyright

(a) INITIAL OWNERSHIP.—Copyright in a work protected under this title vests initially in the author or authors of the work. The authors of a joint work are coowners of copyright in the work.

(b) WORKS MADE FOR HIRE.—In the case of a work made for hire, the employer or other person for whom the work was prepared is considered the author for purposes of this title, and, unless the parties have expressly agreed otherwise in a written instrument signed by them, owns all of the rights comprised in the copyright.

(c) CONTRIBUTIONS TO COLLECTIVE WORKS.—Copyright in each separate contribution to a collective work is distinct from copyright in the collective work as a whole, and vests initially in the author of the contribution. In the absence of an express transfer of the copyright or of any rights under it, the owner of copyright in the collective work is presumed to have acquired only the privilege of reproducing and distributing the contribution as part of that particular collective work, any revision of that collective work, and later collective work in the same series.

(d) TRANSFER OF OWNERSHIP.—

(1) The ownership of a copyright may be transferred in whole or in part by any means of conveyance or by operation of law, and may be bequeathed by will or pass as personal property by the applicable laws of intestate succession.

(2) Any of the exclusive rights comprised in a copyright, including any subdivision of any of the rights specified by section 106, may be transferred as provided by clause (1) and owned separately. The owner of any particular exclusive right is entitled, to the extent of that right, to all of the protection and remedies accorded to the copyright owner by this title.

(e) INVOLUNTARY TRANSFER.—When an individual author's ownership of a copyright, or of any of the exclusive rights under a copyright, has not previously been transferred voluntarily by that individual author, no action by any governmental body or other official or organization purporting to seize, expropriate, transfer, or exercise rights of ownership with respect to the copyright, or any of the exclusive rights under a copyright, shall be given effect under this title, except as provided under title 11.

§ 202.   Ownership of copyright as distinct from ownership of material object

Ownership of a copyright, or of any of the exclusive rights under a copyright, is distinct from ownership of any material object in which the work is embodied. Transfer of ownership of any material object, including the copy or phonorecord in which the work is first fixed, does not of itself convey any rights in the copyrighted work embodied in the object; nor, in the absence of an agreement, does transfer of ownership of a copyright or of any exclusive rights under a copyright convey property rights in any material object.

§ 203.   Termination of transfers and licenses granted by the author

(a) Conditions for Termination.—In the case of any work other than a work made for hire, the exclusive or nonexclusive grant of a transfer or license of copyright or of any right under a copyright, executed by the author on or after January 1, 1978, otherwise than by will, is subject to termination under the following conditions:

(1) In the case of a grant executed by one author, termination of the grant may be effected by that author or, if the author is dead, by the person or persons who, under clause (2) of this subsection, own or are entitled to exercise a total of more than one-half of that author's termination interest. In the case of a grant executed by two or more authors of a joint work, termination of the grant may be effected by a majority of the authors who executed it; if any of such authors is dead, the termination interest of any such author may be exercised as a unit by the person or persons who, under clause (2) of this subsection, own and are entitled to exercise a total of more than one-half of that author's interest.

(2) Where an author is dead, his or her termination interest is owned, and may be exercised, by his widow or her widower and his or her children or grandchildren as follows:

(A) the widow or widower owns the author's entire termination interest unless there are any surviving children or grandchildren of the author, in which case the widow or widower owns one-half of the author's interest;

(B) the author's surviving children, and the surviving children of any dead child of the author, own the author's entire termination interest unless there is a widow or widower, in which case the ownership of one-half of the author's interest is divided among them;

(C) the rights of the author's children and grandchildren are in all cases divided among them and exercised on a per stirpes basis according to the number of such author's children represented; the share of the children of a dead child in a termination interest can be exercised only by the action of a majority of them.

(3) Termination of the grant may be effected at any time during a period of five years beginning at the end of thirty-five years from the date of execution of the grant; or, if the grant covers the right of publication of the work, the period begins at the end of thirty-five years from the date of publication of the work under the grant or at the end of forty years from the date of execution of the grant, whichever term ends earlier.

(4) The termination shall be effected by serving an advance notice in writing, signed by the number and proportion of owners of termination interests required under clauses (1) and (2) of this subsection, or by their duly authorized agents, upon the grantee or the grantee's successor in title.

(A) The notice shall state the effective date of the termination, which shall fall within the five-year period specified by clause (3) of this subsection, and the notice shall be served not less than two or more than ten years before that date. A copy of the notice shall be recorded in the Copyright Office before the effective date of termination, as a condition to its taking effect.

(B) The notice shall comply, in form, content, and manner of service, with requirements that the Register of Copyrights shall prescribe by regulation.

(5) Termination of the grant may be effected notwithstanding any agreement to the contrary, including an agreement to make a will or to make any future grant.

(b) Effect of Termination.—Upon the effective date of termination, all rights under this title that were covered by the terminated grants revert to the author, authors, and other persons owning termination interests under clauses (1) and (2) of subsection (a), including those owners who did not join in signing the notice of termination under clause (4) of subsection (a), but with the following limitations:

(1) A derivative work prepared under authority of the grant before its termination may continue to be utilized under the terms of the grant after its termination, but this privilege does not extend to the preparation after the termination of other derivative works based upon the copyrighted work covered by the terminated grant.

(2) The future rights that will revert upon termination of the grant become vested on the date the notice of termination has been served as provided by clause (4) of subsection (a). The rights vest in the author, authors, and other persons named in, and in the proportionate shares provided by, clauses (1) and (2) of subsection (a).

(3) Subject to the provisions of clause (4) of this subsection, a further grant, or agreement to make a further grant, of any right covered by a terminated grant is valid only if it is signed by the same number and proportion of the owners, in whom the right has vested under clause (2) of this subsection, as are required to terminate the grant under clauses (1) and (2) of subsection (a). Such further grant or agreement is effective with respect to all of the persons in whom the right it covers has vested under clause (2) of this subsection, including those who did not join in signing it. If any person dies after rights under a terminated grant have vested in him or her, that person's legal representatives, legatees, or heirs at law represent him or her for purposes of this clause.

(4) A further grant, or agreement to make a further grant, of any right covered by a terminated grant is valid only if it is made after the effective date of the termination. As an exception, however, an agreement for such a further grant may be made between the persons provided by clause (3) of this subsection and the original grantee or such grantee's successor in title, after the notice of termination has been served as provided by clause (4) of subsection (a).

(5) Termination of a grant under this section affects only those rights covered by the grants that arise under this title, and in no way affects rights arising under any other Federal, State, or foreign laws.

(6) Unless and until termination is effected under this section, the grant, if it does not provide otherwise, continues in effect for the term of copyright provided by this title.

§ 204. Execution of transfers of copyright ownership

(a) A transfer of copyright ownership, other than by operation of law, is not valid unless an instrument of conveyance, or a note or memorandum of the transfer, is in writing and signed by the owner of the rights conveyed or such owner's duly authorized agent.

(b) A certificate of acknowledgement is not required for the validity of a transfer, but is prima facie evidence of the execution of the transfer if—

(1) in the case of a transfer executed in the United States, the certificate is issued by a person authorized to administer oaths within the United States; or

(2) in the case of a transfer executed in a foreign country, the certificate is issued by a diplomatic or consular officer of the United States, or by a person authorized to administer oaths whose authority is proved by a certificate of such an officer.

§ 205. Recordation of transfers and other documents

(a) CONDITIONS FOR RECORDATION.—Any transfer of copyright ownership or other document pertaining to a copyright may be recorded in the Copyright Office if the document filed for recordation bears the actual signature of the person who executed it, or if it is accompanied by a sworn or official certification that it is a true copy of the original, signed document.

(b) CERTIFICATE OF RECORDATION.—The Register of Copyrights shall, upon receipt of a document as provided by subsection (a) and of the fee provided by section 708, record the document and return it with a certificate of recordation.

(c) RECORDATION AS CONSTRUCTIVE NOTICE.—Recordation of a document in the Copyright Office gives all persons constructive notice of the facts stated in the recorded document, but only if—

(1) the document, or material attached to it, specifically identifies the work to which it pertains so that, after the document is indexed by the Register of Copyrights, it would be revealed by a reasonable search under the title or registration number of the work; and

(2) registration has been made for the work.

(d) PRIORITY BETWEEN CONFLICTING TRANSFERS.—As between two conflicting transfers, the one executed first prevails if it is recorded, in the manner required to give constructive notice under subsection (c), within one month after its execution in the United States or within two months after its execution outside the United States, or at any time before recordation in such manner of the later transfer. Otherwise the later transfer prevails if recorded first in such manner, and if taken in good faith, for valuable consideration or on the basis of a binding promise to pay royalties, and without notice of the earlier transfer.

(e) PRIORITY BETWEEN CONFLICTING TRANSFER OF OWNERSHIP AND NONEXCLUSIVE LICENSE.— A nonexclusive license, whether recorded or not, prevails over a conflicting transfer of copyright ownership if the license is evidenced by a written instrument signed by the owner of the rights licensed or such owner's duly authorized agent, and if—

(1) the license was taken before execution of the transfer; or

(2) the license was taken in good faith before recordation of the transfer and without notice of it.

CHAPTER 3—DURATION OF COPYRIGHT

§ 301. Preemption with respect to other laws

(a) On and after January 1, 1978, all legal or equitable rights that are equivalent to any of the exclusive rights within the general scope of copyright as specified by section 106 in works of authorship that are fixed in a tangible medium of expression and come within the subject matter of copyright as specified by sections 102 and 103, whether created before or after that date and whether published or unpublished, are governed exclusively by this title. Thereafter, no person is entitled to any such right or equivalent right in any such work under the common law or statutes of any State.

(b) Nothing in this title annuls or limits any rights or remedies under the common law or statutes of any State with respect to—

(1) subject matter that does not come within the subject matter of copyright as specified by sections 102 and 103, including works of authorship not fixed in any tangible medium of expression; or

(2) any cause of action arising from undertakings commenced before January 1, 1978; or

(3) activities violating legal or equitable rights that are not equivalent to any of the exclusive rights within the general scope of copyright as specified by section 106.

(c) With respect to sound recordings fixed before February 15, 1972, any rights or remedies under the common law or statutes of any State shall not be annulled or limited by this title until February 15, 2047. The preemptive provisions of subsection (a) shall apply to any such rights and remedies pertaining to any cause of action arising from undertakings commenced on and after February 15, 2047. Notwithstanding the provisions of section 303, no sound recording fixed before February 15, 1972, shall be subject to copyright under this title before, on, or after February 15, 2047.

(d) Nothing in this title annuls or limits any rights or remedies under any other Federal statute.

(e) The scope of Federal preemption under this section is not affected by the adherence of the United States to the Berne Convention or the satisfaction of obligations of the United States thereunder.

(f)(1) On or after the effective date set forth in section 610(a) of the Visual Artists Rights Act of 1990, all legal or equitable rights that are equivalent to any of the rights conferred by section 106A with respect to works of visual art to which the rights conferred by section 106A apply are governed exclusively by section 106A and section 113(d) and the provisions of this title relating to such sections. Thereafter, no person is entitled to any such right or equivalent right in any work of visual art under the common law or statutes of any State.

(2) Nothing in paragraph (1) annuls or limits any rights or remedies under the common law or statutes of any State with respect to—

(A) any cause of action from undertakings commenced before the effective date set forth in section 610(a) of the Visual Artists Rights Act of 1990;

(B) activities violating legal or equitable rights that are not equivalent to any of the rights conferred by section 106A with respect to works of visual art; or

(C) activities violating legal or equitable rights which extend beyond the life of the author.

§ 302. Duration of copyright: Works created on or after January 1, 1978

(a) IN GENERAL.—Copyright in a work created on or after January 1, 1978, subsists from its creation and, except as provided by the following subsections, endures for a term consisting of the life of the author and fifty years after the author's death.

(b) JOINT WORKS.—In the case of a joint work prepared by two or more authors who did not work for hire, the copyright endures for a term consisting of the life of the last surviving author and fifty years after such last surviving author's death.

(c) ANONYMOUS WORKS, PSEUDONYMOUS WORKS, AND WORKS MADE FOR HIRE.—In the case of an anonymous work, a pseudonymous work, or a work made for hire, the copyright endures for a term of seventy-five years from the year of its first publication, or a term of one hundred years from the year of its creation, whichever expires first. If, before the end of such term, the identity of one or more of the authors of an anonymous or pseudonymous work is revealed in the records of a registration made for that work under subsections (a) or (d) of section 408, or in the records provided by this subsection, the copyright in the work endures for the term specified by subsection (a) or (b), based on the life of the author or authors whose identity has been revealed. Any person having an interest in the copyright in an anonymous or pseudonymous work may at any time record, in records to be maintained by the Copyright Office for that purpose, a statement identifying one or more authors of the work; the statement shall also identify the person filing it, the nature of that person's interest, the source of the information recorded, and the particular work affected, and shall comply in form and content with requirements that the Register of Copyrights shall prescribe by regulation.

(d) RECORDS RELATING TO DEATH OF AUTHORS.—Any person having an interest in a copyright may at any time record in the Copyright Office a statement of the date of death of the author of the copyrighted work, or a statement that the author is still living on a particular date. The statement shall identify the person filing it, the nature of that person's interest, and the source of the information recorded, and shall comply in form and content with requirements that the Register of Copyrights shall prescribe by regulation. The Register shall maintain current records of information relating to the death of authors of copyrighted works, based on such recorded statements and, to the extent the Register considers practicable, on data contained in any of the records of the Copyright Office or in other reference sources.

(e) PRESUMPTION AS TO AUTHOR'S DEATH.—After a period of seventy-five years from the year of first publication of a work, or a period of one hundred years from the year of its creation, whichever expires first, any person who obtains from the Copyright Office a certified report that the records provided by subsection (d) disclose nothing to indicate that the author of the work is living, or died less than fifty years before, is entitled to the benefits of a presumption that the author has been dead for at least fifty years. Reliance in good faith upon this presumption shall be a complete defense to any action for infringement under this title.

§ 303. Duration of copyright: Works created but not published or copyrighted before January 1, 1978

Copyright in a work created before January 1, 1978, but not theretofore in the public domain or copyrighted, subsists from January 1, 1978, and endures for the term provided by section 302. In no case, however, shall the term of copyright in such a work expire before December 31, 2002;

and, if the work is published on or before December 31, 2002, the term of copyright shall not expire before December 31, 2027.

§ 304. Duration of copyright: Subsisting copyrights

(a) COPYRIGHTS IN THEIR FIRST TERM ON JANUARY 1, 1978.—Any copyright, the first term of which is subsisting on January 1, 1978, shall endure for twenty-eight years from the date it was originally secured: *Provided,* That in the case of any posthumous work or of any periodical, cyclopedic, or other composite work upon which the copyright was originally secured by the proprietor thereof, or of any work copyrighted by a corporate body (otherwise than as assignee or licensee of the individual author) or by an employer for whom such work is made for hire, the proprietor of such copyright shall be entitled to a renewal and extension of the copyright in such work for the further term of forty-seven years when application for such renewal and extension shall have been made to the Copyright Office and duly registered therein within one year prior to the expiration of the original term of copyright: *And provided further,* That in the case of any other copyrighted work, including a contribution by an individual author to a periodical or to a cyclopedic or other composite work, the author of such work, if still living, or the widow, widower, or children of the author, if the author be not living, or if such author, widow, widower, or children be not living, then the author's executors, or in the absence of a will, his or her next of kin shall be entitled to a renewal and extension of the copyright in such work for a further term of forty-seven years when application for such renewal and extension shall have been made to the Copyright Office and duly registered therein within one year prior to the expiration of the original term of copyright: *And provided further,* That in default of the registration of such application for renewal and extension, the copyright in any work shall terminate at the expiration of twenty-eight years from the date copyright was originally secured.

(b) COPYRIGHTS IN THEIR RENEWAL TERM OR REGISTERED FOR RENEWAL BEFORE JANUARY 1, 1978.—The duration of any copyright, the renewal term of which is subsisting at any time between December 31, 1976, and December 31, 1977, inclusive, or for which renewal registration is made between December 31, 1976, and December 31, 1977, inclusive, is extended to endure for a term of seventy-five years from the date copyright was originally secured.

(c) TERMINATION OF TRANSFERS AND LICENSES COVERING EXTENDED RENEWAL TERM.—In the case of any copyright subsisting in either its first or renewal term on January 1, 1978, other than a copyright in a work made for hire, the exclusive or nonexclusive grant of a transfer or license of the renewal copyright or any right under it, executed before January 1, 1978, by any of the persons designated by the second proviso of subsection (a) of this section, otherwise than by will, is subject to termination under the following conditions:

(1) In the case of a grant executed by a person or persons other than the author, termination of the grant may be effected by the surviving person or persons who executed it. In the case of a grant executed by one or more of the authors of the work, termination of the grant may be effected, to the extent of a particular author's share in the ownership of the renewal copyright, by the author who executed it or, if such author is dead, by the person or persons who, under clause (2) of this subsection, own and are entitled to exercise a total of more than one-half of that author's termination interest.

(2) Where an author is dead, his or her termination interest is owned, and may be exercised, by his widow or her widower and his or her children or grandchildren as follows:

(A) the widow or widower owns the author's entire termination interest unless there are any surviving children or grandchildren of the author, in which case the widow or widower owns one-half of the author's interest;

(B) the author's surviving children, and the surviving children of any dead child of the author, own the author's entire termination interest unless there is a widow or widower, in which case the ownership of one-half of the author's interest is divided among them;

(C) the rights of the author's children and grandchildren are in all cases divided among them and exercised on a per stirpes basis according to the number of each author's children represented; the share of the children of a dead child in a termination interest can be exercised only by the action of a majority of them.

(3) Termination of the grant may be effected at any time during a period of five years beginning at the end of fifty-six years from the date copyright was originally secured, or beginning on January 1, 1978, whichever is later.

(4) The termination shall be effected by serving an advance notice in writing upon the grantee or the grantee's successor in title. In the case of a grant executed by a person or persons other than the author, the notice shall be signed by all of those entitled to terminate the grant under clause (1) of this subsection, or by their duly authorized agents. In the case of a grant executed by one or more of the authors of the work, the notice as to any one author's share shall be signed by that author or his or her duly authorized agent or, if that author is dead, by the number and proportion of the owners of his or her termination interest required under clauses (1) and (2) of this subsection, or by their duly authorized agents.

(A) The notice shall state the effective date of the termination, which shall fall within the five-year period specified by clause (3) of this subsection, and the notice shall be served not less than two or more than ten years before that date. A copy of the notice shall be recorded in the Copyright Office before the effective date of termination, as a condition to its taking effect.

(B) The notice shall comply, in form, content, and manner of service, with requirements that the Register of Copyrights shall prescribe by regulation.

(5) Termination of the grant may be effected notwithstanding any agreement to the contrary, including an agreement to make a will or to make any future grant.

(6) In the case of a grant executed by a person or persons other than the author, all rights under this title that were covered by the terminated grant revert, upon the effective date of termination, to all of those entitled to terminate the grant under clause (1) of this subsection. In the case of a grant executed by one or more of the authors of the work, all of a particular author's rights under this title that were covered by the terminated grant revert, upon the effective date of termination, to that author or, if that author is dead, to the persons owning his or her termination interest under clause (2) of this subsection, including those owners who did not join in signing the notice of termination under clause (4) of this subsection. In all cases the reversion of rights is subject to the following limitations:

(A) A derivative work prepared under authority of the grant before its termination may continue to be utilized under the terms of the grant after its termination, but this privilege does not extend to the preparation after the termination of other derivative works based upon the copyrighted work covered by the terminated grant.

(B) The future rights that will revert upon termination of the grant become vested on the date the notice of termination has been served as provided by clause (4) of this subsection.

(C) Where the author's rights revert to two or more persons under clause (2) of this subsection, they shall vest in those persons in the proportionate shares provided by that clause. In such a case, and subject to the provisions of subclause (D) of this clause, a further grant, or agreement to make a further grant, of a particular author's share with respect to any right covered by a terminated grant is valid only if it is signed by the same number and proportion of the owners, in whom the right has vested under this clause, as are required to terminate the grant under clause (2) of this subsection. Such further grant or agreement is effective with respect to all of the persons in whom the right it covers has vested under this subclause, including those who did not join in signing it. If any person dies after rights under a terminated grant have vested in him or her, that person's legal representatives, legatees, or heirs at law represent him or her for purposes of this subclause.

(D) A further grant, or agreement to make a further grant, of any right covered by a terminated grant is valid only if it is made after the effective date of the termination. As an exception, however, an agreement for such a further grant may be made between the author or any of the persons provided by the first sentence of clause (6) of this subsection, or between the persons provided by subclause (C) of this clause, and the original grantee or such grantee's successor in title, after the notice of termination has been served as provided by clause (4) of this subsection.

(E) Termination of a grant under this subsection affects only those rights covered by the grant that arise under this title, and in no way affects rights arising under any other Federal, State, or foreign laws.

(F) Unless and until termination is effected under this subsection, the grant, if it does not provide otherwise, continues in effect for the remainder of the extended renewal term.

CHAPTER 4—COPYRIGHT NOTICE, DEPOSIT, AND REGISTRATION

§ 401. Notice of copyright: Visually perceptible copies

(a) GENERAL PROVISIONS.—Whenever a work protected under this title is published in the United States or elsewhere by authority of the copyright owner, a notice of copyright as provided by this section may be placed on publicly distributed copies from which the work can be visually perceived, either directly or with the aid of a machine or device.

(b) FORM OF NOTICE.—If a notice appears on the copies, it shall consist of the following three elements:

(1) the symbol © (the letter C in a circle), or the word "Copyright", or the abbreviation "Copr."; and

(2) the year of first publication of the work; in the case of compilations, or derivative works incorporating previously published material, the year date of first publication of the compilation or derivative work is sufficient. The year date may be omitted where a pictorial, graphic, or sculptural work, with accompanying text matter, if any, is reproduced in or on greeting cards, postcards, stationary, jewelry, dolls, toys, or any useful articles; and

(3) the name of the owner of copyright in the work, or an abbreviation by which the name can be recognized, or a generally known alternative designation of the owner.

(c) POSITION OF NOTICE.—The notice shall be affixed to the copies in such manner and location as to give reasonable notice of the claim of copyright. The Register of Copyrights shall prescribe by regulation, as examples, specific methods of affixation and positions of the notice on various types of works that will satisfy this requirement, but these specifications shall not be considered exhaustive.

(d) EVIDENTIARY WEIGHT OF NOTICE.—If a notice of copyright in the form and position specified by this section appears on the published copy or copies to which a defendant in a copyright infringement suit had access, then no weight shall be given to such a defendant's interposition of a defense based on innocent infringement in mitigation of actual or statutory damages, except as provided in the last sentence of section 504(c)(2).

§ 404. Notice of copyright: Contributions to collective works

(a) A separate contribution to a collective work may bear its own notice of copyright, as provided by sections 401 through 403. However, a single notice applicable to the collective work as a whole is sufficient to invoke the provisions of section 401(d) or 402(d), as applicable with respect to the separate contributions it contains (not including advertisements inserted on behalf of persons other than the owner of copyright in the collective work), regardless of the ownership of copyright in the contributions and whether or not they have been previously published.

(b) With respect to copies and phonorecords publicly distributed by authority of the copyright owner before the effective date of the Berne Convention Implementation Act of 1988, where the person named in a single notice applicable to a collective work as a whole is not the owner of copyright in a separate contribution that does not bear its own notice, the case is governed by the provisions of section 406(a).

§ 405. Notice of copyright: Omission of notice on certain copies and phonorecords

(a) EFFECT OF OMISSION ON COPYRIGHT.—With respect to copies and phonorecords publicly distributed by authority of the copyright owner before the effective date of the Berne Convention Implementation Act of 1988, the omission of the copyright notice described in sections 401 through 403 from copies or phonorecords publicly distributed by authority of the copyright owner does not invalidate the copyright in a work if—

(1) the notice has been omitted from no more than a relatively small number of copies or phonorecords distributed to the public; or

(2) registration for the work has been made before or is made within five years after the publication without notice, and a reasonable effort is made to add notice to all copies or phonorecords that are distributed to the public in the United States after the omission has been discovered; or

(3) the notice has been omitted in violation of an express requirement in writing that, as a condition of the copyright owner's authorization of the public distribution of copies or phonorecords, they bear the prescribed notice.

(b) EFFECT OF OMISSION ON INNOCENT INFRINGERS.—Any person who innocently infringes a copyright, in reliance upon an authorized copy or phonorecord from which the copyright notice has been omitted and which was publicly distributed by authority of the copyright owner before the effective date of the Berne Convention Implementation Act of 1988, incurs no liability for actual or statutory damages under section 504 for any infringing acts committed before receiving actual notice that registration for the work has been made under section 408, if such person proves that he or she was misled by the omission of notice. In a suit for infringement in such a case the court may allow or disallow recovery of any of the infringer's profits attributable to the infringement, and may enjoin the continuation of the infringing undertaking or may require, as a condition or[1] permitting the continuation of the infringing undertaking, that the infringer pay the copyright owner a reasonable license fee in an amount and on terms fixed by the court.

(c) REMOVAL OF NOTICE.—Protection under this title is not affected by the removal, destruction, or obliteration of the notice, without the authorization of the copyright owner, from any publicly distributed copies or phonorecords.

§ 407. Deposit of copies or phonorecords for Library of Congress

(a) Except as provided by subsection (c), and subject to the provisions of subsection (e), the owner of copyright or of the exclusive right of publication in a work published in the United States shall deposit, within three months after the date of such publication—

(1) two complete copies of the best edition; or

(2) if the work is a sound recording, two complete phonorecords of the best edition, together with any printed or other visually perceptible material published with such phonorecords.

Neither the deposit requirements of this subsection nor the acquisition provisions of subsection (e) are conditions of copyright protection.

(b) The required copies or phonorecords shall be deposited in the Copyright Office for the use or disposition of the Library of Congress. The Register of Copyrights shall, when requested by the depositor and upon payment of the fee prescribed by section 708, issue a receipt for the deposit.

(c) The Register of Copyrights may by regulation exempt any categories of material from the deposit requirements of this section, or require deposit of only one copy or phonorecord with respect to any categories. Such regulations shall provide either for complete exemption from the deposit requirements of this section, or for alternative forms of deposit aimed at providing a satisfactory archival record of a work without imposing practical or financial hardships on the depositor, where the individual author is the owner of copyright in a pictorial, graphic, or sculptural work and (i) less than five copies of the work have been published, or (ii) the work has been published in a limited edition consisting of numbered copies, the monetary value of which would make the mandatory deposit of two copies of the best edition of the work burdensome, unfair, or unreasonable.

(d) At any time after publication of a work as provided by subsection (a), the Register of Copyrights may make written demand for the required deposit on any of the persons obligated to make the deposit under subsection (a). Unless deposit is made within three months after the demand is received, the person or persons on whom the demand was made are liable—

(1) to a fine of not more that $250 for each work; and

(2) to pay into a specially designated fund in the Library of Congress the total retail price of the copies or phonorecords demanded, or, if no retail price has been fixed, the reasonable cost of the Library of Congress of acquiring them; and

(3) to pay a fine of $2,500, in addition to any fine or liability imposed under clauses (1) and (2), if such person willfully or repeatedly fails or refuses to comply with such a demand.

(e) With respect to transmission programs that have been fixed and transmitted to the public in the United States but have not been published, the Register of Copyrights shall, after consulting with the Librarian of Congress and other interested organizations and officials, establish regulations governing the acquisition, through deposit or otherwise, of copies or phonorecords of such programs for the collections of the Library of Congress.

(1) The Librarian of Congress shall be permitted, under the standards and conditions set forth in such regulations, to make a fixation of a transmission program directly from a transmission to the public, and to reproduce one copy or phonorecord from such fixation for archival purposes.

(2) Such regulations shall also provide standards and procedures by which the Register of Copyrights may make written demand, upon the owner of the right of transmission in the United States, for the deposit of a copy or phonorecord of a specific transmission program. Such deposit may, at the option of the owner of the right of transmission in the United States, be accomplished by gift, by loan for purposes of reproduction, or by sale at a price not to exceed the cost of reproducing and supplying the copy or phonorecord. The regulations established under this clause shall provide reasonable periods of not less than three months for compliance with a demand, and shall allow for extensions of such periods and adjustments in the scope of the demand or the methods for fulfilling it, as reasonably warranted by the circumstances. Willful failure or refusal to comply with the conditions prescribed by such regulations shall subject the owner of the right of transmission in the United States to liability for an amount, not to exceed the cost of reproducing and supplying the copy or phonorecord in question, to be paid into a specially designated fund in the Library of Congress.

(3) Nothing in this subsection shall be construed to require the making or retention, for purposes of deposit, of any copy or phonorecord of an unpublished transmission program, the transmission of which occurs before the receipt of a specific written demand as provided by clause (2).

(4) No activity undertaken in compliance with regulations prescribed under clauses (1) or (2) of this subsection shall result in liability if intended solely to assist in the acquisition of copies or phonorecords under this subsection.

§ 408. Copyright registration in general

(a) REGISTRATION PERMISSIVE.—At any time during the subsistence of copyright in any published or unpublished work, the owner of copyright or of any exclusive right in the work may obtain registration of the copyright claim by delivering to the Copyright Office the deposit specified by this section, together with the application and fee specified by sections 409 and 708. Such registration is not a condition of copyright protection.

(b) DEPOSIT FOR COPYRIGHT REGISTRATION.—Except as provided by subsection (c), the material deposited for registration shall include—

(1) in the case of an unpublished work, one complete copy or phonorecord;

(2) in the case of a published work, two complete copies or phonorecords of the best edition;

(3) in the case of a work first published outside the United States, one complete copy or phonorecord as so published;

(4) in the case of a contribution to a collective work, one complete copy or phonorecord of the best edition of the collective work.

Copies or phonorecords deposited for the Library of Congress under section 407 may be used to satisfy the deposit provisions of this section, if they are accompanied by the prescribed application and fee, and by any additional identifying material that the Register may, by regulation, require. The Register shall also prescribe regulations establishing requirements under which copies or phonorecords acquired for the Library of Congress under subsection (e) of section 407, otherwise than by deposit, may be used to satisfy the deposit provisions of this section.

(c) ADMINISTRATIVE CLASSIFICATION AND OPTIONAL DEPOSIT.—

(1) The Register of Copyrights is authorized to specify by regulation the administrative classes into which works are to be placed for purposes of deposit and registration, and the nature of the copies or phonorecords to be deposited in the various classes specified. The regulations may require or permit, for particular classes, the deposit of identifying material instead of copies or phonorecords, the deposit of only one copy or phonorecord where two would normally be required, or a single registration for a group of related works. This administration classification of works has no significance with respect to the subject matter of copyright or the exclusive rights provided by this title.

(2) Without prejudice to the general authority provided under clause (1), the Register of Copyrights shall establish regulations specifically permitting a single registration for a group of works by the same individual author, all first published as contributions to periodicals, including newspapers, within a twelve-month period, on the basis of a single deposit, application, and registration fee, under the following conditions:

(A) if the deposit consists of one copy of the entire issue of the periodical, or of the entire section in the case of a newspaper, in which each contribution was first published; and

(B) if the application identifies each work separately, including the periodical containing it and its date of first publication.

(3) As an alternative to separate renewal registrations under subsection (a) of section 304, a single renewal registration may be made for a group of works by the same individual author, all first published as contributions to periodicals, including newspapers, upon the filing of a single application and fee, under all of the following conditions:

(A) the renewal claimant or claimants, and the basis of claim or claims under section 304(a), is the same for each of the works; and

(B) the works were all copyrighted upon their first publication, either through separate copyright notice and registration or by virtue of a general copyright notice in the periodical issue as a whole; and

(C) the renewal application and fee are received not more than twenty-eight or less than twenty-seven years after the thirty-first day of December of the calendar year in which all of the works were first published; and

(D) the renewal application identifies each work separately, including the periodical containing it and its date of first publication.

(d) CORRECTIONS AND AMPLIFICATIONS.—The Register may also establish by regulation, formal procedures for the filing of an application for supplementary registration, to correct an error in a copyright registration or to amplify the information given in a registration. Such application shall be accompanied by the fee provided by section 708, and shall clearly identify the registration to be corrected or amplified. The information contained in a supplementary registration augments but does not supersede registration augments but does not supersede that contained in the earlier registration.

(e) PUBLISHED EDITION OF PREVIOUSLY REGISTERED WORK.—Registration for the first published edition of a work previously registered in unpublished form may be made even though the work as published is substantially the same as the unpublished version.

§ 409. Application for copyright registration

The application for copyright registration shall be made on a form prescribed by the Register of Copyrights and shall include—

(1) the name and address of the copyright claimant;

(2) in the case of a work other than an anonymous or pseudonymous work, the name and nationality or domicile of the author or authors, and, if one or more of the authors is dead, the dates of their deaths;

(3) if the work is anonymous or pseudonymous, the nationality or domicile of the author or authors;

(4) in the case of a work made for hire, a statement to this effect;

(5) if the copyright claimant is not the author, a brief statement of how the claimant obtained ownership of the copyright;

(6) the title of the work, together with any previous or alternative titles under which the work can be identified;

(7) the year in which creation of the work was completed;

(8) if the work has been published, the date and nation of its first publication;

(9) in the case of a compilation or derivative work, an identification of any preexisting work or works that it is based on or incorporates, and a brief, general statement of the additional material covered by the copyright claim being registered;

(10) in the case of a published work containing material of which copies are required by section 601 to be manufactured in the United States, the names of the persons or organizations who performed the processes specified by subsection (c) of section 601 with respect to that material, and the places where those processes were performed; and

(11) any other information regarded by the Register of Copyrights as bearing upon the preparation or identification of the work or the existence, ownership, or duration of the copyright.

§ 410. Registration of claim and issuance of certificate

(a) When, after examination, the Register of Copyrights determines that, in accordance with the provisions of this title, the material deposited constitutes copyrightable subject matter and that the other legal and formal requirements of this title have been met, the Register shall register the claim and issue to the applicant a certificate of registration under the seal of the Copyright Office. The certificate shall contain the information given in the application, together with the number and effective date of the registration.

(b) In any case in which the Register of Copyrights determines that, in accordance with the provisions of this title, the material deposited does not constitute copyrightable subject matter or that the claim is invalid for any other reason, the Register shall refuse registration and shall notify the applicant in writing of the reasons for such refusal.

(c) In any judicial proceedings the certificate of a registration made before or within five years after first publication of the work shall constitute prima facie evidence of the validity of the copyright and of the facts stated in the certificate. The evidentiary weight to be accorded the certificate of a registration made thereafter shall be within the discretion of the court.

(d) The effective date of a copyright registration is the day on which the application, deposit, and fee, which are later determined by the Register of Copyrights or by a court of competent jurisdiction to be acceptable for registration, have all been received in the Copyright Office.

§ 411. Registration and infringement actions

(a) Except for actions for infringement of copyright in Berne Convention works whose country of origin is not the United States and an action brought for a violation of the rights of the author under section 106A(a), and subject to the provisions of subsection (b), no action for infringement of the copyright in any work shall be instituted until registration of the copyright claim has been made in accordance with this title. In any case, however, where the deposit, application, and fee required for registration have been delivered to the Copyright Office in proper form and registration has been refused, the applicant is entitled to institute an action for infringement if notice thereof, with a copy of the complaint, is served on the Register of Copyrights. The Register may, at his or her option, become a party to the action with respect to the issue of registrability of the copyright claim by entering an appearance within sixty days after such service, but the Register's failure to become a party shall not deprive the court of jurisdiction to determine that issue.

(b) In the case of a work consisting of sounds, images, or both, the first fixation of which is made simultaneously with its transmission, the copyright owner may, either before or after such fixation takes place, institute an action for infringement under section 501, fully subject to the remedies provided by sections 502 through 506 and sections 509 and 510, if, in accordance with requirements that the Register of Copyrights shall prescribe by regulation, the copyright owner—

(1) serves notice upon the infringer, not less than ten or more than thirty days before such fixation, identifying the work and the specific time and source of its first transmission, and declaring an intention to secure copyright in the work; and

(2) makes registration for the work, if required by subsection (a), within three months after its first transmission.

§ 412.   Registration as prerequisite to certain remedies for infringement

In any action under this title, other than an action brought for a violation of the rights of the author under section 106A or an action instituted under section 411(b), no award of statutory damages or of attorney's fees, as provided by sections 504 and 505, shall be made for—

(1) any infringement of copyright in an unpublished work commenced before the effective date of its registration; or

(2) any infringement of copyright commenced after first publication of the work and before the effective date of its registration, unless such registration is made within three months after the first publication of the work.

CHAPTER 5—COPYRIGHT INFRINGEMENT AND REMEDIES

§ 501.   Infringement of copyright

(a) Anyone who violates any of the exclusive rights of the copyright owner as provided by sections 106 through 118, or of the author as provided in section 106A(a), or who imports copies or phonorecords into the United States in violation of section 602, is an infringer of the copyright or the right of the author, as the case may be. For purposes of this chapter (other than section 506), any reference to copyright shall be deemed to include the rights conferred by section 106A(a).

(b) The legal or beneficial owner of an exclusive right under a copyright is entitled, subject to the requirements of section 411, to institute an action for any infringement of that particular right committed while he or she is the owner of it. The court may require such owner to serve written notice of the action with a copy of the complaint upon any person shown, by the records of the Copyright Office or otherwise, to have or claim an interest in the copyright, and shall require that such notice be served upon any person whose interest is likely to be affected by a decision in the case. The court may require the joinder, and shall permit the intervention, of any person having or claiming an interest in the copyright.

(c) For any secondary transmission by a cable system that embodies a performance or a display of a work which is actionable as an act of infringement under subsection (c) of section 111, a television broadcast station holding a copyright or other license to transmit or perform the same version of that work shall, for purposes of subsection (b) of this section, be treated as a legal or beneficial owner if such secondary transmission occurs within the local service area of that television station.

(d) For any secondary transmission by a cable system that is actionable as an act of infringement pursuant to section 111(c)(3), the following shall also have standing to sue: (i) the primary transmitter whose transmission has been altered by the cable system; and (ii) any broadcast station within whose local service area the secondary transmission occurs.

(e) With respect to any secondary transmission that is made by a satellite carrier of a primary transmission embodying the performance or display of a work and is actionable as an act of infringement under section 119(a)(5), a network station holding a copyright or other license to transmit or perform the same version of that work shall, for purposes of subsection (b) of this section, be treated as a legal or beneficial owner if such secondary transmission occurs within the local service area of that station. [Subsection (e) is scheduled to terminate Dec. 31, 1994.]

§ 502. Remedies for infringement: Injunctions

(a) Any court having jurisdiction of a civil action arising under this title may, subject to the provisions of section 1498 of title 28, grant temporary and final injunctions on such terms as it may deem reasonable to prevent or restrain infringement of a copyright.

(b) Any such injunction may be served anywhere in the United States on the person enjoined; it shall be operative throughout the United States and shall be enforceable, by proceedings in contempt or otherwise, by any United States court having jurisdiction of that person. The clerk of the court granting the injunction shall, when requested by any other court in which enforcement of the injunction is sought, transmit promptly to the other court a certified copy of all the papers in the case on file in such clerk's office.

§ 503. Remedies for infringements: Impounding and disposition of infringing articles

(a) At any time while an action under this title is pending, the court may order the impounding, on such terms as it may deem reasonable, of all copies or phonorecords claimed to have been made or used in violation of the copyright owner's exclusive rights, and of all plates, molds, matrices, masters, tapes, film negatives, or other articles by means of which such copies or phonorecords may be reproduced.

(b) As part of a final judgment or decree, the court may order the destruction or other reasonable disposition of all copies or phonorecords found to have been made or used in violation of the copyright owner's exclusive rights, and of all plates, molds, matrices, masters, tapes, film negatives, or other articles by means of which such copies or phonorecords may be reproduced.

§ 504. Remedies for infringement: Damages and profits

(a) IN GENERAL.—Except as otherwise provided by this title, an infringer of copyright is liable for either—

(1) the copyright owner's actual damages and any additional profits of the infringer, as provided by subsection (b); or

(2) statutory damages, as provided by subsection (c).

(b) ACTUAL DAMAGES AND PROFITS.—The copyright owner is entitled to recover the actual damages suffered by him or her as a result of the infringement, and any profits of the infringer that are attributable to the infringement and are not taken into account in computing the actual damages. In establishing the infringer's profits, the copyright owner is required to present proof only of the infringer's gross revenue, and the infringer is required to prove his or her deductible expenses and the elements of profit attributable to factors other than the copyrighted work.

(c) STATUTORY DAMAGES.—

(1) Except as provided by clause (2) of this subsection, the copyright owner may elect, at any time before final judgment is rendered, to recover, instead of actual damages and profits, an award of statutory damages for all infringements involved in the action, with respect to any one work, for which any one infringer is liable individually, or for which any two or more infringers are liable jointly and severally, in a sum of not less than $500 or more than $20,000 as the court considers just. For the purposes of this subsection, all the parts of a compilation or derivative work constitute one work.

(2) In a case where the copyright owner sustains the burden of proving, and the court finds, that infringement was committed willfully, the court in its discretion may increase the award of statutory damages to a sum of not more than $100,000. In a case where the infringer sustains the burden of proving, and the court finds, that such infringer was not aware and had no reason to believe that his or her acts constituted an infringement of copyright, the court in its discretion may reduce the award of statutory damages to a sum of not less than $200. The court shall remit statutory damages in any case where an infringer believed and had reasonable grounds for believing that his or her use of the copyrighted work was a fair use under section 107, if the infringer was: (i) an employee or agent of a nonprofit educational institution, library, or archives acting within the scope of his or her employment who, or such institution, library, or archives itself, which infringed by reproducing the work in copies or

phonorecords; or (ii) a public broadcasting entity which or a person who, as a regular part of the nonprofit activities of a public broadcasting entity (as defined in subsection (g) of section 118) infringed by performing a published nondramatic literary work or by reproducing a transmission program embodying a performance of such a work.

§ 505. Remedies for Infringement: Costs and attorney's fees

In any civil action under this title, the court in its discretion may allow the recovery of full costs by or against any party other than the United States or an officer thereof. Except as otherwise provided by this title, the court may also award a reasonable attorney's fee to the prevailing party as part of the costs.

§ 506. Criminal offenses

(a) CRIMINAL INFRINGEMENT.—Any person who infringes a copyright willfully and for purposes of commercial advantage or private financial gain shall be punished as provided in section 2319 of title 18.

(b) FORFEITURE AND DESTRUCTION.—When any person is convicted of any violation of subsection (a), the court in its judgment of conviction shall, in addition to the penalty therein prescribed, order the forfeiture and destruction or other disposition of all infringing copies or phonorecords and all implements, devices, or equipment used in the manufacture of such infringing copies or phonorecords.

(c) FRADULENT COPYRIGHT NOTICE.—Any person who, with fraudulent intent, places on any article a notice of copyright or words of the same purport that such person knows to be false, or who, with fraudulent intent, publicly distributes or imports for public distribution any article bearing such notice or words that such person knows to be false, shall be fined not more than $2,500.

(d) FRAUDULENT REMOVAL OF COPYRIGHT NOTICE.—Any person who, with fraudulent intent, removes or alters any notice of copyright appearing on a copy of a copyrighted work shall be fined not more than $2,500.

(e) FALSE REPRESENTATION.—Any person who knowingly makes a false representation of a material fact in the application for copyright registration provided for by section 409, or in any written statement filed in connection with the application, shall be fined not more than $2,500.

(f) RIGHTS OF ATTRIBUTION AND INTEGRITY.—Nothing in this section applies to infringement of the rights conferred by section 106A(a).

§ 507. Limitations on actions

(a) CRIMINAL PROCEEDINGS.—No criminal proceeding shall be maintained under the provisions of this title unless it is commenced within three years after the cause of action arose.

(b) CIVIL ACTIONS.—No civil action shall be maintained under the provisions of this title unless it is commenced within three years after the claim accrued.

§ 510. Remedies for alteration of programing by cable systems

(a) In any action filed pursuant to section 111(c)(3), the following remedies shall be available:

(1) Where an action is brought by a party identified in subsections (b) or (c) of section 501, the remedies provided by sections 502 through 505, and the remedy provided by subsection (b) of this section; and

(2) When an action is brought by a party identified in subsection (d) of section 501, the remedies provided by sections 502 and 505, together with any actual damages suffered by such party as a result of the infringement, and the remedy provided by subsection (b) of this section.

(b) In any action filed pursuant to section 111(c)(3), the court may decree that, for a period not to exceed thirty days, the cable system shall be deprived of the benefit of a compulsory license for one or more distant signals carried by such cable system.

CHAPTER 7—COPYRIGHT OFFICE

§ 707. Copyright Office forms and publications

(a) CATALOG OF COPYRIGHT ENTRIES.—The Register of Copyrights shall compile and publish at periodic intervals catalogs of all copyright registrations. These catalogs shall be divided into parts in accordance with the various classes of works, and the Register has discretion to determine, on the basis of practicability and usefulness, the form and frequency of publication of each particular part.

(b) OTHER PUBLICATIONS.—The Register shall furnish, free of charge upon request, application forms for copyright registration and general information material in connection with the functions of the Copyright Office. The Register also has the authority to publish compilations of information, bibliographies, and other material he or she considers to be of value to the public.

(c) DISTRIBUTION OF PUBLICATIONS.—All publications of the Copyright Office shall be furnished to depository libraries as specified under section 1905 of title 44, and, aside from those furnished free of charge, shall be offered for sale to the public at prices based on the cost of reproduction and distribution.

§ 708. Copyright Office fees

(a) The following fees shall be paid to the Register of Copyrights:

(1) on filing each application for registration of a copyright claim or a supplementary registration under section 408, including the issuance of a certificate of registration if registration is made, $20;

(2) on filing each application for registration of a claim to renewal of a subsisting copyright in its first term under section 304(a), including the issuance of a certificate of registration if registration is made, $12;

(3) for the issuance of a receipt for a deposit under section 407, $4;

(4) for the recordation, as provided by section 205, of a transfer of copyright ownership or other document covering no more than one title, $20 for additional titles, $10 for each group of not more than 10 titles;

(5) for the filing, under section 115(b), of a notice of intention to obtain a compulsory license, $12;

(6) for the recordation, under section 302(c), of a statement revealing the identity of an author of an anonymous or pseudonymous work, or for the recordation, under section 302(d), of a statement relating to the death of an author, $20 for a document covering no more than one title; for each additional title, $2 additional;

(7) for the issuance, under section 706, of an additional certificate of registration, $8;

(8) for the issuance of any other certification, $20 for each hour or fraction of an hour consumed with respect thereto;

(9) for the making and reporting of a search as provided by section 705, and for any related services, $20 for each hour or fraction of an hour consumed with respect thereto;

(10) for any other special services requiring a substantial amount of time or expense, such fees as the Register of Copyrights may fix on the basis of the cost of providing the service. The Register of Copyrights is authorized to fix the fees for preparing copies of Copyright Office records, whether or not such copies are certified, on the basis of the cost of such preparation.

(b) In calendar year 1995 and in each subsequent fifth calendar year, the Register of Copyrights, by regulation, may increase the fees specified in subsection (a) by the percent change in the annual average, for the preceding calendar year, of the Consumer Price Index published by the Bureau of Labor Statistics, over the annual average of the Consumer Price Index for the fifth calendar year preceding the calendar year in which such increase is authorized.

(c) The fees prescribed by or under this section are applicable to the United States Government and any of its agencies, employees, or officers, but the Register of Copyrights has discretion to waive the requirement of this subsection in occasional or isolated cases involving relatively small amounts.

(d) All fees received under this section shall be deposited by the Register of Copyrights in the Treasury of the United States and shall be credited to the appropriation for necessary expenses of the Copyright Office. The Register may, in accordance with regulations that he or she shall prescribe, refund any sum paid by mistake or in excess of the fee required by this section.

CHAPTER 8—COPYRIGHT ROYALTY TRIBUNAL

§ 801. Copyright Royalty Tribunal: Establishment and purpose

(a) There is hereby created an independent Copyright Royalty Tribunal in the legislative branch.

(b) Subject to the provisions of this chapter, the purposes of the Tribunal shall be—

(1) to make determinations concerning the adjustment of reasonable copyright royalty rates as provided in sections 115 and 116, and to make determinations as to reasonable terms and rates of royalty payments as provided in section 118. The rates applicable under sections 115 and 116 shall be calculated to achieve the following objectives:

(A) To maximize the availability of creative works to the public;

(B) To afford the copyright owner a fair return for his creative work and the copyright user a fair income under existing economic conditions;

(C) To reflect the relative roles of the copyright owner and the copyright user in the product made available to the public with respect to relative creative contribution, technological contribution, capital investment, cost, risk, and contribution to the opening of new markets for expression and media for their communication;

(D) To minimize any disruptive impact on the structure of the industries involved and on generally prevailing industry practices.

(2) to make determinations concerning the adjustment of the copyright royalty rates in section 111 solely in accordance with the following provisions:

(A) The rates established by section 111(d)(1)(B) may be adjusted to reflect (i) national monetary inflation or deflation or (ii) changes in the average rates charged cable subscribers for the basic service of providing secondary transmissions to maintain the real constant dollar level of the royalty fee per subscriber which existed as of the date of enactment of this Act: *Provided,* That if the average rates charged cable system subscribers for the basic service of providing secondary transmissions are changed so that the average rates exceed national monetary inflation, no change in the rates established by section 111(d)(1)(B) shall be permitted: *And provided further,* That no increase in the royalty fee shall be permitted based on any reduction in the average number of distant signal equivalents per subscriber. The Commission may consider all factors relating to the maintenance of such level of payments including, as an extenuating factor, whether the cable industry has been restrained by subscriber rate regulating authorities from increasing the rates for the basic service of providing secondary transmissions.

(B) In the event that the rules and regulations of the Federal Communications Commission are amended at any time after April 15, 1976, to permit the carriage by cable systems of additional television broadcast signals beyond the local service area of the primary transmitters of such signals, the royalty rates established by section 111(d)(1)(B) may be adjusted to insure that the rates for the additional distant signal equivalents resulting from such carriage are reasonable in the light of the changes effected by the amendment to such rules and regulations. In determining the reasonableness of rates proposed following an amendment of Federal Communications Commission rules and regulations, the Copyright Royalty Tribunal shall consider, among other factors, the economic impact on copyright owners and users: *Provided,* That no adjustment in royalty rates shall be made under this subclause with respect to any distant signal equivalent or fraction thereof represented by (i) carriage of any signal permitted under the rules and regulations of the Federal Communications Commission in effect on April 15, 1976, or the carriage of a signal of the same type (that is, independent, network, or noncommercial educational) substituted for such permitted signal, or (ii) a television broadcast signal first carried after

April 15, 1976, pursuant to an individual waiver of the rules and regulations of the Federal Communications Commission, as such rules and regulations were in effect on April 15, 1976.

(C) In the event of any change in the rules and regulations of the Federal Communications Commission with respect to syndicated and sports program exclusivity after April 15, 1976, the rates established by section 111(d)(1)(B) may be adjusted to assure that such rates are reasonable in light of the changes to such rules and regulations, but any such adjustment shall apply only to the affected television broadcast signals carried on those systems affected by the change.

(D) The gross receipts limitations established by section 111(d)(1)(C) and (D) shall be adjusted to reflect national monetary inflation or deflation or changes in the average rates charged cable system subscribers for the basic service of providing secondary transmissions to maintain the real constant dollar value of the exemption provided by such section; and the royalty rate specified therein shall not be subject to adjustment; and

(3) to distribute royalty fees deposited with the Register of Copyrights under sections 111, 116, and 119(b), and to determine, in cases where controversy exists, the distribution of such fees.

In determining whether a return to a copyright owner under section 116 is fair, appropriate weight shall be given to—

(i) the rates previously determined by the Tribunal to provide a fair return to the copyright owner, and

(ii) the rates contained in any license negotiated pursuant to section 116A of this title.

(c) As soon as possible after the date of enactment of this Act, and no later than six months following such date, the President shall publish a notice announcing the initial appointments provided in section 802, and shall designate an order of seniority among the initially-appointed commissioners for purposes of section 802(b).

§ 802.   Membership of the Tribunal

(a) The Tribunal shall be composed of three Commissioners appointed by the President, by and with the advice and consent of the Senate. The term of office of any individual appointed as a Commissioner shall be seven years, except that a Commissioner may serve after the expiration of his or her term until a successor has taken office. Each Commissioner shall be compensated at the rate of pay in effect for level V of the Executive Schedule under section 5316 of title 5.

(b) Upon convening the commissioners shall elect a chairman from among the commissioners appointed for a full seven-year term. Such chairman shall serve for a term of one year. Thereafter, the most senior commissioner who has not previously served as chairman shall serve as chairman for a period of one year, except that, if all commissioners have served a full term as chairman, the most senior commissioner who has served the least number of terms as chairman shall be designated as chairman.

(c) Any vacancy in the Tribunal shall not affect its powers and shall be filled, for the unexpired term of the appointment, in the same manner as the original appointment was made.

§ 803.   Procedures of the Tribunal

(a) The Tribunal shall adopt regulations, not inconsistent with law, governing its procedure and methods of operation. Except as otherwise provided in this chapter, the Tribunal shall be subject to the provisions of the Administrative Procedure Act of June 11, 1946, as amended (c. 324, 60 Stat. 237, title 5, United States Code, chapter 5, subchapter II and chapter 7).

(b) Every final determination of the Tribunal shall be published in the Federal Register. It shall state in detail the criteria that the Tribunal determined to be applicable to the particular proceeding, the various facts that it found relevant to its determination in that proceeding, and the specific reasons for its determination.

§ 804.   Institution and conclusion of proceedings

(a) With respect to proceedings under section 801(b)(1) concerning the adjustment of royalty rates as provided in sections 115 and 116, and with respect to proceedings under section 801(b)(2)(A) and (D)—

(1) on January 1, 1980, the Chairman of the Tribunal shall cause to be published in the Federal Register notice of commencement of proceedings under this chapter; and

(2) during the calendar years specified in the following schedule, any owner or user of a copyrighted work whose royalty rates are specified by this title, or by a rate established by the Tribunal, may file a petition with the Tribunal declaring that the petitioner requests an adjustment of the rate. The Tribunal shall make a determination as to whether the applicant has a significant interest in the royalty rate in which an adjustment is requested. If the Tribunal determines that the petitioner has a significant interest, the Chairman shall cause notice of this determination, with the reasons therefor, to be published in the Federal Register, together with notice of commencement of proceedings under this chapter.

(A) In proceedings under section 801(b)(2)(A) and (D), such petition may be filed during 1985 and in each subsequent fifth calendar year.

(B) In proceedings under section 801(b)(1) concerning the adjustment of royalty rates as provided in section 115, such petition may be filed in 1987 and in each subsequent tenth calendar year.

(C)(i) In proceedings under section 801(b)(1) concerning the adjustment of royalty rates as provided in section 116, such petition may be filed in 1990 and in each subsequent tenth calendar year, an at any time within 1 year after negotiated licenses authorized by section 116A are terminated or expire and are not replaced by subsequent agreements.

(ii) If negotiated licenses authorized by section 116A come into force so as to supersede previous determinations of the Tribunal, as provided in section 116A(d), but thereafter are terminated or expire and are not replaced by subsequent agreements, the Tribunal shall, upon petition of any party to such terminated or expired negotiated license agreement, promptly establish an interim royalty rate or rates for the public performance by means of a coin-operated phonorecord player of nondramatic musical works embodied in phonorecords which had been subject to the terminated or expired negotiated license agreement. Such interim royalty rate or rates shall be the same as the last such rate or rates and shall remain in force until the conclusion of proceedings to adjust the royalty rates applicable to such works, or until superseded by a new negotiated license agreement, as provided in section 116A(d).

(b) With respect to proceedings under subclause (B) or (C) of section 801(b)(2), following an event described in either of those subsections, any owner or user of a copyrighted work whose royalty rates are specified by section 111, or by a rate established by the Tribunal, may, within twelve months, file a petition with the Tribunal declaring that the petitioner requests an adjustment of the rate. In this event the Tribunal shall proceed as in subsection (a)(2), above. Any change in royalty rates made by the Tribunal pursuant to this subsection may be reconsidered in 1980, 1985, and each fifth calendar year thereafter, in accordance with the provisions in section 801(b)(2)(B) or (C), as the case may be.

(c) With respect to proceedings under section 801(b)(1), concerning the determination of reasonable terms and rates of royalty payments as provided in section 118, the Tribunal shall proceed when and as provided by that section.

(d) With respect to proceedings under section 801(b)(3), concerning the distribution of royalty fees in certain circumstances under section 111, 116, or 119, the Chairman of the Tribunal shall, upon determination by the Tribunal that a controversy exists concerning such distribution, cause to be published in the Federal Register notice of commencement of proceedings under this chapter.

(e) All proceedings under this chapter shall be initiated without delay following publication of the notice specified in this section, and the Tribunal shall render its final decision in any such proceeding within one year from the date of such publication.

§ 805. Staff of the Tribunal

(a) The Tribunal is authorized to appoint and fix the compensation of such employees as may be necessary to carry out the provisions of this chapter, and to prescribe their functions and duties.

(b) The Tribunal may procure temporary and intermittent services to the same extent as is authorized by section 3109 of title 5.

§ 806.   Administrative support of the Tribunal

(a) The Library of Congress shall provide the Tribunal with necessary administrative services, including those related to budgeting, accounting, financial reporting, travel, personnel, and procurement. The Tribunal shall pay the Library for such services, either in advance or by reimbursement from the funds of the Tribunal, at amounts to be agreed upon between the Librarian and the Tribunal.

(b) The Library of Congress is authorized to disburse funds for the Tribunal, under regulations prescribed jointly by the Librarian of Congress and the Tribunal and approved by the Comptroller General. Such regulations shall establish requirements and procedures under which every voucher certified for payment by the Library of Congress under this chapter shall be supported with a certification by a duly authorized officer or employee of the Tribunal, and shall prescribe the responsibilities and accountability of said officers and employees of the Tribunal with respect to such certifications.

§ 807.   Deduction of costs of proceedings

Before any funds are distributed pursuant to a final decision in a proceeding involving distribution of royalty fees, the Tribunal shall assess the reasonable costs of such proceeding.

§ 808.   Reports

In addition to its publication of the reports of all final determinations as provided in section 803(b), the Tribunal shall make an annual report to the President and the Congress concerning the Tribunal's work during the preceding fiscal year, including a detailed fiscal statement of account.

§ 809.   Effective date of final determinations

Any final determination by the Tribunal under this chapter shall become effective thirty days following its publication in the Federal Register as provided in section 803(b), unless prior to that time an appeal has been filed pursuant to section 810, to vacate, modify, or correct such determination, and notice of such appeal has been served on all parties who appeared before the Tribunal in the proceeding in question. Where the proceeding involves the distribution of royalty fees under sections[3] 111 or 116, the Tribunal shall, upon the expiration of such thirty-day period, distribute any royalty fees not subject to an appeal filed pursuant to section 810.

§ 810.   Judicial review

Any final decision of the Tribunal in a proceeding under section 801(b) may be appealed to the United States Court of Appeals, within thirty days after its publication in the Federal Register by an aggrieved party. The judicial review of the decision shall be had, in accordance with chapter 7 of title 5, on the basis of the record before the Tribunal. No court shall have jurisdiction to review a final decision of the Tribunal except as provided in this section.

Appendix A6

Other Federal Laws
Affecting Copyrights

UNITED STATES CODE TITLE 18

[as amended through Dec. 31, 1990]

§ 2319. Criminal infringement of a copyright

(a) Whoever violates section 506(a) (relating to criminal offenses) of title 17 shall be punished as provided in subsection (b) of this section and such penalties shall be in addition to any other provisions of title 17 or any other law.

(b) Any person who commits an offense under subsection (a) of this section—

(1) shall be fined not more than $250,000 or imprisoned for not more than five years, or both, if the offense—

(A) involves the reproduction or distribution, during any one-hundred-and-eighty-day period, of at least one thousand phonorecords or copies infringing the copyright in one or more sound recordings;

(B) involves the reproduction or distribution, during any one-hundred-and-eighty-day period, of at least sixty-five copies infringing the copyright in one or more motion pictures or other audiovisual works; or

(C) is a second or subsequent offense under either of subsection (b)(1) or (b)(2) of this section, where a prior offense involved a sound recording, or a motion picture or other audiovisual work;

(2) shall be fined not more than $250,000 or imprisoned for not more than two years, or both, if the offense—

(A) involves the reproduction or distribution, during any one-hundred-and-eighty-day period, of more than one hundred but less than one thousand phonorecords or copies infringing the copyright in one or more sound recordings; or

(B) involves the reproduction or distribution, during any one-hundred-and-eighty-day period, of more than seven but less than sixty-five copies infringing the copyright in one or more motion pictures or other audiovisual works; and

(3) shall be fined not more than $25,000 or imprisoned for not more than one year, or both, in any other case.

(c) As used in this section—

(1) the terms "sound recording", "motion picture", "audiovisual work", "phonorecord", and "copies" have, respectively, the meanings set forth in section 101 (relating to definitions) of title 17; and

(2) the terms "reproduction" and "distribution" refer to the exclusive rights of a copyright owner under clauses (1) and (3) respectively of section 106 (relating to exclusive rights in copyrighted works), as limited by sections 107 through 118, of title 17.

487

Appendix A7
Copyright Forms

On the following pages, instructions and application forms for copyright registration are reproduced. They include:

- Circular 45: Copyright Registration for Motion Pictures including Video Recordings
- Form PA: Application for Copyright Registration for a Work of the Performing Arts
- Form RE: Application for Renewal Registration
- Copyright Fees Increase Notification

Copyright Registration for Motion Pictures Including Video Recordings

Copyright Registration for Motion Pictures IncludingVideo Recordings

GENERAL INFORMATION

Statutory Definition

Motion pictures are **audiovisual works** consisting of a series of related images which, when shown in succession, impart an impression of motion, together with any accompanying sounds. They are typically embodied in film, videotape, or videodisk.

How Copyright Is Secured

Copyright in a motion picture is automatically secured when the work is created and "fixed" in a copy. The Copyright Office registers claims to copyright and issues certificates of registration, but does not "grant" or "issue" copyrights.

Only the expression (camera work, dialogue, sounds, etc.) fixed in a motion picture is protectible under copyright. Copyright does not cover the idea or concept behind the work or any characters portrayed in the work.

Works that do not constitute a fixation of a motion picture include:

● A live telecast that is not fixed in a copy.

● A screenplay or treatment of a future motion picture. Once the motion picture is made or fixed, the screenplay, to the extent it is embodied in the motion picture, is considered to be an integral part of the motion picture.

Publication

Publication of a motion picture takes place when one or more copies are distributed to the public by sale, rental, lease or lending, or when **an offering** is made to distribute copies to a group of persons (wholesalers, retailers, broadcasters, motion picture distributors, and the like) for purposes of further distribution or public performance. Offering to distribute a copy of a motion picture for exhibition during a film festival may be considered publication of that work. For an offering to constitute publication, copies must be made and be ready for distribution. The **performance** itself of a motion picture (for example, showing it in a theater, on television, or in a school room) **does not** constitute publication.

Publication of a motion picture publishes all of the components embodied in it, including the music, the script, and the sounds. Thus, if a motion picture made from a screenplay is published, the screenplay is published to the extent it is contained in the published work.

COPYRIGHT NOTICE

For works published on and after March 1, 1989, use of the copyright notice is optional, though highly recommended. Works first published before March 1, 1989, **must** bear a notice of copyright or risk loss of copyright protection. The Copyright Office takes no position and offers no advice regarding use of the notice on **reprints** distributed March 1, 1989, or later of works first published **with notice** before March 1, 1989.

Use of the notice is recommended because it informs the public that the work is protected by copyright, identifies the copyright owner, and shows the year of first publication. Furthermore, in the event that a work is infringed, if the work carries a proper notice, the court will not allow a defendant to claim "innocent infringement"—that is, that he or she did not realize that the work is protected. (A successful innocent infringement claim may result in a reduction in damages that the copyright owner would otherwise receive.)

The use of the copyright notice is the responsibility of the copyright owner and does not require advance permission from, or registration with, the Copyright Office.

Form of Notice for Visually Perceptible Copies

The notice for visually perceptible copies should contain all of the following three elements:

1. **The symbol** © (the letter C in a circle), or the word "Copyright," or the abbreviation "Copr."; and

2. **The year of first publication** of the work. In the case of compilations or derivative works incorporating previously published material, the year date of first publication of the compilation or derivative work is sufficient.

3. **The name of the owner of copyright** in the work, or an abbreviation by which the name can be recognized, or a generally known alternative designation of the owner.

Example: © 1990 John Doe

The notice should be affixed to copies of the work in such a manner and location as to "give reasonable notice of the claim to copyright." The three elements of the notice should ordinarily appear together on the copies. The Copyright Office has issued regulations concerning the form and position of the copyright notice in the *Code of Federal*

2

Regulations (37 C.F.R. Part 201.20). For more information, request Circular 3 from the Publications Section, LM-455, Copyright Office, Library of Congress, Washington, D.C. 20559.

> **NOTE:** The notice requirements for works first published before 1978 are governed by the previous copyright law. See page 7 for such works.

COPYRIGHT REGISTRATION

Advantages of Registration

Registration in the Copyright Office establishes a public record of the copyright claim. Before an infringement suit may be filed in court, registration is necessary for works of U.S. origin and for foreign works not originating in a Berne Union Country. (For more information on when a work is of U.S. origin, request Circular 93.) Timely registration may also provide a broader range of remedies in an infringement suit. Request Circular 1, "Copyright Basics," for more information on the benefits of registration.

How to Apply for Registration

To register either a published or unpublished motion picture, send the following to the Copyright Office:

1. A signed application on Form PA;

2. One complete copy of the motion picture being registered (see page 5 for specific requirements);

3. A separate written description of the contents of the motion picture; and

4. A nonrefundable filing fee of $10 for each application in the form of a check or money order payable to the **Register of Cop rights. Effective January 3, 1991, the filing fee increases to $20.**

Send the application, deposit and fee **in the same package** to:

> **Register of Copyrights**
> **Library of Congress**
> **Washington, D.C. 20559**

If it is impossible or highly impractical to send the deposit (for example, a 35mm film) in the same package with the other registration material, include a letter with each set of materials indicating that the missing element(s) are being sent under separate cover.

For forms or circulars, call the Forms Hotline (20 707-9100 and leave a recorded request. To speak with an information specialist, call (202) 479-0700.

Completing Form PA

NOTE: These points do not cover all of the required information on the application. Be sure to refer to the instructions on the Form PA before completing the application.

Space 1:

Nature of This Work: "Motion picture" is generally the appropriate term. If the motion picture is a part of a multimedia kit or other larger work and you are claiming in the entire work, you should indicate that in this space. For example, you could state "multimedia kit, including motion picture and workbook," if applicable.

Space 2:

Name of Author, "Work Made for Hire," and "Nature of Authorship": Ordinarily, a number of individuals contribute authorship to a motion picture, including the writer, director, producer, camera operator, editor, and others. These individuals are not always considered the "authors," however, because a motion picture is frequently a "work made for hire." In the case of a work made for hire, the **employer** — not the individuals who actually created the work—is considered the author for copyright purposes.

Under the copyright law, a "work made for hire" is defined as "a work prepared by an employee within the scope of his or her employment; or...a work specially ordered or commissioned for use...as a part of a motion picture or other audiovisual work...if the parties expressly agree in a written instrument signed by them that the work shall be considered a work made for hire." (Request Circular 9 for more information about works made for hire.)

Before completing space 2, you should determine whether part or all of the motion picture was made for hire.

1. If the entire work was made for hire, name the employer as author and answer "Yes" to the work-made-for-hire

3

question. Under "Nature of Authorship," state "entire motion picture."

2. If no part of the work was made for hire, name the individuals who made the motion picture as the authors and answer "No" to the work-made-for-hire questions. Under "Nature of Authorship," briefly describe what each person did, for example, "director," "producer," "writer," etc.

3. If part of the work was made for hire and part was not, complete each section of space 2 accordingly. You may need to give the same name twice in separate sections of

space 2, with the work-made-for-hire question answered "Yes" in one part and "No" in the other.

Space 3:

Year in Which Creation of This Work Was Completed: Give the year in which the motion picture as a whole was completed. If the motion picture is a new version, give the year of completion of the version being registered.

Date and Nation of First Publication: If the work is published, give a complete date (month, day, year) and nation of first publication. If the work is not published at the time the application is submitted, leave the publication lines blank.

Space 4:

Copyright Claimant(s): For copyright purposes, a claimant must be either an author, or a person or organization that has legally acquired the copyright originally owned by the author(s).

Transfer: If any claimant is not an author, give a statement describing how the claimant acquired the copyright. Copyright must be transferred by means of a written agreement or by operation of law. Therefore, **"by written agreement"** is generally an acceptable statement.

Space 5:

Previous Registration: If the motion picture contains a

4

substantial amount of previously registered material, answer "Yes," to the first question and also check the box that shows the reason for this registration. You should include the registration number and year of the previously registered material in the spaces provided. If no part of the work was previously registered, answer "No" to the first question and leave the rest of the space blank.

Space 6:

Derivative Work or Compilation: Complete this space **only** if the work contains a substantial amount of previously registered, previously published, or public domain material. If it does, complete **both** parts of space 6, describing both the preexisting material and the added material. The following are examples of acceptable statements in space 6:

1. Feature film based on a screenplay that was registered separately:

previously registered screenplay

Motion picture dramatization

2. New version of a training video that was registered previously:

previously registered video production

revisions and some new cinematographic material

3. Television documentary:

some previously published footage and photographs

editing, narration, and some new footage

Space 8:

Certification: Check the box showing under what authority you are filing the application. Provide an **original signature** and a **current date** certifying that the facts as stated on the application are correct.

> **NOTE:** If this work is published, the certification date must be on or after the publication date given in space 3.

DEPOSIT REQUIREMENTS FOR REGISTRATION

In addition to the application and fee, you must send a copy and a description of the work being registered. The nature of the copy and description may vary, depending upon the factors indicated below:

Published Motion Pictures

1. A separate description of the work: In general, a brief summary will suffice. If the work is a theatrical film or major television production, the description should be as complete as possible (for example, a shooting script, a continuity, or a pressbook); and

2. One complete copy: A copy is complete if it is clear, undamaged, and free of splices and defects that would interfere with viewing the work.

● **For motion pictures first published in the U.S.:**

One complete copy of the best edition. Where two or more editions are published in the United States, the best edition is the one preferred by the Library of Congress. Currently, the Library accepts in descending order of preference:

Film rather than another medium

1. Preprint material, by special arrangement
2. Most widely distributed film gauge
3. 35mm
4. 16mm
5. 8mm
6. Special formats (such as 65mm) only in exceptional cases
7. Open reel rather than cartridge or cassette

5

Videotape

1. Most widely distributed tape gauge
2. 2-inch reel
3. 1-inch reel
4. 3/4-inch cassette
5. 1/2-inch cassette (VHS rather than Beta)

Videodisk

- **For motion pictures first published abroad:**

One complete copy as first published.

> NOTE: For the deposit requirement for works published before Jan. 1, 1978, see page 7.

Unpublished Motion Pictures

1. **A separate description** of the work; and

2. **A complete copy** of the work containing all the visual and aural elements covered by the registration.

Alternative Deposit for Unpublished Motion Pictures

It is advisable to send a copy of the complete work. If you cannot, you may send as an alternative deposit either a recording of the complete sound track or reproductions of images from each 10-minute segment of the work. For an alternative deposit, the written description must contain:

1) the title, including any episode title;
2) a summary of the work;
3) the date the work was fixed;
4) the date the work was first telecast, if applicable, and whether telecast was simultaneous with fixation;
5) the running time; and
6) the credits, if any.

Requirements for Motion Pictures That Cannot Be Viewed by the Copyright Office Staff

The Examining Division does not have equipment to view motion pictures in certain formats, including 2-inch and 1-inch tapes, PAL and SECAM 3/4-inch videocassettes, and 8mm videocassettes. If you send one of these formats the separate written description must provide all the information required in items 1 through 6 in the immediately preceding paragraph, including the copyright notice, if any.

EXCEPTIONS TO THE NORMAL DEPOSIT REQUIREMENT

Special Relief

Where it is unusually difficult or impossible to comply with the deposit requirement for a particular motion picture, you may submit a written request for special relief from the normal requirement. The request, addressed to the **Chief of the Examining Division, U.S. Copyright Office**, must state why you cannot provide the required copy, and describe the nature of the substitute copy being deposited. This letter should be included with the registration material.

The Copyright Office may or may not grant special relief in a particular case, depending upon the difficulty of providing a required copy, the acquisitions policies and archival considerations of the Library of Congress, and the examining requirements for registration.

Motion Picture Agreement

The Motion Picture Agreement establishes several alternative deposit procedures for published motion pictures. This agreement may not be in the interest of every applicant. It is most useful in registering theatrical films. For detailed information request the Motion Picture Agreement Leaflet and a copy of the agreement from the **Copyright Acquisitions Division, Library of Congress, Washington, D.C. 20559** or call (202) 707-7125.

MANDATORY DEPOSIT FOR WORKS PUBLISHED IN THE UNITED STATES

Requirement Under Mandatory Deposit

The owner of copyright or the owner of the exclusive right of publication of a motion picture published in the United States has a legal obligation to deposit in the Library of Congress within 3 months of publication in the United States one complete copy of the best edition and a description of the work. Failure to deposit this copy after the Library demands it can result in fines and other penalities.

Satisfying Mandatory Deposit Through Registration

Depositing the required copy with an application and fee

for copyright registration simultaneously satisfies any mandatory deposit requirement for the motion picture. Satisfying the mandatory deposit requirement alone does not provide the benefits of copyright registration.

THE MOTION PICTURE COLLECTION AT THE LIBRARY OF CONGRESS

The Library of Congress is the nation's central collection of books, recordings, photographs, maps, audiovisual works, and other research materials. Many of the Library's acquisitions are obtained through copyright deposits. The material acquired by this means is critical to the Library's recognized success in maintaining superior and comprehensive collections.

Motion pictures form an essential part of the Library's holdings. As feature films, television programs, videos, and other audiovisual media become increasingly popular as a means of communication, education, and entertainment in our society, they also form a greater part of our historical record. The preservation facilities and bibliographic control provided by the Library insure that these works will be available to future generations.

MOTION PICTURES FIRST PUBLISHED BEFORE 1978

Motion pictures first published before 1978 are governed in part by the provisions of the 1909 Copyright Act. These provisions affect the notice requirement, the term of copyright, the deposit requirement, and certain information in the registration record.

Copyright Notice

For a work first published before 1978, copyright was secured if all published copies bore a copyright notice in the proper form and position. The elements of the notice generally are 1) the symbol © (the letter C in a circle), the word "copyright," or the abbreviation "Copr."; 2) the year in which copyright was secured; and 3) the name of the owner of copyright at the time of publication. If published copies did not bear a valid notice, copyright was lost and could not be restored.

The absence of a year date in the notice for motion pictures published before 1978 would not result in the loss of copyright. If a year date is included, however, it should be correct.

Term of Copyright

Works first published with notice before 1978 are protected for an initial term of 28 years, computed from the date of first publication or the year date in the notice, whichever is earlier. Registration must be made during this period and a renewal claim filed within the 28th year to gain a second 47-year term (totaling 75 years). Otherwise, the work enters the public domain after the initial 28-year term.

Deposit Requirement

To register a claim in a motion picture first published before 1978, you should deposit **one copy of the work as first published**, that is, one of the first prints or tapes made from the master and distributed. If it is impossible to send such a copy, you may request special relief from the requirement (see the previous section above on **"Special Relief"**). In this case, you must include with the substitute copy a letter confirming that the copy is identical to the copies as first published, **including the copyright notice.** In considering a special relief request, the Copyright Office may require more information about the facts of first publication.

Registration Record

The application for a work first published before 1978 must name as claimant the person or organization that was the owner of copyright **at the time of first publication.** This name must agree with the name that appears in the copyright notice.

EFFECTIVE DATE OF REGISTRATION

A copyright registration is effective on the date the Copyright Office receives all of the required elements in acceptable form, regardless of how long it then takes to process the application and mail the certificate of registration. The time the Copyright Office requires to process an application varies, depending on the amount of material the Office is receiving and the personnel available. Additionally, it may take several days for mailed material to reach the Copyright Office and for the certificate of registration to reach the recipient.

If you apply for copyright registration, you will **not** receive an acknowledgement that your application has been received (the Office receives more than 600,000 applications annually), but you can expect:

7

- A letter or telephone call from a copyright examiner if further information is needed;
- A certificate of registration to indicate the work has been registered; or
- If registration cannot be made, a letter explaining why it has been refused.

Please allow 120 days to receive a letter or certificate of registration.

If you want to know when the Copyright Office receives your material, send it by registered or certified mail and request a return receipt.

About the cover:

The motion pictures mentioned on the cover of this circular are among the first 25 films named by the Librarian of Congress to the National Film Registry. Congress created the National Film Registry, in part to select examples of great American filmmaking and to preserve these national treasures.

Films on the list but not mentioned on the cover are *The Best Years of Our Lives, The Crowd, High Noon, The Learning Tree, Mr. Smith Goes to Washington, On the Waterfront, The Searchers, Singin' in the Rain, Snow White and the Seven Dwarfs, Some Like It Hot,* and *Sunset Boulevard.*

Copyright Office • Library of Congress • Washington, D.C. 20559

■ October 1990—60,000   ☆U.S. GOVERNMENT PRINTING OFFICE: 1990: 282-171/20,011

Filling Out Application Form PA

Detach and read these instructions before completing this form. Make sure all applicable spaces have been filled in before you return this form.

BASIC INFORMATION

When to Use This Form: Use Form PA for registration of published or unpublished works of the performing arts. This class includes works prepared for the purpose of being "performed" directly before an audience or indirectly "by means of any device or process." Works of the performing arts include: (1) musical works, including any accompanying words; (2) dramatic works, including any accompanying music; (3) pantomimes and choreographic works; and (4) motion pictures and other audiovisual works.

Deposit to Accompany Application: An application for copyright registration must be accompanied by a deposit consisting of copies or phonorecords representing the entire work for which registration is to be made. The following are the general deposit requirements as set forth in the statute:

Unpublished Work: Deposit one complete copy (or phonorecord).

Published Work: Deposit two complete copies (or phonorecords) of the best edition.

Work First Published Outside the United States: Deposit one complete copy (or phonorecord) of the first foreign edition.

Contribution to a Collective Work: Deposit one complete copy (or phonorecord) of the best edition of the collective work.

Motion Pictures: Deposit *both* of the following: (1) a separate written description of the contents of the motion picture; and (2) for a published work, one complete copy of the best edition of the motion picture; or, for an unpublished work, one complete copy of the motion picture or identifying material. Identifying material may be either an audiorecording of the entire soundtrack or one frame enlargement or similar visual print from each 10-minute segment.

The Copyright Notice: For works first published on or after March 1, 1989, the law provides that a copyright notice on a specified form "may be placed on all publicly distributed copies from which the work can be visually perceived." Use of the copyright notice is the responsibility of the copyright owner and does not require advance permission from the Copyright Office. The required form of the notice for copies generally consists of three elements: (1) the symbol "©", or the word "Copyright," or the abbreviation "Copr."; (2) the year of first publication; and (3) the name of the owner of copyright. For example: © 1989 Jane Cole. The notice is to be affixed to the copies "in such manner and location as to give reasonable notice of the claim of copyright." Works first published prior to March 1, 1989, **must** carry the notice or risk loss of copyright protection.

For information about notice requirements for works published before March 1, 1989, or other copyright information, write: Information Section, LM-401, Copyright Office, Library of Congress, Washington, D.C. 20559.

LINE-BY-LINE INSTRUCTIONS

1 SPACE 1: Title

Title of This Work: Every work submitted for copyright registration must be given a title to identify that particular work. If the copies or phonorecords of the work bear a title (or an identifying phrase that could serve as a title), transcribe that wording *completely* and *exactly* on the application. Indexing of the registration and future identification of the work will depend on the information you give here. If the work you are registering is an entire "collective work" (such as a collection of plays or songs) give the overall title of the collection. If you are registering one or more individual contributions to a collective work, give the title of each contribution, followed by the title of the collective work. Example: "'A Song for Elinda' in *Old and New Ballads for Old and New People*."

Previous or Alternative Titles: Complete this space if there are any additional titles for the work under which someone searching for the registration might be likely to look, or under which a document pertaining to the work might be recorded.

Nature of This Work: Briefly describe the general nature or character of the work being registered for copyright. Examples: "Music"; "Song Lyrics"; "Words and Music"; "Drama"; "Musical Play"; "Choreography"; "Pantomime"; "Motion Picture"; "Audiovisual Work."

2 SPACE 2: Author(s)

General Instructions: After reading these instructions, decide who are the "authors" of this work for copyright purposes. Then, unless the work is a "collective work," give the requested information about every "author" who contributed any appreciable amount of copyrightable matter to this version of the work. If you need further space, request additional Continuation Sheets. In the case of a collective work, such as a songbook or a collection of plays, give information about the author of the collective work as a whole.

Name of Author: The fullest form of the author's name should be given. Unless the work was "made for hire," the individual who actually created the work is its "author." In the case of a work made for hire, the statute provides

that "the employer or other person for whom the work was prepared is considered the author."

What is a "Work Made for Hire"? A "work made for hire" is defined as: (1) "a work prepared by an employee within the scope of his or her employment"; or (2) "a work specially ordered or commissioned for use as a contribution to a collective work, as a part of a motion picture or other audiovisual work, as a translation, as a supplementary work, as a compilation, as an instructional text, as a test, as answer material for a test, or as an atlas, if the parties expressly agree in a written instrument signed by them that the work shall be considered a work made for hire." If you have checked "Yes" to indicate that the work was "made for hire," you must give the full legal name of the employer (or other person for whom the work was prepared). You may also include the name of the employee along with the name of the employer (for example: "Elster Music Co., employer for hire of John Ferguson").

"Anonymous" or "Pseudonymous" Work: An author's contribution to a work is "anonymous" if that author is not identified on the copies or phonorecords of the work. An author's contribution to a work is "pseudonymous" if that author is identified on the copies or phonorecords under a fictitious name. If the work is "anonymous" you may: (1) leave the line blank; or (2) state "anonymous" on the line; or (3) reveal the author's identity. If the work is "pseudonymous" you may: (1) leave the line blank; or (2) give the pseudonym and identify it as such (for example: "Huntley Haverstock, pseudonym"); or (3) reveal the author's name, making clear which is the real name and which is the pseudonym (for example: "Judith Barton, whose pseudonym is Madeline Elster"). However, the citizenship or domicile of the author must be given in all cases.

Dates of Birth and Death: If the author is dead, the statute requires that the year of death be included in the application unless the work is anonymous or pseudonymous. The author's birth date is optional, but is useful as a form of identification. Leave this space blank if the author's contribution was a "work made for hire."

Author's Nationality or Domicile: Give the country of which the author is a citizen, or the country in which the author is domiciled. Nationality or domicile must be given in all cases.

Nature of Authorship: Give a brief general statement of the nature of this particular author's contribution to the work. Examples: "Words"; "Co-Author of Music"; "Words and Music"; "Arrangement"; "Co-Author of Book and Lyrics"; "Dramatization"; "Screen Play"; "Compilation and English Translation"; "Editorial Revisions."

3 SPACE 3: Creation and Publication

General Instructions: Do not confuse "creation" with "publication." Every application for copyright registration must state "the year in which creation of the work was completed." Give the date and nation of first publication only if the work has been published.

Creation: Under the statute, a work is "created" when it is fixed in a copy or phonorecord for the first time. Where a work has been prepared over a period of time, the part of the work existing in fixed form on a particular date constitutes the created work on that date. The date you give here should be the year in which the author completed the particular version for which registration is now being sought, even if other versions exist or if further changes or additions are planned.

Publication: The statute defines "publication" as "the distribution of copies or phonorecords of a work to the public by sale or other transfer of ownership, or by rental, lease, or lending"; a work is also "published" if there has been an "offering to distribute copies or phonorecords to a group of persons for purposes of further distribution, public performance, or public display." Give the full date (month, day, year) when, and the country where, publication first occurred. If first publication took place simultaneously in the United States and other countries, it is sufficient to state "U.S.A."

4 SPACE 4: Claimant(s)

Name(s) and Address(es) of Copyright Claimant(s): Give the name(s) and address(es) of the copyright claimant(s) in this work even if the claimant is the same as the author. Copyright in a work belongs initially to the author of the work (including, in the case of a work made for hire, the employer or other person for whom the work was prepared). The copyright claimant is either the author of the work or a person or organization to whom the copyright initially belonging to the author has been transferred.

Transfer: The statute provides that, if the copyright claimant is not the author, the application for registration must contain "a brief statement of how the claimant obtained ownership of the copyright." If any copyright claimant named in space 4 is not an author named in space 2, give a brief, general state-

ment summarizing the means by which that claimant obtained ownership of the copyright. Examples: "By written contract"; "Transfer of all rights by author"; "Assignment"; "By will." Do not attach transfer documents or other attachments or riders.

5 SPACE 5: Previous Registration

General Instructions: The questions in space 5 are intended to find out whether an earlier registration has been made for this work and, if so, whether there is any basis for a new registration. As a general rule, only one basic copyright registration can be made for the same version of a particular work.

Same Version: If this version is substantially the same as the work covered by a previous registration, a second registration is not generally possible unless: (1) the work has been registered in unpublished form and a second registration is now being sought to cover this first published edition; or (2) someone other than the author is identified as copyright claimant in the earlier registration, and the author is now seeking registration in his or her own name. If either of these two exceptions apply, check the appropriate box and give the earlier registration number and date. Otherwise, do not submit Form PA; instead, write the Copyright Office for information about supplementary registration or recordation of transfers of copyright ownership.

Changed Version: If the work has been changed, and you are now seeking registration to cover the additions or revisions, check the last box in space 5, give the earlier registration number and date, and complete both parts of space 6 in accordance with the instructions below.

Previous Registration Number and Date: If more than one previous registration has been made for the work, give the number and date of the latest registration.

6 SPACE 6: Derivative Work or Compilation

General Instructions: Complete space 6 if this work is a "changed version," "compilation," or "derivative work," and if it incorporates one or more earlier works that have already been published or registered for copyright, or that have fallen into the public domain. A "compilation" is defined as "a work formed by the collection and assembling of preexisting materials or of data that are selected, coordinated, or arranged in such a way that the resulting work as a whole constitutes an original work of authorship." A "derivative work" is "a work based on one or more preexisting works." Examples of derivative works include musical arrangements, dramatizations, translations, abridgments, condensations, motion picture versions, or "any other form in which a work may be recast, transformed, or adapted." Derivative works also include works "consisting of editorial revisions, annotations, or other modifications" if these changes, as a whole, represent an original work of authorship.

Preexisting Material (space 6a): Complete this space and space 6b for derivative works. In this space identify the preexisting work that has been recast, transformed, or adapted. For example, the preexisting material might be: "French version of Hugo's 'Le Roi s'amuse'." Do not complete this space for compilations.

Material Added to This Work (space 6b): Give a brief, general statement of the additional new material covered by the copyright claim for which registration is sought. In the case of a derivative work, identify this new material. Examples: "Arrangement for piano and orchestra"; "Dramatization for television"; "New film version"; "Revisions throughout; Act III completely new."

If the work is a compilation, give a brief, general statement describing both the material that has been compiled and the compilation itself. Example: "Compilation of 19th Century Military Songs."

7,8,9 SPACE 7, 8, 9: Fee, Correspondence, Certification, Return Address

Deposit Account: If you maintain a Deposit Account in the Copyright Office, identify it in space 7. Otherwise leave the space blank and send the fee of $10 with your application and deposit.

Correspondence (space 7): This space should contain the name, address, area code, and telephone number of the person to be consulted if correspondence about this application becomes necessary.

Certification (space 8): The application cannot be accepted unless it bears the date and the **handwritten signature** of the author or other copyright claimant, or of the owner of exclusive right(s), or of the duly authorized agent of the author, claimant, or owner of exclusive right(s).

Address for Return of Certificate (space 9): The address box must be completed legibly since the certificate will be returned in a window envelope.

MORE INFORMATION

How To Register a Recorded Work:
If the musical or dramatic work that you are registering has been recorded (as a tape, disk, or cassette), you may choose either copyright application Form PA or Form SR, Performing Arts or Sound Recordings, depending on the purpose of the registration.

Form PA should be used to register the underlying musical composition or dramatic work. Form SR has been developed specifically to register a "sound recording" as defined by the Copyright Act—a work resulting from the "fixation of a series of sounds," separate and distinct from the underlying musical or dramatic work. Form SR should be used when the copyright claim is limited to the sound recording itself. (In one instance, Form SR may also be used to file for a copyright registration for both kinds of works—see (4) below.) Therefore:

(1) File Form PA if you are seeking to register the musical or dramatic work, not the "sound recording," even though what you deposit for copyright purposes may be in the form of a phonorecord.

(2) File Form PA if you are seeking to register the audio portion of an audiovisual work, such as a motion picture soundtrack; these are considered integral parts of the audiovisual work.

(3) File Form SR if you are seeking to register the "sound recording" itself, that is, the work that results from the fixation of a series of musical, spoken, or other sounds, but not the underlying musical or dramatic work.

(4) File Form SR if you are the copyright claimant for both the underlying musical or dramatic work and the sound recording, and you prefer to register both on the same form.

(5) File both forms PA and SR if the copyright claimant for the underlying work and sound recording differ, or you prefer to have separate registration for them.

"Copies" and "Phonorecords":
To register for copyright, you are required to deposit "copies" or "phonorecords." These are defined as follows:

Musical compositions may be embodied (fixed) in "copies," objects from which a work can be read or visually perceived, directly or with the aid of a machine or device, such as manuscripts, books, sheet music, film, and videotape. They may also be fixed in "phonorecords," objects embodying fixations of sounds, such as tapes and phonograph disks, commonly known as phonograph records. For example, a song (the work to be registered) can be reproduced in sheet music ("copies") or phonograph records ("phonorecords"), or both.

FORM PA
UNITED STATES COPYRIGHT OFFICE

REGISTRATION NUMBER

PA   PAU

EFFECTIVE DATE OF REGISTRATION

Month   Day   Year

DO NOT WRITE ABOVE THIS LINE. IF YOU NEED MORE SPACE, USE A SEPARATE CONTINUATION SHEET.

1 TITLE OF THIS WORK ▼

PREVIOUS OR ALTERNATIVE TITLES ▼

NATURE OF THIS WORK ▼ See instructions

2 NAME OF AUTHOR ▼

a

DATES OF BIRTH AND DEATH
Year Born ▼   Year Died ▼

Was this contribution to the work a "work made for hire"?
☐ Yes
☐ No

AUTHOR'S NATIONALITY OR DOMICILE
Name of Country
OR { Citizen of ▶
     Domiciled in ▶

WAS THIS AUTHOR'S CONTRIBUTION TO THE WORK
Anonymous?   ☐ Yes ☐ No
Pseudonymous? ☐ Yes ☐ No

If the answer to either of these questions is "Yes," see detailed instructions

NATURE OF AUTHORSHIP Briefly describe nature of the material created by this author in which copyright is claimed. ▼

NOTE

Under the law, the "author" of a "work made for hire" is generally the employer, not the employee (see instructions). For any part of this work that was "made for hire" check "Yes" in the space provided, give the employer (or other person for whom the work was prepared) as "Author" of that part, and leave the space for dates of birth and death blank.

NAME OF AUTHOR ▼

DATES OF BIRTH AND DEATH
Year Born ▼   Year Died ▼

Was this contribution to the work a "work made for hire"?
☐ Yes
☐ No

AUTHOR'S NATIONALITY OR DOMICILE
Name of country
OR { Citizen of ▶ _____
Domiciled in ▶ _____

WAS THIS AUTHOR'S CONTRIBUTION TO THE WORK
Anonymous?   ☐ Yes ☐ No
Pseudonymous? ☐ Yes ☐ No
If the answer to either of these questions is "Yes," see detailed instructions.

NATURE OF AUTHORSHIP Briefly describe nature of the material created by this author in which copyright is claimed. ▼

NAME OF AUTHOR ▼

DATES OF BIRTH AND DEATH
Year Born ▼   Year Died ▼

Was this contribution to the work a "work made for hire"?
☐ Yes
☐ No

AUTHOR'S NATIONALITY OR DOMICILE
Name of Country
OR { Citizen of ▶ _____
Domiciled in ▶ _____

WAS THIS AUTHOR'S CONTRIBUTION TO THE WORK
Anonymous?   ☐ Yes ☐ No
Pseudonymous? ☐ Yes ☐ No
If the answer to either of these questions is "Yes," see detailed instructions

NATURE OF AUTHORSHIP Briefly describe nature of the material created by this author in which copyright is claimed. ▼

3

YEAR IN WHICH CREATION OF THIS WORK WAS COMPLETED This information must be given in all cases.
▼ Year

DATE AND NATION OF FIRST PUBLICATION OF THIS PARTICULAR WORK
Complete this information ONLY if this work has been published.
Month ▶ _____ Day ▶ _____ Year ▶ _____
◀ Nation

4

See instructions before completing this space.

COPYRIGHT CLAIMANT(S) Name and address must be given even if the claimant is the same as the author given in space 2.▼

TRANSFER If the claimant(s) named here in space 4 are different from the author(s) named in space 2, give a brief statement of how the claimant(s) obtained ownership of the copyright. ▶

APPLICATION RECEIVED

ONE DEPOSIT RECEIVED

TWO DEPOSITS RECEIVED

REMITTANCE NUMBER AND DATE

DO NOT WRITE HERE
OFFICE USE ONLY

MORE ON BACK ▶ • Complete all applicable spaces (numbers 5-9) on the reverse side of this page.
• See detailed instructions.   • Sign the form at line 8.

DO NOT WRITE HERE
Page 1 of _____ pages

EXAMINED BY

FORM PA

CHECKED BY

☐ CORRESPONDENCE
  ☐ Yes

FOR
COPYRIGHT
OFFICE
USE
ONLY

DO NOT WRITE ABOVE THIS LINE. IF YOU NEED MORE SPACE, USE A SEPARATE CONTINUATION SHEET.

PREVIOUS REGISTRATION Has registration for this work, or for an earlier version of this work, already been made in the Copyright Office?

☐ **Yes** ☐ **No** If your answer is "Yes," why is another registration being sought? (Check appropriate box) ▼

☐ This is the first published edition of a work previously registered in unpublished form.

☐ This is the first application submitted by this author as copyright claimant.

☐ This is a changed version of the work, as shown by space 6 on this application.

If your answer is "Yes," give: **Previous Registration Number** ▼   **Year of Registration** ▼

5

DERIVATIVE WORK OR COMPILATION Complete both space 6a & 6b for a derivative work; complete only 6b for a compilation.

a. **Preexisting Material** Identify any preexisting work or works that this work is based on or incorporates. ▼

b. **Material Added to This Work** Give a brief, general statement of the material that has been added to this work and in which copyright is claimed. ▼

6

See instructions
before completing
this space.

DEPOSIT ACCOUNT If the registration fee is to be charged to a Deposit Account established in the Copyright Office, give name and number of Account.
Name ▼   **Account Number** ▼

7

CORRESPONDENCE Give name and address to which correspondence about this application should be sent. Name/Address/Apt/City/State/Zip ▼

Area Code & Telephone Number ▶

Be sure to
give your
daytime phone
▼ number

8

CERTIFICATION* I, the undersigned, hereby certify that I am the

Check only one ▼

☐ author
☐ other copyright claimant
☐ owner of exclusive right(s)
☐ authorized agent of
_____
Name of author or other copyright claimant, or owner of exclusive right(s) ▲

of the work identified in this application and that the statements made
by me in this application are correct to the best of my knowledge.

Typed or printed name and date ▼ If this application gives a date of publication in space 3, do not sign and submit it before that date.

_____ date ▶ _____

✍ Handwritten signature (X) ▼

**MAIL
CERTIFI-
CATE TO**

Name ▼

**Certificate
will be
mailed in
window
envelope**

Number/Street/Apartment Number ▼

City/State/ZIP ▼

9

YOU MUST
• Complete all necessary spaces
• Sign your application in space 8

SEND ALL 3 ELEMENTS
IN THE SAME PACKAGE

1. Application form
2. Non-refundable $10 filing fee
   in check or money order
   payable to Register of Copyrights
3. Deposit material

MAIL TO
Register of Copyrights
Library of Congress
Washington, D.C. 20559

* 17 U.S.C. § 506(e): Any person who knowingly makes a false representation of a material fact in the application for copyright registration provided for by section 409, or in any written statement filed in connection with the application, shall be fined not more than $2,500.

FORM RE

UNITED STATES COPYRIGHT OFFICE
LIBRARY OF CONGRESS
WASHINGTON, D.C. 20559

APPLICATION
FOR
Renewal Registration

HOW TO REGISTER A RENEWAL CLAIM:

- **First:** Study the information on this page and make sure you know the answers to two questions:

  (1) What are the renewal time limits in your case?

  (2) Who can claim the renewal?

- **Second:** Turn this page over and read through the specific instructions for filling out Form RE. Make sure, before starting to complete the form, that the copyright is now eligible for renewal, that you are authorized to file a renewal claim, and that you have all of the information about the copyright you will need.

- **Third:** Complete all applicable spaces on Form RE, following the line-by-line instructions on the back of this page. Use typewriter, or print the information in dark ink.

- **Fourth:** Detach this sheet and send your completed Form RE to: Register of Copyrights, Library of Congress, Washington, D.C. 20559. Unless you have a Deposit Account in the Copyright Office, your application must be accompanied by a check or money order for $6, payable to: *Register of Copyrights*. Do not send copies, phonorecords, or supporting documents with your renewal application.

WHAT IS RENEWAL OF COPYRIGHT? For works originally copyrighted between January 1, 1950 and December 31, 1977, the statute now in effect provides for a first term of copyright protection lasting for 28 years, with the possibility of renewal for a second term of 47 years. If a valid renewal registration is made for a work, its total copyright term is 75 years (a first term of 28 years, plus a renewal term of 47 years). Example: For a work copyrighted in 1960, the first term will expire in 1988, but it renewed at the proper time the copyright will last through the end of 2035.

SOME BASIC POINTS ABOUT RENEWAL:

(1) There are strict time limits and deadlines for renewing a copyright.

(2) Only certain persons who fall into specific categories named in the law can claim renewal.

(3) The new copyright law does away with renewal requirements for works first copyrighted after 1977. However, copyrights that were already in their first copyright term on January 1, 1978 (that is, works originally copyrighted between January 1, 1950 and December 31, 1977) **still have to be renewed** in order to be protected for a second term.

TIME LIMITS FOR RENEWAL REGISTRATION: The new copyright statute provides that, in order to renew a copyright, the renewal application and fee must be received in the Copyright Office "within one year prior to the expiration of the copyright." It also provides that all terms of copyright will run through the end of the year in which they would otherwise expire. Since all copyright terms will expire on December 31st of their last year, all periods for renewal registration will run from December 31st of the 27th year of the copyright, and will end on December 31st of the following year.

To determine the time limits for renewal in your case:

(1) First, find out the date of original copyright for the work. (In the case of works originally registered in unpublished form, the date of copyright is the date of registration; for published works, copyright begins on the date of first publication.)

(2) Then add 28 years to the year the work was originally copyrighted.

Your answer will be the calendar year during which the copyright will be eligible for renewal, and December 31st of that year will be the renewal deadline. Example: a work originally copyrighted on April 19, 1957, will be eligible for renewal between December 31, 1984, and December 31, 1985.

WHO MAY CLAIM RENEWAL: Renewal copyright may be claimed only by those persons specified in the law. Except in the case of four specific types of works, the law gives the right to claim renewal to the individual author of the work, regardless of who owned the copyright during the original term. If the author is dead, the statute gives the right to claim renewal to certain of the author's beneficiaries (widow and children, executors, or next of kin, depending on the circumstances). The present owner (proprietor) of the copyright is entitled to claim renewal only in four specified cases, as explained in more detail on the reverse of this page.

CAUTION: Renewal registration is possible only if an acceptable application and fee are received in the Copyright Office during the renewal period and before the renewal deadline. If an acceptable application and fee are not received before the renewal deadline, the work falls into the public domain and the copyright cannot be renewed. The Copyright Office has no discretion to extend the renewal time limits.

INSTRUCTIONS FOR COMPLETING FORM RE

SPACE 1: RENEWAL CLAIM(S)

• **General Instructions:** In order for this application to result in a valid renewal, space 1 must identify one or more of the persons who are entitled to renew the copyright under the statute. Give the full name and address of each claimant, with a statement of the basis of each claim, using the wording given in these instructions.

• **Persons Entitled to Renew:**

A. The following persons may claim renewal in all types of works except those enumerated in Paragraph B, below:

1. The author, if living. State the claim as: *the author.*

2. The widow, widower, and/or children of the author, if the author is not living. State the claim as: *the widow (widower) of the author* . . . . (Name of author)

and/or *the child (children) of the deceased author* . . . . (Name of author)

3. The author's executor(s), if the author left a will and if there is no surviving widow, widower, or child. State the claim as: *the executor(s) of the author*

. . . . (Name of author)

4. The next of kin of the author, if the author left no will and if there is no surviving widow, widower, or child. State the claim as: *the next of kin of the deceased author* . . . . *there being no will.* (Name of author)

B. In the case of the following four types of works, the proprietor (owner of the copyright at the time of renewal registration) may claim renewal:

1. Posthumous work (a work as to which no copyright assignment or other contract for exploitation has occurred during the author's lifetime). State the claim as: *proprietor of copyright in a posthumous work.*

2. Periodical, cyclopedic, or other composite work. State the claim as: *proprietor of copyright in a composite work.*

3. "Work copyrighted by a corporate body otherwise than as assignee or licensee of the individual author." State the claim as: *proprietor of copyright in a work copyrighted by a corporate body otherwise than as assignee or licensee of the individual author.* (This type of claim is considered appropriate in relatively few cases.)

4. Work copyrighted by an employer for whom such work was made for hire. State the claim as: *proprietor of copyright in a work made for hire.*

SPACE 2: WORK RENEWED

• **General Instructions:** This space is to identify the particular work being renewed. The information given here should agree with that appearing in the certificate of original registration.

• **Title:** Give the full title of the work, together with any subtitles or descriptive wording included with the title in the original registration. In the case of a musical composition, give the specific instrumentation of the work.

• **Renewable Matter:** Copyright in a new version of a previous work (such as an arrangement, translation, dramatization, compilation, or work republished with new matter) covers only the additions, changes, or other new material appearing for the first time in that version. If this work was a new version, state in general the new matter upon which copyright was claimed.

• **Contribution to Periodical, Serial, or other Composite Work:** Separate renewal registration is possible for a work published as a contribution to a periodical, serial, or other composite work, whether the contribution was copyrighted independently or as part of the larger work in which it appeared. Each contribution published in a separate issue ordinarily requires a separate renewal registration. However, the new law provides an alternative, permitting groups of periodical contributions by the same individual author to be combined under a single renewal application and fee in certain cases.

If this renewal application covers a single contribution, give all of the requested information in space 2. If you are seeking to renew a group of contributions, include a reference such as "See space 5" in space 2 and give the requested information about all of the contributions in space 5.

SPACE 3: AUTHOR(S)

• **General Instructions:** The copyright secured in a new version of a work is independent of any copyright protection in material published earlier. The only "authors" of a new version are those who contributed copyrightable matter to it. Thus, for renewal purposes, the person who wrote the original version on which the new work is based cannot be regarded as an "author" of the new version, unless that person also contributed to the new matter.

• **Authors of Renewable Matter:** Give the full names of all authors who contributed copyrightable matter to this particular version of the work.

SPACE 4: FACTS OF ORIGINAL REGISTRATION

• **General Instructions:** Each item in space 4 should agree with the information appearing in the original registration for the work. If the work being renewed is a single contribution to a periodical or composite work that was not separately registered, give information about the particular issue in which the contribution appeared. You may leave this space blank if you are completing space 5.

• **Original Registration Number:** Give the full registration number, which is a series of numerical digits, preceded by one or more letters. The registration number appears in the upper right hand corner of the certificate of registration.

• **Original Copyright Claimant:** Give the name in which ownership of the copyright was claimed in the original registration.

• **Date of Publication or Registration:** Give only one date. If the original registration gave a publication date, it should be transcribed here; otherwise the registration was for an unpublished work, and the date of registration should be given.

SPACE 5: GROUP RENEWALS

• **General Instructions:** A single renewal registration can be made for a group of works if **all** of the following statutory conditions are met: (1) all of the works were written by the same author, who is named in space 3 and who is or was an individual (not an employer for hire); (2) all of the works were first published as contributions to periodicals (including newspapers) and were copyrighted on their first publication; (3) the renewal claimant or claimants, and the basis of claim or claims, as stated in space 1, is the same for all of the works; (4) the renewal application and fee are "received not more than 28 or less than 27 years after the 31st day of December of the calendar year in which all of the works were first published"; and (5) the renewal application identifies each work separately, including the periodical containing it and the date of first publication.

• **Time Limits for Group Renewals:** To be renewed as a group, all of the contributions must have been first published during the same calendar year. For example, suppose six contributions by the same author were published on April 1, 1960, July 1, 1960, November 1, 1960, February 1, 1961, July 1, 1961, and March 1, 1962. The three 1960 copyrights can be combined and renewed at any time during 1988, and the two 1961 copyrights can be renewed as a group during 1989, but the 1962 copyright must be renewed by itself, in 1990.

• **Identification of Each Work:** Give all of the requested information for each contribution. The registration number should be that for the contribution itself if it was separately registered, and the registration number for the periodical issue if it was not.

SPACES 6, 7 AND 8: FEE, MAILING INSTRUCTIONS, AND CERTIFICATION

• **Deposit Account and Mailing Instructions (Space 6):** If you maintain a Deposit Account in the Copyright Office, identify it in space 6. Otherwise, you will need to send the renewal registration fee of $6 with your form. The space headed "Correspondence" should contain the name and address of the person to be consulted if correspondence about the form becomes necessary

• **Certification (Space 7):** The renewal application is not acceptable unless it bears the handwritten signature of the renewal claimant or the duly authorized agent of the renewal claimant.

• **Address for Return of Certificate (Space 8):** The address box must be completed legibly, since the certificate will be returned in a window envelope.

FORM RE

UNITED STATES COPYRIGHT OFFICE

REGISTRATION NUMBER

EFFECTIVE DATE OF RENEWAL REGISTRATION

(Month) (Day) (Year)

DO NOT WRITE ABOVE THIS LINE. FOR COPYRIGHT OFFICE USE ONLY

RENEWAL CLAIMANT(S), ADDRESS(ES), AND STATEMENT OF CLAIM: (See Instructions)

1 Renewal Claimant(s)

1
Name
Address
Claiming as
(Use appropriate statement from instructions)

2
Name
Address
Claiming as
(Use appropriate statement from instructions)

3
Name
Address
Claiming as
(Use appropriate statement from instructions)

(2) Work Renewed

TITLE OF WORK IN WHICH RENEWAL IS CLAIMED:

RENEWABLE MATTER:

CONTRIBUTION TO PERIODICAL OR COMPOSITE WORK:

Title of periodical or composite work: ....

If a periodical or other serial, give: Vol. .... No. .... Issue Date ....

(3) Author(s)

AUTHOR(S) OF RENEWABLE MATTER:

(4) Facts of Original Registration

ORIGINAL REGISTRATION NUMBER: ....

ORIGINAL COPYRIGHT CLAIMANT:

ORIGINAL DATE OF COPYRIGHT:

• If the original registration for this work was made in published form,
give:

DATE OF PUBLICATION: ....
        (Month)   (Day)   (Year)

OR

• If the original registration for this work was made in unpublished form,
give:

DATE OF REGISTRATION: ....
        (Month)   (Day)   (Year)

EXAMINED BY: ....

CHECKED BY: ....

CORRESPONDENCE
☐ Yes

DEPOSIT ACCOUNT
FUNDS USED:
☐

RENEWAL APPLICATION RECEIVED:

REMITTANCE NUMBER AND DATE:

FOR
COPYRIGHT
OFFICE
USE
ONLY

DO NOT WRITE ABOVE THIS LINE. FOR COPYRIGHT OFFICE USE ONLY

RENEWAL FOR GROUP OF WORKS BY SAME AUTHOR: To make a single registration for a group of works by the same individual author published as contributions to periodicals (see instructions), give full information about each contribution. If more space is needed, request continuation sheet (Form RE/CON).

⑤ **Renewal for Group of Works**

1
Title of Contribution: ....
Title of Periodical: .... Vol. ... No. ... Issue Date ...
Date of Publication: ... (Month) ... (Day) ... (Year) ... Registration Number: ...

2
Title of Contribution: ....
Title of Periodical: .... Vol. ... No ... Issue Date ...
Date of Publication: ... (Month) ... (Day) ... (Year) ... Registration Number: ...

3
Title of Contribution: ....
Title of Periodical: .... Vol. ... No. ... Issue Date ...
Date of Publication: ... (Month) ... (Day) ... (Year) ... Registration Number: ...

4
Title of Contribution: ....
Title of Periodical: .... Vol. ... No. ... Issue Date ...
Date of Publication: ... (Month) ... (Day) ... (Year) ... Registration Number: ...

5
Title of Contribution: ....
Title of Periodical: .... Vol. ... No. ... Issue Date ...
Date of Publication: ... (Month) ... (Day) ... (Year) ... Registration Number: ...

6

Title of Contribution: ....
Title of Periodical: .... Vol. .... No. .... Issue Date ....
Date of Publication: ....
(Month)   (Day)   (Year)   Registration Number: ....

Title of Contribution: ....
Title of Periodical: .... Vol. .... No. .... Issue Date ....
Date of Publication: ....
(Month)   (Day)   (Year)   Registration Number: ....

7

DEPOSIT ACCOUNT: (If the registration fee is to be charged to a Deposit Account established in the Copyright Office, give name and number of Account.)

Name: ....

Account Number: ....

CORRESPONDENCE: (Give name and address to which correspondence about this application should be sent.)

Name: ....

Address: ....
     (Apt.)
....
(City)   (State)   (ZIP)

(6) Fee and Correspondence

CERTIFICATION: I, the undersigned, hereby certify that I am the: (Check one)
☐ renewal claimant   ☐ duly authorized agent of: ....
       (Name of renewal claimant)
of the work identified in this application, and that the statements made by me in this application are correct to the best of my knowledge.

Handwritten signature: (X) ....

Typed or printed name: .... Date: ....

(7) Certification (Application must be signed)

MAIL
CERTIFICATE
TO

(Certificate will
be mailed in
window envelope)

....
(Name)
....
(Number, Street and Apartment Number)
....
(City)   (State)   (ZIP code)

(8) Address for Return of Certificate

☆U.S. GOVERNMENT PRINTING OFFICE: 1989—262-306/10

March 1989—10,000

CONTINUATION SHEET FOR FORM RE

FORM RE/CON

UNITED STATES COPYRIGHT OFFICE

REGISTRATION NUMBER

EFFECTIVE DATE OF RENEWAL REGISTRATION

....
(Month)   (Day)   (Year)

CONTINUATION SHEET RECEIVED

Page _____ of _____ pages

INSTRUCTIONS

- Use this sheet only if you are making a single renewal registration for a group of works, and you need more space to continue the listing started in Space 5 of Form RE. Use as many additional continuation sheets as you need.

- Follow the instructions accompanying Form RE in filling out this continuation sheet. Number each line in Space B consecutively.

- Submit this continuation sheet with the basic Form RE and the other continuation sheets, if any. Clip (do not tape or staple) and fold all sheets together before submitting them.

DO NOT WRITE ABOVE THIS LINE. FOR COPYRIGHT OFFICE USE ONLY

(A)

Identification of Application

IDENTIFICATION OF CONTINUATION: This sheet is a continuation of Space 5 of the application for renewal registration on Form RE, submitted for the following:

- TITLE OF FIRST OF GROUP OF WORKS IN WHICH RENEWAL IS CLAIMED: (Give first title as given in Space 5 of Form RE)

- RENEWAL CLAIMANT AND ADDRESS: (Give the name and address of at least one renewal claimant as given in Space 1 of Form RE)

B Continuation of Space 5	☐	Title of Contribution: .... Title of Periodical: .... Vol. .... No. .... Issue Date .... Date of Publication: .... (Month) .... (Day) .... (Year) .... Registration Number ....
	☐	Title of Contribution: .... Title of Periodical: .... Vol. .... No. .... Issue Date .... Date of Publication: .... (Month) .... (Day) .... (Year) .... Registration Number ....
	☐	Title of Contribution: .... Title of Periodical: .... Vol. .... No. .... Issue Date .... Date of Publication: .... (Month) .... (Day) .... (Year) .... Registration Number ....
	☐	Title of Contribution: .... Title of Periodical: .... Vol. .... No. .... Issue Date .... Date of Publication: .... (Month) .... (Day) .... (Year) .... Registration Number ....
	☐	Title of Contribution: .... Title of Periodical: .... Vol. .... No. .... Issue Date .... Date of Publication: .... (Month) .... (Day) .... (Year) .... Registration Number ....
	☐	Title of Contribution: .... Title of Periodical: .... Vol. .... No. .... Issue Date .... Date of Publication: .... (Month) .... (Day) .... (Year) .... Registration Number ....
	☐	Title of Contribution: .... Title of Periodical: .... Vol. .... No. .... Issue Date .... Date of Publication: .... (Month) .... (Day) .... (Year) .... Registration Number ....
	☐	Title of Contribution: .... Title of Periodical: .... Vol. .... No. .... Issue Date .... Date of Publication: .... (Month) .... (Day) .... (Year) .... Registration Number ....

☐ Title of Contribution: ....
Title of Periodical: .... Vol. .... No. .... Issue Date ....
Date of Publication: .... (Month) .... (Day) .... (Year) .... Registration Number ....

☐ Title of Contribution: ....
Title of Periodical: .... Vol. .... No. .... Issue Date ....
Date of Publication: .... (Month) .... (Day) .... (Year) .... Registration Number ....

☐ Title of Contribution: ....
Title of Periodical: .... Vol. .... No. .... Issue Date ....
Date of Publication: .... (Month) .... (Day) .... (Year) .... Registration Number ....

☐ Title of Contribution: ....
Title of Periodical: .... Vol. .... No. .... Issue Date ....
Date of Publication: .... (Month) .... (Day) .... (Year) .... Registration Number ....

☐ Title of Contribution: ....
Title of Periodical: .... Vol. .... No. .... Issue Date ....
Date of Publication: .... (Month) .... (Day) .... (Year) .... Registration Number ....

☐ Title of Contribution: ....
Title of Periodical: .... Vol. .... No. .... Issue Date ....
Date of Publication: .... (Month) .... (Day) .... (Year) .... Registration Number ....

☐ Title of Contribution: ....
Title of Periodical: .... Vol. .... No. .... Issue Date ....
Date of Publication: .... (Month) .... (Day) .... (Year) .... Registration Number ....

☐ Title of Contribution: ....
Title of Periodical: .... Vol. .... No. .... Issue Date ....
Date of Publication: .... (Month) .... (Day) .... (Year) .... Registration Number ....

(B) (Continued)

☐
Title of Contribution: ....
Title of Periodical: .... Vol. ...... No. ...... Issue Date ......
Date of Publication: ...... (Month) ...... (Day) ...... (Year) Registration Number ......

☐
Title of Contribution: ....
Title of Periodical: .... Vol. ...... No. ...... Issue Date ......
Date of Publication: ...... (Month) ...... (Day) ...... (Year) Registration Number ......

☐
Title of Contribution: ....
Title of Periodical: .... Vol. ...... No. ...... Issue Date ......
Date of Publication: ...... (Month) ...... (Day) ...... (Year) Registration Number ......

☐
Title of Contribution: ....
Title of Periodical: .... Vol. ...... No. ...... Issue Date ......
Date of Publication: ...... (Month) ...... (Day) ...... (Year) Registration Number ......

☐
Title of Contribution: ....
Title of Periodical: .... Vol. ...... No. ...... Issue Date ......
Date of Publication: ...... (Month) ...... (Day) ...... (Year) Registration Number ......

☐
Title of Contribution: ....
Title of Periodical: .... Vol. ...... No. ...... Issue Date ......
Date of Publication: ...... (Month) ...... (Day) ...... (Year) Registration Number ......

☐
Title of Contribution: ....
Title of Periodical: .... Vol. ...... No. ...... Issue Date ......
Date of Publication: ...... (Month) ...... (Day) ...... (Year) Registration Number ......

January 1986—12,000

☆U.S. GOVERNMENT PRINTING OFFICE: 1986—491—560/20,013

Copyright

FEES INCREASE

The Copyright Fees and Technical Amendments Act of 1990 (Public Law 101-318) increases fees for Copyright Office services effective January 3, 1991. This act marks the first adjustment of the fee schedule since January 1, 1978. The new fee schedule is printed on the reverse side of this announcement.

All fees under the 1978 fee schedule must be received in the Copyright Office on or before January 2, 1991. If the Copyright Office receives insufficient funds after January 2, 1991, the remitter will be contacted for additional fees due.

All fees should be sent in the form of a check, money order, or bank draft payable to: **Register of Copyrights**.

The Copyright Office cannot assume responsibility for the loss of cash sent in payment of copyright fees. If you are submitting material from outside the United States, please arrange for your fees to be payable in United States dollars. Your fees may be in the form of an International Money Order or a draft on a United States bank. We cannot accept a check drawn on a foreign bank.

If a check received in payment of the registration fee is returned to the Copyright Office as uncollectible, the Copyright Office will cancel the registration and will notify the remitter.

The fee for registration of an original, supplementary, or renewal claim is nonrefundable, whether or not copyright registration is ultimately made.

The Copyright Fees and Technical Amendments Act of 1990 (Public Law 101-318) amends the Copyright Act of 1976 by increasing fees for Copyright Office services, effective January 3, 1991. Citations below are to sections of the Copyright Act of 1976, as amended by Public Law 101-318.

	Fees through 1/2/91	Fees effective 1.3.91	
REGISTRATION OF COPYRIGHT CLAIMS (Forms TX, VA, PA, SR, CA, SE or GR/CP)	$10.00	$20.00	For each registration and renewal you will receive a certificate bearing the Copyright Office seal.
Form SE/Group (minimum fee $20)	N/A	$10 issue	
Form MW	$20.00	$20.00	
Form RE	$6.00	$12.00	
RECORDATION OF DOCUMENTS Recordation, under section 205, of a document of six pages or less listing no more than one title.	$10.00	$20.00	A document which relates to any disposition of a copyright, such as a transfer, will, or license, may be recorded in the Copyright Office. When processing is completed, the submitted document(s) will be returned to you, along with a certificate of recordation for each document.
Additional pages: each	$.50	N A	
Additional titles: each	$.50	N A	
Additional titles: each group of 10 or fewer	N/A	$10.00	
CERTIFICATIONS Additional certificates: each	$4.00	$8.00	Certified copy of the record of registration, including certifications of Copyright Office records. NOTE: fees are cumulative; certification fees are in addition to any other applicable fees, i.e., search, photoduplication, etc.
Any other certification: each	$4.00	$20 hr. or fraction	
SEARCHES Reports from official records: per hour or fraction.	$10.00	$20.00	The Copyright Office will, upon request, estimate the fee required for a search; the fee must be received before the search is undertaken.
Locating Office records: per hour or fraction	$10.00	$20.00	
FILING OF NOTICE OF INTENTION TO MAKE AND DISTRIBUTE PHONORECORDS	$6.00	$12.00	For the filing, under section 115(b), of notice of intention to make and distribute phonorecords.
RECEIPT FOR DEPOSITS each receipt	$2.00	$4.00	For the issuance under section 407, mandatory deposit for the Library of Congress, of a receipt for deposit.
SPECIAL HANDLING FEE Registration (plus registration or renewal fee) (see above)	$200.00	$200.00	Special handling is granted at the discretion of the Register of Copyrights in a limited number of cases as a service to those who have compelling reasons for the expedited service. For further information on special handling, you may call (202) 707-9100 and record your request for ML-319 (registration of claims) or ML-341 (recordation of documents).
Additional Fee For each claim given special handling if a single deposit copy covers multiple claims and special handling is requested only for one. This charge may be avoided by submitting a separate deposit copy.	$50.00	$50.00	
Recordation of a Document (plus recordation fee)(see above)	$200.00	$200.00	
FULL-TERM RETENTION OF COPYRIGHT DEPOSITS For the full-term retention of copyright deposits under section 704(e).	$135.00	$135.00	For information on full-term retention, you may call (202) 707-9100 and record your request for Circular 96, Section 202.23.

Fees remitted to the Copyright Office for registration, including those for supplementary or renewal registrations and for special handling, will not be refunded. Payments made in excess of the statutory fee will be refunded, but refunds of $5 or less will not be refunded unless specifically requested.

Copyright Office • Library of Congress • Washington, D.C. 20559

SL-4 September 1990 — 400,000   ○U.S. GOVERNMENT PRINTING OFFICE: 1990: 262-309/20,007

TO SAVE YOU TIME AND MONEY,

WE HAVE LISTED BELOW SOME OF THE MORE FREQUENTLY ASKED

QUESTIONS ABOUT COPYRIGHT REGISTRATION.

PLEASE TAKE A FEW MINUTES TO READ THIS SHEET

BEFORE YOU CALL OR WRITE THE COPYRIGHT OFFICE.

HOW WILL I KNOW IF MY APPLICATION WAS RECEIVED?

You will not receive an acknowledgement that your application has been received—the Office receives more than 650,000 applications annually—but you can expect **within 16 weeks of submission:**

- A certificate of registration to indicate the work has been registered, or

- A letter or telephone call from a copyright examiner if further information is needed; or, if the application cannot be accepted, a letter explaining why it has been rejected.

If you want to know when the Copyright Office receives your material, send it by registered or certified mail and request a return receipt from the Postal Service. Due to the large volume of mail received by the Office daily, **you should allow at least 3 weeks for the return of your receipt.**

WHAT IS THE STATUS OF MY APPLICATION?

We cannot provide free information about the status of applications that have been in the Copyright Office fewer than 16 weeks. If you must have this information sooner, contact the Certifications and Documents Section, which can provide this information upon payment of applicable fees.

WHEN IS MY REGISTRATION EFFECTIVE?

A copyright registration is effective on the date that all the required elements (application, fee, and deposit) in acceptable form are received in the Copyright Office, regardless of the length of time it takes the Copyright Office to process the application

and mail the certificate of registration. You do not have to receive your certificate before you publish or produce your work, nor do you need permission from the Copyright Office to place a notice of copyright on your material.

HOW MANY FORMS MAY I RECEIVE?

Because of budget reductions we can no longer send unlimited quantities of our application forms and publications. If you need additional application forms or circulars, you may order a limited supply by calling the Copyright Office Hotline anytime day or night at (202)707-9100 and leaving a message on the recorder. We encourage you to photocopy our circulars and other informational material. You may also photocopy blank application forms; however, photocopied forms submitted to the Copyright Office must be clear, legible, on a good grade of 8 1/2-inch by 11-inch white paper. The forms should be printed, preferably in black ink, head to head (so that when you turn the sheet over, the top of page 2 is directly behind the top of page 1). **Forms not meeting these requirements will be returned.** Please allow 2-3 weeks for delivery of your order.

WHAT IS THE COPYRIGHT OFFICE'S ADDRESS?

Please use the following address when sending us mail. You should include your own ZIP code in your return address:

Register of Copyrights
Copyright Office
Library of Congress
Washington, D.C. 20559

Include your nonrefundable filing fee, your completed application form, and your nonreturnable deposit (copies, phonorecords, or identifying material) **in the same package.**

Appendix A8

Address for Additional Copyright Forms and Information

Original forms must be used when applying for a copyright. They can be obtained by writing to:

> United States Copyright Office
> Library of Congress
> Washington, D.C. 20559

or by calling Forms Hot-line 202-707-9100.

Also available at the same address are the following publications on copyrights:

Circular 1:	Copyright Basics
Circular 7d:	Mandatory Deposit of Copies
Circular 8:	Corrections and Amplifications of Existing Registrations
Circular 12:	Recordation of Transfers and Other Documents
Circular 15a:	Duration of Copyright
Circular 15t:	Extension of Copyright Terms
Circular 22:	How to Investigate the Copyright Status of a Work
Circular 38a:	International Copyright Relations of the U.S.

General copyright information can also be obtained by phone at 202-479-0700.

Appendix A9

New York Civil Rights Law §§ 50, 51

§ 50. Right of privacy

A person, firm or corporation that uses for advertising purposes, or for the purposes of trade, the name, portrait or picture of any living person without having first obtained the written consent of such person, or if a minor of his or her parent or guardian, is guilty of a misdemeanor.

§ 51. Action for injunction and for damages

Any person whose name, portrait or picture is used within this state for advertising purposes or for the purposes of trade without the written consent first obtained as above provided may maintain an equitable action in the supreme court of this state against the person, firm or corporation so using his name, portrait or picture, to prevent and restrain the use thereof; and may also sue and recover damages for any injuries sustained by reason of such use and if the defendant shall have knowingly used such person's name, portrait or picture in such manner as is forbidden or declared to be unlawful by section fifty of this article, the jury, in its discretion, may award exemplary damages. But nothing contained in this article shall be so construed as to prevent any person, firm or corporation from selling or otherwise transferring any material containing such name, portrait or picture in whatever medium to any user of such name, portrait or picture, or to any third party for sale or transfer directly or indirectly to such a user, for use in a manner lawful under this article; nothing contained in this article shall be so construed as to prevent any person, firm or corporation, practicing the profession of photography, from exhibiting in or about his or its establishment specimens of the work of such establishment, unless the same is continued by such person, firm or corporation after written notice objecting thereto has been given by the person portrayed; and nothing contained in this article shall be so construed as to prevent any person, firm or corporation from using the name, portrait or picture of any manufacturer or dealer in connection with the goods, wares and merchandise manufactured, produced or dealt in by him which he was sold or disposed of with such name, portrait or picture used in connection therewith; or from using the name, portrait or picture of any author, composer or artist in connection with his literary, musical or artistic productions which he has sold or disposed of with such name, portrait or picture used in connection therewith.

Appendix A10

California Civil Code §§ 3344, 990

§ 3344. Use of Another's Name, Voice, Signature, Photograph, or Likeness in Advertising or Soliciting Without Prior Consent

(a) Any person who knowingly uses another's name, voice, signature, photograph, or likeness, in any manner, on or in products, merchandise, or goods, or for purposes of advertising or selling, or soliciting purchases of, products, merchandise, goods or services, without such person's prior consent, or, in the case of a minor, the prior consent of his parent or legal guardian, shall be liable for any damages sustained by the person or persons injured as a result thereof. In addition, in any action brought under this section, the person who violated the section shall be liable to the injured party or parties in an amount equal to the greater of seven hundred fifty dollars ($750) or the actual damages suffered by him or her as a result of the unauthorized use, and any profits from the unauthorized use that are attributable to the use and are not taken into account in computing the actual damages. In establishing such profits, the injured party or parties are required to present proof only of the gross revenue attributable to such use, and the person who violated this section is required to prove his or her deductible expenses. Punitive damages may also be awarded to the injured party or parties. The prevailing party in any action under this section shall also be entitled to attorney's fees and costs.

(b) As used in this section, "photograph" means any photograph or photographic reproduction, still or moving, or any videotape or live television transmission, of any person, such that the person is readily identifiable.

(1) A person shall be deemed to be readily identifiable from a photograph when one who views the photograph with the naked eye can reasonably determine that the person depicted in the photograph is the same person who is complaining of its unauthorized use.

(2) If the photograph includes more than one person so identifiable, then the person or persons complaining of the use shall be represented as individuals rather than solely as members of a definable group represented in the photograph. A definable group includes, but is not limited to, the following examples: a crowd at any sporting event, a crowd in any street or public building, the audience at any theatrical or stage production, a glee club, or a baseball team.

(3) A person or persons shall be considered to be represented as members of a definable group if they are represented in the photograph solely as a result of being present at the time the photograph was taken and have not been singled out as individuals in any manner.

(c) Where a photograph or likeness of an employee of the person using the photograph or likeness appearing in the advertisement or other publication prepared by or in behalf of the user is only incidental, and not essential, to the purpose of the publication in which it appears, there shall arise a rebuttable presumption affecting the burden of producing evidence that the failure to obtain the consent of the employee was not a knowing use of the employee's photograph or likeness.

(d) For purposes of this section, a use of a name, voice, signature, photograph, or likeness in connection with any news, public affairs, or sports broadcast or account, or any political campaign, shall not constitute a use for which consent is required under subdivision (a).

(e) The use of a name, voice, signature, photograph, or likeness in a commercial medium shall not constitute a use for which consent is required under subdivision (a) solely because the material containing such use is commercially sponsored or contains paid advertising. Rather it shall be a question of fact whether or not the use of the person's name, voice, signature, photograph, or likeness was so directly connected with the commercial sponsorship or with the paid advertising as to constitute a use for which consent is required under subdivision (a).

(f) Nothing in this section shall apply to the owners or employees of any medium used for advertising, including, but not limited to, newspapers, magazines, radio and television networks and stations, cable television systems, billboards, and transit ads, by whom any advertisement or solicitation in violation of this section is published or disseminated, unless it is established that such owners or employees had knowledge of the unauthorized use of the person's name, voice, signature, photograph, or likeness as prohibited by this section.

(g) The remedies provided for in this section are cumulative and shall be in addition to any others provided for by law.

§ 990. Deceased Personality's Name, Voice, Signature, Photograph, or Likeness in Advertising or Soliciting

(a) Any person who uses a deceased personality's name, voice, signature, photograph, or likeness, in any manner, on or in products, merchandise, or goods, or for purposes of advertising or selling, or soliciting purchases of, products, merchandise, goods, or services, without prior consent from the person or persons specified in subdivision (c), shall be liable for any damages sustained by the person or persons injured as a result thereof. In addition, in any action brought under this section, the person who violated the section shall be liable to the injured party or parties in an amount equal to the greater of seven hundred fifty dollars ($750) or the actual damages suffered by the injured party or parties, as a result of the unauthorized use, and any profits from the unauthorized use that are attributable to the use and are not taken into account in computing the actual damages. In establishing these profits, the injured party or parties shall be required to present proof only of the gross revenue attributable to the use and the person who violated the section is required to prove his or her deductible expenses. Punitive damages may also be awarded to the injured party or parties. The prevailing party or parties in any action under this section shall also be entitled to attorneys' fees and costs.

(b) The rights recognized under this section are property rights, freely transferable, in whole or in part, by contract or by means of trust or testamentary documents, whether the transfer occurs before the death of the deceased personality, by the deceased personality or his or her transferees, or, after the death of the deceased personality, by the person or persons in whom such rights vest under this section or the transferees of that person or persons.

(c) The consent required by this section shall be exercisable by the person or persons to whom such right of consent (or portion thereof) has been transferred in accordance with subdivision (b), or if no such transfer has occurred, then by the person or persons to whom such right of consent (or portion thereof) has passed in accordance with subdivision (d).

(d) Subject to subdivisions (b) and (c), after the death of any person, the rights under this section shall belong to the following person or persons and may be exercised, on behalf of and for the benefit of all of those persons, by those persons who, in the aggregate, are entitled to more than a one-half interest in such rights:

(1) The entire interest in those rights belong to the surviving spouse of the deceased personality unless there are any surviving children or grandchildren of the deceased personality, in which case one-half of the entire interest in those rights belong to the surviving spouse.

(2) The entire interest in those rights belong to the surviving children of the deceased personality and to the surviving children of any dead child of the deceased personality unless the deceased personality has a surviving spouse, in which case the ownership of a one-half interest in rights is divided among the surviving children and grandchildren.

(3) If there is no surviving spouse, and no surviving children or grandchildren, then the entire interest in those rights belong to the surviving parent or parents of the deceased personality.

(4) The rights of the deceased personality's children and grandchildren are in all cases divided among them and exercisable on a per stirpes basis according to the number of the deceased personality's children represented; the share of the children of a dead child of a deceased personality can be exercised only by the action of a majority of them. For the purposes of this section, "per stirpes" is defined as it is defined in Section 240 of the Probate Code.

(e) If any deceased personality does not transfer his or her rights under this section by contract, or by means of a trust or testamentary document, and there are no surviving persons as described in subdivision (d), then the rights set forth in subdivision (a) shall terminate.

(f)(1) A successor-in-interest to the rights of a deceased personality under this section or a licensee thereof may not recover damages for a use prohibited by this section that occurs before the successor-in-interest or licensee registers a claim of the rights under paragraph (2).

(2) Any person claiming to be a successor-in-interest to the rights of a deceased personality under this section or a licensee thereof may register that claim with the Secretary of State on a form prescribed by the Secretary of State and upon payment of a fee of ten dollars ($10). The form shall be verified and shall include the name and date of death of the deceased personality, the name and address of the claimant, the basis of the claim, and the rights claimed.

(3) Upon receipt and after filing of any document under this section, the Secretary of State may microfilm or reproduce by other techniques any of the filings or documents and destroy the original filing or document. The microfilm or other reproduction of any document under the provision of this section shall be admissible in any court of law. The microfilm or other reproduction of any document may be destroyed by the Secretary of State 50 years after the death of the personality named therein.

(4) Claims registered under this subdivision shall be public records.

(g) No action shall be brought under this section by reason of any use of a deceased personality's name, voice, signature, photograph, or likeness occurring after the expiration of 50 years from the death of the deceased personality.

(h) As used in this section, "deceased personality" means any natural person whose name, voice, signature, photograph, or likeness has commercial value at the time of his or her death, whether or not during the lifetime of that natural person the person used his or her name, voice, signature, photograph, or likeness on or in products, merchandise or goods, or for purposes of advertising or selling, or solicitation of purchase of, products, merchandise, goods or service. A "deceased personality" shall include, without limitation, any such natural person who has died within 50 years prior to January 1, 1985.

(i) As used in this section, "photograph" means any photograph or photographic reproduction, still or moving, or any videotape of live television transmission, of any person, such that the deceased personality is readily identifiable. A deceased personality shall be deemed to be readily identifiable from a photograph when one who views the photograph with the naked eye can reasonably determine who the person depicted in the photograph is.

(j) For purposes of this section, a use of a name, voice, signature, photograph, or likeness in connection with any news, public affairs, or sports broadcast or account, or any political campaign, shall not constitute a use for which consent is required under subdivision (a).

(k) The use of a name, voice, signature, photograph, or likeness in a commercial medium shall not constitute a use for which consent is required under subdivision (a) solely because the material containing such use is commercially sponsored or contains paid advertising. Rather it shall be a question of fact whether or not the use of the deceased personality's name, voice, signature, photograph, or likeness was so directly connected with the commercial sponsorship or with the paid advertising as to constitute a use for which consent is required under subdivision (a).

(l) Nothing in this section shall apply to the owners or employees of any medium used for advertising, including, but not limited to, newspapers, magazines, radio and television networks and stations, cable television systems, billboards, and transit ads, by whom any advertisement or solicitation is violation of this section is published or disseminated, unless it is established that such owners or employees had knowledge of the unauthorized use of the deceased personality's name, voice, signature, photograph, or likeness as prohibited by this section.

(m) The remedies provided for in this section are cumulative and shall be in addition to any others provided for by law.

(n) This section shall not apply to the use of a deceased personality's name, voice, signature, photograph, or likeness, in any of the following instances:

(1) A play, book, magazine, newspaper, musical composition, film, radio or television program, other than an advertisement or commercial announcement not exempt under paragraph (4).

(2) Material that is of political or newsworthy value.

(3) Single and original works of fine art.

(4) An advertisement or commercial announcement for a use permitted by paragraph (1), (2), or (3).

Appendix A11
Lanham Act, Section 43(a): Excerpt

§ 1125. False designations of origin and false descriptions forbidden

(a) Any person who, on or in connection with any goods or services, or any container for goods, uses in commerce any word, term, name, symbol, or device, or any combination thereof, or any false designation of origin, false or misleading description of fact, or false or misleading representation of fact, which—

(1) is likely to cause confusion, or to cause mistake, or to deceive as to the affiliation, connection, or association of such person with another person, or as to the origin, sponsorship, or approval of his or her goods, services, or commercial activities by another person, or

(2) in commercial advertising or promotion, misrepresents the nature, characteristics, qualities, or geographic origin of his or her or another person's goods, services, or commercial activities,

shall be liable in a civil action by any person who believes that he or she is or is likely to be damaged by such act.

Appendix A12

Address for Trademark Forms and Information

Original trademark forms can be obtained by writing to:

U.S. Department of Commerce
Patent and Trademark Office
Washington, D.C. 20231

Filing requirements and forms are available in a patent and trademark office publication entitled *Basic Facts About Trademarks.*

General trademark information is also available by phone 703-557-INFO.

Appendix A13

Address for the Federal Trade Commission

Federal Trade Commission
Pennsylvania Avenue at 6th Street, N.W.
Washington, D.C. 20580
202-326-2222
Advertising: 202-326-3131

Appendix B
CONTRACTS

User's Guide to the Contract Forms

Appendix B is devoted to contract forms and related materials. These forms cover many of the kinds of deals that an independent producer, actor, director, writer, or other television professional will have to make. For the most part, we have not included contracts relating to station or cable system operations, on the theory that such entities are more likely to have the benefit of regular legal counsel to help educate them and initiate any drafting. We have also left out most long-form or otherwise complicated contracts, for similar reasons.

To highlight the important issues and customary terms of the deals, each section begins with an issue checklist, to be used as a reminder when negotiating or drafting. These include issues that may not have been addressed in the short-form agreements which we have included. The contracts themselves are meant more as educational tools than as specific models to be copied *verbatim*.

Should you wish to use the contract forms as the basis for actual agreements, we urge you to proceed with caution. The match between the form in the book and your actual circumstance may be less than perfect. For instance, most of the agreements we have included are relatively short and somewhat simplified. While this makes them more accessible and allows us to keep the weight of the book under some control, there are, by necessity, possible concerns which have not been addressed. Variations in applicable law may also require changes to the basic form. We recommend that you consult with an attorney about any specific application.

Appendix B1

Rights Acquisition:
Issue Checklist

1. What rights are being granted?

   - Rights in a pre-existing property?
   - Rights in a life story?
   - Rights in a newly-created work, like a script?
   - Rights of privacy and publicity?
   - Rights to use name, likeness, and biography in advertising?
   - Rights in a title?
   - Rights to change, alter, and edit?
   - Rights in any successor work?
   - Is the grant exclusive?
   - Is the grant irrevocable?
   - Is there any obligation to use the material?

2. Are there any reserved rights?

   - Live stage rights?
   - Publication rights?
   - Any holdbacks?

3. What markets and media are covered?

   - All television, film, and related rights?
   - Broadcast television?
   - Standard cable?
   - Pay cable?
   - Home video?
   - Business and educational video?
   - Direct broadcast satellite?
   - Other new technologies?

- Theatrical film?
- Book publishing?
- Merchandising?

4. What territories are covered?

   - The whole universe?
   - The U.S., its territories, and possessions?
   - North America?
   - English-speaking countries?
   - Europe?
   - Japan?
   - Other specific territories?

5. Is the deal an option?

   - How long is the option?
   - Can it be extended?
   - Will force majeure extend it?
   - Are there successive dependent options?
   - How is the option exercised?

6. Is it a firm deal?

   - Are there any preconditions?
   - Is it pay-or-play?

7. What payments must be made for the rights?

   - Is there an option payment?
   - Is there an option extension payment?
   - Do the option payment(s) apply against the purchase price?
   - What is the purchase price?
   - When is it paid?
   - What uses does the purchase price cover?
   - Are there additional payments due for additional uses or subsequent productions?
   - Is there a profit share or other back-end participation being granted?
   - Are there any expenses to reimburse?

8. What representations and warranties should be given?

   - Is the work either original or in the public domain?
   - Does the grantor own the rights and have the rights to grant them?

- Does the work contain any libelous or slanderous material?
- Does the work violate any rights of privacy or publicity?
- Does either the work or its intended use violate any rights of any third parties?

9. Is either party giving an indemnity?

- Does the indemnity cover alleged breaches, or only actual breaches?
- Does the indemnity cover attorney's fees and costs?
- Who controls the defense and settlement of any claim?

10. Are the agreement and the rights granted assignable?

- If so, does the original purchaser remain liable?

11. Does the grantor get a credit?

- Is it in the lead or tail credits?
- Is it on a single card or is it shared?
- Is it a verbal credit?
- Is there any credit obligation in advertising and promotion?
- Are the consequences of a failure to give credit limited in the customary way?

12. Are there limitations on the grantor's remedies?

- Are injunctions prohibited?
- Is recision prohibited?

13. Is there any union or guild involved?

- If so, what impact does it have?

Appendix B2
Submission Release Letter

[Producer Letterhead]

[Date]

[Name and Address]

Dear _____:

As you know, _____ ("Producer") is engaged in the production of television programs for exploitation in any and all entertainment media. In this context, Producer reviews various source ideas, stories and suggestions. Such material may relate to format, theme, characters, treatments and/or means of exploiting a production once completed. In order to avoid misunderstandings, Producer will not review or discuss ideas, scripts, treatments, formats or the like submitted to it on an unsolicited basis by persons not in its employ without first obtaining the agreement of the person submitting the material to the provisions of this letter.

By signing the enclosed copy of this letter and returning it to us, you hereby acknowledge and agree as follows:

1. You are submitting to Producer the following material for its review: _____

_____

_____

_____.

2. You warrant that you are the sole owner and author of the above described material and that you have the full right and authorization to submit it to Producer, free of any obligation to any third party.

3. You agree that any part of the submitted material which is not novel or original and not legally protected may be used by Producer without any liability on its part to you and that nothing herein shall

place Producer in any different position with respect to such non-novel or original material by reason hereof.

4. Producer shall not be under any obligation to you with respect to the submitted material except as may later be set forth in a fully executed written agreement between you and Producer.

5. You realize that Producer has had and will have access to and/ or may independently create or have created ideas, identical to the theme, plot, idea, format or other element of the material now being submitted by you and you agree that you will not be entitled to any compensation by reason of the use by Producer of such similar or identical material.

Very truly yours,
[Producer]

By: _____

AGREED TO AND ACCEPTED:

By: _____

Date: _____

Appendix B3
Personal Release

PERSONAL RELEASE

1. BASIC INFORMATION

Program: _____

Production Company: _____

Its Address: _____

Individual Giving Release: _____

His/Her Address: _____

His/Her Age (check one): Over 18 ____ Under 18 ____

2. RELEASE

The undersigned individual hereby grants to the above named Production Company, and its successors, licensees and assigns, the perpetual and irrevocable right to use the undersigned's name, likeness, voice, biography and history, factually or otherwise, and under a real or a fictitious name, in connection with the production, distribution and exploitation of the Program, and of any elements of the Program and any remakes or sequels based on the Program. Such grant includes use in advertising in connection with the foregoing, and use in any and all media, whether now existing or hereafter devised, throughout the universe. It also includes the right to make such changes, fictionalizations and creative choices as the Production Company may decide in its sole discretion.

The undersigned individual: (i) agrees not to bring any action or claim against the Production Company, or its successors, licensees and assigns, or to allow others to bring such an action or claim, based on the Program or the depiction of the undersigned in the Program or the use of material relating to the undersigned in the Program or as otherwise described above, and (ii) releases the Production Company, its successors, licensees and assigns, from any and all such actions or claims which the undersigned may have now or in the future.

The undersigned acknowledges the receipt of good and valuable consideration for the release and other grants and agreements made herein, and understands that the Production Company is relying on them in proceeding with the production and exploitation of the Program and elements thereof as authorized above. The undersigned warrants that the use of the rights granted hereunder and of any material supplied by the undersigned will not violate the rights of any third party.

3. *SIGNATURE AND DATE.*

Signature: _____

Date: _____

Appendix B4
Short-Form Rights Option Agreement

Dear ___[Author]___ :

This letter, when signed by you, will confirm our agreement for an option for us to acquire the exclusive television, film, and allied rights in the work written by you (the "Work"), and described in the attached Exhibit A, on the following terms:

1. In return for $_____, you are giving us the exclusive option for _____ months from the date of this letter to acquire the exclusive television, film, and allied rights for the Work, in perpetuity, for exploitation worldwide in all media.

2. Should we exercise our option, we will give you notice and pay you a fee of $_____, less the amount described in Paragraph 1 above.

3. If we exercise our option, we will have the right to produce or co-produce one or more projects based on the Work, adapted as we feel necessary, or to license the production to any other producer, broadcaster, etc. We will have the right to use your name and likeness in publicizing any such production.

4. You do not grant us any literary publishing rights in the Work, other than the right to use customary excerpts and synopses in connection with productions. You warrant that the grant of rights you are making will not infringe on the rights of any third party.

5. It is our intention to enter into a longer agreement containing these and other terms customary in the entertainment industry, but unless and until such a longer agreement is fully signed by both you and us, this letter will be the complete agreement between us.

Yours sincerely,
[Production Company]

By:_____

[Producer]

AGREED TO AND ACCEPTED:

_____

[Author]

[Note: Attach Exhibit A describing the Work]

Appendix B5

Development, Distribution, and Finance Agreements: Issue Checklist

1. What media are covered?

    - All television, film, and related rights?
    - Broadcast television?
    - Standard cable?
    - Pay cable?
    - Home video?
    - Business and educational video?
    - Direct broadcast satellite?
    - Other new technologies?
    - Theatrical film?
    - Book publishing?
    - Merchandising?

2. What territories are covered?

    - The whole universe?
    - The U.S., its territories, and possessions?
    - North America?
    - English-speaking countries?
    - Europe?
    - Japan?
    - Other specific territories?

3. Are there any holdbacks or restrictions on rights or territories not granted?

4. What is the term of the distribution contract?

    - Is it for a term of years?
    - Is it for the life of the copyright?
    - Can it be canceled if the distributor defaults?

5. Is the distributor providing production finance?

   - If so, what is the schedule of funding?
   - Will the distributor have a financial representative on the set?
   - Will the distributor take a security interest in the program and all related rights?
   - Will the distributor require a completion bond?
   - Will the distributor have the right to take over the production if the producer goes over budget?
   - How will the investment be recouped?
   - What share of profits or other back-end participation will be paid for this finance?
   - Is a bankable pick-up guaranty being provided instead of cash advances?

6. What input will the distributor have into the production process? (In general, the more finance being provided, the more the input.)

   - What production elements (writer, script, director, cast, designers, director of photography, music) are subject to distributor approval?
   - What business elements (locations, facilities, labs) are subject to approval?
   - Is the budget subject to approval?
   - Are any individual agreements subject to approval?
   - Are the producer's fees and overheads subject to approval?
   - Is there a distributor overhead factor or production fee?
   - Will the distributor bring the production in-house?

7. What are the required delivery items?

   - What are the technical items, tape masters, etc.?
   - Is a lab letter needed?
   - What are the non-technical items, such as script, publicity materials, cue sheets, cast lists, credit lists, residual schedules, E&O insurance certificate?

8. What input does the producer have into the distribution process?

   - Will there be consultation or approval over publicity?
   - Does the producer approve the deals?
   - Are there minimum targets?
   - Does the producer approve any subdistributors?
   - Is there any obligation to distribute, or termination for inactivity?

9. When does revenue start to be counted?

- On actual receipt in the U.S.?
- On receipt by a subsidiary or affiliate?
- How are blocked funds in foreign countries handled?
- Are there any deductions for taxes or other charges off the top?

10. What is the distributor's fee?

- Is it the customary percentage of gross revenues?
- Does it vary by territory and medium?
- Is it inclusive of the fees of any subdistributors, particularly affiliates?

11. What expenses can the distributor deduct?

- Are there any caps?
- Are the costs of physical distribution covered (tapes, satellite time, etc.)?
- Are the costs of publicity and marketing covered?
- Are there any limits on conference, sales-market, and other travel and entertainment costs?
- Can the distributor deduct for interest, taxes, and a distribution overhead?
- Does the distributor pay and recover residuals, reuse fees, and music performance license costs?
- Who pays for initial and ongoing E&O insurance coverage?
- Who pays any litigation and collection costs?

12. How does the distributor recoup any advances and share in profits?

- Does the distributor recoup in the first position, or does it share, pari passu or by some other formula, with other financing sources?
- Is any interest taken?
- How are profits determined?
- Does the distributor, producer, or any other party share in revenues on a different basis (gross, adjusted gross, etc.)?

13. What kinds of reports and accountings are given?

- How frequently?
- How detailed?
- What are the rights to audit these statements and the distributor's books and records?
- When do statements become unchallengeable?

14. What representations and warranties should be given?

   - Is the program original and protected by copyright?
   - Have all the necessary rights and clearances, including music rights, been obtained?
   - Does the producer own the rights that are being granted free and clear, and does he/she have the right to grant them?
   - Does the program contain any defamatory material?
   - Does the program violate any rights of privacy or publicity?
   - Does the program or its intended distribution violate any other rights of any third parties?

15. Is either party giving an indemnity?

   - Does the indemnity cover alleged breaches, or only actual breaches?
   - Does the indemnity cover attorney's fees and costs?
   - Who controls the defense and settlement of any claim?

16. Are the agreement and the rights granted assignable?

   - If so, does the original distributor remain liable?
   - Are subdistributors permitted?

17. Are there limitations on the producer's remedies?

   - Are injunctions prohibited?
   - Can the rights revert on termination, or is recision prohibited?

18. Are there any rights with respect to further projects, such as sequels, remakes, series, spin-offs, etc.?

Appendix B6

Short-Form
Development Deal

This agreement between _____ ("Purchaser") and _____ ("Producer") sets forth the terms of the agreement between them concerning the development and production of the television project tentatively entitled _____ (the "Program"):

1. *The Program:* The Program as currently envisioned consists of:

2. *Development Steps:* Upon the authorization of Purchaser as indicated for each successive step, Producer will take the following development steps:

   (a) *Step 1:*

   Action: [indicate step or steps to be taken, e.g. treatment, budget, script, re-write, etc.]

   Completion Dates:

   Approval Dates: [date for Purchaser to approve and commission next step, require a re-write (if applicable), or cancel; date typically tied to completion date of step]

   Personnel: [i.e. a named writer or production person or person to be designated by one or both parties at the time]

   Fees and Expenses Paid by Purchaser: [can be a fixed amount, all approved costs, a mixture of the two, or some other approach; list payment schedule]

   Other Agreed Points:

   (b) *Step 2:*

   [Same list. Repeat as necessary for additional steps.]

3. *Production Commitment:* Upon the completion and approval of the final step set forth above, or at any other time during the development process mutually agreed between Purchaser and Producer, Purchaser shall have the exclusive right to commission the production of the Program by Producer, in accordance with the terms and conditions set out in the Agreement attached as Exhibit A. All major business and

creative elements, including, without limitation, the budget, production schedule, facilities and locations, cast, production manager, director, writer, and heads of technical departments, will be subject to the mutual approval of Purchaser and Producer. Such approvals may be given at any time in the development process. Should Purchaser and Producer fail to agree on any such points within a reasonable time after good-faith negotiation, then such failure to agree shall constitute a cancellation of development.

4. *Cancellation and Turn-Around:* Should development be canceled, either by a failure by Purchaser to approve and commit to the next step under Paragraph 2 within the required time or by a failure to agree on a major business or creative element under Paragraph 3, then all rights in the program will revert to Producer, subject only to the right of the Purchaser to receive the following amounts should there be a production of the Program or of any other project substantially based on, or directly derived from, the Program:

(a) from the production budget, upon the first day of taping, shooting or principal photography, Purchaser shall be reimbursed for all fees and expenses paid by Purchaser to Producer under this agreement, together with interest at the rate of ____% per year on the balance of such fees and expenses outstanding from time to time (such interest not to exceed, in the aggregate, 100% of such fees and expenses); and

(b) the following interest in the net profits, adjusted gross, or other "back-end" formula from the revenues of the project, calculated and paid on a favored-nations basis with all other recipients of such a revenue interest, including the Producer and financing entity of the project, expressed as a percent of one-hundred percent of such revenue interest:

> if Step 1 is completed, ____%;
> if Step 2 is completed, ____%;
> [etc.].

5. *Development Process:* During the development process (i.e. for so long as Purchaser has continuing rights under Paragraph 2), Purchaser may approach any third parties concerning finance, transmission or any other aspect of distribution of the Program. If any of such approach leads to a "pitch" or other formal presentation of the Program, Purchaser will involve Producer directly, and Producer will provide all reasonable assistance. Purchaser will pay the reasonable expenses of a representative of Producer attending a formal presentation which occurs outside of the _____ metropolitan area. During the development process, neither party will make any third party commitment on any matter relating to the Program requiring mutual approval without the agreement of the other.

6. *Representations and Warranties:* Producer represents and warrants that (i) it is free to enter into and to perform this agreement; and (ii) the Program and any material to be included in the Program (other than material provided by Purchaser) is and will be either owned by Producer, or in the public domain, or fully cleared with respect to all applicable rights, and their use and exploitation as contemplated hereunder will not violate the rights of any third party. Purchaser represents and warrants that (i) it is free to enter into and to perform this agreement; and (ii) any material provided by it to be included in the Program is and will be either owned by Purchaser, in the public domain, or fully cleared with respect to all applicable rights, and their use and exploitation as contemplated hereunder will not violate the rights of any third party.

7. *Miscellaneous:*

(a) The addresses, including phone and fax, of each of the parties are as follows:

Purchaser:

Producer:

(b) Notices and other communications hereunder may be sent by certified mail, personal delivery, courier service or fax, to the address specified above or such other address as may be specified by notice and will be effective upon delivery at such address or upon return, if undeliverable at such address.

(c) This agreement will be subject to the laws of the State of _____ applicable to contracts signed and to be performed solely within such state. It sets forth the full and complete agreement of the parties relating to the Program. It may not be modified except by a writing signed by the party against which the change is asserted.

(d) All payment to Producer hereunder will be sent to:

IN WITNESS WHEREOF, the parties have executed this agreement as of the date set forth below.

DATE: _____

[Purchaser]   [Producer]

By: _____   By: _____

Title: _____   Title: _____

[Note: Exhibit A should consist of the applicable form of production finance/distribution agreement or license. The form in Appendix B7, which follows and is part of this agreement, may be used.]

Appendix B7

Television Distribution/ Finance Agreement

Term Sheet

1. PARTIES:

Distributor: _____
(hereinafter "Distributor")

Producer: _____
(hereinafter "Producer")

2. ADDRESSES (with phone and fax):

Distributor: _____

_____

_____

Producer: _____

_____

_____

3. PROGRAM(S):

_____

_____

_____

(hereinafter the "Program(s)").

4. MEDIA (strike out anything nonapplicable):

(a) all television (including video); (b) theatrical; (c) any and all other media, now existing or hereafter invented; (d) licensing and merchandising; and (e) except for: _____

_____.

5. TERRITORY:

The whole universe except for: _____

_____.

6.   TERM:

_____

_____, thereafter terminable per the Standard Terms.

7.   PRODUCTION FINANCE/ADVANCE (if any):

_____

_____

8.   PRODUCTION PROCEDURES (attach additional sheet(s), if necessary):

Distributor Approvals: _____

_____

Approved Elements: _____

_____

Credits: _____

_____

Schedule: _____

_____

Budget: _____

_____

Overheads: _____

_____

Music Rights: _____

_____

Production Insurance: _____

_____

Completion Bond: _____

_____

Other Requirements: _____

_____

9.   REPORTING PERIODS: _____

_____

10. DELIVERY ITEMS AND DATES (attach additional sheet(s), if necessary): _____

_____

11. STANDARD TERMS:

The attached Standard Terms are hereby incorporated by reference into this Agreement, subject only to any express modifications or additions set forth in this Term Sheet, including the following (attach additional sheet(s) if necessary):

_____

_____

_____

12. COMPLETE AGREEMENT: This Term Sheet, together with the attached Standard Terms and any Exhibits, constitutes the sole and complete agreement between the parties concerning the Program(s).

13. APPLICABLE LAW: This agreement shall be construed according to the laws of the following State applicable to contracts made and wholly to be performed therein: _____.

14. SIGNATURES:

Distributor: Producer:

By: _____   By: _____

Name: _____   Name: _____

Title: _____   Title: _____

STANDARD TERMS

1. *GRANT OF RIGHTS*

Producer hereby grants to Distributor the exclusive right to distribute, license, market and exploit the Programs and all elements thereof in the Media and in the Territory. These rights include the rights to dub the Programs into foreign languages, and to make cuts and edits to meet standards and practices, censorship and time segment requirements, provided that Distributor shall not delete the credits or copyright notice as they may appear in the Programs.

2. *MEDIA*

The licensed media (the "Media") shall be those set forth in the Term Sheet. The grant of television rights shall permit Distributor to exploit the Programs and all elements thereof in all forms of television now or hereafter known, including but not limited to free television, cable television, pay cable television, pay-per-view television, subscription television, over-the-air pay television, closed circuit television, master antenna television, direct broadcast satellite television, armed forces, in-flight use, video cassettes and video discs for home use, and non-theatrical educational sales (collectively "Television Rights").

3. LICENSED TERRITORY

The territory described in paragraph 5 of the Term Sheet shall constitute the "Licensed Territory."

4. TERM

The initial term of this Agreement is as set forth in paragraph 6 of the Term Sheet. The Agreement shall thereafter renew itself automatically for further periods of one (1) year, which renewal periods shall be subject to the right of termination by either party, at the end thereof, by the giving at least of ninety (90) days written notice to the other party.

5. DISTRIBUTION

Distributor shall seek in good faith, subject to Distributor's reasonable business judgment, to maximize the exploitation of the rights granted hereunder. Notwithstanding the foregoing, Distributor shall have the sole control over all distribution activities, and may at any time suspend or resume active distribution of the Programs, as it deems fit, without any penalty.

6. DELIVERY

Producer shall deliver to Distributor the delivery items described in paragraph 10 or in the Term Sheet and any other elements of each of the Programs which may be reasonably necessary for Distributor to perform Distributor's services hereunder. Except as pre-approved in the Term Sheet, the Programs as delivered shall be subject to Distributor's sole approval for acceptance.

7. DISTRIBUTION FEES

(a) In consideration for the services Distributor is rendering to Producer hereunder, Distributor shall retain as its sole and exclusive property from all exploitation of the Programs the distribution fees described on Exhibit A attached hereto.

(b) In calculating such fees, "gross sales" shall be defined to mean all revenue (without any deductions), generated by the exploitation of the Programs by Distributor, including the gross amounts received by any of its subsidiaries or affiliates acting as sub-distributors, sub-licensees and agents. The commissions indicated above are maximum commissions for Distributor and any such subsidiaries or affiliates. If Distributor uses unaffiliated sub-distributors, sub-licensees, agents, etc., however, the fees of such entities shall not be subject to any limitation, but shall be deducted prior to calculating gross sales. Distributor and its subsidiaries and affiliates may take fees for additional services undertaken by them connected with the distribution of the Program, including fees for placing advertising in connection with syndication, provided that such fees shall not exceed those customary in the industry and shall not be subject to the limitations set forth above and shall be deducted before calculating gross sales.

(c) To the extent that Distributor may grant benefits longer then the term of this Agreement or, if this Agreement shall be terminated early for any reason, Distributor shall be entitled to receive commissions due to it in respect of all agreements, and extensions and renewals thereof, for exploitation of the Program in the Licensed Territory, and made by or on behalf of the Producer between the dates of the commencement and termination of the rights granted to Distributor hereunder.

8. *DISTRIBUTION COSTS AND EXPENSES*

After deduction of the fees described in paragraph 7 above, Distributor shall recoup from gross sales of the Programs all distribution costs and expenses which have been advanced or incurred by Distributor in connection with the distribution of the Programs hereunder.

The foregoing distribution costs and expenses shall include, without limitation, a pro-rata share of festival and market expenses, costs incurred in connection with promotional cassettes, sales and withholding taxes, shipping of promotional material, the manufacture of prints and videotapes, music and effects tracks, script duplication, publicity material, bank transfer charges, dubbing and production of foreign language tracks, advertising expenses and legal and agent fees.

Producer shall bear the cost of all rerun, reuse, residual and other similar payments required by any applicable union or guild agreement relative to persons performing services in the production of the Programs. Producer shall supply distributor with an accurate list of all recipients and rates of residuals and other similar payments. Distributor shall supply Producer with all necessary reports and information required to calculate and make such payments.

9. *RECOUPMENT OF ADVANCES*

After the deduction of the amounts set forth in paragraphs 7 and 8 above, Distributor shall recoup from the remaining proceeds to it from the Programs the Production Advance, together with interest thereon, as specified in paragraph 13 hereof.

10. *REPORTS, PAYMENTS AND ACCOUNTINGS*

(a) Distributor shall report and account to Producer in writing within forty-five (45) days after the end of each reporting period as set forth in the Term Sheet. A separate report will be issued for each of the Programs, although a series may be reported as a single unit. The reports shall contain reasonable detail and shall conform with customary industry practice.

(b) After retaining Distributor's fees and recouping the distribution costs and production finance as provided in paragraphs 7, 8, 9 and 13 hereof, Distributor shall attach to the report(s) a check payable to Producer in the appropriate amount for the balance of gross sales received during the period covered by the report(s). With respect to blocked or restricted funds, Distributor will report such funds to Producer and, to the extent permitted by applicable law, Producer will have the right to require Distributor to deposit Producer's share of such funds in a bank account established by Producer in the country where such funds are blocked or restricted.

(c) Distributor shall keep true, complete and accurate books of account and records pertaining to all financial transactions in connection with the performance of Distributors's obligations under this Agreement. Such books and records shall be available for inspection by Producers or its representatives at Distributor's place of business during normal business hours at a time or times mutually acceptable. No more than one such inspection shall occur within any twelve (12) month period, and no inspection shall be made as to any given statement more than once. Producer or its representatives shall have the right to make copies of the pertinent parts of all such books and records that directly relate to such financial transactions.

11. *COPYRIGHT AND COPIES*

(a) Producer shall ensure that its copyright in each of the Programs is properly protected and registered, if required, in any market in which the Programs are distributed.

(b) Distributor will not duplicate or otherwise reproduce the Programs in any manner, nor permit any of its sublicensees to do so, except specifically in connection with the distribution of the Programs as permitted hereunder. Distributor will provide in all license agreements that its licensees will return any prints or tapes distributed by Distributor, or submit an affidavit of erasure or destruction, promptly after the expiration of the period of use permitted to any of such licensees. Distributor will use its reasonable efforts to obtain the return of such items or the submission of such affidavit.

12. *WARRANTY AND INSURANCE*

(a) Producer warrants that it has the right to enter into this agreement and that it has the right to grant Distributor the rights granted herein and that Distributor's exercise of those rights will not infringe or violate the rights of any third party.

(b) Producer warrants that it has obtained the necessary music synchronization licenses for the exploitation of the Programs as contemplated herein; and that all musical compositions in the Programs are controlled by ASCAP, BMI or another performing rights society having jurisdiction, or are in the public domain, or are controlled by Producer (in which case licenses therefor are hereby granted at no cost to Distributor).

(c) Producer will maintain a standard Errors and Omissions insurance policy for the Programs during the term hereof having limits of not less than One Million Dollars ($1,000,000) for any single occurrence and of not less than Three Million Dollars ($3,000,000) for all occurrences taking place in any one year. Such insurance shall provide for coverage of Distributor, its affiliated companies and the officers, directors, agents and employees of the same.

(d) Distributor warrants that it has the right to enter into this Agreement.

13. *PRODUCTION FINANCE*

(a) As used herein, "Production Advance" shall refer to all sums advanced or paid by Distributor in connection with the production of the Programs, including (but not limited to) all amounts advanced to Producer under the Term Sheet and any residuals, royalties and/or clearance costs, insurance premiums, attorneys' fees and/or any other production costs paid or advanced by Distributor in its sole discretion.

(b) Interest shall accrue on the Production Advance from time to time outstanding until repaid or recouped at a rate equal to the Prime Rate declared by Distributor's principal bank from time to time plus two percent (2%).

(c) Producer shall deliver the Programs as set forth in the Term Sheet. Producer shall be solely responsible for any costs relating to the Programs which exceed the amount of the Production Advance agreed to in the Term Sheet for the Programs.

(d) In the event Producer fails to deliver any of the Programs as provided in this agreement or is otherwise in material breach of this Agreement, then without limiting any other right or remedy of Distributor, Distributor shall be entitled to demand, and Producer shall immediately thereupon pay to Distributor, the then outstanding amount of the Production Advance on any Program not yet delivered at the time of such demand, together with interest thereon as set forth above.

(e) To secure Producer's full and complete performance hereunder and any and all amounts owing to Distributor hereunder, Producer hereby grants Distributor a first priority lien and security interest in all right, title and interest in and to the Programs and each Program, and all elements, properties and proceeds thereof, whether now in existence or hereafter coming into being, and wherever located, including (but not limited to):

(i)   the copyright in and to each Program;

(ii) all film, sound and/or videotape copies and/or elements of or relating to the Programs whether now or hereafter in existence and wherever located;

(iii) all literary property rights and ancillary rights as specified herein in relation to the Programs including, without limitation, all right, title and interest of Producer in the teleplays of the Programs;

(iv) all right, title and interest of Producer in the music used in the Programs to the extent of Producer's rights therein;

(v) all contract rights of Producer relating to the Programs in any and all media throughout the world as set forth herein;

(vi) all proceeds of the Programs and of any of the elements of the Programs referred to in (i) through (iv) above, including without limitation all income and receipts derived and to be derived from the marketing, distribution, exhibition, exploitation and sale of the Programs and of said elements thereof, and all proceeds of insurance relating to the Programs and said elements thereof.

Producer agrees to execute such financing statements and/or other instruments as Distributor deems necessary or appropriate to perfect such security interest, and irrevocably appoints Distributor its attorney-in-fact to execute any such instruments in Producer's name should Producer fail or refuse to do so promptly on Producer's request.

(f) In the event Producer is in material default of this Agreement or materially breaches any of its obligations hereunder, then without limiting any other right or remedy of Distributor, Distributor shall have the right, but not the obligation, to take over production of any or all of the Programs, without any obligation to Distributor as to the results of its efforts.

14. *INDEMNIFICATION*

(a) Producer shall indemnify and hold Distributor harmless from and against any demand, claim, action, liability, and expense (including reasonable attorneys' fees) arising out of Producer's breach of any of the representations, warranties, or provisions contained in this Agreement; provided that Distributor shall promptly notify Producer of any such demand, claim, etc., and that Producer shall have the right to control the defense and to approve any settlement thereof.

(b) Distributor shall defend, indemnify, and hold Producer harmless from and against any demand, claim, action, liability and expense (including reasonable attorneys' fees) arising out of Distributor's breach of any of the representations, warranties, or provisions contained in this Agreement; provided, that Producer shall promptly notify Distributor of any such demand, claim, etc., defense and to approve any settlement thereof.

15. *PRODUCER REMEDIES*

The rights granted to Distributor hereunder are irrevocable, and the sole remedy of Producer in the case of a default by Distributor shall be an action for monetary damages.

16. *NOTICES*

Any notice required to be given hereunder shall be given by receipted telefax or by prepaid telegram or certified mail to the parties at their respective addresses set forth in the Term Sheet or at such other address as either party may hereafter notify the other. Any notice sent by telegram or by fax shall be deemed given on the day such notice is faxed or given to the telegraph office. Any notice sent by certified mail shall be deemed given 3 business days after such notice is mailed.

17. *NO PARTNERSHIP*

This agreement shall not be construed so as to constitute a partnership or a joint venture between the parties hereto, and no party is deemed to be the representative or the agent of the other except as herein otherwise provided.

18. *LAB LETTER*

Producer shall supply Distributor with a lab access letter covering all material relating to the Program. Such letter shall be in form acceptable to Distributor in its reasonable discretion.

EXHIBIT A: SCHEDULE OF DISTRIBUTION FEES

1. All Television Rights Except 2 and 3 Below:
   (a) for sales in the United States:
      (i)   ____% of gross sales for a national sale.
      (ii) ____% of gross sales for a syndicated sale.
   (b) for sales in Australia, Canada and/or the United Kingdom:
      (i)   ____% gross sales for a national sale.
      (ii) ____% of gross sales for a syndicated sale.
   (c) for sales in all other counties:
      ____% of gross sales.

2. For armed forces, in-flight and any other ancillary television use:

   ____% of gross sales.

3. For videocassettes and videodiscs and other devices for home use and non-theatrical educational uses:

   ____% of gross sales, provided that if Distributor or its subsidiary or affiliate actually manufactures and distributes the cassettes and/or discs, gross sales shall be deemed to equal 20% of actual retail sales, subject to Distributor's customary adjustments.

4. For theatrical release:

   ____% of gross sales.

5. For licensing and merchandising:

   ____% of gross sales.

Appendix B8
Short-Form Home Video License

This agreement, when executed by the parties identified below as the Licensor and the Licensee, will set forth the terms of the agreement between them concerning the license of home video rights in the Program(s) described below.

1. *Licensor Name, Address, Phone and Fax:*

2. *Licensee Name, Address, Phone and Fax:*

3. *Title and Description of the Program(s):*

4. *Distribution, Licensed Media; Territory; Term:* The Licensor hereby grants to the Licensee the exclusive right to distribute the Program(s) in all aspects of home video, including tape, disc, chip and any other similar tangible medium capable of being played by an individual consumer on a home viewing device without transmission from a remote point:

    (a) subject to the following exclusions (if any):

    (b) in the following territories:

    (c) and for the following term:

Except as expressly provided in paragraph 9, Licensee will have sole control over the exercise of its home video rights hereunder, provided, however, that if Licensee ceases to actively distribute the Program(s) hereunder, and fails to recommence active distribution within 3 months of a written request to do so from the Licensor, then the rights granted hereunder to Licensee shall terminate and revert to Licensor.

5. *Advance and Royalties:* The Licensee will pay to the Licensor the following consideration for the license granted hereunder:

    (a) An advance in the amount of $_____, payable upon delivery of the items specified in Exhibit A hereto.

    (b) A royalty at the rate of _____%, to be calculated and paid in accordance with the procedures specified in Exhibit B hereto.

6. *Publicity and Advertising:* During the term hereof, Licensee will have the right to use the names, likeness and other attributes of personality of the performers appearing in the Program(s) and of the producer, director, writer, and other principal off-screen contributors to the program in connection with advertising and publicity for the distribution of the Program(s) hereunder. Licensee agrees not to alter the titles and credits contained in the Program(s) (other than to add its own credit as video distributor at the very beginning and/or end of the Program(s)), and will abide by (and will require, as a matter of contract, all subdistributors and other entities in the chain of distribution to abide by) all of the credit requirements specified in Item 2 of Exhibit A. No inadvertent or third-party failure to abide by such credit requirements will be a breach of this agreement provided that Licensee takes all reasonable steps to correct any such failure upon learning of it.

7. *Warranties:* The Licensor warrants that (i) it is free to enter into and to perform this agreement; and (ii) the Program(s) and any material contained in the Program(s) is either owned by Licensor, or in the public domain, or fully cleared with respect to all applicable rights, and their use and exploitation as contemplated hereunder will not violate the rights of any third party. In this regard, the Licensor agrees to pay any and all residuals, reuse, music or other similar rights fees or costs related to the exploitation and distribution of the Program(s) hereunder, except as may be expressly provided in Paragraph 9.

The Licensee warrants that it is free to enter into and to perform this agreement.

8. *Limits on Remedies:* Except as otherwise expressly provided in this agreement, all grants of rights hereunder are irrevocable during the Term, and Licensor waives all rights to any equitable relief in connection with any breach or termination of this agreement. The foregoing shall not apply in the case of a breach of this agreement by the Licensee, not subject to unresolved litigation or dispute in good faith, which continues uncured for a period of one month following written notice of such breach to Licensee from Licensor.

9. *Additional Provisions:* The following additional provisions shall apply (include any agreements on approvals of the distribution process, designs, rights payments, and any other further agreements; if none, write "none"):

10. *Miscellaneous:* This agreement will be subject to the laws of the State of _____ applicable to contracts signed and to be performed solely within such state. It sets forth the full and complete agreement of the parties relating to the license described herein. It may not be modified except by a writing signed by the party against which the change is asserted.

Dated: _____

LICENSOR   LICENSEE

By: _____   By: _____

Title: _____   Title: _____

EXHIBIT A

[Insert delivery requirements here]

EXHIBIT B

ROYALTIES:

Royalties will be calculated and paid in accordance with the following provisions:

1. Retail Price and Sale Date. Subject to the adjustments set forth below, the royalty will be calculated based on the suggested retail price of the Program(s) sold. In the case of a direct retail sale by Licensee or its affiliates, the retail price will be that actually received. A sale will be deemed to have occurred, and a royalty will be payable, upon receipt by the Licensee or an affiliate of the purchase price for the item sold (or upon the accrual of any offset or other non-cash consideration), but reasonable amounts may be held in a good faith reserve for returns, if permitted, for a period not to exceed 6 months.

2. Adjustments. The retail price will be adjusted in the case of sales made at discount, remainder or other bona fide exceptions to Licensee's normal practices. In such a case, the retail price will be deemed to be twice the amounts actually received by Licensee or its affiliates from such a sale at wholesale, or, if Licensee or an affiliate makes the retail sale in such a circumstance, the retail price will be the amount actually received.

3. Payments and Reports. Licensee will provide written reports of sales, income, and the royalty payable at the following intervals:

All accrued royalties will first be applied to the recoupment of any advance paid on the Program(s), and then will be paid by check included with the applicable statement.

4.   Accountings. Licensee will keep complete and accurate records of the financial transactions relating to the Program(s), and shall not destroy such records for at least five years. Licensor will have the right to conduct an inspection of such books and records of the Licensee to verify the accuracy of the reports at Licensee's normal business premises during normal business hours, once within any twelve-month period. No report can be challenged any later than two years after it has been received by Licensor.

Appendix B9

Sales Representative Letter Agreement

[Producer Letterhead]

⎡ Sales Representative ⎤
⎣ Name and Address ⎦

Dear _____ :

This letter, when signed by you, will set forth the agreement between us concerning your acting as a sales representative for us in connection with the Programs described below, on the following terms:

1. *Programs Covered.* This agreement covers the following programs (the "Programs"):

2. *Markets and Media Covered.* This agreement covers sales and licenses of the Programs in the following markets (the "Markets") and media (the "Media") (describe the degree of exclusivity, if any, for each):

3. *Term.* The term of this agreement is as follows:

4. *Sales Duties.* You agree to use your best efforts to seek potential buyers and licensees (collectively "Buyers") for the Programs in the Markets and Media. Once you have identified a prospective Buyer, you will inform us of its identity and degree of interest. Although you will assist us in pursuing the possible sale or license, you will have no authority to finalize or enter into any agreement with the Buyer on our behalf, except as we may expressly grant by a separate written authorization.

5. *Compensation.* If we close a sale or license, either during the Term or within _____ months of the end of the Term, of any of the Programs with a Buyer introduced to us by you hereunder for any of the Media and Markets, we will pay you a fee of _____% of the amounts actually received by us during the Term and any time thereafter from

such sale or license. We will pay you this fee within _____ days of our receipt of good funds on the payment to which it relates. Such fee shall be calculated and paid net of (describe any deductions which come off the top or from the sales representative's share):

6. *Limits on Sales Representative.* Nothing in this agreement will constitute you our agent or attorney in fact. You will not hold yourself out as having any greater authority with respect to the Programs and our business generally than has been expressly granted to you by us in this agreement.

7. *Further Provisions.* This agreement is subject to the following additional provisions [include any further agreements on such topics as expenses, excluded contracts or other matters]:

8. *Miscellaneous.* This agreement will be subject to the laws of the State of _____ applicable to contracts signed and to be performed solely within such state. It sets forth the complete understanding of the parties relating to the sales representation described above. It may not be modified except by a writing signed by the party against which the change is asserted.

Please confirm that the foregoing accurately reflects our understanding on this matter by signing the enclosed copy of this letter and returning it to me.

Yours sincerely,

[Producer]

Accepted and Agreed:

_____

[Sales Representative]

Appendix B10

Insurance: E&O Application

TRANSAMERICA ENTERTAINMENT INSURANCE

Radio, Television, and Motion Picture Producers'
Liability Insurance Schedule and Application

TRANSAMERICA INSURANCE COMPANY (herein called "the Company")

Notice: *This is an application for a* **CLAIMS MADE POLICY.** *Except to such extent as may be provided otherwise herein any insurance policy which may issue hereafter will be limited to liability for only those* **CLAIMS THAT ARE FIRST MADE AGAINST THE INSURED DURING THE POLICY PERIOD.** *Please read and review this application carefully and discuss the coverage with your insurance agent, broker or representative.*

1. NAME OF INSURED	2. ADDRESS

3. INSURED IS
☐ An individual   ☐ A corporation
☐ A partnership or joint venture

4. NAMES & TITLES OF PRINCIPAL OFFICERS, PARTNERS OR INDIVIDUALS

5. TITLE OF PICTURE, PROGRAM OR SERIES	6. NAMES OF AUTHORS & WRITERS *(INCLUDING WORKS, SCREENPLAYS, ETC.)*

7. NAME OF INDIVIDUAL PRODUCER	8. NAME OF INDIVIDUAL EXECUTIVE PRODUCER

9. HAS A TITLE REPORT BEEN OBTAINED FROM ANY TITLE CLEARANCE SERVICE?
☐ Yes *(If yes, attach copy)*   ☐ No

10. NAME, ADD & TEL. NO. OF APPLICANT'S ATTY *(IF FIRM, NAME INDIVIDUAL AT FIRM)*

11. HAS APPLICANT'S ATTY. READ & AGREED TO USE HIS BEST EFFORTS TO ASSURE THAT THE "CLEARANCE PROCEDURES" ATTACHED HERETO, ARE FOLLOWED?
☐ Yes   ☐ No *(If no, explain)*

12. DESIRED EFF. DATE *(FOR THE TERM OF ONE YEAR)*

13. LIMITS FOR WHICH QUOTATION DESIRED

ANY ONE CLAIM	AGGREGATE	DEDUCTIBLE
$	$	$

14. THE PRODUCTION IS:
☐ Motion picture for theatrical release
☐ Motion picture for television release
☐ Television pilot
☐ Television special
☐ Music/variety/comedy
☐ Dramatic
☐ Other: Explain _____
☐ Other: *(Describe Fully)* _____
_____
_____

☐ Television series
   No. of episodes _____
☐ Television "mini series"
☐ Television documentary
☐ Radio program
   No. of programs each week ____
   No. of weeks _____

Progam or running time of production _____
Initial release or air date _____

15. Will any film clips be used in this production? ☐ Yes ☐ No If yes, have all necessary licenses and consents been obtained with respect to material contained in the clips, including for music, sync, underlying literary rights and performers?
☐ Yes ☐ No (If no, explain:)

16. Is the name or likeness of any living person used in the production? ☐ Yes ☐ No If yes, have clearances been obtained?
☐ Yes ☐ No (If no, explain:)

17. Is there a plausible risk that a living person could claim (without regard to the merits) to be identifiable in the production (whether or not the person's name or likeness is used or the production purports to be fictional)? ☐ Yes ☐ No If yes, has a release been obtained from each such person? ☐ Yes ☐ No If no, explain

18. Is the name or likeness of any deceased person used in the production? ☐ Yes ☐ No
If yes, have clearances been obtained from personal representatives heirs or owners of such rights? ☐ Yes ☐ No
If no, explain

E 560

COMPANY COPY
Page 1 of 4
(Continued)

Radio, TV and MP Liab. App.   4-89

561

Radio, Television, and Motion Picture Producers'
Liability Insurance Schedule and Application

19. Has applicant or any of its agents been unable to obtain or refused an agreement or release after having (a) negotiated for any rights in literary, musical or other materials, or (b) negotiated for releases from any persons in connection with the production?
☐ Yes ☐ No If yes, explain:

20. Is the production:
☐ Entirely fictional?
☐ Entirely fictional, but inspired by specific events and/or occurrences?
☐ A portrayal of actual facts which includes significant fictionalization?
☐ A true portrayal of actual facts or happenings?
☐ Other than above (Explain):

21. Is the production based upon another work or works? ☐ Yes ☐ No If yes, explain:

22. Are there any ambiguities, gaps or problems in the copyright chain of title. ☐ Yes ☐ No If yes, explain:

Have copyright reports been obtained? ☐ Yes ☐ No

23. Brief description of plot or nature of production:

24. The time frame for the setting of the plot is (e.g. the present; ten years in the future; within the last 20 years, etc.):

25. Have the following musical rights been cleared: performing, recording and syncronization rights? ☐ Yes ☐ No
If no, explain:

26. Has the production been previously insured for similar coverage? ☐ Yes ☐ No If yes, attach copy of previous policy.

27. Have the production or applicant been refused, or discussed with representatives of another carrier, the issuance of similar insurance coverage? ☐ Yes ☐ No If yes, explain:

28. Applicant represents and warrants that neither its counsel nor any of its partners, officers, directors, senior employees or it or its partners have any knowledge, actual or constructive:

(a) Of any claims or legal proceedings made or commenced against applicant, or any of its officers, directors, partners, agents, or subsidiary or affiliated corporations, within the last three (3) years for invasion of privacy, infringement or copyright (statutory or common law), defamation, unauthorized use of titles, formats, characters, plots, ideas, other program material embodied in any production, or breach of implied contract arising out of alleged submission of any literary or musical material.
☐ No exceptions. ☐ Except as follows:

(b) Of any existing or threatened claims or legal proceedings of any kind based on the production to be insured or any material contained in or upon which such production is based, that would be covered by the policy sought by applicant.
☐ No exceptions. ☐ Except as follows:

(c) Of any inquiry, fact, circumstance or prior negotiation which might reasonably be expected to lead to a claim or legal proceeding instituted against the applicant that would be covered by the policy sought by applicant.
☐ No exceptions. ☐ Except as follows:

CLEARANCE PROCEDURES

Insured's attorney should assure himself of the following before first exhibition of the insured production:

1. A copyright report must be obtained, covering domestic and foreign copyright, as well as all extensions and renewals thereof, for all literary material (other than original and unpublished) contained in the production. If the Insured is acquiring the production as a completed work (such as a pick-up of a motion picture) a copyright report must also be obtained covering the completed work. In the case of an unpublished original work, the origin of the work must be traced in order to ascertain that the Insured has all required rights in the work.

2. Written agreements must exist between the Insured and the creators, authors, writers and owners of all material, including quotations from copyrighted works, used in the insured production, authorizing the Insured to use the material in the insured production.

3. If the production is in any way based on actual facts, it must be ascertained if the source materials is primary (e.g. direct interview, court records) and not secondary (e.g. another copyrighted work). Use of secondary sources may be permissible, but full details must be provided to Company in an attachment to the application.

4. Written releases must be obtained from all persons who are recognizable or who might reasonably claim to be identifiable in the insured production, or whose name, image or likeness is used, and if such person is a minor, the minor's consent must be legally binding. If the recognizable or identifiable person is deceased, releases must be obtained from the personal representative of such person. Releases of the type described in the preceding two sentences may not be required in certain instances, but full details must be provided Company in an attachment to the application. Releases are not necessary if the recognizable person is part of a crowd or background shot and his image is not shown for more than a few seconds or given special emphasis.

5. Where the work is fictional in whole or in part, the names of all characters must be fictional. In certain limited instances, particular names need not be fictional, but full details must be provided Company in an attachment to the application.

6. Where scenes are filmed depicting or referring to distinctive businesses, personal property or products identifiable with any person, firm or corporation, or depicting or referring to distinctive real property of any person, firm or corporation, written releases must be obtained from such person, firm or corporation granting the Insured the right to film and use such property in the insured production. In ceratin instances releases may not be required, but full details must be provided Company in an attachment to the application. Releases are not necessary if property is non-distinctive background only.

7. All releases must give the Insured the right to edit, modify, add to and/or delete any or all of the material supplied by the releasor. Releases from recognizable persons must grant the Insured the right to fictionalize the Insured's portrayal of the releasor.

8. All contracts and releases must give the Insured the right to market the production for use in all media and markets (e.g. video discs, cassettes, supplemental markets), except to the extent the Insured qualifies the application to exclude insurance coverage for particular media.

9. Synchronization and performance licenses must be obtained from the composer or copyright owner of all music used in the insured production. Licenses are unnecessary if the music (and its arrangement) is in the public domain. Licenses must also be obtained for the use of previously recorded music.

10. If the production contains any film clips, the Insured must obtain authorization to use the film clip from the owner of the clip who has the right to grant such authorization and must obtain authority from the appropriate persons for "secondary use" of all material contained in the film clip, e.g. underlying literary and musical rights, performances of actors and musicians.

11. A report (generally known as a "title report") covering the title of the production must be obtained from a recognized source setting forth prior uses of the same or similar titles, and the title of the production must be changed to avoid any conflict.

12. It must be determined whether the applicant, or any of its officers, directors, partners or agents received any submission of any similar material or production, and if so, Company must be fully advised of all circumstances relating to each such occurrence, in an attachment to the application.

13. It must be determined that the insured production does not contain any material which constitutes defamation, invasion of privacy or violation of the right of publicity or of any other right of any person, firm or corporation.

14. Prior to any public exhibition of the production, it must be previewed to assure that the Clearance Procedures have been followed.

15. To the extent that any information required to be furnished pursuant to these Clearance Procedures is not known at the time of the application, such information must be furnished in writing to Company as soon as known.

The foregoing Clearance Procedures should not be construed as exhaustive; nor do they cover all situations which may arise, given the great variety of productions. Rather, applicant and its counsel must continually monitor the production at all stages, and in light of any special circumstances, to make certain that the production contains no material which could give rise to a claim.

Radio, Television, and Motion Picture Producers'
Liability Insurance Schedule and Application

If there is sufficient space to respond fully to any of the questions contained herein, Applicant shall continue such responses by an attachment to the application.

Applicant will use best efforts to procure from third parties from whom it obtains material for the production to be insured written warranties and indemnities against all claims arising out of any use of such material.

Applicant and its counsel will use due dilligence to determine whether any portrayal, matter of materials used in the production to be insured violates the right of any person or entity, and, where necessary, applicant will obtain from such person or entity, the right to use the same in connection with the insured production.

Applicant warrants and represents:

(i) that the information supplied herein is in all respects true, and material to the issuance of an insurance policy, and that no information has been omitted, suppressed or misstated: and

(ii) that Applicant and its counsel have supplied Company with all information required to be furnished pursuant to the Clearance Procedures, and to the extent such information is not known at the time of the application, such information will be furnished in writing to the Company as soon as known.

If pursuant to (ii) above, information is hereafter furnished to Company, Company shall have the right to limit the insurance coverage in its discretion.

This application and all attachments will be attached to, and form part of, any policy which may be issued as a result of this application. The signing of this application does not bind the applicant or the Company to compete the insurance unless and until a Policy of Insurance is issued in response to this application. All exclusions in any policy which may be issued by Company shall apply regardless of any answers or statements in this application. Applicant understands that the limit of liability and deductible under any policy which may be issued by Company shall include both loss payment and claim expenses, as defined in the policy.

"Any person who knowingly and with intent to defraud any insurance company or other person files an application for insurance containing any false information, or conceals for the purpose of misleading, information concerning any fact material thereto, commits a fraudulent insurance act, which is a crime."

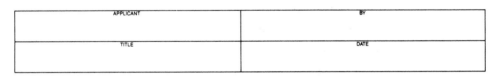

APPLICANT	BY
TITLE	DATE

You have given us a copy of the Transamerica Clearance Procedures which you recommended be utilized in connection with the above production and we have sent to our clients a copy of such procedures. Our clients have authorized us to inform you that we will take such steps to endeavor to comply with those procedures which are applicable, as and to the extent we are engaged by our clients so to do.

Upon request from you or any other representative of the insurance carrier, we will provide you with any available information concerning the subject matter of the application which such carrier may reasonably require in connection with reviewing the application to the extent our clients authorize us so to do.

_____   _____
ATTORNEY'S SIGNATURE   DATE

COMPANY COPY

Page 4 of 4   Radio, TV and MP Liab. App.

Appendix B11

Talent and Service Agreements: Issue Checklist

1. What services are to be performed?

   - Is the contract for acting, writing, directing, or some other creative service?
   - Is it for producing, finance-raising, or some other business service?
   - Is it for a mixture of services?
   - Is the service being provided as an employee or as an independent contractor (see #2)?
   - Are the services exclusive to the producer or the production?

2. How are the services to be performed?

   - Are they subject to the producer's direction and control?
   - Are they at locations designated by producer?
   - Does the service provider retain any approvals or controls over the project as a whole, over his/her work process, or over the product?
   - Are there special facilities, accommodations, transport, or other amenities being provided?

3. What are the dates for the services?

   - Are there dates for the delivery of certain items?
   - Are the dates tied to the production process?
   - Are they set to particular dates?
   - Can they be extended or altered?
   - Will a talent provider be available for post-production services, such as dubbing or looping?
   - What is the effect of force majeure or the disability of the service provider?

- What are the arrangements for rehearsals, wardrobe, travel, post-production publicity, and other additional services?

4. What rights are being granted?

   - Rights in newly-created product, like a script, direction, acting, etc.?
   - Rights to use name, likeness, and biography in exploitation of the project, including advertising?
   - Rights to change, alter, and edit?
   - Is the work product a work for hire?
   - Is the grant exclusive?
   - Is the grant irrevocable?

5. Are there any reserved rights?

6. What markets and media are covered?

   - All television, film, and related rights?
   - Are there any restrictions?
   - Is merchandising and print publishing included?

7. What territories are covered?

   - The whole universe?
   - Any specific territories included or excluded?

8. Is the deal contingent or pay-or-play?

   - What are the contingencies or option aspects?
   - How long is the option?
   - Can it be extended?
   - Will force majeure extend the option?
   - Are there successive dependent options?
   - How is the option exercised?
   - Is it a firm, pay-or-play deal?
   - Are there any preconditions?
   - Is the pay-or-play commitment for the full amount?
   - Is there any obligation to use the services?

9. What is the compensation for the services?

   - Is there an option payment or holding fee?
   - Is there an option extension payment?
   - What is the basic fee?

- Is it set to any union or guild rate?
- When is it paid?
- What is the fee for any overtime or work beyond the basic dates? (The producer should set this in advance.)
- Are there additional payments, such as residuals or other agreed-upon amounts due for additional uses or subsequent productions?
- Are there any expenses to reimburse?
- Is there a profit or other back-end participation?
- What is the definition of such a participation?
- Is there most-favored-nation protection on the definition?

10. What representations and warranties should be given?

- Is any creative work either original and subject to copyright, or in the public domain?
- Does the service provider have the right to enter into the contract?
- Does the work product of the service provider contain any libelous or slanderous material?
- Does the work product violate any rights of privacy or publicity?
- Does either the work product or its intended use violate any other rights of any third parties?

11. Is either party giving an indemnity?

- Does the indemnity cover alleged breaches, or only actual breaches?
- Does the indemnity cover attorney's fees and costs?
- Who controls the defense and settlement of any claim?

12. Are the agreement and the rights granted assignable?

- If so, does the original producer remain liable?

13. Does the service provider get a credit?

- Is it in the lead or tail credits?
- Is it on a single card or is it shared?
- Is it a verbal credit?
- Is there any credit obligation in advertising and promotion?
- Are the consequences of a failure to give credit limited in the customary way?
- Are there any union or guild requirements?

14. Are there limitations on the service provider's remedies?
    - Are injunctions prohibited?
    - Is recision prohibited?
15. Is there any union or guild involved?
    - If so, what impact does it have?
    - Have its minimums been met?
    - Does the producer retain the maximum benefits available to it?

Appendix B12
Short-Form Services Agreement

This agreement, when executed by the parties identified below as the Employer and the Employee, will set forth the terms of the employment agreement between them.

1. *Employer Name, Address and Tax Identification Number:*

2. *Employee Name, Address and Social Security Number:*

3. *Duties and Services of Employee; Term:* The Employee will have the following duties and will perform the following services:

All of the Employee's services and duties will be performed subject to the direction and control of the Employer and at such times and places as the Employer may designate. The term of the employment will be as follows [can be day-to-day or for a set period]:

The Employer will not be obliged to actually use any of Employees services or workproduct, but the failure to use such services or workproduct will not in itself relieve Employer of the obligation to pay the compensation set forth herein.

4. *Compensation:* The Employer will pay the Employee the following compensation [include any bonus, overtime, benefits, or other agreed provisions]:

The Employer will also reimburse the out-of-pocket expenses of the Employee relating to his/her employment, provided they are approved in advance by the Employer and customary documentation is presented.

5. *Warranties:* The Employee warrants that (i) she/he is free to enter into and to perform this agreement; and (ii) any material which she/he creates or adds to any project or production during the course of her/his employment will be either original or in the public domain and its use and exploitation will not violate the rights of any third party. The

Employer warrants that it is free to enter into and to perform this agreement.

6. *Legal Requirements:* The Employee will abide by all applicable laws and regulations, including those under Section 507 of the Communications Act of 1934 prohibiting the undisclosed acceptance of consideration for the inclusion of material in a television program.

7. *Grant of Rights; No Equitable Relief for Employee:* The Employee grants all rights of every kind in the fruits and proceeds of his/her employment hereunder to the Employer and its licensees, successors and assigns. Any copyrightable material created by Employee hereunder will be treated as a work for hire, and the Employer will be the author thereof. The Employee also grants to Employer and its licensees, successors and assigns, the right to use his/her name, likeness, voice and biography in connection with the exploitation of any project or program with which the Employee has been involved through his/her services hereunder. All grants of rights hereunder are irrevocable and perpetual, and Employee waives all rights to any equitable relief in connection with any breach or termination of this agreement.

8. *Additional Provisions:* The following additional provisions shall apply [include any agreements on credits, any applicable unions and guilds, any locally-required provisions and any other further agreements; if none, write "none"]:

9. *Miscellaneous:* This agreement will be subject to the laws of the State of _____ applicable to contracts signed and to be performed solely within such state. It sets forth the full and complete agreement of the parties relating to the employment described herein. It may not be modified except by a writing signed by the party against which the change is asserted.

Dated: _____

EMPLOYER   EMPLOYEE

By: _____   _____

Title: _____

Appendix B13
Service Description Clauses

The following clauses describe typical services required of a variety of production employees, and may be used in conjunction with the agreement in Appendix B17. Other service descriptions may be drafted following the same general model.

Producer:
Employee will provide all of the services customarily provided by the producer of a television program, including, without limitation, overseeing the business aspects such as budgets, finance and banking, the production aspects such as facilities, equipment and creative and technical staff, the rights acquisitions, and the creative aspects such as scripts, director and casting. Employee recognizes that all such matters will be subject to the ultimate approval of the Employer.

Director:
Employee will provide all of the services customarily provided by the director of a television program, including, without limitation, involvement in the pre-production aspects such as script writing, casting, rehearsals and the selection of designers and music; directing the filming, taping or other production steps; and overseeing the editing and other post-production steps. Employee recognizes that except to the extent expressly otherwise agreed hereunder or as may be provided by applicable union agreement, all such matters will be subject to the ultimate approval of the Employer.

Writer:
Employee will provide the following services customarily provided by a writer in the television industry: [specify what is to be written, what editing, re-write or other general services are to be provided, and any applicable deadlines]. Employee recognizes that all such matters will be subject to the ultimate approval of the Employer.

Actor:

Employee will provide all of the services customarily provided by an actor in a television production, including rehearsals, make-up, wardrobe, and on-camera appearance, at mutually convenient times and places subsequent to production, dubbing, looping, retakes and publicity support. Employee will play the role of _____.

Appendix B14

Performer Contract: Deal Memo

TO: _____
   [Performer]

   _____
   [Agent]

FROM: _____
   [Producer]

DATE: _____

The following has been agreed between the parties listed above for the services of the Performer to perform as an actor in production company's television production entitled "_____". Performer grants Producer all rights in his performance for exploitation throughout the universe in all media in perpetuity.

Role: _____

Start Date: _____

Compensation: _____
   [Total]

   _____
   [Pro-rata per week]

Guaranteed Term: _____

Other matters (if not applicable put 'NA'): _____

Expenses: _____

_____

_____

Travel: _____

Lodging: _____

Union/Guild: _____

Other Arrangements: _____

Billing: _____

_____

Location: _____

Estimated Schedule: _____

_____

Personal Information:

     Address:_____

     Telephone:_____

     SS #:_____

Agent Information:

     Address:_____

     Telephone:_____

     SS #:_____

Producer Information:

     Address:_____

     Telephone:_____

     SS #:_____

Signatures:

_____   _____

Performer   Producer

Appendix B15

Performer Contract:
Pre-Test Option and
Series Option Clauses

[Pre-test option clause]

This letter will confirm that _____ ("Artist") has agreed to test for the role of _____ (the "Role") in "_____" (the "Series"), a one-hour dramatic weekly series to be produced in _____ and such other locations as Producer may designate, by _____ (the "Producer"). The time and place for the test will be determined by mutual agreement. On the basis of this test, the Producer shall have the exclusive and irrevocable option to cast Artist in the Role by giving written notice to that effect to Artist's or Artists' agent on or before _____, 199___. Should Producer exercise this option, Artist agrees to render his/her acting services to the Series, and the following terms shall govern Artist's employment in the Series.

[Series option clause]

Dates/Options. If Producer exercises the initial option granted to it herein, Producer shall have five further consecutive exclusive and irrevocable options, in each case exercisable no later than _____, to obtain Artist's acting services hereunder in episodes to be produced in the immediately following production year. The base commitment to Artist for each production year for which any option is exercised is for _____ (___) episodes. In each production year, including the initial year, Producer shall have the further option, exercisable no later than [December 1] in such year, to employ Artist's services in connection with no fewer than _____ (___) or more than _____ (___) additional episodes for such production year, the number to be designated by Producer at time of exercise. Each production year hereunder will run from [June 15 to June 14], with the initial production year beginning June 15, 199___.

Appendix B16

SAG Day Player Form Contract

**THE ARTIST MAY NOT WAIVE ANY PROVISION OF THIS CONTRACT
WITHOUT THE WRITTEN CONSENT OF SCREEN ACTORS GUILD, INC.**

SCREEN ACTORS GUILD

**DAILY CONTRACT
(DAY PERFORMER)
FOR TELEVISION MOTION PICTURES OR VIDEOTAPES**

Company _____   Date _____

Date Employment Starts _____   Actor Name _____

Role _____   Address: _____

Production Title _____   Telephone No.: (_____) _____

Production Number _____   Social Security No. _____

Daily Rate $ _____

Weekly Conversion Rate $ _____

Complete for "Drop-And-Pick-Up" Deals ONLY:

Firm recall date on _____ or

on or after* _____

("On or after" recall only applies to pick-up as Weekly Performer.)

As ☐ Day Performer   ☐ Weekly Performer

*Means date specified or within 24 hours thereafter

Wardrobe supplied by Actor _____ Yes _____ No

If so, number of outfits _____ @ $ _____

(formal) _____ @ $ _____

Date of Actor's next engagement _____

THIS AGREEMENT covers the employment of the above-named Performer by _____
in the production and at the rate of compensation set forth above and is subject to and shall include, for the benefit of the Performer and the Producer, all of the applicable provisions and conditions contained or provided for in the current Screen Actors Guild Television Agreement (herein called the "Television Agreement"). Performer's employment shall include performance in non-commercial openings, bridges, etc., and no added compensation shall be payable to Performer so long as such are used in the role and episode covered hereunder in which Performer appears; for other use, Performer shall be paid the added minimum compensation, if any, required under the provisions of the Screen Actors Guild agreements with Producer.

Producer shall have all the rights in and to the results and proceeds of the Performer's services rendered hereunder, as are provided with respect to "photoplays" in Schedule A of the Producer-Screen Actors Guild Codified Basic Agreement and the right to supplemental market use as defined in the Television Agreement.

Producer shall have the unlimited right throughout the world to telecast the film and exhibit the film theatrically and in supplemental markets in accordance with the terms and conditions of the Television Agreement.

If the motion picture is rerun on television in the United States or Canada and contains any of the results and proceeds of the Performer's services, the Performer will be paid for each day of employment hereunder the additional compensation prescribed therefor by the Television Agreement, unless there is an agreement to pay an amount in excess thereof as follows:

_____

_____

_____

_____

If there is foreign telecasting of the motion picture as defined in the Television Agreement, and such motion picture contains any of the results and proceeds of the Performer's services, the Performer will be paid in the amount in the blank space below for each day of employment hereunder, or if such blank space is not filled in, then the Performer will be paid the minimum additional compensation prescribed therefor by the Television Agreement.

If the motion picture is exhibited theatrically anywhere in the world and contains any of the results and proceeds of the Performer's services, the Performer will be paid $ _____ , or if this blank is not filled in, then the Performer will be paid the minimum additional compensation prescribed therefor by the Television Agreement.

If the motion picture is exhibited in supplemental markets anywhere in the world and contains any of the results and proceeds of the Performer's services, then Performer will be paid the supplemental market fees prescribed by the applicable provisions of the Television Agreement.

If the Performer places his initials in the box, he thereby authorizes Producer to use portions of said television motion picture as a trailer to promote another episode or the series as a whole, upon payment to the Performer of the additional compensation prescribed by the applicable provisions of the Television Agreement.

SPECIAL PROVISIONS:

PRODUCER _____   PERFORMER _____

Production time reports are available on the set at the end of each day. Such reports shall be signed or initialed by the Performer.

Attached hereto for your use are the following: (1) Declaration Regarding Income Tax Withholding ("Part Year Employment Method of Withholding") and (2) Declaration Regarding Income Tax Withholding. You may utilize the applicable form by delivering same to Producer. Only one of such forms may be used.

NOTICE TO ACTOR: IT IS IMPORTANT THAT YOU RETAIN A COPY OF THIS CONTRACT FOR YOUR PERMANENT RECORDS.

AFTRA Day Actor Contract, Prime Time Dramatic Television

AFTRA PRIME TIME DRAMATIC TELEVISION (EXHIBIT A)
EMPLOYMENT OF DAY ACTOR

Company _____ Dated _____

Date Employment Starts	Name
Part	Address
Production Title	Telephone No.
Production Number	Social Security No.
Daily Rate	Weekly Conversion Rate

THIS AGREEMENT covers the employment of the above-named performer by _____ in the production and at the rate of compensation set forth above and is subject to and shall include, for the benefit of the performer and the Producer, all of the applicable provisions and conditions contained or provided for in the AFTRA 1988–91 National Code of Fair Practice for Network Television Broadcasting (herein called the "Code"). Performer's employment shall include performance in noncommercial openings, closings, bridges, etc., and no added compensation shall be payable to performer so long as such are used in the role and episode

---

covered hereunder in which performer appears; for other use, performer shall be paid the added minimum compensation, if any, required under the provisions of AFTRA's agreements with Producer.

Producer shall have all the rights in and to the results and proceeds of the performer's services rendered hereunder, as are provided with respect to programs in Exhibit A of the Code and the right to Supplemental Market use as defined in Exhibit D of the Code.

Producer shall have the unlimited right throughout the world to telecast the program and exhibit the program theatrically and in Supplemental Markets in accordance with the terms and conditions of Exhibits A and D of the Code.

If the program is rerun on television in the United States or Canada and contains any of the results and proceeds of the performer's services, the performer will be paid for each day of employment hereunder the additional compensation prescribed therefor by Exhibit A of the Code, unless there is an agreement to pay an amount in excess thereof as follows:

_____

_____

_____

_____

_____

_____

_____

If there is foreign telecasting of the program as defined in Exhibit A of the Code, and such program contains any of the results and proceeds of the performer's services, the performer will be paid the amount in the blank space below for each day of employment hereunder, or if such blank space is not filled in, then the performer will be paid the minimum additional compensation prescribed therefor by Exhibit A of the Code.

If the program is exhibited theatrically anywhere in the world and contains any of the results and proceeds of the performer's services, the performer will be paid for each day of employment hereunder $_____, or if this blank is not filled in, then the performer will be paid the minimum additional compensation prescribed therfor by Exhibit A of the Code.

If the program is exhibited in Supplemental Markets anywhere in the world and contains any of the results and proceeds of the performer's services, the performer will be paid the Supplemental Market fees prescribed by the applicable provisions of Exhibit D of the Code.

If the performer places his initial in the box he thereby authorizes Producer to use portions of said television program as a trailer to promote another episode or the series as a whole, upon payment to the performer of the additional compensation prescribed by the applicable provisions of Exhibit A of the Code.

Initial

By ————————————————

Producer

————————————————

Performer

NOTICE TO PERFORMER: IT IS IMPORTANT THAT YOU RETAIN A COPY OF THIS CONTRACT FOR YOUR PERMANENT RECORDS.

Production time reports are available on the set at the end of each day, which reports should be signed or initialed by performer.

Appendix B18

WGA Standard Form Free-Lance Television Writer's Employment Contract

Agreement entered into at _____, this _____ day of _____, 199____, between _____, hereinafter called "Company", and _____, hereinafter called "Writer".

WITNESSETH:

1. Company hereby employees the Writer to render services in the writing, composition, preparation and revision of the literary material described in subparagraph 2 hereof, hereinafter for convenience referred to as the "work". The Writer accepts such employment and agrees to render his/her services hereunder and devote his/her best talents, efforts and abilities in accordance with the instructions, control and directions of the Company.

2. FORM OF WORK:

(   ) Plot outline (based on _____).

(   ) Story (based on _____).

(   ) Story and teleplay (based on _____).

(   ) Teleplay (based on _____).

(   ) Rewrite (of _____).

(   ) Polish (of _____).

(   ) Other material (described as _____).

3. DELIVERY:

If the Writer has agreed to complete and deliver the work, and/or any changes and revisions, within a certain period or periods of time, then such agreement will be expressed in this paragraph as follows:

4. RIGHT TO OFFSET:

With respect to Writer's warranties and indemnification agreement, the Company and the Writer agree that upon the presentation of any claim or the institution of any action involving a breach of warranty, the party receiving notice thereof will promptly notify the other party in regard thereto. Company agrees that the pendency of any such claim or action shall not relieve the Company of its obligation to pay the Writer any monies due hereunder, and the Company will not have the right to withhold such monies until it has sustained a loss or suffered an adverse judgment of decree by reason of such claim or action.

5.   COMPENSATION:

As full compensation for all services to be rendered hereunder, the rights granted to the Company with respect to the work, and the undertakings and agreements assumed by the Writer, and upon condition that the Writer shall fully perform such undertakings and agreements, Company will pay the Writer the following amounts:

(a) Compensation for services: $_____

(b) Advance for television reruns: $_____

(c) Advance for theatrical use: $_____

No amounts may be inserted in (b) or (c) above unless the amount set forth in (a) above is at least twice the applicable minimum compensation set forth in the Writers Guild of America Theatrical and Television Basic Agreement of 1988 (herein "Basic Agreement") for the type of services to be rendered hereunder.

If the assignment is for story and teleplay or teleplay the following amounts of the compensation set forth in (a) above will be paid in accordance with the provisions of Article 13.B. of said Basic Agreement.

(1) $_____ following delivery of story.

(2) $_____ following delivery of first draft teleplay.

(3) $_____ following delivery of final draft teleplay.

In the event Writer receives screen credit on the television motion picture based on the above work and said motion picture is exhibited theatrically, Company shall pay to the Writer the additional sum of $_____ as provided in Article 15.B.13 of the Basic Agreement.

6.   MINIMUM BASIC AGREEMENT:

The parties acknowledge that this contract is subject to all of the terms and provisions of the Basic Agreement and to the extent that the terms and provisions of said Basic Agreement are more advantageous to Writer than the terms hereof, the terms of said Basic Agreement shall supersede and replace the less advantageous terms of this agreement. Writer is an employee as defined by said Basic Agreement and Company has the right to control and direct the services to be performed.

7.   GUILD MEMBERSHIP:

To the extent that it may be lawful for the Company to require the Writer to do so, Writer agrees to become and/or remain a member of Writers Guild of America in good standing as required by the provisions of said Basic Agreement. If Writer fails or refuses to become or remain a member of said Guild in good standing, as required in the preceding sentence, the Company shall have the right at any time thereafter to terminate this agreement with the Writer.

IN WITNESS WHEREOF, the parties hereto have duly executed this agreement on the day and year first above written.

By: _____
            Company

      _____
            Writer

(The foregoing Freelance Television Writer's Contract may contain any other provisions acceptable to both Writer and Company and not less favorable to, inconsistent with or violative of any of the terms or provisions of the Basic Agreement above mentioned.)

NOTE: This contract may *only* be utilized if the employer is a signatory to the WGA Theatrical and Television Basic Agreement, as the many provisions of the WGA agreement are incorporated into this form contract. The WGA recommends that writers only accept employment with or sell or option literary material to signatories to the WGA Agreement (Guild members cannot do otherwise).

Appendix B19
Music: Issue Checklist

[See the issue checklists for Rights Acquisitions and for Talent and Service Agreements for general considerations applicable to music-related rights and services.]

1. What compositions and recordings are covered?

   - Pre-existing music?
   - Pre-recorded music?
   - Specially commissioned music?
   - Specially recorded music?

2. What rights are being granted?

   - Synchronization rights?
   - Small or grand performance rights?
   - Master use rights in the recording?
   - Rights to use name, likeness, and biography in advertising?
   - Rights in a title?
   - Rights to change, alter, and edit?
   - Do the rights include the right to use the music in advertising and publicity?
   - Are publishing rights being granted?
   - Is the composition a work for hire?
   - Is the grant exclusive?
   - Is the grant irrevocable?

3. What media are covered?

   - All television, film, and related rights?
   - Are there any specifically included or excluded media?

4. What territories are covered?

   - The whole universe?
   - Are there any specifically included or excluded territories?

5. Does the producer participate in the music publishing?

   - Who is the publisher?
   - What is the split—traditional 50/50, or some form of co-publishing?
   - Are there any administrative, overhead, or expense deductions?
   - How are decisions on other uses and administrative matters made?

6. Are composing services being supplied?

   - What music is to be supplied?
   - What is the approval process?
   - What are the delivery dates?
   - Is parts copying and arranging included?

7. Are recording services being supplied?

   - What music is being recorded?
   - Who handles and pays for booking the facilities and hiring the musicians?
   - Are union players being used?
   - Are real players or a synthesizer being used?
   - What kind of finished product is being delivered, and in what technical format?

8. Are mixing and post-production services being supplied?

9. What payments must be made for the rights and services?

   - What is the composing fee?
   - What is the recording fee and expense payment?
   - When are they paid?
   - What uses do these prices cover?
   - Are there additional payments due for additional uses in subsequent productions or a series?
   - Are there any expenses to reimburse?

10. What representations, warranties, and indemnities should be given?

11. What credit does the composer get?

12. Are there limitations on the composer's remedies?

13. Is there any union or guild involved? If so, what impact does it have?

Appendix B20

Composer Deal Letter

[Producer's Letterhead]

[Date]

[Composer Name and Address]

Re: [Name of Program]

Dear _____:

This letter, when executed by you (the "Composer"), will set forth the agreement between the Composer and _____ (the "Producer") relating to the original music and recordings thereof (the "Music") for Producer's television series currently entitled "_____" (the "Series") and a pilot for the Series (the "Pilot").

1. *Ownership of Copyright.* Producer and Composer will own jointly the copyright in the Music composed by Composer and all rights, title and interest therein (the "Rights") throughout the universe in perpetuity. In particular, producer will own fifty percent (50%) of the copyright in the Music and Rights and Composer will own fifty percent (50%) of the copyright in the Music and Rights.

2. *Use of Music.* Producer will use the Music in the Series unless the network or other primary licensee objects to the use thereof. Composer will provide the copy of appropriate masters of the Music to Producer. Composer will provide additional masters to Producer on a cost basis if and when required by Producer.

3. *Compensation.* For all rights to use the Music in the Pilot and, if produced, the Series, Producer will pay the following compensation to Composer:

(a) The sum of $_____ payable upon the signing of the agreement for the direct, out-of-pocket recording costs of the master tape for the Pilot.

(b) The sum of $_____ if the Series is produced and the Music is used therein.

(c) The sum of $_____ if the Series is produced and the Music is not used therein pursuant to Paragraph 2 hereof.

Composer shall be solely liable for any third party talent payments due at any time with respect to any use of the Music or the Rights hereunder.

4. *Small performance rights.* Customary small performance royalties will be shared as and when received through performance rights organizations. Producer, or a company designated by Producer, will act as publisher for this purpose and Producer and Composer will each take fifty percent (50%) respectively of the Publisher's share and the Composer will receive one hundred percent (100%) of the writer's share.

5. *Credit.* Composer will receive on-screen credit in the closing titles of each program of the Series in substantially the following form:

Music By

_____

6. *Decisions.* Administrative decisions, licensing arrangements and other business decisions relating to the Music and the Rights and not otherwise discussed herein will be resolved by the mutual consent of Composer and Producer.

7. *Representations and Warranties.* Composer hereby represents and warrants that:

(a) Composer is free to enter into this Agreement and are able to comply with their obligations and agreements hereunder. Composer has not made, and will not make, any commitment or agreement which could or might materially interfere with the full and complete performance of Composer's obligations and agreements hereunder or which could or might in any way diminish the value of Producer's full enjoyment of the rights or privileges of Producer hereunder.

(b) All material which Composer may write, prepare, compose and/or submit in connection with the Music (except any such material in the public domain) shall be wholly original with Composer, and no such material shall be copied in whole or in part from any other work or shall infringe upon or violate any right of privacy of, constitute a libel against or violate any right of any entity.

Please indicate your acceptance of these terms by signing the enclosed counterpart copy on the indicated lines below and returning it to the undersigned. While we will, in all likelihood, enter into a more detailed agreement containing additional provisions customary in the entertainment industry, unless and until such agreement is executed by us, this letter shall constitute the binding agreement between us relating to the Music in the Series and Pilot.

Yours sincerely,
[Producer]

By: _____

Title: _____

AGREED TO AND ACCEPTED:

_____

[Composer]

Appendix B21
Performer Release

The undersigned Performer hereby releases the above specified Producer and its successors, licensees and assigns from any and all claims, actions and damages relating to or arising out of the use in any context and in any form by Producer, its successors, licensees and assigns, of the musical compositions described below and any recorded performances thereof in which Performer may have participated.

Performer assigns to Producer any and all rights which he/she may have to such compositions and performances, and agrees that any matter subject to copyright which he/she may have created in connection therewith will be a work for hire, with Producer deemed to be the author. Producer, and its successors, licensees and assigns, may change or edit any aspect of such compositions and performances as it sees fit, and may exploit them throughout the universe in any medium now known or hereafter discovered in perpetuity.

Performer acknowledges that she/he has received good and valuable consideration for the agreements set out above, and that Producer is relying on these agreements in connection with its exploitation of the compositions and performances.

Signed: _____

Performer's Name, Address,
and Social Security Number:

_____

_____

Dated: _____

Compositions: _____

_____

_____

Appendix B22

AFM Personal Service Contract

Union Copy

Personal Service Contract Blank

AMERICAN FEDERATION OF MUSICIANS
of the United States and Canada

For all Videotape/Live Television

THIS CONTRACT for the personal services of musicians, made this
_____ day of _____, 19____.

between the undersigned Producer (hereinafter called the Producer) and_____
_____ musicians (hereinafter called
(Number including leader)

Employees), represented by the undersigned representative (leader, composer or orchestra manager).

WITNESSETH, That the Producer employs the personal services of the Employees, as musicians severally and the Employees severally, through their representative, agree to render collectively to the Producer services as musicians in the orchestra under the leadership of _____

Conditions of Employment shall be in accordance with the provisions contained in the Wage Scales, Hours of Employment and Working Conditions in the basic agreement executed between the A. F. of M. and the Producer.

Network _____	Station _____
Tape Date _____	
Air Date _____	
Re-use Date _____ Domestic ____ Foreign ____	
Network Videotape	☐
Syndicated Videotape	☐
new use	☐
reuse	☐
Other _____	☐

SIGNATORY TO A.F. OF M. AGREEMENT

Name _____
Address _____
Telephone _____

NAME OF PROGRAM

GUEST STARS OR TITLE OF SEGMENT

REHEARSALS/PRE-RECORD/TAPE USE					MEMO	PAY SCHEDULE
Date	Start	Dism'd	Hours	Span		

PAY SCHEDULE

- Air & Min. Reh. $_____
- Add. Reh./Pre-Rec._____
- Use of Track_____
- Span_____
- Meal Pen._____
- Wrd. bs/Make-up_____
- Mult. Span._____
- Total Base._____

#	EMPLOYEE'S NAME (As On Social Security Card) LAST FIRST INITIAL	DOUBLES	HOME ADDRESS (Give Street, City and State)	Local Union No.	SOCIAL SECURITY NUMBER	SCALE WAGES	AFM-EPW	H. & W.
	LEADER							
1								
2								
3								
4								
5								
6								
7								
8								
9								
10								
11								
12								
13								
14								
15								
16								
17								

Make check payable to "AFM & EPW FUND" $_____

BY:_____
(Officer of Company)

SIGNED_____
Orchestra Manager

B-6—REV. 5/78

Reprinted by permission of the American Federation of Musicians.

590

2

ADDITIONAL TERMS AND CONDITIONS

The Producer shall at all times have complete control of the services which the employees will render under the specifications of this contract. The Producer will distribute to the musicians, including leader, composer or orchestra manager, not less than the prescribed union scale for their services. He may do this directly or through the leader, composer or orchestra manager. All such payments are to be made in accordance with the provisions of the basic agreement.

1. The Producer hereby authorizes the Leader, Composer or Orchestra Manager to replace any Employee who by illness, absence, or for any other reason does not perform any or all of the services provided for under this contract. The agreement of the Employees to perform is subject to proven detention by sickness, accidents, or accidents to means of transportation, riots, strikes, epidemics, acts of God, or any other legitimate conditions beyond the control of the Employees.

2. To the extent that their inclusion and enforcement are not prohibited by a valid federal or state statute, the rules, laws and regulations of the American Federation of Musicians and the rules, laws and regulations of the Local in whose jurisdiction the musicians perform, insofar as they are not in conflict with those of the Federation, are made part of this contract, and to such extent nothing in this contract shall ever be construed as to interfere with any obligation which any employee hereunder may owe to the American Federation of Musicians pursuant thereto.

3. Any member or members who are parties to or affected by this contract, whose services thereunder or covered thereby, are prevented, suspended or stopped by reason of any strike, ban, unfair list order or requirement of the Federation shall be free to accept and engage in other employment of the same or similar character, or otherwise, for other employers or persons without any restraint, hinderance, penalty, obligation or liability whatever, any other provisions of this contract to the contrary notwithstanding.

4. This contract shall not become effective unless and until it shall be approved by the Federation or an authorized representative.

5. This contract is ineffective and invalid unless the Producer is signatory to a basic agreement with the American Federation of Musicians.

6. All the terms and provisions set forth in the basic agreement between the Producer and the American Federation of Musicians shall be deemed part of this agreement with the same force and effect as though fully set forth herein and nothing herein contained shall be deemed to amend or supersede any provision of such basic agreement.

7. In consideration of the common interests of all the members of the A. F. of M. in the terms and conditions of this personal service contract and the basic agreement between the Producer and the A. F. of M., incorporated herein, the Employees authorize the A. F. of M. exclusively and irrevocably to take any and all steps and procedings in its name and behalf and/or the Employees' behalf and/or in behalf of any of its members for the enforcement of all rights under this contract and/or the said basic agreement, all of which rights of the Employees are hereby assigned to the A. F. of M., and said A. F. of M., in behalf of any of its members is irrevocably authorized to agree to any change, modification and/or the said basic agreement, except that nothing herein contained shall deprive the Employees of any money compensation agreed to be paid to such Employees for services in connection with the making of such motion picture and sound track.

8. The employer agrees that he shall be liable for loss or damage to musical instruments, accessories (pedals, benches, or seats, that come with instruments, drum sticks, castanets, maracas, etc.), music (sheet music, manuscripts, folios, arrangements and/or orchestrations and/or any music of any type whatsoever) amplifiers, microphones, speakers, and any other supplies or equipment necessary for the performance, or used by the musicians and/or entertainers, performing under this contract, while all the, or any of, the aforementioned instruments, amplifiers, music supplies, etc. are on his premises. This includes any loss resulting from accident, malicious mischief, burglary, theft, fire, or any other event that causes the aforementioned loss.

AMERICAN FEDERATION OF MUSICIANS' and EMPLOYERS' PENSION WELFARE FUND
(AFM & EPW FUND)

733 THIRD AVENUE , NEW YORK, N. Y. 10017

TELEVISION VIDEO TAPE

Effective May 1, 1978 Employer shall contribute 8 percent of all earnings of whatever nature covered by this agreement. computed at scale, to the American Federation of Musicians' and Employers' Pension Welfare Fund. Employer shall be bound by the Trust Agreement of the AFM & EPW Fund dated October 2, 1959.

Such payments shall be made in accordance with the conditions of the applicable Labor Agreement with a copy of the letter transmitting the payment simultaneously mailed to the Federation Studio Representative. The trustees may agree with contributors upon different dates of payment.

NOTICE TO EMPLOYER:

There are 6 copies of this contract.

a. You should retain employer copy for your files, and send all other copies to the Local Union with your separate checks for the pension contribution and H&W contribution.

b. The remaining 5 copies will be distributed by the Local Union as follows:

One copy to be retained by the Local Union.

One copy to AFM-EPW.

One copy to H&W.

One copy to the American Federation of Musicians, 1500 Broadway, New York, N.Y. 10036.

One copy to the Leader.

Contracts covering the reuse shall be distributed in the same manner as above. Pension contributions and H&W for a reuse shall also be made as above.

Appendix B23

Video Synchronization and Distribution License

THIS AGREEMENT made and entered into this _____ day of _____ by and between _____ ("Publisher") and _____ ("Licensee")

WHEREAS Publisher owns or controls the musical composition ("Composition") entitled _____, written by _____; and

WHEREAS Licensee desires to utilize the Composition in that certain production entitled _____ ("Production"), and to reproduce the Production and Composition in videocassettes and videodiscs (both devices being referred to herein as "Videograms");

NOW THEREFORE the parties hereto do hereby mutually agree as follows:

1. In consideration of the royalties to be paid hereunder by Licensee to Publisher and the other covenants herein on the part of the Licensee, the Publisher hereby grants to Licensee the nonexclusive right and license to reproduce and make copies of the Composition in Videogram copies of the Production and to distribute the Videograms to the public by sale or other transfer of ownership.

2. No right to rent Videograms is hereby granted. If Licensee wishes to utilize Videograms via rental Licensee shall advise Publisher in writing and the parties hereto shall negotiate in good faith the compensation or other participation to be paid to Publisher in respect of rental receipts.

3. This license and grant is for a term of _____ years only, commencing on the date of this agreement. At the expiration of earlier termination of such period, all rights and licenses granted hereunder shall cease and terminate.

4. The rights granted hereunder are limited solely to the territory of _____ (the "licensed territory").

Reprinted from *This Business of Music,* by permission.

5. As compensation to the Publisher, Licensor agrees to pay to the Publisher the following royalties:

a) As to each copy of a videodisc sold in the licensed territory and paid for and not returned _____, and

b) As to each copy of a videocassette sold in the licensed territory and paid for and not returned _____.

6. Accountings shall be rendered by Licensee to Publisher within sixty (60) days after the close of each calendar quarter, showing in detail the royalties earned, and any deductions taken in computing royalties. Publisher shall be responsible for paying royalties to writers and any third party by reason of the grant and license hereunder. No statement shall be due for a period in which Videograms are not sold. All royalty statements shall be binding upon Publisher and not subject to any objection by Publisher for any reason unless specific objection in writing, stating the basis thereof, is given to Licensee within one (1) year from the date rendered.

7. Publisher shall have the right to inspect and make abstracts of the books and records of Licensee, insofar as said books and records pertain to the performance of Licensee's obligations hereunder; such inspection to be made on at least ten (10) days written notice, during normal business hours of normal business days but not more frequently than once annually in each year.

8. The rights and license granted hereunder may not be assigned or transferred, either affirmatively or by operation of law, without Publisher's written consent.

9. Publisher warrants and represents that it has full right, power and authority to enter into and to perform this agreement.

10. This agreement shall be deemed made in and shall be construed in accordance with the laws of the State of New York. The agreement may not be modified orally and shall not be binding or effective unless and until it is signed by both parties hereto.

IN WITNESS WHEREOF the parties have entered into this agreement the day and year first above written.

Publisher

By _____

Licensee

By _____

Appendix B24

Television Film Synchronization License

To: _____ TV Lic. #_____ Date _____

Composition: _____

1. In consideration of the sum of _____ payable upon the execution hereof, we grant you the non-exclusive right to record on film or video tape the above identified musical composition(s) in synchronization or timed relation with a single episode or individual program entitled ____ _____ for television use only, subject to all of the terms and conditions herein provided.

2. (a) The type of use is to be _____

(b) On or before the first telecast of the said film, you or your assigns agree to furnish to us a copy of the Cue Sheet prepared and distributed in connection therewith.

3. The territory covered by this license is the world.

4. (a) This license is for a period of _____ from the date hereof.

(b) Upon the expiration of this license all rights herein granted shall cease and terminate and the right to make or authorize any further use or distribution of any recordings made hereunder shall also cease and terminate.

5. This is a license to record only and does not authorize any use of the aforesaid musical composition(s) not expressly set forth herein. By way of illustration but not limitation, this license does not include the right to change or adapt the words or to alter the fundamental character of the music of said musical composition(s) or to use the title(s) thereof as the title or sub-title of said film.

6. Performance of the said musical composition(s) in the exhibition of said film is subject to the condition that each television station over which the aforesaid musical composition(s) is (are) to be so performed

shall have a performance license issued by us or from a person, firm, corporation, society, association or other entity having the legal right to issue such performance license.

7.   No sound records produced pursuant to this license are to be manufactured, sold and/or used separately or independently of said film.

8.   The film shall be for television use only and may not be televised into theatres or other places where admission is charged.

9.   All rights not herein specifically granted are reserved by us.

10. We warrant only that we have the legal right to grant this license and this license is given and accepted without other warranty or recourse. If said warranty shall be breached in whole or in part with respect to (any of) said musical composition(s), our total liability shall be limited either to repaying to you the consideration theretofore paid under this license with respect to such musical composition to the extent of such breach or to holding you harmless to the extent of the consideration theretofore paid under this license with respect to such musical composition to the extent of said breach.

11. This license shall run to you, your successors and assigns, provided you shall remain liable for the performance of all of the terms and conditions of this license on your part to be performed and provided further that any disposition of said film or any prints thereof shall be subject to all the terms hereof, and you agree that all persons, firms or corporations acquiring from you any right, title, interest in or possession of said film or any prints thereof shall be notified of the terms and conditions of this license and shall agree to be bound thereby.

_____
(Licensor)

By   _____

Appendix B25
Performance License

Program: _____

Producer: _____

Composition: _____

Type of Use: _____

Duration of Use: _____

Composer: _____

Lyricist: _____

Publisher: _____

Medium of Use: _____

Territory of Use: _____

Dates of Use: _____

Number of Repeats: _____

Consideration: _____

License Grantor: _____

2. *GRANT OF LICENSE.*

All capitalized terms used in this license refer to those items specified in the Basic Information set forth above. Provided that the Consideration is paid in full upon signing hereof, the undersigned License Grantor hereby grants Producer, and its licensees and assigns, the right to perform the Composition publicly through television in connection with the exhibition of the Program through the Medium of Use and throughout the Territory of Use. This license shall only cover the Type of Use and Duration of Use specified above, and shall only apply during the Dates of Use and only for the specified Number of Repeats. Producer represents and warrants that it has received a valid synchronization licensee for this use. The License Grantor represents and warrants that the License Grantor has the power to grant this performance license, and that the performance of the Composition in accordance with this license will not violate the rights of any third party. This license is subject to the receipt by the License Grantor from the Producer, on or about the first performance authorized hereunder, of a copy of the complete musical cue sheet for the Program.

3. SIGNATURE AND DATE.

License Grantor: _____

Signature: _____

Name and Title: _____

Date: _____

Appendix B26

Sample Television Film Cue Sheet

[Production Company Name]

[Program Title]

NO. SELECTION	COMPOSER	PUBLISHER
REELS 1 & 2		
1. Medley consisting of:		
(a) SIGNATURE	JANE DOE	XYZ
(b) JUNIPER	JANE DOE	XYZ
2. COWBOYS	MIKE ROE	ABC
3. Medley consisting of:		
(a) JUNIPER	JANE DOE	XYZ
(b) COWBOYS	MIKE ROE	ABC
(c) JUNIPER	JANE DOE	FGH
(d) THE BOYS	IRV GROW	XYZ
4. THE GIRLS	MAY JOE	ABC
5. THE BIRDS	MAY JOE	ABC
REELS 3 & 4		
6. KERMITS	MAY LOE	ABC
7. KERMITS	MAY LOE	XYZ
8. Medley consisting of:		
(a) JUNIPER	JANE DOE	XYZ
(b) CLEO	BOB SMITH	ABC
(c) KERMAC	MAY LOE	ABC
9. KERMAC	MAY LOE	ABC
10. Medley consisting of:		
(a) JUNIPER	JANE DOE	ABC
(b) COWBOYS	MIKE ROE	ABC
(c) JUNIPER	JANE DOE	XYZ
(d) COWBOYS	MIKE ROE	ABC
(e) JUNIPER	JANE DOE	XYZ
(f) COWBOYS	MIKE ROE	ABC

Adapted from *This Business of Music,* by permission

[Date]

EXTENT	HOW USED	TIME
ENTIRE	BKG. INST.	0.07
ENTIRE	VIS. VOC.	5.37
PARTIAL	BKG. INST.	0.34
PARTIAL	BKG. INST.	0.09
ENTIRE	BKG. INST.	0.45
PARTIAL	BKG. INST.	0.38
PARTIAL	BKG. INST.	0.47
ENTIRE	BKG. INST.	0.05
ENTIRE	VIS. VOC.	2.45
ENTIRE	VIS. VOC	2.09
PARTIAL	BKG. INST.	0.23
PARTIAL	BKG. INST.	1.40
ENTIRE	VIS. VOC.	1.50
ENTIRE	BKG. INST.	1.30
ENTIRE	VIS. VOC.	1.25
PARTIAL	BKG. INST.	0.24
PARTIAL	BKG. INST.	0.24
PARTIAL	BKG. INST.	0.12
PARTIAL	BKG. INST.	0.14
PARTIAL	BKG. INST.	0.30
PARTIAL	BKG. INST.	0.45

Appendix B27

Design/Location:
Issue Checklist

[Note: See the checklists for Rights Acquisition and for Talent and Service Agreements for general considerations applicable to design and location agreements.]

1. How are the design services being handled?

   - What is to be designed?
   - What is the approval process?
   - Who arranges for, and oversees, construction and fabrication?
   - What are the delivery dates?
   - What are the ongoing responsibilities of the designer?
   - What is the initial compensation of the designer?
   - What is the ongoing compensation of the designer?
   - Are there residuals or reuse fees?
   - Who owns the designs?
   - Is there an applicable union or guild?

2. How is the location being arranged?

   - Is a location manager or outside location service being used?
   - Are you dealing with an owner or leasor who has the power to grant both the right of access and any necessary media rights?
   - What are the times of access?
   - Who is responsible for damages?
   - Who is responsible for carrying insurance; what types and how much?
   - Are changes and construction permitted?
   - What maintenance staff is required, and who pays for it?
   - What compensation is payable for the location use and any media rights?

Appendix B28

United Scenic Artists: Free-Lance Television Agreement, Art Director

AGREEMENT made this _____ day of _____, 19____ between _____ hereinafter called ART DIREC-TOR and _____ hereinafter called EMPLOYER.

THE EMPLOYER AGREES to engage the services of the Art Director and the Art Director agrees to design the television production known as _____ to be telecast or otherwise exhibited on the _____ day of _____, 19____, and subsequently on _____ (state additional dates and number of shows in the case of a Series) _____

NOTE: The terms TELEVISION PRODUCTION and TELECAST used in this agreement refer to live television broadcasts as well as to reproductions by means of any mechanical or electronic processes, including so-called "pilot" versions intended for previewing by prospective sponsors or advertisers but excluding motion pictures produced for use on television. Designs for motion pictures must be executed under the terms and conditions of the Local 829 Feature Motion Picture Contract.

THE ART DIRECTOR AGREES to render the following services where required in connection with said production:

(a)   Submit sketches and/or models and prepare working drawings, story boards, continuity sketches, perspective drawings, color sketches, color schemes, floor plans, elevations and full size details, select decorative wall coverings, draperies and set dressings. Design and select matte shots, gobos and other transitional change-of-scene effects and other such visual effects as are required.

(b)   Supervise the assembling of physical production in the studio.

I. *Single Production.* The Employer agrees to pay the Art Director the sum of $_____ for the production representing _____ weeks.

Reprinted by permission of United Scenic Artists Local 829.

II. *Series* (more than one (1) production within the same program). The Employer agrees to pay the Art Director the sum of $_____ per week (payable each week) for the duration of the program.

III. *Minimum Scales*

   A. The minimum rate for Art Director shall be no less than $2,000. per week. A week shall be any five (5) consecutive days. The sixth and seventh days, if required, shall each be paid at 3/10 of the weekly rate ($600).

   B. For continuing programs not requiring any design changes a minimum daily rate of $400.00 shall be charged for supervision at the studio which would include minor maintenance refurbishing.

IV. *Assistants.* Assistants to the Art Director, if any, shall be hired at no less than the United Scenic Artists prevailing daily rates and conditions.

V. *Pension and Welfare.* In addition to the salaries stipulated in this agreement, the Employer shall pay a sum equal to 12% of all monies due to a special trust fund designed to provide various types of pension and welfare to the member employed hereunder. Such payments shall be made by separate checks, made out to the United Scenic Artists Pension and Welfare Fund at 575 Eighth Avenue, New York, N.Y. 10018, at the end of each month during which salaries are due, except that the first payment of 12% shall be due upon signing of this agreement.

VI. *Expenses.* The Employer agrees to pay the Art Director necessary and actual out-of-pocket expenses upon delivery of valid accounting of bills for local transportation, including taxi fares, artists' material, prints of working drawings, etc., in connection with said production.

   The Employer agrees to provide the Art Director and/or Assistants, if any, with first-class round-trip transportation and hotel expenses whenever the Art Director and/or Assistant is required by the Employer to travel outside of New York City in connection with the services hereunder. The Employer furthermore agrees to pay the Art Director and/or Assistant not less than $79.00 per day for living expenses for each and every day that the Art Director and/or Assistant are required to be outside of New York City in connection with the production.

VII. *Postponement.* Where an Employer postpones the production for more than two (2) weeks, the Employer and Art Director agree to fulfill all of the provisions of this agreement without change, except for adjustment of dates of production. Where the postponement exceeds four (4) weeks, the production shall be deemed abandoned and payments based upon the adjusted amount shall be made in accordance with the Abandonment Provision herein, unless the parties by mutual agreement and with the consent of the Union, enter into a new agreement.

VIII. *Abandonment.* Should the production be abandoned after the Art Director has completed drawings and/or color sketches, Art Director shall be entitled to full payment of the herein stipulated amount. If Art Director has not fully completed his/her drawings and/or sketches, he/she shall receive not less than 50% of the amount stipulated herein.

IX. *General Provisions*

   A. Whenever Air Credit is given to the director of a program, the Employer shall give the Art Director credit on a single frame in the same size, quality and format as for the director. Such credits shall be given in the following forms:

   "Art Director _____"

or

   "Art Direction by _____"

   Where there is a Production Designer, his/her credit shall be in the form:

   "Production Designer _____"

or

   "Production Designed by _____"

   B. The Employer agrees not to alter or substitute changes in the settings or properties as provided by the Art Director for said production at any time without the approval of the Art Director, and that the Art Director shall have exclusive jurisdiction over, and ultimate authority to design, select or approve all props and visual effects in connection with said production to which he/she is hereby assigned.

   C. Under no circumstances may any of the designs prepared under this agreement be used by any party or parties in any other manner or for any other purpose except for the production as specified in this agreement.

   D. The designs and/or the production so designed under this agreement may not be used for re-telecasting by means of any photographic, mechanical or electronic processes at any subsequent date without the written consent by the Art Director and the Union and payment to the Art Director of sum no less than 25% of the original payment for each subsequent telecast, except that in the case of a "live" re-telecast a new agreement must be entered into. Employer must notify the Union of each and any re-telecast.

   E. The continuing use of a permanent set will be $184.00 per week.

   F. The repeat of a series will be $184.00 per week. A repeat is defined as a single showing or multiple showings in one single week.

   G. The obligations of the Art Director are not subject to delays caused by strikes, accidents, acts of God, fire or other causes beyond the control of the Art Director. The Art Director is not responsible for any failure or inability on the part of contractors, builders, and painters to execute the designs and/or plans prepared by the Art Director.

H. The title to all drawings, designs and specifications prepared by the Art Director under this contract shall at all times remain the property of the Art Director. They may not be reproduced at any time without his/her consent or used for another production.

I. It is agreed that the Employer will execute and file with the Union, in accordance with the Union's working rules, a television Costume Designer's contract covering the costume requirements for the production referred to in this agreement.

J. In case of a dispute between the Union and the Employer the parties agree to make every attempt to settle such matter promptly, amicably and in good faith. If the dispute cannot be so adjusted, the party initiating the dispute may ask the American Arbitration Association to appoint an arbitrator and the arbitration shall proceed in accordance with the rules of that agency.

The decision of the arbitrators shall be final and binding upon all parties. Since time is of the essence in any arbitration, any hearing shall be held on five (5) working days' notice and shall be concluded within fourteen (14) consecutive days from the first hearing unless otherwise ordered by the arbitrator. The award by the arbitrator shall be made within seven (7) consecutive days after the close of the hearing. The cost of the arbitration shall be shared equally by both parties.

K. The original Art Director shall have the right of first refusal for any subsequent reproduction. The Art Director shall be given a minimum of two weeks to so decide.

ACCEPTED: ACCEPTED:

By: _____   By: _____

For United Scenic Artists   For: _____
    Local 829   Producer
    575 Eighth Avenue
    New York, NY 10018   Address: _____

                                                    _____

Date: _____   Date: _____

                                                    ACCEPTED:

                                                    By: _____
                                                            Art Director

                                                    Address: _____

                                                    _____

                                                    Date: _____

Appendix B29
Location Release

Owner/Tenant: _____

Producer: _____

Premises: _____

Program: _____

The undersigned Owner/Tenant hereby agrees to permit the Producer to use the Premises, both exterior and interior, for the purpose of filming, photographing and/or otherwise recording scenes for the Program. Producer and its licensees and assigns shall have the right to use the film, photographs and/or other recording made on and showing the Premises in any manner throughout the world in perpetuity without any limitations or restrictions.

Producer will have the right to film, photograph and/or otherwise record in and around the Premises for _____ days, commencing _____, (subject to change due to adverse weather conditions).

Producer will leave the Premises in the same condition as existed prior to use, and Producer will indemnify and hold the Owner/Tenant harmless from all claims for damages occurring during its use of the Premises which arose out of its activities.

Owner/Tenant acknowledges that it has received good and valuable consideration for this grant and warrants that it has the authority to grant the rights granted herein with respect to the Premises.

OWNER/TENANT

By: _____

Title: _____

_____
[Producer]

Appendix B30
Production: Issue Checklist

1. What production facilities will be used?

   - Which studio?
   - Which location(s)?
   - Which mobile unit (truck)?
   - Does the facility offer sufficient technical and staging resources for the production? Can rentals fill in the gaps?

2. Does the facility provide adequate non-technical support?

   - Are dressing rooms, make-up and hair, and wardrobe provided, or must facilities be rented?
   - Is an audience holding area needed? Is it available on the premises, or must other rental arrangements be made?
   - Is office space available for the production staff, or must it be rented? What is the cost of renting it from the facility? Is this a fair price?
   - Is parking available, or must arrangements be made?
   - Are dining facilities available nearby, or must catering be arranged?

3. On what basis will the facilities be rented?

   - Hourly?
   - Daily?
   - Weekly?
   - Monthly?
   - On a bulk rate, based on multiple uses?

4. What equipment and other facilities will be included in the studio or soundstage rental package?

   - Will lighting equipment be provided? How many instruments? What types? What are the capabilities of the lighting board?

- Does the facility have adequate power and air conditioning to service the production?
- How many cameras will be provided? How many hand-helds, how many pedestal cameras, how many with special mounts (such as cranes)?
- Will audio be handled by the house, or by an outside contractor?
- How many microphones will be provided? What types? Any special mountings? Are there any special charges, or special technical issues, related to the use of RF wireless microphones? What are the limitations of the house PA system?
- What type of equipment will be used to record and to mix the program?
- What audio playback facilities come with the package?
- How many videotape machines will be provided? What are the formats? What is the cost of additional machines?
- What is the make and model of the video switcher? Does it offer the flexibility needed for the production?
- What type of computer graphics devices (including character generator, DVE, still-store) are available?
- What are the capabilities and limitations of the communications system?
- Is the facility available after hours for the scenic crew?
- What is the overall quality of the technical facility? Is the equipment relatively new, and properly maintained? Does the facility offer the flexibility needed for the production?

5. Technical Crew:
   - Who will hire the crew?
   - Will the crew work under union rules? Which union?
   - What are the hourly or daily rates for each individual crew member? What are the overtime charges?
   - Are there any special work rules for crew members, such as guaranteed meal breaks or rest periods? Are there penalties associated with breaking these rules?
   - Who will the key crew members be? Can the director approve these crew members? Can the director replace them?

6. Stage Crew:
   - Who will hire the stagehands?
   - Do they belong to a union?
   - What are the rates and work rules?

- How many people will be needed to set up, run, and strike the production?

7. Financial Arrangements:

- Is a payment required to reserve the facility? Is it refundable? Under what circumstances?
- On what basis will the facility be billed?
- How often will the studio bill (for a series)?
- Will outside rentals and free-lance personnel be billed through the facility (at a mark-up), or hired directly by the producer?
- Does the facility carry adequate insurance?
- What is the cost of using the facility's phones, copier, and fax machine? For a big project, can the production install its own phone system?
- If the program is a pilot, is there any further responsibility to the facility regarding the series?

Appendix B31
Lab Letter

[Name and Address of Laboratory]

Gentlemen:

The undersigned, _____ ("Producer") has entered into an agreement (the "Agreement") with _____ ("Distributor") under which Agreement Distributor has been granted certain distribution rights in and to the television programs entitled "_____" (the "Programs").

For good and valuable consideration, receipt of which is hereby acknowledged, it is hereby agreed, for the express benefit of Distributor, as follows:

1. You now have in your possession in the name of Producer the materials ("Materials") listed in Exhibit A attached hereto for said Programs; you certify that all materials are ready and suitable for the making of commercially acceptable release copies and duplicating material, including visual elements and soundtracks.

2. You will retain possession of all Materials at your laboratory located at _____ and you will not deliver any of said Materials to anyone without the written consent of Producer and Distributor.

3. Distributor and its designees shall at all times have access to said Materials.

4. You will at all times perform all laboratory services requested by Distributor or its designers relating to the Programs, which laboratory services will be performed by you at prevailing rates at Distributor's sole expense.

5. Neither Distributor nor Producer shall have any liability for any indebtedness to you incurred by the other.

6. You presently have no claim or lien against the Programs or the Materials, nor, insofar as Distributor is concerned, will you assert any claim or lien against the Programs or the Materials except for your charges for services rendered for and materials furnished to Distributor.

7. This Agreement is irrevocable and may not be altered or modified except by a written instrument executed by Distributor and Producer.

Please signify your agreement to the foregoing by signing where indicated below.

Very truly yours,
[Producer]

By: _____

AGREED TO:

[Name of Laboratory]

By: _____

CONSENTED TO:

[Distributor]

By: _____

EXHIBIT A

[For Videotape Productions]

(a) the fully edited, titled and assembled electronic master of each Program on SMPTE 1-inch Type C format videotape with fully synchronized sound;

(b) all videotape footage shot or created in connection with each Program including all title and credit sequences;

(c) all separate dialog tracks, sound effects tracks and music tracks recorded on magnetic media; and

(d) any scripts, notes and logs relating to the editing of the Programs.

Appendix B32

Business Entities and Tax: Issue Checklist

1. What kind of business entity is appropriate?

   - Is the economy and simplicity of a sole proprietorship important?
   - Will there be more than one owner, requiring a partnership or corporation?
   - Is the flexibility of a partnership important?
   - If the business is for a limited purpose, would a joint-venture form of partnership be appropriate?
   - Is the limited liability of a corporation important?
   - Would a limited partnership, if available, provide enough limited liability?
   - Are the tax benefits of a partnership important?
   - Would a Sub-Chapter S corporation provide enough tax benefits?
   - Is Sub-Chapter S treatment available?
   - Is the corporate form too expensive to set up and maintain?
   - Would a partnership of corporations be too expensive or unwieldy?

2. What is the most advantageous state in which to establish the business?

   - The state where the headquarters of the business will be located?
   - Some other state where there will be a significant business presence?
   - A state with flexible and attractive corporate or partnership laws and taxes, such as Delaware or Nevada?

3. If a sole proprietorship, partnership, or joint venture, have the usual filings been made?

   - The "doing business as" or "fictitious name" certificate?
   - The federal taxpayer identification number?

- The employment-related filings at the state and federal level?
- If a limited partnership, has the limited partnership certificate been filed and any publishing requirement been met?

4. If a corporation, have the usual filings been made?

- The certificate or articles of incorporation?
- The federal tax identification number?
- The employment-related filings at the state and federal level?
- The federal and any state Sub-Chapter S filing, if applicable?

5. Have matters of governance and management been decided?

- Who are the officers or managing partners?
- Who are the directors?
- How are officers, directors, and managing partners elected?
- How are day-to-day and major decisions made?
- Who has banking authority?
- Who decides to admit new partners or sell more stock?
- Who approves mergers, sales of the business, major loans, other significant business events?
- Who designates the lawyers, accountants, and other major service providers?

6. Have matters of finance been determined?

- Who is contributing to capital?
- In cash?
- In kind?
- Who is loaning money or other property?
- What is the return on these investments?
- Is there a priority return through contract recoupment, debt, or preferred stock?
- Has a budget estimate showing working capital needs been prepared?

7. How have management and financial matters been established?

- By default, as a matter of applicable law?
- If a joint venture or partnership, in a written agreement?
- If a corporation, in the certificate of incorporation, in the By-Laws, or in a shareholders agreement?
- Through a loan agreement and notes?

8. Have a lawyer and an accountant been consulted?

Appendix C
OTHER RESOURCES

Appendix C1
Selected Bibliography

Andorka, Frank H. *A Practical Guide to Copyrights and Trademarks*. New York: Pharos Books, 1989.

Battersby, Gregory J., and Charles W. Grimes. *The Law of Merchandise and Character Licensing*. New York: Clark Boardman, 1989.

Becker, Benjamin M., David M. Becker, and David L. Gibberman. *Legal Checklists, 1990 Cumulative Supplement*. Deerfield, Illinois: Callaghan & Company, 1990.

Bovee, Courtland L., and William F. Arens. *Contemporary Advertising*. Chicago: Irwin, 1986.

Brenner, Daniel. "Cable Television and Freedom of Expression." *First Amendment Law Handbook*, James L. Swanson and Christian L. Castle, eds. New York: Clark Boardman, 1990.

Brenner, Daniel. "Uncertain Renewal Conditions in the Cable Industry in the Mid to Late 1970s." *1990 Entertainment, Publishing and the Arts Handbook*, John David Viera and Robert Thorne, eds. New York: Clark Boardman, 1990.

Brown, Les. *The New York Times Encyclopedia of Television*. New York: Times Books, 1977.

Capogrosso, Eric. *The IDC Labor Guide 1990, Eighth Edition*. Burbank, California: IDC Services, Inc., 1990.

Castleman, Harry, and Walter J. Podrazik. *The TV Schedule Book: Four Decades of Network Programming from Sign-On to Sign-Off*. New York: McGraw-Hill, 1984.

Castleman, Harry, and Walter J. Podrazik. *Watching TV: Four Decades of American Television*. New York: McGraw-Hill, 1982.

Collyer, Michael. "Television and Television Program Development." *Entertainment Law*, Howard Siegel, ed. Albany: New York State Bar Association, 1989.

Dunlap, William H., ed. *1990 INTV Census.* New York: VIEW Communications, Ltd., 1990.

Fireman, Judy, ed. *TV Book: The Ultimate Television Book.* New York: Workman Publishing Company, 1977.

Freedman, Robert I. "Part III—Television." *Entertainment Industry Contracts: Negotiating and Drafting Guide, Volume 2,* Donald C. Farber, ed. Los Angeles: Times Mirror Books, 1990.

Gerdes, Ted F. "The Special Problems of Docudramas: No Shortcuts in the Clearance Process." *1990 Entertainment, Publishing and the Arts Handbook,* John David Viera and Robert Thorne, eds. New York: Clark Boardman, 1990.

Goodale, James C. *All About Cable: Legal and Business Aspects of Cable and Pay Television.* New York: Law Journals Seminars Press, 1989.

Hawes, James E. *Copyright Registration Practice.* New York: Clark Boardman, 1990.

Head, Sydney W. *World Broadcasting Systems: A Comparative Analysis.* Belmont, California: Wadsworth Publishing Company, 1985.

Head, Sydney W., and Christopher H. Sterling. *Broadcasting in America: A Survey of Electronic Media, Sixth Edition.* Boston: Houghton Mifflin, 1990.

Henn, Harry G. *Copyright Law: A Practitioner's Guide, Second Edition.* New York: Practising Law Institute, 1988.

Kent, Felix H., and Elhanan C. Stone. *Legal and Business Aspects of the Advertising Industry 1989.* New York: Practising Law Institute, 1989.

Lindey, Alexander. *Lindey on Entertainment, Publishing and the Arts: Agreements and the Law.* New York: Clark Boardman, 1990.

London, Mel. *Getting into Video: A Career Guide.* New York: Ballantine Books, 1990.

McCarthy, J. Thomas. *The Rights of Publicity and Privacy.* New York: Clark Boardman, 1990.

Mitz, Rick. *The Great TV Sitcom Book, Expanded Edition.* New York: Perigee Books, 1983.

National Association of Broadcasters. *Legal Guide to Broadcast Law and Regulation, Third Edition.* Washington, D.C., 1988.

Nelson, Harold L., and Dwight L. Teeter, Jr. *Law of Mass Communications: Freedom and Control of Print and Broadcast Media, Sixth Edition.* Mineola, New York: The Foundation Press, 1989.

Nimmer, Melville B., and David Nimmer. *Nimmer on Copyright: A Treatise on the Law of Literary, Musical and Artistic Property, and the Protection of Ideas.* Los Angeles: Times Mirror Books, 1990.

Roman, James W. *Cablemania: The Cable Television Sourcebook.* Englewood Cliffs, New Jersey: Prentice-Hall, 1983.

Sanford, Bruce W. *Libel and Privacy: The Prevention of Defense of Litigation.* Prentice Hall Law and Business, 1987.

Selz, Thomas D., Melvin Simensky, and Patricia Acton. *Entertainment Law: Legal Concepts and Business Practices.* Colorado Springs, Colorado: Shepards/McGraw-Hill, Inc., 1990.

Shemel, Sidney, and M. William Krasilovsky. *This Business of Music, Sixth Edition.* New York: Billboard Books, 1990.

Television Business International's World Guide '90. New York: Act III Publishing, 1990.

Trubow, George B., editor-in-chief, Jay M. Cohen, Richard E. Ehlke, Paul B. Rasor, Daniel L. Skoler, and Charles R. Trumper. *Privacy Law and Practice, Volume I.* Los Angeles: Times Mirror Books, 1989.

Ward, Peter C. *Federal Trade Commission: Law, Practice and Procedure.* New York: Law Journal Seminars-Press, 1986.

Williams, Huntington. *Beyond Control: ABC and the Fate of the Networks.* New York: Atheneum, 1989.

Willis, John W., editor-in-chief. *Radio Regulation, Second Series.* Bethesda, Maryland: Pike & Fisher, Inc., 1990.

Winship, Michael. *Television.* New York: Random House, 1988.

Yeldell, Eric B. *The Motion Picture and Television Business.* Beverly Hills: Entertainment Business Publishing Co., 1987.

Additional Publications of Interest:

Billboard. New York: Billboard Publishing Inc. Published weekly. Includes coverage of home video.

Comm/ent: Hastings Communications and Entertainment Law Journal. San Francisco: Hastings College of the Law, University of California. Published quarterly.

Electronic Media. Chicago: Crain Communications, Inc. Published weekly.

Entertainment Law Reporter. Santa Monica, California: Entertainment Law Reporter, Inc. Published monthly.

The Hollywood Reporter. Los Angeles: The Hollywood Reporter, Inc. Published daily.

Media Law Reporter. Washington, D.C.: The Bureau of National Affairs, Inc. Published weekly.

Television Business International. London: Act III Publishing, UK, Ltd. Published monthly.

Variety. New York: Variety, Inc. Published daily and weekly.

Video Business. New York: Fairchild Publishing. Published weekly.

Appendix C2

Source Directories for Further Information

The Hollywood Reporter Blu-Book
617 Sunset Boulevard
Hollywood, California 90028
213-464-7411 Fax: 213-461-6020

> Comprehensive annual directory to Hollywood entertainment industry, including suppliers of production and post-production services as well as network executive rosters.

The IDC Labor Guide
IDC Services, Inc.
2600 West Olive Avenue
Burbank, California 91505
818-569-5100 Fax: 818-569-5184

> Annual publication summarizing all major guild and union agreements, wage scales, working conditions, and insurance.

Motion Picture, TV, and Theatre Directory
Motion Picture Enterprises Publications, Inc.
P.O. Box 276
Tarrytown, New York 10591
212-245-0969 Fax: 212-245-0974

> Annual directory of services and products used in industry.

New York Commercial & Television Guide
Jonas Publishing
3220 Arlington Avenue
Riverdale, New York 10463
212-409-1300 Fax: 212-518-0809

> Annual handbook giving rates and working conditions for all major unions involved in television production in New York; with local supplier directory.

The Producer's Masterguide
330 West 42nd Street, 16th Floor
New York, New York 10036-6994
212-465-8889 Fax: 212-465-8880

Annual international production manual for motion picture, television, commercial, cable and videotape industry including current labor contract wage scales, information on major awards, guidelines and bidding procedures for commercial production, and directory of suppliers.

Appendix C3
Guilds & Unions

National Offices

American Federation of Musicians (AFM)
1501 Broadway, Suite 600
New York, New York 10036
212-869-1330 Fax: 212-764-6134

> Union headquarters for all local AFM musician unions. Representation for local musician unions in the interpretation of agreements, negotiations, and settlements.

American Federation of Television and Radio Artists (AFTRA)
260 Madison Avenue
New York, New York 10016
212-532-0800 Fax: 212-545-1238

> Union representing performers and news people in the fields of videotape, television, radio, commercials, and phonograph recordings.

American Guild of Musical Artists (AGMA)
1727 Broadway
New York, New York 10019-5284
212-265-3687

> Representing ballet dancers, opera singers, and other concert performers.

Directors Guild of America (DGA)
7950 Sunset Boulevard
Los Angeles, California 90046
213-289-2000 Fax: 213-289-2024

All descriptions of guilds and unions reprinted by permission of the 1990 *Hollywood Blu Book.*

The work of DGA members is represented in theatrical motion pictures; television (filmed, live, or taped); radio, industrial, educational, and government films; and commercials.

International Alliance of Theatrical Stage Employees (IATSE)
1515 Broadway, Suite 601
New York, New York 10036
212-730-1770 Fax: 212-921-7699

Represents pre-production, production, and post-production; technical and artistic (behind-the-camera) workers in the motion picture and television industries.

National Association of Broadcast Employees and Technicians (NABET)
7101 Wisconsin Avenue, Suite 800
Bethesda, MD 20814
301-657-8420 Fax: 301-657-9478

Represents pre-production, production, and post-production; technical and artistic (behind-the-camera) workers in the motion picture and television industries.

Screen Actors Guild (SAG)
7065 Hollywood Boulevard
Hollywood, California 90028-6065
213-465-4600 Fax: 213-856-6671

Trade union which negotiates minimum wages and working conditions for professional screen actors who perform in theatrical motion pictures, prime time television, commercial, industrial films, and music videos.

Screen Extras Guild (SEG)
3629 Cahuenga Boulevard
West Los Angeles, California 90068
213-851-4301 Fax: 213-851-0262

Union representing extras in the entertainment industry.

Writers Guild of America (WGA)
555 West 57th Street
New York, New York 10019
212-245-6180 Fax: 212-582-1909

8955 Beverly Blvd., Penthouse D
Los Angeles, California 90048
213-550-1000

Union representing screen, television, and radio writers for the purpose of collective bargaining. The WGA's service also covers the enforcement and administration of agreements made from collective bargaining negotiations.

California

Affiliated Property Craftspersons (IATSE Local 44)
11500 Burbank Boulevard
North Hollywood, California 91601
818-769-2500

>   Members consist of prop makers, coordinators, property masters, set decorators, and special effects personnel.

American Federation of Guards, Local 1
4157 West Fifth Street, Suite 220
Los Angeles, California 90020
213-387-3127

>   Representing security guards, policemen, and firemen for the entertainment industry.

American Federation of Musicians (AFM)
1777 North Vine Street, Suite 401
Hollywood, California 90028
213-461-3441 Fax: 213-432-8340

American Federation of Television and Radio Artists (AFTRA)
6922 Hollywood Boulevard
Hollywood, California 90028-6128
213-461-8111 Fax: 213-463-9041

American Guild of Musical Artists (AGMA)
15060 Ventura Boulevard, Suite 490
Sherman Oaks, California 91403
818-907-8986

Association of Film Craftsmen (NABET Local 531)
1800 North Argyle Street, Suite 501
Los Angeles, California 90028
213-462-7484 Fax: 213-462-3854

>   Exclusive bargaining agent for engineers and other technicians at several Southern California television stations.

Broadcast TV Recording Engineers & Communication Technicians (IBEW Local 45)
6255 Sunset Boulevard, Suite 721
Los Angeles, California 90028
213-851-5515

>   Representing broadcast recording engineers and technicians.

Costume Designers Guild (IATSE Local 892)
14724 Ventura Boulevard, Penthouse C
Sherman Oaks, California 91403
818-905-1557

Directors Guild of America, Inc. (DGA)
7920 Sunset Boulevard
Los Angeles, California 90046
213-289-2000 Fax: 213-289-2029

IATSE & MPMO International (AFL-CIO)
13949 Ventura Boulevard, Suite 300
Sherman Oaks, California 91432
818-905-8999 Fax: 818-905-6297

Illustrators & Matte Artists (IATSE Local 790)
14724 Ventura Boulevard, Penthouse B
Sherman Oaks, California 91403
818-784-6555

> Representing illustrators and matte artists who create scenes using photographic prints together with live action footage.

International Brotherhood of Electrical Workers Local 40
5643 Vineland Avenue
North Hollywood, California 91601
213-877-1171

> Studio responsibilities: electrical construction and maintenance, power distribution, handling generators for power supply, house panel hook-ups, repairs of electronic equipment and air conditioning.

International Photographers (Cameramen) (IATSE Local 659)
7715 Sunset Boulevard, Suite 300
Los Angeles, California 90046
213-876-0160

> Representing people who direct photography and operate camera/photographic equipment.

International Sound Technicians, Cinetechnicians, Studio Projectionists & Video Projection Technicians (IATSE 695)
11331 Ventura Boulevard, Suite 201
Studio City, California 91604
818-985-9204

> Labor union representing people who operate sound equipment, transparency process, and projection equipment, and who maintain

and rebuild camera and other equipment used for picture projection. These people do not operate the movieolas used for editing and/or cutting.

Laboratory Film-Video Technicians (Local 683)
2600 West Victory Boulevard, P.O. Box 7429
Burbank, California 91505
818-955-9720 Fax: 818-955-5834

Representing people who handle all phases of film processing for motion pictures and television.

Make-Up Artists and Hair Stylists (IATSE Local 706)
11519 Chandler Boulevard
North Hollywood, California 91601
818-984-1700

Representing people who apply make-up and style hair.

Motion Picture & Television Editors Guild (Film Editors) (IATSE Local 776)
7715 Sunset Boulevard, Suite 220
Hollywood, California 90046
213-876-4770

Representing the people who edit and/or cut positive prints for motion pictures, serials, short films, and trailers. This includes people who assemble and synchronize sound or sound effects on film tracks.

Motion Picture & Video Projectionists (IATSE Local 150)
2600 Victory Boulevard
Burbank, California 91505
818-842-8900

Representing theater projectionists and video technicians.

Motion Picture Costumers (IATSE Local 705)
1427 North LaBrea Avenue
Los Angeles, California 90028
213-851-0220

Representing people who supervise and operate the wardrobe department, test shooting, script breakdown and research (in regards to costumes), requisition, fitting, handling, manufacturing, and wardrobe storage.

Motion Picture Craft Service (IATSE Local 727)
14629 Nordhoff Street
Panorama City, California 91402-1816
818-891-0717

Representing on-location personnel, production-oriented unskilled labor. Responsibilities include assisting members of other crafts, supplying, moving and/or maintaining benches/tables, and opening/closing stage doors.

Motion Picture First Aid Employees (IATSE Local 767)
8303 Gustav Lane
Canoga Park, California 91324
818-884-8894

Representing people who give medical treatment to crews, instruct and/or train in first-aid techniques, and assist or advise on medical-related set decoration and/or procedures.

Motion Picture Screen Cartoonists (IATSE Local 839)
4729 Lankershim Boulevard
North Hollywood, California 91602
818-766-7151

Has jurisdiction over the entire animation process: animation writing, storyboard, layout, background, animation, checking and ink-and-pen.

Motion Picture Set Painters & Sign Writers (IATSE Local 729)
11365 Ventura Boulevard, Suite 202
Studio City, California 91604
818-984-3000

Representing people who paint, decorate, and make signs for sets.

Motion Picture Sound Editors (MPSE)
P.O. Box 8306
Universal City, California 91606
818-762-2816

Motion Picture Studio Grips (IATSE Local 80)
6926 Melrose Avenue
Los Angeles, California 90038
213-931-1419

Representing people who build, handle, maintain, load, unload, and store grip equipment, including camera perching and installation. Also represents people who rig, strike, build, and move equipment on sets and backlots.

Musicians Union AFM Local 47
817 North Vine Street
Los Angeles, California 90038
213-462-2161

National Association of Broadcast Employees & Technicians (NABET)
NABET Local 53
1918 West Burbank Boulevard
Burbank, California 91506
818-846-0490 Fax: 818-842-7154

Office & Professional Employees (OPEIU Local 174)
5643½ Vineland Avenue
North Hollywood, California 91601
818-508-5333

Representing office, clerical, and professional employees.

Ornamental Plasterers & Sculptors Local 755
14724 Ventura Boulevard, Penthouse 5
Sherman Oaks, California 91403
818-379-9711

Representing modelers, sculptors, and plasterers for the entertainment industry.

Production Office Coordinators & Accountants Guild (IATSE Local 717)
14724 Ventura Boulevard, Penthouse Suite
Sherman Oaks, California 91403
818-906-9986

Production office coordinators set up and run the production offices, working in conjunction with the unit production manager to coordinate all aspects of the production from shooting schedule through rental of equipment to daily production reports. Production accountants set up and maintain a full set of general ledger books, handling all aspects of accounting on the production.

Publicists Guild (IATSE Local 818)
14724 Ventura Boulevard, Penthouse
Sherman Oaks, California 91403
818-905-1541

Scenic & Title Artists (IATSE Local 816)
14724 Ventura Boulevard, Penthouse 5
Sherman Oaks, California 91403
818-906-7822

Representing scenic artists, set painters, graphic designers, title designers, courtroom illustrators, portrait artists, electronic graphic artists, and video illustrators.

Screen Actors Guild (SAG)
7065 Hollywood Boulevard
Hollywood, California 90028-6065
213-465-4600 Fax: 213-856-6671

Screen Extras Guild, Inc. (SEG)
3629 Cahuenga Boulevard West
Los Angeles, California 90068
213-851-4301 Fax: 213-851-0262

Screen Story Analysts (IATSE Local 854)
14724 Ventura Boulevard, Penthouse B
Sherman Oaks, California 91403
818-784-6555

Representing people who read, synopsize, and/or comment on literary and/or dramatic properties. This includes critique, editorial, analytical breakdown, legal comparison, foreign translation, and synopsis.

Script Supervisors (IATSE Local 871)
7061-B Hayvenhurst Avenue
Van Nuys, California 91408
818-782-7063

Representing people who break down scripts for motion pictures, television, and commercials. This includes recording timings, verification of actor's lines, and assistance with scene blocking and continuity.

Set Designers & Model Makers (IATSE Local 847)
14724 Ventura Boulevard, Penthouse B
Sherman Oaks, California 91403
818-784-6555

Representing people who prepare layouts, set models, working drawings, miniatures, and backgrounds.

Society of Motion Picture & Television Art Directors (IATSE Local 876)
14724 Ventura Boulevard, Penthouse Suite
Sherman Oaks, California 91403
818-905-0599

> Representing people who prepare sketches, set design, and backgrounds, and who oversee the execution of designs, set decoration, and/or backgrounds for motion pictures and television.

Studio Electrical Lighting Technicians (IATSE Local 728)
14629 Nordhoff Boulevard
Panorama City, California 91402
213-851-3300

> Representing people who handle all on-set electrical equipment and apparatus.

Studio Teachers (IATSE Local 884)
14724 Ventura Boulevard, Penthouse
Sherman Oaks, California 91403
818-905-1175

> Representing certified teachers with experience in welfare supervision that work with minors (on-set) employed in the entertainment field.

Studio Transportation Drivers (Teamsters Local 399)
4747 Vineland Avenue, Suite E
North Hollywood, California 91602
818-985-7374 Fax: 818-985-8305

> Representing chauffeurs and truck drivers of all rolling stock, automotive service (other than mechanical repair), dispatchers, wranglers (men employed in connection with the handling and feeding of livestock), and animal trainers.

Studio Utility Employees Local 724
6700 Melrose Avenue
Hollywood, California 90038
213-938-6277

> Representing labor used in construction of new sets, and for the sweeping and cleaning around sets where active construction is taking place. This includes maintenance of streets, landscapes, and lawns; washing windows; hauling refuse from construction area.

Theatre Authority West Inc. (Charity Clearing House)
6464 Sunset Boulevard, Suite 640
Hollywood, California 90028
213-462-5761 Fax: 213-462-1930

> Administers and regulates the free appearances of performers and provides assistance to members of the theatrical community.

Theatrical & Television Stage Employees (IATSE Local 33)
1720 West Magnolia Boulevard
Burbank, California 91506
818-841-9233

> Representing people who handle props, electrical, and grip for television, cable and video productions.

Theatrical Wardrobe Union (IATSE 763)
14724 Ventura Boulevard, Penthouse D
Sherman Oaks, California 91403
818-789-8735

Writers Guild of America West (WGA)
8955 Beverly Boulevard
Los Angeles, California 90048
213-550-1000

Chicago

American Federation of Musicians (AFM)
175 West Washington Street
Chicago, Illinois 60602
312-782-0063

American Federation of Television & Radio Artists (AFTRA)
307 North Michigan Avenue
Chicago, Illinois 60601
312-372-8081 Fax: 312-372-5025

Directors Guild of America (DGA)
520 North Michigan Avenue, Suite 1026
Chicago, Illinois 60611
312-644-5050 Fax: 312-644-5776

Screen Actors Guild (SAG)
307 North Michigan Avenue
Chicago, Illinois 60601
312-372-8081 Fax: 312-372-5025

New York

American Federation of Musicians (AFM)
1501 Broadway, Suite 600
New York, New York 10036
212-869-1330 Fax: 212-764-6134

American Federation of Television and Radio Artists (AFTRA)
1350 Avenue of the Americas
New York, New York 10019
212-265-7700 Fax: 212-545-1238

American Guild of Musical Artists (AGMA)
1727 Broadway
New York, New York 10019-5284
212-265-3687

Cinematographers, Local 644
505 Eighth Avenue, 16th Floor
New York, New York 10018

> Representing people who direct all photography and operate all photographic (camera) equipment.

Directors Guild of America, Inc. (DGA)
110 West 57th Street, 2nd Floor
New York, New York 10019
212-581-0370 Fax: 212-581-1441

International Brotherhood of Electrical Workers Local 1212
230 West 41st Street
New York, New York 10036
212-354-6770

Make-Up Artists Local 798
31 West 21st Street
New York, New York 10010
212-627-0660

> Representing people who style hair and apply make-up.

Motion Picture Editors Local 771
535 West 48th Street, Fifth Floor
New York, New York 10036
212-581-0771

Musicians Union Local 802
330 West 42nd Street
New York, New York 10036
212-239-4802

Screen Actors Guild (SAG)
1515 Broadway, 44th Floor
New York, New York 10036
212-944-1030 Fax: 212-944-6774

Screen Cartoonists, Local 841
505 Eighth Avenue, 16th Floor c/o Local 644
New York, New York 10018
212-244-4699 Fax: 212-643-9218

Script Supervisors Local 161
1697 Broadway, Suite 902
New York, New York 10019
212-956-5410

> Representing people who break down wardrobe and props, do
> rough timing, and supervise the continuity of a script. This includes
> handling production reports, daily notes for the editor, and the
> combined continuity from composite print.

Studio Mechanics Local 52
326 West 48th Street
New York, New York 10036
212-399-0980

> Representing people like sound monitors, recordists, boom men,
> recording engineers, video technicians, electricians, grips, and
> shop craftsmen; property, drapery, and generator men; and special-
> effects workers.

Theatrical State Employees (IATSE Local 1)
320 West 46th Street, 3rd Floor
New York, New York 10036
212-333-2500

> Representing stagehands in television production studios.

Theatrical Teamsters Local 817
1 Hollow Lane
Lake Success, Long Island, New York 11042
516-365-3470

Representing chauffeurs and truck drivers of all rolling stock, automotive services (other than mechanical repairs), and dispatchers. This includes all pick-up, delivery, or hauling of any description performed by or for the company in a vehicle.

United Scenic Artists Local 829
575 Eighth Avenue
New York, New York 10018
212-736-4498 Fax: 212-736-4681

Representing art directors responsible for the design and production of all illustrations and sketches, scenery and sets, props and set dressing. Scenic artists prepare and apply all texturing and/or painting or coloration on sets, scenery, and props. They also do all lettering and sign work, sculpturing, portraits, or special artwork.

Wardrobe Attendants Local 764
1501 Broadway, Suite 1313
New York, New York 10036
212-221-1717

Representing people who supervise the general operation of the wardrobe department, including the maintenance, fittings, manufacturing, remodeling, alterations of all costumes/wardrobe and accessories used in production.

Writers Guild of America East (WGA)
555 West 57th Street
New York, New York 10019
212-245-6180 Fax: 212-582-1909

Appendix C4
Music Organizations

Music Performance Rights Organizations

American Society of Composers, Authors and Publishers (ASCAP)
1 Lincoln Plaza
New York, New York 10023
212-595-3050 Fax: 212-724-9064

Broadcast Music, Inc. (BMI)
320 West 57th Street
New York, New York 10019
212-586-2000 Fax: 212-956-2059

Broadcast Music, Inc. (BMI)—West Coast
8730 Sunset Boulevard, 3rd Floor
Los Angeles, California 90069-2211
213-659-9109 Fax: 213-657-6947

SESAC
156 West 56th Street, 24th Floor
New York, New York 10019
212-586-3450 Fax: 212-397-4682

Music Synchronization Licensing Agency

Harry Fox Agency
205 East 42nd Street, 18th Floor
New York, New York 10017
212-370-5330 Fax: 212-953-2384

Appendix C5
Producer Organizations

Alliance of Motion Picture & Television Producers (AMPTP)
14144 Ventura Boulevard
Sherman Oaks, California 91423
818-995-3600 Fax: 818-789-7431

> A service organization that handles labor negotiations and monitors legislation for television and film producers.

American Academy of Independent Film Producers
2067 South Atlantic Avenue
Los Angeles, California 90040
213-264-1422

Association of Independent Commercial Producers (National Office)
100 East 42nd Street
New York, New York 10017
212-867-5720 Fax: 212-986-8851

> Serving commercial producers for the purpose of exchanging information and ideas, as well as strengthening the relationships between clients and suppliers.

Association of Independent Commercial Producers (West Coast Office)
2121 Avenue of the Stars, Suite 2700
Los Angeles, California 90067-5010
213-557-2900 Fax: 818-763-2427

Producers Guild of America
400 South Beverly Drive, Suite 211
Beverly Hills, California 90212
213-557-0807

> Represents executive producers, associate producers, and producers for motion pictures and television.

Appendix C6
Trade Organizations

Academy of Motion Picture Arts & Sciences (AMPAS)
8949 Wilshire Boulevard
Beverly Hills, California 90211
213-278-8990 Fax: 213-859-9619

Academy of Television Arts & Sciences
3500 West Olive Avenue, Suite 700
Burbank, California 91505-4628
818-953-7575

Action for Children's Television (ACT)
20 University Road
Cambridge, Massachusetts 02138
617-876-6620

Actors Advisory Board
9000 Sunset Boulevard, Suite 905
Los Angeles, California 90069
213-550-7104

The Advertising Council Inc.
1717 North Highland Avenue, Suite 910
Los Angeles, California 90028
213-462-0988

American National Academy of Performing Arts
10944 Ventura Boulevard
Studio City, California 91604
818-763-4431

American Association of Advertising Agencies (AAAA)
666 Third Avenue
New York, New York 10017
212-682-2500 Fax: 212-658-6825

8383 Wilshire Boulevard, Suite 342
Beverly Hills, California 90211
213-658-5750

American Film Institute
2021 North Western Avenue
Los Angeles, California 90027
213-856-7600 Fax: 213-467-4578

American Film Marketing Association (AFMA)
10000 Washington Boulevard, Suite S-226
Culver City, California 90232-2728
213-558-1170 Fax: 213-558-0560

American Guild of Variety Artists (AGVA)
4741 Laurel Canyon Boulevard, Suite 208
North Hollywood, California 91607
818-508-9984

American Society of Cinematographers (ASC)
P. O. Box 2230
Hollywood, California 90078
213-876-5080 Fax: 213-876-4973

The Art Directors Club of Los Angeles
7080 Hollywood Boulevard, Suite 410
Los Angeles, California 90028
213-465-1787

ASIFA Hollywood International Animated Film Society
5301 Laurel Canyon Boulevard, Suite 250
North Hollywood, California 91607
818-508-5224

Association of Freelance Professionals, Inc. (AFP)
3607 West Magnolia Boulevard, Suite K
Burbank, California 91505
818-842-7797

Association of Independent Television Stations (INTV)
1200 18th Street N.W. Suite 502
Washington, DC 20036
202-887-1970

Association of Talent Agents
9255 Sunset Boulevard, Suite 318
Los Angeles, California 90069
213-274-0628

Association of Visual Communicators
7440 North Figueroa, Suite 103
Los Angeles, California 90041
213-340-1540

Broadcast Promotion & Marketing Executives
6255 Sunset Boulevard, Suite 624
Los Angeles, California 90028
213-465-3777 Fax: 213-469-9559

Cable Advertising Bureau (CAB)
757 Third Avenue, 5th Floor
New York, New York 10017
212-751-7770

Cable Alliance for Education
1211 Connecticut Avenue, NW, Suite 700
Washington, DC 20036
202-822-8822

Cable Television Administration & Marketing Society (CTAM)
635 Slaters Lane #250
Alexandria, Virginia 22214
703-549-4200

Cable Television Information Center (CTIC)
1700 Shaker Church Road NW
Olympia, Washington 98502
206-866-2080

Cable Television Public Affairs Association (CTPAA)
1660 Inverness Drive West
Englewood, Colorado 80112
303-799-1200

Casting Society of America (CSA)
6565 Sunset Boulevard, Suite 306
Los Angeles, California 90028
213-463-1925

Direct Broadcast Satellite Association (DBSA)
2000 L Street, NW Suite 702
Washington, DC 20036

Electronic Industries Association (EIA)
1722 Eye Street, NW Suite 300
Washington, DC 20006
202-457-4900

Hollywood Foreign Press Association
292 South La Cienega Boulevard, Suite 316
Beverly Hills, California 90211
213-657-1731 Fax: 213-657-5576

Hollywood Press & Entertainment Industry Club
P.O. Box 3381
Hollywood, California 90028
213-466-1212

Hollywood Women's Press Club
342½ North Sierra Bonita Avenue
Los Angeles, California 90036
213-960-5725

Independent Feature Project/West (IFR)
5550 Wilshire Boulevard, Suite 204
Los Angeles, California 90036
213-937-4379 Fax: 213-937-4038

International Documentary Association
1551 South Robertson Boulevard, Suite 201
Los Angeles, California 90035
213-284-8422

Motion Picture Association of America (MPAA)
14144 Ventura Boulevard, Suite 210　　1133 Avenue of the Americas
Sherman Oaks, California 91423　　New York, New York 10036
818-995-3600　　212-840-6161

Motion Picture & Television Credit Association
1653 Beverly Boulevard
Los Angeles, California 90026
213-250-8278

Motion Picture Sound Editors (MPSE)
P.O. Box 8306
Universal City, California 91608-0306
818-762-2816

Musicians Contact Service
7315 Sunset Boulevard
Hollywood, California 90046
213-851-2333

National Academy of Cable Programming
1724 Massachusetts Avenue, NW
Washington, DC 20036
202-775-3611

National Association of Broadcasters (NAB)
1771 N Street, NW
Washington, DC 20036
202-429-5300

National Association of College Broadcasters
Brown University Box 1995
Providence, Rhode Island 02912
401-863-2225

National Association of Public Television Stations
1919 M Street
Washington, DC 20036
202-632-7000

National Association of Telecommunications Officers and Advisors
1301 Pennsylvania Avenue, NW #600
Washington, DC 20004
202-626-3160

National Association of Television Program Executives (NATPE)
10100 Santa Monica Boulevard, Suite 300
Los Angeles, California 90067
213-282-8802 Fax: 213-282-0760

National Broadcasters Editorial Association (NBEA)
6223 Executive Boulevard
Rockville, Maryland 20852
301-468-3959

National Cable Forum
1724 Massachusetts Avenue NW
Washington, DC 20036
202-775-3629

National Cable Television Association (NCTA)
1724 Massachusetts Avenue NW
Washington, DC 20036
202-775-3550

National Cable Television Institute
Box 27277
Denver, Colorado 80227
303-761-8554

National Conference of Personal Managers
10707 Camarillo Street, Suite 308   210 East 51st Street
North Hollywood, California 91602   New York, New York 10022
818-766-0114 Fax: 818-980-8212   212-421-2670 Fax: 212-838-5105

National Federation of Local Cable Programmers (NFLCP)
P.O. Box 27290
Washington, DC 20038
202-829-7186

National Satellite Cable Television Association
888 16th Street NW
Washington, DC 20036
202-659-2928

Radio and Television News Directors Association (RTNDA)
1717 K Street, NW Suite 615
Washington, DC 20006
202-659-6510

Satellite Broadcasting & Communications Association (SBCA)
225 Rienekers Lane
Alexandria, Virginia 22314
703-549-6990

Screen Composers of America
2451 Nichols Canyon Road
Los Angeles, California 90046-1798
213-876-6040

Scriptwriters/Filmmakers Book Club
8033 Sunset Boulevard, Suite 306
Hollywood, California 90046
818-769-2811

Society of Cable Television Engineers
669 Exton Commons
Exton, Pennsylvania 19341
215-363-6888

Society of Motion Picture & Television Engineers (SMPTE)
595 West Hartsvale Avenue
White Plains, New York 10607
914-761-1100 Fax: 914-761-3115

Society of Professional Stuntwomen
818-785-8988

Stuntmen's Association of Motion Pictures Inc.
11020 Ventura Boulevard, Suite G
Studio City, California 91604
818-766-4334

Stuntwomen's Association of Motion Pictures Inc.
202 Vance Road
Pacific Palisades, California 90272
213-462-1605

Subscription Television Association
8200 Greensboro Drive
McLean, Virginia 22102
703-556-9250

Television Movie Awards
415 Route 10 P.O. Box 1000
Mount Freedom, New Jersey 07970
201-366-6691 Fax: 201-361-1391

Theatre Equipment Association
244 West 49th Street, Suite 305
New York, New York 10019
212-246-6460

Video Software Dealers Association (VSDA)
3 Eves Drive, Suite 307
Marlton, New Jersey 08053
609-596-8500

Videotex Industry Association
8403 Cloesville Road, Suite 865
Silver Springs, Maryland 20910
301-495-4955

Wireless Cable Association
2000 L Street, NW Suite 702
Washington, DC 20036
202-452-7853

Western States Advertising Association (WSAA)
2410 Beverly Boulevard, Suite 1
Los Angeles, California 90057
213-387-7432 Fax: 213-380-6277

Women in Cable
500 North Michigan Avenue, Suite 1400
Chicago, Illinois 60611
312-661-1700
Washington, DC office: 202-737-3220

Women in Film (WIF)
6464 Sunset Boulevard, Suite 660
Los Angeles, California 90028
213-463-6040

Youth in Film/Television International
5632 Colfax Avenue
North Hollywood, California 91601
818-761-4007

Appendix C7

Federal Government Agencies and Legislative Committees

Armed Forces Radio and Television Service
601 North Fairfax Street
Alexandria, Virginia 22314
703-274-4824

Board for International Broadcasting
1201 Connecticut Avenue NW
Washington, DC 20036
202-254-8040

Copyright Royalty Tribunal
1111 20th Street NW, Suite 450
Washington, DC 20036
202-653-5175

Corporation for Public Broadcasting
1111 16th Street NW
Washington, DC 20036
202-293-6160

Department of Justice
10th & Constitution Avenue NW
Washington, DC 20530
202-633-2000

Department of Labor
200 Constitution Avenue NW
Washington, DC 20210
202-523-6666

Equal Employment Opportunity Commission
2401 E Street NW
Washington, DC 20507
202-634-6922

Federal Communication Commission
1919 M Street NW
Washington, DC 20554
202-632-7000

Federal Trade Commission
Pennsylvania Avenue at 6th Street NW
Washington, DC 20580
202-326-2222
202-326-3131 Advertising

Food and Drug Administration
5600 Fishers Lane
Rockville, Maryland 20857
301-443-1544

House of Representatives Subcommittee on Telecommunications
   and Finance
House Office Building Annex No.2, Room H2-316
Washington, DC 20515-6119

National Telecommunications and Information Administration
US Department of Commerce
H.C. Hoover Building, Room 4890
Washington, DC 20230
202-377-1800

Senate Subcommittee on Communications
Hart Senate Office Building, Room 227
Washington, DC 20510-6125

US Copyright Office
Library of Congress
1st and Independence Avenue SE
Washington, DC 20540
202-479-0700

US Trademark Office Information
1755 Jefferson Davis Highway
Arlington, Virginia 22202
703-557-3551

Voice of America
330 Independence Avenue SW
Washington, DC 20547
202-485-6231

Appendix C8

Broadcast Networks, Public Broadcasters, and Cable Networks

Broadcast Networks

American Broadcasting Companies, Inc.
1330 Avenue of the Americas
New York, New York 10019
212-887-7777

4151 Prospect Avenue
Los Angeles, California 90027
213-557-7777

Columbia Broadcasting System, Inc.
51 West 52nd Street
New York, New York 10019
212-975-4321

7800 Beverly Boulevard
Los Angeles, California 90036
213-852-2345

Fox, Inc.
40 West 57th Street
New York, New York 10019
212-977-5500

10201 West Pico Boulevard
Los Angeles, California 90035
213-277-2211

National Broadcasting Company
30 Rockefeller Plaza
New York, New York 10020
212-664-4444

3000 West Alameda Avenue
Burbank, California 91505
818-840-4444

Public Broadcasters

Corporation for Public Broadcasting
1111 16th Street NW
Washington, DC 20036
202-293-6160

Public Broadcasting Service (Executive Headquarters)
1320 Broddock Place
Alexandria, Virginia 22314
703-739-5000

Public Broadcasting Service
1790 Broadway
New York, New York 10019-1412
212-708-3000

Cable Networks

Arts and Entertainment Network (A&E)
555 Fifth Avenue
New York, New York 10017
212-661-4500 Fax: 212-697-0753

Bravo Cable Network
150 Crossways Park West
Woodbury, New York 11797
516-364-2222 Fax: 516-364-2297

Cable News Network (CNN)
One CNN Plaza
Atlanta, Georgia 30348-5366
404-827-1500

Cinemax Cable Pay Television
1100 Avenue of the Americas
New York, New York 10036
212-512-1000

The Comedy Channel
120A East 23rd Street
New York, New York 10010
212-512-8900

Cable Satellite Public Affairs Network (C-SPAN)
444 North Capitol Street NW
Washington, DC 20001
202-737-3220

Cable Value Network (CVN)
1405 Xenium Lane North
Minneapolis, Minnesota 55441
612-559-8000

The Discovery Channel
8201 Corporate Drive, Suite 1200
Landover, Maryland 20785
301-577-1999 Fax: 301-577-0733

The Disney Channel
3800 West Alameda Avenue
Burbank, California 91505
818-569-7711 Fax: 818-845-3742

ESPN, Inc.
605 Third Avenue
New York, New York 10158
212-916-9200 Fax: 212-916-9325

The Family Channel
1000 Centerville Turnpike
Virginia Beach, Virginia 23463
804-523-7151 Fax: 804-523-7880

Home Box Office, Inc. (HBO)
1100 Avenue of the Americas   2049 Century Park East
New York, New York 10036   Los Angeles, California 90067
212-512-1000 Fax: 212-512-8700   213-201-9200

Lifetime Television
Kaufman Astoria Studios   10880 Wilshire Boulevard,
36-12 35th Avenue   Suite 201
Astoria, New York 11106   Los Angeles, California 90024
718-706-3503 Fax: 718-706-0373   213-850-0373

Madison Square Garden Television (MSG)
4 Pennsylvania Plaza
New York, New York 10001
212-563-8000

MTV Networks
1515 Broadway
New York, New York 10036
212-258-8000 Fax: 212-719-7199

The Nashville Network (TNN)
1451 Elm Hill Pike
Nashville, Tennessee 37210
615-361-0366

Nickelodeon
1515 Broadway
New York, New York 10036
212-258-7500

Prime Network International
250 Steele Street, Suite 300
Denver, Colorado 80206
303-355-7777 Fax: 303-377-3973

Shop Television Network (STN)
Hollywood Center Studios
5842 Sunset Boulevard, Building 11
Los Angeles, California 90028
213-871-8380 Fax: 213-960-2455

Sportschannel
150 Media Crossways
Woodbury, New York 11797
516-364-3650

Showtime Entertainment Corporation (The Movie Channel)
1633 Broadway   10900 Wilshire Boulevard
New York, New York 10019   Los Angeles, California 90024
212-708-1600   213-208-2340

Turner Broadcasting System, Inc. (TNT, TBS)
One CNN Plaza P.O. Box 105366
Atlanta, Georgia 30348-5366
404-827-1700

USA Network
1230 Avenue of the Americas
New York, New York 10020
212-408-9100 Fax: 212-408-3606

Appendix C9

Television Syndicators, Television Distributors, and Video Distributors

Television Syndicators and Distributors

ABC Distribution Company (Div. of Capital Cities/ABC)
825 Seventh Avenue
New York, New York 10019
212-887-1725 Fax: 212-877-1708

2040 Avenue of the Stars
Century City, California 90067
213-557-6600 Fax: 213-557-7925

All American Television
304 East 45th Street
New York, New York 10017
212-818-1200 Fax: 212-661-0396

Carolco Films International Limited
432 Park Avenue South
New York, New York 10016
212-685-6699 Fax: 212-213-3598

CBS Broadcast International
51 West 52nd Street
New York, New York 10019
212-975-8585 Fax: 212-975-7452

7800 Beverly Boulevard
Los Angeles, California 90036
213-852-2345 Fax: 213-651-5900

Columbia Pictures International Television
711 Fifth Avenue
New York, New York 10022
212-751-4400 Fax: 212-702-6206

Columbia/Embassy Television
Columbia Plaza
Burbank, California 91505
818-954-6000

D.L. Taffner, Ltd.
31 West 56th Street
New York, New York 10019
212-245-4680

Films Around the World, Inc.
685 Fifth Avenue, 10th Floor
New York, New York 10022
212-752-5050 Fax: 212-838-9642

Fox/Lorber Associates and Gaga Communications Inc.
432 Park Avenue South
New York, New York 10016
212-686-6777 Fax: 212-685-2625

Fremantle Corporation Limited
660 Madison Avenue
New York, New York 10021
212-421-4530 Fax: 212-207-8357

Fries Distribution Company
6922 Hollywood Boulevard
Hollywood, California 90028
213-466-2266 Fax: 213-464-6082

Genesis Entertainment
5743 Corsa Avenue
Westlake Village, California 91362
818-706-6341

Hearst Entertainment (formerly King Features Entertainment)
235 East 45th Street
New York, New York 10017
212-455-4000 Fax: 212-983-6379

ITC Distribution
12711 Ventura Boulevard
Studio City, California 91604
818-760-2110 Fax: 818-506-8189

King World Productions, Inc.
1700 Broadway, 35th Floor
New York, New York 10019
212-315-4000 Fax: 212-418-3010

Lorimar Telepictures
15303 Ventura Boulevard
Sherman Oaks, California 91403
818-986-3600

MCA TV
100 Universal City Plaza
Universal City, California 91608
818-777-1000 Fax: 818-777-6276

MGM/UA Telecommunications
10000 West Washington Boulevard
Culver City, California 90232
213-280-6000 Fax: 213-280-0359

MTM TV
4024 Redford Avenue
Studio City, California 91604
818-760-5000

Multimedia Entertainment
75 Rockefeller Plaza
New York, New York 10019
212-484-7993

NBC International
30 Rockefeller Plaza
New York, New York 10019
212-644-6606 Fax: 212-333-7546

New World International
115 East 57th Street
New York, New York 10022
212-755-8600 Fax: 212-755-0041

Orbis Communications
432 Park Avenue South
New York, New York 10016
212-685-6699

Orion Television International
1325 Avenue of the Americas, Sixth Floor
New York, New York 10019
212-956-3800 Fax: 212-956-7235

Paramount Pictures Corporation
5555 Melrose Avenue
Los Angeles, California 90038
213-956-5858 Fax: 213-956-3938

Paramount Television
One Gulf + Western Plaza
New York, New York 10023
212-333-4600

Pathe/Cannon International
8670 Wilshire Boulevard
Beverly Hills, California 90211
213-967-2225 Fax: 213-652-3397

Public Television International
1790 Broadway, 16th Floor
New York, New York 10019-1412
212-708-3048 Fax: 212-708-3045

Republic Pictures Corporation
12636 Beatrice Street
Los Angeles, California 90066
213-306-4040 Fax: 213-301-0142

Samuel Goldwyn Company
10203 Santa Monica Boulevard
Los Angeles, California 90067
213-552-2255 Fax: 213-284-9108

The Silverbach-Lazarus Group
9911 West Pico Boulevard, Penthouse M
Los Angeles, California 90035
213-552-2660 Fax: 213-552-9039

Television Program Enterprises
1155 Avenue of the Americas
New York, New York 10022
212-759-8787

Tribune Entertainment Co.
435 North Michigan Avenue, Room 1429
Chicago, Illinois 60611
312-222-4484

Turner International
1050 Techwood Drive
Atlanta, Georgia 30318
404-827-2085 Fax: 404-824-2373

Twentieth Century-Fox Television
10201 West Pico Boulevard
Los Angeles, California 90213
213-277-2211

Viacom International
1515 Broadway
New York, New York 10036
212-258-6552 Fax: 212-258-6391

The Walt Disney Company/Buena Vista International
350 South Buena Vista Street
Burbank, California 91521
818-840-1000 Fax: 818-841-3225

Warner Bros. International Television Distribution
4000 Warner Boulevard, Towers Building Suite 1449
Burbank, California 91522
818-954-5491 Fax: 818-954-4040

Westinghouse Broadcasting International, Group W Productions
3801 Barham Boulevard, Second Floor
Los Angeles, California 90068
213-850-3877 Fax: 213-851-9185

Worldvision Enterprises, Inc.-A Unit of Spelling Entertainment, Inc.
660 Madison Avenue, 3rd Floor
New York, New York 10021

Video Distributors

CBS/Fox Video
1211 Avenue of the Americas, 2nd Floor
New York, New York 10036
212-819-3200 Fax: 212-819-3286

Time Life Video
777 Duke Street
Alexandria, Virginia 22314
703-838-7003 Fax: 703-838-6915

Index

THIS BUSINESS OF TELEVISION—ON COMPUTER DISKETTE

Most of the agreements in this book are now available on floppy diskette. You can use these agreements in your word processor as the basis for your own agreements, saving time and money. To order a diskette, please send the information shown below along with a check for $100, payable to "This Business of Television."

- Your name
- Company name
- Address
- Telephone
- Format (specify only one for each order): Macintosh 3½-inch diskette or IBM 3½-inch diskette

Mail this information and your check to This Business of Television, P.O. Box 668, Newtown, PA 18940. Allow 4–6 weeks for delivery. For multiple copies, deduct 10% from your entire order. Prices subject to increase after 1992.